INDUSTRIAL TRAFFIC MANAGEMENT

INDUSTRIAL
TRAFFIC MANAGEMENT

Thurman W. Van Metre, Ph.D., L.H.D.

Professor Emeritus of Transportation
Graduate School of Business
Columbia University

McGRAW-HILL BOOK COMPANY, INC.

NEW YORK   TORONTO   LONDON

1953

INDUSTRIAL TRAFFIC MANAGEMENT

Preface

In preparing a book of limited size on such a broad subject as industrial traffic management, the author often feels much as the guide must feel who accompanies a group of tourists on a motor vehicle sightseeing journey. Traveling on main roads, he can give an extended account of only a few of the imposing and important edifices and other objects of interest seen along the way. However, he can call fleeting attention to many objects of lesser import as well as to intersecting branch roads and byways which, though not subject to immediate examination, may excite enough interest and curiosity among his listeners to impel some of them to return some day to undertake a thorough and leisurely exploration.

This means that the author finds himself under the necessity of picking and choosing the subjects to which he will devote major attention. Moreover, after he has chosen these subjects, he must exercise still further his selective judgment in the matter of the emphasis accorded to the topics which he singles out for more or less extended treatment. It goes without saying that there will not be universal approval of his choices and his judgment, but since what is done is done, he can say only that he regrets any failure to satisfy all expectations and preferences, and rejoices if some of his readers are in substantial agreement with his decisions.

The author has tried to explain what industrial traffic management means; he has pointed out the chief problems with which the industrial traffic manager is likely to be confronted; he has discussed at some length many of the technical features of traffic management, such as rates, tariffs, bills of lading, claims, insurance, routing, demurrage, terminal services, and the rules of practice of administrative boards; and he has endeavored to give to the student of traffic management, as well as to the professional traffic manager, some conception of the knowledge and training he must have in order to attain proficiency in his chosen calling. At no point in the discussion has the author failed to emphasize the fact that while reading, the study of books, and attendance in traffic courses of an educational institution can do much to illuminate and interpret experience, they are never to be regarded as a substitute for experience.

This is not a work on transportation as such. It deals with the physical

v

operation of transportation facilities and the business practices and policies of the transportation industry only to the extent that they affect the consumer, the purchaser of transportation service. Although the economics of transportation and such topics as the theory of rates are touched upon, the treatment is in the nature of a hasty review of what the would-be traffic manager should have studied elsewhere, though some of it is presented, perhaps, from an unfamiliar angle of vision. Here we are concerned primarily with the practical aspects of traffic management, with the day-to-day duties of the professional traffic manager.

Inevitably, in such a work as this, the author must devote the major portion of its pages to the business relations between shippers and railroads, for railroads are still by far the most important carriers of our domestic commerce. Moreover, because of its peculiar physical characteristics, railroad transportation presents the industrial traffic manager with a larger number and a greater variety of technical problems than water, highway, or air transportation. The purely "business" problems arising between shipper and carrier are much the same, regardless of the type of carrier selected to perform a transportation service, and space is saved and repetition minimized by calling attention to the differences between railroad and other kinds of transportation rather than by giving full consideration to all.

The author has included chapters which give a brief digest of our leading transportation laws primarily for the benefit of those who do not possess complete copies of the statutes and those who do not care to wade through the entire texts of these laws. He has indicated where the printed statutes may be purchased or consulted.

Following this preface there is a note on study materials. The student of traffic should have some laboratory material in the course of his inquiries, and perhaps the minimum amount of the tools and equipment with which he should be supplied is set forth. The author has not endeavored to prepare an extensive bibliography, but has included a brief bibliographical note at the end of the text, primarily for the use of those who wish to do additional reading on the history and general features of the transportation industry.

The author should like to extend here his thanks to a few friends upon whom he has called for assistance in the preparation of this book. Needless to say, he is deeply indebted to hundreds of writers who have contributed to the rich and voluminous literature of transportation, to the legislators, commissions, courts, and members of other governmental agencies who have had so much to do with shaping transportation policy, and to numerous transportation and other business agencies from whose headquarters proceeds a constant flow of books, booklets, bulletins, and special studies dealing with current transportation problems. But the acknowledgments made here are to individual claimants to his gratitude. His former student and successor in the Graduate School of Business of Columbia University, Dr. Ernest Williams, has given much of his time to friendly consultation on knotty problems; Ludwell Larzelere, assistant traffic manager of the Luckenbach Steamship Company, also one of his former students and for the past several years a teacher of traffic management in the Graduate School of Business of Columbia University, has responded in person to many requests for help. He has also read portions of the manuscript and made numerous suggestions for its improvement. The author has taken advantage of his many years of friendship with Russell B. James, of the legal staff of the Chicago, Burlington, and Quincy Railroad, to obtain expert advice on many legal and other technical problems. Edward M. Barnet, instructor in marketing in the Graduate School of Business at Columbia University, has read most of the manuscript and offered many thoughtful comments. The author acknowledges his great indebtedness also to Miles O. Price, the law librarian of Columbia University, and to his capable assistant, Miss Virginia H. Gray, both of whom, on his numerous and prolonged visits to the library, have guided him unerringly to sources of information for which he was seeking. In typing the manuscript, Miss Agnes Fabbroni has displayed not only an uncommon mastery of the typewriter but an extraordinary and much needed knowledge of orthography.

Thurman W. Van Metre

NEW YORK, N.Y.
OCTOBER, 1952

Contents

x   *Contents*

Study Materials

The serious student of industrial traffic management, especially the one who is just beginning the study, will be greatly aided by having at his command, either through ownership or in an accessible library, certain documentary material, forms, and reference works. The following list of such materials represents probably a minimum of what is needed.

1. Tariffs and Forms

The Consolidated Freight Classification and the Uniform Freight Classification, both procurable from the Consolidated Classification Committee, Union Station, Chicago. Although the Uniform Classification will eventually replace the Consolidated Classification, the transition will take some years for completion.

Some freight rate tariffs, certainly of railroads and, if possible, of water carriers, motor carriers, and air carriers. The collection of tariffs should include tariffs containing both class and commodity rates, local and joint, both individual and agency issues. A demurrage and storage tariff, a *Leland's List of Open and Prepay Stations,* a Railway Equipment Register, a New York Lighterage Tariff, and some agency tariff of "exceptions" would all be helpful. It is not necessary that tariffs be currently in effect. Tariffs can be secured by application to carriers and to industrial traffic managers. Many traffic departments have numerous obsolete, canceled tariffs, of which they are willing to dispose.

Bill of lading forms, both straight and order, used by railroads and other carriers.

Standard forms for the presentation of claims for overcharges and claims for loss and damage.

2. Government Publications

The Interstate Commerce Act, the Civil Aeronautics Act, *Tariff Circular* No. 20, tariff circulars for the use of other carriers, the Rules of Practice of the Interstate Commerce Commission and of the Civil Aeronautics Board. The student can obtain for the asking, from the Superintendent of Documents, Washington, D.C., the price lists of documents dealing respectively with aviation, transportation and roads, and interstate commerce. These price lists include not only the documents just mentioned but many others which the student may wish to examine.

The Interstate Commerce Acts Annotated. This highly valuable work, now running to the fourteenth volume, contains, in addition to the Acts themselves, a complete history and analysis of the Interstate Commerce Act and related statutes. The manner in which the law has been interpreted by the Interstate Commerce Commission is given in detail, and references are made to thousands of decisions of the Commission and of our courts.

The Interstate Commerce Commission Reports, the Reports of the Supreme Court of the United States, and the reports of the lower Federal courts and state courts, all of which are available in good law libraries, and in whole or in part in many general libraries.

3. *Reference Works*

There are many good reference works dealing with the subject of traffic management. One of the best single volumes is the bulky *Freight Traffic Red Book*, published at frequent but irregular intervals by the Traffic Publishing Company in New York. This work contains the Interstate Commerce Act and many other statutes, the tariff circulars of various carriers, the rules of practice of a few commissions, copies of rate scales, explanations of rate structures, innumerable rules and regulations which carriers and government agencies have published, sample tariffs, many important court decisions, dozens of traffic forms, and an extended discussion of traffic problems and practices, all accompanied by abundant references to leading court and commission decisions. In 1943, the same company published a *Motor Traffic Red Book*, which has not been reissued. Although somewhat out of date, it is still useful.

The Hawkins Publishing Company, in Washington, has published a number of volumes dealing with a variety of traffic practices and problems, including tables of the cases which have been decided by the Interstate Commerce Commission. The Traffic Service Corporation, in Washington, publishes a number of manuals and studies on traffic management.

4. *Periodicals*

The one periodical which no professional traffic manager can afford to do without, and with which all students of traffic management should be familiar, is *Traffic World*, published weekly by the Traffic Service Corporation. For those interested in the technical aspects of transportation, *Railway Age*, published in New York by the Simmons-Boardman Publishing Corporation, is recommended.

CHAPTER I

The Function of the Industrial Traffic Manager

What is traffic management? The word "traffic," like so many words in our language, has a variety of meanings. Of Latin origin, it came down to us through French and Norman parentage, as both a noun and a verb. At first, it was a synonym for trade, barter, or exchange. In Genesis, Joseph promises his brothers the privilege to "traffick" in the land of Egypt. The prophets Jeremiah and Ezekiel both spoke of the rich "traffick" of the ancient city of Tyre.

As time went on, the word "traffic," though retaining its meaning as trade or barter, began to carry the connotation of transportation, and eventually this meaning became tied to it more closely than trade. However, we still meet the word frequently in its original meaning, as when we speak of the "liquor traffic," the "traffic in narcotics," or the "white-slave traffic."

TRAFFIC AS TRANSPORTATION

In its meaning as transportation rather than as trade, the word has diverse uses. It may refer merely to the movement of goods or persons, it may refer to the vehicles by which this movement is accomplished, or it may refer to the persons and things which are moved. When, on our return from a Sunday or holiday excursion in our motorcars, we complain about the "heavy traffic," we are thinking of the large number of vehicles which challenged us for the right of way on the roads; when we speak of "traffic congestion" and of the "traffic problem" of our urban centers, both large and small, we are likewise thinking of the huge number of vehicles which crowd our thoroughfares. But, when we speak of the "traffic cop" who directs the movement of motorcars at highway crossings or of "traffic signals" or of "traffic control," it is not so much the vehicles themselves of which we are thinking as it is their movement, their actual operation. Finally, the word is used frequently to refer to the volume of business which a carrier performs. A railroad's "passenger traffic" is measured by the number of passengers carried or the number of passenger-miles of service performed; similarly, we measure a railroad's "freight traffic" in tons or ton-miles.

It is an interesting fact that carriers in America use the word "traffic" primarily to indicate what is transported, while carriers in European and other foreign nations are more likely to employ the word to indicate movement, or the act of transporting. A "director of traffic" on a European railroad is an official whose primary duty is to supervise the movement of trains. He is an operating man, comparable to a division superintendent or a general manager in this country. The traffic manager on a railroad in the United States is not an operating official and has no duty in connection with train movements. He is concerned with the passengers or goods which the trains carry from place to place. He solicits business for his railroad and makes the rates which the railroad charges for its transportation service. This difference between nations in the use of the word "traffic" is likely to create some confusion in the minds of foreign students making a study of transportation in American schools, unless they are properly enlightened at the beginning of their work.

TWO KINDS OF TRAFFIC MANAGEMENT

When we speak of "traffic management," we are again using an expression which may be said to have a double meaning. This is because we have two kinds of "traffic managers," one representing the carriers who produce transportation and the other representing shippers who consume transportation. The traffic manager of a railroad, motor trucking company, or steamship line is the selling agent of the carrier which employs him. Although he may, and usually does, have other duties, his chief function is to try to obtain the patronage of the shippers whom his employer is able to serve. Because of this, he thinks in terms of the commodity to be hauled rather than of the operation of trains, trucks, or boats by which the service is performed. The very titles given to the traffic manager of a railroad are significant. We have "freight traffic managers" and "passenger traffic managers," and in some of the large railroad systems we find traffic managers or their subordinate agents, whose interests are confined to certain kinds of freight, designated by such titles as "coal traffic manager," "export freight agent," or "foreign freight manager."

A traffic manager who is employed by consumers instead of producers of transportation may represent the interests of a single shipper, or he may represent the interests of a group of shippers or a shippers' organization. A traffic manager who works for an industrial firm is usually called an "industrial traffic manager," while one who represents a group or an organization is usually known as a "commercial traffic manager." In this volume, we are interested primarily in the work of the industrial traffic manager.

THE INDUSTRIAL TRAFFIC MANAGER

The industrial traffic manager is often called a specialized purchasing agent whose function is to buy or otherwise provide transportation services for his employer. This definition is much too narrow, as the industrial traffic manager has many other duties. Broadly speaking, the traffic manager of an industrial or commercial establishment supervises the details of the transportation service, which his plant requires, through all stages of production, beginning with the movement of raw materials and supplies into the plant and ending with the delivery of finished products to their purchasers. A list of the functions of an industrial traffic manager would include as his most important duties:

1. Purchase of transportation
2. Receipt of materials and supplies
3. Shipping products out of the plant
4. Audit of transportation accounts
5. Adjustment and settlement of claims
6. Exercise of rights and privileges under the law

Each of these duties or functions involves numerous activities. We shall discuss each one, in summary form, in this chapter. The remaining chapters are for the most part devoted to an elaboration of these functions and to a discussion of the other duties of the industrial traffic manager. The discussion will be confined almost entirely to domestic commerce, since traffic management in foreign trade, both export and import, is a subject large enough to be worthy of an entirely separate study.[1]

ECONOMIC SIGNIFICANCE OF TRAFFIC MANAGEMENT

It is only within comparatively recent years that industrial traffic management has assumed a position of outstanding importance in the operation of a business enterprise. During most of the nineteenth century, the producers of the United States were engaged primarily in extractive industry, in the exploitation of the soil, the forests, and various subsoil resources. While transportation was necessary to get the products of field, forest, and mine to market, shippers did not have great need for the services of a transportation specialist. Goods were simply turned over to a carrier, who did the rest. Loss and damage claims were likely to be settled in a haphazard fashion, if settled at all, and rates were largely a matter of bargaining—often secret bargaining—between shippers, especially the larger shippers, and carriers. In an industrial plant, a shipping clerk was supposed to be able to take care of the paper work and other duties connected with the plant's transportation service.

With the industrialization of the United States, this situation began to change. An enormous flow of manufactured products began to reach a market that was continental and even world-wide in scope. The competition of rival producers began to result in a closer scrutiny of the costs of

---

[1] The best discussion of traffic management in foreign commerce is to be found in Morris S. Rosenthal, "Techniques of International Trade" (1950).

production; survival in a highly competitive economy became largely a matter of eliminating unnecessary costs and reducing those which could not be avoided. Producers finally made the discovery of a fact, well known to armchair political economists, that there was something more to the process we call "production" than the mere forming or fashioning of raw materials into a consumable article. It was recognized that transportation, too, was a part of the process of production, that what the economists called "place utility" and "time utility" were just as important as "form utility," and often more important. An article is not "produced" until it is in the possession of the ultimate consumer, and the costs of assembling raw materials and distributing finished products are just as much a part of production costs as the cost of manufacturing.

Wide-awake managers of business enterprise came to realize that the proper supervision of transportation service was just as necessary as the adequate supervision of manufacturing processes, accounting, financial operations, or selling. Moreover, it soon became apparent to the successful business manager that the supervision of a plant's transportation service demanded the constant attention of an expert. Thus the traffic manager took his place in business organization beside the production manager, the sales manager, the controller, and the treasurer. The traffic department was added to the older and more familiar departments of the conventional business organization.

RELATION OF TRAFFIC MANAGER TO OTHER DEPARTMENTS

Needless to say, the traffic manager maintains close contact with the managers of other departments of his organization. He advises the purchasing agent and the sales manager concerning the kinds of transportation service available for securing needed supplies and for distributing finished products, and likewise he informs them with regard to transportation costs. He keeps a watchful eye on the transportation services and costs of his employer's competitors, endeavoring to secure the removal of any unfair or unjust advantage which any competitor may have, and safeguarding the competitive position to which his employer is fairly entitled. In cooperation with the production manager, he plans intraplant transportation and keeps a careful watch that the receipt and disposition of freight at the plant are efficiently supervised without waste of time or money.

VARIETY IN MODERN TRANSPORTATION

When industrial traffic management began to assume some degree of importance as a function in business enterprise, the varieties of transportation available in domestic commerce were much fewer than at present. Long-distance commercial transportation, except in limited areas where shippers could take advantage of coastwise shipping or the services of the few carriers operating on inland waterways, both natural and artificial, was a monopoly of the steam railroad. Local transportation—this was before the day of the motor vehicle—was cared for by horse-drawn drays and vans. We still use the term "team track" to designate a certain variety of railroad siding, although today one seldom sees any team near such a track.

Today, a shipper may make use of the steam railroad or of the limited possibilities for water transportation still to be found in the United States, but in addition he has a vast and varied system of highway transportation of comparatively recent growth and a still younger system of transportation by air.

Such has been the development of transportation methods that many shippers find it possible to run and operate their own facilities. Thousands of the motor trucks which speed along our streets and highways are owned by the owners of the commodities which they carry. Not a few industrial concerns have their own airplanes for the carriage of both passengers and freight, though the amount of transportation service rendered by such planes is quite small. There are many shipper-owned barges, tankers, and other boats on our rivers, lakes, and coastal waters. Some large industries run and operate their own little railway systems for intraplant switching. For the most part, however, the owners of transportation facilities are not the owners of the articles transported. Transportation, like nearly all other business functions, is a highly specialized activity, and by far the most of the transportation services of this country are performed for hire by an agency separate and distinct from the shipper.

COMMON AND CONTRACT CARRIERS

The carriers which serve the public for hire are of two kinds, common and contract. A common carrier is one that offers to serve the public in general, to the extent of its ability; a contract carrier affords service only to those shippers with which it has made special contractual arrangements. Our railroads are virtually all common carriers which carry for hire, as are most of our nonprivate water carriers and carriers by air. On the other hand, many motor haulage companies perform contract services. Many of our chain stores employ contract motor carriers for the distribution of merchandise among their various branches. Large quantities of milk and petroleum products and road-building materials are also transported by contract carriers.

It might be said here that regulating bodies have occasionally had difficulty in determining the exact difference between a contract and a common carrier.[2] Contract carriers by motor vehicle and by water are not

[2] In obtaining an understanding of the difficulties involved in distinguishing between a private carrier, a contract carrier, and a common carrier, the following

subject to the detailed regulation to which common carriers by motor vehicle and by water are subjected. It has happened occasionally that certain carriers by motor vehicle have "signed up" a considerable number of shippers, and while their service has purported to be that of a contract carrier, the scale and character of their operations have differed little from those of a common carrier representing itself as willing to serve anyone.

MIDDLEMEN IN TRANSPORTATION

Instead of employing private carriers—facilities owned by the shippers—or dealing directly with carriers for hire, either common or contract, the traffic manager may deal with a middleman, that is, an agency which provides little or no transportation itself but which engages to obtain transportation services for the shippers. The freight forwarder is such an agency, and so is the Railway Express Agency. The student of transportation is usually surprised to discover how extensively middlemen enter into the transportation business, in both domestic and foreign trade. These middlemen employ all types of carriers, both common and contract, operating land, water, and air facilities. Some of them even own and operate transportation facilities of their own.

Another carrier of merchandise which the traffic manager employs today is the government. Our domestic parcel-post service has been in existence since 1913, and we have a very extensive service extending to all corners of the globe. The postal service also cares for the transportation of great quantities of newspapers and periodicals which enter into our second-class mail. In a sense, the postal service also plays the part of a middleman, since the amount of mail transportation performed directly by the government is relatively small, most of the work being done by privately operated common or contract carriers by land, water, and air.

CHOICE OF AGENCY

The important fact to keep in mind is that today the industrial traffic manager has a much wider range of choice than his predecessor had a

---

decisions of the Interstate Commerce Commission, dealing with applications for permits and certificates authorizing motor vehicle operation, will be helpful: N. S. Craig, 28 M.C.C. 629 (1941); Hunter Motor Freight Inc., 27 M.C.C. 51 (1940); George Luck, 27 M.C.C. 283 (1941); Lucy F. Zimmerman, 28 M.C.C. 233 (1941); Ray C. Kline, 26 M.C.C. 741 (1940); Charles Bleich, 27 M.C.C. 9 (1940); McNamee J. Buscher, 32 M.C.C. 485 (1942); Gallagher Transfer and Storage Co., 32 M.C.C. 669 (1942); Casper Werner, 27 M.C.C. 793 (1941); Enterprise Trucking Corporation, 27 M.C.C. 264 (1941); McKown Transportation Co., 42 M.C.C. 792 (1943); Zimmerman Trucking Service, 43 M.C.C. 22 (1943); Overland Freight Lines Inc., 42 M.C.C. 261 (1943); John S. Teeter and Sons Inc., 43 M.C.C. 200 (1944); John Toussaint, 41 M.C.C. 200 (1942); Motor Convoy, Inc., 41 M.C.C. 143 (1942).

half-century ago. The variety of services available gives him a larger opportunity for the practice of efficiency and economy for, like any other agency which buys in an open market, he must exercise judgment in his selection of methods of transportation, his decision being governed by those familiar considerations of quality of service, direct cost of service, and such supplementary costs as may be encountered.

The traffic manager must know many things about the various available services and must base his choice on numerous factors. Is speed the chief consideration? Is safety? Is the service offered given from "door to door," or are deliveries to a carrier and collections from a carrier or his agent separate transactions? To what extent must packing requirements be taken into consideration in determining the total cost of transportation? What about the matter of insurance if he contemplates making use of a carrier by water?

TRAFFIC MANAGER MUST KNOW RATES

Above everything else, however, in his purchase of transportation the traffic manager must know transportation charges, or rates. He must be a good "rate man." There are many reasons for this, but at this point we shall mention only one. The shipper of goods by a common carrier in this country is, in most cases, himself responsible for a knowledge of rates. For example, if a railroad freight agent should, upon inquiry, tell a traffic manager that the rate of transportation for a certain shipment was 50 cents a hundred pounds, and it turned out later that the agent had made an error—that the correct rate was $1.50 a hundred pounds—could the shipper hold the carrier responsible for any loss that might have been incurred because of the incorrect rate quotation? Not at all. The shipper would be obliged to pay the correct rate—in fact, if he refused, the carrier would be forced by law to endeavor to collect it by legal process— and he would have no basis for a claim for damages because of the misinformation. In other words, the shipper is "presumed" to have a knowledge of the rate, since a railroad's schedules of charges are by law matters of "public" information, available to all interested persons. In consequence, nearly all industrial traffic departments keep a complete file of the tariffs in which to find the proper rates for the transportation of the articles in which they have an interest. The alert traffic manager must have a thorough knowledge of the rates on the commodities received and shipped out by his plant, and in addition he should be familiar with the rates which competing plants are required to pay.

RECEIPT OF RAW MATERIALS AND SUPPLIES

One is likely to make the mistake of thinking that the chief concern of the industrial traffic manager is the safe, expeditious, and economical distribution of the products of the business enterprise by which he is employed. Very often, however, the supervision of the movement of incoming materials and supplies may be of just as much importance as directing the movement of outbound traffic. It is the duty of an industrial traffic manager to give shipping instructions with regard to the movement of the commodities which his concern has purchased. These instructions may relate to the type of carrier selected by the vendor and even to the precise carrier to be employed. If more than one carrier is to be employed, the traffic manager may want to indicate the particular carriers which are to share in the movement. It may often be desirable and necessary that specific directions be given with regard to the place of delivery of incoming shipments. The lack of proper "billing" instructions to carriers may frequently result in needless delay and expense at the point of destination.

If an industrial plant has a siding on a particular railroad, it goes without saying that instructions should be given designating that railroad as the delivering carrier. If such instructions are not given, and the goods arrive at destination on another line, time is lost in a switching movement. The necessary switching movement may involve additional transportation expense to the receiver of the shipment. Delivery instructions should often be given even in connection with less carload shipments which a railroad unloads at a freight station. A railroad may have numerous freight stations in a single city. One of these stations may be so near the plant of the consignee that cartage charges between plant and station are comparatively small. But, if incoming shipments are not billed to that particular station, they may be—and usually are—delivered to a station so much farther away that cartage charges make the total transportation costs much heavier.

The selection of the carrier or the route which a traffic manager desires inbound shipments to take may not always be solely a matter of speed or economy. While businessmen are usually reluctant to talk about it freely, what we call "reciprocity" is involved in numerous business transactions. While the practice of mutual accommodation has been subjected to abuse on various occasions, there is no good reason why it should be universally condemned. There is nothing unethical in extending patronage to a carrier or to any other business concern which is the purchaser and user of your own product, if the practice does not involve waste and extravagance and does not mean the extension of special favors and privileges which are forbidden by law or which, though not illegal, nevertheless violate generally accepted codes of business conduct. Mutually advantageous relationships, carefully cultivated and firmly established, are highly useful to any kind of business and may often constitute a substantial portion of that somewhat intangible but highly valuable asset we call good will.

It is the duty of the traffic department to check incoming goods against the copy of the carrier's bill of lading or other shipping documents, to see that articles listed as shipped are actually received. Should there be a shortage, a proper notation made upon the freight bill will greatly facilitate the adjustment of a subsequent claim for loss. All incoming shipments should also be inspected for damage, and if any injury is observed the fact should likewise be noted on the freight bill. In case of concealed loss or damage, which cannot be perceived immediately upon the receipt of a shipment, it is the duty of the traffic manager's staff to secure the affidavits and prepare the documents necessary to substantiate any claim for damage.

For all shipments which are not delivered directly by the carrier, the traffic department must make the necessary arrangements for cartage from the carrier's receiving station, either by the plant's own trucks or by other vehicles or by common or contract carrier vehicles which can be employed to perform local service. Whenever the purchasing department of the plant decides, because of market conditions or for other reasons, to create a stock pile of materials and supplies so much beyond current needs that extra storage space must be found, it is the function of the traffic department to make arrangements for warehousing.

OUTBOUND SHIPMENTS: PACKING

The duties of the traffic department in connection with the shipment of products from a plant are more numerous and varied than the operations relating to inbound movements. The first duty, if the outbound product is a manufactured article, is to see that it is properly packed for shipment. There is no traffic function which has been subjected to more scientific study and research in recent years than the art of packing goods for transportation. It must be understood that "packing for transportation" is not the same as "packaging" for sale to the consumer. The latter function is also highly important, and the traffic manager may often be called into consultation with the sales manager and the production manager to help decide what makes the most suitable retail "container."

Packing for transportation, however, is the task solely of the traffic department. There is probably no other traffic function in which the alert traffic manager has a greater opportunity to save transportation costs and at the same time promote the efficiency of distribution of his plant's products. Proper packing means, first of all, adequate protection for the article to be shipped. But "adequate" protection can be provided in many ways, with wide variations in expense. Variations may arise not only from differences in the costs of containers and other packing materials but also from differences in the costs of transportation, for the container in which an article is shipped is subjected to the same freight rate as the article it contains. It may frequently be found that the saving accomplished by using a cheaper container may be more than offset because of greater transportation costs.

The same type of packing is not necessary for articles carried by different transportation agencies. By and large, goods shipped by railroad require more protection against possible breakage and other damage than goods shipped by other carriers. It is a well-known fact that highway carriers have been able to secure much traffic that was once hauled almost exclusively by rail partly because of the savings shippers are able to make by reason of less expensive packing requirements. Not only may the cost of packing be low, but since less sturdy containers are likely to be of less bulk, their use means that a greater volume of actual freight may be loaded into a vehicle than would be possible if packing materials took up large amounts of space. It is often found that the expense of packing goods shipped in carload quantities is lower than that of the same goods shipped in less carload quantities, because the latter are likely to be subjected to rougher and more frequent handling. Every traffic manager knows, too, that the rates charged by a carrier may vary according to the way shipments are packed. When we come to the study of freight classification, we shall find that many articles are given different ratings when shipped "loose," in "crates," or in "boxes."

The traffic manager whose plant produces articles for sale in foreign countries soon learns that it is wise to become familiar with the packing regulations which foreign governments adopt with regard to imports. He will learn also that in our domestic commerce the packing of "explosives" and many so-called "dangerous articles" is strictly regulated by law.

MARKING

After goods are properly packed for shipment, they must be plainly marked to indicate their point of origin and their intended destination. One of the chief causes of the loss of freight transported by commercial carriers is faulty marking. Despite the detailed rules which all carriers lay down on this subject, hundreds of shipments go astray each year because packages are marked inaccurately, illegibly, or in a fashion which lacks necessary durability. Export shipments must show not only the names and addresses of shipper and consignee but also identifying "symbols," and the same thing is true for domestic shipments carried under an "order" bill of lading.

ORDERING CARS; PRIVATE CARS

The traffic manager of the plant which ships goods in carload quantities has the responsibility of ordering the cars needed for outbound shipments.

If the commodity to be shipped is one whose carload minimum weight varies according to the length of car employed in its transportation, the traffic manager finds that ordering cars for his plant's needs requires more thought and attention than merely telling the railroad agent the number of cars desired and the dates on which they will be needed. Many industrial concerns find it desirable to own at least a part of the freight car equipment they employ, and some plants also lease privately owned freight cars either from car companies or from other shippers. The traffic manager participates in all decisions concerning the purchasing or lease of cars, and it is his duty—often a somewhat complicated one—to supervise the movement of these private cars, keeping them in service as nearly continuously as possible and checking their mileage, both loaded and empty, in order to make financial settlements with the railroads which use the equipment.

SHIPPING PAPERS

Another highly important responsibility of the traffic manager, in connection with outbound shipments, is the preparation of "shipping papers," the most important of which is the "bill of lading." This document, which we shall later study at some length, is the "contract" with the carrier. It is made out in triplicate, an original and two copies. One copy is the "shipping order," which becomes the carrier's original record of a shipment, and a "memorandum" copy is usually sent by the shipper to the consignee of the shipment. The bill of lading is the most important of all shipping documents; needless to say, its preparation requires the highest degree of accuracy. It contains the names and addresses of shipper and consignee, a complete description of the shipment it covers, routing instructions to the carrier, the rate of freight to be paid, the total charges, and a notation to indicate if the charges are "prepaid" or "collect." If the bill is for a carload shipment by rail, it also gives the initials and number of the car in which the shipment is to be transported. In the shipment of many articles of a special character, it may be necessary to make other notations on the face of the bill of lading, and a place is provided on the bill where the shipper may indicate that he is not to be held responsible for freight charges because of the failure of the carrier to collect the charges from the consignee. Bills of lading for ordinary merchandise shipments are of two kinds, "straight" and "order," the latter being "negotiable." We shall discuss the nature of these two kinds of bills in a later chapter and explain the duties and responsibilities under each type.

LOADING INSTRUCTIONS

It is the traffic department which prepares the loading rules and regulations for the direction of the men who work in the shipping room, rules with regard to checking and counting packages and the proper stowage of freight in railroad cars or other vehicles.

TRACING

When a shipment appears to be lost or strayed in transit, the traffic department sets in motion the machinery by which the endeavor is made to locate the missing articles. In times of emergency, when speed and regularity of transportation are matters of great urgency, the "tracing" and "expediting" of freight, to keep it moving steadily toward its destination, may become one of the most pressing duties of an industrial traffic manager.

AUXILIARY TRANSPORTATION SERVICES

Many carriers, and railroads in particular, may offer services in addition to transportation. Among the supplementary services, those which go under the general name of "transit privileges" are the most numerous and most important. Many carload shipments are "diverted" or "reconsigned" in transit. For example, a whole trainload of bananas may start northward from New Orleans without the final destination of a single car being known when the train begins its journey. By the time the train reaches some large freight yard along the way, say in Cairo, the shipper has provided the railroad with instructions for the completion of the journey of each car, and the shipments go to final destination under the "through" rate from New Orleans, and not a rate made by a combination of the sum of the rates from New Orleans to Cairo and from Cairo to final destination. Every day in the year, hundreds of carloads of freight are thus reconsigned. Under such a practice, the movement of traffic is expedited and the total transportation charges kept at a lower level.

There are many other transit privileges, such as "storage-in-transit," "milling-in-transit," "fabrication-in-transit," and "feeding-in-transit." Thousands of bushels of wheat are stored in elevators located at some point between the grain field and the port of export, to be held until orders are received for the movement seaward to be continued. Wheat, oats, corn, and other grains may be stopped at mills to be converted into flour or other products and then shipped on to destination at a single through rate instead of the combination of two rates—one to the milling point and one from milling point to final destination. Logs are converted into lumber in transit, ties and other timbers are subjected in transit to a preservative treatment of creosote; steel bars are sawed, numbered, and bent in transit to prepare them to be members of the framework of a building; cattle, hogs, and other animals are unloaded for fattening before their final journey to the slaughter pens. The carriers sometimes exact a small charge for the transit privilege, but it is much less than the difference between the applicable through rate and the combination based on the transit point. The traffic department of the big flour milling companies and other producers of foodstuffs find that the checking of transit services and the computation of transit rates and charges constitute a large portion of their work. Many industrial concerns, of course, find it necessary to make use of transit privileges only on rare occasions.

INTRAPLANT TRANSPORTATION

The intraplant movement of necessary raw materials and outbound products is usually supervised by the production department, though even in this movement the traffic department may be and often is consulted. It is the business of the traffic department to see that demurrage charges— the penalty charges imposed by a carrier for failure to load or unload cars or other equipment within a specified amount of "free time"—are kept to a minimum. The traffic manager can give advice with respect to the scheduling of loading and unloading operations and can effect the prompt release of empty equipment. Too often, a plant superintendent in charge of production either knows little or nothing about the subject of demurrage or is so intent upon carrying out a certain scheme of plant operation that he forgets that demurrage charges, unnecessarily incurred, may overbalance the savings effected by the adoption of operating methods which do not take into account the desirability of releasing transportation equipment with the least possible delay. There may be many ways in which the traffic manager can bring a greater degree of efficiency and economy into intraplant transportation. After all, the traffic manager is trained to be an expert in the movement of goods, and he should be able to detect wastes of lost motion which are not apparent to less observant eyes.

AUDITING

The auditing or verification of transportation bills is one of the most important duties and responsibilities of the industrial traffic manager. Carriers which serve a plant for hire, bringing in raw materials and supplies and taking finished products away, present bills for their services. These bills must be checked and verified, before payment is made if possible. But if, after payment is made, an error in a freight bill is discovered, its prompt correction must be sought by the traffic department.

In the preparation of freight bills and bills for other transportation services, the clerical forces of carriers for hire have abundant opportunity to make mistakes. They are honest mistakes, indeed, but mistakes nevertheless, and it is the duty of the industrial traffic manager to detect them. The errors which creep into transportation bills arise from many causes. There may be a mistake in the weight, in the classification, or in the rate.

Errors in multiplication and addition are frequently found. In the traffic department of a plant which handles thousands of shipments in the course of a month, the work of auditing freight bills may be heavy enough to require the constant attention of several clerks, who must be familiar with transportation rates and practices and must also be accurate accountants.

In some establishments, the work of auditing freight bills is not done by the traffic department but is turned over to an outside agency, known generally as a freight auditing bureau, which checks freight bills and recovers overcharges, either on a straight fee basis or for a percentage of the overcharges it is able to collect from carriers. The traffic department of one of the large American mail-order houses makes a practice of auditing only those transportation bills which amount to $5 or more. All bills for amounts less than $5 are audited by an independent freight bureau.

OVERCHARGE CLAIMS

The Interstate Commerce Act provides for a limitation of the time in which claims for overcharges on interstate shipments may be presented to carriers or complaints to the Interstate Commerce Commission or suits at law may be filed for their recovery. In general, the claim must be made or the complaint or suit filed within two years after the cause of action occurs, but if a claim is filed with the carrier within the two-year period, the period in which the shipper may file suit for recovery is extended to include six months after the carrier has given notice in writing of a disallowance of the claim or any part thereof. The shipper is thereby protected against "stalling" tactics on the part of a carrier.

LOSS AND DAMAGE CLAIMS

In a later chapter we shall discuss at length the liability of different types of carriers for the shipments which are entrusted to their care. In the case of land carriers, this liability is almost that of an insurer; the liability of a carrier by water is not nearly so great as that of a carrier by land; and the liability of a carrier by air has not yet been defined by statute. Railroads and motor carriers are responsible to the shipper for the full amount of the loss the shipper may sustain if freight is lost or damaged, except under a few certain conditions. It goes without saying that in handling millions of shipments these carriers may lose some of them by theft, fire, flood, or misadventure, and likewise many shipments are damaged, often so greatly as to destroy their entire value.

It is the duty of a traffic department to prepare and present to carriers claims for redress because of lost or damaged shipments. Each claim must be supported by adequate proof that the shipment in question was actually made and by proper evidence with reference to the amount of the loss incurred by reason of the carrier's failure to perform its contractual duty. It is also the duty of the traffic department to see that shipments turned over to a carrier by water are properly insured against risks and losses for which the carrier itself is not responsible.

The amount of claim work which an industrial traffic department has to do will depend in a large measure on the type of commodity shipped. Losses on crude raw materials or heavy semifinished manufactures are not likely to be numerous. But on many kinds of manufactured products and retail merchandise, especially those often shipped in comparatively small quantities or packaged in fragile containers, such as cigarettes and tobacco, liquors, glass-enclosed fruit and vegetable products, drugs, and cameras, the number of claims for loss and damage is likely to be fairly large. Some articles are more likely to be subject to pilferage than others; some articles are more susceptible to breakage than others.

CLAIMS FOR DAMAGES DUE TO DELAY

Carriers are liable not only for loss or damage of a physical nature. They are also liable for unreasonable delay in the transportation of property entrusted to their care. Many products are "perishable," especially products of animals and of horticulture, and if not transported to their destination with reasonable dispatch will become unmarketable because of deterioration and decay. It may occur, too, that while perishable products arrive at destination in good condition, they have been unreasonably delayed so long that when they finally reach the market the shipper is compelled, because of a fall in price, to accept a much smaller amount of money for his shipment than he would have received had the shipment been forwarded with reasonable promptness and dispatch. For a loss of this kind, too, the carriers are responsible.

LIMITATION

Claims arising from loss and damage, like claims because of alleged overcharges, are subject to limitation with respect to time. Claims for loss or damage suffered by interstate shipments must be filed within nine months after goods have reached destination or within nine months after a reasonable time for their arrival has elapsed. A suit at law for recovery on any claim must be filed within two years and one day after the carrier with which the claim was filed has disallowed the claim in writing either in whole or in part.

There are many other legal rules and regulations with respect to lost or damaged freight, some of them derived from the common law and some imposed by statutory enactment. These rules will be discussed at length in a subsequent chapter.

LEGAL OBLIGATIONS OF SHIPPER AND CARRIER

It has already been indicated that there are numerous laws dealing with the various relationships between shippers and carriers. Over the years, it has been recognized that both shippers and carriers should be subjected to certain legal restrictions, that both have certain duties and obligations which, for the proper conduct of the transportation service, should be defined by law. Clearly, it is incumbent upon the industrial traffic manager to know his own rights, obligations, and privileges under the law, and it is equally important that he should have a comprehensive knowledge of the duties and obligations which the carriers have toward the shipper of which he is the duly qualified representative. The traffic manager who understands the nature of the legal relations between shippers and carriers is in a position at all times to guard with confidence the interests of his employer, and he is not likely to become involved in expensive, fruitless controversies.

It is chiefly in the Interstate Commerce Act that one finds defined the legal rights and duties of shippers and carriers in their business relations. It occasionally becomes necessary for a shipper to appeal to the Interstate Commerce Commission to obtain remedial action if his rights have been violated in the past, and to secure the proper observation of his rights for the future.

APPEARANCE BEFORE INTERSTATE COMMERCE COMMISSION

Though persons who represent complainants before the Interstate Commerce Commission are required to possess certain qualifications and pass certain tests before being authorized to practice before that body, they are not required to have the legal training which is required of lawyers who represent clients before our courts of justice, both state and Federal. Some of the best known and most successful practitioners before the Commission are industrial traffic managers who have had little formal legal education. Members of the legal profession, desirous of securing the exclusive right to represent complainants before the Interstate Commerce Commission, as well as before various other government bodies, have tried on various occasions to induce Congress to enact a statute to give them what amounts to a monopoly of such practice. Fortunately, Congress has not yielded yet to these importunities. There is no reason why a qualified industrial traffic manager cannot represent a shipper before the Commission as well as a member of the bar of state or Federal courts. In fact, there is every reason to believe that an experienced traffic manager has training and technical knowledge which enable him to represent a shipper more competently than the average lawyer, whose activities call him into so many fields remote from the intricacies of traffic procedure and practice. Moreover, to require a shipper to employ a lawyer to represent him in all cases before the Interstate Commerce Commission would entail much additional expense, for inevitably the lawyer would have to rely upon the knowledge and experience of the traffic manager. A law which would give lawyers a monopoly of practice before the Interstate Commerce Commission would doubtless inure to the financial benefit of the legal profession, but it is difficult to see how such a law could benefit shippers, serve the public interest, or promote the cause of justice.

A good industrial traffic manager should know when he has just reason to lodge a complaint before the Interstate Commerce Commission because some carrier has been guilty of an infraction of the Interstate Commerce Act. He should be able to file the complaint properly, set forth his evidence expeditiously and clearly before the examiner or commissioner who hears the case, prepare a brief in support of his contentions, and, if necessary, make an oral argument. There are many industrial traffic managers who regard their practice before the Interstate Commerce Commission as a regular, and indeed a most interesting and important, part of their work.

ORGANIZATION OF INDUSTRIAL TRAFFIC DEPARTMENTS

The organization of an industrial traffic department depends, first of all, upon the size of the plant which the department serves and the volume of work which the department is required to perform. There are thousands of business establishments in the United States in which the entire organization is centered in a single individual, who contains within himself the duties of production, purchasing, selling, accounting, financing, and traffic management. Then there are thousands of "small business enterprises" in which these various functions are divided among several individuals, many of them having one or more helpers. In such a concern, the traffic manager often does all of the traffic work—rates, claims, receipt of goods, shipping of goods, preparation of documents, and auditing. But there are many plants in which the traffic work, like the work of other departments, is entirely too voluminous for a single person to perform, and there are numerous huge industrial and commercial establishments in which the traffic department alone, as well as each of the conventional departments, is much larger than the entire organization of the small business establishment.

In those plants where the traffic department has a great amount of detailed work to do, the department must be organized and the work divided among many individuals, just as the work of producing, selling, or accounting must be divided and subdivided. The exact form of organization which the large traffic department must adopt depends upon the character of the work to be done. In one department, it may be that freight claims demand the attention of a staff of workers, in another the matter of freight claims may be of minimum importance. The same situation holds with respect to other functions, such as rates, auditing, preparation of documents, and maintenance of records and accounts.[3]

It follows that there can be no "typical" organization for the traffic department of a particular business enterprise to follow. The functions which a traffic department should fulfill are the same for all business concerns, but because of the wide variations in the character of the work to be performed there must inevitably be variations of departmental organization.

Of course the traffic manager is the head of the department. Sometimes there are huge corporations which operate many plants scattered hither and yon over the country. It may be that such a corporation has a "general traffic manager," who supervises the traffic work of the entire business, and a traffic "manager" for each individual plant. But the traffic manager is the head of the organization which has charge of transportation services. Under his supervision are subordinate officials and employees who conduct the traffic department's different duties. A division of duties which is found in many traffic departments gives rise to the following subdivisions: rates, claims, billing, shipping, accounts, and records. Each of the divisions may be subdivided in turn. There may be two claims divisions, one dealing with overcharge and another with loss and damage. In the rates division, one group of employees may work with rates on outbound shipments and another group with rates on incoming freight. The shipping department may have one force of men who work exclusively with outbound movements and another which confines its work to the proper receipt of incoming shipments. The organization chart of such a traffic department can be easily constructed, as well as the charts for traffic department organizations in which the division of traffic functions follows a different pattern.

TRAFFIC MANAGEMENT AS A PROFESSION

Though industrial traffic management is a recognized profession and those who engage in it should have professional training, it does not have the status which attaches to such well-known professions as law, medicine, and public accounting. There are no laws which define the qualifications or prescribe an educational and training program for those who would become traffic managers, and there is no law which requires a person to

[3] A function of many traffic departments, which has not been discussed here because it has nothing to do directly with the movement of goods, is the purchase of passenger tickets and the making of hotel and train reservations for officers and employees who find it necessary to travel on company business. To this chore is added, in some traffic departments, the task of procuring tickets for theatrical performances and sporting events for the use of out-of-town officers, employees, and guests.

be duly licensed, after proper examination, in order to enter the profession and call himself a "traffic manager." In some states, attempts have occasionally been made to secure the enactment of statutes for the licensing of traffic managers and for prescribing a course of study and practical training which must be followed before taking the examination for a license, but so far no such statutes have been enacted.

Perhaps the chief reason for the lack of statutory regulation is that the great majority of traffic managers are in the private employment of individual business concerns. Lawyers, doctors, and certified public accountants, for the most part, serve the public at large, and it has been thought necessary, in the public interest, to take such precautions that only duly qualified persons are authorized to follow a professional career in these fields of activity. There are many accountants, privately employed, who are not certified and licensed, many people act as their own doctors—often to their sorrow—and all good businessmen should have a sufficient knowledge of business law to know when they need a practicing lawyer—as well as to know if the one they have is competent. But the doctors and lawyers whose office doors are open to all patients and clients are engaging in a public activity, as it were, and have consequently been subjected to a certain degree of public control and regulation.

There is, it is true, a large number of consulting traffic managers who work for numerous clients, both private and public. But the number is small compared with the number of traffic managers privately employed by individual business firms; so far, at least, the work of the public or consulting traffic managers has not been such as to create any public demand that they be duly licensed to practice their profession. What little demand has been made for statutory regulation in connection with the profession of traffic management has come almost entirely from professional traffic managers themselves, who, like the members of labor unions and other exclusive groups, are not averse to some limitation of competition in their particular field of employment. It should be noted that doctors, lawyers, certified accountants, and members of other professional groups have also been active in endeavors to limit competition, by requiring more extensive training and by imposing more rigorous tests, but the chief source of the demand for the licensing of professional groups has been the public at large, for the protection of public interest.

Undoubtedly, it would be advantageous in some respects if the profession of traffic management received legal recognition and its public practice were subjected to some degree of regulation. In the first place, it would serve to emphasize, to those persons who desire to become traffic managers, the necessity of securing adequate training in order to become proficient. Even traffic managers in private employment would endeavor to secure certificates or licenses, as evidence of their ability, just as many accountants endeavor to obtain certification although their activities are confined to teaching or to private employment. The certificate or license is a badge of proficiency.

Moreover, the licensing of traffic managers would result in raising the level of ability among all members of the traffic profession, including those who are engaged only in private employment. Unhappily, the general managers of many business establishments do not know if the traffic managers they employ are entirely competent to perform the duties which go with their position. Traffic management is a highly specialized, extremely technical field of work, and many general managers of business enterprises large enough to employ traffic managers are not sufficiently acquainted with the functions of traffic management, or with the possibilities of the economy and efficiency which first-class traffic management could add to the operation of a business enterprise, to know whether their own firms are being adequately served by their traffic departments. The real answer to this difficulty is that every general manager of an enterprise should know as much about traffic management as he knows about law, accounting, finance, and production. Unfortunately, however, the study of transportation is required in a very few colleges of business administration, and the great majority of top executives in our business world—though not all of them, by any means—have had little actual contact with traffic work. They must take their traffic managers on trust and hope that they are efficient and competent, but the only way of checking on their ability is to call in an outside consultant, a procedure which many executives are reluctant to adopt. In employing as head of a traffic department only a duly licensed traffic manager, a business executive would have some degree of assurance that the transportation problems of his enterprise would receive expert attention.

Another advantage which would come from the statutory professionalization of traffic management is that the traffic work of all business enterprises would be handled with a greater measure of skill and competence. It is a somewhat disturbing fact to learn that a great many business leaders and executives in American enterprise seem to have a rather low opinion of the importance of traffic management and confine the activities of their traffic departments, if they have any, to conducting only a small part of the duties which should belong to a traffic manager. One large American corporation, for example, permits its traffic department to do nothing beyond checking freight rates and auditing freight bills. Packing, marking, ordering cars, tracing, claim adjustments, and other traffic duties are scattered among other departments. The wise executive understands that traffic management has to do with transportation, with the *movement* of goods, and that every phase of this highly important part of the process of production should receive the close supervision of a trained and experienced specialist. A wider recognition of the importance of traffic management would undoubtedly tend to raise the level of competence among those who choose this profession as a career. At the same time, it would ensure that the transportation services of business as a whole would be conducted with a higher degree of efficiency and economy.

REMUNERATION

Because of the wide variation to be found in the character of the work assigned to traffic departments, the remuneration of traffic managers varies greatly. The traffic man who has complete charge of the transportation services of his plant, who really performs all the work that is a part of traffic management, is regarded as an executive holding rank equal with that of the sales manager, the controller, the purchasing agent, or the production manager, and he is compensated accordingly. On the other hand, the traffic manager who, except for his title, is little more than a shipping clerk, and subordinate in his position to the production manager, purchasing agent, or some other official, is not likely to receive a high salary, and moreover is likely to find his position somewhat precarious. Too many business executives are likely to list their subordinate company officers much as items are listed on a balance sheet. Some of them are listed mentally as assets, others as liabilities. The assets include those who seem to bring in money to the enterprise—they are the sales managers and production managers. But accountants, treasurers, and traffic managers are expense items in the business ledger. The nearsighted executive cannot discern any tangible contribution which they make to the enterprise as a whole. They are necessary, of course, to the conduct of the business, but they are a sort of necessary evil, and although indispensable, are often not compensated as well as the officers who are regarded as "producing" members of the organization.

TRAINING FOR TRAFFIC MANAGEMENT

There is a very close similarity between the kind of training required of those persons who become professional traffic managers and those persons who enter such professions as law, accounting, and medicine. One cannot become a traffic manager simply by reading books, taking correspondence-school courses, or studying the subject of traffic management in a university college of business administration, any more than a doctor, lawyer, or accountant can become proficient in his chosen calling by going to school. While education is indispensable, it must be supplemented by practical experience in the world of affairs. Indeed, in most states, doctors, lawyers, and certified public accountants are not permitted to hang out a shingle as practitioners until they have had a specified amount of practical work, in hospitals, offices of practicing lawyers, and accounting firms, respectively. Although in the profession of traffic management there are no statutory rules requiring a minimum amount of practical experience, such experience is indispensable for the person who is ambitious to become a competent traffic manager. It is only by observation, by participation in the actual work of traffic management, by coming into contact with carriers and dealing with the host of problems that arise each day, that the traffic manager can find the essential training he must have. He can and must learn much from books and other printed material, he must read widely and intelligently to keep up with the developments in his chosen field of endeavor, but he must realize that no amount of reading and study can take the place of experience.

The good traffic manager must have an educational background which far transcends the study of traffic alone. He should know the fundamentals of economics, be familiar with the broad principles of accounting, finance, management, and business law, and have a knowledge of the history of his country and of its commercial and industrial geography. He should know something of literature, and by all means he should be able to give expression to his thoughts, either orally or in writing, in language that is clear, concise, and readily intelligible. He should be logical in his thinking and, of course, be able to get along with people, for in the traffic profession he will come into daily contact with persons who are active in many walks of life.

A formal course in traffic management, for which a book such as this serves as a guide or manual, should be preceded by one or more courses in the fundamentals of transportation. The teacher of traffic management in the United States presupposes a certain amount of knowledge on the part of his students. They should be familiar with the history of transportation and should know in a general way how the business of transportation is conducted. They should have a mental picture of the leading transportation facilities of the United States, land, water, and air, and though they cannot be expected to know the name and location of every railroad or truck line, they should be familiar with the names and locations of leading railroad systems, leading highway and air routes, the chief avenues of water transportation, and something of the character, direction, and volume of the great currents of trade which make up the nation's domestic commerce. They should understand what is meant by "government regulation" of the transportation industry. They should know that domestic carriers by land and water—railroads, motor vehicles, carriers by water, pipelines, sleeping car companies, express agencies, and freight forwarders—come under the jurisdiction of the Interstate Commerce Commission whereas carriers by air are subject to regulation by a separate agency, the Civil Aeronautics Board. They should know what are the chief powers and duties of these bureaus, and something of the manner in which their work is accomplished. They should have some acquaintance with the theory of rates and realize that it is a highly specialized portion of the general theory of prices. While all of these topics will be alluded to frequently in this study, they will not be treated with the detail that is employed in beginning general courses in transportation.

The student should know how to make use of a library and be able to look up references to the decisions of courts and commissions and consult other works of reference. He should endeavor to follow, in newspapers and periodicals, all current developments in transportation, whether technical or mechanical changes or new departures in transportation service or in transportation law. A word of warning is needed here. The student must read the accounts of current happenings with discriminating care. Traffic management is a technical subject; unfortunately, many errors creep into the articles about traffic and transportation which are to be found in the pages of most of our newspapers and "popular" business magazines.[4] Many writers make glib use of the vocabulary of traffic management without having adequate knowledge of the meaning of the terms they employ. The thoughtful student will not be misled by technical errors, and in case of doubt will endeavor to check on the accuracy of statements about which he has any question.

[4] For an illustration of some of the misinformation distributed by publishers who should be more careful, see *Newsweek,* Mar. 20, 1950, in which a correspondent is told that "under the Reed-Bulwinkle Act, two or more railroads may set up joint through rates without fear of prosecution under the Sherman Antitrust Act." Not only have railroads never had any reason to fear prosecution under the Sherman Antitrust Act or any other statute, for setting up "joint through rates," but they are informed in the Interstate Commerce Act that it is their "duty" to establish such rates. In case of their refusal to do so, when the Interstate Commerce Commission thinks that the public interest warrants such action, the Commission itself may order such rates to be established and even prescribe the amount of revenue each participant in the joint rate should receive. The Reed-Bulwinkle Act has to do with the establishment of competitive rates. It permits railroads and other carriers, under certain conditions, to enter into price-fixing agreements, which come under the general condemnation of antitrust laws.

CHAPTER II

The Publication and Filing of Rates [1]

In the first chapter, mention was made of the fact that carriers engaged in providing transportation service which crosses state lines are required by law to publish all their rates and charges and file schedules of such rates with the proper governmental agency, either the Interstate Commerce Commission or the Civil Aeronautics Board. These published rates are matters of public information. It was pointed out that the shipper himself is presumed to have a knowledge of the published rate and cannot hold a carrier accountable for damages in case he suffers a loss because the agent of a carrier misquotes a rate.

AUTHORITY OF THE COMMISSION OVER TARIFF PUBLICATION

When the original Act to Regulate Commerce was passed in 1887, it required railroads engaged in interstate commerce to publish and file schedules of rates with the Interstate Commerce Commission, but unfortunately the law did not give the Commission sufficient authority to compel observance of the provisions respecting publication.[2] For many years after the Act was passed, the carriers did pretty much as they pleased in the matter of publishing and filing rates. There was no uniformity in the matter of publishing—some tariffs were vest-pocket size, some were as large

[1] In connection with the study of this chapter, the reader will find it helpful to have at hand a copy of the Interstate Commerce Commission's *Tariff Circular* No. 20, and perhaps a copy of *Tariff Circular* M.F. No. 3. These can be purchased from the Superintendent of Documents, Washington, D.C. The student should also have at hand one or more freight tariffs.

[2] An amendment to the Act to Regulate Commerce, passed in 1889 (25 Stat. L. 855), gave the Commission slightly greater powers in tariff publication than it had had under the original law. However, at that time railroads were required to "post" for public inspection only their local rates. If railroads established joint rates and fares, the tariffs containing them had to be filed with the Commission, but they were made public only to the extent that the Commission thought necessary. Furthermore, until 1906 the Commission was without adequate power to obtain the observance of its orders. Under the Hepburn Amendment of that year, the Commission received full authority over rate publication, and joint rates were required to be published and filed in the same manner as local rates. For the various orders the Commission issued, dealing with the matter of the preparation of tariffs, immediately preceding and following 1906, see *Interstate Commerce Acts Annotated,* Vol. 2, pp. 1469–1471.

as old-fashioned school atlases, some were long rolled sheets, some resembled memorandum pads—and there was as much variation in typographical style as in the size and shape of the publications. Since, however, it was impossible to secure any satisfactory regulation of rates under the law framed in 1887, the confused and confusing methods of rate publication were of relatively small importance. Anyway, it was seldom that a railroad observed its published rates before the enactment of the Elkins Act of 1903. The actual rates charged on most of our railroad traffic were matters of agreement, usually secret, between shippers and carriers; under such conditions, the manner in which rates were published and filed was of little significance to the shipping public.

With the passage of the Hepburn Amendment to the Act to Regulate Commerce in 1906, the publication and filing of rates came under strict control. This amendment at last put teeth into the law, and henceforth railroad rates were to be subject to effective regulation. Moreover, the Interstate Commerce Commission received the authority it needed to make its regulative powers workable, and one feature of this authority was the unqualified right to prescribe the methods which railroads should employ in publishing, posting, and filing their schedules of rates and fares.

As the Interstate Commerce Act was expanded to include provisions for the regulation of express companies, sleeping car companies, pipelines, motor vehicle carriers, water carriers, and freight forwarders, the provisions with respect to the publication and filing of rates were extended to these carriers, too. In this chapter, we shall confine our discussion largely to rail carriers, but it must be borne in mind that the rules applicable to the publication of rates of motor vehicle and other carriers subject to the jurisdiction of the Interstate Commerce Commission are virtually identical with the rules and regulations applicable to railroads. Moreover, the statutory provisions of the Civil Aeronautics Act and the rules of the Civil Aeronautics Board with respect to the publication and filing of rates and fares follow the pattern long ago adopted in connection with rail carriers.

SECTION 6 OF THE INTERSTATE COMMERCE ACT (PART I)

The statutory provisions dealing with the publication of railroad rates are found in section 6, part I, of the Interstate Commerce Act. This section declares in one paragraph that "no carrier, unless otherwise provided by this part, shall engage or participate in the transportation of passengers or property, as defined in this part, unless the rates, fares and charges upon which the same are transported by said carrier have been filed and published in accordance with the provisions of this part." The duty to publish and file is unavoidable. One of the great difficulties which the Interstate Commerce Commission encountered when it began to regulate highway carriers a dozen or more years ago was to "educate" the thousands of operators of motor vehicles, to make them acquainted with the fact that they must obtain proper authorization for operation and must publish and file their charges. The first paragraph of section 6 states:

That every common carrier subject to the provisions of this part shall file with the Commission created by this part and print and keep open to public inspection schedules showing all the rates, fares and charges for transportation between different points on its own route and between points on its own route and points on the route of any other carrier by railroad, by pipe line, or by water, when a through route and joint rate have been established. If no joint rate over the through route has been established, the several carrriers in such through route shall file, print and keep open to public inspection as aforesaid, the separately established rates, fares and charges applied to the through transportation. The schedules printed as aforesaid by any such common carrier shall plainly state the places between which property and passengers will be carried, and shall contain the classification of freight in force, and shall also state separately all terminal charges, storage charges, icing charges, and all other charges which the Commission may require, all privileges or facilities granted or allowed and any rules or regulations which in any wise change, affect, or determine any part of the aggregate of such aforesaid rates, fares, and charges, or the value of the service rendered to the passenger, shipper, or consignee. Such schedules shall be plainly printed in large type, and copies for the use of the public shall be kept posted in two public and conspicuous places in every depot, station or office of such carrier where passengers or freight, respectively, are received for transportation, in such form that they shall be accessible to the public and can be conveniently inspected.

RULES GOVERNING POSTING OF TARIFFS

It was originally the idea of Congress that there should be a public tariff file, open freely to everyone, in each railroad freight and passenger station. It soon became obvious that the proper maintenance of such public files would be impossible, and the law was amended to permit the schedules of charges to be "published, filed and posted in such form and manner as the Commission by regulation shall prescribe." One can observe, in any railroad station, a notice stating that the tariffs containing the rates and fares applicable from that station are on file with the agent and can be consulted upon proper application of interested parties. Moreover, the Commission in a general order governing the posting of tariffs requires carriers to keep at designated points a complete file of all tariffs to which they are parties. There is, of course, a complete file of tariffs in the office of the Interstate Commerce Commission in Washington. The rooms in which the tariffs are filed resemble the large stack rooms of a library.

One of the most important of the changes that have been made in the Interstate Commerce Act since the original law was enacted in 1887 has been the steady enlargement of the discretionary powers of the Interstate Commerce Commission. Its power to "prescribe" the methods for posting, filing, and publishing rates has a parallel power, embodied also in section 6, to permit carriers to file new rates which shall become effective on less than the thirty days' notice which was once mandatory by statute. Very frequently, the Commission permits new rates to become effective on ten or five days' or even one day's notice, if in its opinion the shortening of the statutory period is consonant with the public interest.

The Commission publishes detailed rules which the carriers are obliged to follow in preparing and publishing their tariffs. Before entering on a discussion of these rules, however, it will be well to give some definition and description of the kinds of rates and charges which railroads publish.

RATE PUBLICATION A HUGE TASK

It must be immediately apparent that the publication of rates for a railroad system as large as that of the United States is a monumental task. Our railroads handle thousands of commodities each day, between thousands of stations. On each commodity handled there is a published freight rate applying to its transportation between each freight station and all other freight stations in the country. If all articles carried were charged an identical rate per hundred pounds, the tariff for a single station would have to be as large as a good-sized mail-order catalogue. But instead of one article, there are probably as many as 30,000 for which freight rates must be made. Moreover, a single article may have several rates for the same haul. Usually, when an article is shipped in less carload quantities, the rate is different from the rate applicable to carload shipments of the same article. Again, the same commodity will often have rates which vary according to the condition in which it is shipped (for example, set up or knocked down) or according to the way in which it is offered for shipment (in boxes, in crates, in bundles, or loose). Then there may be many—perhaps several thousand—routes between two freight stations, with rates applicable over each separate route. So it comes about that there are literally millions upon millions of freight rates on the articles which go to make up the huge commerce of the United States. Once in a while a person who is unfamiliar with the complexity and the volume of freight rates asks if he can find a "book" giving the freight charges applicable to railway traffic in the United States, and he is quite surprised when told that instead of a book it takes an entire library to contain all of these rates.

The work which railroads and many other carriers have done over many years to simplify the staggering task of making and publishing rates gave rise long ago to the development of two kinds of rates with respect to articles transported. It is these two kinds we shall discuss first. They are "class rates" and "commodity rates." These are the first purely technical traffic words to be defined in our work, and they are of high importance. They will be followed, of course, by many others.

CLASS RATE DEFINED

A class rate is a rate given to a certain article because it is listed in a particular group, or "class," of articles. The first step in the simplification of rate making and rate publication is the "classification" of freight. The thousands of articles to be transported are divided into a limited number of groups, or classes, and everything in the same class receives the same rate for any particular haul. The principle is the same as that followed in job classification or in the classification of students in a school. The entire purpose of classification, wherever it is employed, is to simplify the process by which large numbers of individual persons or things are dealt with. When a carrier divides some 30,000 articles into, say, ten classes, and provides that all articles in the same class shall be rated alike, the effect is to reduce the number of articles upon which actual rates are named from 30,000 to ten. It is obviously a much easier task to compile a tariff with rates on only ten articles than a tariff giving rates on a vastly greater number.

In the next three chapters, we shall discuss at length the subject of freight classification, its methods, its principles, and how it is carried out in the United States. Here we shall be content with only the definition of a class rate—a rate that is applicable to a group, or class, of articles rather than to a single one.

COMMODITY RATES

While a great many articles of freight are transported subject to class rates, not all freight is so carried. Many articles receive specific rates, applicable to the article as named. These rates are called "commodity rates." While the number of shipments charged class rates is much greater than the number of· shipments that are charged commodity rates for their transportation, the volume of traffic moving under commodity rates is far greater than the volume of traffic moving under class rates. Nearly all of our heavy, bulky raw materials, such as coal, ore, and forest products, and many of our finished heavy manufactured articles, such as iron and steel products and building materials, which usually move in quantity and make up much more than half of the total freight traffic of the United States, are given commodity rates. On the other hand, nearly all less carload shipments and many carload shipments of highly finished manufactured products receive class rates.

While all articles of freight are "classified," and, in the absence of commodity rates, are subject to class rates, whenever an article is given a commodity rate for a certain haul, the commodity rate is the one which must be applied to the shipment, except in a few cases where alternative use of rates is specifically permitted. In other words, commodity rates, with few exceptions, have precedence over class rates. For any particular shipment of freight, there can be only one legal rate. If a carrier were permitted to alternate freely between class and commodity rates, the practice not only would result in much confusion with respect to rates but might give rise to a great deal of unjust discrimination.

LOCAL AND JOINT RATES

Railroad freight rates must also be considered with regard to the roads by which the transportation is performed. Though we have more than seven hundred operating railroads in the United States, these lines are all linked together in one huge railroad system. With only a few exceptions, all of our railroads have a common gauge (4 feet 8½ inches), and the practice of car interchange among the numerous railroads of the country is well-nigh universal. Nearly every freight train one sees on an American railroad is composed of cars belonging to several railroads, giving visible evidence that railroad operation in America is in some respects a joint, cooperative undertaking.

Just as railroads cooperate in the operation of their lines, they also cooperate in rate making. This cooperation has resulted in the emergence of another twofold pattern of rates: local rates and joint rates. A local rate is a rate applicable between stations on a single railroad; a joint rate is a single rate applicable from a station on one railroad to a station on some other railroad. It must be made by voluntary agreement among the railroads concerned, or, lacking such agreement, by order of the Interstate Commerce Commission. Two, three, or even a dozen railroads may be participants in a single joint rate. In other words, there may be one or more "intermediate" roads between the road on which a shipment subject to a joint rate originates and the road having the station of the shipment's final destination.

COMBINATION RATES

Although joint rates are applicable to a vast amount of the joint or interline traffic hauled by American railroads, there are many instances in which connecting railroads do not have these cooperative rates. When no joint rate is available to be applied to an interline shipment, the shipment receives a "combination rate," made by adding together various component rates which cover the route over which the shipment moves. These component rates may be all local rates, all joint rates, or a combination of local and joint rates.

Joint rates and local rates may be either class or commodity rates. Since this is true, it may happen that a combination rate is made up of both class and commodity rates.

Here we come again to another technicality concerning transportation rates. Whenever a joint rate is established on a shipment between any two stations, this joint rate becomes the legally applicable rate, and a combination rate cannot be employed. Even though a combination rate may be found which is lower than the joint rate, the joint rate is the only legally applicable rate. There are some exceptions to this general rule, in situations where the Interstate Commerce Commission has given special permission for a shipper to use a "lower applicable combination rate" than an applicable joint rate, but the exceptions are very few. The existence of a joint rate exceeding the sum of applicable intermediate rates is technically illegal, unless it has been specifically approved by the Interstate Commerce Commission, and it may serve as the basis of a claim for reparation on the part of the shipper who has been required to pay it as well as the basis for a complaint asking for its reduction to an amount not greater than the sum of the intermediate rates.

In the absence of a joint rate, the combination rate to which the shipper is entitled is the "lowest combination" applying over the route of movement of the shipment. When several railroads are employed to transport a shipment to which a combination rate must be applied, it may require considerable study of intermediate rates to find the components which, added together, will produce the lowest combination. Occasionally, a combination rate will be found which includes component rates of several kinds, class and commodity, joint and local.

VALUE OF JOINT RATES TO SHIPPERS

The publication of joint rates in America has been beneficial both to carriers and to shippers. It has simplified the process of rate publication, it has brought about a greater degree of certainty with respect to the exact amount of charges a shipper must pay, and it has led to a lessening of discrimination among shippers. In the development of our transportation service, we have come a long way from the time in which every railroad was operated independently, and traffic passing over the lines of two or more carriers had to be transferred from the vehicles of one carrier to those of another at each junction or point of connection.

The revenues derived from joint rates are divided among the carriers participating in the joint hauls, according to an agreement among the carriers. In times past, carriers have been unable to agree upon the division of joint rates, with the result that joint rates have not been established or existing joint rates have been canceled. The manifest convenience of such rates, however, caused Congress to amend the Interstate Commerce Act in such a way as to give the Interstate Commerce Commission, under certain restrictions, the power to establish joint rates where none were initiated by the voluntary action of the carriers, and even to prescribe the amount of the joint rate to be received by each of the participating carriers.

Ordinarily a joint rate, when established, is lower than any available combination rate, though this is not always true. But it is usually found that carrier rates per mile decrease with the distance of the haul, the decrease arising from the fact that the component of the total rate representing terminal charges is fixed, and as it is "spread" over large distances the average revenue per mile shows a decrease. A freight rate covering a 20-mile haul, for example, will show a much higher average charge per mile than a rate covering a 200-mile haul because, even though the actual charge per mile of haul is the same, the fixed component representing terminal costs is the same for both hauls, and is spread out more thinly for the long haul.

PROPORTIONAL RATES

The commonly accepted belief that the average charge per mile should decrease with distance has resulted in the establishment on many railroads of "proportional" rates. The first thing to be remembered about a proportional rate is that it never stands alone. It is used invariably as a "part" of a combination rate. A proportional rate between two points is invariably lower than the local or joint rate applying to traffic moving only between those same two points. Proportional rates not only serve to reduce the average charge per mile over routes where combination rates are applied, but they are often employed to equalize the competitive positions of rival commercial and industrial centers or the competitive positions of rival railroads serving the same center. For example, the Illinois Central Railroad gives a proportional rate from Chicago to Cairo which is lower than the local rate. The proportional rate applies, however, only as a part of a combination rate on traffic bound for the southeastern part of the United States. This proportional rate is offered to equalize the Illinois Central with the New York Central and other lines which operate between Chicago and Cincinnati and which have, because of the lesser distance, lower local rates between those two cities than the local rate from Chicago to Cairo.

EXPORT AND IMPORT RATES

American railroads have long followed the practice of giving special rates on imported goods and upon goods intended for export, which are lower than the same rates applicable to the same goods produced by our home industries and intended for sale in the domestic market. These rates are really a special kind of proportional rate. They have been justified often, on the theory that the domestic haul of the traffic constitutes only a "part" or a "proportion" of the haul between the domestic point of origin and the foreign port, and consequently the rate to or from shipside should be reduced to bring down somewhat the average charge per mile for the total haul. In other words, the theory of the export and import rate is the same as that which has been applied in the establishment of proportional rates on domestic traffic.

Export and import rates have been employed, too, to equalize the competitive positions of rival seaports, as well as of the railroads serving the different ports. All Atlantic ports except New York and all ports on the Gulf of Mexico have numerous special export and import rates, both class and commodity, to give them a better opportunity to share in handling the nation's foreign trade as well as to give the railroads serving each port a "fair share" of the traffic which makes up the nation's large overseas commerce. New York City, too, has a great many export and import rates, though not so many as the other Atlantic ports. There has at times been much complaint about these special rates—about import rates because they had a tendency to neutralize the effect of tariff duties designed to protect American producers against foreign competition, about export rates because they represented an unfair discrimination against American consumers of American products—but these complaints have never resulted in the elimination of the practice of carriers of giving export and import rates. At one time, Congress made an ill-advised attempt to aid American shipping by providing that special export and import rates should apply only to traffic carried in American flagships, but the confusion and friction which promised to result from such action resulted in the abandonment of this particular method of providing an indirect subsidy for the merchant marine, before it went into operation.

It is necessary for railroads to "police" traffic to which special export rates have been applied and see that it is actually shipped to a foreign destination. Should the shipper of export freight, to which the railroad gives a special rate, change his mind before the traffic is loaded on a ship and decide to sell the shipment in the domestic market, it would be necessary for the railroad collecting the freight charges to see that the shipper paid the applicable domestic rate. One reason for abandoning the plan to apply export and import rates only to traffic carried in American flagships was that it would have added greatly to the "policing" work of the railroads.

THROUGH RATES

The expression "through rate" is frequently employed. To a great many people, a through rate is the same as a joint rate or a combination rate, that is, it is regarded as the total rate applying to interline or "through" traffic. However, the term, according to the Interstate Commerce Commission, has no genuinely technical significance. A through freight rate is simply the total rate from point of origin to point of destination, whether it is a local rate, a joint rate, or a combination of rates.

COLUMN RATES

In many tariffs, rates are published which are certain percentages of other rates, usually of the first-class rate. At one time, it was customary for the railroad agent to perform the arithmetical calculation which would give the exact amount of the rates so published. The Interstate Commerce Commission requires that in tariffs now containing rates which are percentages of other rates, the proper rates shall be given, each rate opposite its given percentage. This practice in rate publication has produced parallel columns of rates, and they are often referred to as "column rates." But they are not a special variety of rate, such as a class rate or commodity rate may be said to be. The term refers only to the method by which the rate is ascertained and published.[3]

SPECIAL SERVICE TARIFFS

Although transportation—the carriage of persons and property—is the chief function of carriers, they also perform other functions for which charges are made, and consequently schedules of such charges must be published and filed. The tariffs in which these schedules are published are usually known as "special service tariffs," and the leading kinds issued by rail carriers are icing and heating (protective service) tariffs, storage, demurrage, wharfage, lighterage, switching, loading, and unloading (terminal service) tariffs, and milling, fabricating, compressing, and reconsigning (transit privilege) tariffs.

WHO PUBLISHES TARIFFS

The various tariffs which contain the schedules of charges which carriers receive for their services are published by the carriers themselves or by duly authorized agents of the carriers. A tariff published by a carrier is known as an "individual tariff," one published by an agent as an "agency tariff."

It is well known that railroads for many years have not competed much in making rates, and in the Reed-Bulwinkle Act of 1948, passed over presidential veto, they were authorized by Congress to cooperate in making competitive rates without being in danger of prosecution under the

[3] The railroads are now publishing class-rate tariffs governed by the new Uniform Classification, which will be described in the immediately ensuing chapters. When this classification comes into general use by all railroads, column rates, as they now exist, will probably disappear, or perhaps it would be better to say that all class rates will be column rates, since all classes except Class 100 are published as percentages of that class. It will be some years before the Uniform Classification becomes applicable throughout the United States.

antitrust laws of the nation. The result of this long cooperation, both before and after it was formally made legal, was that competing railroads, having fairly equal facilities and parallel routes, followed the practice of charging identical rates for services between competitive points. So far as rates were concerned, the shipper's selection of a rail carrier was a matter of indifference.

For a long time, it was customary for each railroad to publish its own schedules of rates. Since this separate publication of many identical rates involved much unnecessary labor and expense, numerous railroad companies eventually joined in issuing single tariffs to which all the companies were parties. A great many of these tariffs are published on behalf of various American railroads, the publication being effected through agents armed with proper authority from each interested carrier. It must be understood that the agent is not authorized to *make* rates for any railroad for which he publishes tariffs. His function is purely that of compilation, publication, and filing. In theory, each railroad makes its own rates, and though numerous railroads "agree" upon what competitive rates shall be, nevertheless each railroad reserves the right of independent action and is not subject to coercion by any other railroad or group of railroads.

There is no uniform rule which railroads follow with regard to who shall publish their tariffs. Many railroads publish their own local rates; many joint tariffs, too, are published by railroads. For the most part, the rates published in agency tariffs are joint rates, but some of these tariffs may also contain local rates.

ICC TARIFF CIRCULARS

It was pointed out previously that the Interstate Commerce Commission strictly supervises the publication of the tariffs of those carriers which are subject to the Commission's jurisdiction. The rules and regulations with respect to tariff publications are issued by the Commission in booklets known as "tariff circulars." The Commission puts out separate circulars for the different kinds of carriers—railroads, motor vehicle operators, water carriers, and freight forwarders—and ordinarily the rules for the publication of passenger fares and freight rates are contained in different circulars.

Even before the passage of the Hepburn Amendment in 1906, the Commission had issued several tariff circulars making various suggestions to railroads as to how their rate schedules should be published. Though these circulars had little effect upon tariff-publishing practice, because the Commission's powers to enforce its orders were sadly deficient, they had a certain measure of educational value, and in a sense prepared the Commission and the railroads, too, for the day when the Commission would have the authority to see that its acts were felt and its words obeyed. The tariff circulars that have appeared since 1906 were issued with the knowledge that the instructions they contained must be observed. Not only are carriers penalized by fines for failing to obey publication and filing instructions given them by the Commission, but the Commission has the right to refuse any tariff that shows a failure of a carrier to comply fully with the rules and regulations which the Commission has promulgated. Since a carrier subject to the Commission's jurisdiction can charge only such rates that are published and filed in accordance with the law, it is not difficult to understand why the Commission's instructions on tariff publication are carefully observed.

TARIFF CIRCULAR NO. 20

The tariff circular containing the "regulations issued by the Interstate Commerce Commission, under authority of section 6, part I of the Interstate Commerce Act, as amended, to govern the construction and filing of freight rate schedules and classifications, and pipe line schedules, by common carriers, as defined in said Act, part I," is known as *Tariff Circular* No. 20. It was first issued in 1928, to succeed *Tariff Circular* No. 18–A. Five "supplements" have been added to the circular since it was first issued, the fifth supplement now containing all changes and additions.[4]

Since *Tariff Circular* No. 20, together with the Commission's administrative rulings governing freight tariffs and rates, constitutes a book of more than a hundred pages, we are not going to discuss all the features of the circular in detail, but only enough to give some idea of its scope and purpose.

It must be remembered that although this circular should be of some interest to the industrial traffic manager, it is compiled and issued primarily for the guidance of those persons in the traffic department of a railroad or other interested carrier, or of tariff-publishing agents, whose duty it is to compile and supervise the publication of the many schedules of rates and other charges which must be filed with the Interstate Commerce Commission.

On the first page of the circular, one finds the definitions of such terms as "local rates," "local tariffs," "joint rates," "joint tariffs," and "through rates."

The first rule of the circular says that all tariffs must be in "book,

[4] The Commission's rules and regulation governing the preparation, construction, and filing of the rates of common carriers by motor vehicle are published in ICC *Tariff Circular* M.F. No. 3. *Tariff Circular* M.F. No. 2 contains instructions for the publication and filing of the charges of contract motor carriers, and M.P. No. 3 shows how the tariffs containing rates for the transportation of passengers and express by motor vehicle should be prepared.

pamphlet or loose-leaf form of size 8 by 11 inches, and must be printed on hard calendered or No. 1 machine finished book paper of durable quality," and type of stipulated sizes must be used. Uniformity in the size of tariffs makes the work of filing much easier, and uniformity in style of construction makes the examination of tariffs a simpler task.

Each tariff must have a bare margin of not less than ⅝ inch at the binding edge. When numerals are shown in tables, pages containing the numerals must be ruled from top to bottom. In all printed tables, there must be a break of at least one space across the page or a ruled line appearing after each sixth line or less.

Certain uniform symbols must be used to indicate changes which have been made in previously published tariffs. The following symbols are prescribed; they can be used in a tariff for no other purpose than that indicated.

- ⁴ to indicate reductions
- ⁺ to denote increases
- ▲ to denote changes in wording which result in neither increases nor reductions in charges
- ● to denote no change in rate
- ⁕ to denote prepay stations or points
- ⁺ to denote intrastate application only
- ▢ to denote reissued matter

The use of symbols to indicate changes in a tariff is a great help to the tariff staff of the Interstate Commerce Commission, who examine all new tariffs submitted for inclusion in the Commission's files. Without the symbols, it would be necessary to compare each new tariff, item by item, with the tariff preceding it, in order to ascertain whether any changes had been made. Likewise, the symbols call the attention of shippers to tariff changes which they might not have observed had they been required to make an actual comparison of old and new tariffs.[5]

The rules regarding the make-up of the title page of a tariff are full and explicit. These rules ensure the uniformity of appearance which facilitates filing, indicating to filing clerks the nature of the tariff, its territorial application, and the carriers or agents who have been responsible for compilation.

TARIFF TITLE PAGE

With a few exceptions, the title page of every tariff and the title page of every supplement to a tariff must contain the following items:

[5] The symbols employed in the tariffs of common carriers by motor vehicle are slightly different from those prescribed for railroad tariffs, and it is permissible in the motor carrier tariffs to use the letters R, A, and C to denote respectively reductions, increases, and changes involving neither reductions nor increases.

1. On upper left-hand corner of tariffs of five pages or less and on tariffs issued in loose-leaf form, the words: "No supplement to this tariff will be issued except for purpose of canceling the tariff unless otherwise specifically authorized by the Commission."

2. ICC number of the tariff or supplement. Immediately thereunder must appear the numbers of the tariffs or supplements canceled. If the number of tariffs or supplements canceled is so large as to make it impracticable to list them on the title page, they must be listed in the body of the tariff, immediately following its table of contents, and a reference to the page where the cancellation notice may be found must be given on the title page.

3. Corporate name of issuing carrier or name of issuing agent or agency.

4. Whether tariff or supplement contains local, joint, proportional, export or import rates, or a combination of the same, and whether the rates are class or commodity or a combination of both.

5. A brief statement indicating the geographical territory, states, or points to which the rates apply.

6. Reference by name and ICC number to the classification, classification exceptions, or other tariff publications, if any, by which the tariff or supplement is governed.

7. Date of issue and effective date.

8. Notice as to authorization, with date, by the Commission for the publication of rates on less than statutory notice, or for the publication of rates which, by permission of the Commission, constitute exceptions to the general rules of the Interstate Commerce Act.

9. Name, title, and address of the officer or agent by whom the tariff or supplement is issued.

BODY OF TARIFF

Tariff Circular No. 20 contains the same explicit instructions regarding the construction of the body of a tariff or supplement as it does concerning the form and content of the title page. In the body there must be, among other things, a table of contents, the names of participating carriers, a complete index of articles upon which commodity rates are named, with cross references to other commodity tariffs, an alphabetical index of names of stations "from which" rates apply and a similar index of stations "to which" rates apply, an explanation of symbols, reference marks, and abbreviations employed, a list of any exceptions to the governing classification, "such explanatory statements in clear and explicit terms regarding rates and rules contained in the tariff as may be necessary to remove all doubt as to their proper application," and, most important of all, "an explicit statement of the rates, in cents or in dollars and cents, per 100 pounds, per ton, per car, or other unit, together with the names or designation of the places from and to which they apply, all arranged in a simple and systematic manner."

TARIFF COMPLEXITY

There are many shippers and traffic experts who are inclined to believe that the Commission has not yet reached the goal it sought when it required an "explicit statement" of rates. It must be admitted that a great many of the bulky tariffs which railroads and other carriers issue, however "systematic" they may be, can scarcely be characterized as "simple." On the other hand, there has been steady progress in simplification, as well as in systematization.[6] At least the modern tariff is not like so many of those published almost a half-century ago, which permitted favored shippers who were "in the know" to take advantage of obscure and subtly concealed provisions enabling them to obtain rates which were substantially lower than the rates which the public at large was required to pay.

One reason, of course, for the complexity and volume of many tariffs is the fact that we have so many railroad systems in the United States. A huge joint tariff participated in by three or four hundred carriers is likely to have so many special rules, routing instructions, and exceptions that the mere mass of detail they contain confuses and bewilders the novice in traffic management. Should the railroads of the United States ever be consolidated into a few systems or into a single system, the construction of rates and the calculation, compilation, and publication of rate schedules could be very greatly simplified.

CONCURRENCES

In times past, there was much difficulty over the publication of joint rates. Railroads were once accustomed to publish joint rates applying over their own lines and the lines of other carriers without obtaining the consent of the other carriers. This practice caused confusion and uncertainty, and at the same time opened the door for much unreasonable discrimination. The Hepburn Amendment of 1906 provided that

[6] On Aug. 3, 1951, it was announced that because of the mounting concern of the chief railroad traffic officials of America over the increasing complexity of freight tariffs, as well as because of the growing difficulties which shippers' representatives had in interpreting tariffs, the railroads had appointed a Railroad Research Group on Freight Tariffs. This group, with headquarters in Washington, has the function of recommending ways in which tariffs may be published in more readily understandable form. The leading shippers' organization of the United States, the National Industrial Traffic League, heartily endorsed the action of the railroads, and has appointed committees to cooperate with the Research Group. See *Traffic World*, Aug. 4, 1951, p. 17.

. . . the names of the several carriers which are parties thereto, other than the one filing the same, shall file with the Commission such evidence of concurrence therein or acceptance thereof as may be required or approved by the Commission, and where such evidence of concurrence or acceptance is filed it shall not be necessary for the carriers filing the same to also file copies of the tariffs in which they are named as parties.

Tariff Circular No. 20 gives the various forms of concurrence used by connecting carriers to signify their acceptance of rates published and filed for them by another carrier. These concurrences differ in the extent of the authority conferred. There are separate concurrence forms which railroads give to tariff-publishing agents, corresponding in scope and content to the concurrences running from railroad to railroad. The circular also gives a form of power of attorney which a railroad gives to the agent authorized to publish its tariffs.

A joint tariff contains the ICC numbers of the concurrences which have been filed with the Commission covering that particular tariff. An agency tariff lists not only concurrences but also the powers of attorney which interested railroads have executed.

There is nothing to prevent a railroad from filing a tariff which shows another railroad as a party even though proper authority has not been obtained. If this is done, the nonconcurring carrier receives its full lawful rate for its part of any joint haul; the shipper is "protected" in the rate; and the loss of revenue, if any, falls upon the filing carrier, which is also required to correct its error either by cancellation of the unauthorized rate or by securing proper authorization.

The circular makes provision for the cancellation of concurrences in those cases where railroads disagree upon the division of revenue or other matters. A concurrence can be canceled, however, only upon sixty days' notice, giving the filing carrier time to provide substitute rates within the statutory limit of thirty days.

ADVANTAGES OF JOINT RATES ON INTERLINE TRAFFIC

One of the very great advantages which shippers derive from joint rates should be mentioned once more. It is a single rate from point of origin to destination, regardless of the number of carriers which participate in the haul. No separate charges must be imposed upon either a carload or a less carload shipment when it is transferred from the rails of one participating carrier to those of another. Even if one of those carriers performs only what is known as an "intermediate switching" service, that is, transfers a shipment from the line of one railroad to the line of another, and takes no part in the line haul itself, the joint transportation rate covers this switching movement. *Tariff Circular* No. 20 is very clear on this matter. One of the rules (9c) has the following to say:

A joint through rate from a point on the line of one carrier to a point on the line of another carrier includes switching, drayage, or other transfer service at intermediate interchange points, and no part of such charges may be added to the joint rate on shipments handled through and not stopped for special services at such intermediate interchange points. Carriers performing intermediate switching services in connection with joint rates should be shown as participating carriers in the joint rate; but if this is not done, the carrier performing the switching service must have on file with the commission a tariff naming its charges for the intermediate switching service and the line-haul carriers parties to the joint rate must file tariffs providing for the payment of all such charges to the switching road.

The rule goes on to say that a tariff containing joint rates must carry a statement to the effect that all transfer charges are covered by the joint rates.

A combination rate may include one or more switching charges, for either direct or intermediate switching, as component parts of the total combination. Such charges must be published and filed, of course, just as all other charges which a carrier makes for its services.

TARIFF SUPPLEMENTS

Nearly all tariffs of rates and charges, as well as freight classifications, are changed many times before they are canceled by the issuance of a new tariff or classification. Such changes are made in supplements to the currently effective tariff, and these supplements are constructed and filed in much the same way that tariffs themselves are made and filed. It may be that several dozen supplements are printed and filed before a new tariff is issued. Supplements are numbered consecutively. Since it would manifestly be burdensome upon the shipper to have to consult a large number of supplements in order to find out whether any changes had been made in the original schedules, the Commission limits the number of supplements which can be in effect at any one time. When a new supplement is to be filed which would go beyond the permissible number, it must repeat the changes carried in one or more of the preceding supplements, and the supplements whose material is repeated are canceled. Each supplement contains a notice on its title page indicating the numbers of the supplements which are in effect. *Tariff Circular* No. 20 contains complete directions regarding the compilation and filing of supplements. There is a limit, too, to the amount of material which can be included in the supplements to a single tariff; when this limit is reached, no more supplements can be filed, and if further changes must be made the tariff must be reissued.

CONCLUSION

The foregoing brief discussion of the rules of tariff publication is enough to indicate that the Interstate Commerce Commission has endeavored to fulfill adequately its function to see that rates are properly published and filed in accordance with the law. The many regulations which the Commission has imposed, while they may seem complicated and in some respects onerous, have done much to simplify and facilitate the Commission's work of rate regulation, and they have also served to give the shipping public a larger measure of protection against the arbitrary, unreasonable, and unduly discriminating practices to which at one time it was unjustly subjected.

CHAPTER III

Freight Classification [1]

Freight classification, as we have said before, is the process of dividing articles of freight into a limited number of groups, or classes, for the purpose of simplifying the task of making freight rates. All articles in the same class are charged alike for their transportation, that is, for identical hauls. In other words, the rates are made upon the various classes instead of upon the individual articles, and the rate which a particular article pays is the rate which is applicable to its class.

The various classes are usually, though not invariably, designated by number or by letter, and it is customary in the United States for railroads to apply higher rates to the classes having higher numbers or letters. That is, first-class rates are higher than second-class rates, Class 90 rates higher than Class 40 rates, Class A rates higher than Class B rates, and so on. [2]

A classification book contains, primarily, a long list of articles and indicates the class to which each article belongs. A modern freight classification contains other information, which will be discussed later, but the original and still the chief purpose of a freight classification is to list various articles of freight to be transported and assign them to their respective groups.

DEVELOPMENT OF CLASSIFICATION

The classification of freight for the purpose of simplifying the process of making and quoting transportation rates did not begin with the steam railroad. Many early canal transportation companies and wagoners had a primitive method of classifying the articles which they carried into sepa-

---

[1] The student should, if possible, have copies of the Consolidated Freight Classification and the Uniform Freight Classification for use in connection with this chapter. A copy of a classification that has been superseded and canceled may be used, though the classification currently in effect would be more satisfactory. Both current classification books may be purchased from the Consolidated Classification Committee, 202 Chicago Union Station, Chicago 6.

[2] It should be noted that there is a distinction in meaning between the word "rating" and the word "rate." A rating indicates the class to which an article belongs; it is a classification term. A rate is the amount of the freight charge applicable to a shipment; it is given in cents or in dollars and cents per hundredweight, ton, or other unit. These words must not be confused.

rate groups, with a rate applicable to each class or group. The first railroads merely continued the practice which their predecessors had adopted, though in time they developed a much more elaborate and comprehensive system of classification.

Originally, it was customary for each railroad to make and publish its own classification. The number of classes was small, usually not more than four, and the number of articles actually listed in the classification, though larger than the number which had been listed by canal companies and teamsters, was comparatively small. All articles not listed in the classification, if offered for transportation, were lumped into one class, usually the first, which carried the highest rate, or were given specific rates, corresponding to our modern commodity rates.

Sometimes the freight classifications of the early American railroads were included in the annual reports of their presidents. The annual reports of the president of the Pennsylvania Railroad, for example, during the early 1850's included a copy of the freight classification which that road employed in making rates on its lines between Harrisburg and Pittsburgh.

As the American railroad net grew and the number of railroads serving common points increased, it became apparent that the publication of separate classifications involved much duplication of effort. As the railroads sought, by means of rate agreements, pools, and other devices, to eliminate strenuous competition among themselves, they came to see that one method by which they could bring about a greater degree of equality among the rates charged over competing routes was to adopt and use a common freight classification. Consequently, between 1885 and 1888, the railroads of the East, the South, and the West joined in making common classifications in their respective territories. Thus the three "classification territories," which we still have, came into existence: the Official (or Eastern) Territory, the Southern, and the Western.

CLASSIFICATION TERRITORIES

The Official Classification Territory lies north of the Ohio and James Rivers between the Atlantic seaboard, the Great Lakes, and a line extending in a southwesterly direction from Chicago to St. Louis. The Southern Classification Territory lies in the region south of Official Territory and east of the Mississippi River; the Western Classification Territory occupies all that great stretch of country lying west of the other two territories.

For many years the classifications of the three territories were published in separate volumes. When the Federal government was operating the railroads of the United States during the First World War, the Director General of the railroad administration ordered the publication of all three classifications in a single volume, which was known as the Consolidated Freight Classification. When the railroads were returned to their owners, the practice of publishing the three classifications in one volume was continued. The classification has been issued twenty times since 1918. The current issue—Consolidated Freight Classification No. 20—contains Official Classification No. 64, Southern Classification No. 63, and Western Classification No. 75. It became effective October 15, 1951.

THE ILLINOIS CLASSIFICATION

The three major classifications for a long time applied primarily to interstate traffic, though they were also used for much intrastate traffic. In addition to the major classifications, there were at one time many state classifications. Most of these classifications have long since been discontinued. One of them, however, the Illinois Classification, still remains. Since 1933, it has been published with the three major classifications, so that the Consolidated Classification now contains, in addition to the Official, Southern, and Western Classifications, Illinois Classification No. 28.

THE PROBLEM OF UNIFORM CLASSIFICATION

The question arises very naturally why we have three or more freight classifications for American railroad freight traffic. Why not have a single uniform classification for all our railroads? France, Great Britain, Canada, and many other countries have single, uniform classifications.

In order to understand why uniformity of classification has not yet been attained here, it is necessary to keep in mind that classification of freight does not have so much to do with the actual freight rates which railroads charge as it has to do with *relative* freight rates. The classification contains no freight rates; class rates are found in the various class-rate tariffs which railroads or their agents publish.

Although there is much similarity in the traffic of the three major classification territories, there is also much diversity. Many articles which constitute a highly important part of the freight hauled in one territory may not be so important in the other two. The purpose of classification is to put into a single class or group, as nearly as may be, the articles which are alike from a transportation standpoint. It can readily be seen that two articles which may be regarded as sufficiently similar from a transportation standpoint to be put in the same class in Official Territory may be regarded in Southern Territory as sufficiently dissimilar to justify putting them in different classes. A study of the Consolidated Classification will show that by far the most of the articles classified are grouped in the same fashion in the different territories, but we will also find that there is much divergence of treatment.

The combination of the three classifications into a single volume, though it did not produce uniformity of grouping, did produce uniformity in other respects. The "descriptions" of all articles listed became uniform, so that it was no longer necessary, as once it had been, to give two descriptions of a shipment in the same bill of lading in order to obtain the proper rate on one article which bore a combination of class rates governed by two separate classifications. Moreover, the "rules" of the classification, which we will discuss in some detail later, were made almost completely the same for all territories. In other words, the Consolidated Classification represented a long step toward uniformity, even if it did not go all the way.

PROGRESS TOWARD UNIFORMITY

The railroads of the country have cooperated sincerely with one another in an effort to secure a higher degree of classification uniformity, but the consensus of opinion among railroad officials for many years was that complete uniformity was undesirable, if not unattainable. The Interstate Commerce Commission, however, had other ideas on the subject. For a long time, it cooperated with the carriers in the effort to reach uniformity, and it finally took the position that complete uniformity was entirely feasible. Finally, in 1945, the Commission, in the Class Rate Investigation case decided that year, ordered the railroads to proceed forthwith to prepare for publication a uniform freight classification to be used throughout the United States.[3] Representatives of the carriers began to work assiduously on the project, but as may be imagined, they found that there were many differences of opinion among shippers and carriers which they had to try to iron out before an even partially satisfactory uniform freight classification could be prepared. However, they made enough progress in the course of some five years so that the Commission thought it should establish a deadline for the completion of the task. Accordingly, on July 31, 1951, the Commission issued an order directing that the new classification be completed and filed within four months.[4] Although the

[3] Class Rate Investigation, 1939, 262 I.C.C. 447–766 (1945). This voluminous decision not only decides an important controversy, but it deals at length with the whole subject of freight classification in the United States, its history, principles, and practices. The Commission has handed down many decisions on classification matters, but this one probably gives a more elaborate discussion of the various phases of classification procedure than any of the others.

[4] The Commission's order was modified in some particulars in supplementary proceedings. 264 I.C.C. 41 (1945); 268 I.C.C. 577 (1947); 281 I.C.C. 213 (1951); 281 I.C.C. 329 (1951). The order issued on July 31, 1951, made a few modifications, but its purpose was primarily to bring the long-drawn-out investigation with respect to uniform classification to an end, as well as to settle finally the controversy which had arisen because of differences in the class rates of the three classification territories.

officials in charge of preparing the uniform classification had to secure an extension of time, the work was finally finished. On February 1, 1952, Uniform Freight Classification No. 1 was issued, to become effective on May 30, 1952. For the time being, class rates governed by the new classification are to be published only for the territory east of the Rocky Mountains. Class rates in the region of the Far West are still under investigation by the Commission; until this investigation is completed, all class rates in that area will still be subject to the Consolidated Classification.

But even in the eastern region, it will take some time to have the Consolidated Classification entirely replaced by the new Uniform Classification. Some new class tariffs were published and filed at the same time that the new classification was made public, but they do not apply universally throughout the eastern region.

This means that for a time, at least, the two classifications must exist together. But this will cause no confusion. The class-rate tariffs will indicate the classification to which the classes are subject, just as they have always done. It must be remembered that once a rate is published, it remains in effect until it is canceled. Consequently, all class tariffs, the rates in which are governed by the Consolidated Classification, will remain effective until new tariffs subject to the Uniform Classification are issued. The Uniform Classification does not "cancel" the Consolidated Classification, and for some time all cancellations will be only in class tariffs. It may be several years before the class rates in the Far West are brought under the Uniform Classification, but it is likely that the displacement of the Consolidated Classification in the region east of the Rocky Mountains will be completed within a couple of years.

The new Uniform Classification carries the names of the older major classifications just as the Consolidated Classification does, except that the numbering is different. The constituent classifications in the new book are called Official Classification No. 1–A, Western Uniform Classification No. 1–A, Southern Classification No. 1–A, and Illinois Classification No. 1–A. It is probable that when the Uniform Classification comes into general use, the names of the old classifications will be dropped entirely, though this is not necessarily true. The three classification territories will still be recognized as rate-making territories, and the names may persist for a long time.

CLASSIFICATION COMMITTEES

The work of preparing freight classifications is entrusted to "classification committees," the members of which are selected and compensated by the interested railroads and other carriers which are parties to the classifications. The chairmen of the three major classification committees and the Illinois Classification Committee constitute a Consolidated Classification Committee. It is the duty of this committee to bring together, organize, and publish the work of the four committees which they serve. They also act as agents through which the classification is filed with the Interstate Commerce Commission, the Board of Transport Commissioners for Canada, the Federal Maritime Board (which has replaced the former United States Maritime Commission), and the many state public service or public utility commissions with which the classification must be filed.

It was this Consolidated Classification Committee which had a leading part, along with many aids and advisers, in framing the Uniform Classification No. 1, and it too has been filed by them as agents with the various national and state regulatory bodies.

At one time, the members of the classification committees were designated traffic officials of various railroads, who took time off from their regular duties with their respective companies to perform the work of freight classification. This plan of operation did not work well, because it was found to be extremely difficult for the officers selected for classification work to give adequate time and attention to both of the positions they held. Either their work for their respective railroads suffered or the classification work did not receive the careful consideration it deserved. Consequently, classification committees were formed composed of men who gave their entire time to the single task. Classification of freight is not a simple undertaking; it requires concentrated effort and study and the exercise of fair and impartial judgement. It requires the services of men who by long experience have become genuine experts in their work.

HOW CLASSES ARE DESIGNATED

The first task in preparing to classify the articles to be accepted for transportation is to decide upon the number of classes into which the articles will be divided. The three major classifications which make up the Consolidated Classification are not alike in this respect, and the Uniform Classification employs a system which is entirely different from that followed in the Consolidated Classification. Moreover, the classes now provided in the three older major classifications are not the same, either in number or in designation, that they once were.

The Official Classification has seven classes, six of them numbered from one to six, and another class known as Rule 26 Class. Originally there were only six Official classes. A greater subdivision being desired, it was decided that instead of increasing the numbered classes, which would have meant shifting many articles from the class numbers with which they had long been associated, new classes would be provided for by rules. At one time there were three such classes, Rules 25, 26, and 28. Rule 25 created an extra class between the second and third classes, Rule 26 an extra class between the third and fourth, and Rule 28 an extra class between the fourth and fifth. For many years, the rates charged under these rule classes were percentages of the preceding class. The calculation of the actual rates under the rules was left to the railroad freight agents and, as one may well imagine, an abundance of errors crept into freight bills covering shipments subject to the rules. The Interstate Commerce Commission finally ordered that the rates applicable to articles classed under the rules should be stated in dollars and cents just as the rates for articles grouped under the numbered classes were stated. Two of the rule classes were eventually dropped, Rule 28 going first and Rule 25 following. Rule 26 Class still remains as one of the seven classes of the Official Classification, as given in the Consolidated Classification.

The Southern Classification formerly had ten classes, one to six and A, B, C, and D. The Interstate Commerce Commission completely overhauled the southern class-rate structure in the early 1920's and made provision for twelve numbered classes which the Southern Classification, as published in the Consolidated Classification, still contains. For many years there were a few ancient tariffs in the South which were still governed by the classification containing both numbered and lettered classes, making it necessary in the current classification to indicate the numbered class which was the equivalent of a class formerly designated by letter. These tariffs eventually disappeared, giving way to class tariffs quoting rates on the prescribed twelve classes.

The Western Classification, as given in the Consolidated Classification, has ten classes, five numbered one to five and five lettered A to E. The Illinois Classification is much like the Official Classification, and only in the case of a relatively few items are there some differences.

All of the three major classifications of the Consolidated Classification provide for some extra or additional classes, which are higher than first, by giving to certain articles ratings which are $1\frac{1}{4}$, $1\frac{1}{2}$, 2, $2\frac{1}{2}$, 3, $3\frac{1}{2}$, and 4 times first class. Moreover, a great many articles are listed as "percentages" of first class. These percentages have made it necessary to include in many class-rate tariffs the so-called "column rates" previously mentioned.

The Uniform Classification presents a completely new departure in the manner of designating the class to which an article belongs. Though the classes are designated by number, the system resembles a table of what we call "index numbers," with the base equivalent to 100. Class 100 corresponds roughly to first class in the Consolidated Classification. Then there are thirty other classes represented by numbers ranging from 13 to 400, each number being merely a percentage of the base Class 100. In many class tariffs subject to the Consolidated Classification, the rates on classes below first class are definite percentages of the first-class rate, but the practice of making them so has not been universal, and percentages, where employed, have not been uniform throughout the country. But when all of our class tariffs are subject to the Uniform Classification, the rates on the different classes will bear a definite and unvarying relationship to the rate on Class 100. Though in class tariffs governed by the Uniform Classification there will be more classes than provided for in any of the three major classifications of the Consolidated Classification, the work of constructing class rates will be simplified because of the greater degree of systematization.

HOW ARTICLES ARE LISTED

Once the number of classes is determined, it is the duty of the classification committee to assign various articles to their proper classes. This is done simply by listing the articles and giving each one its class rating or ratings in columns at the right of the page. In the body of the classification—the part where the class of each article is indicated—the articles are not listed in alphabetical order but are often grouped under major headings. Automobiles, for example, are not listed under the letter A, but under V, the initial for "vehicles." This kind of grouping renders it necessary for the classification to have an alphabetical index, which tells the place in the body of the classification where each article's rating may be ascertained. There are not many longer lists of nouns than that to be found in a freight classification index, and some crossword puzzle designers find the index a highly useful source of raw material.

C.L. AND L.C.L. RATINGS

Since the class ratings of most articles when shipped in carload quantities are different from the ratings when shipped in less carload quantities, the pages of the Consolidated Classification and of the Uniform Classification give a column to each type of rating—l.c.l. and c.l.[5] In the Consolidated Classification the ratings may be for any one or all of the four constituent classifications, but in the Uniform Classification there is only a single rating in each column.

[5] An interesting example of how changes in the English language may develop is to be found in the term "less carload." Formerly, the hyphenated expression "less-than-carload" was used to designate the smaller freight shipments. The expression "less carload" is now in common use, and will be employed in this work. The Consolidated Freight Classification and the Uniform Classification use the term "less carload," though in some of the rules of the classification, the wording of which has not been revised for several years, the expression "less than carload," can still be found, though not hyphenated. See Rule 10. In the "explanation of abbreviations," the letters l.c.l. are still said to stand for less than carload. Another example of variation in spelling is found in the word, or words, "livestock." In some documents it is one word, in others two. The Interstate Commerce Act makes it one word; the Commission has had it both ways; the classification has it as two words.

CARLOAD MINIMUM WEIGHTS

Any article which has a carload rating must also have a "carload minimum weight," the least weight for which a carrier will accept payment on a shipment billed as a carload. The carload minimum weights, in both classifications, are listed in a third column standing between the columns in which the ratings are shown. Even in the Consolidated Classification, the committees were able to secure almost complete uniformity in carload minimum weights; in the Uniform Classification, full uniformity has been achieved.

THE BASES OF CLASSIFICATION

How does a classification committee decide in which class a certain article must be placed? There are many factors to be taken into consideration. The classification committees work for the railroads, and it is only natural that they should want to classify articles in a way that will produce the greatest possible revenue for the carriers. This purpose would of course be defeated if ratings were made so high that traffic could not bear the resulting transportation charges. The classification committees desire to encourage, not stifle, the productive activities of the patrons of the carriers. Moreover, the classification committees, like the authorities who make the actual rates, are bound by the injunction of the law requiring all rates and classifications to be reasonable and not unduly discriminatory. The Interstate Commerce Commission has jurisdiction over the classification of freight just as it has over the rates published in carrier tariffs; if a shipper feels that his product has been classified in such a way as to cause him to pay unreasonably high charges, to subject him to unduly discriminatory charges, or both, he has a right to appeal to the Commission to change the classification of his product in such a manner as to protect him from unlawful injury.

THE COST FACTOR

There are many factors which a classification committee takes into consideration in determining the ratings which an article shall receive. By far the most important factor is the "cost of service," the amount which it costs a carrier to transport a given commodity. Obviously a carrier is bound, in its own interest, when competitive conditions permit, to charge higher rates for the transportation of those articles the cost of whose transportation is higher; to a certain degree, this higher charge can be effected through classification.

This does not mean that the classification committee or the carrier can calculate with mathematical exactitude the cost of carriage of each shipment it transports. We shall discuss later the reasons why it is impossible to make such an exact calculation. But the classification committee and the carrier can often determine whether it costs more to transport a certain article than it costs to transport another. The committee, other things being equal, will give a higher rating to the article which it costs more to transport.

We have mentioned the fact that when shipped in carload quantities nearly all articles receive a lower classification rating than when shipped in less carload quantities.[6] This differentiation is plainly due to differences in the cost of service. It costs the carrier more per hundred pounds or per ton to transport less carload shipments than to transport carload shipments of the same commodity. Carload shipments are, with few exceptions, loaded by the shipper and unloaded by the consignee, while the loading and unloading of less carload shipments are performed by the carrier. Less carload shipments often have to be transferred from car to car one or more times during the course of their transportation. The carrier must often provide space for a limited free storage of less carload shipments. The "paper work" which the carrier must perform for a less carload shipment consumes about the same time and effort that is spent on the paper work for a carload shipment.

WEIGHT AND BULK

It must be remembered that the "earning unit" of a railroad is the car in which freight is carried; for other carriers, too, the earning unit is the vehicle in which goods are conveyed from place to place. A railroad car earns revenue for its owner only when it is moving and under load. Since rates are almost all quoted in cents or dollars and cents per hundred pounds or per ton, it is plain that a car loaded to its capacity in pounds earns more than one which is loaded only to a fraction of that capacity. But there are many articles so light in proportion to their bulk that under no circumstances could enough of them be packed into a car to bring its load up to its weight capacity. Therefore it costs the railroad much more per hundred pounds to transport such articles than to transport articles so heavy in proportion to the space they occupy that they can fill a car to the limit of its weight capacity. The light, bulky articles take up the earning space of the carrier's equipment, and the only way in which a carrier can secure revenue which adequately reflects the cost of transporting such articles is to make a high charge per hundred pounds for

[6] There is no uniform relationship between the carload and less carload ratings applied to the same article. A difference of two classes is most commonly employed in the Consolidated Classification, that is, articles shipped in less carload quantities are given ratings two classes higher than the same articles shipped in carload quantities. But in many cases the difference is more than two classes, in many other cases the difference is only one class, and a few items have an A.Q. rating, that is, the rating applicable to carload and less carload shipments is the same.

their transportation. Consequently, the classification committee gives high ratings to articles which are light in proportion to the space they occupy in a car. Such articles as canoes and boats, set-up furniture, and airplane bodies are much more costly to transport, pound for pound, than grain, coal and ore, lumber, steel billets, books, or most fruits and vegetables. An examination of the classification will disclose that light and bulky articles invariably receive higher ratings than articles of equal weight which take up less space. Nearly all of the articles which have ratings of three and four times first class are very bulky for their weight.

This same principle of giving higher ratings to light, bulky articles lies behind the practice of giving higher ratings to less carload shipments. Articles shipped in carload quantities are of a homogeneous nature and can be loaded in such a way as to take up a car's entire cubic capacity. Less carload shipments, both because of the wide diversity in their size and shape and because of the fact that they must often be loaded in a car according to their destination, are usually not loaded so "heavily" in a car as carload shipments. In other words, a car of less carload freight is likely to have less weight than a car of carload freight, and in terms of the space occupied earns much less for a railroad. The only way in which the carrier can obtain equivalent earnings from the less carload shipments is to charge them more per hundred pounds for carriage. This higher charge is accomplished in part by stepping up the classification of freight when carried in less carload amounts.

Again, the same principle operates when a carrier gives a lower rating to an article "knocked down" than to the same article "set up." Pails, buckets, and other receptacles which are shipped "nested" have a lower rating than the same articles "not nested." The classification of paper boxes affords an interesting illustration of how closely a classification committee studies the relation of bulk to weight.

LOSS AND DAMAGE INSURANCE

There are many factors other than weight in proportion to bulk which clearly affect the cost of transportation service. Since a carrier is liable for lost and damaged freight, every freight rate must contain an element of insurance premium. On goods which are the most susceptible to damage caused by breakage, leakage, or abrasion, the rates must be higher than on goods the transportation of which entails small risk. This "insurance" is one of the carrier's costs, and it must be recovered in freight charges. Fragile articles receive higher ratings than sturdy ones. In the same way, the classification varies the ratings on the same article according to the method of packing that has been employed in preparing it for shipment. The stronger and less liable to damage the container, the lower the class rating an article may receive. The same principle appears in the higher ratings given to articles which are most likely to be lost through pilferage.

One reason for the elaborate and complex system of classification employed by railroads and other land carriers should now become apparent. Their rates are quoted virtually entirely upon a weight basis: so much per hundred weight or per ton. The difference in the density of the thousands of articles which a railroad carries makes the detailed classification unavoidable.

WEIGHT OR MEASUREMENT RATES ON WATER TRAFFIC

Many carriers by water, especially those engaged in foreign trade, avoid the necessity of employing an elaborate classification of freight by using an alternative system of making freight charges. An article is charged either on the basis of its avoirdupois weight or on the basis of its cubical content. Weight is equated to volume. A "ton" of cargo of ocean freight is a ton "by weight" of either 2,000 or 2,240 pounds, or a ton "by measurement" of 40 cubic feet. On general cargo, the traffic department of a steamship line may quote a rate for a certain haul at $20 per ton W/M/SO (weight or measurement, ship's option). A shipment weighing only two tons but occupying 160 cubic feet of space in a ship's hold would pay $80 in freight charges, while a shipment weighing four tons, even though it occupied only 60 cubic feet of space, would also have to pay $80. In the same way, steamships often quote alternative rates by the hundred pounds or by the cubic foot, and collect charges on the basis which provides the greatest revenue.

A few years ago, a number of metropolitan newspapers carried a big "publicity" story for an American air line, to the effect that it was not going to make use of the long and complicated "classification" which caused so much confusion and difficulty in railroad rates. The air line, it was said, was going to make "the same rate of charge on all shipments," whatever they were. No classification, no differentiation; air cargo rates were to be something like postage rates on first-class mail, so much a pound for everything, though of course charges would increase with distance. This was a preposterous story. No carrier could afford to transport all freight at the same rate per pound or hundredweight. It took only a brief examination of the air cargo tariff, upon which the story was based, to find that everything was charged at the same rate per pound only if a pound by weight occupied a space of 400 cubic inches or less. If it occupied more than 400 cubic inches, a pound became a "measurement" pound. The air line had simply adopted the weight or measurement practice long followed by many ocean carriers, but no mention was made of this fact in the newspaper stories which declared that there was to be no cumbersome classification to bewilder prospective shippers by air.

VALUE AS A FACTOR IN CLASSIFICATION

Although cost of service is by far the most important factor in the determination of class ratings, it is not always the controlling factor. There are many articles carried by American railroads and other transportation agencies that are charged higher rates than other articles whose cost of transportation is no greater, simply because they can "afford" to pay more. Long ago, the Interstate Commerce Commission recognized the validity of a rate theory which justified the imposition of higher charges on certain articles than the charges imposed upon other articles, which, though similar from a transportation standpoint, were of considerably less market value.[7] We have mentioned the fact that a higher charge on the more valuable article is justified on the ground that the rate must cover insurance against loss and damage. However, many commodities have rates based on value which are considerably higher than rates necessary merely to take care of the risk involved in their transportation.

RELEASED VALUE

For many years, railroads have taken steps to reduce by contract their liability for loss and damage to freight. We shall have much more to say, in later chapters, concerning the liability of carriers and how it may be limited. Here we shall mention only the fact that the Interstate Commerce Commission has the power under the law to permit carriers to base rates on what is known as "released value." Such released value marks the maximum amount which a shipper may recover from a carrier in case of loss or damage. Released value rates may not be made upon shipments of "ordinary livestock" or upon any other commodity without the express consent and approval of the Commission. One finds quite a few articles in both the Consolidated and the Uniform Classifications which have ratings graded according to the released value given to them by the shipper. In all cases, there is a note calling attention to the order of the Commission authorizing the ratings. Among the articles having such ratings are household goods, rugs, chinaware, moving-picture films, crucibles, livestock valuable for breeding or exhibition purposes (but not ordinary livestock), and certain kinds of ore. The Uniform Classification goes somewhat further than the Consolidated in providing released value ratings. For example, a large number of drug and pharmaceutical products, which have ratings without regard to value, have lower ratings if released to a value of less than 50 cents a pound.

---

[7] Ever since the Interstate Commerce Commission was established and organized, it has taken the position that cost of service is not the only matter to be taken into consideration in determining the reasonableness of a rate. "While cost is of importance in determining the measure of rates, it has never been the sole consideration." Baltimore Chamber of Commerce v. Ann Arbor R.R., 159 I.C.C. 691 (696) (1929).

In addition to released value rates, railroads publish a few rates based on "actual value." Such rates do not require authorization by the Commission. In both the Consolidated and the Uniform Classifications, field glasses and glassware, noibn (not otherwise indexed by name), have ratings based on actual value. In a former issue of the Consolidated Classification, fur and fur-lined clothing was given ratings dependent upon actual value; in both classifications, such clothing now has released value ratings. It might be pointed out, too, that when a certain maximum value is reached on many articles having released value ratings they are "not taken."

The Interstate Commerce Commission permits released value rates on all merchandise express traffic. The usual rate is applied to articles declared by the shipper to have a value of not more than $50 or on shipments weighing more than 100 pounds, a value not in excess of 50 cents a pound. If a shipper declares a higher value, he must pay a higher rate.

It must be emphasized, however, that these released value ratings and rates are for the purpose of minimizing or limiting the risk or the liability of the carrier in case shipments are lost or damaged. In ordinary rates and ratings, the amount of the charge supposedly takes care of the risk factor. Indeed, in passing upon the "reasonableness" of rates, the Commission frequently takes into consideration the amount of the risk which the carrier must assume and scrutinizes the past record of loss and damage suffered in the transportation of various articles.

But let it be said once more that in many cases the difference between the ratings and rates applicable to valuable and less valuable articles is more than enough to take care of the risk element many times over. The valuable articles are "taxed," as it were, to provide a greater revenue for the carriers. The sole justification of this method of rate making seems to be that many articles could not enter our domestic commerce unless they received a concession in the way of low transportation rates. While the carrier does not suffer an absolute loss in the transportation of the commodities receiving low rates, it gets only a small part of its overhead, or fixed costs, from such traffic and is compelled to make up the discrepancy by exacting a disproportionately higher share of these costs from articles which can "afford" to pay higher rates because of their greater value. In this way, the commerce of the United States is developed and encouraged, more commodities become available for general consumption, and the people of the nation can enjoy a higher standard of living.

TRAFFIC VOLUME

All carriers have a tendency to grant lower rates to freight which moves regularly in large volume or gives promise of a rapid and steady growth. This practice is quite understandable and corresponds to the practice which manufacturers and merchants frequently follow of giving quantity discounts. However, a railroad or other common carrier cannot discriminate between its patrons who produce the same commodity. Freight rates must be the same for everybody. What the carrier studies, in reaching a decision as to whether to give a somewhat lower rating or rate to articles which move in large quantities, is the traffic—the freight—itself, and not the shippers.

The practice of taking the volume of traffic into consideration when determining the class rating a particular kind of traffic should receive was in part responsible for the lack of uniformity among the three major classifications which make up the Consolidated Classification. A particular commodity may provide a very substantial volume of freight in one territory and be relatively insignificant in another territory. There is a strong feeling among carriers that this commodity should not be classified the same in both territories but should receive a lower rating in that territory where it moves in large volume. The Interstate Commerce Commission has chosen to disregard this matter in requiring the preparation and publication of the Uniform Classification, though doubtless the territorial differences still present a difficult problem, and some kind of adjustment may have to be made before the Uniform Classification fully justifies its name.

Each of the major classification committees is constantly busy. Almost every day, some new article is produced and offered for transportation. It must be classified, and it is the business of the traffic manager of the concern producing a new article—if it has a traffic manager—to see that the new product is properly classified. Then, too, many attempts are made to bring about changes in the classification. Carriers ask that some articles be shifted to a higher class; shippers frequently appeal to have their products placed in a lower class.

COMMITTEE DOCKETS AND HEARINGS

Although the classification committees have permanent headquarters and offices, they all hold hearings at various places in their respective territories. All the requests for changes in classification, both up and down, and requests for the classification of new articles are carefully filed, and a "docket" is prepared for stated hearings at specified points. This docket constitutes the "agenda" for a meeting—to use a word seen quite frequently now that the diplomats who represent the various nations of the world gather so frequently. On the days the hearings are held, the representatives of shippers and carriers come before the committees, present their views upon docketed topics in which they are interested, and put forward the arguments they have in justification of their demands.

The most interesting part of the hearing before a classification committee is that part having to do with the classification of a new article which has just been placed or is about to be placed on the market. The committee hears statements from the representatives of both shippers and carriers. By its questions, it shows that in trying to arrive at a fair decision with respect to the new product it is keeping in mind the various principles of classification, including the ones we have discussed: cost of service, value of the commodity, and volume of traffic promised. The proceedings before the classification committee bear a strong resemblance to proceedings before the Interstate Commerce Commission or before one of its examiners.

CLASSIFICATION LARGELY A MATTER OF COMPARISON

The consideration upon which a classification committee leans most heavily in reaching a decision as to what rating an article should receive is comparison. The whole process of classification is largely one of comparison, and the object of the committee is to put into the same class articles which from a transportation point of view are alike. It is impossible to make any hard and fast rules which a committee can follow in reaching a decision. The members must use their best collective judgment and endeavor to the best of their ability to give each article a rating which is fair and reasonable and which does not involve any unjust discrimination against some other article. If ratings and rates were governed solely by the cost of service, by the value of service to a shipper, or by the value of the commodity, their task would be somewhat easier, but all of these factors must be taken into consideration and, as it has already been pointed out, there are many occasions when the principle of cost of service must give ground to the principle of the value of the commodity. A decision which gives more weight to the value of the commodity than to the cost of service necessarily means that from the standpoint of cost of service alone the decision creates a discrimination in favor of one article whose rating is determined more nearly in accord with the cost of service. But —and here is a good place for this to be mentioned—discrimination is not unlawful. Only that discrimination is unlawful which is undue or unjust, and the Commission has said many times that the value of an article may be given great weight in determining its classification. It is at all times difficult to draw the line between discrimination which is unjust and discrimination which is not unjust. All a classification committee can do— and the same is true of the Interstate Commerce Commission—is to exercise its best judgment and endeavor to reach a fair and honest decision.

CLASSIFICATION BY OTHER CARRIERS

It has already been pointed out that carriers other than railroads follow the practice of classifying traffic and making class rates. Many highway carriers, carriers by water, and freight forwarders are parties to both the Consolidated and the Uniform Classifications, have long published rates governed by the former document, and are now in the process of publishing class rates governed by the latter. On the other hand, many trucking companies and carriers by water use other freight classifications.

The most important highway freight classification is the National Motor Freight Classification, first issued in 1936 and reissued ten times since then. This classification, which governs the tariffs of hundreds of motor carriers operating throughout the United States, was compiled and published through the American Trucking Associations, with headquarters in Washington, D.C. Like the railroads' much older classification, it provides different ratings in the East, the South, and the West, on many articles, and it also gives lower ratings on volume shipments than on small less than truckload shipments. Though this motor freight classification is the one most widely used, there are a few minor highway freight classifications used locally in certain regions, the best known being classifications adopted by numerous motor trucking concerns operating in New England. It is not unlikely that the motor trucking industry will in time follow the example of the railroads and publish a Uniform Motor Freight Classification.

EXPRESS CLASSIFICATION

The Railway Express Agency, the successor of the American Railway Express Company, which was itself a merger of a number of great express companies which once served the nation, has a classification which dates back to 1913, when the Interstate Commerce Commission overhauled the entire rate structure of the express business.[8] The express classification does not list many articles. Express traffic is nearly all divided into two classes, the second class including food and drink except alcoholic beverages, and the first class including other kinds of merchandise. A third class covers various kinds of printed matter, and a money class applies to bullion, currency, securities, and other highly valuable instruments. The express classification lists a number of articles which for one reason or another are not embraced in these classes. For the most part, these articles are of high value or can be carried only at considerable risk, and are therefore classified at some multiple of first class. The express agency, like the railroads, quotes commodity rates on many shipments, usually applicable to produce or merchandise which moves in considerable volume, often as carload shipments.

WATER CARRIERS

Domestic carriers by water, if publishing class rates at all, make use of the Consolidated and the Uniform Classifications. All the intercoastal lines

---

[8] In the Matter of Express Rates, Practices, Accounts and Revenues, 24 I.C.C. 381–541 (1912), 28 I.C.C. 131 (1913).

are parties to these classifications, as are some of the lines carrying traffic on the Great Lakes and other inland waterways. Many barge lines, which carry only bulk freight consisting of a relatively few commodities, do not publish class tariffs at all, but apply only commodity rates to the tonnage they transport.[9]

THE TRAFFIC MANAGER AND CLASSIFICATION

It is incumbent upon every traffic manager whose firm distributes products carried at class rates to see that the descriptions of the articles shipped correspond to the descriptions given in the classification. Otherwise, he may discover that his traffic is being carried at higher rates than necessary. Many articles are classified according to the way they are packed or according to the condition in which they are shipped. Some secondhand or used articles receive lower ratings than the same articles "new." It is the business of the traffic manager to see that his transportation charges are those which his traffic is legally entitled to pay, and one way of avoiding what might be an unnecessarily high rate is to see that classification descriptions are carefully followed.

The description of an article is entered on the bill of lading, the contract of carriage between the shipper and carrier. A copy of this bill of lading, known as the shipping order, is retained by the carrier. It is the carrier's original record of the transaction with the shipper. From the information given in the shipping order, the carrier's billing clerk makes out the "waybill," which contains, in addition to the information contained in the shipping order, the shipping instructions which govern the movement of a shipment. The waybill of a freight shipment is comparable to the ticket of a passenger.

What many shippers may not know is that the billing clerk who makes out the waybill often does not actually see the freight listed in the shipping order, upon which the waybill is based. He is bound, therefore, by the description given in the shipping order. If the shipper has neglected to give the proper description of his freight, and if it happens that it carries different ratings, according to the manner of its packing, the billing clerk, to be on the safe side, will give the shipment the highest rating which the classification provides. The shipper may subsequently file a claim for "overcharges" if he discovers that he has neglected to give the proper description of his shipment. But he may remain in ignorance of his error. Even if he should find out the mistake, he must take the time and trouble

[9] Until 1947, each air carrier which accepted cargo for transportation published its own tariffs, consisting of a modest classification and a schedule of charges. In 1947, the certificated air lines of the United States published three agency "consolidated tariffs," consisting of a rules tariff, a pickup and delivery tariff, and a rate tariff. Many "exceptions" to these tariffs have been filed by individual air carriers.

to prepare and file a claim and pursue it until he is reimbursed for the overcharge. It is much better to avoid the waste of time and energy involved in collecting a claim by writing the correct description of all shipments in the original bill of lading.

PUBLICATION OF CLASSIFICATIONS

Thus far, our discussion has been confined to the theory and practice of classification, or the division of various articles of merchandise into groups or classes. Though this is the primary, and most important, object of the Consolidated Freight Classification and the Uniform Freight Classification, they both contain much more information with which the trained traffic manager must be familiar.

It is worth while to note, on the first examination of either or both of these two classification books, that they are made up like any other tariff publication. The Consolidated Classification follows scrupulously the rules and instructions contained in the Commission's *Tariff Circular* No. 20, but there are a few unimportant deviations from those rules in the Uniform Classification.[10]

Both books are 8½ by 11 inches in size, they are printed on good paper, and the rules of typography are observed. The title page of the Consolidated Classification follows the prescribed pattern, with filing numbers, cancellation notices, brief description, issuing and effective dates, and the names of the issuing agents. The title page of the Uniform Classification, of course, does not have any cancellation notices; the filing numbers are omitted, though attention is called to the fact that they may be found on the second page; and it looks quite bare in comparison with the title page of the Consolidated Classification. Inside the covers of both books may be found their tables of contents as well as the names of the members of the four classification committees who prepared and compiled the volumes.

Both books have the long lists of participating carriers, divided into groups—railroads, water carriers, motor carriers, and freight forwarders. In the Consolidated Classification, the water carriers and rail carriers are listed in the same group; in the Uniform, they are listed separately. In the Consolidated Classification, the power of attorney or the concurrences of all the participating carriers are indicated by file number; in the Uniform, both space and labor have been saved by omitting the long list of documentary evidences of participation and stating merely that the necessary powers of attorney and concurrences "are on file with the Interstate Commerce Commission." In both books, it is interesting to notice, one can find

---

[10] Because of the need for haste, the Uniform Freight Classification No. 1 was prepared without complete adherence to the rules of *Tariff Circular* No. 20. A brief notice on the inside of the front cover of the classification calls attention to the lack of full compliance with the Commission's tariff rules and mentions the order by which the deviations were authorized.

in alphabetical order the names of all the railroads of the United States. The first railroad bears the euphonious name of Aberdeen and Rockfish. How many traffic managers and traffic students know where this little railroad is located?

Both books include sample copies of all the various forms of the bills of lading used by railroads and some participating carriers and a complete explanation of all the signs, symbols, and abbreviations used in the classifications. At the end of each book, nearly fifty pages are devoted to a description of the "authorized packages or shipping containers" and other "authorized forms of shipment specified in connection with the description of articles and ratings" given in the body of the classification.

Finally, each classification book contains a body of "rules" which, next to the descriptions and ratings, are the most important part of a classification, so important that we shall devote all of the following two chapters to the discussion of their terms, purpose, and significance.

CLASSIFICATION EXCEPTIONS

One would think, after an examination of the Consolidated and Uniform Classifications and a study of their contents, that they were all that interested carriers need as a basis for their numerous class tariffs. Unhappily, this is not true.

It has already been mentioned that a carrier may give an article a specific commodity rate, which has the effect of removing it from the classification. The railroads and other carriers publish a very large number of commodity tariffs. But the class tariffs based on current classification and the commodity tariffs—thousands in number—have not been sufficient to provide for all the variations in the rates which carriers think it necessary to offer to the public.

In a great many instances, railroad traffic officials have found themselves in a kind of dilemma. They have not wanted to give some articles a specific commodity rate applicable between the stations in a certain region or territory, or between stations on particular parts of a railroad system, but at the same time they have not wanted to observe the classification of the article as provided in the Consolidated Classification. For example, the "volume" of some article of traffic may have been so large that a carrier felt justified in giving it a fourth-class rating, though in the Consolidated Classification it had a third-class or even a higher rating.

The railroads solved this problem by issuing an "exception" to the controlling classification, Official, Southern, or Western, whose rating it was desired to modify. Virtually every railroad in the country has issued such exceptions. Some of them are "individual" publications of single systems, but there are also many exception tariffs issued jointly by several railroads. Some of the volumes containing the exceptions are nearly as large as the Consolidated Classification itself.

The exceptions now in effect are, for the most part, exceptions to the Consolidated Classification. Unquestionably, one thing the Interstate Commerce Commission had in mind, when it required the preparation of a "uniform" classification, was to get rid of some of the exceptions to governing classifications. But even when the Consolidated Classification disappears completely, and the Uniform Classification prevails throughout the entire country, there will probably still be many exceptions. In other words, while complete uniformity has an appealing appearance in theory, complete uniformity in practice seems to offer too many difficulties to be successfully achieved.

While the exceptions have to do, for the most part, with the ratings provided for different articles, there are also exceptions to the rules of a classification. For example, one rule of both the Consolidated and Uniform Classifications provides that carload shipments must be loaded by consignors and unloaded by consignees. A railroad may issue an exception to this rule, stipulating that at certain stations, because of the limitation of space and other reasons, the loading and the unloading of carload freight will be performed by the carrier. It is difficult to see how an exception of this kind cannot be made with respect to the new Uniform Classification. It will be a long time, in all probability, before all exceptions are abolished and we have only commodity rates and class rates based upon a classification to which there are no exceptions.

RATE PRECEDENCE

The exception to a classification, when properly and lawfully issued, takes precedence over the classification. All class tariffs will show, on their cover, that they are "governed" by one of the major classifications, and possibly by "exceptions thereto," as indicated in the tariff.

We are already beginning to see that transportation rates are a somewhat complicated subject of study. We know that any article transported has a published rate applicable between any pair of stations in the United States. If there is a single applicable through rate, either joint or local, that is the rate to apply. If a commodity rate exists, it is the legal rate. If there is no commodity rate, then the shipment is subject to a class rate. Before looking up the rate in the proper class tariff, one must first ascertain the class to which the article belongs. Ordinarily, its class would be indicated in the Consolidated or Uniform Classification. But it may be that an exception to the classification has been published and filed by the railroad or railroads over which the shipment is to move. If this is true, then it is the exception which names the applicable class.

If there is no single through rate, we must search for the proper combination rate, remembering always that our article is entitled to the lowest combination rate found to be applicable. If the shipment is to move over several railroads before it reaches its destination, it may be necessary to consult many commodity tariffs and many classification exceptions before we find the lowest available combination. The study of railroad rates begins to take on a somewhat formidable—even forbidding—appearance. The successful industrial traffic manager must master a highly technical subject in the study of transportation rates alone, and the knowledge of rates is only a small, albeit a highly important, part of his professional equipment.

One could hardly find fault with the student who is just beginning the study of traffic management if he admits to some confusion created by the simultaneous existence of two major classifications. But let him be reassured. Though the form and the title of freight classifications will change from year to year, the practice and the principles of freight classification will still remain, and they will undergo but little change. What he needs to know is what "classification" means, what its purpose is, and why we must have it. It does not make much difference if he uses for illustration Consolidated Classification No. 20, Uniform Classification No. 1, or any one of the numerous classifications of which these are the lineal descendants. And let him remember that Uniform Classification No. 1, in the years to come, will be replaced by No. 2 and No. 3 and many others, not to mention hundreds of supplements which will be issued before the classification itself is remodeled and published under a new number. But with all these changes, the fundamental features of freight classification will remain pretty much the same. These he will master by study and by reading; the knowledge and understanding of the superficial changes which are bound to appear will come as a part of his experience in actual traffic work.

Note. After the issuance on February 1, 1952, of Uniform Classification No. 1, and of the class-rate tariffs to be governed by it, numerous petitions were filed with the Interstate Commerce Commission protesting many provisions of the new publications and asking that they be "suspended," pending further investigation and study. However, the Commission was adamant in its determination to bring the new system of class rates into effect at the date it had chosen, and in a decision handed down May 23, 1952, it denied all applications for suspension and ordered the new tariffs to take effect, as planned, on May 30, 1952. On that date, consequently, Uniform Classification No. 1 and class-rate tariffs governed by that Classification became effective for rail traffic in that part of the United States east of the Rocky Mountains. The new class-rate tariffs were compiled and published by agents in various rate territories. They have taken the place of literally thousands of individual and agency class-rate tariffs and exceptions formerly in effect. They represent a long step forward in the simplification of freight tariffs.

On May 19, 1952, the Commission handed down a decision requiring the joint ocean-rail class rates applicable to traffic of the eastern seaboard to be revised, the rates to be governed by Uniform Classification No. 1 and patterned after the new all-rail class rates scheduled to take effect on May 30. The ocean-rail rates were to take effect July 22, 1952, but, more time being needed for the compilation of the tariffs, the Commission issued an order on June 20, 1952, postponing the effective date to September 20, 1952.

CHAPTER IV

Rules 1 to 10 of the Consolidated and the Uniform Classifications

The rules of a freight classification have to do with certain conditions that the participating carriers make with respect to all shipments which they accept for transportation, and with certain duties and obligations which are imposed upon all shippers. There are few printed documents dealing with transportation which contain more vital information concerning the relations that obtain between shippers and carriers than these rules. It is the duty of the trained traffic manager to acquaint himself fully with their provisions.

While the descriptions and the ratings shown in a classification book are employed for the most part to help in ascertaining the charges which carriers make for the transportation of the traffic carried at class rates, the rules apply to commodity tariffs as well as to class tariffs.

In framing the new Uniform Classification, the committees took over, almost unchanged, all the rules of the Consolidated Classification, omitting one but adding two rules which do not appear in the older publication. Even the numbers given to the rules common in both publications are the same. It will be understood, therefore, in the following discussion, that we are talking about the rules of both books. Where there has been any important variation in the rules, it will be mentioned, and of course attention will be called at the proper point to the two new rules found in the Uniform Classification.

The rules of the Consolidated Classification have varied in number from time to time, and doubtless, as time goes along, there will be additions to and cancellation of rules of the Uniform Classification. Carriers are adept in thinking up new conditions which should be attached to their business relations with their customers, and of course new shipping practices and new transportation methods may require changes in the rules. Consolidated Classification No. 20, which is the one currently in effect, has forty-eight rules. Consolidated Classification No. 19 had forty-nine, but one of them carried a notice of cancellation in the classification itself. No rules are assigned to the numbers 33 and 37, so that a hasty glance might give the impression that the Consolidated Classification had fifty rules instead of forty-eight. Likewise, in the Uniform Classification, no rule is assigned to the numbers 33 and 37. Moreover, the Uniform Classification omits Rule 44 of the Consolidated Classification. The two rules of the Uniform Classification No. 1 which do not appear in the Consolidated Classification are numbered 52 and 53. No rule is assigned to the number 51, which means that the Uniform Classification contains forty-nine rules.

The rules of our major freight classification have been modified many times since they were first published. We have already mentioned the fact that in the Official Classification, Rules 25, 26, and 28 once were ratings. While we still have a Rule 26 Class in Official Territory, for class tariffs subject to the Consolidated Classification there is also a Rule 26 which is not a class rating.

When one reads the present classification rules, one is inclined to believe that the classification authorities, like lawyers and landlords, think that the more words employed in framing a document the more impressive and "legal" the document becomes, and one is inclined to wish that the language of many of the rules could be overhauled in the interest of simplicity and clarity. As a matter of fact, rules have at times been published in such involved and muddy language that it has been impossible for all interested parties to agree upon their precise meaning. But even though the language of the present rules seems to be involved and cumbersome, there is no current dispute as to the meaning of any of them.

The rules of Consolidated Classification No. 20 take up twenty-eight pages of the classification book; in Uniform Classification No. 1, because of some alterations and the addition of two new rules, thirty-four pages are required. The pages of both books are large, and many of them carry printing in fine type and closely arrayed lines. We shall not endeavor to discuss all the rules in detail. Of some of them we shall merely state their purpose and not try to describe their provisions at all. Some we shall deal with in more detail than others.

It should be mentioned again that the rule numbers which follow are the numbers employed in both the Consolidated and the Uniform Classifications, unless otherwise indicated.

Rule 1. The first rule calls attention to the "uniform" bills of lading which carriers employ, sample copies of which are to be found in the classification book, just following the rules. The shipper is informed that if he does not want to accept the conditions of any one of these bills of lading under which his property is to be transported, but wants his goods to be transported under "carrier's liability, limited as provided by common law," or by state and Federal statutes, then he must ship under another form of bill of lading and pay 10 per cent additional freight charges.

This particular provision of the first rule is for the most part sheer nonsense at the present time with respect to domestic freight. It was adopted and included in the classification at a time when the carriers had the right, under the common law, greatly to limit a "carrier's liability, limited as provided by common law." For years, it was the practice of railroads to insert provisions in their bills of lading by which their common law liability for loss and damage was substantially reduced. The courts recognized the validity of these limiting provisions. Consequently, when a shipper signed the bill of lading customarily employed by the carrier, he was bound to accept the limitations of liability set forth in the bill. If he did not want to accept these limitations, he could demand a bill providing for full common law liability on the part of the carrier, but if he shipped under such a bill, his freight charges were advanced 10 per cent.

We shall discuss in a later chapter the nature of the liability of a common carrier for the loss of or damage to property entrusted to its care. Suffice it to say here that, under present Federal statutes regulating surface transportation by land in interstate commerce, a carrier may not limit by contract its common law liability, except under special conditions and circumstances, and then only under strict supervision, regulation, and control. A contract for the limitation of the carrier's liability, even though signed by both carrier and shipper, is legally null and void. In a certain sense, the liability of the carrier is greater now than it was when the matter of liability was governed entirely by the rules of common law. Then the carrier could limit his liability by contract with the shipper. Now he cannot do so. Under these circumstances, it is difficult to see why a shipper should prefer to pay 10-per-cent higher charges on a shipment merely for the sake of an empty and largely meaningless phrase. The liability provisions of the rule simply carry along some conditions that meant something when the rule was first adopted and for many years thereafter, but it is highly doubtful if at the present time any shipper pays any attention to them.

There are two sections of Rule 1, however, that are of some importance. One tells the shipper that he must assume the cost of any marine insurance taken out on his shipments unless otherwise specifically provided for in tariffs.

The other makes provision for what is known as a "short form" of the uniform straight bill of lading. Many shippers secure their bill of lading forms from the carrier. Such a form usually bears upon its face the name of the carrier from which it is obtained, and the back of the bill of lading contains the somewhat lengthy statement of the contractual obligations of the bill. On the other hand, many shippers like to print their own bills of lading, putting the firm name on the face and writing in the name of the carrier. A shipper may even have bills of lading on which is printed a list of the commodities he customarily ships from his plant. The first rule of the classification permits the shipper to employ a short form of the straight bill of lading, and provides that the contractual terms which appear on the back of the railroad's own bill of lading may be omitted, though it is clearly stated on the face of the short form that the shipper understands the terms and conditions of the uniform bill of lading and agrees to be bound by them. This concession to the shipper may save him considerable trouble and expense, and aid in expediting the paper work which must be done for the shipments he sends out.[1]

Rule 2. This rule advises the shipper that the descriptions of articles entered in the bill of lading and shipping order should conform to the descriptions given in the classification or in a tariff. Attention is called to the tariff and exceptions thereto containing special rules with respect to the shipment of explosives. An important part of this rule provides that carriers have the right to "inspect" shipments, if deemed necessary, to find out whether they have been properly described and given lawful ratings.

Unhappily, some shippers have shown a disposition to "chisel." In order to escape proper and legal freight charges, they have described their shipments incorrectly. If done with deliberate intent to defraud a carrier, this offense is punishable by fine and imprisonment. But whether the offense is deliberate or unintentional, the carrier has the right to examine any shipment to see if it has been properly described and rated. In times past, many carriers have created joint "weighing and inspection bureaus," whose agents made a business of checking freight shipments in order to discover whether there were any fraudulent or incorrect statements in the billing with respect to weight, description, or rate. The reason for the creation of the joint bureaus was that carriers occasionally entered into collusive arrangements with favored shippers for the misbilling of their shipments in such a manner that a favored shipper would receive a concealed rebate. The joint bureaus, independently operated, represented an effort by the carriers to keep watch on one another. As time passed, the efforts of carriers to increase their business by dishonest methods declined, and at the present time nearly every carrier does its own work of inspecting traffic. Shippers, too, have been educated over the years, some of them the hard way, and it is very seldom that any of them resort to fraudulent practices, either independently or collusively, for the purpose of avoiding the payment of legal rates.

[1] It should be pointed out that by the inclusion of the bill of lading forms in the classification or in tariffs, the bill of lading becomes a part of every contract between a shipper and a carrier, even though one has not actually been issued. In paragraph (11), section 20, part I, of the Interstate Commerce Act, which says that a carrier subject to that part "shall issue a receipt or bill of lading" to a shipper, it is also said that the carrier shall be liable for loss or damage "whether such receipt or bill of lading has been issued or not." The provisions of this part apply also to other surface carriers by land. In motor vehicle transportation, it often happens that receipts or bills of lading are not issued, but the carrier and the shipper are bound just the same by the terms of the bills of lading shown in classifications or tariffs.

Rule 3. This rule notifies the shipper that the carrier employing this classification will not accept for transportation articles of "extraordinary value," and names some of the articles which will be refused under the rule, including metallic and paper money, precious metals, jewelry, and antiques.

Immediately after the First World War, the United States had a boom period, which was characterized by extravagant expenditures for various luxuries. It was occasionally called the "silk-shirt" era of the economy. Because of excessive demand, the price of silk, both natural and artificial, soared to a fantastic level, and so many shipments were lost in whole or in part because of pilferage that the railroads added this commodity to the list of "valuable articles" which would not be accepted for shipment as freight. One of the manufacturers of artificial silk brought suit in a Federal court to have the action of the carriers set aside. After some months of argument and appeal the manufacturer was told that he had approached the wrong tribunal for the correction of what he thought was an unlawful injury and that he should first have gone to the Interstate Commerce Commission. This decision followed a line of decisions made in former years, in which the courts had taken a similar stand. By the time the final decision of the Supreme Court on the artificial-silk controversy was handed down, the boom had turned into bust, and the price of silk had collapsed. It was therefore withdrawn from the list of forbidden articles of value, and neither the complaining shipper nor the public ever found out what the attitude of the Interstate Commerce Commission might have been on the matter.

Rule 4. This very short rule provides that the carrier may accept and receipt for, "subject to delay for suitable equipment," any freight which might damage carrier equipment or other freight, or may, because of lack of suitable equipment, refuse to carry the proffered goods.

Rule 5. This is a long and detailed rule dealing with the manner in which shipments are packed for transportation. It stipulates, first of all, that "articles tendered for transportation will be refused unless in such condition and so prepared for shipment as to render the transportation thereof reasonably safe and practicable." This represents a form of protection against loss to which the carrier is justly entitled. One of the most prolific sources of loss of and damage to freight shipments is improper packing. One often wonders why carriers do not enforce more rigorously the part of this rule which gives them the right to refuse shipments turned over to them in such condition that the possibility of their safe transportation is extremely uncertain.

The remainder of the rule has to do mostly with alternatives a shipper has with regard to packing. In the classification, packing "specifications" are provided for a great many listed articles, especially when they are shipped in less carload quantities. This rule provides for an alternative choice of containers. In case the selected container offers less promise of safety in transportation than the specified container, there is an increase in the charges for transportation. When the shipment is in a container of the kind specified in the classification, of course no question arises as to the rating or rate to be applied. But if the container is of the kind specified, but does not conform to the rules of construction provided in the classification, the freight charges are advanced 20 per cent on less carload shipments and 10 per cent on carload shipments. When "articles are in containers of a kind or a shipping form of a kind, which is not specifically provided for in the description of such articles," there may be an increase in the transportation charges. A table is given, showing what the charges are to be in case of the use of a container of a kind "not specifically provided for." For example, if the description provides for shipment "in boxes," and the article is tendered "in barrels," the transportation charges are the same, it being thought that a barrel affords as much protection as a box. But if this shipment is tendered "in crates," the charges are 20 per cent higher l.c.l. and 10 per cent higher c.l. than in barrels or boxes.

Rule 6. While this rule is not nearly so long as some of the others, it is a very important one, and its careful observance by all shippers would do much to reduce the amount of claims for lost freight which carriers receive each year. The primary purpose of the rule is to give instructions on how to mark less carload freight for shipment. Carload freight, a shipment of which occupies the capacity of a car, or a shipment weighing 6,000 pounds or more or which is declared by the shipper to weigh 6,000 pounds and is so charged by the carrier, does not have to be marked. But freight shipped at l.c.l. or "any quantity" ratings which are beneath the 6,000-pound limitation should be marked as this rule indicates.

The most pronounced difference between this rule and the rules which precede it lies in the frequent use of the word "must." In the first five rules, the directions and instructions are conveyed with the expressions "should be," "shall be," "will be," and "would be." The word "must" is seldom encountered. But the sixth rule, in language at least, is plainly mandatory, though it must be admitted that carriers are not overly severe in insistence upon compliance with their orders.

In the first place, if the container of freight is one that is being reused, all old consignment marks must be removed or effaced. Each package or bundle of freight in the shipment must be plainly stenciled or otherwise "plainly and durably marked," showing the name of the consignee and the name of the station and state to which the goods are destined. The addition of the street address is helpful in expediting proper delivery. When consigned to a place of which there are two or more in the same state, the name of the county must be shown. Shipments consigned "to order" must have, in addition to the above information, an identifying symbol or number, which must also be shown on the bill of lading. Packages containing fragile articles must be marked FRAGILE—HANDLE WITH CARE. The rule gives specifications for shipping tags and states that all labels must be securely attached with a good adhesive substance.

Although a railroad or other carrier has a right to refuse shipments not marked in accordance with this rule, all too frequently the terms of the rule are not observed. Many shipments go astray each year because of faulty marking. Writing and stenciling are illegible, old marks are not effaced, labels are not fastened securely, shipping tags of inferior material are used, and often the tags are lost because they have been insecurely fastened to the package.

One of the chief faults of which too many shipping departments are guilty is the use of abbreviations in the addresses placed on packages and on shipping papers. This is particularly true with respect to the names of our forty-eight states. Illegible or careless writing then creates confusion. Mass. is frequently made to look like Miss., Cal. becomes Col., and Nev. is read as Neb. The most amazing of all errors in the abbreviations of state names arises from the fact that when written hastily in longhand the abbreviation for Maryland is practically indistinguishable from the abbreviation for Indiana. Many letters and packages have gone astray because of the similarity of these abbreviations.

Not so many years ago, a prominent Englishman made a trip to the United States, partly on a political errand, and in the course of his stay visited several of our eastern cities. When he returned to England, he wrote an account of his trip to the United States for a well-known British periodical, in which he stated that on his way from Washington to New York he had stopped off at Aberdeen, Ind., to visit the Navy's ordnance proving ground. A New York newspaper editor got hold of this article, and castigated the poor Englishman in blistering terms for displaying such an abysmal ignorance of American geography. It was easy enough to see that the Englishman had made the error of writing the abbreviation of Maryland to look as if it were the abbreviation for Indiana. The typographical error in the printed article was not discovered, and the New York editor unfortunately did not know that there was any resemblance in the abbreviations of two words phonetically so far apart as Maryland and Indiana.

Avoidance of the use of abbreviations is a good habit to cultivate. Like all other rules, this one has its exceptions, but not very many. Usually the person who uses abbreviations freely in his writing has a streak of indolence in his make-up.

Rule 7. The chief purpose of this rule is to indicate the conditions under which shipments will be delivered when shipped under an order bill of lading and when shipped under a straight bill of lading. With a few indicated exceptions, the name of only one shipper, one consignee, and one destination shall appear on one bill of lading, except that the bill may specify the name of a party to be "notified" at the same destination. We shall discuss all the terms of bills of lading in a subsequent chapter.

This rule shows that under ordinary circumstances the consignee of an "order" shipment receives the goods only upon presentation of the original bill of lading properly endorsed. Goods shipped on a straight bill of lading are deliverable to the person named in the bill, or upon his written order. It sometimes happens that bills of lading are lost, accidentally destroyed, or so delayed in transit that they reach the consignee or person to be notified long after the goods have reached their destination. This rule shows how, by the posting of bonds or otherwise, the person actually entitled to receive the goods may obtain possession of them without the presentation of bill of lading or written order.

Rule 8. Except as provided in tariffs, a carrier will not "advance" any charges to shippers, owners, consignees, their agents, or their draymen or warehousemen. Shippers occasionally ask originating carriers, for example, to pay a drayage bill and add the sum to the freight bill to be collected from a consignee, or even to advance all or part of the value of a shipment. The carrier will not make such advances. Once in a while an interline shipment travels over a route where there is no joint rate, and no through billing arrangement, whereby the originating or the delivering carrier collects all freight charges. It is customary in such a case for one carrier to advance the charges of the preceding carrier, if the shipment is "collect," and the delivering carrier bills the consignee for the amounts advanced. Railroads seldom advance the charges of motor vehicle common carriers.

Rule 9. All charges must be prepaid or guaranteed on shipments which in the judgment of the agent of the carrier would not at a forced sale bring in enough money to pay the charges at the point of destination.

Rule 10. This famous rule is known as the "mixed carload rule." There are thousands of commodities for which different ratings are given according to whether they are shipped in carload or in less carload quantities. The distinction offers no problem as long as a single carload shipment consists of a single commodity. But suppose a shipper has a few thousand pounds each of a half-dozen commodities which he wants to ship to a single consignee. Each of the commodities has a carload rating, or perhaps a commodity carload rate, but each may have a carload rating or rate and a carload minimum weight which differs from the ratings or rates and the minimum weights applicable to the other articles. The total weight of all the articles together is enough to make a carload shipment, and they can all be loaded into a single car. The railroad is quite willing to accept them as a carload shipment. But the question arises: what shall be the rating or rate and the carload minimum weight for the entire shipment? Rule 10 answers this question.

First, the rule stipulates that

. . . when a number of articles for which the same or different ratings or rates are provided when in straight carloads, are shipped at one time by one consignor to one consignee and destination in a carload, they will be charged at the straight carload rate applicable to the highest classed or rated article contained in the carload and the carload minimum weight will be the highest provided for any article in the carload.

If all the articles were rated as sixth class, for example, and all had the same carload minimum of 60,000 pounds, it is easy to see that the entire shipment would take the sixth-class rate with a 60,000-pound minimum weight. Suppose, however, that one article was rated fifth class, minimum weight 40,000 pounds, and another sixth class, minimum weight 60,000 pounds. Then the fifth-class rate and the 60,000-pound minimum would be applicable to the shipment. If there were three articles—one fourth class, 30,000 pounds minimum; one fifth class, 40,000 pounds minimum; one sixth class, 60,000 pounds minimum—and a fourth article with a commodity rate of 30 cents a hundred pounds, 40,000 pounds minimum weight, then the applicable minimum weight would obviously be 60,000 pounds, and the applicable rate would be the fourth-class rate, unless the fourth-class rate were less than 30 cents a hundredweight, in which case the rate of 30 cents would apply.

The rule goes on to say that "when the aggregate charge upon the entire shipment is made lower by considering the articles as if they were divided into two or more separate carloads, the shipment will be charged for accordingly." It also says that when the aggregate charge on the entire shipment is less on the basis of carload rate and minimum weight for one or more of the articles and of the less carload rates for the other article or articles, the shipment will be charged for accordingly. Sometimes it may be necessary to calculate the total charges for a mixed carload of freight in several ways in order to ascertain the proper amount to be collected for its transportation. Let us suppose that we have three articles which we want to ship as a mixed carload. The rates on the three articles are respectively 50 cents, 40 cents, and 20 cents a hundred pounds. The carload minimum weight for the first two articles is 20,000 pounds and for the third, 36,000 pounds. The first article weighs 15,000 pounds, the second 4,000 pounds, and the third 16,000 pounds. Considering the shipment as one carload, and applying the provisions of the rule, the shipment will be charged for at the rate of 50 cents a hundred pounds. The weight charged for, since the total weight is 35,000 pounds, will be the minimum weight of 36,000 pounds. The total charges, on this basis, would be $180.

But suppose we consider the shipment as two separate carloads, instead of one. The third article, taken as a carload, with a minimum of 36,000 pounds, and a rate of 20 cents, would bear a total charge of $72. The other two articles, also taken as a single carload, with a minimum of 20,-000 pounds and the highest rate, 50 cents a hundredweight, would bear a charge of $100. Obviously the shipment, considered as two separate carloads, would bear a charge $8 less than if it were shipped as a single carload.

Let us take a shipment where the conditions present further complications. We shall assume that the class rates applicable for a certain haul, for six classes, are as follows:

Class	1	2	3	4	5	6
Rate, cents per cwt.	100	85	70	50	35	28

Then we shall assume that we have four different articles to ship, all taking class rates. We shall designate the commodities by letters, and the actual weights, ratings, and minimum weights shall be as follows:

Article	Weight, pounds	Class rating, l.c.l.	Class rating, c.l.	Carload, min. wt., pounds
A	7,000	1	4	24,000
B	10,000	3	5	30,000
C	4,000	4	6	36,000
D	12,000	3	5	30,000

The total weight is 33,000 pounds, which comes within the highest minimum. Should the shipment go as a single carload, it would be charged for at the rate of 50 cents a hundredweight for 36,000 pounds, the total amount of the charge being $180. It is not possible to figure out a lower charge considering the shipment as two or more separate carloads. But suppose we take articles A, B, and D as a single carload and include article C as a less carload shipment. The carload would go at the rate of 50 cents a hundredweight, 30,000 pounds (since the combined weight of A, B, and D is 29,000 pounds), giving a total charge of $150. At the fourth-class rate of 50 cents a hundred pounds, article C would have a charge of $20. The total charge on the entire shipment, figured on this basis, would be $170, or $10 less than if the. shipment were taken as a single carload. It sometimes takes considerable thought for a shipper to figure out what the lowest possible charges on a mixed carload shipment will be.

There has in times past been much controversy over the mixed carload rule. There are many retailers in the country who cannot readily dispose of a straight carload of a certain kind of merchandise but can easily manage to sell a carload of varied articles. For example, a retailer of agricultural implements might not be able to sell in a single season a carload each of plows, harrows, cultivators, mowers, and reapers, though he could dispose of a mixed carload made up of all these implements. With a liberal "mixing rule," he can buy directly from a manufacturer of agricultural implements, and add to his profits both through a saving in freight rates and through his opportunity to buy at the manufacturer's price. If there is no liberal mixing rule, the retailer is compelled to buy from a wholesaler, who can buy carload quantities of each of several kinds of farm machinery. It can readily be seen that the retailer favors a liberal rule on mixed carloads, while the wholesaler would like to see the rule abolished entirely. When shipments must travel for long distances from the manufacturer's plant to the consuming center, the freight charges constitute a very substantial item of cost. One cannot blame the retailer for wanting to reduce his total costs, nor can one blame the wholesaler for wanting to do as large a business as possible.

In former years, the eastern railroads, occupying a region where the shipping distances were somewhat short, had a very liberal mixing rule, much more liberal than the one now found in the Consolidated Classification. In the South, the mixing rule was much less liberal, and in the West, the rule was least liberal of all. When the Consolidated Classification was first published, the tenth rule was not uniform for all three classifications, the eastern railroads offering more generous terms than the roads of the South and West. As years passed, each side made certain concessions, and eventually a uniform mixing rule was adopted.

However, with the advent of strong motor vehicle competition, the railroads were under strong pressure to make the mixing rule more liberal. The result has been that the carriers of the East and South have abandoned Rule 10 as it appears in the Consolidated Classification and have published, in "exceptions" to the classification, a mixing rule which varies to a considerable extent from the one we have been discussing. Western railroads, for the most part, still use Rule 10 as it appears in the classification.

The mixing rule now observed by eastern and southern railroads states that

. . . when a number of articles for which the same or different ratings or rates are provided when in straight carloads are shipped at one time by one consignor to one consignee and destination, in a carload . . . they will be charged at the actual or authorized estimated weight and at the straight carload class or commodity rate . . . applicable to each article. . . . The carload minimum weight will be the highest provided for any article in the mixed carload, and any deficit in the minimum weight will be charged for at the highest carload rating applicable to any article in the mixed carload.

Just as in Rule 10 of the classification, various articles are listed to which the provisions of the rule in the exceptions do not apply. The rules to be observed when the shipment is considered as two or more separate carloads are the same.[2]

It will be seen at once that this exception rule is much more liberal to shippers than the regular Rule 10. Each article in the mixture is carried at its own carload rate, and all articles are not subject to the rate applicable to the highest rated article in the carload. However, the carload minimum weight is the highest for any article in the mixture, and if the total weight of the shipment is less than the applicable minimum weight, the deficit or difference between actual weight and the carload minimum bears the rate applicable to the highest rated article in the shipment.

It will now be interesting to go back and study the examples previously given to show how Rule 10 works, and see what charges would be applicable under the modified rule employed by our eastern and southern carriers. In the first example, in which all articles are sixth class and all have a carload minimum weight of 60,000 pounds, there would be no difference in the charges. In the second example, where we had one article fifth class, 40,000 pounds minimum, and another sixth class, 60,000 pounds minimum, the carload minimum weight of the shipment would still be 60,000 pounds, but each article would carry its own rate. If the total weight of the two articles were less than 60,000 pounds, the deficit would be charged for at the fifth-class rate. In the third example, in which the mixture consisted of four articles, each would take its own applicable rate, and the minimum weight would be 60,000 pounds, with the deficit, if any, bearing the highest rate of any one of the articles.

In the fourth example, it will be found that it will not pay the shipper to consider the shipment as two separate carloads, though the charges would be a trifle less than they would be under Rule 10 as it was computed. If each article were charged its own applicable carload rate, the amount for each part of the shipment would be respectively $75, $16, and $32. To this sum must be added $5, since there is a deficit of 1,000 pounds to be charged for at the 50-cent rate. The total charges would be $138, or $34 less than the total charges applicable under the unmodified rule.

---

[2] Although Rule 10 of the Uniform Freight Classification is the same as Rule 10 of the Consolidated Freight Classification, the first tariffs of class rates to be published showing the ratings given in the Uniform Classification contained the exception which has been in effect for some time in the East and South. See, for example, Southern Freight Tariff Bureau, Freight Tariff No. S-1011, C. A. Spaninger, Agent, effective May 30, 1952, Item 20, p. 6. It is thought quite generally that when the Uniform Classification becomes applicable in the West the "exception" will become the "rule," and all parts of the country will have the more liberal "mixing" privilege.

In the fifth example, the total charges, after the proper carload rate was applied to each part of the shipment, with a minimum weight of 36,000 pounds being employed (deficit, 3,000 pounds at the fourth-class rate of 50 cents), would be $138.20. But if we again take articles A, B, and D as a carload (charges, A, $35; B, $35; D, $42; deficit, 1,000 pounds at 50 cents, or $5) and C as a less carload shipment ($20), we get a total charge of $137, which is less than the charges when the carload rate is applied to each article and the minimum is 36,000 pounds.

It should be mentioned here that another way in which rail carriers have endeavored to meet the competition of the motor haulage industry is by giving "all-commodity" rates in various parts of the country. Such rates enable a shipper to load whatever he pleases into a car and have the entire shipment transported at a single rate.

It is probable that freight forwarders make more use of Rule 10 than any other shippers. Their business is to consolidate a number of less carload shipments and ship them as a carload. Many of them could not carry on their business without a mixing rule. In a later chapter, we shall discuss at length the business of the freight forwarder, or "carloading company."

CHAPTER V

Rules 11 to 52 of the Consolidated and the Uniform Classifications

Rule 11. Unless otherwise provided, freight charges shall be computed on gross weights, except where estimated weights are authorized. This simply means that the containers in which merchandise is packed, or any pallets, platforms, or other contrivances on which freight may be loaded, are charged for at the same rate as the merchandise. Many a traffic manager has saved his employer large sums of money by devising containers which are lighter in weight than containers previously used but which give just as much protection against damage.

Rule 12. It frequently occurs that a shipper tenders to a carrier as a single shipment several packages of merchandise not all of which have the same class rating. Or it may be that a single shipment consists of packages containing articles belonging to different classes. This rule tells how such shipments are to be billed and rated. Single l.c.l. shipments of two or more classes, when each class is in a separate package, are charged for at the rating applicable to each class. The charge for a package containing articles classed or rated differently is the charge applicable to the highest classed or rated article in the package. When such a shipment is made, it is not necessary for the shipper to list the separate articles contained in the package. He names in the bill of lading only one of the articles taking the highest rate or rating, and makes on the bill of lading the notation: "And other articles classified or rated the same or lower." The same procedure is followed when a carload shipment is made of packages containing articles which are classified or rated differently. This is the second instance in which the classification rules have called attention to the need for a special notation on the bill of lading.

Rule 13. Nearly all carriers, whatever their rates for transportation services, make a minimum charge for a single shipment. Many other public utilities, such as electric light companies, water companies, telephone companies, and the like, follow the same practice. The thirteenth rule of the Consolidated Classification and of the Uniform Classification has to do with the minimum charges per shipment imposed by the carriers who are parties to this document. First of all, there is, for less carload and carload shipments, a flat minimum charge. As given in Uniform Classification No. 1, the minimum charge for a less carload shipment is $1.43, but by authority of the Interstate Commerce Commission this amount has been advanced. The minimum given for a carload shipment is $28.60 per car, which has also been advanced, though the minimum does not apply to the movement of a number of specified commodities.[1] When one reflects that shortly before the First World War the minimum charges for a less carload shipment was 25 cents, one has a better realization of what the forces of inflation have done to prices.

The flat minimum charge in dollars and cents is not, however, the only figure for a minimum charge. And here, for almost the first time, we meet with the need for distinguishing between the language of the rules of the Consolidated Classification and of the rules of the Uniform Classification. The Consolidated Classification states that on any less carload shipment from one consignor to one consignee on one bill of lading, the minimum charge, if the shipment is classified first class or lower, is the charge for 100 pounds at the class or commodity rate applicable to the shipment. If the shipment is classified higher than first class, the minimum charge is the first-class rate for 100 pounds.

Since the Uniform Classification does not have a "first" class, this part of Rule 13 in that classification says that the minimum charge on a single l.c.l. shipment, if classified Class 100 or lower, is the charge for 100 pounds at the applicable class or commodity rate; if classified higher than Class 100, the minimum charge is that for 100 pounds, Class 100.

It will be seen that the wording, in effect, identifies "first class" under Consolidated Classification with "Class 100" under Uniform Classification.

The multiple minimum charge scheme in both classifications sometimes overtakes the shipper going and coming. If the rate on a shipment bearing a first-class (or Class 100) rating is 50 cents and the weight of the shipment is 200 pounds, the total charge is not $1, but $1.43. If the first-class (or Class 100) rate happens to be $4 and the shipment weighs 50 pounds, the total charge is not $2, but $4. For articles which are classified as a multiple of first class (or Class 100), there is a bit more consideration for the shipper. An article classified at four times first class, for example, if the

---

[1] It has been utterly impossible for carriers to reissue their classifications and tariffs rapidly enough to keep up with the increases in rates and ratings which the Interstate Commerce Commission has authorized during this inflationary period of our economy. All tariffs and classifications have been modified from time to time by supplementary "master" tariffs which show the increases which the Commission has approved. The Consolidated Classification No. 20 shows that it is subject to tariffs of increased rates and charges, X-168-B and X-175. The Uniform Classification No. 1 is subject to the increased charges given in the "master tariff" X-175. Needless to say, the publication of the master tariffs authorizing general increases in virtually all rates has not made the task of ascertaining the proper rate to apply to a particular shipment any easier.

first-class rate were $4, and the shipment weighed only 50 pounds, would bear a total charge of $8. But if the shipment weighed only 10 pounds, it would have to pay $4, since on the basis of weight at $16 a hundredweight the charge would be only $1.60.

At one time the railroads, eager to improve their revenues, endeavored to apply the minimum charge rule to each part of an interline movement over which a combination rate was applicable. The Interstate Commerce Commission came to the rescue of the shippers, however, and declared that the minimum charge should apply to the continuous through movement, despite the absence of a joint rate, and not to each separate factor. Accordingly, it is so provided in this rule.

Rules 14, 15, and 16. Rule 14 defines a carload shipment and states that unless otherwise provided, carload freight is to be loaded by the shipper and unloaded by the consignee. Rule 16 defines a less carload shipment. Rule 15 states that with indicated exceptions the charge on a less carload shipment must not exceed the charge for a minimum carload of the same freight at the carload rate. The rule stipulates, however, that if a shipment has been tendered as a less carload shipment and it is found, after it has been loaded, transported, and unloaded by the carrier, that it is entitled to the carload rate and if under the tariff rules loading and unloading are to be done by the shipper and consignee, then the carrier is entitled to receive extra compensation, at the rate of 6½ cents a hundred pounds for loading and the same for unloading.

Rule 17. Every once in a while, a new article is tendered to a carrier for transportation, and it is found that the article is not mentioned either in the classification or in any commodity tariff. Nor is it identifiable as an article listed noibn. Since a carrier may not engage to transport a shipment for which no rate is available, it is necessary to make some kind of provision for such an unexpected shipment. This rule, which is sometimes called the "analogous rule," takes care of this situation. The carrier applies the classification which is applicable to articles which are analogous, that is, articles which most nearly resemble the unclassified and unrated article. The agent who classifies an article by analogy must notify the freight department of his employer at once, however, in order that the new article may be properly classified as soon as possible.

Rule 18. When two or more articles are combined, and the combination is not specifically classified, it will be charged for at the rating provided for the highest classed article in the combination. Such an article might be a combination chair and stepladder or hatrack and mirror.

Rules 19 *and* 21. It was mentioned previously that many articles receive a lower rating when knocked down than when set up, and when nested than when not nested, because when knocked down or nested they occupy less space in the car. Rule 19 provides that an article will receive a knocked-down rating only when it has been taken apart in such a manner as materially to reduce the space it occupies. Merely separating it into parts, without reducing its bulk, does not mean "knocking down." In a similar fashion, Rule 21 says that nesting of three or more articles means there must be a substantial reduction of the space occupied, and it stipulates the way in which articles must fit together in order to be entitled either to a "nested" or a "nested-solid" rating.

Rule 20. A shipment consisting of the parts or pieces of a complete article is charged for at the rate provided for the complete article. If a manufacturer is shipping an elaborate soda fountain, he must be careful to make separate shipments of its parts or he will find that he is obliged to pay on the heavy marble slabs of the counter the rate which may apply to the shiny faucets.

Rule 22. On the theory that the value of an article should be a factor in determining its classification and that the risk of damage is also an important consideration, the classification provides different ratings for many articles according to the state of their processing for use. Many wooden articles are rated according to whether they are "in the rough," "in the white," or "finished." This rule tells the meanings of these terms as employed in the classification of different wooden articles.

Rule 24. This rule is a highly important one for the shippers of many commodities transported in carload quantities. It is sometimes called the "overflow rule" and sometimes the "follow lot rule." It has to do with the rating of carload freight in excess of the amount that can be loaded into a single car. It applies only to freight the authorized minimum weight for which is 30,000 pounds or more. It does not apply to bulk freight or to livestock. It does not apply to freight requiring protective care (heating, icing, ventilation) at the time of shipment or to freight the minimum carload weights for which are subject to Rule 34 (to be discussed later).

The shipment must be made from one station, by one shipper, in one calendar day, on one shipping order and bill of lading, to one consignee and one destination. Each car into which the shipment may be loaded, except the car carrying the "overflow," must be loaded as heavily as conditions permit, and each of such cars is charged for at the carload rate and minimum weight applicable.

The excess over the quantity that can be loaded in or on one car will be charged, if loaded in a closed car, at the rate applicable to the carload portion of the shipment, subject to a minimum weight of 6,000 pounds. If loaded on an open car, the minimum charge is for 4,000 pounds at the carload rate. The excess freight must be marked as required for less carload freight, as provided in Rule 6. The waybill for each car transporting the shipment, whether full carload or excess, must give a reference to the waybill used for each other car used.

Rules 25, 26, 27, and 28. Rule 25, which used to be a "class" in Official Territory, declares that "unless the contrary appears," the terms "iron" and "steel" are interchangeable as to meaning in the classification, and that where reference is made to the "gauge" of a metal, if not otherwise provided, it means the United States Standard Gauge. Rule 26 admonishes shippers not to load freight in the ice bunkers of refrigerator cars. Rule 27 requires shippers and consignees to load and unload freight carried at carload ratings or rates, except where the carrier's tariff provides otherwise, and contains a few instructions to shippers with respect to the loading and unloading of shipments of various kinds. Rule 28 indicates that the word "rubber" as used in the classification refers to artificial and synthetic as well as natural rubber.

Rule 29. There are many articles of freight such as steel girders, wooden poles, and even logs which, because of their length, cannot be transported on a single car. Such articles are supported on one car, and the excess length is cared for by an "idler" car or possibly by two or three added cars. This rule tells how a railroad charges for such freight when shipped either in carload or in less carload quantities. It also tells of the minimum charges applicable to articles of such dimensions that they cannot be loaded through the side door of a closed car without making use of end doors or windows.

Rule 30. This rule is labeled "Dunnage." In order to make certain kinds of carload freight safe for transportation, it is often necessary to employ temporary blocking and bracing materials or such contrivances as racks, stakes, special flooring, or temporary bulkheads. This bracing material, which keeps freight from shifting as a car moves to its destination, goes under the name of "dunnage." It does not include excelsior, shavings, sawdust, straw, or other packing materials. We have already discussed the rule under which a railroad charges freight at its gross weight, that is, it makes the same charge for the container that it makes for the merchandise contained. This is not true with respect to dunnage. For the braces, props, stakes, and other such materials used in rendering carload shipments safe for transportation, the railroads make a certain "allowance" to the shipper, or relieves him from having to pay for the transportation of a certain portion of dunnage used. Rule 30 explains in detail what this allowance is and how it is computed for open and for closed cars.

Rules 31 and 32. The first of these rules calls attention to the fact that the ratings in the classification do not include the expenses for protective services of icing or heating. These services, when provided by the carrier, are paid for according to special tariffs which the railroads issue. The second of these two rules provides that no charge is made for the transportation of ice which shippers may place in the bunkers of refrigerator cars, unless the ice is taken out of the bunker by the consignee, in which case it is charged for at the rate applicable to the freight it has served to protect. All ice not taken by the consignee becomes the property of the carrier. No charge is made for ice placed in the body of the car for the protection of freight, but ice placed in the same package with freight is charged for at the rate applicable to the rest of the package.

Rule 34. There is no Rule 33 in Consolidated Classification No. 20 or in Uniform Classification No. 1. A rule under this number was in effect during the course of the Second World War, having to do with the multiple loading of carload freight in a single car, the freight being owned by different consignors. It was canceled shortly after the war ended.

Rule 34 represents the nearest approach which railroads make to adopting the "weight or measurement" method of making freight charges such as many ocean steamship companies employ. It provides, in effect, for a "sliding scale" of carload minimum weights, the minimum varying in accordance with the length of the car used in transportation. In many cases, the carload minimum weight indicated in the classification is followed by the letter R. This means that the minimum weight is subject to the conditions of Rule 34. When an article is "subject to Rule 34," the carload minimum weight specified in the classification is applicable only if the freight is loaded in a closed car 40 feet 7 inches or less in length. If loaded in a longer car, the minimum weight is increased in accordance with a table of weights given in the third section of the rule. There is a similar provision with respect to freight loaded on open cars, and a corresponding table of the varying minimum weights.

However, if a shipper orders a closed car not less than 40 feet in length, and the carrier is unable to furnish a car of the length ordered and instead furnishes a longer car, the minimum weight applicable will be that of the car ordered, unless the car supplied is loaded to capacity, in which case the minimum weight will be that applicable to the car used. If a shipper orders a car more than 40 feet 7 inches in length, and the carrier is unable to furnish a car of the length ordered or a longer car, the carrier may furnish two cars. The rule explains how the minimum weight is calculated in case two cars are provided. The provisions of the rule with regard to open cars are similar in principle to the regulations applicable in connection with closed cars.

It is extremely important for shippers dealing in articles subject to Rule 34 to be familiar with all the provisions of this rule. They must not just order "a car" from a carrier, but must specify a car of the length desired, if excess freight charges are to be avoided. It should be remembered that ignorance of the terms of the rule is no defense against its strict application. In fact, the carrier is bound to observe the terms of the rule just as it is bound to observe strictly the provisions of any published tariff. And, as it was pointed out before, the shipper is presumed to have knowledge of the rules, regulations, and charges of the tariffs under which his goods are transported.

One thing more about this rule should be noted. It provides that the length of cars referred to is based on the platform measurement of flat cars and the inside measurement of all other cars, except in the case of refrigerator cars with built-in bunkers, which are measured between the inner sides of the bunkers. Then the rule calls attention to a very important publication which is issued as an official tariff on behalf of virtually all the railroads of the country. As a matter of fact, this publication is referred to several times in the classification rules. It is the Official Railway Equipment Register, published by M. A. Zenobia as agent for the carriers. This important publication gives the measurements of all the freight cars used on American railroads.

Everyone knows that railroad cars are numbered. The numbering process reminds one somewhat of the methods which manufacturers employ in designating automobiles. Each manufacturer may turn out several "models," and each model has a certain descriptive number or combination of numbers and letters. The freight cars of a single railroad company consist of a number of different types, or models. Each model falls within a certain series of numerals. For instance, all boxcars of a certain length and type may be numbered from 30,001 to 60,000, another type may take another series, and so on. Such a method of numbering makes it relatively simple to present car measurements in the Equipment Register. In case of a dispute between carrier and shipper as to the length of a car which has been used to transport any article, it is easy to appeal to the information contained in the Register.

The average traffic man knows that the Register contains other information of high value to the shipper. Perhaps the most valuable item, next to giving the measurements of freight cars, is the list of all the junction points where any railroad makes physical connection with another. With the aid of the Register, one can find all the available rail routes that exist between any pair of freight stations in the United States, routes, that is, over which carloads of traffic may be moved without the necessity of transfer of lading from car to car.

Rule 35. This rather long rule has to do with freight carried in tank cars. Most of these cars are "private cars," that is, they are owned by industrial concerns or car companies and not by railroads. A carrier, according to this rule, is not obligated to furnish shippers with tank cars, though many of them do so voluntarily. This rule deals with minimum weights, the conversion of gallons into pounds, and certain safety measures which must be taken in connection with the movement of some tank car freight. Here again we have references to other publications, including the Railway Equipment Register which gives the measurements of privately owned tank cars, as well as to certain tariffs giving the gallonage capacities of tank cars and the weights per gallon of various liquids.

Rules 36 *and* 38. The first of these two rules tells how fractions are disposed of in computing rates which are proportions or multiples of other rates. A rate that is $1\frac{1}{4}$ times the first-class rate may turn out to have a fractional component. The rule followed is the one generally employed in many business transactions. If the fraction is less than half a cent, it is dropped; if half a cent or more, it is increased to the next whole figure.

There is no Rule 37, the former rule carrying that number having been dropped and no other rule assigned. Rule 38 calls attention to the precedence of a commodity rate over a class rate.

Rule 39. Railroads and other carriers in the United States transport a great many articles which are explosive or dangerous to handle. Long ago, the Interstate Commerce Commission was authorized to prescribe rules and regulations governing the transportation of these articles. At one time, the Commission's rules were published as a part of the classification, but they are now published as an agency tariff by H. A. Campbell, a separate tariff being issued by him on behalf of the three types of surface carriers, railroads, motor vehicles, and carriers by water. Rule 39 calls attention to these tariffs, the terms of which must be observed by all shippers, in accordance with orders of the Interstate Commerce Commission. These tariffs deal extensively with the methods of packing explosives and dangerous articles and also tell how packages containing such articles must be marked to indicate the nature of their contents.

Rules 40 *and* 41. These rules answer some very important questions. When, as the word is used in the classification, is a box a box? When is a barrel a barrel? The same question is answered with respect to such containers as crates, pails, firkins, kits, tubs, casks, drums, hogsheads, kegs, and tierces.

Older people can remember when virtually all containers in which freight was shipped by rail were made of wood. Boxes in which groceries and other merchandise were shipped, sugar barrels, salt and vinegar barrels, beer kegs, kerosene barrels, and many other containers were all made of wood. Boxes were carefully nailed, and sometimes strapped with steel. Barrels and kegs were held securely with strong hoops. The research of chemical engineers, the genius of inventors, and the steady cheapening of the processes by which steel, aluminum, and other metals could be made led to the introduction of new types of containers, just as strong, just as durable, affording just as much protection against loss or damage as the wooden containers, and frequently much lighter in weight and much cheaper to make.

The most common type of container which has replaced the wooden box is the container made of "fiberboard," which comes from the processed fibers of wood, straw, or various other vegetable substances. These fiberboard containers, solid or corrugated, are the subject of Rule 41, which is by far the longest rule in the Consolidated and the Uniform Classifications.

Rule 40 says that boxes must be made of iron, steel, or wood (except as provided in Rule 41) or of "hydraulically pressed wood or cane fiberboard not less than ⅛ inch thick, all ends, sides, tops and bottoms to be framed with wooden strips, stapled and stitched to each panel." Similar specifications are indicated for other types of containers, such as barrels, drums, and firkins. It is interesting to note how many kinds of material may now be employed to make containers which are acceptable to carriers under the terms of the classification. An amazing amount of research, study, and experimentation has been devoted in the last half-century to the development of shipping containers which resemble in little but size and shape the containers in general use a half-century ago. The brewery delivery truck of today, propelled by a powerful internal combustion motor, and loaded to the top with tier after tier of aluminum beer kegs, certainly has little in common with the delivery truck loaded with stout, ironbound oaken kegs and drawn by a matched four-horse team of huge Percheron horses, which rumbled and rattled over the streets in the gay nineties. Nor do the boxes one sees in grocery stores, shoe stores, and other retail establishments today look much like the boxes in which nearly all merchandise was packed for shipment a few dozen years ago, when pine wood was plentiful and the art of making fiberboard was in its infancy.

Rule 41 covers in detail the rules and regulations under which merchandise of various kinds can be shipped in solid or corrugated fiberboard boxes and other containers and the containers can be considered proper receptacles within the terms and descriptions of the Consolidated or Uniform Classification. It is stipulated in the very first section of the rule that when articles are tendered for shipment in fiberboard boxes and the requirements and specifications of the rule are not fully complied with, "freight charges will be increased 20% LCL or any quantity and 10% CL" above the charges applicable if the boxes are such as the rule requires. Similar increases are specified on freight in other fiberboard containers which do not comply with the specifications of the rule.

These specifications have to do with the character of the fiberboard employed in the construction of the various containers and the weight of the merchandise they contain. Several tables are given showing the dimensions, the weight of the material, the resistance to a bursting test the material must have, and the maximum weight which a container and its contents may have. A container must bear the certificate of its manufacturer stating that it conforms "to all the construction requirements of Consolidated Freight Classification," followed by a statement of its bursting strength, its size limit, and its gross weight limit.[2] Moreover, when a shipper uses containers such as are specified in Rule 41, as well as a few of the containers specified in Rule 40, he must certify in the bill of lading and shipping order that each container conforms to the specifications set forth in the certificate of the container's maker and to all other requirements of the Consolidated (or Uniform) Classification. The rules formerly required that each container bear a statement describing its contents, but this requirement was later dropped because it was thought to lead to pilferage.

Rule 42. This rule says that reshipping documents, invoices, and assembly and operating instructions may be included with freight shipments, either carload or less carload, at the rate applicable to the articles they accompany.

Rule 43. Many articles of freight, including all kinds of livestock, have attendants in charge during their transportation. Carriers do not accept liability for accidents to such attendants unless the accident is due to carrier negligence. Consequently, they require an attendant traveling by freight train to sign a contract relieving the carrier from liability for personal injuries. The contract with an attendant caring for livestock of any kind is to be found on the uniform livestock contract, which is the bill of lading under which livestock is shipped. Rule 43 provides the form of contract which attendants accompanying shipments other than livestock, live wild animals, or ostriches are required to sign. If a prospective attendant refuses to sign the contract, he will not be accepted for transportation. If an individual tariff item requires a certain shipment to be accompanied by an attendant, and the attendant refuses to sign the release, the shipment will not be accepted for transportation.

Rule 44 (*In Consolidated Classification only*). The fourth section of the Interstate Commerce Act forbids railroads to charge a higher rate for a short haul than for a long haul over the same route and in the same direction, the shorter haul included within the longer; it also forbids a railroad to charge a rate which is higher than the aggregate of the intermediate rates over the same route. These prohibitions are not, however, without qualification, for the Interstate Commerce Commission is authorized to grant "relief" from the provisions of the fourth section and permit the carriers to charge rates which, if charged without the Commission's permission, would be in violation of the fourth section.

In Fourth Section Order 144, the Commission authorized the carriers to make changes in the three major classifications and in the Illinois Classi-

---

[2] Of course, Uniform Classification No. 1 says that the containers must comply with the construction requirements of the Uniform Freight Classification. This classification has more detailed and elaborate rules about containers than its predecessor.

fication, without observing the prohibitions of the fourth section of the Interstate Commerce Act, where the existing rates were already protected by outstanding fourth section orders or applications. In the preparation of the revised classification, the committees found that there might be certain violations of the fourth section which were not authorized by Order 144. This rule, which was published at the Commission's order, says that such violations will be corrected on one day's notice and that the carriers will make prompt application for permission to make reparation to shippers who have been required to pay technically illegal rates.

Rule 45. It is customary for many manufacturers to furnish to merchants who distribute their products various kinds of advertising matter such as window signs, cards, and folders. Many products are accompanied by "premiums" for the consumer, the premium enclosed in the package in which the product is dispensed. This rule tells what and how much in the way of advertising matter and premiums may be shipped with merchandise at the same rate as the merchandise itself. Here again, the shipper must indicate on the bill of lading the amount of advertising matter or premiums which accompanies the shipment.

Rule 46. This rule explains the meaning of the terms "and," "or," "rate," "rating," and "column" as used in the classification, and also tells how indentations and parentheses appearing in the classification are to be interpreted. The classification items dealing with paper boxes affords a good illustration of the manner in which the terms "and" and "or" are used. It has already been indicated that the term "rate," as used in the classification, refers to the amount of a freight charge in money, while "rating" has reference to the numerals or letters employed in the classification to indicate the "class" to which an article belongs. Rates, of course, are found only in freight tariffs and not in the classification.

Rule 47. For many years, railroads did not accept C.O.D. shipments; that is, they would not contract to collect the selling price of an article from a consignee on behalf of a shipper, though the express business has followed the practice almost from its inception, and even the parcel-post service provides for the transmission of packages C.O.D. The competition of motor vehicle carriers and other agencies for the transportation of a great deal of the small lot, less carload shipments, which once went almost exclusively by rail, finally led the railroads to offer their customers a C.O.D. service. This rule explains the conditions under which such service will be rendered, and also indicates the charges which the railroad will exact for performing this comparatively new function. The service applies only to shipments moving at less carload or any quantity ratings, which are consigned to an "open" station, that is, a station at which the carrier maintains an agent. Here again, we come to a mention of one of the more important auxiliary documents of the railroads, Agent A. P. Leland's *List of Open and Prepay Stations,* which has the standing of an official tariff and is published and filed as other tariffs are published and filed.

Rule 48. This is a short rule which states that reference in the classification or in any of its supplements to any items, pages, or rules in this classification includes reference to reissues of such items, rules, and pages. It has already been explained that because of the limitation which the Interstate Commerce Commission puts upon the number of supplements to a tariff that can be effective at any one time, it is often necessary that supplementary material contained in some supplements be "reissued" in a succeeding supplement. This rule also states that any reference in the classification to other publications includes reference to supplements or successive issues of those publications.

Rule 49. It will be remembered that, under the terms of Rule 5 and Rule 41, certain increases in charges were made when merchandise was not shipped in prescribed containers. Occasionally a shipper or a container manufacturer develops a new type of container which it is believed will give as much protection as some container which would be subject to a lower rating. This rule permits, under certain conditions, an experimental or test shipment of merchandise in the new container, without any advance in freight charges which might technically be applicable. The chairman of one of the major classification committees must issue a permit for a test shipment, and of course the bill of lading must contain a reference to Rule 49 and indicate the number of the permit which has been issued.

Rule 50. Because of the common necessity of reconditioning and repacking certain commodities shipped in carload quantities, shippers may include with a shipment a number of empty containers of the kind in which the merchandise in the car is packed. This rule states that empty containers not exceeding a total weight of 25 pounds may be included in straight or mixed carload shipments of articles employing the same kind of containers. The rate applicable to the empty containers is the highest carload rate or rating of any commodity in such shipping containers included in the carload, but the weight of the extra containers shall not be counted in ascertaining if the carload exceeds or surpasses the applicable minimum carload weight.

Rules 51 *and* 52 *of the Uniform Freight Classification.* These two rules, which do not appear in the Consolidated Classification, give the weights to a gallon of liquefied petroleum gas and of butadiene, when transported in tank cars, according to their specific gravity at 60 degrees Fahrenheit and according to the time of year in which shipment takes place.

GENERAL OBSERVATIONS

This brings us to the end of the rules of the two great freight classifications. The rules are a highly important part of the intricately interwoven fabric of freight rates, and their close and careful study is an imperative task for all industrial traffic managers. It should be emphasized once more that the rules as printed in the classifications may be subject to many exceptions. These exceptions are to be found in various tariffs, both class and commodity, which are governed by one or the other of the classifications, or in the numerous exception tariffs which have been issued in profusion either individually or jointly by the nation's carriers.

It should always be borne in mind that a freight classification does not "stand alone." It contains virtually no rates; it is to be used in connection with the tariffs "governed" by the classification as indicated. The beginner in the study of traffic is sometimes puzzled about the question of "which classification to use." There is no danger of making an error in this matter, for the tariff in which the rate is sought will always name the governing classification. The same tariff cannot be subject to more than one classification.

It must be remembered that the Consolidated Freight Classification is not one single classification, but four. The same is true, nominally at least, of the Uniform Freight Classification. Class and commodity tariffs, which are to be used in conjunction with the Consolidated Classification, invariably tell whether they are governed by the Official, the Southern, the Western, or the Illinois Classification. The question arises as to what must be done about classifying traffic which moves from one classification territory into another. If there is a joint rate from point of origin to point of destination, though one cannot be sure, until seeing the tariff, which classification applies, one can always be sure that it will be only one of the classifications. In the publication of their joint class rates, railroads have followed different practices with respect to the governing classification. Sometimes it is the classification in general use in the territory of the point of origin; sometimes it is the one in use in the territory of the point of destination. It may be that some tariffs will be governed by one of these classifications, and some by the other. Rates on transcontinental freight—that is, freight shipped between points east of the Rocky Mountains and points on the Pacific Coast and in Intermountain Territory—have long been governed by Western Classification, and the existence of the new Uniform Classification will not, for the time being, disturb this practice. Freight passing between Official and Southern Territories is governed in some tariffs by the Southern Classification and in others by the Official.

If no joint rates exist on shipments moving between two territories, the traffic must move on a combination rate, and the classifications of both territories must be used, each with its proper tariff. It is entirely possible that a shipment may move on a combination rate through all three of the major classification territories, in which case all three classifications may have to be consulted in order to find the lowest applicable combination.

When the Uniform Classification comes into general use, it is unlikely that rate tariffs will refer to the four component classifications, nominally existent though they still may be. Since ratings and rules will all be the same, nothing would be gained by carrying along the names of the old territorial classifications. It is probable that in time even the names will be dropped, and in the distant future perhaps forgotten. Certainly the use of a single name and a single uniform classification will be of help to the compiler of tariffs and to the rate clerk who desires to ascertain the charges on a shipment.

In a previous part of this chapter, it was pointed out that motor carriers are participants in the Consolidated and the Uniform Classifications, and they also have freight classifications of their own. This will make understandable how a single carrier may be a participant in two or more freight classifications. It is the tariff that counts—the publication in which the actual rates are found—and it is quite possible for a motor vehicle carrier to have some tariffs subject to one classification and some to another. Freight forwarding companies may be parties to classifications of railroads, motor carriers, water carriers, and air lines. But each tariff will show its own governing classification.

CHAPTER VI

Freight Rate Tariffs

One qualification which every competent traffic manager must possess is the ability to read and understand the tariffs which carriers issue showing their rates for the transportation of freight and charges for other services they perform. Skill in the interpretation of tariffs is largely a matter of practice and must come from the study of tariffs themselves. An understanding of the general principles and of the patterns which tariff-publishing authorities employ in the preparation of schedules of charges may, however, be helpful to those who are just beginning the study of traffic management. In this chapter, we shall set forth a brief description of the methods followed by carriers in their efforts to present "an explicit statement of the rates, in cents or in dollars and cents, per 100 pounds, per ton, per car, or other unit, together with the names or designation of the places from and to which they apply, all arranged in a simple and systematic manner." It must be remembered that we are considering only the mechanics of tariff publication, not the manner or method by which the amount of a rate is determined. Though we shall deal primarily with railroad tariffs, it must be borne in mind that the rates of other carriers are compiled and published in a manner similar to that which the railroads follow.

TARIFF A PRICE LIST

A tariff is, of course, only a price list, showing in printed form the charges which a carrier exacts for its services. Like any other price lists, tariffs vary widely in volume and complexity according to the number of prices quoted. A manufacturing establishment may issue a price list on a small number of articles on a single printed page. A mail-order house which sells and distributes a vast number of articles may issue a price list which requires a volume of several hundred pages.

POSTAL TARIFF

Nearly everybody is familiar with one very common price list for transportation service. This is the list of the rates we pay for postage on matters which the government accepts as mail. All mail matter used to be carried at a flat rate for all distances, though there was a difference in the charges for different "classes" of mail, and the total charge varied with the weight of the letter or publication carried. When the government finally established a parcel-post system, in 1913, it was deemed advisable to have parcel rates vary with distance as well as with weight. As a consequence, the price list for mail matter had to be considerably enlarged. Even so, the system adopted was relatively simple, and the "United States postal rates" which one can find in dozens of publications still do not require much space for their printing. The post-office clerk or the traffic manager who wants to know the exact charge for a parcel-post shipment from a certain point must have a "guide" by which he ascertains the "zone" of the point of destination, so the "tariff" of the rates on parcel post is a bit more complicated than the familiar statement of charges given in almanacs, many memorandum books, and other compendiums of miscellaneous information.

When the parcel-post system was inaugurated, the postal clerk used a map to determine the zone location of any destination point for which he might receive a parcel for transportation. The continental United States was divided into "units," each 30 minutes square and numbered in a systematic manner. For each of these units, a map was printed, having a series of concentric circles which marked the boundaries of eight postal zones. A parcel-post guide showed the "unit location" of each post office in the country. Once the unit location of a destination office was known, it was easy enough for the postal employee to find the zone of that office by consulting the map. It was not long until zone keys were printed for each unit. A key gave directly the zone location of all other post offices and made the use of the map unnecessary.

RAILWAY EXPRESS TARIFF

Another fairly simple transportation price list was that which the Interstate Commerce Commission prescribed for the express system of the United States, in 1912, and which is still in use, though the rates have been changed greatly, and the various express companies which existed in 1913 have long since been merged into a single organization, now owned by the railroads themselves. Under this rate pattern, the United States was divided into a number of "blocks," each one degree square, or four times as large as the units employed in the parcel-post rate scheme. Each block was subdivided into sixteen subblocks. A Directory of Express Stations gave the block location of all express stations in the country. A "Rate Table I" gave the block location of each station, and a "Rate Table II" showed for each block the number of a "rate scale" applicable to shipments from any one block to all other blocks. The numbered rate scales showed the actual charges to be imposed according to the weight of the shipment. A similar scheme was employed to indicate the rates between the subblocks of a single block and between the subblocks of one block and those of adjacent blocks.

Railroads have never adopted—and it is difficult to see how they could adopt—a simplified system of rate publication such as that employed by the express business and by the parcel post. The variety and volume of traffic are much too great, and numerous competitive situations make it impossible to carry simplification so far. They have long followed and still follow the practice of quoting rates from station to station. It was pointed out in a previous chapter how the large number of stations and the large number of articles carried as railroad freight made the task of rate publication a highly complicated matter. It was shown how the process was simplified, to some extent at least, by introducing the practice of freight classification.

SIMPLE FREIGHT TARIFFS

Some freight tariffs are very simple and easy to read. There are many commodity tariffs, for example, which quote rates on a single commodity from a single station to a relatively small number of destination stations. Obviously, the problem of compiling or reading a tariff of this kind presents no difficulty. Such a tariff may take up only one page. The destination stations are given in a column at the left of the page, and opposite the name of each station is given the rate from the single point of origin.

Some class tariffs have been compiled which are almost equally simple. Rates on various classes are given from a single station to a number of other stations. Here again, the rates may be read directly. The stations of destination are listed at the left of the page—there may be several pages—and in appropriate columns the rates on the different classes are given opposite the name of each station. Many railroads have compiled local tariffs after this pattern. Such tariffs are as simple as a manufacturer's price list; the rates are read directly in a single step; there are no complications to be dealt with.

The chief objection to simplified tariffs of this kind is that they can be used only at single stations, and if a carrier has a large number of stations and is obliged to print a separate tariff for each one, the process involves a great deal of unnecessary labor and expense. A railroad which has a large number of stations usually prints a local tariff of class rates which can be used at any one of its stations, to ascertain the rates to all other stations on the road. So the process of complication in tariff publication begins.

TARIFF COMPILATION

The usual method of compiling tariffs which can be used at all local stations is to list stations "from which" at the left of a page and stations "to which" across the top of the page. Vertical lines are drawn enclosing the names of the stations "to which," while horizontal lines enclose the names of the stations "from which." Where these lines cross, small squares are formed, and in each square is inserted a "rate reference number," [1] under which, in another part of the tariff, may be found the actual rates applicable to each class of freight. The page of such a tariff, with its intersecting lines and squares, resembles the schedules of the games of the two major baseball leagues which are printed in all newspapers each spring, and they are similar also to the mileage charts or tables which one finds on nearly all road maps obtainable at gasoline filling stations. The rate reference numbers correspond to the distances between various pairs of cities on a road-map distance table.

If there are many stations between which rates are to be quoted in a single tariff, it is necessary to repeat, perhaps several times, the names of a group of stations "from which," in order that a rate reference or rate base number can be given for all of the stations to be listed at the top of the page as stations "to which." When the first group of stations "from which" has been repeated until a rate base number is supplied for all the stations "to which," another group of stations "from which" is listed, rate base numbers given in the same manner, and so on, until a number has been supplied for all pairs of stations. The greater the number of stations to be paired, the more rate base numbers there will be. These numbers are all listed on designated pages of the tariff, and opposite each number is the rate applicable to each class of freight which may be hauled between the pair of stations to which that reference number has been assigned.

It will be seen at once that this type of tariff can be used only when the number of stations between which rates are to be given is somewhat limited. But suppose a carrier having a very large system or a group of carriers desired to publish rates between a thousand or two thousand or even ten thousand pairs of stations. It is obvious that to follow such a plan of publication would require a volume of such size as to make a large mail-order catalogue look, by comparison, like a thin pamphlet. Here the tariff-publishing authorities must resort again to a process of simplification, and it is interesting to note that the process employed bears a close resemblance to what is done in the classification of freight. The process makes the ascertainment of rates a slightly more complicated matter, but it certainly reduces the volume of material to be printed.

[1] The expression "rate reference number" is not used in all tariffs. The numbers under which the rates are found at the proper place in a tariff are sometimes called rate scale numbers, rate base numbers, or rate basis numbers. It is probable that "rate base number" is used most frequently.

TARIFFS WITH GROUP RATES

The tariff compiler, in effect, "classifies" the stations named in a tariff, though not on the same basis that articles are classified in a freight classification. The classification or grouping of stations is purely geographical. In other words, stations of origin and stations of destination are divided into groups, and the rates from all stations of origin in a single group to all stations of destination in a single group are the same. The process of grouping, it will be seen, has the same result, as far as tariff publication is concerned, as the process of freight classification. It reduces, as it were, the number of stations between which rates are to be quoted. If, for example, a tariff naming ten thousand stations of origin, and an equal number of stations of destination, divided both kinds of stations into ten groups, the effect would be the same as reducing the number of stations to twenty, ten "from which" and ten "to which."

Many tariffs are constructed on this plan. The groups into which stations are divided are designated by letters, by figures, or in some other manner.[2] All stations of origin are listed in an index, as required by *Tariff Circular* No. 20, and each is assigned to a certain group. The same thing is done with the stations of destination. Then the rates, either class or commodity, instead of being given directly from one station to another, are given from group to group. This plan necessitates an additional step in reading such a tariff. Before looking for the base number, under which the actual rate is to be found, in the case of a class-rate tariff, the person reading the tariff must first ascertain the groups to which the stations of origin and destination belong, between which it is desired to find the proper rate.

TERRITORIAL DIRECTORIES

Some of the tariffs constructed so as to show rates between groups of stations rather than directly between individual stations may apply to several thousand stations, and the indexes of stations may take up as many pages of the tariff as the rates, rules, and other matter which the tariffs contain. If the indexes of stations appear in the body of such a tariff, each time the tariff is reissued a very large amount of material must be reprinted in which there has been no substantial change since the edition

[2] There are numerous ways in which the stations belonging to a single group may be designated. Very often the names of "key points" are used. For example, a rate from "New York" is given, and other points of origin shown as taking "New York" rates. But whether letters, figures, city names, or other devices are used, the scheme of grouping points of origin and destination, for the purpose of tariff simplification, is the same in all tariffs where it is impracticable to publish "station-to-station" rates.

to be canceled has been published. As a measure of economy as well as convenience—since such a tariff may be very large—the indexes of stations may be published in a separate volume known as a "territorial directory of stations," a procedure which is permissible under the Commission's rules. A territorial directory, with perhaps a few thin supplements, may outlast a half-dozen or more issues of the tariff, and the saving in printing charges and in the labor of publication is very considerable.

FIRST STEPS IN TARIFF READING

It must be remembered that every tariff is likely to have its own special rules and regulations, and nearly all class tariffs are subject to certain designated exceptions to the ruling classification. The larger the tariff, as a rule, the greater becomes the number of special rules and directions for the use of the tariff. The first step to be taken in the study of any tariff is to examine carefully the table of contents, in order to ascertain exactly what divisions the tariff contains and the nature of the subject matter it deals with.

Every footnote, every reference mark, every special rule or regulation in a tariff must be observed carefully and its meaning comprehended. Many tariffs contain routing instructions indicating the routes over which the rates in the tariffs are applicable; some will contain provisions for the "alternative" use of certain sections of the tariffs; many will contain notes to the effect that certain general provisions of the tariffs are not applicable at certain stations or on certain routes or parts of routes; many tariffs have notices to the effect that they contain rates concerning which the issuing lines have obtained "fourth section relief," and indicating the number of the order of the Interstate Commerce Commission in which such relief was granted.

INTERMEDIATE POINTS RULE

The rules of the Interstate Commerce Commission provide that tariffs must be filed at all stations from which the rates included in the tariff apply. There are many commodity tariffs published containing rates which are not applicable from certain intermediate stations which are not specifically named, because there is not one chance in a thousand that the commodity or commodities upon which the rates are given will ever be shipped from the small intermediate stations from which rates are not published. Such a tariff is likely to contain a notice based upon the so-called intermediate rule, found in Rule 27 of the Commission's *Tariff Circular* No. 20. It provides, with certain conditions, that

. . . from any point of origin from which a commodity rate on a given article to a given destination and via a given route is not named in this tariff, which point is intermediate to a point from which a commodity rate on said article is published in this tariff via a route through the intermediate point over which such commodity rate applies to the same destination, apply from such intermediate point to such destination and via such route the commodity rate in this tariff on said article from the next point beyond from which a commodity rate is published herein on that article to the same destination via the same route.

This is the intermediate rule for obtaining a commodity rate *from* an intermediate station; there is a similar rule for obtaining a commodity rate *to* an intermediate station to which no rate specifically applies.

As an example of how it might become necessary to apply the intermediate rule, let us suppose that there is a center we shall designate as A where some junk dealer, because of the character of local industry, has been able to build up a very considerable business in the collection and sale of scrap iron, which he sells to a steel mill 100 miles away. He secures a commodity rate on the scrap iron, but since at no point between A and the steel mill is there another scrap-iron business, the commodity rate is published only from A, and not from any "intermediate" station. Then some enterprising individual at B, 40 miles closer than A to the steel mill, gathers up enough scrap iron for a carload and sells it to the steel mill. When he goes to ship it, he finds that the only rate in effect on scrap iron from B to the mill is a class rate, perhaps twice as much as the commodity rate which the junk dealer at A must pay on his shipments to the steel mill. Obviously, if the railroad imposes the class rate, it is guilty of violating the fourth section of the Interstate Commerce Act, which forbids a railroad, without the consent of the Commission to charge more for a short haul than for a long haul, over the same route and in the same direction, the shorter haul being included in the longer. If the railroad has protected itself with an intermediate provision in its tariff, it can give the new junk dealer a commodity rate which is no higher than the rate from A.

There are a few "conditions" attached to the intermediate rule. If the class rate from or to the intermediate point happens to be lower than the commodity rate from or to the next most distant point, of course the class rate will be applicable. When, because of diverging routes or branch lines, there are two or more "next beyond" points, the commodity rate applicable to or from the intermediate point will be the lowest charge applicable from the various "beyond points." Or it may be that the intermediate point lies between two points from which commodity rates apply on the article to be shipped, and for some reason the Interstate Commerce Commission has given permission for the point at the greater distance from the destination to charge a lower rate than the rate applicable from the nearer point. In this case, the intermediate point will take the higher of the two rates. The same condition attaches if one is seeking a rate "to" an intermediate point situated between two points having different commodity rates.

ARBITRARIES

Very often, one will find in the "notes" of a tariff a number of items known as "arbitraries." They are found, for the most part, in tariffs which contain rates applying from one group of stations to another group. There may be a number of outlying stations which, because of distance or other reasons, are not included in any group. If the number of such stations is so small as not to justify the creation of another group, their rates are made by the addition of certain amounts to the rates applicable to the stations of the nearest group. These small amounts are called arbitraries. Occasionally, one may find a tariff where both points of origin and points of destination are listed as taking arbitraries. In many large tariffs, one will find a footnote number after the names of numerous stations and, upon consulting the note to which a number refers, will discover that an arbitrary is to be added to some designated rate to procure the rate to the station the name of which carries a footnote reference. The notes in a tariff may mean many other things, and they must always be consulted when reference is made to them. One may find that this station handles only inbound freight, and that one only outbound; that this station handles only carload freight, and that one only less carload; that this station is equipped with cranes for unloading heavy objects from flat cars. There is a seemingly endless number of items of special information with which the reader of a tariff must familiarize himself.

CROSS REFERENCES

Many tariffs carry references to other tariffs, and can be understood only in conjunction with these other publications. It is plain that any class-rate tariff would be of no use unless read in conjunction with its governing classification and exceptions, but it often happens that publications other than classifications must be consulted in order to understand the meaning of all the provisions of a particular tariff.

Enough has been said to indicate that the development of an ability to read railroad tariffs intelligently requires much study and practice. But if one finds that learning to read tariffs readily is a task of considerable difficulty, there may be some consolation in reflecting upon the fact that the task of compiling tariffs and preparing them for publication is a task of much greater magnitude.

THE NEED FOR ACCURACY

The first requisite in the compilation of a tariff is accuracy. The mere work of proofreading a tariff during the course of its printing requires the careful, painstaking efforts of many persons. If an error is made in a rate, the rate still stands until a correction can be made. If a rate of 73 cents, for example, is inadvertently changed to read 37 cents, the shipper is entitled to the use of the lower rate until a supplement can be published in which the mistake is corrected.[3]

The rules and regulations of the Interstate Commerce Commission must be scrupulously followed and, as has previously been indicated, these rules are numerous and detailed. The language employed in the tariff must be such that it is susceptible to only one interpretation. If a tariff contains ambiguous language, that is, if it contains clauses that can fairly be interpreted in different ways, the shipper is entitled to the benefit of the interpretation which is most favorable to him. Tariffs must not contain any "double talk."

It is not often that errors of importance creep into railroad tariffs, but occasionally they do. And quite frequently carriers and shippers have grave differences of opinion about the interpretation of the passages of a freight tariff, differences which the Interstate Commerce Commission may be called upon to settle.

TARIFFS EFFECTIVE UNTIL CANCELED

Once in a while it may happen that a railroad decides to change the location of certain rates in its tariff publications. That is, it is decided that rates which have been published in one tariff shall for the future be published in another tariff. The rates are changed accordingly. But it is discovered subsequently that the carrier has neglected to cancel the rates as they formerly appeared. If there is no change in the rates, no harm ensues, but suppose the rates have been either increased or lowered. Then we apparently have two different rates for the same transportation service. Obviously, this is an impossible situation. The question naturally arises as to which rate is the legal rate. The rule in this case is very simple. A rate once published remains in effect until it is canceled, and the new rates cannot become effective until the carrier retraces its steps and effects a cancellation of the older rates.

It was explained in a former chapter that tariffs may be published by the carriers themselves as "individual" tariffs, or they may be published and filed by agents duly authorized by carriers to perform the task. Each individual carrier maintains a tariff bureau, large or small, according to

[3] If, as in this case, the mistake favors the shipper, the railroad cannot recover for any loss in revenue due to the error in the tariff. But if a rate of 73 cents is published, when 37 cents was intended, the shipper, though having to pay the higher rate until it is canceled, can secure reparation from the carrier. The reparation will usually be paid without question, though the formal consent of the Commission is necessary.

the number of publications it compiles and issues, and the agents which publish tariffs likewise maintain a force of expert compilers.

HISTORICAL NATURE OF TARIFFS

There are several reasons why the work of the bureau which prepares rate publications is not so formidable as it may at first seem to be. In the first place, not many "new" tariffs are compiled. Most of them are revisions of former publications, and these in turn followed predecessors of their own. The "historical" nature of railroad rates must never be forgotten. This is true whether we are thinking of the amount of the rate or of the manner and methods of compilation and publication. Virtually every tariff is a product of long years of growth and development. If our present transportation system were suddenly destroyed and forgotten about, and then in some distant age it should suddenly be reproduced in a very short time, the work of constructing a rate system and publishing it would indeed be formidable. But complicated things do not spring full-blown into existence. We should stop and remember once in a while that our railroad system had a very modest start, in a line only a few miles long, over a hundred years ago; that our amazing system of communication by wire had an equally modest start with a line between Baltimore and Washington just a little more than a century ago; that our motor vehicles, our airplanes, our highways, our stupendous factories for mass production, all had feeble and often most unpromising beginnings. Many people are still able to remember our first earphone radios and the lively controversy over the benefits of the so-called "loud-speaker"; some can remember when all moving pictures were of the silent variety (and perhaps wish they still were); and everybody has followed with interest the painful progress of television. Everything we see is a product of a longer or shorter period of growth. Indeed, the greatest scientific theory advanced during the nineteenth century was that all forms of living matter were the result of untold ages of gradual evolution and development. There is not much under the sun that can be called new.

RATE STRUCTURES

Another thing that makes the work of the tariff compiler much easier than it might otherwise be is that nearly all rates are made after a definite pattern. The work of dressmaking is made easier by the use of patterns, and so is the work of building a steamship made easier by the employment of templates in the mold loft. Over the years the railroads, in cooperation with one another, have agreed on the pattern which rates should follow in a certain territorial district, and though the particular types of patterns employed have been subject to more or less change, the use of patterns still persists. The rates of a certain region, which have been made after a prescribed pattern, are known collectively as a "rate structure," and the experienced traffic manager invariably has a close acquaintance with one or more of the rate structures that are in use throughout the United States.

To work out a rate structure satisfactory to all the railroads in a certain territory, it was necessary for the railroads to "organize." This they did by the creation of what we call "traffic associations," which are nothing more or less than railroad "trade associations" similar to those found among many industries, though the railroad associations are much older. In fact, industry seems to have gotten the idea of developing trade associations from a study of the activities of the traffic associations of the railroads.

TARIFFS AND TRAFFIC ASSOCIATIONS

In the beginning, the work of these railroad traffic associations was carried on openly, without danger of being called to account for violation of the law. For while the rate agreements they worked out could not be enforced at law, because they were "contracts in restraint of trade" and therefore not recognizable as binding under the common law, they nevertheless did not constitute a violation of any statute. In 1887, the Act to Regulate Commerce (which has become our present Interstate Commerce Act) declared railroad pools to be illegal, and for a time brought an end to the practice which the railroads had followed of making agreements with respect to competitive freight rates and passenger fares. The traffic associations, however, soon found a way to enter into rate agreements without the use of pools to enforce their terms. But the Supreme Court, in two notable decisions handed down in 1897 and 1898, declared that these formal rate agreements were illegal because they violated the provisions of the Sherman Antitrust law of 1890.[4] These decisions brought an end to formal rate agreements, but the railroads maintained their traffic associations, and by "informal" action managed to secure just as great a degree of agreement on competitive rates as they had been able to achieve when pools were not unlawful. After the Interstate Commerce Act was amended in 1906 and again in 1910, and the Interstate Commerce Commission obtained plenary powers to regulate railroad rates, little attention was given to the activities of the traffic associations, because it was thought they could do no harm in view of the fact that the Commission had ample powers to prevent them from raising or otherwise modifying rates by arbitrary action. During the First World War, while the government was operating the railroads, these associations were used by the government itself to settle controversies over rates; when government control ended, the railroads continued to operate their associations in the open, even going to the extent of having "public" hearings on proposals which

---

[4] United States v. Trans-Missouri Freight Association, 166 U.S. 290 (1897); United States v. Joint Traffic Association, 171 U.S. 505 (1898).

shippers or carriers brought forward with respect to changes in the rates.

These activities on the part of traffic associations were doubtless illegal, because the Sherman Law condemns, without any equivocation or circumlocution, "all" contracts in "restraint of trade." But for years the Department of Justice took no action against the associations, and there was no public clamor demanding that the traffic associations be prosecuted for violation of Federal statutes. It was true that their activities might be technically illegal, but since the Interstate Commerce Commission had ample power to protect the public from any abuses of which the traffic associations might be thought guilty, there was no use in "getting technical" about the law. The time eventually came, however, when the Department of Justice changed its views on the matter and brought suit against certain railroad associations for what it claimed to be violations of the antitrust laws. At almost the same time, the sovereign state of Georgia, abetted and aided by other southern states, brought proceedings in the Supreme Court of the United States charging that there was a "conspiracy" among certain railroads and bankers to throttle economic progress in the South by subjecting southen products to higher rates than were imposed upon competing products originating in the eastern states and other parts of the country.

Alarmed by a fear that the successful prosecution of these various suits would bring an end to cooperation among railroads in making competitive rates, the carriers inaugurated an impressive publicity campaign designed to convince the public that the "conference" method of rate making was a desirable and wholesome practice, and at the same time they appealed to Congress to enact a measure authorizing them to employ the conference method without being held guilty of violating Federal law.

REED-BULWINKLE ACT

After considerable hesitation and delay, Congress finally passed, in June, 1948, over a presidential veto, the so-called Reed-Bulwinkle Act, granting the request of the troubled railroads. This law, which constitutes Section 5a of the Interstate Commerce Act, authorizes carriers, under certain conditions and always contingent upon the consent and approval of the Interstate Commerce Commission, to enter into agreements with respect to competitive rates, and declares that the "parties to any agreement approved by the Commission . . . are hereby relieved from the operation of the antitrust laws with respect to the making of such agreement." Lawful agreements can be made between carriers of one class only, that is, railroads can enter into arrangements with other railroads with regard to competitive rates, but not with other carriers. This prohibition does not apply, however, to agreements with respect to joint rates and through routes, which can legally be negotiated by the different classes of carriers.

The Reed-Bulwinkle Act saved the traffic associations of the railroads and of other carriers, and they are now able to do, without fear of prosecution, what they had long been doing anyway. The Supreme Court, after the enactment of the new law, dismissed the conspiracy charges which the state of Georgia had brought against the railroads, and while the charges brought by the Department of Justice have not yet been formally dismissed, the judge who listened to testimony and argument has indicated that the enactment of the Reed-Bulwinkle measure will doubtless have a pronounced effect on any decision he may eventually render.

There are many traffic associations and other organizations maintained by railroads and by other carriers. The organizations have different names, the water lines preferring to designate theirs as "conferences." But whether called a conference, an association, a league, a bureau, or a federation, the purpose of all the organizations is the same—to endeavor by discussion and conference to reach a mutually satisfactory understanding of common problems and to iron out the difficulties which arise from competition.

LEADING TRAFFIC ASSOCIATIONS

The leading freight traffic associations maintained by the railroads are given in the following list. The name of the association indicates the geographical area to which its activities are confined. All of these associations and many others have filed "articles of organization and procedure" with the Interstate Commerce Commission, as required by law.

New England Railroad Association
Trunk Line Territory Railroads (eastern trunk lines)
Central Territory Railroads
Southern Freight Association
Western Trunk Line Committee
Southwestern Freight Bureau
North Pacific Coast Freight Bureau
Pacific Southwest Freight Bureau
Trans-Continental Freight Bureau

There are numerous smaller associations having jurisdiction over the traffic of a single state or of two states, or over the traffic of a few strategic cities or river crossings, and a few associations may deal with certain kinds of commodities, such as coal. The railroads maintain passenger traffic associations which parallel their freight associations. There are numerous freight and passenger associations which have been organized by the operators of trucks and buses, and there are several conferences of water carriers, the best known being the Intercoastal Steamship Freight

Association, which deals with the rates and operating practices of vessels operating in that part of our domestic commerce which passes through the Panama Canal.

TRAFFIC ASSOCIATIONS AS AGENTS

The "agency" tariffs, of which we have spoken, are issued in the main by these various associations. Sometimes the association, or the tariff bureau of an association, is named as the "agent" by which the tariff is issued, and sometimes the agent is an individual, usually the chairman of a traffic association under whose auspices the rates are compiled. Because both individuals and bureaus act as agents, some writers make a distinction between an "agency's tariff" and an "agent's tariff," but it is a distinction without a difference. They are all treated alike by the Interstate Commerce Commission. Even when a bureau appears as an agent, there must be an individual appearing as "attorney-in-fact" for the publication of the tariff.

It is through these associations that most of the rate structures of the country have been originated and developed. We shall deal in more detail with these rate structures in the following chapters, in which the amount of the freight rates charged will be discussed. It is necessary here only to call attention to the fact that these agencies have made "rate patterns," and once a pattern is devised, which the rates of a particular region must follow, the task of compiling and publishing rates is greatly simplified. Many of the patterns which were formerly in effect have been greatly transformed by orders of the Interstate Commerce Commission. Even so, a pattern still remains as guide to the employees of a tariff bureau, either of a carrier or of a carrier association, in determining the character of the rate schedules which make up any particular tariff.

WHO READS TARIFFS

The two principal groups of individuals who devote much of their time to the reading and interpretation of tariffs are industrial traffic managers and their employees and the freight agents of various carriers. There are certain circumstances which tend to make the work of both these groups somewhat easier than a beginner in the study of traffic management might assume. The industrial traffic manager, while he may have to familiarize himself with rates from several points of origin and to many points of destination, is likely to be concerned with only a limited number of products—the raw materials which his plant consumes and the finished products which it distributes. He does not have to have an extended knowledge of the rates on all the commodities which carriers transport, but of the rates on a relatively small number of them. On the other hand, the freight agent, whose business it is to look up rates on the traffic which passes through his station, though he must learn about the rates on many articles, is concerned chiefly with the rates from a single station. He does not have to be familiar with the great web of rates which encompasses the entire country. The work of both these groups, therefore, is simplified by the nature of their particular employment. It is interesting to watch an experienced rate clerk in a railroad freight office write down the rates on shipping orders for the use of the billing clerk who prepares the way-bills. He is so familiar with the rates applicable from his station that he writes most of them from memory. Only once in a while will he lay a shipping order to one side without marking the rate. This one has to do with a shipment to a place with which he is not familiar, or a shipment of a commodity which is rarely handled through his station. For the rate, he must consult a tariff in order that the proper notation may be made on the shipping order.

There are individuals who must have a wider knowledge of rates than that possessed by the average traffic manager or railway station agent. Such persons are the rate clerks of freight auditing bureaus, who may be called upon to check freight bills from many parts of the country, and the employees of the Interstate Commerce Commission or other government bureaus, state or federal, whose duty it is to check the rates mentioned in complaints which are submitted for adjudication. Some rate clerks may be asked questions about a rate from some obscure point in southern California to a still more obscure point in the wilds of Maine. It is obvious that they cannot always depend on memory. What are the steps which a clerk takes in an endeavor to check a rate between places of which he has never heard?

HOW TO LOCATE STATIONS

Obviously, the first thing the clerk must know is the railroad location of the points named. He has the names of the stations and the states, but he does not necessarily know on which railroads the stations are located. The best publication in which to obtain this information is *Leland's List of Open and Prepay Stations,* which has already been referred to. It is the best publication because it is an official tariff, from which the clerk can work with complete confidence. There is also another publication which is known to all traffic managers and widely used to discover on what railroad or railroads a particular station is located. This publication is *The Official Guide of Railways and Steam Navigation Lines in the United States,* published monthly by the National Railway Publication Company, in New York City. It is strictly a "private" publication, that is, it has no official standing, such as a railroad tariff has. Its chief function is to give information about passenger train service in the United States, and it lists all the passenger train timetables of all American railroads. If you want to make a tour about the country by rail, you can plan your itinerary and your schedule by consulting this interesting and useful publication.

The Official Guide contains a complete index of all the passenger stations in the United States, tells what railroads they are served by, and if a particular point is served by different roads with different passenger stations, it even tells how far apart the stations are. Many industrial traffic managers and their rate clerks use this guide to obtain information about the location of various railroad stations, or rather to determine on what railroad a particular station may be located. But the guide is not infallible. It is an odd fact that many places in the United States have one name as a passenger station and another name as a freight station. A few have had even a third name as a post office. But, for the most part, the guide is an entirely satisfactory document for a traffic manager to use when he wants to know what railroad or railroads reach a particular point.

TARIFF INDEXES

If the inquirer who is in search of a rate finds that the point of origin and the point of destination involved in his inquiry are both located on the same railroad, he knows at once that his task does not present much more difficulty. Obviously a local rate will be available, and all he has to do is find out in what tariff the rate is published. How does he do this? Among the rules which the Interstate Commerce Commission has included in *Tariff Circular* No. 20, there is one which we have not previously mentioned. It is a rule which requires every railroad to publish and file a complete "index" of its tariffs. This index will show all the tariffs—local, joint, proportional, class, commodity, export, and import—to which the carrier is a party. It will indicate the kind of publication, whether individual or agency, and will tell the names of the carriers who participate in joint tariffs.

With such an index, our rate clerk can soon ascertain the identity of the local class and commodity tariffs which contain rates between the two stations in which he is interested. We have previously explained that if there is no commodity rate applicable on the article to be shipped, it must move under a class rate. If, after consulting applicable exceptions, our clerk finds that the article in question is not named therein, he will go to the effective classification to obtain the proper class of the article to be transported and then consult the local class tariff for the proper rate.

If, after consulting either *The Official Guide* or *Leland's List,* our clerk finds that the stations between which he seeks a rate are located on different railroads, his task becomes a little more complicated. If the two railroads are located so as to have junction points, in all likelihood there is a joint rate, class or commodity, applicable to the shipment, and the index will reveal in what tariff the rate may be found. If the railroads are far apart, the index may reveal that notwithstanding the separation the railroad on which the point of origin is located has joint rates applicable on classes or commodities or both, maintained in connection with the railroad upon which the point of destination is located. A little more search, and the applicable rate will be found.

FINDING COMBINATION RATES

Finally, the most difficult case arises, that in which there are no joint rates whatever between the point of origin and the point of destination. It is necessary to look up an applicable combination rate, remembering at all times that the lowest combination rate applicable is the one to which the shipper is lawfully entitled. After having found the railroads upon which his shipping points are located, and finding too perhaps that the railroad of the point of origin does not make any direct connection with the road of the point of destination, the rate clerk must determine the route which the shipment must follow in its journey. A traffic manager of even average ability and experience should have enough knowledge of the geography of the United States and of the railroad network of the country to be able to designate the route or routes over which a combination rate is to be calculated. But if one or both of the stations are located on little "jerk-water" roads, which he has never heard of even by name, his cause is still not hopelessly lost. He can refer to the Railway Equipment Register, which we have mentioned previously, and with the exercise of a little ingenuity he will soon be able to figure out the route over which the shipment will most readily move. He will look up the junction points of the roads of origin and destination, as listed in the Register, and in very little time will obtain a connection with a well-known road. Once the problem of finding a route has been solved, the task of finding the applicable combination rate is a matter of search among possible applicable tariffs.

There are many other helps which are available to traffic managers in their rate work. Numerous private agencies issue "guides" which tell about routing and railroad services, and some of their publications give the freight rates applicable over many of the leading railroads of the country. Similar guides are available which discuss traffic law and keep the traffic manager up to date on changes in the law as well as in the administrative policies and practices of the Interstate Commerce Commission.

TARIFF FILES

All large traffic departments maintain a file of tariffs in which may be found the rates and rules applicable to the traffic which the various departments handle. The tariffs are obtained by applying to the railroad companies on whose behalf they are issued either by the railroads themselves or by agents. The railroads of England and various other European countries have long followed the practice of selling their tariffs for enough to pay for the cost of their publication and distribution. In the United States, the Consolidated and the Uniform Classifications, and some of the more important agency tariffs can be purchased from the bureaus through which they are issued. But for the most part, American railroad tariffs are distributed gratuitously to interested shippers. The expense of publication and distribution is considerable, and one wonders why American railroads which complain chronically of their desperate financial situation do not follow the example of European carriers and make a modest charge for their rate schedules.

Some industrial traffic departments, once having obtained the necessary tariffs, have followed the practice of making a card index of the rates most frequently employed. This method of cataloguing rates so that they can be referred to quickly has suffered some discouragement in recent years because nearly all railroad rates have been changed so frequently. A card index has barely been completed when it has had to be completely revised because rates have been increased to a new level. Many firms which once maintained card indexes of transportation rates have abandoned the practice. Their traffic departments rely directly upon tariffs for rate information.

TRAFFIC BULLETIN AND TRAFFIC WORLD

A traffic manager must always be on the alert for changes or proposed changes in rates. He may not always be supplied with information by the carriers who upon proper application supply him with tariffs. One of the valuable private publications which many traffic managers subscribe to is the *Traffic Bulletin,* published by the Traffic Service Corporation of Washington, D.C. This weekly bulletin carries information with respect to all rate changes proposed to or filed with the Interstate Commerce Commission. The Traffic Service Corporation is also the publisher of *Traffic World,* a weekly magazine with which few industrial traffic managers can afford not to have an intimate acquaintance. It contains numerous articles of interest to members of the traffic profession; it contains either a verbatim report or an excellent summary of all decisions of the Interstate Commerce Commission, as well as a summary of the decisions of courts, state and Federal, and of state commissions, dealing with transportation controversies. In its question-and-answer column, one may find illuminating discussions of many knotty traffic problems, all of them bolstered with references to laws and court decisions. The advertisements keep the wide-awake traffic manager aware of all the current developments in the field of traffic work, from the services of transportation agencies to technical improvements in all the facilities with which a progressive traffic manager should be familiar.

"MASTER TARIFFS"

For the past few years, the work of finding correct railroad rates has been made much more difficult because of the frequency with which the Interstate Commerce Commission has permitted the railroads to make "blanket" increases in virtually all of their transportation charges. It is obviously impracticable for the carriers to revise at once all their tariffs when a general increase or reduction of rates takes effect. The Commission has permitted them to use "special supplements" to indicate the changes in rates. In one column of such a supplement will be given the amount of the old rate, and in a parallel column will be given the amount of the new rate. These "master supplements" modify all the tariffs previously published, which means that the rate clerk must take still another step in finding the correct rate for a particular shipment. After finding the rate published in a tariff, he must turn to the supplement to find what change in the rate has been made because of some blanket increase. Since the increases have not been the same for all rate territories—for example, the percentage of increase in Official Territory may be greater than in Western —the rate clerk who has to seek out a new combination rate may find that he has a formidable task ahead of him.

SUMMARY

The statement that the work of reading American railroad freight tariffs is difficult, complicated, exacting—and often exciting—will bear repeating once more. There are many persons who believe that if the railroads and the Interstate Commerce Commission worked on the problem with a little more perseverance and assiduity they could bring about a great deal of improvement in rate publications in the direction of simplification. But it must be admitted that—with the large number of operating railroads we have, with their thousands of stations; with the much larger number of shippers, with their thousands upon thousands of commodities to be shipped; with each railroad having its own particular interest to serve; with each shipper keeping a wary eye on his actual or potential competitors; with new forms of transportation cropping up to disturb competitive relationships between older carriers, between shippers, and between shippers and carriers—simplification is not nearly so easy as it may sound to those who are unfamiliar with the practical problems involved in rate making. Rates for the transportation of freight in a country with the vast expanse and diversified products of the United States can not be made like the rates for the transportation of mail or telegraphic messages. In the next two chapters, we shall find out why this has been true and still is true.

CHAPTER VII

Freight Rates under Conditions of Competition

If any single subject has received more attention than others in economic treatises, that subject is prices. What makes prices what they are? How do they come to be what they are? What causes them to change? The central core of the subject of political economy, on which so much has been written and is still being written, is the theory of prices.

OUR ECONOMY BASED ON TRADE

After all, we live in a world in which trade, commerce, or exchange is the most vital and important of all economic functions. While production and consumption receive many pages of discussion in our books on economic science, it takes only a little reflection to realize that in an organized economic society such as ours there would be no production and consumption such as that we are familiar with if we did not have our complicated process of exchange in which everything that enters into our material well-being, as well as the physical and mental labor which we perform, must be bought and sold in some kind of market place. It is perfectly true that we do not produce to consume in the modern world. We produce first of all to sell; there are few things consumed which have not previously been bought and sold—the food and drink which sustain our life, the clothing and houses which give us shelter, the luxuries with which we gratify our desires for pleasure, the vast paraphernalia of machines and structures which are employed in the production and transportation of our consumption goods, and the labor of our minds and bodies.

We pick up a newspaper and find that usually more than half of it is devoted to the advertisement of things to sell; the financial pages are replete with tables of security prices and observations on the state of the "market" for stocks, bonds, and commodities here and abroad; column after column is devoted to the problem of wages and to the effort of laborers to get ever more for the one commodity they bring to the market place; just now we read—many of us somewhat fearfully—of the specter of inflation, and wonder what our present economic policies, both of private enterprise and of the government, are going to do to our price structure unless an effort is made to establish some system of arbitrary control.

TRANSPORTATION RATES ARE PRICES

Transportation rates—the charges which carriers impose for their services in taking goods and persons from place to place—are a species of prices, and over the years have been subject to the same influences and forces which have been important in the determination of other prices. But in more recent times, transportation rates, and the rates charged by other industries which go by the name of "public utilities," have been determined largely in a manner quite different from that determining the prices of most of the articles bought and sold by private enterprise in the public market place. They have been subject to a high degree of governmental control.

SUPPLY AND DEMAND

Many persons are fond of saying somewhat glibly that in the free market the prices of commodities are determined by the "law of supply and demand," and that "competition" is the all-important force which brings prices to a proper level. The mainspring of private business enterprise is the desire for profit; without profit there would be no private enterprise. All private business must have profits if it is to continue in existence. How prices reach their level is explained very simply. If profits mount too high, new competitors will enter the field, and competition will bring prices—and consequently profits—down. If extreme competition causes prices to drop to a level where profits tend to diminish to the vanishing point, the weakest producers will go to the wall, supply will diminish in relation to demand, and the "law of supply and demand" will cause prices to rise to a point where production is once more profitable. The whole price structure, in fact the entire economic system, is self-regulating, as it were; the irrepressible forces of the free market operate constantly to give form and shape to our complex economy.

IMPERFECT COMPETITION

This much oversimplified description of what happens in the world of business has one fatal defect. It presumes that competition is an all-pervasive, constantly active force in the economy. It assumes that our complex economic structure is completely fluid and that, under the impulse of the forces which act upon it, it maintains a constant level, just as water in a vessel will maintain an even horizontal surface regardless of how the vessel may be tilted this way or that. Unfortunately—or perhaps fortunately—our economic system does not work this way. It is not fluid; it does not readjust itself rapidly to the action of the many influences and forces to which it is subject; labor is not perfectly mobile; capital goods are even less mobile than labor; supply does not adjust itself readily to changes in demand, or demand to changes in supply; competition is not all-pervasive in the market place; in fact, there is much more writing in economic science today devoted to the "imperfections" of competition than to the traditional assumptions of what happens when "perfect competition" is imagined to exist. In our economic literature of today, we constantly encounter words such as monopoly, oligopoly, monopsony— word which were seldom employed by or even known to the armchair economists of past generations.

From time immemorial, governments have interfered with the free play of so-called economic forces. There never has been a time during recorded history when government bounties, subsidies, "protective" tariffs, regulations of production, regulations of prices, licensing systems, prohibitions, and taxes have not intervened to produce conditions in national and international economy which would not have developed had "free" competition been permitted to operate. Whether we like it or not, the interposition of government in economic affairs is greater today perhaps than it has ever been, and gives promise of becoming a still more important factor in the business activities of the world.

Governments have not been the only agencies to interfere with the operations of a "free" market. Business enterprise—private business enterprise—has done its share of interfering with the law of supply and demand, under which a freely competitive system is supposed to operate successfully. The sins of "engrossing," "forestalling," and "monopolizing" are as old as business itself, and they are by no means unknown in the business world today, even in this country, if the activities of the Department of Justice are not all based upon misconceptions of what is taking place in our economic system. Of course, the business community is inclined to resent with some bitterness and a great deal of asperity all attempts by the government to "interfere" with private business enterprise, but one has only to study a little economic history to realize how necessary this interference has been and to wonder what conditions in the business world would be today had there never been any intervention in business affairs on the part of the government. Those who are acquainted with the transportation business in America must occasionally have difficulty in repressing a smile when listening to some railroad president bitterly condemning the "subsidized" competition to which the railroads are subjected, just after he has participated in a strenuous campaign to have Congress pass a law under which the railroads can, without fear of prosecution, suppress competition among themselves.

FIXED COSTS AND PRICES

But the force which has led to the greatest interference with the operations of the free market has been neither that of the government nor that of the individuals who direct our business enterprise. It has been a self-generated force arising out of the methods by which nearly all productive industries of the modern world are conducted. We live in an "industrialized" world. The great change which has come about in virtually all forms of industry since the steam engine was invented and electric and internal combustion motors were perfected is that virtually all the processes of productive industry have been mechanized. This has meant the creation of an almost unbelievable amount of what we call "fixed capital"—the innumerable machines, the vast power plants, the mammoth structures, the tremendous assemblages of equipment, with which we turn out the never ending, rushing stream of goods which go to satisfy our daily wants.

There was a time, long ago, when production was direct; nearly all power employed in industry was muscular power, either of man himself or of a few domesticated animals; except for a few "machines," such as the potter's wheel, the stones of a gristmill, spinning wheels, hand looms, and a few cumbersome contrivances for shaping metals, our fixed capital consisted for the most part of tools, such as those long employed in agriculture, and they were operated almost entirely by human hands.

The outstanding transformation which the shift from hand industry to mechanized production brought about was the emergence of "fixed costs" as a factor of highly increased importance in the total cost of producing the things the world consumes. When production was simple and direct, nearly all costs were "variable"; they rose and fell with the scale of production. But with the progress of mechanization, a larger and larger proportion of the total costs of things produced was independent of the rate or volume of production. The costs involved in establishing, and much of the costs involved in maintaining, and even a substantial part of the costs involved in operating, heavily mechanized industry kept accumulating whether the plants which were mechanized kept on producing at full speed, produced at a greatly slackened rate, or stopped producing altogether. In a plant adapted to and fitted for machine production, the unit cost of a product came to be a function of the volume of production. In a plant operating to capacity, the fixed or constant costs were spread over all units produced; in the same plant operating at half capacity, these same constant costs were spread over half as many units, thereby greatly increasing unit cost; and the unhappy producer who was forced for one reason or another to close his plant entirely was confronted with the dismal fact that the interest charges upon his investment in plant and equipment, as well as many operating costs, went ahead just the same as when his business was operating full blast.

FIXED COSTS IN RAILROAD TRANSPORTATION

Railroad transportation was one of the first industries to be designated by the term "big business," and it was one of the first to have an unhappy experience with the misfortunes that may overtake an industry which, because of thorough mechanization, is possessed of a large amount of fixed property in the form of capital goods and is consequently saddled with a heavy burden of costs that are fixed or constant. The building of railroad tracks and terminals, the procurement of locomotives, freight cars, and passenger cars, in other words, the construction of the railroad physical plant, called for an investment which was very heavy in proportion to the investment in fixed capital to which industry had previously been accustomed. The investors who were prevailed upon to put their savings into railroads quite naturally hoped for a return on their investment, and if the funds for construction were borrowed, as they often were, the return to the investor became legally a "fixed charge" against the railroad he had helped to build. But whether a legal charge or not, a fair return on all the the capital prudently invested in a railroad could properly be regarded from an economic standpoint as a fixed cost, the amount of which was measured by the passage of time and not by the performance of the railroad. Railroad managers found out, too, that many operating costs were independent of the amount of traffic carried. The deterioration of a railroad track, which necessitated regular maintenance, was due as much to weather as to the passage of trains, and the cost went on regardless of how much revenue-yielding passenger and freight traffic the railroad was able to obtain. Some costs could be cut down as traffic dwindled. Train service could be curtailed and the cost of fuel and labor reduced. Even so, it might not be possible to shrink train costs in proportion to the shrinkage in traffic. It costs little less to operate a passenger train half filled with passengers than to operate one in which all the seats are occupied, and the cost of operating a freight train weighing only half as much as the load which the locomotive is able to draw is only a little less than the cost of operating a train with a full load. Business made the discovery of the great paradox of our modern economy—that it may be cheaper to operate an enterprise at a loss than not to operate at all. If revenues are sufficient to cover operating costs and one-half the fixed charges, the loss for the time being is less than if the business suspends and must still support the burden of all its fixed costs.

CUTTHROAT COMPETITION

The managers of business enterprise of a newly industrialized world found out quickly that competition was not the same as it had been under more primitive conditions of production. They found that, since unit costs were closely related to volume, it might be more profitable for an enterprise to sell goods at low prices than at high prices, if by selling at low prices a plant could be operated at or near full capacity. There was an ever present temptation to reduce prices in order to secure full production and consequently larger profits. But invariably a competitor who was also saddled with high fixed charges responded to the price reductions with even greater reductions, and almost before rivals were aware of what was occurring they were involved in a price war of such a nature that there were no profits for anybody. They discovered that "cutthroat competition" was ruinous, and yet they were constantly subject to an almost irresistible temptation to precipitate a struggle which would inevitably have a disastrous effect on all warring competitors.

When a business enterprise became involved, either willingly or unwillingly, in a bitter and unrelenting price war, it found that it could not suspend operation and wait until the smoke of battle cleared away. If it suspended, its fixed costs continued, and its losses might be greater than if it continued in operation and took part in the struggle. Competition was entirely different from what it had once been. It was not like the competition between grocers, which Arthur T. Hadley, once president of Yale University, who wrote the first notable American textbook on railroad transportation, described concisely in a paragraph which has been quoted many times:

> If Grocer A sells goods below cost, Grocer B need not follow him, but simply stops selling for a time. For (1) this involves no great loss to B. When his receipts stop most of his expenses stop also. (2) It does involve present loss to A. If he is selling goods below cost, he loses more money the more business he does. (3) He cannot continue indefinitely. If A returns to paying prices, B can again compete. If A continues to do business at a loss, he will become bankrupt, and B will find the field clear again.

EFFECT OF EARLY RAILROAD COMPETITION IN AMERICA

The early railroads of America did not meet with much competition. They had no fear of stagecoaches and wagons, and they were soon able to demonstrate a large measure of superiority over canals for the transportation of both passengers and freight. Nearly every one of the early small roads had a virtual monopoly and was able to charge rates and fares which yielded handsome profits. Some of the smaller lines in New York and in other middle Atlantic states proved to be veritable gold mines. Of course, the inevitable happened. The huge profits of the first comers attracted others to the field, and the days of undisturbed monopoly came to a speedy end. It was not long until competing lines began to slash rates in the hope of building up traffic volume at the expense of competitors, and the railroad business of America entered into a period of competitive warfare which is still regarded as an outstanding example of what happens to business enterprise having high fixed charges when it engages in a relentless price war. Many once prosperous lines were forced into bankruptcy, and others saw their profits vanish. A bankrupt road did not give up the competitive struggle; in fact, it was in a better position than ever to keep it up, since for the time being it was relieved of any obligation to meet the interest upon its debts. It was obvious that if railroad transportation in America was ever to become reasonably prosperous, something had to be done to curb competitive warfare among rival lines.

EARLY RATE AGREEMENTS: POOLS

The first thing the rival carriers did was to get together and make "rate agreements," in which they would promise one another to abide by rates which all had agreed to charge. These first rate agreements ended in failure, because there was no way in which they could be enforced at law and because the temptation to cut rates for the purpose of building up traffic was too great for many of the competing lines to resist. Some device was needed by which observance of a rate agreement could be obtained. The carriers were not long in finding such a device. It was called a pool. Under a pooling agreement, either all the traffic or all the revenue from the traffic was divided among competing lines according to a mutually satisfactory ratio. If any one railroad secured more than its allotted share during a certain period, it was supposed to turn over the excess receipts, if the pool was a "money pool," or the revenues from excess traffic, if the pool was a "traffic pool," to the carriers which had not received their share. Since these contracts also were "in restraint of trade," and not enforceable at law, some members of early pools, once they had obtained possession of revenue in excess of their proper share, refused to surrender any of it to their fellow members. This little impediment to the possible success of a pool was soon removed, however, when all members were required to pay in advance, to the pool's treasurer, a sum deemed sufficient to take care of any discrepancies which might occur because all members did not receive their allotted share of business.

The early railroad pools were highly successful. Pooling agreements were negotiated throughout the railroad business, and they brought an end to the destructive rate wars which had demoralized the railroad business during former years. While it seems that they did not result in the charging of excessive rates, they kept rates from falling occasionally to ridiculously low levels, as they had done during the days of cutthroat competition, and they tended to stabilize rates, to eliminate the wide fluctuations which had characterized the period when competition was rampant.

EFFECT OF POOLS ON DISCRIMINATION

There was one thing, however, that pools did not do. They did not bring an end to unjust discrimination in rates. During the days of competitive warfare among the railroads, the only shippers who derived any benefit from the rate wars were the shippers at "competitive points." Each railroad had many customers who did not have access to a rival line, and these customers obtained nothing in the way of a rate reduction when rival lines engaged in a competitive struggle. In fact, many railroads tried to recoup some of their losses on competitive traffic by making substantial increases in the rates on noncompetitive traffic. Unjust discrimination became a characteristic feature of railroad rates, and there was much complaint on the part of many communities. After rate wars came to an end, because of the organization of railroad pools, it was found that competitive points were still able to secure, on the whole, a lower level of rates than noncompetitive points. In other words, the evil of unjust discrimination persisted even after the railroads succeeded in making peace with one another.

POOLING BECOMES ILLEGAL

The resentment of the public against unjust discrimination, and a belief in many quarters that railroads were also taking advantage of their monopolistic organizations to charge rates which were unreasonably high, led to a demand that railroad rates be subjected to public regulation and control. State governments first embarked upon a program of railroad regulation, but it soon became apparent that if effective regulation was to be accomplished it had to be done by the Federal government. After several years of somewhat fruitless agitation, Congress was prevailed upon to act, and the first Federal law for the regulation of railroads was passed in February, 1887. It was originally called an Act to Regulate Commerce. It has always been known, however, as the Interstate Commerce Act, and that is now its legal title. As was previously explained, it has been enlarged and amended many times since its original enactment.

For some reason, the framers of the Act of 1887, however much they may have been impressed by the higher degree of stability which pools had brought about in railroad rates, were convinced that these pools were in part responsible for much of the unjust discrimination which prevailed in rates throughout the country and that they were also responsible for the fact that some rates were unduly high. The members of the Congress which passed the first railroad law were old-fashioned in their economic thinking and still had a belief in the virtue of open competition even among business enterprises which were possessed of large amounts of fixed capital equipment. Consequently, they decreed in the fifth section of the Act to Regulate Commerce that railroad pooling agreements should be brought to an end. Pooling contracts were declared to be illegal and railroads were forbidden to make use of them.

BINDING RATE AGREEMENTS

Deprived of their effective instrument for controlling unbridled competition, the railroads returned to the wars, but they soon found that the

conflicts were ruinous to all who engaged in them. A new method of securing rate agreements was not long in forthcoming. This time, there
were "binding" agreements with penalties for violation. The lessons which
years of warfare had brought made the carriers more circumspect about
observing their promises, and competition was once more brought under
control.

THE SHERMAN ANTITRUST ACT

Meanwhile, other types of big business had followed the example of the
railroads and fostered monopolistic agreements among themselves for the
control of prices. The "trust" problem became a burning political and
economic issue; Congress, still wedded to the theories of the eighteenth
century with respect to competition, enacted the Sherman Antitrust law
of 1890, which forbade "all" agreements in restraint of trade among the
several states and with foreign nations, and sternly forbade the creation
of monopolies.

Since railroad managers and their lawyers did not seem to believe that
the Sherman law applied to railroad rate agreements (at least that was the
defense they submitted when the agreements gave rise to prosecution),
the railroad traffic associations went boldly ahead in their activities. Eventually, the Department of Justice caught up with them. The Supreme
Court, declaring that there was nothing in the Sherman law to indicate
that the railroads were exempt from the provisions of the statute which un-
qualifiedly condemned all combinations in restraint of trade, in 1897 and
1898 held the rate agreements to be illegal.

The formal rate agreements having fallen under the ban of the law,
the railroad magnates of the country endeavored to bring the evils of
competition to an end by the consolidation of the leading railroads of
the country into a small number of rich and powerful systems and by the
establishment of "communities of interest" among these systems through
"interlocking directorates." The story of railroad consolidation in the
United States during the latter years of the nineteenth and the first few
years of the twentieth century constitutes a dramatic chapter in the economic history of the United States. But once more the carriers ran afoul
of the Sherman law. In the famous Northern Securities case, decided in
1904, the Supreme Court declared a combination of the Great Northern,
the Northern Pacific, and the Burlington railroads under common control to be in violation of the law, and ordered its dissolution. Subsequent
decisions were rendered to break up the Union Pacific–Southern Pacific
combination. Under the influence of these decisions, the march toward
general consolidation was halted; some of the combinations that had
been organized were dissolved without any intervention on the part of
the government.

TRAFFIC ASSOCIATIONS AND RAILROAD RATES

The traffic associations, however, continued to function, without any governmental hindrance for a time, and while the agreements that were reached were of an informal nature and had no binding effect, the experience which the carriers had had in the past with rate wars was sufficient to keep them in line. There was little in the way of open warfare. Eventually, though, the railroads got too bold. In 1910, there was a simultaneous declaration on the part of eastern and western carriers that they were going to increase all freight rates by 10 per cent, and tariffs to this effect were filed with the Interstate Commerce Commission. There did not seem to be any way at the time to prevent the proposed rates from taking effect within the statutory period of thirty days, and there was a vigorous public outcry against the monopolistic policy which the carriers were pursuing. The Department of Justice got busy and applied for an injunction to keep the rates from going into effect, on the grounds that the simultaneous filing of the increases by all roads was indicative of the existence of an unlawful "combination in restraint of trade." Fearful that the successful prosecution of the suit would mean the end of their traffic associations, the railroads withdrew the tariffs of increased rates, Congress hastily enacted a measure to give the Interstate Commerce Commission power to "suspend" proposed changes in rates, pending an investigation of their "reasonableness," and the Department of Justice dropped its suit. The traffic associations remained undisturbed in their activities for many years. They now function under the protection of the Reed-Bulwinkle law, the terms of which were described in the preceding chapter.

PLANNED CONSOLIDATION IN 1920

To a certain extent, the relaxation of legal attacks against what were once considered monopolistic practices on the part of railroads was due to the fact that members of Congress were beginning to take a more realistic view of the modern economic organization. Some of them had finally come to the conclusion that business enterprise, as it is conducted at the present time, can have too much competition, just as it can have too little, a fact which for a long time had been apparent to students of economics as well as to leaders in the business world. With respect to railroad transportation, Congress eventually reversed its former position to the extent of including in the Transportation Act of 1920 clauses legalizing pools and providing for the consolidation of all the railroads of the United States into a limited number of large, equally strong systems after a "plan" to be devised by the Interstate Commerce Commission. Although the Commission drew up such a plan, Congress neglected to make its adoption compulsory, and the railroads never displayed any inclination to adopt it voluntarily. The provisions of the law with respect to consolidation in accordance with a master plan were repealed in 1933, but the Commission still retains the power to permit any railroad consolidation to take place that is thought to be in the public interest. Under the terms of the law as it now stands, railroads are permitted to do without fear of prosecution many things which were once sternly condemned by statute and judicial decisions.

THE SPREAD OF MONOPOLY

Let it not be thought that the railroads were the only agencies of business enterprise that adopted a program of combination with one another for the purpose of controlling prices. Monopolistic practices eventually became the order of the day in all kinds of business activity. The ease with which combinations can be organized and maintained depends as a rule on the numbers who try to participate in agreements to dictate price policies. Labor unions among highly skilled workers are likely to be more effective than unions among unskilled workers, because the number in a group is much smaller. Railroads found combination easier than farmers for the same reason, although it cannot be said that farmers did not try to develop organizations for the elimination of competition in prices. With the active aid or the lack of interference of a complaisant government, much of the competition which once activated business policies is a thing of the past. Farmers secure price supports which guarantee a "floor" under the prices of many agricultural products, but nobody ever hears of a ceiling. Labor unions enforce their demands with paralyzing strikes in key industries. Producers of steel, automobiles, and other articles play the game of follow the leader as the spiral of prices mounts upward. Once in a while, there may be an old-fashioned competitive struggle between gasoline dispensers in New Jersey, but somehow it never lasts long. Barbers get together and calmly inform the public that the prices of a haircut and of other tonsorial ministrations are going to be five or six times what they were a few years ago, while the tavern keepers assemble in meeting and agree to lift the price of a glass of beer by 50 per cent or more. There is little wonder that economists regard with increasing doubt the validity of the old-fashioned theory that prices are, on the whole, determined by competition in a "free market."

RAIL AND WATER COMPETITION

So far, we have been discussing only one type of competition with which the railroads had to contend. That was competition among themselves. In many parts of the United States, the railroads also had water competition to reckon with in their efforts to obtain a lion's share of available commercial traffic. Until the government intervened, American railroad management treated water competition in ruthless fashion, waging relentless and disastrous rate wars until the weaker water lines were compelled to give up the ghost or consent to absorption by their stronger rail competitors. The great Mississippi River steamboats, which for so many years were the pride and glory of the Father of Waters, were tied up to decay at their mooring posts; traffic on the famous Erie Canal, which at one time rivaled in volume the traffic of the Mississippi, dwindled away and vanished; the steamship lines of the Great Lakes and the Atlantic Coast for the most part passed into railroad hands; intercoastal competition was throttled. It was not until after the Panama Canal Act of 1912 was passed that any substantial measure of competition between railways and waterways was restored, but even the partial recovery of domestic water transportation under the protection of the government has not lifted it to the position of relative importance which it once occupied.

INDUSTRIAL AND COMMERCIAL COMPETITION

There were other varieties of competition, however, with which the railroads had to contend in their early days, and which they have never at any time been able to eliminate. There is a competition which does not involve a struggle between parallel carriers trying to secure control of the same traffic, but a struggle between carriers widely separated and serving different regions and markets. It is a competition which has an effect upon rates just as real as direct competition between parallel lines of transportation. Such a competition is industrial competition, which is the competition of rival producing regions for the same market; in another form, it is called commercial competition, which is the competition of rival markets for the products or traffic of a single region. Some of the bitterest and most prolonged competitive struggles among railroads which the country has witnessed have been due to industrial competition. The famous lake cargo coal rivalry was an excellent example. The boats which bring iron ore from the head of Lake Superior to various ports of Lake Erie for shipment to steel-producing centers such as Youngstown and Pittsburgh return to Duluth and Superior with cargoes of coal for the northwestern states of the United States. There are mines in Kentucky, Ohio, West Virginia, Virginia, and Pennsylvania, the owners of which are eager to supply the coal for the returning ore carriers. It happens that each of the mining fields is served by a different railroad, and of course each railroad would be glad to have its own mining field provide all the lake cargo coal. It is inevitable that the coal rates charged by one railroad have an influence upon the rates charged by others, though the roads are not competing for the same traffic. Other examples of industrial competition are readily brought to mind. The rates on citrus fruits from Florida to the great consuming markets of New England and the middle Atlantic states affect the rates on citrus fruits from Texas and California, though the railroads that are involved in the competitive contest are widely separated from one another. In the same way, the sugar refined in Boston, New York, Philadelphia, Baltimore, and New Orleans must compete with the sugar refined in San Francisco and in various beet-sugar-producing areas. The salt from New York, Michigan, Kansas, and Louisiana competes for the custom of the great meat-packing plants of Chicago, St. Louis, St. Paul, Indianapolis, and Sioux City. The "balancing" of the rates to the satisfaction of rival producing centers and the railroads which serve these centers is a task which calls for diplomatic negotiation of a high order. When diplomacy fails, as it has done sometimes in the past, the only recourse is to a rate war.

Perhaps the best illustration of commercial competition is what happens when several seaports engage in a contest for the export trade of a producing or marketing region. American seaports along the Atlantic and Gulf Coasts each would like to have a large share of the export grain traffic which originates in the central states, and each seaport has one or more railroads, none of which is averse to hauling the grain between primary marketing centers and the seaboard. The struggles of rival ports and rival railroads to obtain this traffic, as well as other available export traffic, have left a deep impression on the railroad rate structures of the country.

COMPETITION OF COMMODITIES

Another kind of competition which affects railroad rates is the competition of commodities. Many articles can be and are used for the same purpose. Gypsum and clay may both be employed in the manufacture of tile; containers of various liquid products and of canned meat, fruit, and vegetables may be made either of glass or of metal; a wide variety of products is used in the manufacture of boxes and other shipping containers; there are numerous materials which compete for favor in the construction of buildings. It is obvious that the rates on competing products have something to do with their selection for a particular purpose, and since each carrier is desirous of building up its own traffic it will endeavor to see that its particular product does not get rates so high as to exclude it from the competitive market.

HIGHWAY AND AIR COMPETITION

In recent years, the railroads have met with the competition of new agencies of transportation. For many years, the railroads had a virtual monopoly of long-distance transportation of the commerce of the United States, except the relatively small part that moved by water, but now the highway motor vehicle and the airplane are demanding and obtaining a part of the business which the railroads long regarded as their exclusive possession. For long-distance travel either within the limits of the United

States or to lands overseas, the airplane offers a speed of service with which no surface carrier can hope to compete, and some of the passenger business of railroads and steamships has been lost, never to be recovered. Though the amount of freight transported by airplanes is relatively small, nevertheless these new agencies carry substantial quantities of mail and express which surface carriers used to transport, and the carriage of freight which once yielded high revenues to railroads and steamships is furnishing each year a larger and larger portion of the earnings of the air lines.

When highway transportation by motor vehicle began in a small way at the close of the nineteenth century, nobody dreamed that it would reach its present magnitude. The inhabitants of cities were acquainted with paved streets, but nobody imagined that within a half-century the United States would be covered by a vast network of hard-surfaced highways over which millions of self-propelled vehicles would move with the speed of a railroad train. Privately owned automobiles have taken more than half the passenger traffic the railroads once hauled, and the taxi and small truck have driven the once familiar horse-drawn cabs and delivery wagons from the streets of all urban centers. When intercity truck transportation began in a small way during the First World War, it was commonly thought that trucks would be confined to the transportation of only light and comparatively valuable merchandise, and that their use would be uneconomical for distances above 50 miles. There is no kind of freight which motor trucks do not carry today, and there is no limit to the distances which they can traverse. Many of our trucks carry for hire, either as common carriers or as contract carriers, but most of them are private carriers, the owner of the vehicle and of the freight transported being the same. When truck transportation was in its infancy, the railroads were urged to adopt this new facility of transportation which was obviously so well adapted for the carriage of goods which the railroads had been least successful in transporting, but bound by tradition and stubborn in the belief that their competitive position was impregnable for all time to come, the railroads haughtily refused to entertain such suggestions. In other hands, the motor truck has become a powerful and challenging rival of the railroad, and each year sees it come to occupy a stronger and more important place in our transportation system. It has compelled the abandonment of thousands of miles of branch line and main line railroads throughout the country, and has brought about a virtual revolution in the merchandising methods and distributive systems of many business establishments. The motor bus has also made inroads on railroad passenger traffic, has driven hundreds of miles of interurban electric railways out of business, and has replaced the electric trolley cars of hundreds of our cities.

Needless to say, the highway motor vehicle has had a pronounced effect upon the rates of the railroads and other older transportation facilities. Together, the airplane and the highway motor vehicle have restored to transportation in America something that for a long time was virtually absent—the active force of competition among rival carriers. Industrial and commercial competition and the competition of commodities had never been suppressed, of course, and they were all that prevented a railroad from having a virtually absolute monopoly in the territory it served. However, the new competition bears little resemblance to the competition which prevailed when the railroads indulged in bitter and relentless conflict with one another. The days of open and uncontrolled cutthroat competition among transportation agencies have come to an end. All transportation for hire in the United States is under a certain degree of government control, and one power which the Interstate Commerce Commission now possesses over surface carriers in interstate commerce is to name the minimum as well as the maximum rates which these carriers may charge. The Commission has the power to prevent a destructive rate war from taking place; if one should get started, it has the power to bring it to a speedy end by the control which it exercises over the rates of rival carriers.

PUBLIC POLICY AND THE NEW COMPETITION

Motor transportation on highways is still so new that no fixed policy with respect to what should be done to protect one type of carrier from savage onslaughts by other types has been worked out. The railroad interests would like to see highway competition eliminated entirely; they spend a great deal of money on publicity campaigns designed to convince everybody that they are being subjected to what amounts to economic persecution because of what they term the "subsidized" competition of other forms of transportation. Highway transportation interests and air transportation interests, too, have boldly met the challenge, and demand their right to existence, even evincing a willingness to leave the matter to a competitive contest, without government interference and with no holds barred. Congress has adopted a piously worded "national transportation policy," which now appears as a preamble to the Interstate Commerce Act, and states that the purpose of the government is to

. . . provide for fair and impartial regulation of all modes of transportation . . . so administered as to recognize and preserve the inherent advantages of each . . . to the end of developing, coordinating, and preserving a national transportation system by water, highway and rail, as well as by other means, adequate to meet the needs of the commerce of the United States, of the Postal Service, and of the national defense.

The precise means by which each mode of transportation can be confined to the area of operation in which its "inherent advantages" can best be employed have not yet been devised, and there is no question but that at the present time we find one "mode" of transportation endeavoring to perform a service which common sense indicates could be performed more economically by another mode. We have not done much yet in the way of coordinating our transportation facilities, partly because of the manifest reluctance of any one mode voluntarily to enter into cooperative arrangements with the others, for fear of sacrificing some portion of a peculiar advantage it may be thought to possess, and partly because the government, however willing it may be to promote economy and efficiency in the transportation business, is reluctant to adopt any policy which smacks of regimentation or totalitarianism. We still have a large measure of faith in the virtues of uninhibited competition. We may have a transportation policy in words, but it has not yet been translated into action. We still have a "transportation problem," which in some respects is more serious than the problem we had when transportation facilities were far less complicated and varied than they are at the present time.

RATE STRUCTURES UNDER COMPETITION

We still have to consider the kinds of rate structures which railroads developed during the time when they were settling their own competitive relations and bringing the competition of carriers by water under a large measure of railroad control. The great difference in these rate structures depended on the extent to which distance was taken into consideration in determining the amount of a rate, or perhaps it might be better to say that the most interesting feature of the rate structures was the manner in which the competition of rival interests compelled distance to be neglected as the most important factor in the determination of satisfactory rates. Many of the American rate structures were the subject of much writing and comment. Travelers from Europe, where governments exercised a potent influence in rate making long before the United States government did, found the rate systems here a peculiarly interesting object of study, and the aberrations which American rates displayed were as well known to European students of the economics of transportation as to American. We shall give a brief description of only a few typical rate structures.

THE EASTERN PERCENTAGE STRUCTURE

The "percentage system" of rates in the eastern region—the rate structure applying to traffic moving between New England and Eastern Trunk Line Territory on one hand and Central Freight Association Territory on the other—was one of the first structures to become fully crystallized. It applied in a region where the railroad mileage was greatest in proportion to area and where railway traffic was the densest to be found in the United States. Here were the nation's strongest railroads; here was the largest part of its population; here were its largest industries; and here were its leading seaports and interior centers of production and distribution. Here, too, was the region in which unbridled railroad competition had wrought its greatest havoc and where the pressure to bring peace among rival lines had been strongest.

When the railroads of the East finally made peace and reached an agreement with respect to rates, which they kept with a laudable, though not always perfect, record of faithfulness to one another, the most striking feature of the pattern which was adopted was that the rates between New York and Chicago became the "yardstick" by which other rates were measured. The system was simplicity itself. Given the rates between New York and Chicago—and the pattern—all other rates could be easily calculated; change the rates between New York and Chicago, and all the other rates changed automatically.

Once the rates between New York and Chicago were established, the rates between New York and all other points in Central Freight Association Territory were calculated as a percentage of the New York–Chicago rates, the percentage being roughly the ratio which the distance between New York and any point in question bore to the distance between New York and Chicago. Central Freight Association Territory was subdivided into comparatively small "zones," to each of which was given a number corresponding to its proper percentage distance. The zones were not in the shape of concentric circles, like the later parcel-post zones, but had certain irregularities dictated by the location of various railroads and by the competitive influence of the larger cities, which were always eager to shift the zone boundary in such a manner as to get into a lower rated zone. Rates were not always the same in both directions, so that it was necessary to have different zones for eastbound and westbound traffic.

THE SEABOARD DIFFERENTIALS

This arrangement took care of the rates of Central Freight Association Territory to and from New York City. It was, on the whole, a fair and equitable arrangement so far as relative rates were concerned, because differences in rates corresponded roughly to differences in distance, and there were no glaring instances of unjust discrimination. After the rates from and to New York were given a satisfactory pattern, the next task was to make a proper adjustment of rates between Central Freight Association points and other points in New England and Trunk Line Territories. Here it was that competition raised its head, and it was found that a percentage system, with distance as the determining factor, could not be employed, chiefly because of the rivalry of the North Atlantic seaports, Boston, New York, Philadelphia, and Baltimore.

Philadelphia and Baltimore would have been glad to have their rates made on the distance principle, because they were much nearer Chicago by rail than was the City of New York; Boston, on the other hand, had no liking for the distance principle, especially on export traffic, because she was considerably farther from Chicago than her rival ports. New York, not to be outdone in making claims to preferential treatment, urged that, because of her preeminence as a commercial center and railroad terminal, not to mention the fact that she had a water route to Chicago via the Erie Canal and the Great Lakes, she was entitled to rates certainly no higher than those of Philadelphia and Baltimore and somewhat lower than those of Boston. The controversy, in which both the cities and the railroads involved participated, each with becomingly zealous solicitude for its own selfish interest, was solved by a compromise which brought into existence rates which went by the name of "seaboard differentials." On westbound domestic traffic, Boston and all of New England received New York rates, putting the manufacturers of that territory on an equal competitive footing. Eastbound rates on domestic traffic to Boston were higher than the rates to New York by certain "differentials," or differences, while export rates to Boston were on a parity with those of her more powerful rival. The rates of Philadelphia and Baltimore were lower than the rates of New York by small differentials, Baltimore rates being slightly less than those of Philadelphia. Had distance been the controlling factor in the rates, both Philadelphia and Baltimore rates would have been lower than the rates established by the compromise. The rates to and from inland places were lower than the rates to and from the coast cities.

The rates which made up this structure, or pattern, remained in effect for many years. Even when the series of general increases in rates began, in 1914, the differentials on domestic traffic were left undisturbed, much to the satisfaction of New York, because the higher a rate goes the less importance an unchanged differential assumes. None of the seaboard cities ever expressed complete satisfaction with the structure, each claiming that it was being treated unfairly. The fact that all of them complained and protested is probably fair evidence that the arrangement was as good as could have been made. Had any city or railroad expressed complete satisfaction with the structure, there would have been good reason to think that there was something wrong with it.

THE SOUTHERN BASING POINT SYSTEM

The rate structure of the South which grew out of the compromises of the competing railroads and cities bore little resemblance to the structure

adopted in the eastern region. In the South, distance was not acknowledged to be such an important factor in the determination of the relationship of rates, and the most striking characteristic of southern rates was
the extent to which "place discrimination" was practiced. The structure
of southern rates for many years went by the name of the "basing point
system."

Unlike the eastern region of the United States, the South had numerous rivers flowing into the Atlantic Ocean and the Gulf of Mexico.
In the days before railroads were built throughout the southern states,
these rivers were navigated by numerous steamboats which carried the
cotton, lumber, and other products to coastal ports. So well did river
navigation serve the South that there was a belief on the part of many
people that railroads could not be built to compete with the steamboats,
and for this reason railroad construction in the South lagged far behind
railroad development in the North in the years preceding the Civil War.
When railroad construction did begin in the South on a substantial scale,
the new facilities found that they were confronted with fairly strong
competition, and the basing point system was devised to meet, and eventually dispose of, this competition.

A railroad between two ports on a river, in order to get what it regarded as a fair share of the traffic between those ports, had to meet the
steamboat rate. But it was not necessary for the railroad to take direct
steamboat competition into account when making the rates to local points
intermediate to the river ports but inland from the navigable water. The
rates to these points, which had no water competition, were invariably
higher than the port-to-port rates, though the practice of charging the
higher rates often involved charging more for the short than for the long
haul. In other words, it resulted in discrimination against the "local"
points, a discrimination which was widely regarded to be unjust and unfair, but about which the shippers who paid the higher rates could for
many years do nothing of a remedial nature. As time went on, the leading
river ports, and later leading railroad centers in the South, such as Atlanta,
Birmingham, and Knoxville, were designated as basing points. The rates
between these points showed the effects of competition, both between rail
and water lines and between rival rail lines. Rates to local points were
constructed by adding to the rates to a basing point the rates from the
basing point to the local points. It made no difference whether the distance was shorter or longer, but if shorter, the local point became the
victim of discrimination. A graph of the rates from basing point to basing
point, which included the rates applicable to intermediate points, looked
like the apex of a triangle, and the graph of rates over a route that included several basing points resembled the outline of the serrated teeth of
a crosscut saw.

THE TRANSCONTINENTAL RATE STRUCTURE

An even more extraordinary rate structure than the southern basing point system was the structure of transcontinental rates on traffic westbound from the eastern part of the United States to points on the Pacific Coast and in the Rocky Mountain area, which went under the name of Intermountain Territory. The first transcontinental railroad to reach the Pacific Coast over its own trackage had its eastern terminal at Chicago. When it came to consider the rates to be imposed upon traffic westbound from Chicago to the coast, it had to take into consideration the rates applicable to traffic which went over an all-ocean route between the Atlantic and Pacific Coast ports except for a short rail haul across Panama or Nicaragua. The intercoastal rate by water set the rail rate. Since cities farther east than Chicago were interested in the development of trade with the Pacific Coast area, they demanded, and secured, through the cooperation of the eastern railroads, rates which were no higher than those previously given to traffic originating in Chicago. The "group" rates thus established covered such a wide stretch of territory that they became known as "blanket rates," and eventually the blanket spread as far west as Denver. It was commonly said that railroads hauled eastern traffic to Denver for nothing, and "charged for it the rest of the way" to the Pacific Coast. There have probably never been any railroad rates in which the element of distance was such an unimportant factor. It could truly be said that the railways of the United States were faithfully fulfilling their mission of overcoming distance instead of yielding to it.

This claim on behalf of the railroads might have been more praiseworthy, however, had it not been for the manner in which Intermountain Territory was treated. This region was not on the coast, and the railroads had no direct water competition to meet. They followed the practice which had been employed by the southern roads in building up the basing point system. A rate was established to an intermountain destination from the "blanketed" East by adding the rate to the coast to the rate from the coast eastward to the intermountain point. It cost a great deal more to ship a carload of merchandise from New York, Pittsburgh, Chicago, St. Louis, or Kansas City to Spokane, Reno, or Phoenix than to Seattle, San Francisco, or Los Angeles.

The railroads justified this discrimination with the same reasoning they employed to justify the discrimination against the local points in the South. The rates were compelled by water competition. It was true that the rates for longer distances were not so remunerative as the rates for shorter distances. But if the rates to the competitive points on the coast were increased, the railroads would lose the traffic. The track, locomotives, and cars were in existence—fixed capital in which invested funds had already been sunk. While the rates to the coastal points might not pay all the fixed charges fairly attributable to the service, they yielded more than operating expenses and contributed something toward fixed costs. If rates graded according to distance were applied to intermountain stations, the railroads would soon become bankrupt; if the rates to the coast points were raised, the railroads would lose the business, and the intermountain points traffic would have to be subjected to even higher rates in order that the total amount of fixed costs could be met.

However plausible this argument may have been, it was not possible to convince an intermountain consignee at Reno that it was fair for a railroad to charge him as much on a shipment from Chicago as if the shipment were sent all the way to San Francisco and then back to Reno. Western receivers and shippers added their complaints to those of the southern shippers who felt they were being victimized by the basing point system. Their chorus was augmented by the loud and vigorous expressions of resentment poured forth by farmers of the great central wheat and corn belt, who were not only indignant because of the discriminatory character of the rates they were forced to pay if living in noncompetitive territory but were thoroughly convinced that the level of railroad rates for the entire country was altogether too high. There was less clamor in the eastern region, where the level of rates was somewhat lower than it was in the rest of the country and where the practice of discrimination, confined for the most part to secret favors to important shippers, was not so open and glaring as it was in the South and West. A swelling demand for the regulation of railroad rates by the Federal government finally compelled a reluctant Congress to frame and pass the Interstate Commerce Act. In the next two chapters, we shall examine some of the principles upon which this law was based and see how its enforcement eventually brought about some striking changes in the railroad rate structures which had been painfully reared in response to the action of competitive forces.

CHAPTER VIII

Freight Rates under Regulation: Reasonable Rates

Previous to the enactment of Federal legislation in 1887 for the regulation of railroad rates, several states had endeavored to deal with the problems which had arisen with the development of railroad transportation. A few western states had enacted laws for the regulation of rates by state commissions, and some maximum rate and fare laws applicable to intrastate traffic had also been placed on the statute books. For a time, it was thought that even though the Federal Constitution entrusted the regulation of interstate and foreign commerce to Congress, as long as Congress did not act, each state had the right to regulate that part of an interstate haul which took place within the state. In 1886, the Supreme Court declared that the regulation of railroad rates on interstate traffic was one of those fields in which Congress had "exclusive" jurisdiction, after which the states were confined to the regulation of purely intrastate traffic. It was this decision that turned the balance in Congress in favor of passing the original Act to Regulate Commerce.

RAILROAD REGULATION AND THE CONSTITUTION

The railroads were vigorously opposed to any rate regulation whatever, and were not slow in challenging state regulatory laws in the Federal courts on the theory that they invaded the "constitutional" rights and privileges of the railroad companies. They declared that the laws for the regulation of rates, enacted by the states, deprived them of their property without "due process of law," in violation of the Fourteenth Amendment of the Federal Constitution, and that the charters under which they operated were "contracts," the obligations of which a state was forbidden by the Constitution to impair.

During the years between 1876 and 1899, the Supreme Court handed down a number of noteworthy decisions dealing with the right of the government to regulate railroad rates. As a result of these decisions, the following principles of constitutional law and procedure were established.[1]

[1] The decisions which were landmarks in the development of the Supreme Court's ideas about the constitutionality of railroad regulation and the limitations imposed by the Constitution upon the authority of state and Federal legislative bodies to control the prices which railroads could charge for their services were:

First of all, the Court held, in a divided opinion, that the legislative branch of the government has the right to regulate the charges which a railroad may exact for its services, on the theory that the railroads were "clothed with a public interest," which transcended any private privilege or immunity which the railroads might claim under the Constitution. This right, however, the Court declared, was "not without limit," and the legislature could not by statute destroy the property of a railroad. In its action, the legislature could impose only such rates as were reasonable, and the determination of what was reasonable was eminently a "judicial question." The legislature could not be arbitrary in its acts, and the railroads had the right to question in the courts the validity of any legislative rule or regulation, whether enunciated directly or through a properly authorized administrative commission. If, in the opinion of the judiciary, the rule or regulation objected to involved an invasion of the constitutional rights of the complainant, the rule or regulation would be set aside. In other words, the Supreme Court made it plain that in setting aside rates, fixed by the railroads, on the grounds that they were unreasonably high, the legislative arm of the government could not, under the Constitution, compel the railroads to substitute rates which were unreasonably low—so low as to effect the "confiscation" of railroad property.

The decisions which brought the Supreme Court to this point left it with the extremely knotty problem of how to determine when a rate should be considered as being reasonable. What was the limit to which the legislative arm of the government could go? What was the measure of "reasonableness"? In a memorable decision handed down in 1898,[2] the Supreme Court declared that a railroad was fairly entitled to rates which would cover its cost of service but that the shipper was entitled to rates which did not exceed the value of the service. "What the company is entitled to ask is a fair return on that which it employs for public convenience. On the other hand, what the public is entitled to demand is that no more be exacted from it for the use of a public highway than the services rendered by it are reasonably worth." A railroad was entitled to rates

---

Munn v. Illinois, 94 U.S. 113; Chicago, Burlington and Quincy R.R. v. Iowa, 94 U.S. 155; Peik v. Chicago and North Western R.R., 94 U.S. 164; Winona and St. Peter R.R. v. Blake, 94 U.S. 180. (These four decisions, coming in 1877, marked the outcome of the so-called "granger cases." The first decision, Munn v. Illinois, dealt with the regulation of grain elevators, and not railroads, but the principles enunciated in the decision were followed in the railroad cases.) Stone v. Wisconsin, 94 U.S. 181 (1877); Stone v. Farmers' Loan and Trust Company (Mississippi Railroad Commission Cases), 116 U.S. 307 (1886); Chicago, Milwaukee and St. Paul Ry. v. Minnesota, 134 U.S. 418 (1890); Reagan v. Farmers Loan and Trust Company, 154 U.S. 362 (1894); Smyth v. Ames, 169 U.S. 466 (1898).

[2] Smyth v. Ames, 169 U.S. 466 (1898).

which would pay operating costs and leave enough over to yield a fair return on the "fair value of the property being used by it for the convenience of the public."

THE PROBLEM OF VALUATION

Having gotten this far, the Court found that though it might have pushed the problem of finding a "reasonable rate" one step further, it immediately had to answer another question—how does one determine the value of the property of a railroad company? Admitting that the question presented some difficulty, the Court declared that in ascertaining the value of the property of a business enterprise many things must be taken into consideration.

The original cost of construction, the amount expended in permanent improvements, the amount and market value of its bonds and stocks, the present as compared with the original cost of construction, the probable earning capacity of the property under particular rates prescribed by statute, and the sum required to meet operating expenses are all matters for consideration, and are to be given such weight as may be just and right in each case.

Just to be sure that no other element of value might possibly be neglected, the Court added, "We do not say that there may not be other matters to be regarded in estimating the value of the property."

A long span of years was to pass, many legislative acts, many decisions of administrative commissions, and many decisions of courts were to be propounded before the Supreme Court finally admitted that some of its reasoning in the decision of 1898 had been of the variety labeled as "circular," and that in a "going concern" prices are a determinant of value just as much as value is a proper basis for a reasonable price. Once "earning power" is admitted as an element of "value," it becomes obvious that any legislative action which reduces earning power destroys a part of the value of the business whose earning power has been lessened. Once the truth of this premise is granted, it becomes apparent that any legislative act which has for its purpose the reduction of rates is confiscatory in its effect and therefore indefensible, and that a railroad can justify any increase of rates for the purpose of preserving the value of its property.

Legislatures, commissions, and courts tried to get around the implications of the decision of 1898 by seeking to establish the value of the "tangible property" of a railroad and to use this value as a base upon which to establish "reasonable rates." But once more the problem was just pushed a step further along. How does one ascertain the "value" even of tangible property for rate-making purposes? Is it "original cost less depreciation," "cost of replacement," "prudent investment"? These things are not only difficult to ascertain, but replacement cost, for which the railroads contend most forcibly as the proper measure of value, especially during a period of rising prices, changes from day to day and from year to year. However acceptable it may appear, it is obviously possessed of too much instability to be employed as a workable standard. Moreover, any of these standards leaves out the factor of earning power, which the Supreme Court explicitly stated to be one of the elements of the value of property devoted to the public service. Despite objections, in 1913, Congress amended the Interstate Commerce Act by adding a "valuation" law, under which the Interstate Commerce Commission was to make a complete inventory of railroad property and ascertain its "value." The Commission proceeded, at a large expense to both the government and the railroads, to make the inventory.

THE RULE OF RATE MAKING OF 1920

When the Transportation Act of 1920 was passed, just previous to the termination of railroad operation by the government, a section 15a was added to the Interstate Commerce Act. This section was a "rule of rate making" for the guidance of the Commission, and directed that body to initiate and maintain a system of railroad rates which would enable the railroads as a whole, or in such groups as the Commission might designate, to earn a fair return on the "value" of their property devoted to transportation. Congress stipulated that for two years 5½ per cent should be taken as the fair rate of return, to which the Commission might, in its discretion, add ½ per cent (which the Commission proceeded to do), and after the expiration of the two-year period the Commission should fix the rate. Under the impulse of this mandate, the Commission authorized, late in 1920, the largest single blanket increase of railroad rates the carriers have ever received.[3] Ostensibly, the Commission did this to enable the railroads to get a fair return on the value of their property. But the value upon which calculations were based was not a value that had been ascertained by the application of some standard of measurement, but an "estimated" value adopted by the Commission, based in part, however, upon the valuation work which the Commission had begun a few years before. The law also provided for the "recapture" by the government of half the net earnings any one railroad might obtain in excess of 6 per cent.

Despite the greatly increased level of rates, a sharp depression prevented the carriers as a whole from earning the fair rate of return stipulated in the rule of rate making (on the estimated value adopted by the Commission), but in the face of this failure the Commission ordered a blanket reduction of railroad rates of 10 per cent, early in 1922,[4] for the

---

[3] In the Matter of Applications of Carriers in Official, Southern and Western Classification Territories for Authority to Increase Rates, 58 I.C.C. 220 (1920).

[4] Reduced Rates, 68 I.C.C. 676 (1922).

purpose of hastening business recovery. Though the railroads were reasonably prosperous for a few years following, they at no time earned the "fair rate of return" upon the valuation which they claimed for themselves, and the Commission did not endeavor to juggle rates in such a manner as to give the railroads a net income which presumably the law said they should have. It did not at any time set forth in definite figures the value of the railroads, to be used as a rate base, though it proceeded with its valuation work. When the great depression overtook the nation in 1929, railroad traffic was soon cut in half, and it was obvious to anybody that no system of rates which might be put into effect would enable the carriers to earn more than a bare fraction of the fair return on their own assumed value of their physical property. One had only to glance at the parade of bankruptcies and the prices of railroad stocks and other securities to be convinced that whatever standard might be adopted for the valuation of physical property, the value of a railroad in the market place was nevertheless much more closely related to its earning power than to its physical property in the form of track, terminals, and rolling stock.

VALUE AND RECAPTURE OF EXCESS EARNINGS

The Commission managed to avoid coming to grips with the problem of establishing a value to be regarded as a base upon which the fair rate of return for the railroads as a whole should be computed, even though the railroads complained with some bitterness that the Commission was dodging its duty under the law. But the Commission also had another duty to perform under the new rule of rate making. This was the "recapture" of the excess earnings of any single railroad which was deemed to be having a net income in excess of 6 per cent of its "value." To administer the recapture clause, the Commission was compelled to cease dallying with the problem of valuation and actually assign a value to any railroad a part of whose earnings was thought to be subject to recapture. The Commission tried.[5] It is unnecessary to discuss here the precise method of valuation which the Commission adopted in order to compel a carrier to disgorge some of its profits, for the method it employed was promptly condemned by the Supreme Court as being illegal because it did not take into consideration to a sufficient degree all the "elements" which go to make up the total value of a railroad's property.[6] The Commission backed up and manfully tried again. But before the second effort could be fully tested by the judiciary, the economic depression, into which the nation had plunged in 1929, had reached such depths that the railroad system was gasping for the breath necessary for survival. Congress came to the rescue of the railroads as it endeavored to come to the aid of the farmers,

[5] Excess Income of St. Louis and O'Fallon Ry. 124 I.C.C. 3 (1927).
[6] St. Louis and O'Fallon Ry. v. United States, 279 U.S. 461 (1929).

manufacturers, and other economic interests. An "emergency" transportation act was passed in 1933. Among its provisions were the repeal of the rule of rate making adopted in 1920 and of the recapture clause. The repeal of the recapture clause was made retroactive; any railroad which had voluntarily paid a portion of its excess earnings to the Commission had the money returned, and those who had received large excess earnings, but had made no effort to share them with the government, were left in undisturbed possession of their accumulations.

THE NEW RULE OF RATE MAKING

The rule of rate making adopted in 1933 made no mention of a "fair rate of return" or "value of property." It stated that, in the exercise of its power to prescribe reasonable rates, the Commission should give due consideration to

. . . the effect of rates on the movement of traffic . . . to the need, in the public interest, of adequate and efficient railway transportation service at the lowest cost consistent with the furnishing of such service; and to the need of revenue sufficient to enable the carriers, under honest, economical and efficient management, to provide such service.

Under this rule, it was no longer necessary for the Commission to embark upon elaborate calculations for the purpose of establishing the value of railroad property which it should regard as a rate base, nor was it incumbent upon the Commission to enter into speculative investigations in an effort to determine what particular rate of return should be considered a fair rate of return upon a particular base.

It must be borne in mind that the rule of rate making of 1920, as well as the one that replaced it in 1933, had to do with the general "level of rates" and not with the rates on particular articles of traffic. It was a rule which the Commission should employ when endeavoring to determine if the income of railroads as a whole (or in large territorial groups) was sufficient to meet the requirements of the law. In all the time the rule of 1920 was in effect, no definite value of railroad property to be used as a rate base was ever promulgated by the Commission, and the only effort it made to establish the value of a single railroad for the purpose of applying the recapture clause was rejected by the Supreme Court as having a result which was at variance with the law. Since the railroads constantly maintained that they were receiving a return which was less than fair, presumably they had the right to secure an order from a Federal court directing the Commission to carry out the mandate of the Act of 1920. But the railroads never took such action, though one or two leading railroad officials, who felt outraged because they believed the Commission to be derelict in its duty, threatened to start judicial proceedings. As a consequence, though the Commission, when it authorized several general increases in freight rates and passenger fares, mentioned the "value" of railroad property, this value at no time had any "legal" standing, and at no time did the Commission, in any of its decisions authorizing general rate advances, endeavor to figure out mathematically that the increases authorized were calculated to bring in revenues sufficient to give the railroads a specific rate of return on an assumed property value. It was only in its effort to administer the recapture clause that the Commission actually tried to give effect to the letter of the law with respect to railroad value and, as we have stated previously, this effort came to nought.

After the rule of rate making of 1920 was repealed, the Commission continued, in its decisions having to do with the general level of rates, to make statements concerning the "value" of the railroads, but it never asserted that any particular value was to be regarded as a rate base nor did it indulge in any speculation with respect to the problem of "fair return." It studied the income and expenses of the railroads; if it thought that the gap between them was too narrow, and if at the same time it was convinced that the internal commerce of the country could "stand" an advance of rates without undue injury, it authorized the railroads to advance their charges. Since the end of the Second World War, the process of inflation, with its alternating advances of wages and prices, has led the Commission to authorize railroads to make general rate increases no less than ten times. In no increase, however, was a particular amount of net return expressly mentioned as a goal, and at no time have the railroads had a rate of return which they think that in fairness they should receive. The Commission has endeavored to the best of its ability to maintain the solvency of the railroads, but at the same time has tempered the wind to protesting shippers.

For many years, despite the failure of the railroads to receive what they considered to be a fair return, they were nevertheless supposedly under the protection of the Supreme Court decision of 1898, which declared unequivocally that they were entitled to earnings which would cover their costs and give them a fair return on the value of their property. It is an interesting fact that, during all these years, no general rate orders of the Commission were ever challenged in the courts, nor was any attempt made to compel the Commission, through judicial process, to initiate a level of rates which would give the railroads any particular rate of return. As far as railroads were concerned, though the law and the decisions of courts said one thing, the Commission was undisturbed in its efforts to do the best it could for the struggling carriers, regardless of the fact that the carriers did not believe that the Commission's best was good enough.

PUBLIC UTILITY RATES BASED ON VALUE

If the railroads and the Interstate Commerce Commission did not become ensnared in the numerous entanglements of judicial theorizing about the matters of fair value and fair return, the same could not be said of other public utility enterprises and the boards and bureaus which had supervision over their rates and practices. Water companies, gas companies, telephone companies, street railway corporations, and other utilities kept the courts busy dealing with controversies arising from charges that public service commissions had been guilty of "confiscation" because of improper decisions they had made with respect to the values of utility properties or with respect to the rates of return they declared to be fair. Case after case reached the Supreme Court with the demand that it require regulatory commissions to obey the injunction of the Court's famous decision of 1898—to permit the complaining utility to enjoy rates which would give it a fair return upon the value of its property devoted to public service, a value to be ascertained by the proper consideration of all the "elements" which the Court had said in 1898 should be given adequate weight in the establishment of the rate base upon which a fair return was to be computed. The Court never adopted any single standard of valuation applicable to all utilities, nor did it ever fix upon a certain standard rate of return as being "fair." Each case was decided on its own merits, in accordance with the views of the Court as it was constituted at the time the case was heard. A fair rate of return might be 5 or 6 per cent in some cases, and 8 or 10 in others. In one case, the cost of reproduction might be given the most weight in ascertaining the value of a public service corporation's property; in another case, original cost might be accepted as the proper standard. The chief result of the often contradictory and irreconcilable positions the Court took was a vast stimulation of theorizing among economists, public utility "experts," lawyers, and politicians on the question of "value" and related problems, but however painstaking and persistent the cultivation of the soil, it can hardly be said that the harvest was a fruitful one.

THE HOPE CASE

In 1944, the Supreme Court suddenly made an about-face movement that took the theorists by surprise and left many critics worse confounded than before.[7] In a notable decision with respect to rates prescribed by the Federal Power Commission on natural gas sold in interstate commerce, the Court in effect repudiated the decision of 1898, to which it had for so many years endeavored to adhere; admitted that the reasoning in that decision and in other decisions in which it had virtually ignored the rela-

[7] Federal Power Commission v. Hope, 320 U.S. 591 (1944).

tionship between value and earning power was "circular" reasoning; and admitted that an administrative commission's activities in rate making do not necessarily start from some arbitrary conception of "fair value" but that this value may become the end product of rate decisions. It seemed to adopt the common-sense view that in a going concern net earnings are the chief determinant of value; that value is not something which can be separated from earning power and employed as a standard for the establishment of reasonable prices which will produce a "fair return." Any administrative or statutory action which reduces the prices which a utility may charge may have the effect of reducing the value of the utility in the market place. But this did not mean, in the opinion of the Court, that the fixing of prices was invalid under the Constitution. It is the "impact" of the rate which counts, the Court declared, and not the particular theory upon which the rate was established, and if that impact is such as to result in "rates which enable the company to operate success-fully, to maintain financial integrity, to attract capital, and to compensate investors for the risks assumed," such rates cannot "be condemned as invalid even though they might produce only a meager return on the so called 'fair value' rate-base." In the search for "reasonableness," it was entirely proper for an administrative body to make certain "pragmatic adjust-ments," and if these adjustments were of such a character as to maintain an equitable balance between public welfare and private advantage, no wrong had been committed, however much the owners of a utility might have thought they had been outraged by bureaucratic officiousness. "If the total effect of the rate order can not be said to be unjust and unrea-sonable, judicial inquiry is at an end."

It must be remembered that this case had to do with the sale of gas and not with railroad rates, and it is not our purpose here to enter into a pro-longed discussion of the theories of public utility rate regulation. But it may be worth while to point out that what the Court declared in this case to be reasonable conduct on the part of an administrative commission was precisely the conduct which for a score of years had characterized the work of the Interstate Commerce Commission in dealing with the "general level" of railroad rates. Only once, in the advanced rate de-cision of 1920, had it endeavored to set up a value of railroad property and establish rates which it was hoped would yield the return declared by statute to be fair. In all the numerous rate orders that followed, the Commission had made "pragmatic adjustments," endeavoring to hold a fair balance between railroad owners and railroad users, though, it must be said, seldom to the satisfaction of either party. It had clearly been swayed more by what it thought would be the impact of its rate orders than by any elaborate theory of rate making. It had followed no precise formula; it had merely endeavored to exercise good judgment, after giving careful consideration to all the circumstances with which it was confronted in the midst of trying and difficult economic conditions.

RATES ON PARTICULAR COMMODITIES

While the industrial traffic manager is bound to be interested in rate decisions and rate investigations bearing upon the general level of rates, both because of the effect they may have upon his transportation costs and because, as a good citizen, he has an interest in the economic welfare of his country, he is likely to be more concerned with the rates on the commodities, the transportation of which it is his duty to provide for and direct. It is on particular rates and not on the general level of rates that he is most likely to concentrate his professional attention, and it is with particular rates that he will have most to do in his professional capacity. The Interstate Commerce Commission has many more cases involving particular rates than cases involving the rate level. While its decisions making changes in all the rates of the entire country or of a large section of it are likely to create the largest newspaper headlines, it has to make many more decisions in the pursuit of its duty to see that the rates charged by carriers for particular hauls of particular articles of commerce are neither unreasonable nor unjustly discriminatory.

THE HOCH-SMITH RESOLUTION

The same theory which has been adopted with regard to the general rate level—that rates should cover the cost of service and not exceed the value of service—applies to the rates exacted for the transportation of single commodities offered for transportation. The Supreme Court has held, on various occasions, that each article carried, or each class of traffic, should bear its proper share of the total transportation costs of the country's carriers. In 1925, Congress passed the so-called Hoch-Smith Resolution, which stated that it is "hereby declared to be a true policy of rate making to be pursued by the Interstate Commerce Commission in adjusting freight rates, that the conditions which at any given time prevail in our several industries should be considered in so far as it is legally possible to do so, to the end that commodities may freely move." It directed the Commission to "effect with the least practicable delay such lawful changes in the rate structure of the country as will promote the movement by common carriers of the products of agriculture affected by the depression, including livestock, at the lowest possible rates compatible with the maintenance of adequate transportation service."

This was nothing more or less than an effort on the part of the agricultural interests in Congress to bring "relief" to agriculture, either at the expense of the railroads or at the expense of industries whose products would have to pay higher transportation rates to make up for the losses which the railroads might suffer by reason of granting depressed rates on farm products. The railroads were to be employed as an economic balance wheel, by which the little new wealth that was created during a period of depression might be "shared" by the agricultural interests. Of course, the language was somewhat cloudy—so cloudy, in fact, that the Supreme Court was not entirely sure what the resolution meant. But the Court did not hesitate to say that if Congress intended that the Interstate Commerce Commission should establish rates on the products of depressed industries so low that the revenue would not cover the costs of transportation, it was directing the Commission to take action which would clearly be in violation of the Constitution. Neither Congress nor the Commission had the right to make rates on particular commodities lower than what the "nature and cost of the transportation service" required.[8]

THE ZONE OF REASONABLENESS

On the other hand, the Supreme Court has never said that a rate which "exceeded" the cost of service would necessarily be an unreasonable rate. Rates below the cost of service are unreasonably low, but rates are not necessarily unreasonably high until they exceed the "value" of the service. Between the cost of service and the value of service, there is a "zone of reasonableness," and with respect to many commodities this zone may have considerable width. As the Supreme Court once declared, "rates are reasonable from the standpoint of the shipper . . . though their net product furnishes more than a fair return to the carrier."[9] It is within this zone of reasonableness that the Commission makes those pragmatic adjustments of particular rates in a manner designed to do no violence either to the rights of the carrier or to the rights of the shipper.

VALUE OF SERVICE AS A STANDARD

That such pragmatic adjustments offer the only sensible method of dealing with the problem of establishing a reasonable rate becomes apparent when one considers the difficulties involved in any effort to ascertain either the cost of a particular service to a carrier or the value of a particular service to a shipper. It takes but a little reflection to realize that the value of a transportation service cannot be measured with precision. It will differ from day to day, and it will be different at the same time for many users of transportation. A bandit who is two jumps ahead of a sheriff's posse is likely to set more store on a good horse than a farmer riding to the local post office for his daily mail. When some catastrophe such as a flood, fire, or military invasion occurs, the value of transportation service may become immeasurable.

[8] Ann Arbor R.R. v. United States, 281 U.S. 658 (1930).
[9] Dayton–Goose Creek Ry. v. United States, 263 U.S. 456 (1924).

EXACT COSTS IMPOSSIBLE OF CALCULATION

We have already discussed briefly some of the difficulties which theorists encountered in endeavoring to establish a level of rates based on the cost of service. The difficulties met with in any attempt to ascertain the cost of a particular transportation service are even more baffling. They are so baffling, in fact, that it is impossible for an administrative commission, court, or rate "expert" to determine with precision the exact cost of hauling any commodity to a carrier which offers a general transportation service, in which passengers, express, and many kinds of freight are hauled from place to place.

The reasons why it is impossible to discover with mathematical exactitude the cost of a particular transportation service are not hard to find. Here again, we take our example from the railroad, though the same considerations apply to the services of carriers by water, highway, and air. Very little of the total expenses of a railroad can be definitely assigned to the transportation of any single shipment. A railroad's expenses are "composite." They are incurred jointly for many different services. These expenses are often referred to as "joint costs," though they are not joint costs in the strictest sense of the term. But they are incurred for many services, and it is impossible to segregate them completely and say that this expense is incurred for this shipment and that expense for that. It is impossible even to separate all of the expenses of a railroad's passenger service from the expenses for freight service. Some expenses, such as the wages of train crews, the cost of fuel, the costs of terminal operations, and the money spent in acquiring and maintaining equipment, can be accurately divided between the two branches of service, but the costs of maintaining tracks, operating and maintaining signals, and general supervision of all services and a host of other expenses cannot be so divided. If they are divided at all, it must be upon the basis of some more or less arbitrary "allocation" or "apportionment." If it is impossible to say with any degree of accuracy what proportion of total railroad expense is definitely attributable to the freight or to the passenger service, how much less fruitless would be the effort to calculate the exact cost of transporting a single passenger or a single less carload shipment of freight.

A second reason why it is impossible to find out accurately the cost of hauling particular shipments is that so many railroad expenses are constant, or "fixed," and, as was pointed out previously, continue to be borne regardless of the amount of business the railroad enjoys. How can one say with confidence that a particular carload of freight was chargeable with a certain amount of the fixed expenses of a railroad, when those fixed expenses would have been precisely the same had this particular carload of freight never been transported? The only expenses for which this carload, if it were actually hauled, was accountable, were the added expenses of operation, or what are called the "out-of-pocket" expenses, for which it was obviously responsible. Of course a railroad would not survive long if it exacted from all its traffic only these out-of-pocket expenses. To continue in operation, it must secure revenue sufficient to cover its fixed expenses as well as its variable expenses. The problem in rate making is how to divide these fixed charges among the different kinds of traffic without injustice to passengers and shippers. Here the rate maker, whether he is a railroad traffic manager or an administrative official of the government, must operate within the zone of reasonableness, making those pragmatic adjustments which serve the public interest without violating private rights.

COMPARATIVE COSTS

Though unable to escape the fact that the exact costs of individual transportation services are impossible of ascertainment, we soon discover, in any study of railroad rate making, that the cost of service has more to do with the determination of the exact amount of a railroad rate than any other factor, whether the rate is made by the traffic manager of a railroad or by an administrative body which seeks to make all rates "reasonable." This is the paradox of rate making and of rate-making theory. For the question immediately arises—if it is impossible to ascertain the cost of a transportation service, how can it be that cost is used as a deciding factor in the establishment of a rate? We must once more remember that the entire structure of transportation rates must be considered historically; it did not spring into existence full-blown, but is the result of many years of patient observation and experimentation. Experience has shown, over the years, that rate relationships are much more important in the practical operations of rate making than the exact amount of the rates on particular articles of commerce. Once a rate structure has been established for a certain number of commodities, the rates for additional commodities offered for transportation are made largely on the basis of comparison with rates previously established for other commodities.[10] We do not know the cost of transporting each of the articles the carrier has been accustomed to carry, and we cannot find out the exact cost of carrying the additional articles that are offered. But we can tell, with a reasonable degree of certainty, whether the new articles will cost less or more to transport than the ones

[10] The Interstate Commerce Commission has employed the principle of comparison in thousands of cases involving the reasonableness of rates on individual articles. "We have long adhered," the Commission once said, "to the principle that the best test of the reasonableness of a rate is a comparison of the assailed rate with other rates in effect on like traffic moving in the same general territory." Pan Handle Lumber Company v. Fort Worth and Denver City Ry., 210 I.C.C. 353 (1935).

that have been carried. Rate making becomes a matter of comparison rather than of cost finding. It becomes a question of less or more.

If a carrier has a monopoly, it is likely to think of "less or more" only in connection with the value of service, and exact rates on different articles which are at wide variance with the comparative costs of service. But when competition begins, or when the government steps in to see that shippers are charged only rates that are reasonable, then the matter of costs, and particularly of relative costs, becomes a factor of high importance.

THE LEADING COST FACTORS

It is necessary to have only the most cursory acquaintance with the rate structure of the railroads of the United States to understand how much attention has been given to the matter of relative costs in the process of rate making. Though there are many elements that enter into the cost of transporting a particular commodity, there are only three elements of outstanding importance. These are weight in proportion to bulk, actual weight, and the distance of the haul. We have already shown how, in the process of freight classification, articles which are bulky in proportion to their weight are assigned, as a rule, to higher classes, and therefore receive higher rates than articles having a greater density. There is no rule-of-thumb method of establishing the rate relationships that arise because of the difference of density of different articles. But other things being equal, it is almost the invariable practice of railroads to impose higher charges on those articles which, in proportion to their weight, take up more space in a freight car.

In the same way, a railroad charges more to carry a heavier than a lighter shipment of the same commodity. Indeed, virtually all the freight rates of American railroads are quoted as so much per hundred pounds or so much per ton. The reason for charging more for the larger weight is simply that the greater the weight, the higher the cost of transportation. We do not need to know how much it costs to carry a shipment weighing a hundred pounds to know that it must cost approximately twice as much to carry a shipment of the same commodity weighing two hundred pounds. Consequently, the charge for the latter shipment is twice as great as for the former.

The element of relative cost appears again in the matter of the distance of a haul. Other things being equal, the longer the haul, the greater the total charge. We shall discuss the exceptions to this practice later, and try to find out why they are made without violating the rule of reasonableness.

Every shipper is familiar with the fact that, as a rule, railroads charge more per hundred pounds for less carload shipments than they charge for carload shipments. Why is this? The reason is plainly because it costs more per hundred pounds to transport the less carload shipments. How much more? We do not know precisely, and we cannot find out. But we know that less carload shipments do not stow so well in a car, that they must often be transferred en route, that they must frequently be stored, that they must be loaded and unloaded by the carrier, and that perhaps they must receive other services not accorded to carload shipments. The greater cost of transporting the less carload shipments obviously justifies a greater charge per hundred pounds for their transportation. The amount of the difference in cost cannot be mathematically determined; the difference in the rate is one of those matters which must be decided solely by the exercise of good judgment after a careful consideration of all circumstances and conditions.

SOME OTHER COST FACTORS

There are other costs which affect the relationship between rates. Goods which require refrigeration or other protective service must, as a rule, pay higher charges than goods which, though similar in other respects from a transportation standpoint, do not require special protective care. It has been mentioned before that the element of insurance against loss and damage enters into transportation costs, with the result that the more valuable an article is, the greater the charge for its transportation is likely to be.

RATE MAKING LARGELY A MATTER OF COMPARISON

Thus the effort to establish proper relationships between rates becomes largely a matter of comparison. Other things being equal, articles which are similar to one another, because of that similarity, are bound to have approximately equal costs of transportation and are likely to carry similar rates. The total charges collected for the transportation of different articles are arrived at usually by a rough-and-ready calculation of relative costs.

The emphasis upon rate relationships has long been observed in the rate making of the traffic officials of railroads. In the distant past, when the early railroads had little or no competition to face, rates were closer to the value of the service to shippers. As competition appeared and grew, the pressure of shippers and the rivalry of transportation agencies had the effect of making cost a more and more important consideration in the fixing of rates. Once the railroads had succeeded in bringing competition under a substantial measure of control and began to establish rate structures by voluntary agreement, the relative costs of transporting different products became an increasingly important factor in rate making. While there were many departures and many exceptions, some of which we have previously discussed—exceptions which all too frequently resulted in objectionable discrimination—the cost elements we have noted as being of the most important—weight in proportion to bulk, actual weight, and distance—were the deciding factors in establishing the relationships in the great mass of railroad rates.

OLD RATE STRUCTURES MODIFIED BY THE COMMISSION

When the Interstate Commerce Commission finally received the power to regulate rates effectively in 1906, it began to overhaul many of the rate structures of the country, especially those in which the carrier had given the least observance to relative costs. More and more, as the years have passed and the Commission has brought the rate structures of the country under firm control, the element of relative cost has been emphasized. The famous basing point system of the South, with its numerous instances of violation of the long-and-short-haul principle of rate making, has been completely overhauled—so completely, in fact, that the term "southern basing point system" is no longer encountered except in historical accounts of the development of American railroad rates. Southern rates were put on a "dry-land" basis, and with a few exceptions rates in that region were made to progress with the increase of the distance of the haul. In the same fashion, the system of transcontinental rates, with its wide "blanket" and excessive discrimination against intermountain points, was transformed; while all transcontinental rates do not progress with distance, a great many of them do, and there has been a decided amelioration of the conditions which for so many years aroused the indignation of the inhabitants of the Intermountain Territory. In the East, too, the Commission has brought about extensive changes, especially in the rates on domestic traffic, and Baltimore and Philadelphia have rates which, when compared to New York rates, show a greater degree of recognition of the fact that distance is a matter of primary consideration in the establishment of rate relationships.

MILEAGE SCALES

The most striking example of the efforts of the Commission to bring railroad rates more into line with costs had been its use of "mileage scales" in the establishment of reasonable rates in those areas where, in the opinion of the Commission, the carriers had not created rate structures which conformed to the principles laid down in the Interstate Commerce Act. There are few parts of the country now which do not have class-rate scales worked out in cooperation with carriers and shippers and prescribed in orders of the Commission; many commodity rates progress according to mileage scales which the Commission has ordered to be observed. Class-rate scales are simple in construction. First of all, a percentage relationship is established between the different classes, so that the rates on the classes below first will bear a fixed relationship to the first-class rate. Then the first-class rates are made for different distances according to a system of "progression." Given the relationships of the classes, the first-class rate for the initial distance of the scale, and the method of progression according to distance, the tariff compiler—who, of course, knows the distance between stations on his railroad—has no difficulty in making up rate schedules which conform to the prescribed pattern.

The scales which the Commission has put into effect are by no means the same for all rate territories. Indeed, there may be variations in the scales for different parts of the same territory because the paucity of traffic in one area makes the "cost" of transportation greater than in another area. But there has been steady progress toward uniformity, and as we mentioned before, the Commission hopes eventually to have the new Uniform Freight Classification applicable throughout the length and breadth of the United States and a "mileage scale," according to which all class rates shall be made.

COST OF SERVICE NOT THE SOLE FACTOR IN RATE MAKING

It must not be thought that the Interstate Commerce Commission has adhered in a slavish manner to a cost-of-service theory of rate making, any more than the traffic officials of railroads did in the days before government control of rates began. While in general it may be said that the tendency of Commission policy has been to keep rates fairly close to the lower area of the zone of reasonableness in which rates may fluctuate without becoming unreasonable, there are many instances in which rates have been permitted to approach the upper limit of that zone and instances, too, in which rates have been permitted, because of special circumstances, to become much lower than a strict application of the cost principle would appear to justify. The courts have held that any railroad rate must cover and more than cover the out-of-pocket cost of transportation. That is, a rate must be sufficiently high to reimburse the railroad for the added cost which it incurs by reason of transporting the article to which the rate is applied and at the same time contribute something toward the fixed costs of the carrier. But it is a matter of common knowledge, as well as an established principle in rate making, that some commodities are required to bear a higher portion of fixed charges than others.

In its very first report to Congress, the Interstate Commerce Commission stated that it was only reasonable that the value of a commodity should be taken into consideration in rate making, and that it was only fair that certain articles of high value should bear a higher proportion of railroad costs in order that other commodities could enter the stream of our foreign and domestic commerce. There are still many articles which to a large extent would be excluded from our markets if they had to bear "a relatively equal burden" of the fixed costs of the operation of our great network of transportation facilities, and there are many commodities to which considerably lower rates would be given if the principle of equal apportionment of fixed costs were rigorously applied.

Deviations from the strict application of the cost-of-service principle often result in lower rates than would be applied if there were equality of apportionment. Nearly every railroad finds that it has an unbalanced traffic, requiring the return movement of a number of empty cars. Rates may be made so low as to fill these returning empties with paying loads, and even though the traffic does not bear its full share of the fixed costs of the carrier, it yields enough revenue to cover all out-of-pocket costs and contribute something toward overhead expenses. Motor vehicle carriers frequently make rates which will ensure return loads for trucks which would otherwise travel empty, and shipowners often are glad to have "distress space" filled with low-rated cargo, knowing that it costs virtually as much to send a ship across the ocean with half a cargo as it costs to send it with holds loaded until the vessel sinks to its load line.

COMPETITION STILL IMPORTANT

Perhaps the chief cause for deviation from a rigid application of the cost-of-service principle in rate making is competition. We have many railroads which operate between the same terminals, and while they no longer engage in cutthroat warfare, they must nevertheless often adjust rates in such a manner as to give each an opportunity to share in traffic which any one of the competing lines could carry. The departure from the cost principle is seen usually in the rates of the carrier with the longer route. It must equalize its rates on competitive traffic with the rates of the short line, even though its costs of transportation are larger. It is not at all unusual for the Interstate Commerce Commission to grant "circuitous" lines fourth section relief, permitting them to charge more for short hauls than for longer ones, in order that they may meet the competition of shorter lines at the more distant points. The competition of water lines, either actual or potential, still has a potent influence on many railroad rates, and may cause the Commission to extend fourth section relief to rival carriers by rail.

Just now our railroads are engaged in a tense competitive struggle with motor vehicles, so many of which operate over our highways throughout the country. Thousands of railroad rates have been reduced to meet motor competition, and there are few of these motor-compelled rates which contribute as much proportionally to the total costs of transportation as those rates which are more nearly free from the influence of carrier competition. When the motor vehicle first began to enter the field as an active competitor for the traffic which the railroads had so long monopolized, it found a situation made to order for its effort, because so many valuable articles of railroad traffic were being transported at rates which were very near the upper boundary of the zone of reasonableness.[11] It was this

[11] Joseph B. Eastman, a member of the Interstate Commerce Commission and Federal Coordinator of Transportation under the emergency Act of 1933,

cream of the railroad traffic in which motor vehicles first made their heaviest inroads, and while their operations have been extended to the transportation of many commodities which are much less valuable, they still find a substantial portion of their most profitable traffic in merchandise which has considerable value in proportion to its weight. Needless to say, the shippers of this merchandise have profited greatly because of the advent of this new carrier and because of the competition which it has stimulated. Many traffic managers who once purchased their transportation service almost entirely from railroads now find that by far the largest part of their business goes to the carriers of the highway.

Industrial competition and commercial or market competition likewise may cause railroads and other carriers to swerve from a strict adherence to the cost-of-service principle of rate making, and here again the Interstate Commerce Commission has abstained from a strict application of the cost theory. Rates on many export commodities are "equalized" to different seaports, regardless of the fact that the distances of the rail hauls may vary greatly. The "seaboard differentials" of the North Atlantic ports, which the Commission modified to conform more closely to distance with respect to domestic traffic, were left undisturbed with respect to export traffic in order that no single port should obtain an excessive advantage. Group rates have been made not only to facilitate the work of rate publication but to equalize the competitive opportunities of industries producing the same commodity in a limited area or region. Since all group rates involve charging identical rates for different—often widely different—distances, it is apparent that they represent a departure from the cost-of-service theory of rate making. One of the best examples of how the principle of cost is honored by its nonobservance is found in the rates from Central Freight Association Territory to the port district of New York. It is an inescapable fact that the cost of transporting a carload of merchandise from Chicago to Newark or Jersey City is less than the cost of transporting a carload of the same merchandise from Chicago to New York by way of Newark and Jersey City, necessitating a car ferry haul across the Hudson River. Yet the Commission has consistently refused to permit the establishment of lower rates to the cities on the west side of the Hudson, because of its unwillingness to "divide the port" as an integrated commercial unit. Dozens—hundreds—of other examples of rate equalization may be found, all of which do a certain measure of violence to the cost theory of rate making.

pointed out, in one of his reports dealing with the regulation of highway transportation, that the adherence of the railroads to the value of the service as a proper measure of a reasonable rate had made it possible for the motor vehicle to capture much traffic that the railroads had long been accustomed to haul. House Document No. 89, 74th Congress, 1st Session, p. 120 (1935).

THE QUESTION OF DISCRIMINATION

The question now to be considered is how far a railroad or an administrative body can go in making rates that palpably are out of line with the relative costs of transportation service. Any departure from this principle plainly involves a practice which we call discrimination. In the following chapter, we shall deal with the rules and principles by which discrimination is tested in order to find out if it is undue or unjust, and therefore unlawful.

CHAPTER IX

Freight Rates under Regulation: The Problem of Discrimination

The word "discrimination" has for some reason acquired a rather unsavory character, which it does not at all deserve. It is one of the words which puzzle the student of semantics. In the minds of a great many persons, it has to do with an act which is unwholesome or reprehensible, an act which is properly subject to social condemnation, when all it really means is differentiation, discernment of differences, or exercise of selective judgment.

The word has acquired undeserved and disagreeable connotations because so many writers and speakers have failed to distinguish between discrimination and unjust or unfair discrimination. They frequently use the word as if all discrimination were objectionable and repugnant. But this is not the case. When we say that a woman exercises discriminating taste in the selection of her hats or other articles of apparel, we are giving her a compliment, just as we give a compliment to a man when we say that he displays a fine sense of discrimination in the choice of his friends and companions.

DISCRIMINATION NOT FORBIDDEN BY LAW

We frequently read in books and newspapers that a railroad or other public utility is forbidden by law to charge "discriminatory" rates. This is not true. What a utility is forbidden to charge is rates that are "unjustly," "unfairly," or "unduly" discriminatory. There is a vast and very important difference. It might be said in passing that even Congress has slipped in its use of the word "discrimination." The Interstate Commerce Act condemned only unjust discrimination, but in the Elkins Act of 1903, which was directed against the vicious practice of rebating, in which so many railroads had long indulged, Congress said that:

it shall be unlawful for any person, persons, or corporation to offer, grant, or give, or to solicit, accept or receive any rebate, concession or discrimination in respect to the transportation of any property in interstate or foreign commerce by any common carrier subject to the said Act to Regulate Commerce and the Acts amendatory thereof whereby any such property shall by any device whatever be transported at a less rate than that named in the tariffs published and filed by such carrier, as required by said Act to Regulate Commerce and Acts amendatory thereof, or whereby any other advantage is given or discrimination is practiced.

As first used in this clause of the law, the world "discrimination" has a limited meaning, merely indicating that when a railroad departs from its published rates it is guilty of illegal discrimination. But in the last phrase of the clause, it would appear that all discrimination on the part of a carrier subject to the Interstate Commerce Act, of whatever nature, is unequivocally condemned. Of course it was not the intention of Congress to enact such a sweeping measure, and the courts have quite properly construed the meaning of the word as if it were equivalent to the expression "unjust discrimination," which appears in the second section of the original Act to Regulate Commerce. But even Congress should exercise a little more care in its legislative draftsmanship and endeavor to avoid trifling with the English language.[1]

We have no laws which forbid discrimination. We have only laws which forbid discrimination which, for one reason or another, has come to be regarded as objectionable. We also have laws which compel the exercise of discrimination which is thought to be socially desirable. For example, in some states we have laws for the protection of civil rights, which forbid discrimination in the selection of employees or in the admission of students to educational institutions, if the discrimination is based upon such consideration as race or religion. There is no law which forbids discrimination against an applicant for employment on the grounds

---

[1] Federal judges have also been known to indulge in loose language on the subject of discrimination. One judge declared, "The outstanding purpose of the Commerce Act was to absolutely uproot and destroy all discriminations in interstate commerce regardless of how conceived or by what plan, scheme or device they may be sought to be accomplished." L. M. Kirkpatrick Company v. Illinois Central R.R., 195 Southern 692 (1940).

The Interstate Commerce Commission has never failed to recognize the fact that there can be discrimination in rates which is not undue discrimination. "It is evident," said the Commission, "that every system of group rates must occasion more or less discrimination. The rate to the nearer edge of the group as compared with that to the more distant edge is of necessity discriminatory. The discrimination grows relatively more in proportion as the distance from the group decreases, and plainly there must come a point where the point of origin is so near the group that the discrimination will become undue." W. D. Mitchell v. Atchison, Topeka & Santa Fe Ry., 12 I.C.C. 324 (1907). At another time the Commission said, "We have always recognized that in the application of group rates a discrimination by necessity arose between the near and the far edge of the group; but have felt in many cases this discrimination was not undue and therefore not unlawful." Southwestern Missouri Millers' Club v. Missouri-Kansas-Texas Ry., 22 I.C.C. 422 (1912). See also Atlas Portland Cement Company v. Baltimore and Ohio R.R., 22 I.C.C. 446 (1912); Hammerschmidt & Franzen Co. v. Chicago and North Western Ry., 30 I.C.C. 71 (1914); the Illinois Coal Cases, 32 I.C.C. 659 (1915).

of age, skill, experience, or physical qualifications, and no law which forbids an educational institution to refuse admission to a prospective student on the grounds of inadequate preparation or lack of moral integrity. On the other hand, we have laws and rules which quite properly forbid the employment in public service, or the retention in employment, of Communists and other persons who, because of known disloyal sentiments, are deemed to be bad "security risks."

WHEN DOES DISCRIMINATION BECOME UNJUST?

There is always a great deal of difference of opinion as to what constitutes unfair or unjust discrimination. In the study of social history, we find that certain discriminatory practices which were once considered to be entirely unobjectionable are now regarded as reprehensible in the extreme. For example, human slavery was justified or condoned in various passages in the Old Testament as well as by such respectable Greek philosophers as Plato and Aristotle; it was practiced with approval until comparatively recent times by our own nation and by other countries which were the founders and defenders of "western civilization"; today it is regarded with abhorrence by those nations. With other nations, however, human slavery still exists without social disapprobation. At the present time, the people of our own country are sharply divided over the question of civil rights for members of the Negro race. Some of us believe that segregation, while it obviously involves discrimination, should not be regarded as immoral or unlawful if "equal opportunities and facilities" are impartially provided, while others take the position that segregation in and of itself constitutes unjust discrimination and that such things as Jim Crow cars, separate educational facilities, rental restrictions based upon racial considerations, and all other practices of racial differentiation should be resolutely and sternly forbidden by law. In other words, there are discriminatory practices which are unreservedly condemned by society as a whole, other discriminatory practices which receive almost universal approval, and others about which there is a wide difference of opinion.

PRICE DISCRIMINATION

What we are interested in here is discrimination in prices, particularly discrimination in the prices which carriers charge for transportation service. A dealer or seller who discriminates in prices differentiates in some manner among his customers; he does not accord them all the same treatment. The most common example of price discrimination arises when a seller charges his customers different prices for identical articles. He favors one customer or group of customers over others. But we may have price discrimination in connection with the sale of different articles, though this type of discrimination is not so easily definable and is more difficult to detect. If we start out with the premise that a reasonable price for an article or service should bear some relation to the cost of its production, we can easily draw the conclusion that the relative prices of different articles or services should bear some reasonable relation to the relative costs of their production. We discussed this matter at some length in the preceding chapter, and endeavored to show that reasonable rates are based in part upon relative costs, though not always strictly so. In any event, it is generally conceded that the prices charged by a public service industry should in some manner reflect costs, and when the industry sells a number of commodities or services, the prices should to a certain extent reflect the differences in costs or, as we said before, the relative costs of the different articles sold. When a difference in price is based upon a difference in cost, the discrimination or difference in treatment of different customers is unobjectionable. But if a seller of a product charges different prices which are not fairly related to differences in cost, we may have discrimination that is rightly regarded as unjust. For example, there should be no objection, under ordinary circumstances, to a dealer's granting what is known as a quantity discount. Ordinarily, the unit cost of manufacturing and shipping articles is less when they are produced and distributed in large quantities than when produced and distributed in small quantities, and since the unit cost is less in one case than in the other the practice of making a lower unit price for the article produced at the lower cost is usually regarded as a fair practice, if the difference in price fairly and equitably reflects the difference in cost. But if the producer grants to the large consumer or purchaser a quantity discount that is substantially greater than the difference in cost fairly warrants, we are likely to believe that he is engaging in an unjustly discriminatory practice. We shall see, however, that a rule of this kind does not have universal application. There may be occasions when relative prices which fairly reflect differences in cost are regarded as unjustly discriminatory, and there may be cases when it is not considered unjust for a seller to charge the same or even more for an article or service which has been less costly to produce.

TESTING DISCRIMINATION FOR INJUSTICE

Price discrimination is not and never has been regarded as unlawful, any more than many other kinds of discrimination. It becomes unlawful only when it becomes unjust. Plainly, the problem with which we are confronted in any study of price discrimination is, when does price discrimination become unjust? This is one of those many questions which it is much easier to ask than to answer.

We have already mentioned the fact that Congress declared in the Elkins

Act of 1903 that any carrier which departed from its filed and published rates should be regarded as guilty, by that very act, of unjust discrimination. Congress has promulgated one other unqualified test of discrimination, as well as one qualified test, to serve as a guide in determining if discrimination in transportation rates is or is not unjust and therefore unlawful, but for the most part Congress has left the determination of the character of rate or price discrimination to the judgment of administrative boards and commissions. Hard and fast rules have not been prescribed; it is the duty of the administrative commission to decide, after a consideration of all relevant circumstances, whether a particular discrimination in rates or prices should be condemned as unjust.

SECTION TWO: AN UNQUALIFIED TEST

The unqualified test of injustice which Congress included in the original Act to Regulate Commerce, passed in 1887, was simple. In the second section of the law, Congress declared

. . . that if any common carrier, subject to the provisions of this act shall, directly or indirectly, by any special rate, rebate, or drawback, or other device, charge, demand, collect or receive from any person or persons a greater or less compensation for any service rendered, or to be rendered, in the transportation of persons or property, subject to the provisions of this act, than it charges, demands, collects, or receives from any person or persons for doing for him or them a like and contemporaneous service in the transportation of a like kind of traffic under substantially similar circumstances and conditions, such common carrier shall be deemed guilty of unjust discrimination, which is hereby prohibited and declared to be unlawful.

This was merely a rule to the effect that railroads should charge all customers alike for the performance of the same service. They were to play no favorites; they were not to extend lower rates to one shipper than to another if the services given to both were substantially the same.

SECTION FOUR: A QUALIFIED TEST

The qualified test of injustice in discriminatory rates was embodied in the fourth section of the law. Here Congress was taking into consideration not the matter of actual costs for identical services but the matter of relative costs for services which were not identical. The fourth section stated that

. . . it shall be unlawful for any common carrier subject to the provisions of this act to charge or receive any greater compensation in the aggregate for the transportation of passengers or of like kind of property, under substantially similar circumstances and conditions, for a shorter than for a longer distance over the same line, in the same direction, the shorter being included within the longer distance; but this shall not be construed as authorizing any common carrier within the terms of this act to charge and receive as great compensation for the shorter as for the longer distance; Provided, however, That upon application to the Commission appointed under the provisions of this act, such common carrier may, in special cases, after investigation by the Commission, be authorized to charge less for the longer than for the shorter distance for the transportation of persons or property; and the Commission may from time to time prescribe the extent to which such designated common carrier may be relieved from the operation of this section of the act.

It is worth while to notice carefully the language of the fourth section. Why does it say "over the same line, in the same direction, the shorter being included within the longer distance"? It was surely because Congress had in mind the matter of relative and not actual costs. It stood to reason that the cost of a long haul "over the same line, in the same direction" would be more than the cost of a short haul included within the longer. Whenever a railroad charged a larger amount for the shorter haul, it was plainly guilty of a discrimination in which the difference in price did not reflect the difference in cost. Yet Congress did not make an absolute rule. The violation of the long-and-short-haul principle should not necessarily be considered as unjust under all circumstances and conditions. There was no exception to the rule that all shippers should pay the same price for identical services, but the Commission might, in its discretion, permit deviations from or exceptions to the general rule of the fourth section.

SECTION THREE: ADMINISTRATIVE DISCRETION

Then the law went still further with respect to the discretionary power which the Commission might exercise. The third section of the Act, broad and general in its terms, made it unlawful for a carrier subject to the provisions of the act to give

. . . any undue or unreasonable preference or advantage to any particular person, company, firm, corporation or locality, or any particular description of traffic, in any respect whatsoever, or to subject any particular person, company firm, corporation or locality, or any particular description of traffic, to any undue or unreasonable prejudice or disadvantage in any respect whatsoever.

The law laid down one set of conditions under which a difference in rates should be regarded as unduly discriminatory. It laid down another set of conditions under which a difference of rates might be regarded as prima-facie evidence of unjust discrimination, but authorized the Interstate Commerce Commission to give "relief" from the operation of the rule. Finally, the law condemned all forms of unjust discrimination, prejudice, or preference, but left it to the Interstate Commerce Commission to determine whether a particular differentiation of rates, other than those mentioned in the second and fourth sections, should be regarded as undue and unjust.[2]

Just how can the Interstate Commerce Commission determine whether a particular discrimination in railroad rates is unjust and unlawful? Or how can any other administrative body decide whether a price discrimination is to be condemned as unfair? We have already pointed out the more or less mandatory tests prescribed in the Interstate Commerce Act. But there are many situations, in which undue discrimination in rates is charged, which do not come under the terms of the second and fourth sections, situations in which the Commission must use its judgment. The most common situation in which it is likely to find that unjust discrimination exists is one in which the difference in rates complained of seems far greater than the difference in the costs of transportation reasonably justify. It is a situation comparable to that which arises when a manufacturer gives a large purchaser of his product a quantity discount which is greater than the savings of quantity production warrant.

TEST BY EFFECTS

There are many reasons why discrimination in the treatment of individuals as persons may be considered to be unjust, and perhaps be condemned by law. But when it comes to discrimination in prices, the reasons for condemnation of differentiation are not numerous, and the line between mere discrimination and discrimination which is unjust and unlawful is much more difficult to draw. We have mentioned one test, namely, that differences in price must fairly reflect differences in cost. But there may be other tests. One, at least, has been adopted by various administrative commissions. Instead of riveting its attention on the antecedent conditions which may be considered as sufficient justification for a differentiation in price, that is, upon differences in cost, a commission may look upon the possible results of the discrimination and reach the conclusion that however much the discrimination may be justified on the grounds of relative costs, it may still be held to be unjust and unlawful because of the effects it may have. For example, an administrative board, clothed with the power of correcting what it believes to be unfair methods of competition, may condemn a quantity discount given to a large purchaser not because the discount does not reflect fairly and equitably a difference

[2] It might be thought that sections 2 and 4 of the Interstate Commerce Act represent "special instances" of discrimination which is forbidden by section 3, that is, that it would be impossible to violate section 2 or 4 without violating section 3. However, the Commission has held in a few cases that section 2 can be violated without the violation of section 3. See Ashland Fire Brick Co. v. Southern Ry., 22 I.C.C. 115 (1911); Richmond Chamber of Commerce v. Seaboard Airline Ry., 44 I.C.C. 455 (1917). There was a vigorous dissent in the latter case.

in cost but because it believes that the discount would produce an effect which would be socially undesirable. The government of the United States has always displayed a considerable degree of solicitude for small business, with the result that it has often discouraged business practices which, if pursued too far, would have a tendency to favor unduly the interests of big business and promote the establishment of monopolies.

The Interstate Commerce Commission, in the exercise of its discretionary authority over discriminatory rates and practices, has, in one instance at least, based its decision not on the principle of relative cost but on the possible effect a discriminatory practice, if declared valid, might have. This has been its refusal, except in a very few exceptional cases, to permit railroads to publish rates on "multiple carloads" of traffic. It has not interfered with the practice of differentiating between rates on carload and less carload shipments, though it has on various occasions declared that the amount of the spread has been unjustly discriminatory and ordered the gap to be narrowed. But it has followed the policy of refusing to authorize "trainload rates," even when it has been possible to show that the costs of transporting multiple carload shipments would be less per carload than the cost of transporting single carloads, on the ground that lower rates granted to the larger shipments might unduly favor the large producer at the expense of his smaller competitor. The only exception has been when a competing transportation agency, such as a barge line, has provided a service by which "trainload" quantities of a commodity could be moved.[3]

TESTS IN PARTS II, III, AND IV OF THE ACT

The provisions of the Interstate Commerce Act with respect to discrimination, preference, and prejudice have been added to and modified many times since the original Act was passed in 1887. The new "parts" of the Act dealing respectively with motor vehicle carriers, carriers by water, and freight forwarders prohibit unjust discrimination and undue and unreasonable prejudice or disadvantage, and rebates are specifically forbidden. However, the parts of the law relating to these carriers prescribe no test of discrimination, except rebating and departure from published rates. In parts II and IV of the law, there is nothing comparable to the provisions of sections 2 and 4 of part I. In part III, which provides for the regulation of carriers by water, there is no section comparable to section 2 of part I, but the fourth section of part I now provides that carriers by water, subject to part III, shall be governed by the same long-

---

[3] Molasses from New Orleans, 235 I.C.C. 485 (1939). This decision marked an instance in which the Commission permitted the establishment of multiple carload rates. The decision contains references to many other cases in which the subject had received consideration.

and-short-haul rule of rate making that is applicable to railroads and other carriers subject to part I.

CHANGES IN PART I SINCE 1887

The second section of part I of the Interstate Commerce Act remains virtually as it was when it was originally written in 1887. There have been some changes, however, in section 3. Whereas this section originally forbade undue discrimination only against shippers, passengers, or "any particular description of traffic," and between connecting lines, it now also protects "any association, locality, port, port district, gateway, transit point, region, district, territory" against any undue or unreasonable prejudice or disadvantage. The section also contains a paragraph declaring it to be the "policy of Congress" that shippers of farm products for export "shall be granted export rates on the same principles that are applicable in the case of rates on industrial products for export." Another paragraph, enacted in 1940, directs the Interstate Commerce Commission to make a general investigation of rail and rail-and-water rates on all products moving between the major classification territories, as well as rates on traffic moving within those territories, for the "purpose of determining if the rates are unjust and unreasonable or unlawful in any other respect in and of themselves or in their relation to each other." Another clause added to section 3, about which we have previously spoken, provides that the general terms of the third section with respect to discrimination "shall not be construed to apply to discrimination, prejudice or disadvantage to the traffic of any other carrier of whatever description." The same clause was inserted in the other three parts of the Act. The Commission may not sustain a claim of undue discrimination or prejudice because the rates of one type of carrier differ from the rates of another type of carrier for the same kinds of traffic.

Other paragraphs have been added to the third section of the Act which do not deal with the subject of discrimination but with the matter of the collection of charges by carriers. These provisions of the law will be taken up at a subsequent point, although it might be mentioned here that all carriers subject to the Act are in general required to do a cash business, and can extend credit to their patrons only as they may be authorized to do so by the Interstate Commerce Commission and under such rules and regulations as the Commission may prescribe.

There have been several changes in the fourth section since it was first enacted. The original section became a "dead letter" within a few years after its enactment because of the interpretation the Supreme Court placed upon the phrase "under substantially similar circumstances and conditions." The Court declared that competition between rival carriers at any point created conditions and circumstances which were dissimilar from the conditions and circumstances prevailing at points where there was no carrier competition. Since the only reason the railroads ever had for violation of the long-and-short-haul rule of rate making was to meet competition of rival agencies of transportation, it was plain that the law gave no protection to the victim of the higher rate at the noncompetitive short-haul point, and the place discrimination so prevalent in the basing point system of the South and in the transcontinental rate structure was not subject to remedial action by the Commission.

ADMINISTRATION OF FOURTH SECTION

In 1910, the Mann-Elkins Act amended the fourth section by the elimination of the "weasel words" which had rendered the section ineffective, and thereafter a railroad could discriminate against the short-haul point only with the express consent of the Commission. Needless to say, the Commission was almost immediately overwhelmed with a flood of applications for fourth section relief, and it took a long time to iron out all the unjust discrimination and undue prejudice, created by violations of the long-and-short-haul rule, which had formerly been permitted to flourish. The Commission did not require all violations to come to an end. In many cases, in the years immediately following the amendment of 1910, and in many cases since, the Commission has granted relief, so that in our present railroad rate structures we find many rates that are greater for the short haul than for the long haul over the same line and in the same direction, the shorter included in the longer haul.

At times, Congress has tried to lay down specific rules which the Commission should follow in deciding whether or not to grant requested relief. Even now, the fourth section places certain limitations on the Commission's discretionary authority. It may not "permit the establishment of any charge to or from the more distant point that is not reasonably compensatory for the service performed," and no relief shall be "granted on account of merely potential water competition not actually in existence." At one time (1920), Congress inserted what was called the "equidistant rule" in the fourth section, which stated:

. . . if a circuitous rail line or route is, because of such circuity, granted the authority to meet the charges of the more direct line or route to or from competitive points and to maintain higher charges to or from intermediate points on its line, the authority shall not include intermediate points as to which the haul of the petitioning line or route is not longer than the direct line or route between the competitive points.

This clause was repealed in 1940, leaving solely to the judgment of the Commission the matter of how far back from the competitive point any discrimination in rates should be permitted.

A few years ago, it seemed for a time that Congress was going to repeal the fourth section altogether for the purpose of giving the railroads unrestricted opportunity to meet the competition of the steadily increasing number of highway carriers. A bill for the repeal of the long-and-short-haul rule was adopted by the House of Representatives in 1936 and again in 1937, but in both cases the Senate took no action on the matter. Thereafter, no further bills for the repeal of the fourth section were introduced.

STATE AND FEDERAL CONFLICT IN REGULATION

The second, third, and fourth sections of the Interstate Commerce Act are not the only places in which the subject of unfair discrimination is mentioned in the law. Another place where it is dealt with, in perhaps the most interesting manner, is section 13, which gives the Interstate Commerce Commission a large measure of authority over intrastate railroad rates. For many years, it was assumed that the powers of the states and of the Federal government over commerce were mutually exclusive, that the states had complete power to deal with intrastate commerce and that Congressional power was confined to the regulation of interstate and foreign commerce. The Wabash case, which hastened the passage to the original Act to Regulate Commerce in 1887, seemed to be a confirmation of this view with respect to the division of state and national power.[4] The first section of the original law stated unequivocally that "the provisions of this act shall not apply to the transportation of passengers or property, or to receiving, delivering, storage, or handling of property, wholly within one State."

There is some indication, however, that notwithstanding this section the Federal government and its agency, the Interstate Commerce Commission, under the terms of the third section of the Act had the right to order the removal of any discrimination against interstate commerce which might arise from the fact that an interstate carrier voluntarily gave a preference in rates to an intrastate shipper who might be in competition with an interstate shipper. It does not appear, however, that this belief was ever put to the test, for the record discloses no instance in which a railroad was ever accused of "voluntarily" discriminating unduly against interstate commerce by granting preferential rates to an intrastate shipper. Had such a complaint ever arisen, there seems to be little doubt that the Supreme Court would have sustained any action which the Interstate Commerce Commission might have taken, under the third section, to bring about a correction of the unfair discrimination. Indeed, the Supreme Court said so explicitly in one of its decisions, though the decision had to do primarily not with discriminatory rates which had been voluntarily im-

[4] Wabash, St. Louis and Pacific Ry. v. Illinois, 118 U.S. 557 (1886).

posed by a railroad but with railroad rates on intrastate traffic which had been imposed by state authority.[5]

As railroad regulation both by the Federal government and by the governments of the various states developed, there was bound to come a time when it would be charged by some shipper or shippers' organization that the freight rates which railroads were compelled to charge by some state authority on intrastate traffic created a discrimination against interstate commerce, the rates on which were subject exclusively to Federal control. The Interstate Commerce Commission frankly took the position that there was some doubt as to its authority, "in the present state of the law," to hold the carrier responsible for such discrimination.[6]

[5] In Houston and Texas Ry. v. United States, 234 U.S. 342 (1914), the Supreme Court remarked, "This is not to say that Congress possesses the authority to regulate the internal commerce of a State as such, but that it does possess power to foster and protect interstate commerce, and to take all measures necessary and appropriate to that end, although intrastate transactions of interstate carriers may thereby be controlled."

In the same opinion, the Court said, "That an unjust discrimination in the rates of a common carrier, by which one person or locality is unduly favored as against another, under substantially similar conditions of traffic, constitutes an evil is undeniable, and where the evil consists in the action of an interstate carrier in unreasonably discriminating against interstate traffic over its line, the authority of Congress to prevent it is equally clear. It is immaterial, so far as the protecting power of Congress is concerned, that the discrimination arises from intrastate rates as compared with interstate rates. . . . Nor can the attempted exercise of State authority alter the matter, where Congress has acted, for a State may not authorize the carrier to do that which Congress is entitled to forbid and has forbidden."

A judge in a Federal district court had been even more emphatic: "No practice on their lines [of interstate carriers] can be permitted which favor local commerce at the expense of interstate or foreign commerce. In case of a conflict with a rule for the protection of interstate commerce, which has been duly made by the Interstate Commerce Commission, local Constitutions, statutes, orders of Railway Commissions, and regulations by the carriers all must give way." Chicago and Alton Ry. v. Interstate Commerce Commission, 173 Fed. 930 (1908). Rates were not involved in this case.

[6] See Freight Rates between Memphis and Points in Arkansas, 11 I.C.C. 180 (1905); G. S. Baxter & Co. v. Georgia Southern and Florida Ry., 21 I.C.C. 647 (1911); E. E. Saunders v. Southern Express Co., 18 I.C.C. 415 (1910). In the Baxter case, involving rates imposed by state authority, the Commission said, "While state rates are valuable for comparative purposes in fixing a reasonable charge for a transportation service, the assumption of the complainant that the action of the defendant in this case in maintaining higher transportation rates on interstate than upon intrastate traffic amounts to unlawful discrimination on the part of the carrier is not sound, for upon the record it is shown that the condition is one over which the carrier has no control." In a subsequent case, the Commission stated that formerly some doubt had existed "as to our power to remove unjust discrimination caused by the relation of interstate and intrastate rates." Traffic Bureau of Sioux City v. American Express Co., 39 I.C.C. 703 (1916).

THE MINNESOTA RATE CASE OF 1910

The Commission's doubts about its power to interfere with rates imposed by a state were resolved by the Supreme Court before the Commission itself summoned up enough courage to act on its own initiative. A classic example of how intrastate rates could influence interstate rates came to light in connection with rates on grain from points in southern Minnesota to two ports at the head of Lake Superior, Duluth and Superior, the former port being in Minnesota and the latter in Wisconsin. It was plain that if Minnesota ordered a reduction in grain rates to Duluth, which it had a right to do, within limits, the railroads which hauled grain interstate to Superior, for lake transportation eastward, would be obliged to make a similar reduction in their rates if they were to enjoy any portion of the competitive grain traffic. The state of Minnesota either created a discrimination against the port of Superior or, if the interstate rates to Superior were reduced to meet the rates imposed on Minnesota's intrastate traffic, the state was, in effect, accomplishing the regulation of interstate commerce, which under the Federal Constitution it had no right to do. In a case involving a controversy over the Minnesota intrastate rates, a district Federal court ordered the cancellation of the rates, on the ground that they were so low as to impose a burden on interstate commerce and create an unjust discrimination against points not located in the state of Minnesota.

The Supreme Court of the United States, in review of the lower court's action, reversed the decision, but at the same time held that Congress had the power to regulate intrastate rates, if such action was necessary to remove any unjust discrimination against interstate commerce. Since Congress had not yet exercised its power, and since the intrastate rates could not be held to be confiscatory in themselves, the lower court had erred in ordering their cancellation.[7]

THE SHREVEPORT CASE

The Interstate Commerce Commission did not hesitate to take advantage of the implication of this decision. Congress had already created an agency through which its power could be exercised, and this agency was the Commission itself. All doubt of its authority to prevent discrimination against interstate commerce, brought about by an unjustifiable difference between intrastate rates and interstate rates on competitive traffic, was cast aside, and the Commission proceeded to take action which was soon to lead to some noteworthy litigation as well as to a clearer definition of its power under the law. Its first action was taken in what has

[7] Minnesota Rate Cases, 230 U.S. 352 (1910), *modifying* 184 Fed. 765.

long been known as the Shreveport case,[8] in which it ordered certain Texas carriers to remove a discrimination against interstate traffic passing from Shreveport westward into Texas created by the fact that the intrastate Texas rates, which had been fixed by state authority, were lower than the Shreveport rates, which the Commission declared to be reasonable. In a few other cases, in which merchants doing business in cities located near the border of another state were subjected to unfair discrimination in their attempts to conduct an interstate business because of the contemporaneous existence of low intrastate rates, the Commission took action similar to that it had taken in the Shreveport case.[9] Though it did not endeavor in any of these cases to prescribe higher intrastate rates, it directed that the discrimination against interstate commerce be removed, and in at least one case it ordered that the terms and conditions under which intrastate traffic was moved be "equalized" with the terms and conditions surrounding the movement of interstate traffic.[10]

SECTION 13: AMENDMENT OF 1920

The assumption of power by the Interstate Commerce Commission to remove an unjust discrimination which intrastate rates created against interstate commerce was fully approved by the Supreme Court of the United States in a suit in which the Railroad Commission of Louisiana sought to have the Commission's Shreveport decision overruled.[11] Since some doubt existed as to the authority of the Commission to prescribe an intrastate rate for the purpose of removing a discrimination against interstate commerce, Congress took steps to clarify the situation. In 1920, as a part of the Transportation Act, it inserted an amendment to the thirteenth section of the Interstate Commerce Act which cleared up all doubt on the subject. The amendment provided that the Commission was authorized to investigate, either upon complaint or upon its own initiative, "any rate, fare, charge, classification, regulation or practice, made or imposed by the authority of any state," and provided further that:

Whenever in such investigation the Commission, after full hearing, finds that any such rate, fare, charge, classification, regulation or practice causes any undue or unreasonable advantage, preference, or prejudice as between persons

---

[8] Railroad Commission of Louisiana v. St. Louis Southwestern Ry., 23 I.C.C. 31 (1912).

[9] See Railroad Commission of Louisiana v. St. Louis Southwestern Ry., 34 I.C.C. 472 (1915); Railroad Commission of Louisiana v. Aransas Harbor Terminal Ry., 41 I.C.C. 83 (1916); Missouri River–Nebraska Cases, 40 I.C.C. 83 (1916); Traffic Bureau of Sioux City v. American Express Co., 39 I.C.C. 703 (1916).

[10] Missouri River–Nebraska Cases, 40 I.C.C. 201 (1916).

[11] Houston and Texas Ry. v. United States, 234 U.S. 342 (1914).

or localities in intrastate commerce on the one hand and interstate or foreign commerce on the other hand, or any undue, unreasonable or unjust discrimination against interstate or foreign commerce, which is hereby forbidden and declared to be unlawful, it shall prescribe the rate, fare, charge, or the maximum or minimum, or maximum and minimum, thereafter to be charged, and the classification, regulation or practice thereafter to be observed, in such manner as, in its judgment, will remove such advantage, preference, prejudice or discrimination. Such rates, fares, charges, classifications, regulations, and practices shall be observed while in effect by the carriers parties to such proceedings affected thereby, the law of any state or the decision or order of any state authority to the contrary notwithstanding.

ADMINISTRATION OF SECTION 13

It was not long after its passage that the Commission made use of this addition to the Interstate Commerce Act. Following the Commission's orders in 1920, which authorized a large increase in all interstate rates and fares, some of the states refused to follow the Commission's lead, and insisted that the rates and fares on intrastate traffic should not be advanced. The carriers affected promptly appealed to the Commission, which ordered them to lift the level of intrastate charges to the level of those previously prescribed for interstate traffic, on the theory that the failure of state traffic to contribute a fair share of the total return to which the carriers were by law entitled placed an undue and unjustly discriminatory burden on interstate commerce.[12] Though Senator Cummins, the chief architect of the Transportation Act, declared that it had not been the intention of Congress to give the Commission the power to raise the level of intrastate rates but merely to clothe it with authority to correct rate inequalities in such situations as those presented in the Minnesota and Shreveport controversies, the Supreme Court, applying the letter of the law, upheld the Commission's decision and declared that it had ample authority to deal with the level of intrastate rates when it was necessary to do so for the purpose of removing an unjust discrimination against interstate commerce.[13] The Commission has continued to exercise this power over intrastate railroad charges, even though the rule of rate making, under which it first acted, was repealed in 1933 and replaced with a rule which says nothing about "value" or "fair return."[14]

[12] See Intrastate Fares in Wisconsin, 59 I.C.C. 391 (1920); Rates, Fares and Charges of the New York Central R.R., 59 I.C.C. 290 (1920); Intrastate Rates within Illinois, 59 I.C.C. 350 (1920).

[13] Railroad Commission of Wisconsin v. Chicago, Burlington and Quincy R.R., 257 U.S. 563 (1922).

[14] The Supreme Court declared that the modification of the rule did not alter the Commission's authority over the level of intrastate rates and fares. Florida v. United States, 292 U.S. 1 (1934).

It should be noted that the law gives the Commision power, in express terms, to deal with intrastate rates only when the rates have been "made or imposed" by state authority. But despite the clause in the first section of the Interstate Commerce Act which declares that this part (part I) of the law shall not apply "to the transportation of passengers or property . . . wholly within one State and not shipped to or from a foreign country," there seems to be no doubt that the Commission has the power to modify even the intrastate rates voluntarily made by railroads if the rates create an unfair discrimination against interstate commerce. The Supreme Court's decision in the Shreveport case seems to support this point of view. There was one case in a lower Federal court where the Commission's action in ordering a modification of intrastate rates was challenged on the ground that the rates had been "voluntarily" made by a railroad, but the presiding judge held that these particular rates had been modified by state authority before they were filed. He then went on to say that, independent of the fact that an intrastate Florida rate had been charged or imposed by state authority, "its status as a lawful rate depended upon its allowance by the Florida Commission. It was established as a rate in accordance with and under the laws of Florida, and was for this reason alone made, though not imposed, by the authority of the State." [15] It would appear under this decision that any rate made "voluntarily" by a railroad becomes a state-made rate when duly filed with a state authority, which is only another way of saying that all intrastate railroad rates are made by state authority and consequently are subject, under certain circumstances, to correction by the Interstate Commerce Commission.

STATE DISCRIMINATION IN PARTS II, III, AND IV

There is nothing in parts II and III of the Interstate Commerce Act which gives the Commission authority to interfere with the intrastate rates of the carriers which come under those parts of the law. The second section of part II says that nothing in that part shall be construed "to interfere with the exclusive exercise by each State of the power of regulation of intrastate commerce by motor carriers on the highways thereof." To make doubly sure that intrastate motor vehicle rates shall be free from Federal interference, the law states explicitly that "nothing in this part shall empower the Interstate Commerce Commission to prescribe, or in any manner regulate, the rate, fare or charge for intrastate transportation, or for any service connected therewith, for the purpose of removing discrimination against interstate commerce or for any other purpose whatsoever." Though Congress doubtless has the power to regulate the intrastate rates of motor vehicle carriers to the same degree that it has power

[15] Florida v. United States, 30 F. 2d 116 (1929).

to regulate intrastate railroad rates, in the enactment of the Motor Carrier Act it chose to abdicate its authority and ordered the Interstate Commerce Commission to let intrastate motor vehicle rates severely alone. In part III, one finds the same provisions with respect to intrastate traffic transported by water carriers that part II contains with respect to the intrastate traffic of motor vehicles, though the Commission, under a clause in Part I, apparently has the power to conduct investigations concerning the relationships between interstate rates and the intrastate rates of carriers by water which have been "made and imposed" by state authority.

In part IV, however, we find provisions with respect to the rates and practices of freight forwarders, "made and imposed by state authority," which are identical with the provisions contained in part I with respect to the intrastate rates and rules of railroads and other carriers subject to that part of the Act. Like railroads, freight forwarders may be ordered by the Interstate Commerce Commission to correct any unjust discrimination which their intrastate rates may create against interstate commerce. It would be interesting to know why Congress, in the exercise of its constitutional power over interstate commerce, decided to discriminate so clearly between our different agencies of transportation.

THE PROBLEM OF ADMINISTRATIVE DISCRETION

It is in the exercise of discretionary power by the Interstate Commerce Commission that we find the most interesting field of study of the entire problem of unjust discrimination in rates. When we have an unequivocal rule, such as provided in section 2 of the Interstate Commerce Act, the difficulties of administration are not severe, though even in connection with the interpretation of that section questions may be raised as to the precise meaning of "contemporaneous," "like kind of traffic," and "substantially similar circumstances and conditions." But these questions are not so puzzling as the ones which arise because the third section of the law forbids "undue or unreasonable prejudice or disadvantage in any respect whatsoever," or the ones which arise under the fourth section when the Commission is asked to determine if "relief" shall be granted, and if so, the "extent" to which a carrier shall be "relieved" from the long-and-short-haul rule of rate making.

In its administration of the third section, the Commission relies primarily upon the process of comparison. When a charge of unjust discrimination, preference, or prejudice is made with respect to a certain rate or rate structure, the Commission compares the rates complained of with the rates applicable to other traffic, or, as the case may be, to the rates applicable to other localities, ports, regions, or territories. If costs are fairly comparable, the rates should be comparable. It is not necessary for the Commission to find out the exact costs of transporting the commodities the rates upon which are to be compared. It is again a matter of relative costs, as well as of relative rates, just as it is if the Commission is endeavoring to find out whether a certain rate is unreasonable.

There is an important difference, however, between the situation which arises when the Commission is investigating the reasonableness of a rate and the situation which exists when it is trying, under the third section, to determine whether a rate is to be regarded as unduly discriminatory. In the former case, the Commission is endeavoring to find out simply if the carrier is charging too much for a certain service which it performs. Does the rate under investigation lie within the zone of reasonableness? Does it bear a proper relation to the cost of service, without exceeding the value of the service? In the case of a rate alleged to be unduly and unjustly discriminatory, however, the element of competition between the shipper who is paying the allegedly discriminatory rate and the shipper who is paying a lesser rate enters the picture. There is a comparison of rates on commodities which compete with one another in the market, of the rates which a seaport or an industrial center pays to the rates charged to a competing seaport or industrial center, and of the rates which carriers impose within a certain region or territory to the rates imposed within another region or territory which has competing industries.

REASONABLENESS AND DISCRIMINATION

It often comes about that a certain rate may be entirely reasonable but, at the same time, unjustly discriminatory. Comparison may show that it is not out of line with the rates imposed on other articles which are similar from a transportation standpoint, but comparison may also show that the rate is unduly high when compared to the rate which the carrier imposes upon a competing product which is also similar from a transportation standpoint and consequently must have approximately the same cost of carriage. Both the rates under investigation may be in themselves reasonable, that is, they may both come within the zone of reasonableness, but the shipper who is obliged to pay the higher rate is subjected to undue disadvantage in competition with the shipper who enjoys the lower rate. The shipper placed at a disadvantage because of the higher rate may suffer an actual damage because of the unequal competition.

THE SOUTHERN RATES CONTROVERSY

It was explained in the chapter dealing with freight classification that the Interstate Commerce Commission is in the process of imposing a uniform classification throughout the United States. In its last important general investigation of class rates, instituted in 1939 and reported upon in a lengthy decision in 1945, the Commission held that many of the class rates in effect throughout the United States were unreasonable, and it also sustained a long-standing complaint that shippers and receivers in Southern, Southwestern, and Western Trunk Line Territories had been subject to "undue and unreasonable prejudice and disadvantage," because many of their products were required to pay higher rates, both intra-territorially and interterritorially, than competing products of industries located in Official and Illinois Territories.[16] In this investigation, the Commission's Bureau of Accounts and Cost Finding had prepared some elaborate studies which purported to show that the costs of transportation in the territories which were alleged to be at a disadvantage were no higher than the costs in Official and Illinois Territories, though rates in the South and West were considerably higher. Here was a case in which the element of relative cost was of controlling importance in the conclusions which the Commission reached. Where there were no substantial differences in costs and no substantial differences in the conditions and circumstances of transportation, there could be no justification for a substantial difference in transportation rates on the same articles of commerce. Not only did the Commission order a 10-per-cent reduction in the class rates of those territories which were found to be subjected to undue disadvantage, but it took the unprecedented step of ordering a 10-per-cent advance in the class rates of the territories which were profiting by the undue preference, though no question as to the reasonableness of those rates had been raised during the course of the investigation. Needless to say, the railroads in Eastern Territory accepted this unexpected windfall with ill-disguised enthusiasm, and though the shippers were indignant, they were unsuccessful in their efforts to have the order of the Commission set aside by judicial process. Section 3 of the Interstate Commerce Act condemned undue and unreasonable preference and prejudice "in any respect whatsoever," and under the law the Commission could use whatever methods it thought most suitable to remove the disadvantage which unequal rates might create.

PROBLEM OF FOURTH SECTION RELIEF

In its administration of the fourth section, the Commission is also confronted with the matter of competition, but here it becomes a question not only of competition between shippers but also of competition between rival carriers. Were the selfish interests of the carriers alone consulted, the most widespread discrimination would be permitted; if the selfish interests of shippers and receivers alone were consulted, there would be little if any violation of the long-and-short-haul principle of rate making. It is the duty of the Commission to try, to the best of its ability, to reconcile

[16] Class Rate Investigation, 1939, 262 I.C.C. 447 (1945), *sustained by Supreme Court*, New York v. United States, 331 U.S. 284 (1947).

the conflicting interests and administer the fourth section in such a way as not to do violence to the mandate of the law that there shall be no unjust or unreasonable discrimination. When a railroad wants to meet at a terminal the competition of a water line or of a motor vehicle service, or when a railroad with a circuitous route wants to meet at a terminal the competition of a railroad with a direct and shorter route, it seeks relief from the provisions of the fourth section, that is, it asks permission to make rates which are higher for shorter distances than for longer, over the same route and in the same direction. If the Commission grants relief, it subjects the shipper or receiver at the short-haul points to a certain amount of discrimination. It is compelled to choose, as it were, between protecting the competitive interest of the rail carrier and the competitive interest of a shipper or receiver of freight. Once it has decided to permit a measure of discrimination against the shipper or receiver in order to protect the competitive position of the railroad, it has to decide the "extent" to which discrimination against the shipper or receiver may be permitted before it becomes undue or unreasonable. The administration of the fourth section brings many nice questions to the Commission, questions in the answering of which it must exercise a highly discriminating judgment if it is to succeed in dispensing evenhanded justice to everybody.

Here again, the Commission has no hard and fast rules under which it operates, and by the very nature of the problems with which it is confronted it can have no such rules. It has issued thousands upon thousands of fourth section orders, some granting relief, others denying it, some of them "general orders," but most of them orders dealing with particular situations. It has tried to administer the law impartially and fairly, though, needless to say, many of its decisions have been subjected to criticism, either by carriers or by shippers—by carriers who failed to obtain the relief to which they thought they were entitled or by shippers who thought that the relief granted subjected them to unreasonable prejudice.

From time to time, the Commission has announced some guiding principle which it would follow in the administration of the fourth section. Of course it has been at all times subject to limitations imposed by law, such as the provision that it will not authorize a lower rate to the more distant point which is not "reasonably compensatory," and for a score of years to the limitation contained in the equidistant clause. But the Commission has set some rules for itself, also. It has refused to grant fourth section relief to railroads whose routes were so circuitous that the haul over the route would be a wasteful operation. On a few occasions, the Commission has adopted a pattern with respect to the relief granted to circuitous routes. It has regarded the longer route as unduly circuitous, and therefore not entitled to relief, when the distance via the short line "does not exceed 150 miles and the distance via the circuitous line is more than

70 per cent in excess of the short-line distance; when the distance via the short line exceeds 150 miles but does not exceed 1,000 miles and the distance via the circuitous line is more than 50 per cent in excess of the short-line distance; when the short-line distance exceeds 1,000 miles and the distance via the circuitous line is more than 33⅓ per cent in excess of the short-line distance."

On at least one occasion, the Commission changed its previously adopted policy with respect to relief granted to transcontinental rail carriers because of an "interpretation" which it chose to adopt of a legislative act of Congress. Before the First World War, the Commission had permitted the rail carriers to give reduced rates on transcontinental traffic bound for a Pacific terminal and had permitted a certain measure of discrimination against points in Intermountain Territory.[17] During the war, since virtually all intercoastal transportation through the Panama Canal came to an end because of the government's need for ships for military purposes, the Commission ordered the discrimination against intermountain points to be discontinued.[18] After the war ended and the railroads were again confronted with intercoastal steamship competition, they appealed to the Commission for permission to restore the discrimination against Intermountain Territory. Much to their surprise, the Commission turned down their application, on the ground that the Transportation Act of 1920 had declared it to be the "policy of Congress to promote, encourage, and develop water transportation, service and facilities. . . ." It refused to permit the establishment of a rate structure the purpose of which would be to permit railroads to interfere with the development of water transportation by the capture of intercoastal steamship business.[19]

THE TRAFFIC MANAGER AND RATE THEORY

The competent industrial traffic manager will familiarize himself, through a study of typical cases, with the methods and principles which the Commission employs in reaching its decisions with respect to rates which are alleged to be unreasonable or unduly discriminatory. He will understand that unreasonableness in a rate and undue discrimination in a rate are by no means the same thing, that a rate may be reasonable and still be unduly discriminatory. He will understand that in any effort made to sustain an allegation that a rate is unreasonable, attention must be centered upon the revenue which a carrier derives from the rate, compared with the reve-

[17] Applications for Fourth Section Relief, 21 I.C.C. 329, 400 (1911); Intermountain Rate Cases, 234 U.S. 476 (1911); Commodity Rates to Pacific Coast Terminals and Intermountain Points, 32 I.C.C. 611 (1915).

[18] Transcontinental Rates, 46 I.C.C. 236 (1917), 48 I.C.C. 79 (1918).

[19] Transcontinental Cases of 1922, 74 I.C.C. 48 (1922); Transcontinental Wool Cases of 1922, 74 I.C.C. 48 (1922).

nue derived from the rates imposed upon other commodities which plainly cost the carrier no more to transport. It is not necessary that the commodity subject to the rate alleged to be unreasonable be competitive with the other commodities, the rates on which are used for comparison. The question to be answered is, does the carrier get an unreasonably large revenue for hauling a certain article, in comparison with the revenue it obtains for hauling articles which are of a similar character from a transportation standpoint; in other words, in view of the cost of the service to the carrier and the value of the service to the shipper, is the rate unreasonably burdensome to the shipper?

On the other hand, if there is an allegation of undue discrimination, the rate complained of must be compared to a rate imposed upon a competing commodity or a rate given to a competing city, locality, or region. The question is not so much the revenue derived by the carrier in consideration of the cost of the service or the value of the service performed, but the revenue exacted from the complainant in comparison to the revenue exacted for similar services from the complainant's active competitors. This may mean, of course, that a rate may be reasonable but unduly discriminatory, and that, conversely, a rate may be unreasonable and not unduly discriminatory. Or a rate may be both unreasonable and unduly discriminatory. It is often a fortunate thing for a shipper that the law protects him against both unreasonableness and undue discrimination in the transportation rates he is asked to pay. He very frequently finds that he has two arrows in his quiver, only one of which will hit the mark. But if he is wise, when he goes hunting, he does not leave either arrow at home.

REPARATION

If a shipper succeeds in showing that he has suffered financial loss because he has been subjected to unreasonable or discriminatory charges by a carrier subject to the Interstate Commerce Act, he may be able to obtain reparation for the amount of damage. Under parts I and III of the Act, dealing respectively with railroads, express companies, pipelines, and sleeping car companies and with carriers by water, he may appeal either to the Interstate Commerce Commission or to a Federal district court for reparation, though he cannot under the law exercise both options. Parts II and IV contain no express provisions with respect to the matter of reparation for damages which a shipper might suffer by reason of violation of the Act. If, under parts I and III, the Commission should award reparation, and the offending carrier refuses to comply with the Commission's order, the shipper has the right to appeal to a Federal district court to secure compliance with the award. It goes without saying that a shipper who suffers injury because of noncompliance with the law by a carrier subject to part II or part IV of the law, may seek redress in a Federal court. It may often occur that the Commission refuses to award reparation, even though it finds that a certain rate has been unreasonable or unduly discriminatory. The Commission has asked Congress many times to be relieved of the duty of dealing with the question of reparation, but Congress has not yet seen fit to comply with the Commission's request. A shipper may still "elect" the tribunal before which to file a demand for reparation for damages incurred because a carrier violates the provisions of parts I and III of the Act.

PENALTIES

A carrier which violates provisions of the Interstate Commerce Act may suffer other penalties than the payment of damages to injured shippers. If a carrier "knowingly" violates the law; if it deliberately and intentionally gives rebates to favored shippers; if it willfully and knowingly departs from its published rates; if it enters into collusive arrangements with shippers for the purpose of misbilling or otherwise misrepresenting the services which it performs, whereby the shippers are given rates lower than lawful rates, the carrier is liable to a heavy fine, and its agents are subject even to a penalty of imprisonment. The law insists that a carrier shall collect only reasonable charges for the service it performs and that it shall give no undue preference or advantage to any of its patrons.

UNDUE DISCRIMINATION DIFFICULT TO ERADICATE

It has been a difficult task for the government to eradicate the custom, which nearly all railroads once practiced, of granting unwarranted concessions to favored shippers. Little by little the laws have been tightened up; free transportation, except in special cases, has been forbidden; mere departure from published rates has been branded as an act of unjust discrimination, and if performed knowingly has been severely penalized; all other acts of undue favoritism have been brought under the condemnation of the law. On the whole, the government has been singularly successful in stamping out the evils of undue discrimination and unjust favoritism in the transportation business, though we still sometimes read that a railroad has been indicted for such things as leasing valuable property to a favored shipper for a trifling sum utterly out of proportion to the value of the property; for selling property to a shipper for a mere fraction of its value; for letting a favored shipper evade lawful charges for demurrage, storage, or other services; or for letting certain customers fraudulently violate tariff rules and regulations.

UNDUE DISCRIMINATION STILL EXISTS

Many acts of undue and unjust discrimination have been detected by the agents of the Interstate Commerce Commission, and the guilty parties have been properly penalized for their infractions of the law. Some acts of improper discrimination have been disregarded. For example, during the Second World War it was a common practice of the railroads carrying passengers between Washington and New York to sell as a "parlor car" seat a numbered chair in a club car. It frequently happened that if the purchaser of such a chair temporarily left it, he would, upon his return, find it occupied by some visitor from another car, who was imbibing a highball or some other liquid refreshment, and could be evicted from his place only at the expense of considerable embarrassment to the rightful occupant. There could be no doubt that the carrier, in charging the same price for a chair of uncertain occupancy in the club car that it charged for a comfortable reclining seat in a parlor car, of which the purchaser was reasonably sure of undisputed and undisturbed possession, was guilty of discrimination and of undue and unjust discrimination, at that. Or, if the charge of undue discrimination could not be maintained, because of the lack of the element of "damage," at least there was a distinct act of unreasonableness on the part of the carrier in making the same charge for such vastly unequal accommodations. Of course, nothing was ever done about the abuse. The passenger who had grounds for complaint swallowed his indignation and said nothing, probably glad that he had the chance to sit down in the overcrowded train at least during part of his journey, and the Interstate Commerce Commission, in the absence of any complaint, took no action.

Railroads and other carriers, too, have usually found it to their advantage to treat the traveling and shipping public fairly and equitably. Discrimination, if carried too far, is like all other kinds of crime; it does not pay.

CHAPTER X

The Face of the Bill of Lading [1]

There are many documents employed in the business transactions between shippers and carriers, and there are many documents which are used exclusively by either the shipper or the carrier. Every industrial traffic manager has a large amount of paper work to supervise, and the amount of such work which must be performed by carriers is perhaps even larger. It is not only in the operations of the military and civil services of the government that we meet with an endless stream of forms, reports, and other records which must be made out with meticulous exactitude and carefully filed away for preservation; private enterprise, too, has a burden of elaborate documentation. Neither government nor private enterprise could keep track of the complex and multifarious activities in which both engage without the painstaking maintenance of adequate records. Much of the talk we hear about "red tape" implies a greater concern with a "red herring." In the actions in law and equity, with which the dockets of our courts are crowded, we are likely to find that there is much more difficulty and confusion because of the lack of proper records than because of an addiction to an excess of concern over an authentic and accurate documentary history of business transactions.

THE BILL OF LADING

By far the most important document in which shipper and carrier both have an interest is the bill of lading. We have already discussed briefly the use and importance of the bill of lading; in this chapter and in the two chapters which follow, we shall carry the examination of its functions and significance somewhat further.

What is a bill of lading? First of all, it is a receipt. It is an acknowledgment on the part of the carrier that it has actually received certain property from a shipper. Here we already glimpse a warning that a carrier must heed. It should not issue a bill of lading until the property listed in the bill has passed into the carrier's control. Although it is perfectly true

[1] The Consolidated and the Uniform Freight Classifications both contain the forms of the bills of lading employed by American railroads. If a classification is not available, the reader should obtain copies of a straight and an order bill of lading either from a shipper or from a railroad freight agent.

175

that the "facts" of a situation are controlling in any controversy and that the carrier could usually not be held responsible for property which it could prove it had not received, to sign a bill of lading which misrepresents the actual facts may mean some disagreeable trouble and litigation which, by the exercise of a little care, could have been avoided.

Second, the bill of lading is a contract between the shipper and the carrier, in which the carrier agrees to transport certain specified property from one point to another. Like any other contract, the bill of lading must have those characteristics which students of business law know must be present in all valid contracts. There must, for example, be a "meeting of minds"; there must be a "consideration"; the contract must be for a "lawful purpose"; and the parties to the contract must be legally capable of making the stipulated agreement. Finally, a bill of lading may be, and often is, "documentary evidence of title to goods."

VARIETIES OF BILLS OF LADING

In railroad transportation, as well as in other forms of transportation, we have several forms, or kinds, of bills of lading. Railroads issue "uniform domestic bills of lading," of which there are two varieties, "straight" and "order"; a "uniform livestock contract," employed in the transportation of livestock; and a "through export bill of lading," which covers a shipment originating at some interior point in the country and destined via a particular seaport to a foreign destination. Of the export bill of lading, there are also two varieties, "straight" and "order."

DUTY OF CARRIER TO ISSUE BILLS OF LADING

Congress has enacted a great deal of legislation with respect to bills of lading and their use. Section 20, paragraph (11), part I, of the Interstate Commerce Act says:

That any common carrier, railroad or transportation company subject to the provisions of this part receiving property for transportation from a point in one State or Territory or the District of Columbia to a point in another State, Territory, District of Columbia, or from any point in the United States to a point in an adjacent foreign country shall issue a receipt or bill of lading therefor, and shall be liable to the lawful holder thereof for any loss, damage or injury to such property caused by it or by any common carrier, railroad, or transportation company to which such property may be delivered or over whose line or lines such property may pass within the United States or within an adjacent foreign country when transported on a through bill of lading. . . .[2]

[2] This is substantially the language of the Carmack Amendment to the Interstate Commerce Act, adopted in 1906. This amendment, as well as the two Cummins Amendments mentioned later in this chapter, have to do primarily with the liability of carriers for loss and damage, and will be discussed in detail in the following chapter.

Section 1, paragraph (6), of part I declares that carriers subject to that part have the duty to "establish, observe, and enforce . . . just and reasonable practices and regulations" affecting "the issuance, form, and substance of tickets, receipts and bills of lading."

Parts II and IV of the Interstate Commerce Act make motor carriers and freight forwarders liable to the same provisions with respect to the issuance of bills of lading and common carrier liability that apply to railroads in part I. Although the language of the two parts differs in some respects from the language employed in part I, the carriers subject to those parts are likewise enjoined to establish, observe, and enforce just and reasonable practices "relating to or connected with the transportation of property in interstate or foreign commerce."

The Shipping Act of 1916 provided that carriers by water, engaged in our interstate and foreign commerce, should likewise adopt just and reasonable practices with respect to the issuance of bills of lading. The Transportation Act of 1940—which was made up chiefly of the provisions which now constitute part III of the Interstate Commerce Act, under which domestic carriers by water are regulated—though it repealed a substantial portion of the Shipping Act of 1916, repeated almost word for word the provisions of the earlier statute with respect to bills of lading. The Harter Act of 1893, "relating to the navigation of vessels, bills of lading, and to certain obligations, duties and rights in connection with the carriage of property," provides "that it shall be the duty of the owner or owners, master or agent of any vessel transporting merchandise or property from or between ports of the United States and foreign ports to issue to shippers of any lawful merchandise a bill of lading, or shipping document. . . ." Although the language is a trifle cloudy, it apparently means that carriers by water in domestic as well as in foreign commerce are under a legal obligation to issue a bill of lading or its equivalent to a shipper, and the law provides a penalty for ship operators who refuse, on the demand of a shipper, to issue a proper bill of lading. The Carriage of Goods by Sea Act (1936), under which ocean carriers engaged in the foreign commerce of the United States now operate and under which domestic carriers by water may, at their option, operate with respect to the terms and conditions of bills of lading, specifically provides in unequivocal language that the carrier, after receiving property for transportation, shall, on the "demand of the shipper, issue a bill of lading."

Carriers by air likewise issue bills of lading for the merchandise they transport, although they usually designate their bills of lading as "airbills." The Civil Aeronautics Act makes no mention of bills of lading, and the Civil Aeronautics Board has never prescribed any form of bill of lading for the use of air carriers, though it probably has the power to do so under its general authority to make necessary economic regulations for the conduct of civil aviation. Our aviation companies show in their tariffs the forms of the airbills, or other documents, which embody their contractual relations with shippers, and there is little variation in the forms used by the different companies.

POMERENE BILLS OF LADING ACT

In addition to the clauses relating to bills of lading which are to be found in the several acts for the regulation of our various agencies of transportation, Congress passed, in 1916, the Bills of Lading Act, often known as the Pomerene Act, after the Ohio Senator who introduced it and advocated its enactment. This law applies to all bills of lading "issued by any common carrier for the transportation of goods in any Territory of the United States, or the District of Columbia, or from a place in a State to a place in a foreign country, or from a place in one State to a place in another State, or from a place in one State to a place in the same State through another State or foreign country." While this law deals primarily with the relations between shippers and consignees or sellers and buyers it also has provisions which impose certain responsibilities on the carriers by which the bills are issued. The various features of the law which affect the operations of carriers will be dealt with later.

COMMISSION AUTHORITY OVER BILLS OF LADING

Under its power to investigate any rule or practice which carriers subject to the Interstate Commerce Act may adopt in the conduct of their business, and the power to cause the elimination or modification of any rule or practice found not to be in conformity with the law, the Interstate Commerce Commission has required railroads and other common carriers subject to its jurisdiction to adopt and use the forms of bills of lading under which our commerce now moves. It conducted several "investigations" after the Interstate Commerce Act was amended in 1906 and in 1910, and issued its first decision prescribing bill of lading forms in April, 1919.[3]

Previous to this decision, both the railroads and the Interstate Commerce Commission had endeavored to secure uniformity in bills of lading, but without complete success. In a report issued in June, 1908, the Commission discussed at some length the character of the merchandise bills of lading then in use, and took the position that there was a real need for a greater degree of uniformity.[4] Lacking the necessary power to prescribe the form of bills of lading, the Commission had to content itself with "recommending" that a form which had been prepared by a joint committee of shippers and carriers be adopted by all carriers subject to

---

[3] In the Matter of Bills of Lading, 52 I.C.C. 671 (1919).
[4] In the Matter of Bills of Lading, 14 I.C.C. 346 (1908).

the Interstate Commerce Act. The carriers of the East and West accepted the Commission's recommendation, for the most part, but virtually all the carriers of the South refused to go along. After the enactment of the Mann-Elkins law of 1910, the Commission, deeming that it had the authority to prescribe the form of bill of lading which the carriers should adopt, undertook another investigation of the entire subject. It received numerous suggestions from committees representing both carriers and shippers. Some of these proposals the Commission accepted, but it also rejected some of them, and it insisted upon several changes in the terms and conditions of the bill of lading previously used in interstate commerce.

BILL OF LADING FORMS PRESCRIBED BY COMMISSION

In the decision handed down in April, 1919, the Commission discussed at considerable length the history of the bill of lading and the nature of its provisions. The decision still remains a document which is well worth careful reading and study by anybody who is interested in traffic management, from the standpoint either of a carrier or of a shipper. As a result of its investigation, the Commission prescribed a form of bill of lading to be used in domestic commerce as well as a form of "through export bill of lading," and ordered that they should be adopted and put in use by August 8, 1919. Although the Commission indulged in some discussion of the form of bill of lading to be employed in the transportation of livestock it did not at that time make any order with respect to a uniform livestock contract.

OBJECTIONS OF WATER CARRIERS

As might have been expected, a great many carriers objected to the bill of lading which the Commission had prescribed. The most vigorous objectors were the coastwise carriers, because the Commission had refused to include in the terms of the bill of lading a rule to the effect that a carrier by water engaging in a joint transportation service with a rail carrier was subject to the laws which limited the liability of carriers by water. The Commission held that a through bill of lading for a shipment dispatched over a through rail-and-water route was a contract for transportation under an "arrangement for continuous carriage," and that the part of the haul by water was subject to the terms of the Cummins Amendment of the Interstate Commerce Act to precisely the same degree as the part of the haul by rail, or indeed any all-rail haul, was subject. The Commission stated:

The exemptions from liability which the respondents desire to incorporate in the bill of lading solely on behalf of carriers by water, when they participate in transportation subject to the act, might be proper in respect to transportation from port to port, or to transportation of such character as does not fall within the

Cummins amendment. With such transportation we have nothing to do, but it is our opinion that, as applied to transportation by a water carrier under an arrangement with a railroad for common control and continuous carriage or shipment, the proposed rule would be in contravention of the Cummins amendment and therefore null and void.

In the course of its somewhat long decision, the Commission quoted several passages from the Interstate Commerce Act and from court decisions for the purpose of sustaining the legality of the views which it expressed. Oddly enough, however, it did not, in refusing to give carriers by water the exemption from liability to which these carriers thought they were legally entitled, pay the least attention to a certain provision which had been added to section 15 of the Interstate Commerce Act in 1910 when the Mann-Elkins Act was passed. The new provision gave the Commission the power, under certain conditions, to require railroads to establish through routes and joint rates. It also gave the Commission power to establish through rail-and-water routes in domestic commerce. But the provision said quite plainly: "Nor shall the Commission have the right to establish any route, classification, fare, or charge when the transportation is wholly by water, and any transportation by water affected by this act shall be subject to the laws and regulations applicable to transportation by water."

Whether the Commission chose to ignore this provision of the law (surely it must have known of its existence) or whether it chose to interpret the second part of the clause as applying only to transportation "wholly" by water, there is no way of telling. But whatever its reasons, it refused point blank to permit the inclusion in the bill of lading of any clause giving to the water carriers participating in a joint rail-and-water haul any less degree of liability than that to which the railroads were subjected under the terms of the Carmack and Cummins Amendments. This meant, of course, that the port-to-port commerce of a coastwise steamship line came under the laws having to do with the liability of water carriers in general but that the commerce which a carrier by water handled under a through bill of lading, in cooperation with a rail carrier, was subject to the liability provisions of the Interstate Commerce Act as they applied to rail carriers. However correct the Commission may have been from a technically legal standpoint (and there is room for argument about this), its decision meant that the carrier by water would probably have to maintain a double standard of charges—one for shippers who consigned goods from port to port, for which goods the carrier had a greatly limited liability, and one for those shippers who consigned goods on a through rail-and-water bill of lading and for whose shipments the carrier had to assume the same responsibility that the law imposed upon a railroad.

THE ALASKA STEAMSHIP COMPANY CASE

Several coastwise carriers by water, including the Alaska Steamship Company, appealed to the courts to have the order of the Commission set aside. A three-judge statutory court of the Southern District of New York was convened to hear the complaint. A majority (Judges Ward and Mayer) issued a temporary injunction in July, 1919, to prevent the order from becoming effective, chiefly on the ground that the Commission was "without power" to prescribe the form of bills of lading which carriers should be required to adopt either in domestic or in foreign commerce.[5] The opinion quoted in full the portion of section 15 of the law, given above, which said that transportation by water was to be subject to the laws and regulations applicable to transportation by water—the portion of the law the Commission had chosen to ignore. As if torn by some doubt as to their unqualified affirmation that the Commission had no power to prescribe the form of a bill of lading, the court said that "in any event there was no power to prescribe an inland bill of lading in form or substance depriving carriers of the benefits of a statute limiting the liability of vessel owners and of the Harter Act."

The third member of the court, Judge Learned Hand, followed up the majority decision with a penetrating and vigorous dissent, in which he declared it to be his conviction that the Commission did have the power and authority under the Interstate Commerce Act to prescribe the form and substance of bills of lading which domestic carriers should use. He sustained the legal validity of each and every one of the particular changes which the Commission had held should be made in the bills of lading previously used. When he came to a discussion of the Commission's refusal to permit carriers by water to enjoy the liability which the law regarding such carriers supposedly gave them, he swept away any suggestion that the amendment to section 15, quoted above, made any difference, saying:

. . . the statute does not say that water transportation affected by the act shall be "subject only" to the laws applicable to transportation by water. There is nothing exclusive in the language and the more natural interpretation of it would seem to be "subject also" to the laws and regulations applicable to water transportation. Indeed the language fits better the purpose to make water law applicable whenever it does not conflict than with the purpose to make it supersede the act.

The Commission promptly appealed the decision of the district court to the Supreme Court, which handed down its decision on May 17, 1920.[6] Before the Supreme Court delivered its judgment, however, the Trans-

---

[5] Alaska Steamship Co. v. United States, 229 Fed. 713 (1919).
[6] United States v. Alaska Steamship Co., 253 U.S. 113 (1920).

portation Act of 1920 had been enacted (February 28). In this Act some provisions had been included which obviously would make it necessary for certain changes to be made in the bills of lading as prescribed by the Commission in its order of 1919. Therefore, the high court declared the case to be moot, reversed the decision of the lower court, and dismissed the appeal "without prejudice" to the rights of any complainants to assail any future order of the Commission which might be thought to be beyond the Commission's statutory or constitutional powers. The Supreme Court said that it was not necessary to enumerate the changes effected by the Transportation Act which made "the cause a moot one." It declared that "the complainants do not need an injunction to prevent the Commission from putting in force bills of lading of the form prescribed. The subsequent legislation necessitates the adoption of different forms of bills, in the event that the power of the Commission be sustained." The Court held that it was not yet necessary for it to pass upon the question of whether the Commission had power to prescribe the form of bills of lading which carriers should adopt.

INTERSTATE COMMERCE ACT AMENDED

There were not many provisions of the Transportation Act of 1920 which necessitated changes in the form of bill framed by the Commission in 1919. But there was one of considerable importance to the litigants in this suit. The carriers by water had apparently in some manner persuaded Congress to include a proviso in section 20 of the Interstate Commerce Act, immediately following the terms of the Cummins Amendment, which said plainly, in language that was unmistakable in meaning:

. . . provided, that if the loss, damage, or injury occurs while the property is in custody of a carrier by water the liability of such carrier will be determined by the bill of lading of the carrier by water and by and under regulations applicable to transportation by water, and the liability of the initial or delivering carrier shall be the same as that of such carrier by water.

This meant that the liability of a carrier by water, while conducting its part of a through transportation service over a rail-and-water route, should be subject to the limitations set forth in the Harter Act of 1893, or later in the Carriage of Goods by Sea Act of 1936, if the domestic carrier by water should elect to conduct operations under the terms of the latter statute. Furthermore, the ancient Carmack Amendment was explicitly altered so that the liability of an initial or delivering carrier by rail for the loss of or damage to a shipment while in the possession of a joint carrier by water would be just the same as the liability to the carrier by water. The "relief" given to carriers by water in section 15 was carried along in the law until 1940, when it was eliminated, presumably as being superfluous.

NEW FORMS OF BILL OF LADING ADOPTED

Following the Supreme Court's decision, the Commission went to work once more to frame what it thought would be fair and reasonable bills of lading. In December, 1921, it again prescribed a form of domestic bill of lading, through export bill of lading, and uniform livestock contract. This time, the domestic bill of lading contained a section calling attention to the limited liability of carriers by water who participated in a through rail-and-water shipment.[7] This section still remains in the conditions of the uniform domestic bill of lading and will be discussed later. Oddly enough, the Commission followed the example set by the Supreme Court and did not mention the change made in the Interstate Commerce Act which necessitated its change of attitude.

The water carriers had won their point and did not endeavor to chal-

[7] Bills of Lading, 64 I.C.C. 347 (1921), 64 I.C.C. 257 (1921), 66 I.C.C. 63 (1922). There was one exception which should be mentioned. The Panama Canal Act of 1912 amended section 5 of the Interstate Commerce Act by adding a provision forbidding any common carrier subject to the Act to have any interest, direct or indirect, by lease, stock ownership, or otherwise, in a carrier by water operating through the Panama Canal or elsewhere in the United States, with which the controlling carrier might be in competition. However, it was stipulated that a carrier already operating and controlling a competing water line, except one passing through the Panama Canal, might, if the Commission thought it to be in the public interest and gave its authorization, continue such operation and control. In the event that the Commission gave such permission, the law provided that "the rates, schedules and practices of such water carrier shall be filed with the Interstate Commerce Commission and shall be subject to the Act to Regulate Commerce and all amendments thereto in the same manner and to the same extent as is the railroad or other common carrier controlling such water carrier. . . ." Under the terms of this amended section, the Commission required the "divorce" of numerous rail and water carriers which had long been affiliated, though it also permitted some railroads to continue in control of competing water lines. But the rates and practices of such controlled water carriers remained under the jurisdiction of the Commission (see 32 I.C.C. 690; 63 I.C.C. 867; 81 I.C.C. 312; 123 I.C.C. 203; 211 I.C.C. 601). When the Transportation Act of 1940 was passed, the paragraph of section 5 dealing with the control of water carriers was revised, making it legal for a carrier subject to the Act to "acquire" control of a competing water line (not operating through the Canal), as well as to "continue" in control, if the Commission approved. The provision about rates was omitted, since under the new law the rates and practices of all domestic water carriers came under the Commission's jurisdiction. The matter of carrier's liability was not mentioned, but presumably such controlled water carriers have the same liability as that of railroads and other carriers subject to part I of the Interstate Commerce Act.

lenge the validity of the new bill of lading or question the right of the Commission to prescribe it. The rail carriers of the three major classification territories adopted the new domestic bill as well as the uniform livestock contract, and they became effective March 15, 1922. The Merchant Marine Act of 1920 had provided that any export bill of lading which the Commission might prescribe, before becoming effective, should first receive the approval of the United States Shipping Board. The Board made certain recommendations for changes in the bill originally prescribed. The Commission modified the bill, accordingly, in time for it to become effective July 15, 1922.[8] The authority of the Commission to prescribe bill of lading forms was quietly accepted without further litigation, and the courts have not been asked again to consider the matter. Since 1922, the carriers by land in the domestic commerce of the United States have employed uniform bills in their transactions with the shippers who make use of their services. There have been a few modifications in the forms originally prescribed, necessitated by further changes in the Interstate Commerce Act and because of the extension of the Commission's jurisdiction over other carriers, but there have been no changes of a fundamental nature. Since the enactment of part IV of the Act, in 1942, the Commission has had to exercise its authority in connection with the bill of lading issued by or in behalf of freight forwarders, but its only important order respecting this document did not have to do so much with the terms and conditions of the bill as with the kind of relations that should exist between a forwarder and a carrier.[9]

It might be mentioned here that in the Transportation Act of 1920, Congress, at that time intent upon doing everything which it thought might encourage our export trade and lead to the development of a strong American merchant marine, provided in section 25 of the Interstate Commerce Act that rail carriers, upon the request of shippers, should supply quotations of ocean transportation rates on export traffic, arrange for the reservation of cargo space on ocean carriers, and issue through bills of lading from inland points of the United States to foreign destinations. This section subjected the railroads to a great deal of unrewarded labor, it did not have any significant effect upon our foreign commerce or upon the growth of our merchant marine, and Congress wisely repealed it *in toto,* in 1940. At the present time, some of our railroads do not issue through export bills of lading, though a few still continue to do so. Export traffic is carried to the seaboard on domestic bills and the overseas movement made on a regular ocean bill.

[8] Export Bill of Lading, 66 I.C.C. 687 (1922).
[9] Bills of Lading of Freight Forwarders, 259 I.C.C. 277 (1944).

FACE OF BILL OF LADING

When we examine the printed matter on uniform domestic bills of lading, straight and order, we find that they are almost exactly alike, except for the few words which make one of them negotiable. We shall discuss the matter of negotiability later in this chapter. The face of either kind of bill of lading contains the agreement between the carrier and the shipper; the back of the bill contains, in fairly small print, the "contract terms and conditions" of the bill, most of which have to do with the liability of the carrier for the goods it undertakes to transport.

At the top of the face of the bill is the name of the carrier, if the bill is one which is supplied by a carrier. If the shipper supplies his own bill of lading, his own name or the name of the shipper's company appears at the top, and the name of the carrier is written in a blank space provided for that purpose. There are also blank spaces in which the carrier and the shipper may insert the proper file number which each may want to give the bill of lading.

The first part of the business terms of the bill of lading is the formal receipt, which reads:

RECEIVED, subject to the classifications and tariffs in effect on the date of the issue of this Bill of Lading, at (name of place) (date), from (name of shipper) the property described below, in apparent good order, except as noted (contents and condition of contents of packages unknown), marked, consigned and destined as indicated below, which said company (the word company being understood throughout this contract as meaning the person or corporation in possession of the property under the contract) agrees to carry to its usual place of delivery at said destination, if on its own road or its own water line, otherwise to deliver to another carrier on the route to said destination. It is mutually agreed, as to each carrier of all or any of said property over all or any portion of said route to destination, and as to each party at any time interested in all or any of said property, that every service to be performed hereunder shall be subject to all the conditions not prohibited by law, whether printed or written, herein contained, including the conditions on the back hereof, which are hereby agreed to by the shipper and accepted for himself and his assigns.

Following the receipt are spaces for the name and the mail or street address of the consignee (the address for purpose of notification only unless the shipment is subject to store-door delivery), the station of destination of the property shipped, the route the shipment is to take, the name of the delivering carrier, and the initials and number of the car in which the property is transported. A space is even given for the name of the county in which the destination point is located, to be used if the state of the destination point has another station bearing the same name.

Rule 7 of the Consolidated and the Uniform Classifications provides that only "one shipper, one consignee and one destination shall appear on a shipping order or bill of lading, except that the shipping order and bill of lading may specify the name of a party at the same destination to be notified of the arrival of the shipment." There are certain exceptions, however, which the rule provides. The shipment may be "consigned" to one point, with consignee's address or instructions to notify the consignee or other party, at another point

. . . when the consignee or party to notify or advise is located at a river landing or other point inaccessible to carrier's deliveries; or when the consignee or party to notify or advise is located at a prepay station or on a rural free delivery route or in the interior, in which case the shipment must be consigned to an adjacent open station designated by the shipper; or when the destination station and the consignee's post office address adjacent to such station are differently named.

Some carriers permit "split deliveries," in which case more than one consignee can be named.

The part of the bill of lading in which the property is "described" has spaces for the "number of packages," the "description of the articles, special marks and exceptions," "weight (subject to correction)," "class or rate," and a "check column." A footnote referring to weight calls attention to the fact that if a shipment moves between two ports by a carrier by water, the law requires that the bill of lading shall state whether it is "carrier's or shipper's weight." The law does not compel the insertion of this notice in the bill of lading, and for many years after the passage of the Harter Act of 1893, which provided that either carrier's or shipper's weight should be given in a bill of lading for property to be transported by water, no such notice was given, although the terms of the law were nevertheless binding. The inclusion of the notice, which first appeared in domestic bills of lading in the early 1920's, serves as a warning and helps prevent inadvertent violations of the statute.

On the right-hand margin of the bill of lading, to the right of the spaces we have just described, are spaces in which statements may be given with respect to the payment of freight charges. In one space may be written or stamped the words: "To be prepaid"; in another is a receipt to be signed by the carrier's agent indicating the amount of the charges which has been prepaid; and in another space a notation may be made of any charges which the carrier has "advanced." Probably the most important of these spaces is the first one, in which is found the "nonrecourse" stipulation which, to have any effect, must be signed by the shipper.

LIABILITY FOR CARRIER CHARGES

The law makes both the shipper and the consignee liable for the payment of a carrier's charges, the former as the maker and signer of the contract and the latter as the beneficial owner of the property which is transported. A very large portion of the freight transported by domestic carriers is shipped with charges "collect." Sometimes it may happen that a carrier, either through oversight or through negligence, may deliver a collect shipment to a consignee and fail to request payment of the accrued charges. Several years ago, when the carrier tried to rectify its error and collect charges due from the consignee, it was frequently found that the consignee had become bankrupt or could not be located, whereupon the carrier would turn to the consignor for the payment of the charges; if the consignor was financially able, he was obliged to make payment. This obviously imposed a hardship upon the consignor, through no fault of his own but through the fault of the carrier. As a consequence of many complaints by shippers, the nonrecourse clause was finally placed in the bill of lading. The shipper avoids liability for freight charges by simply signing this clause which states that the carrier shall not make delivery of the shipment without payment of freight charges and all other lawful charges.

At the time the Interstate Commerce Commission was holding the investigation which led to its prescribing the form of bill of lading adopted in 1922, a number of shippers called attention to the fact that when goods shipped under an order bill of lading were reconsigned, and one bill of lading exchanged for a second one, the consignee of the first bill might become the consignor of the second bill, and if the railroad failed to collect lawfully accrued charges from the second consignee, it might endeavor to collect from the original consignee. Should this consignee happen to be merely an agent for the transfer of the shipment from the original owner to a purchaser and to have no beneficial title to the property, he might be subjected to the payment of charges, for which he could be held legally liable, even though he was in no sense a principal in the entire transaction. The Commission refused in its orders of 1919 and 1921 to include any clause in the bill of lading which would give the agent adequate protection from liability for charges for which he was not morally responsible. In 1927, Congress amended section 3 of the Interstate Commerce Act in such a way as to make only the actual principals to a transaction covered by a straight or order bill of lading liable for the charges of the carrier. The enactment of this measure required a change in the contract terms of the bill of lading, and section 7 of these terms was modified to the extent necessary for compliance with the law. As a result, the nonrecourse clause on the face of the bill of lading, which for a long time had been a simple nonrecourse clause and nothing else, now includes the phrase, "subject to Section 7 of conditions," on the back of the bill. We shall discuss the exception more fully when we deal with the present terms of section 7.

RELEASED VALUE SHIPMENTS

Near the bottom of the face of the bill of lading is a space in which the shipper may make a statement concerning the value of the property described in the bill. The Interstate Commerce Act provides that the Commission may, if it deems it advisable, permit railroads and other carriers subject to its jurisdiction to make rates on all articles, except "ordinary" livestock, which are based upon the "released" value of the article carried. In case of loss of or damage to a shipment carried at a rate based upon its released value, the stated value, even though it is much less than actual market value, is the maximum amount which the shipper may recover. The shipper is not to be held guilty of "misrepresentation" of the property for the purpose of securing a lower rate, however, even though he declares the value of the shipment to be lower than its value in the market.

It might be mentioned here once again that the Commission permits railway express companies to base all rates on merchandise express shipments upon declared value. The receipt which the Railway Express Agency employs is not called a bill of lading but merely a "uniform express receipt." The document is nevertheless a bill of lading, containing contract terms and conditions very much like those found in the railroad bill of lading. All merchandise shipments weighing 100 pounds or less are accepted for transportation at an agreed value of not more than $50; if more than 100 pounds, at an agreed value of not more than 50 cents a pound. If the value of an article shipped by express is greater than the limit indicated, and should the shipper want to hold the carrier liable for the actual value in case of loss, he must declare a greater value and consequently be obliged to pay a higher rate. Of course, the express company cannot be held liable for a value greater than the actual market value of a lost or damaged shipment, notwithstanding any overstatement of value on the part of the shipper.

SHORT FORM OF BILL OF LADING; ALTERNATIVE FORM

At the bottom of the page of the face of the bill of lading are spaces for the signatures of shipper and carrier, or of their agents, with a place for writing the permanent address of the shipper.

We have already mentioned the fact that carriers permit the use of a short form of straight bill of lading, which is like the ordinary form except that the "contract terms and conditions" are not printed on the back of the bill, although the shipper acknowledges his acquaintance with these terms and accepts them as fully as if they were explicitly stated.

In addition to the short form of bill of lading, there is an alternative form, both of the straight and of the order bill of lading, which is authorized for the optional use of the shipper. This form contains the same contract terms and conditions on the back of the bill, but the face of the bill contains spaces for a greater amount of information than that given in the form of bill of lading ordinarily used. Space is provided for more detailed information with respect to the weight of a shipment, for better identification of the car in which the shipment moves, for indicating if the car has been ordered subject to Rule 34 of the Consolidated and the Uniform Classifications. There is even a space for indicating the kind of car, whether box, hopper, refrigerator, stock, tank, or other variety, with a list of abbreviations by which each kind of car is designated. The bill also contains a space to be used if the shipment is billed C.O.D., in which the amount to be collected from the consignee, the carrier's fee, and the total amount to be collected may be shown. Finally, there is a space to indicate if the shipment is to be delivered to the consignee's place of business.

LIVESTOCK CONTRACT

The uniform livestock contract under which carriers transport livestock appears only in the form of a straight bill; no negotiable livestock contract is issued. The face of the bill is similar to the face of the uniform domestic bill of lading, except that it calls attention, with considerable detail, to the fact that rates on "ordinary livestock," based upon an agreed value of the animals, are forbidden by law. Consequently, the shipper makes no declaration of value of such stock, but he must sign a statement on the contract that the livestock he is having transported is of the ordinary variety, which is stated to mean "all cattle, swine, sheep, goats, horses and mules, except such as are chiefly valuable for breeding, racing, show purposes or other special uses." Should the shipment consist of livestock having a special value for the reasons mentioned, the shipper must so indicate in a space provided for that purpose on the face of the bill, and he must also make a declaration of the agreed value of the animals. If the declared value is higher than that given in the Consolidated or Uniform Classification as a base value of the various kinds of livestock, the freight rate is increased by an amount prescribed in the classification or in an applicable carrier's tariff. In case of loss of the shipment, the agreed value marks the limit of the amount which can be recovered from the carrier.

The "contract terms and conditions" on the back of the uniform livestock contract are similar in a general way to the terms and conditions of the uniform domestic bill of lading. But, since the loading and unloading of livestock, their care in transit, and the carrier's responsibility with respect to such things as loss, packing, free time, and other matters are so different in the transportation of livestock from the responsibility assumed in the transportation of ordinary merchandise, several of the terms and conditions of the ordinary merchandise bill of lading do not appear at all on the back of the livestock contract. We have already mentioned the fact that the livestock contract has a supplementary contract which must be signed by any man or men in charge of the livestock during the course of transportation. This agreement relieves the carrier of liability for any injury to the traveling caretakers, unless the injury is due to the carrier's negligence.

THROUGH EXPORT BILL OF LADING

We have mentioned previously the three parts of the terms and conditions of the through export bill of lading. The conditions governing the movement of a shipment from an interior point to the port of export are similar to the terms of the uniform domestic bill of lading, although there are some differences arising from the fact that the liability of a carrier for an export shipment moving on a through bill is not the same as its liability for a shipment moving in domestic commerce, and the provisions of the law with respect to the liability of an "agent" for freight charges do not apply to export shipments. The second part of the terms and conditions of the through export bill, which covers transportation from an American port to a foreign port, are similar to the conditions found in nearly all ocean bills of lading, and are governed by the provisions of the Carriage of Goods by Sea Act of 1936. The third part of the bill describes the rights and responsibilities of the ocean carrier in case delivery to a final port of destination for some reason cannot be made, and states that transportation between the port of discharge and the point of final destination of the shipment shall be subject to the conditions of the carrier or carriers completing the transit.

TERMS OF BILLS OF LADING ACT

It has already been noted that there is little difference in the form of the domestic straight and order bills of lading. But this difference is of very great importance both to the carrier and to the shipper. In times past, there was some confusion as well as frequent litigation over the duties and responsibilities of the parties who signed and used bills of lading, with the result that Congress, in the Bills of Lading Act of 1916, gave a more precise definition of the obligations of the various parties to a bill of lading. The law took effect January 1, 1917.

The very first substantive provision of the law, after a clause stating that it applies to all bills of lading used in domestic interstate commerce, consists of definitions of the two kinds of bills of lading. A straight bill is one in which it is "stated that the goods are consigned or destined to a specified person." An order bill is one in which it is "stated that the goods are consigned or destined to the order of any person named in such bill." "Person" is declared later in the Act to include a corporation, a partnership, or "two or more persons having a joint or common interest."

Since the goods covered by an order bill are shipped to "the order of" a named person, the bill possesses the property of negotiability. Some writers call the order bill of lading a negotiable instrument, but such a statement is incorrect, because a negotiable instrument is an order or promise for the payment of a stipulated sum of money, such as a check, note, or draft, and the bill of lading is not such an order or promise. It is nevertheless negotiable, and the Pomerene Act stipulates that any provision in such a bill or "in any notice, contract, rule, regulation or tariff that it is non-negotiable shall be null and void and shall not affect its negotiability within the meaning of this act unless upon its face and in writing agreed to by the shipper." The straight bill of lading is not negotiable, and the Pomerene Act requires that it be plainly marked so.

We explained previously that bills of lading are made out in triplicate, an original bill and two copies, one of which is the carrier's shipping order and the other a memorandum copy for the use of the shipper. As an added precaution against confusing the two kinds of bills, the original order bill is printed on yellow paper and the copies on blue paper, while all copies of the straight bill are printed on white paper.

The law requires the carrier, in the absence of some lawful excuse, to "deliver goods upon a demand made either by consignee named in the bill for the goods, or, if the bill be an order bill, by the holder thereof"; if the demand is accompanied by an offer to pay the carrier's lawful charges, to sign a receipt for the goods if asked to do so by the carrier; and to surrender, properly endorsed, the bill for the goods, if it is an order bill. Under ordinary circumstances, the carrier is "justified" in delivering goods to a person lawfully entitled to their possession, to the consignee named in a straight bill of lading, or to a person holding an order bill of lading properly endorsed. If a carrier sells goods in order to satisfy the lien which it has for its lawful charges, or sells them because they have not been claimed within the proper time or because they are perishable or hazardous, it is not liable subsequently for failure to deliver the goods themselves to the consignee or holder of an order bill for the goods. If a carrier delivers goods to a person not lawfully entitled to receive them, it becomes liable to the lawful owner for the value of the goods.

TITLE TO SHIPMENTS

When goods are shipped under a straight bill of lading, as soon as they pass into the possession of the carrier, the carrier holds them subject to the orders of the consignee, and the only way the shipper can reobtain possession of the goods is by the exercise of the right of "stoppage in transitu," by which he can claim goods destined to a consignee who has become bankrupt after the delivery of the goods to the carrier. In case a shipper wishes to exercise this right, the carrier must be given notice in sufficient time to enable it to prevent the delivery of the goods to the named consignee. Under ordinary circumstances, it is presumed that the title to goods which are shipped on a straight bill of lading passes to the consignee when the goods are turned over to a carrier for transportation.[10] Contractual arrangements between shipper and consignee, as buyer and seller, may provide that the title change at a different time, but even so, the law states plainly that the carrier of goods shipped on a straight bill is "justified" in delivering the goods to the consignee unless it has information that the consignee is not lawfully entitled to receive them. It may happen that the named consignee has sold the goods while they were in transit, and has given an order to the purchaser, whereby the purchaser may claim the goods from the carrier. Should the named consignee, after such a sale, endeavor to secure delivery of the goods to himself, and if the carrier has been notified of the sale of the goods, obviously the carrier would be obliged to make delivery to the lawful owner and would be held liable to that owner in case it knowingly delivered them to the consignee or anybody else not lawfully entitled to their possession.

It often happens that the shipper of goods on a straight bill of lading consigns them to himself, or to another party, with instructions to the carrier to notify some person at destination. Such goods will be delivered to the person to be notified, ordinarily, only upon his presentation to the carrier of a written order by the named consignee. It may happen that such a written delivery order is lost, stolen, or destroyed. The fourth section of Rule 7 of the Consolidated and the Uniform Classifications provides that the carrier may deliver the goods, in advance of the presentation of a written order for delivery, to a person who declares in writing that he is the owner of the goods or is lawfully entitled to their possession, and that the written order for delivery has been lost, destroyed, delayed, or in some other manner made not immediately available. However, the carrier requires, under the rule, that the recipient of the goods must protect the carrier against liability by supplying the carrier with currency, certified check, or bank cashier's check in amount equal to 125 per cent of the value of the goods, or furnish the carrier with a surety

[10] Not a few writers state that the expression "F.O.B." (free on board) has to do with the time of the passage of title to goods turned over to a carrier for transportation under a straight bill of lading, saying that if the goods are shipped "F.O.B. point of origin" the title passes to the consignee at that point, but if they are shipped "F.O.B. point of destination" the shipper retains title until the goods reach the point to which they are consigned. There is no legal justification for such a belief. The term F.O.B. has to do primarily with responsibility for freight charges and is not conclusive as to the time of the passing of title. If a shipper wishes to retain title in goods entrusted to a carrier, he should consign them to himself under a straight bill of lading or ship them under an order bill of lading.

bond in an amount twice the invoice value of the goods. The bond may be specific, applying only to the delivery of the goods in question, or it may be a blanket bond acceptable to the carrier. Any deposit in the form of cash or certified check is returned to the receiver of the goods upon presentation of the missing written order or on the execution of a bond for twice the invoice value of the goods. A bond is subject to cancellation after the expiration of the time—nine months—within which another person asserting ownership of the goods may lawfully file a claim of loss against the carrier, provided no such claim has been presented.

Goods shipped under an order bill of lading belong ordinarily to the one who holds the original bill of lading, properly endorsed. Usually, the goods are shipped to the order of the consignor, who can transfer title to the goods by the delivery of the bill of lading, properly endorsed, to another party. The endorsement may be in blank, that is, made merely by the shipper's writing his name in the space provided on the bill for endorsements, or it may be endorsed to a specified person. The procedure is the same as that followed in the transfer by endorsement of a check or draft, either of which may be endorsed in blank or to a specified person. The same bill of lading may be endorsed and transferred several times before coming into the possession of the party who actually claims the goods from the carrier.

It will be seen at once that the carrier must exercise extraordinary care in the delivery of goods shipped on an order bill and that the shipper or the endorsee of a bill must use every precaution in handling the original bill to see that it gets into the possession only of those rightfully and lawfully entitled to it. Ordinarily, the carrier makes delivery of the goods only upon presentation of the original bill of lading properly endorsed, and when the goods are delivered the carrier takes up the bill and cancels it. It may happen, of course, that an order bill of lading is lost, destroyed, or stolen or that there has been unavoidable delay in its transmission to the endorsee who plans to take delivery of the goods. In case of the loss, theft, or destruction of an order bill, a court may order delivery of the goods upon proof of the theft, loss, or destruction, if the recipient furnishes the carrier with a surety bond of an amount sufficient to protect the carrier or any person injured by such delivery against any loss or liability incurred because the original bill remains outstanding. The third section of Rule 7 of the Consolidated and the Uniform Classifications makes provision for the delivery of goods shipped on an order bill of lading to a person who claims to be the owner, but avers in writing that the original bill has been lost, stolen, destroyed or delayed in transmission, under virtually the same conditions as those described above in connection with the delivery of goods consigned on a straight bill of lading which has been lost, destroyed, or delayed in transit.

It behooves the possessor or an order bill of lading to take good care of it, for the theft of an original order bill of lading may be as disastrous to the owner as the theft of the goods which the bill represents. The law plainly states

. . . that the validity of the negotiation of a bill is not impaired by the fact that such negotiation was breach of duty on the part of the person making the negotiation, or by the fact that the owner of the bill was deprived of possession of the same by fraud, accident, mistake, duress, loss, theft, or conversion, if the person to whom the bill was negotiated, or a person to whom the bill was subsequently negotiated gave value therefor in good faith, without notice of the breach of duty, or fraud, accident, mistake, duress, loss, theft, or conversion.

When an innocent purchaser, in good faith of an order bill of lading which the seller has obtained by theft or fraud, demands the goods from the carrier, he is entitled to receive them. Under the circumstances, either the purchaser of the bill or the one from whom the bill was fraudulently obtained must suffer a loss. The law imposes the loss upon the latter; the law with respect to negotiable instruments has a similar provision.

HOW ORDER BILLS OF LADING ARE USED

The order bill of lading is a highly useful document for facilitating the operations of the vast and far-flung commerce of the United States. It not only makes trading easier but also serves as a means of financing trade and production. The important thing about the order bill of lading is that it is negotiable, and the carrier is under notice to retain control of the goods shipped on such a bill until the document is presented, or in case of loss or delay, until the carrier is adequately secured against any risk or loss. The way in which the bill of lading is employed in trade is comparatively simple. A manufacturer or merchant, who wants to be sure of payment for goods he sells before the buyer obtains possession, maybe because he is uncertain about the credit of the buyer or simply because he does not want to wait for payment, can ship goods subject to his own order and arrange for the delivery of the bill of lading to the buyer only when the latter has paid for the goods. The operation is usually conducted through banks. The seller attaches to the order bill a draft upon the buyer for the purchase price of the goods, and turns both documents over to his own bank. This bank sends the two documents to a correspondent bank in the buyer's city. The correspondent bank notifies the buyer of the arrival of the documents. The buyer makes arrangements for the payment of the draft, receives the bill of lading, and is able to claim the goods from the carrier. Thousands of commercial transactions are expedited by the use of the order bill of lading.

It may be that the person or firm which ships goods on order bills of lading uses them to finance the operations of its business enterprise. Since the bill of lading carries title to the goods, it can be used to obtain loans at a bank, particularly if the goods covered by the bill are standard articles of commerce for which there is a daily market. A cotton buyer or a wheat buyer, for example, can employ a capital of, say, a hundred thousand dollars to buy a million dollars' worth of cotton or wheat, by negotiating bank loans on the order bills of lading which represent his shipments to a primary market. A manufacturer whose working capital has been temporarily depleted is able to borrow funds to meet payrolls and to purchase supplies, by borrowing at a bank, with order bills of lading for the products he has shipped as security for the loans. Order bills of lading are used extensively also in transporting products which are sold en route and reconsigned at some point along the journey. A shipper of fruit or farm produce may start several carloads of his commodities on their way without knowing their ultimate destination at the time the shipment is made. The order bill of lading enables him to retain legal control of the traffic. He can study the market and consign his produce to the point where the price is most favorable. Often, a shipper may start a shipment of produce toward one market, discover that prices have fallen at the destination originally planned, and have the shipment diverted to a market where prices have remained steady or perhaps risen. Some shippers prefer to consign goods to themselves on a straight bill of lading rather than make use of the order bill. Although this enables them to control the movement of the traffic, they lose the advantage of the negotiability of the order bill of lading and must issue orders and instructions to the destination carrier with respect to the final delivery of the goods.

Very frequently, though not invariably, an order bill of lading contains the name of a person to be notified by the carrier when the goods covered by the bill have arrived at their destination. In fact, another difference between the straight and the order bill of lading, which has not previously been mentioned, is that the latter has, below the spaces for the name of the person to whose "order" the goods were shipped and the name of the place of destination, a space in which may be written the name and the address of the person to be notified. Because this space is filled in so often, the order bill of lading is often called an "order-notify" bill of lading. The person to be notified is usually the purchaser of the goods described in the bill, although it may be an agent by whom the goods are to be handled on behalf of the shipper. The arrival notice of the carrier means to the one notified that he may soon expect the original bill of lading, if he has not already received it. If the bill does not arrive quickly enough to enable him to obtain the goods promptly from the carrier, he can obtain them by posting proper security, as previously described, and subsequently recover his bond or cash deposit when the bill of lading comes into his possession.

GOVERNMENT BILL OF LADING

There is one more form of bill of lading employed by our carriers in domestic commerce which, during the past several years, has been widely used by shippers. This is the "government bill of lading" which our Federal government requires to be used in the transportation of government property. With respect to the names and addresses of shippers and consignees, the description of the articles shipped, and other information having to do with the actual movement of the goods, the government bill of lading differs little from the straight or order commercial bill of lading we have described previously in this chapter. But there is no space for a nonrecourse declaration and no space for indicating that charges are prepaid. Government property is shipped collect. There is a space on the bill in which to name the government department, establishment, or bureau of service on whose behalf the shipment is made and to which the freight and other charges are to be billed.

Unlike the other bills of lading we have mentioned, the government bill of lading is retained by the carrier and not by the consignor. There are spaces on the face of the bill in which are entered the names of the consignor and the consignee. After the carrier has delivered the goods, the consignee signs a receipt for them at the proper place on the bill of lading. The bill then becomes the documentary proof that the carrier has rendered the service for which the bill called. The carrier prepares a voucher or bill for its charges, on a blank supplied by the government. A separate voucher is made out for each bill of lading. The bill of lading is attached to the voucher and is presented to the proper government agency for payment. The carrier's liability for loss and damage is the same, of course, as for private property.

LAND-GRANT RATES ABOLISHED

Formerly, it was incumbent upon the officials of the government who made arrangements for the shipment of government purchases and other government property to be familiar with the so-called land-grant rates. A great many western carriers received grants of land from the Federal government, land which was sold to help defray the expenses of railroad construction. In return for the land grants, the railroad recipients agreed to carry government freight at a stipulated discount below the regular commercial rates. It was the duty of government officials to see that, whenever possible, government freight was routed over land-grant railroads in order that advantage might be taken of the lower rates. In 1944, Congress enacted a law abolishing the land-grant rates on government property except that moving for the actual use of the military and naval forces of the United States. The following year, even the discounts on this kind of property were abolished, and the rail transportation of government property, under ordinary conditions, became subject to ordinary commercial rates. However, unlike a private shipper, the Federal government, or a state or local government, may enter into contractual agreements with railroads and other common carriers for the transportation of property at less than the commercial rates. A difference between the rate which a carrier charges the government and the lawfully published rate, which a private shipper is obliged to pay, is not regarded as an unreasonable or unjust discrimination.

CHAPTER XI

Terms and Conditions of the Bill of Lading: Carrier's Liability

We are now ready to turn the bill of lading over and have a look at the several paragraphs of fine print on the back. As explained before, these "terms and conditions" have to do chiefly with the liability of the carrier which issues the bill and any other carriers that participate in a through service, although liability is not the only thing they deal with. Before scrutinizing these contractual terms, it would be well to discuss in a general way the matter of carrier's liability and to sketch briefly the legal and legislative history of this important subject.

In the complex, highly organized economic society in which we live, it is surprising how often we find ourselves entrusting some of our possessions to the care of another person. We send our washing to the laundry, our clothing to the tailor or the cleaner; we check our hats and coats in hotels, restaurants, and clubs; we leave our cars in public garages, or at least some of us do so; we often leave our luggage in hotel rooms; we sublet our houses and apartments, furnished, to various tenants; we store our goods for long or short periods in warehouses; we leave our pets temporarily in animal homes or kennels while we are absent from home and cannot take them with us; we put our money in banks and our securities and other valuables in safe-deposit vaults.

Without doubt, however, the most common example of entrusting property to the care of another is found in the delivery of goods to a carrier for transportation; certainly, the amount of property turned over to the temporary custody of carriers is far greater than the amount turned over to any other commercial agency.

LIABILITY IN GENERAL

The person or company who holds another's property in trust—often designated as a bailee—has a certain measure of responsibility for the care and safekeeping of the property, and in case of its loss or damage is liable, under certain circumstances, to the owner for the amount of the loss. However, the liability of all temporary custodians of property belonging to others is by no means the same. The extent of the liability of the bailee and the measure of the amount recoverable by the owner in case of loss or damage have, over the years, been fixed by law—in part by the common law and in part by statutory law duly enacted by legislative assemblies.

We often hear of a distinction between the liability of a "warehouseman" and the liability of a "common carrier." Indeed, both these kinds of liability are mentioned in our bills of lading. A warehouseman is ordinarily liable for loss and damage only if he has been negligent in guarding and looking after the property entrusted to his care. The liability of many common carriers goes far beyond the liability of a warehouseman; some of them are often said to be insurers of the property they transport, and liable for loss even if they have not been negligent.

CARRIER'S LIABILITY AND THE LAW

The liability of all kinds of carriers is by no means the same. Both under the common law and under statutory enactments, the liability of a carrier by land has been vastly different from the liability of a carrier by water. In the United States, the liability of both these types of carriers has been largely defined by statute.

The liability of a carrier by air in our domestic interstate commerce is different, apparently, from the liability either of carriers by land or of carriers by water. There is no United States statute defining the liability which the carrier by air assumes for the property it transports in interstate commerce. This country is, however, an adherent to the so-called Warsaw Convention for the Unification of Certain Rules Relating to International Transportation by Air. The Convention prescribes the form and content of the "air waybill," which takes the place of the bill of lading, and article 22 of the Convention states that the liability of an air carrier for each passenger transported shall be limited to the sum of 125,000 gold francs, though carrier and passenger may by special contract agree to a higher limit. The liability of the carrier for baggage and goods is limited to the sum of 250 gold francs per kilogram, unless the shipper declares a higher value when the shipment is handed over to the carrier and, if required to do so, pays a "supplementary sum" in addition to the regular transportation charges.

The liability of an air carrier in the domestic interstate commerce of the United States is presumably governed by common law, but there has not been a sufficient number of judicial decisions to enable one to determine with certainty what this common law liability is. It has long been the practice of the various courts of law in this country, both state and Federal, to make their own interpretation of the common law. Consequently, there may be a wide difference of interpretation, and until the Supreme Court of the United States, by virtue of some Federal law, is able to establish a rule of liability under the common law, to be observed in connection with air transportation in our interstate commerce, there may be a complete lack of uniformity of practice in dealing with the responsibilities of aviation companies. The possible divergence could be easily avoided if Congress would enact, as it should enact, a statute defining the liability of our air carriers, just as it has enacted statutes dealing with the liability of other kinds of carriers. So far, however, Congress has taken no action on the subject, and apparently the carriers by air have not been greatly concerned over the lack of legislative action.

LORD HOLT ON CARRIER'S LIABILITY

The practice of imposing a greater degree of responsibility upon a common carrier than upon a mere "warehouseman" goes very far back in our commercial and legal history. One of the early recorded explanations of why the common law liability of a carrier is greater than that of a warehouseman was given early in the eighteenth century by a distinguished English jurist, Lord Holt. His remarks have been quoted many times, and appeared early in the memorable decision which the Interstate Commerce Commission handed down in 1919 in the matter of bills of lading. Said Lord Holt, in language which the Commission described as "quaint" but which was nevertheless unmistakable in its meaning, if "a delivery to carry or otherwise manage" is made

. . . to one that exercises a public employment . . . and he is to have a reward, he is bound to answer for the goods at all events. . . . The law charges this person thus intrusted to carry goods, against all events, but acts of God, and of the enemies of the King. For though the force be never so great, as if an irresistible multitude of people should rob him, nevertheless he is chargeable. And this is a politick establishment, contrived by the policy of the law, for the safety of all persons, the necessity of whose affairs oblige them to trust these sorts of persons, that they may be safe in their ways of dealing; for else these carriers might have an opportunity of undoing all persons that had any dealings with them, by combining with thieves, &c., and yet doing it in such a clandestine manner as would not be possible to be discovered. And this is the reason the law is founded upon that point.[1]

LIABILITY OF LAND CARRIERS AND OF WATER CARRIERS NOT THE SAME

Whatever suspicions Judge Holt might have harbored against "these sorts of persons," who served as common carriers by land in his day, he was only describing in clear language a custom which had prevailed for a long time in British commerce as well as in the commerce of many other nations. At one time in the distant past, it seems that the liability of carriers by water was the same as the liability of carriers by land, but gradu-

---

[1] Coggs v. Bernard, 2 Ld. Raym. 909, 1 Smith's Leading Cases 369, *quoted in* 52 I.C.C. 671 (679) (1919).

ally a distinction came to be made between the two, partly because of the greater dangers inherent in transportation by water, partly because of the rivalry of maritime nations, each anxious to give preference to its own ships, and probably because of the pressure which mercantile and shipping interests, which were much more wealthy and powerful than carriers by land, were able to exert on the governmental agencies charged with the task of determining and establishing public policies. It was because of the greatly limited liability of the carrier by water that the great branch of casualty insurance which we know as marine insurance came into existence, under which a shipper may obtain protection against marine losses comparable in many respects to the losses for which the carrier by land is itself responsible.

As custom and practice hardened into common law, and common law was replaced or bolstered in weak spots by statutory enactments, there was a tendency ever to lighten the responsibility of the carrier by water and to impose a greater and greater degree of liability upon the carrier by land. Today we find that virtually all the clauses in the bills of lading of both carriers by water and carriers by land having to do with liability for loss and damage are clauses which they have been required by law to adopt.

LIMITATION OF CARRIER'S LIABILITY UNDER COMMON LAW

Before proceeding with the discussion of the liability of a carrier as defined in the present bill of lading, it might be well to clear up another point of linguistic difficulty. Any legal rule or any legal contractual agreement by which the carrier in effect diminishes its liability for loss and damage is usually spoken of as a rule for the "limitation" of a carrier's liability. This limitation may have two aspects which are quite different from each other, but unfortunately the term "limited liability" is frequently used to describe both of these aspects. It will therefore be well to understand clearly that there is a difference, and what the difference is.

It might be better if we used two expressions instead of one to denote that a carrier's liability is limited. These expressions would be "exemption from liability" and "limitation of liability." But the latter expression is almost unversally employed to describe both limitation and exemption, which makes it necessary to exercise some discrimination in our thinking when the subject of limitation is under discussion.

A carrier is not invariably liable for loss and damage to the property it transports. We have seen that Lord Holt stated that it was not liable for loss due to an act of God or to the enemies of the King. These two possible causes of loss for which the carrier cannot be held responsible have been added to in the course of time. In other words, there are certain events or acts which may cause a loss for which the carrier is not chargeable. But if the cause is something different from one of those which carries exemption, though the carrier may be liable it may, nevertheless, under certain conditions, "limit" its liability. That is, it may, by contract with a shipper, limit the amount which a shipper may recover in case he suffers a loss.

At one time, it was a regular practice for the railroads of the United States to include in the terms and conditions of their bills of lading certain clauses which exempted them from liability if the loss was due to causes other than those generally accepted under the common law, and they had many more provisions under which they could, by contract with the shipper, limit the amount recoverable by the shipper in case of loss or damage to his property. It frequently became necessary for the courts to construe the terms of the contract under which a carrier limited its liability. Since there was no applicable statute in many cases, the decisions of the courts had to be made under the common law. With each court privileged to interpret the common law as it thought best, it was not surprising that there came to be considerable confusion in the United States with respect to the common law liability of carriers. To make the confusion worse, a number of states enacted statutes for a more precise definition of the liability of carriers, and since a shipper, even in the case of an interstate shipment, in the event of loss or damage had the right to sue in the state in which the loss occurred, it can readily be seen that the pattern of carrier's liability in the United States came to assume an appearance of that household article of comfort and decoration which our feminine ancestors called a crazy quilt.

It will not be necessary to enter into a detailed discussion of the contradictions and complexities once to be found in the practices in the United States with respect to the liability of land carriers, for most of them have been eliminated by statutes which superseded the common law. But before 1915, it was a common practice for railroads to provide for a limitation of their liability by the device known as "released value" agreements in bills of lading. In consideration of a "reduced rate," the shipper would consent to limit to a stipulated sum the amount he could recover in case of loss. Should he want full coverage, he would be obliged to pay a higher rate. The Supreme Court of the United States ruled that such releases were valid under the common law.[2] A few states enacted statutes declaring such contracts to be null and void; if a shipper suffering a loss brought suit in a state having such a statute, he could recover the full value of a lost shipment, regardless of the limited liability contract he had entered into with the railroad.[3] The case which probably called the sharpest attention to the confusion with respect to such contracts arose

[2] Hart v. Pennsylvania R.R., 112 U.S. 31 (1884).
[3] Chicago, Milwaukee & St. Paul Ry. v. Solan, 169 U.S. 133 (1898).

when a race horse valued at $10,000, shipped by rail at a released value of $100, was lost in Pennsylvania in an accident due to negligence. The shipper sued in the Pennsylvania courts, and though that state had no law providing that a limited liability contract was unlawful, the Supreme Court of the state held that the contract was invalid at common law as being contrary to the "settled policy" of that state.[4] Since the horse had been shipped interstate, the carrier promptly took the case to the Supreme Court of the United States, with complete confidence that the Pennsylvania court would be reversed, since the highest Federal court had already declared that a carrier's limited liability contract was good at common law. Much to the surprise of the legal profession as well as the carrier, the Supreme Court declined to reverse the state court's judgment, on the ground that each jurisdiction was entitled to interpret the common law as it saw fit, and a difference between the interpretation followed by one court and the interpretation followed by another, even though it was the Supreme Court of the United States, did not constitute grounds for reversal.[5] So it came about that the ability of a shipper to recover the full value of the property which had been lost while being transported by a railroad under a released value agreement became a matter of which court he applied to for the redress of his injury. If he went directly to a Federal court, he was bound to lose; if he went to a court of a state having a law declaring carrier's released value contracts null and void, he could collect an amount covering his total loss regardless of the contract; if he went to the court of a state having no such statute, it would all depend upon how the judiciary of that state interpreted the common law on the matter. He would win his suit in Pennsylvania if the loss was due to negligence—at least as long as the judiciary of that state did not change its collective mind—but he could not be sure of how he would come out in another state.

THE CARMACK AMENDMENT

Congress eventually changed all of this with respect to interstate railroad commerce, but the interesting fact is that Congress did not know for some time that it had effected any change, and when, on the authority of the Supreme Court, it found out that it had done so, it soon effected another and a more important change.

Before 1906, the shippers of the United States had for many years ex-

[4] Hughes v. Pennsylvania R.R., 202 Pa. 222 (1902). The Pennsylvania Supreme Court did not choose to follow the doctrine enunciated by the Supreme Court of the United States in Hart v. Pennsylvania R.R. The judiciary of Pennsylvania had held for many years that contracts for the limitation of liability for loss due to negligence were "null and void." See Grogan v. Adams Express Company, 114 Pa. 523 (1887).

[5] Pennsylvania R.R. v. Hughes, 191 U.S. 477 (1903).

perienced a great deal of difficulty in obtaining from railroads recompense for through or interline shipments which had been lost or damaged in transit. If the initial carrier, by which the bill of lading was issued, disclaimed responsibility on the ground that the loss or damage had not occurred on its line, it was necessary for the shipper to ascertain upon what carrier's line or route the loss had occurred before he could obtain compensation for his loss. This was at best a difficult task, and many times entirely impossible. The shipper was compelled to swallow his loss—as well as his wrath—bewail his impotence, and indulge in the hope that some day the law would be changed in such a way as to give him adequate protection against "these sorts of persons" who performed his transportation services.

Congress came to the rescue of the shippers when the Hepburn Amendment to the Interstate Commerce Act—the law which for the first time put teeth into the original act—was passed in 1906. One part of this amendment, which was in itself known as the Carmack Amendment, after the Tennessee Senator who introduced it, modified section 20 by providing that a carrier subject to the act should give the shipper a bill of lading, and if the shipment was an interline shipment the initial carrier should be responsible for any loss or damage caused by it or by any connecting carrier by which the shipment might be handled. The law has since been amended to give the shipper the right to hold the delivering as well as the originating carrier responsible for the loss or damage, as well as the carrier on whose line the loss or damage might occur. If the loss does not occur on the line of the carrier which the shipper holds responsible, that carrier has the right, under the law, to obtain reparation from the carrier on whose lines the loss took place.

ADAMS V. CRONINGER

When the Carmack Amendment was passed, it seems that Congress, as well as the shipping public, thought that it made no change in the existing practice and law with respect to carrier's liability beyond imposing responsibility for the loss of through shipments upon the initial carrier. But in a few years it became apparent that Congress had said more than it had perhaps intended to say. A young man in Kentucky sent a diamond ring by Adams Express to his girl friend in another state, accepting from the company a receipt which stipulated a released value for the ring of $50. The express company lost the ring, and the young man sued in a Kentucky state court for the full value of the ring, which was considerably more than $50. Since Kentucky had a law declaring that carrier's contracts for limited liability based upon a released value were null and void, the plaintiff obtained a judgment for the full value of the article lost. The express company carried the case to the Supreme Court, asking that body to scrutinize the provisions of the Carmack Amendment. The Court had to determine what the law meant when it said that the carrier of an interstate shipment should give the consignor a bill of lading and be liable "for any loss, damage, or injury to such property caused by it" or by a connecting carrier. It was the Court's opinion (1913) that this meant that the carrier of an interstate shipment was liable *as at common law* for the loss or damage. Since the Court had already declared that under the common law, as it interpreted such law, a carrier had the right to enter into contracts for the limitation of the amount a shipper could recover for a lost shipment, it reversed the judgment of the Kentucky court, and declared that the young man was entitled to only $50 in compensation for the lost diamond ring.[6] This decision meant that, by reason of the Carmack Amendment, carriers subject to the provisions of the Interstate Commerce Act were now operating under a uniform rule as to their liability for lost or damaged interstate shipments, and that the confusion which had arisen because of conflicting laws and conflicting decisions had come to an end. In a few subsequent cases, the Court emphasized its view, even holding that a shipper was bound by the terms of a tariff which provided for a limitation of carrier's liability for lost baggage, even though he was unacquainted with the terms of the tariff. Under the law, he was presumed to know the contents of a tariff which contained rates and rules applicable to his shipment.[7] After the Court's decision of 1913 as to the meaning of the Carmack Amendment, according to the Interstate Commerce Commission:

From a former policy of compromise, of making the best terms possible with the claimant, which was not wholly disadvantageous to the claimant in many instances, and which, of course, was often discriminatory in its operation, a disposition was developed upon the part of many carriers to stand uncompromisingly upon their rights as defined in the bill of lading.[8]

THE CUMMINS AMENDMENTS

The persistence of the carriers in standing flatfooted upon what was "nominated in the bond" soon brought loud repercussions, which resulted in the enactment by Congress of further amendments to the Interstate Commerce Act designed to tighten up the law with respect to carrier's liability. These amendments were patterned generally after the laws of the states which had declared contracts limiting liability to a released value to be null and void. There were two amendments, both named after Senator Cummins of Iowa—one passed in 1915 and the second the follow-

---

[6] Adams Express Co. v. Croninger, 226 U.S. 491 (1913).
[7] See Boston and Maine R.R. v. Hooker, 233 U.S. 491 (1914); Pierce Co. v. Wells, Fargo & Co., 236 U.S. 278 (1915).
[8] Bills of Lading, 52 I.C.C. 671 (677) (1919).

ing year—to correct some of the difficulties that had been encountered in enforcing the intent, if not the letter, of the earlier amendment. These Cummins Amendments now constitute that part of the Interstate Commerce Act which indicates the extent to which a carrier subject to what is now part I of the law may legally limit the amount of its liability. It has been said previously that the provisions applicable to the carriers subject to part I have been applied to carriers subject to parts II and IV, but not to the water carriers subject to part III.

Section 20, subdivision 11, of the Interstate Commerce Act holds the carrier by rail liable for the "full actual loss, damage or injury" of the property which it transports, notwithstanding "any limitation of liability or limitation of the amount of recovery or representation or agreement as to value" in any receipt or bill of lading, or in any rule or tariff, and "any such limitation, without respect to the manner or form in which it is sought to be made is hereby declared to be unlawful." But there are exceptions. Water transportation is specifically exempted from the terms of the section, and the provisions respecting

. . . liability for full actual loss, damage or injury, notwithstanding any limitation of liability or recovery or representation or agreement or release as to value, and declaring such limitation to be unlawful and void, shall not apply, first to baggage carried on passenger trains or boats, or trains or boats carrying passengers; second, to property, except ordinary livestock, received for transportation concerning which the carrier shall have been or shall hereafter be expressly authorized or required by order of the Interstate Commerce Commission to establish and maintain rates dependent upon the value declared in writing by the shipper or agreed upon in writing as the released value of the property, in which case such declaration or agreement shall have no other effect than to limit liability and recovery to an amount not exceeding the value so declared or released, and shall not, so far as it relates to values, be held to be a violation of section 10 of this part to regulate commerce, as amended; and any tariff schedule which may be filed with the Commission pursuant to such order shall contain specific reference thereto and may establish rates varying with the value so declared and agreed upon; and the Commission is hereby empowered to make such order in cases where rates dependent upon and varying with declared or agreed values would, in its opinion, be just and reasonable under the circumstances and conditions surrounding the transportation.

The first Cummins Amendment provided that if

. . . goods are hidden from view by wrapping, boxing or other means, and the carrier is not notified as to the character of the goods, the carrier may require the shipper specifically to state in writing the value of the goods, and the carrier shall not be liable beyond the amount specifically stated, in which case the Interstate Commerce Commission may establish and maintain rates for transportation, dependent upon the value of the property shipped as specifically stated in writing by the shipper.

The first Cummins Amendment abolished the entire system of "released rates," by the use of which railroads had so long been able to contract for a limitation of their liability for lost and damaged freight; but with respect to goods concealed from view, the carrier had a right to "require" the shipper to state the value of the goods, the Commission could establish rates graded according to the value of such goods, and the stated value would be the maximum amount which the shipper could recover in case the goods were lost. Such rates were "actual value" rates as contrasted with "released value" rates, and it was the duty of the shipper to stay reasonably well within the bounds of truth in any written statement concerning the value of a shipment, hidden from view, in case he were "required" by the carrier to state the value. Since the shipper's stated value was presumably the actual value, it could hardly be said that the purpose of this part of the second amendment was to enable the carrier to limit its liability for "full, actual loss, damage or injury," although if a shipper deliberately undervalued a shipment and no effort was made to change the billing by stating the correct value and assessing the rate based on that value, and in case of loss the shipper made no attempt to collect more than the false stated value, it could be said that the law operated in such a way as to limit the carrier's liability. An interesting situation might have arisen had an undervalued shipment been lost or damaged. Obviously the shipper would have been stopped from recovering more than the value which he had declared, but could he have been required to pay the lawfully applicable rate, and would he have been subject to prosecution for misrepresentation?

With respect to goods not "hidden from view," railroads maintained the right which they had always possessed of charging actual value rates. In case a shipment in this category was lost, the shipper, under the first Cummins Amendment, still had the right to recover an amount equivalent to the full actual loss, even though he had undervalued the shipment. But since there was no question that under such circumstances he would have been subject to prosecution for misrepresenting his property for the purpose of securing a lower rate, he was not likely to attempt to recover any more than the value he had attributed to the lost shipment. Of course, there were not many actual value rates, that is, rates which were graded in accordance with the value of the shipment of some one particular commodity.

The first Cummins Amendment had been in effect only a short time when it became apparent that Congress had gone a little further than it had probably intended to go in denying the right of a carrier to limit its liability for loss and damage. Taking a second, and better, look at the subject, Congress discarded most of the first Cummins Amendment, especially the part dealing with shipments hidden from view, and substituted a second Cummins Amendment, which, with a few relatively unimportant changes, remains a part of subdivision 11 of section 20 of the Act, most of which was quoted above. As can be seen, Congress restored to railroads the right to make rates based on released value, but only with the specific consent and authorization of the Commission. But not even the Commission could authorize a railroad to make rates on ordinary livestock which were based on released value.

COMMISSION INTERPRETATION OF FIRST CUMMINS AMENDMENT

Although it was apparent that the second Cummins Amendment had permitted the restoration of released value rates, except on ordinary livestock, when such rates were duly authorized by the Commission, there seemed to be some difference of opinion about the status of actual value rates under the new legislation. After the enactment of the first Cummins Amendment, there had been much discussion about its precise meaning and a great deal of confusion of counsel, and the Commission had undertaken, on its own responsibility, to give expression to some "tentative views" on the matter.[9] In the course of its statement, it said:

The law does not specifically say that attempts to limit the carrier's liability shall not be resorted to, but declares them to be invalid and unlawful, wherever found and in whatever guise they appear. Obviously, therefore, neither bills of lading or other contracts for carriage, or classifications or rate schedules of the carriers, should contain any provisions which are declared to be unlawful and void.

Moreover, the Commission asserted that while released rates were forbidden, "it is important to keep in mind that the carriers are not prohibited from making different rates depend upon the value of different grades of a given commodity." If such rates were established, it was the shipper's duty, of course, to declare the true value of a shipment to which such rates were applicable; it was the duty of the carrier not to accept a shipment if the shipper's representation as to its value was known to be false. In other words, a commodity might be "reasonably classified according to value, and be subject to different rates applicable to different grades of the same commodity, which is a different matter from limiting the liability to declared value." In one case, at least, the Commission approved of graded rates on livestock which were based upon actual (declared) value and in connection with which there was a plain statement that the carrier's liability was limited to the "actual value."[10]

[9] The Cummins Amendment, 33 I.C.C. 682 (1915).
[10] National Society of Record Assos. v. Aberdeen & Rockfish R.R., 40 I.C.C. 347 (1916).

INTERPRETATION OF SECOND CUMMINS AMENDMENT

After the passage of the second Cummins Amendment, the Commission did not issue any declaration of "tentative" views as to the meaning of the revised version of the statute, but it was not long before it handed down decisions indicating that the second amendment had brought about an important change with regard to actual value rates. The Commission, in effect, placed actual value rates on the same footing with released value rates, declaring that such rates, applicable to ordinary livestock, should not be published under any circumstances and should not be published as applicable to other commodities, without the express authorization of the Commission. It expressly disclaimed authority to establish either released or actual value rates on ordinary livestock,[11] and it decided that certain published ratings on soap, dependent upon the value declared by the shipper, were unlawful because they had been issued without necessary authorization.[12] "One can not fairly or effectively differentiate," declared the Commission, "between released rates and rates based on actual value." In another case, the Commission said: "We can not authorize or sanction rates on ordinary livestock which are dependent upon value,"[13] and again, "The maintenance by defendants of rates on ordinary livestock in terms of value subsequent to the amendment of the Act by the Cummins Amendment of August 9, 1916, was unlawful."[14] In another case, the Commission, although admitting that neither of the Cummins Amendments explicitly forbade the publication of rates based on actual value (since their purpose was to make unlawful attempts on the part of carriers to limit their liability, except under certain specified conditions), declared that a tariff requiring a declaration of value by the shipper, while it "did not directly limit" liability, nevertheless had the same effect, since, had the goods been lost and had the shipper sought to recover on a value in excess of the declared value, he would "have been subject to prosecution" for misrepresentation. "Thus the defendant's liability was indirectly, but effectively, limited" by the declaration of value, and the "limitations as to value attached to the rates were unlawful."[15] The same idea was stated even more emphatically in another case having to do with rates on ordinary livestock. Quoting its former statement to the effect that it

[11] Express Rates, Practices, Accounts and Revenues, 43 I.C.C. 510 (1917).

[12] J. B. Williams v. Hartford & New York Transportation Co., 48 I.C.C. 269 (1918).

[13] Live Stock Classification, 47 I.C.C. 335 (1917).

[14] Wilson & Co. v. Chicago, Milwaukee & St. Paul Ry., 50 I.C.C. 126 (1918). See also Charles F. Carr v. Chicago, Milwaukee & St. Paul Ry., 51 I.C.C. 205 (1918).

[15] U.S. Industrial Alcohol Co. v. Director General, 68 I.C.C. 389 (1922).

could not differentiate between released rates and actual value rates, the Commission ruled that all tariffs which "required declarations of value by shippers of ordinary livestock, and all limitations attached to the rates" were unlawful. The clear implication of the decision was that there could be one rate and one rate only applicable to any single shipment of ordinary livestock, regardless of its actual value,[16] and that the same was true with respect to all other commodities, unless the Commission expressly authorized the publication of rates based upon "released value."

THE DARDEN CASE

It was not long, however, until the Commission felt compelled completely to reverse its attitude. The reversal was the result of a decision handed down by the Supreme Court, in 1924. A certain Darden had shipped a half-dozen race horses by express from Latonia, Kentucky, to Windsor, Ontario. Five of the animals had been killed in transit, because of the negligence of the carrier. The horses had been shipped under a declared "real valuation" of $100 each, but the owner of the horses sued for his "full loss." A jury in a Federal district court awarded him damages to the amount of $32,500. The verdict was upheld in the Circuit Court of Appeals,[17] whereupon the express company took the case to the Supreme Court on a writ of error. The Supreme Court's decision was brief and to the point.[18] The Cummins Amendments forbade the carriers to limit their liability except in the case of specifically authorized released rates. The express company was liable for the actual loss, which was $32,500.[19] It was perfectly true that the horses had been shipped with a "real" valuation of $500, but this valuation did not operate to limit the liability of the car-

[16] North Packing & Provision Co. v. Chicago, Milwaukee & St. Paul Ry., 69 I.C.C. 235 (1922).

[17] Adams Express Co. v. Darden, 286 Fed. 61 (1923).

[18] Adams Express Co. v. Darden, 265 U.S. 265 (1924).

[19] It should be noted that the rate under which the horses were transported was an "actual value" and not a "released value" rate. Had it been a released rate, such as carriers now apply with Commission consent to livestock valuable for racing, breeding, or show purposes, the amount of recovery would have been limited to $500, even though the owner had been unaware that such a limitation was contracted for by the person who actually directed the shipment. The Supreme Court has never abandoned the position which it took in Adams v. Croninger, 226 U.S. 491 (1913). See also Kansas City Southern Ry. v. Carl, 227 U.S. 639 (1913); American Railway Express Co. v. Lundenberg, 260 U.S. 123 (1923); American Railway Express Co. v. Daniel, 269 U.S. 40 (1925). The Circuit Court of Appeals, in Feinberg v. Railway Express Agency, 163 F.2d 998 (1947), reversed a judgment for approximately $5,000 obtained in a district court for the loss of a mink coat shipped by a hotel clerk to the owner, declaring that $50, the released value of the coat, was the maximum amount recoverable. The clerk was said to be the "agent" of the owner, who did not discover that the coat had been shipped with the released valuation until after it had been lost.

rier. Although it might be said that the carrier was guilty of rebating, because of the low rate charged, or that the shipper was guilty of misrepresentation, neither of those considerations operated to defeat the law with respect to the carrier's liability. It was noted in the decision that the owner was not guilty of fraud or deception, but even if he had been, the actual value rate would not have prevented the recovery of the full value of the lost horses, although he might have been subject to prosecution for violation of section 10 of the Interstate Commerce Act.

ACTUAL VALUE RATES

As a result of this decision of the Supreme Court, the Interstate Commerce Commission promptly had a change of mind with respect to actual value rates. It now said that "released rates and actual-value rates may, in our opinion, be fairly and effectively differentiated." Since the Cummins Amendments were not

. . . directly aimed at actual-value rates as to which there is no attempt to limit the liability of the carriers . . . there can no longer be any doubt that shipments under actual-value rates, even upon a declaration of value which is less than the actual value and at the reduced rate, does *not* operate as a limitation upon the shipper's right to recover for the full actual loss, damage or injury.[20]

Commissioner Hall, who had written the ruling opinion in the North Packing and Provision case, took strong exception to the decision of the majority. He was joined in his dissent by Commissioner Eastman.

Subsequent decisions affirmed and reaffirmed the Commission's view that actual value rates could be published and filed, even when applicable to "ordinary livestock," without the specific authorization of the Commission, although such rates were not valid if they were "based on values declared by shippers not required by tariffs to be actual values" or if they were accompanied by the slightest implication that they involved a limitation of liability on the part of the publishing carrier.[21]

Actual value rates, like all other rates, are subject to rejection or revision by the Interstate Commerce Commission. But their filing does not require any previous authorization by the Commission, as is the case with released rates. The number of actual value rates employed by the carriers is not large, and released rates seem to be preferred as the better type of graduated rates. For example, the ratings on certain kinds of fur or fur-lined clothing were for several years carried in the Consolidated

[20] Crown Overall Mfg. Co. v. Director General, 100 I.C.C. 471 (1925).

[21] See Heller Bros. v. Director General, 102 I.C.C. 749 (1925); Cudahy Packing Co. v. Director General, 104 I.C.C. 705 (1925); C. Scherger & Sons v. Boston & Maine R.R., 109 I.C.C. 555 (1926); Armour & Co. v. Director General, 129 I.C.C. 587 (1927), 183 I.C.C. 669 (1932); G. F. Carpenter v. Central Vermont Ry., 93 I.C.C. 309 (1924), *reversed,* 147 I.C.C. 373 (1928).

Classification as actual value ratings, but in the nineteenth edition of the classification they became released ratings, authority for the publication of which had been obtained from the Commission. At the present time there are no actual value rates applicable to ordinary livestock.

SUMMARY

To sum up briefly, the Carmack and the two Cummins Amendments together now make the following provisions with respect to the liability of carriers, subject to part I of the Interstate Commerce Act, for loss, damage, or injury to the property they transport.

1. The carrier receiving property for transportation "from a point in one State or Territory or the District of Columbia to a point in another State, Territory, District of Columbia, or from any point in the United States to a point in an adjacent foreign country" shall issue a bill of lading and be liable to the "lawful holder thereof for any loss, damage or injury to such property caused by it" or by any connecting carrier, and "no contract, receipt, rule, regulation, or other limitation" shall exempt the carrier from this liability. The amount recoverable by the shipper is not to be limited by any agreement or representation as to the value of the property.

2. There are exceptions to this general rule. The first is that if a through shipment is carried part of the way by water, the liability of the carrier by water shall be such as provided in the water carrier's bill of lading or by the laws governing water transportation, and the initial carrier shall be liable only for the loss chargeable to the water carrier if the loss occurred on the line of the carrier by water.

3. The second exception is that the general rule shall not apply to passenger baggage.

4. The Interstate Commerce Commission may authorize the carrier to make rates based upon a declared or released value of the goods shipped. But this permission does not extend to "ordinary live stock." Under no circumstances can the carrier limit the amount which a shipper may recover for the loss of ordinary livestock. With respect to other kinds of traffic, there can be no limitation without the consent of the Commission.

5. If the Commission authorizes the carrier to make rates based upon the declared or released value of any commodity, the value declared is the maximum amount a shipper may recover in case of loss. The shipper is not to be held guilty of "misbilling" if he declares a value which is less than actual value.

EFFECTS OF CUMMINS AMENDMENTS

As may be imagined, the railroads did not greet the Cummins Amendments with any great degree of enthusiasm. Some railroad officials called attention to Rule 1 of the three major classifications which stated that the liability assumed by the carrier was contingent upon the shipper's acceptance of the bill of lading offered by the carrier, and if the shipper demanded "common law liability" his freight charges would be increased 10 per cent. The officials declared that the imposition of a greater degree of liability by the first Cummins Amendment automatically entitled the railroads to a 10-per-cent advance in freight rates. Although the idea reflected some "brilliant" official thinking, it did not make a favorable impression upon the Interstate Commerce Commission, and the carriers were soon disabused of any belief that they could require all shippers to accept a sudden increase of 10 per cent in their freight rates.[22]

The Commission's reflections on the possibility of the first Cummins Amendment's justifying an automatic increase in freight rates appeared in a report which it issued shortly after the amendment was passed. It also called attention to the changes in the law with regard to carrier's liability and stated that it would be necessary for all railroads to make changes in their bills of lading to meet the requirements of the new statute. Especially emphasized was the necessity for modifying the terms of the livestock contracts which the railroads had been accustomed to use.[23] In addition to issuing this report, the Commission went steadily forward with its investigation of the entire subject of bills of lading. This investigation eventually resulted in the order of 1919, prescribing uniform domestic and export bills, which we discussed in the preceding chapter.

BILL OF LADING CONDITIONS: SECTION 1

The first section of the conditions of the uniform domestic bill of lading reads as follows:

Sec. 1. (a) The carrier or party in possession of any of the property herein described shall be liable as at common law for any loss thereof or damage thereto, except as hereinafter provided.

(b) No carrier or party in possession of all or any of the property herein described shall be liable for any loss thereof or damage thereto or delay caused by the act of God, the public enemy, the authority of law, or the act or default of the shipper or owner, or for natural shrinkage. The carrier's liability shall be that of warehouseman, only, for loss, damage, or delay caused by fire occurring after the expiration of the free time allowed by tariffs lawfully on file (such free time to be computed as therein provided) after notice of the arrival of

---

[22] The Cummins Amendment, 33 I.C.C. 682 (1915). This pronouncement of the Commission came before the enactment of the second Cummins Amendment.

[23] Although the Commission has sanctioned the publication of actual value rates on ordinary livestock, the uniform livestock contract still carries the notation: "On shipments of ordinary live stock no declaration of value shall be made by the shipper, nor shall any values be entered in this bill of lading." As a matter of fact, carriers no longer publish actual value rates on ordinary livestock.

the property at destination or at the port of export (if intended for export) has been duly sent or given, and after placement of the property for delivery at destination, or tender of delivery of the property to the party entitled to receive it, has been made. Except in case of negligence of the carrier or party in possession (and the burden to prove freedom from such negligence shall be on the carrier or party in possession), the carrier or party in possession shall not be liable for loss, damage, or delay occurring while the property is stopped and held in transit upon the request of the shipper, owner, or party entitled to make such request, or resulting from a defect or vice in the property, or for country damage to cotton, or from riots or strikes.

Subsection (c), which is somewhat long, has to do with the matter of quarantine. In general, it releases the carrier from obligation for any expense or delay because of the operation of any quarantine law.

It will be interesting to scan closely some of the provisions of this section and to compare them with the provisions of the bill of lading used by the eastern and western railroads before the present form was adopted in 1922. We shall not endeavor to make a comparison between all the parts of the old and new bills of lading, but it will be instructive to examine some of the changes which were brought about by the Commission's insistence that all provisions of the bill should conform to the law.

First of all, it should be noted that the carrier now says it is liable for loss or damage "as at common law." The old bill did not mention common law, but merely said the carrier would be liable for loss or damage "except as hereinafter provided." What we find in the present bill of lading is that virtually all of the "exceptions" to liability as at common law are such as to increase the liability of the carrier above that provided by the common law, while in the old bill the exceptions were such as to lessen the carrier's liability ordinarily imposed by the common law. It will be remembered that the courts of the United States, particularly the Federal courts, recognized the legality of contractual provisions in the bill of lading by which the carrier escaped some of the responsibility which under a strict application of the common law it would have been compelled to assume.

For example, in the old bill of lading, the carrier, instead of exempting itself for liability for any loss due to "natural shrinkage," said that it was not liable for loss due to such shrinkage or for loss due to "discrepancies in elevator weights." A carload of wheat might weigh a thousand pounds less at destination than at the point where it was loaded. Unless the shipper could actually prove that there had been a loss by leakage, theft, or otherwise, the carrier would merely rely upon the exception with regard to discrepancy in elevator weights to avoid liability for the loss.

In the old bill, the carrier said that it was not liable, except as a warehouseman, for loss, damage, or delay due to fire occurring after forty-eight hours after notice of arrival has been duly sent or given. The Commission pointed out several things which might be wrong with this type of exemption. In the first place, the tariffs of various carriers might provide for a period of free time longer than forty-eight hours at certain destinations. Moreover, even though a notice of arrival had been "duly sent or given," the property might not be so placed that the consignee could take possession before the expiration of the forty-eight hours. The present bill of lading gives to the consignee of property the free time permitted in the carrier's tariff and provides that the property must be placed or tendered for delivery.

Another provision of the old bill of lading, of which the carrier took advantage in order to avoid its common law liability, said:

When in accordance with general custom, on account of the nature of the property, or when at the request of the shipper the property is transported in open cars, the carrier or party in possession (except in case of loss or damage by fire, in which case the liability will be the same as though the property had been carried in closed cars) shall be liable only for negligence, and the burden to prove freedom from such negligence shall be on the carrier or party in possession.

There was nothing in the common law which called for a differentiation between property shipped on open cars and property shipped in closed cars. The carrier was adding to the exemptions from liability imposed by the common law. This was something different from entering into a contractual arrangement for the limitation of the amount a shipper might recover in case his property were lost or damaged. The contract for the limitation of the recovery was widely sanctioned by common law up to the time of the enactment of the Cummins Amendments, but the common law concept of a carrier's liability, as expressed by Lord Holt, still prevailed, and there were only a very few commonly accepted causes for loss or damage such as to enable the carrier to escape all responsibility.

The act of God and the act of the public enemy are the oldest such causes, and they are still carried in the bill of lading. An act of God is a violent accident of nature, such as a flood or stroke of lightning, the occurrence of which the carrier could not reasonably be expected to anticipate. A spring flood which washes out a railroad bridge and causes a wreck, with consequent damage to property, is not an act of God if the flood is of a kind that could reasonably be expected to occur. It is only an unprecedented and utterly unpredictable violent manifestation of destructive natural force that can be considered an act of God. The "public enemy" mentioned in the bill of lading is not one of the hoodlums or gangsters who are often so designated these days, but the organized force of a government with which our nation is at war or an organized insurrectionary force within our borders. Once in a while, the courts have a little difficulty in determining the precise character of the destructive forces which have caused loss or damage to property in the possession of a carrier. There would be no question that a catastrophe such as the San Francisco earthquake was an act of God; the famous Johnstown flood, however, was also caused by an act of God, although the immediate cause of the disaster was the breaking of a man-made dam. There was some argument in the courts as to whether the predatory raids which the Mexican rebel chief, Francisco Villa, made across our Texas border were acts of the "public enemy"; there would have been no question about the raid which Morgan and his cavalry made into Ohio and Indiana during the Civil War or about the destruction caused by invading British forces during the War of 1812.

When a shipper requests his shipment to be held in transit pending the receipt of reconsignment orders or other instructions, the carrier's liability becomes that of a warehouseman only; he is liable for loss only in case of negligence. In the same way, if a shipper's property is lost during strikes or domestic riots—there have been frequent instances of heavy damage to property during periods of labor turmoil—the carrier is liable for the loss only if it has been negligent in its endeavors to prevent the loss. The same may be said with respect to loss or damage resulting from a vice or defect of the property carried. The carrier is bound under the law to exercise due diligence in caring for the property which is endangered, and cannot be held responsible for loss if it has exercised such diligence. A carrier may be held liable for damage due to negligence in trying to prevent losses, the primary cause for which might even be an act of God. In other words, the carrier is always expected to take all reasonable precautions to avoid the loss of the property entrusted to its care.

One other kind of loss a carrier is responsible for only if it is negligent is "country damage to cotton." There are many glossaries and dictionaries of traffic terms, but one will search them in vain for the meaning of this expression, though it has been in use in the bill of lading for many years. It is doubtful if one out of a dozen traffic managers whose work is confined largely to the northern states knows what the expression means. The Chairman of the Southern Classification says there is no "official" definition of the term but that it is used generally through the cotton-raising states to describe the damage suffered by cotton between the time it is picked and ginned and the time it is delivered to a carrier for transportation. Because of the inadequacy of storage space on farms and in local warehouses, bales of cotton are left on the ground in the open weather for days and often for weeks, where the cotton is discolored and otherwise damaged by rain, snow, or mildew. Sometimes the cotton is damaged when dumped on the ground near a shipping station before it is actually delivered to the carrier for shipment. The carrier disclaims responsibility for any damage prior to the actual receipt of the cotton, and subsequently also unless it has been negligent in affording adequate protection from the elements.

BILL OF LADING CONDITIONS: SECTION 2

The second section of the conditions of the bill of lading reads:

Sec. 2 (a) No carrier is bound to transport said property by any particular train or vessel, or in time for any particular market or otherwise than with reasonable dispatch. Every carrier shall have the right in case of physical necessity to forward said property by any carrier or route between the point of shipment and the point of destination. In all cases not prohibited by law, where a lower value than actual value has been represented in writing by the shipper or has been agreed upon in writing as the released value of the property as determined by the classification or tariffs upon which the rate is based, such lower value plus freight charges if paid shall be the maximum amount to be recovered, whether or not such loss or damage occurs from negligence.

(b) As a condition precedent to recovery, claims must be filed in writing with the receiving or delivering carrier, or carrier issuing this bill of lading, or carrier on whose line the loss, damage, injury or delay occurred, within nine months after delivery of the property (or, in case of export traffic, within nine months after delivery at the port of export) or, in case of failure to make delivery, then within nine months after a reasonable time for delivery has elapsed; and suits shall be instituted against any carrier only within two years and one day from the day when notice in writing is given by the carrier to the claimant that the carrier has disallowed the claim or any part or parts thereof specified in the notice. Where claims are not filed or suits are not instituted thereon in accordance with the foregoing provisions, no carrier hereunder shall be liable, and such claims will not be paid.

(c) Any carrier or party liable on account of loss of or damage to any of said property shall have the full benefit of any insurance that may have been effected upon or on account of said property, so far as this shall not avoid the policies or contracts of insurance: Provided, That the carrier reimburse the claimant for the premium paid thereon.

This important section has to do in part with the amount recoverable by the shipper or owner of property shipped in case of loss, damage, or delay. It will be noticed that there is no clause under which the amount of loss or damage is to be measured, except in the case of property shipped under a released value agreement. The carrier, in the absence of such an agreement, provided the agreement is of the lawful kind authorized under the terms of the Cummins Amendments, is liable for the full amount of the loss which the shipper or owner of the property has suffered. In the old bill of lading, there was a clause stating, with respect to shipments which had no "agreed value," that "the amount of loss or damage for which any carrier is liable shall be computed on the basis of the value of the property (being the bona fide invoice value, if any, to the consignee, including the freight charges, if prepaid) at the time and place of shipment under this bill of lading."

THE MEASURE OF DAMAGE

Before the Cummins Amendments were passed, a carrier was responsible as at common law for damage to the property it carried. The rule of common law was that the value of the property was the value at destination, "plus interest on such value, from the date when, in general course, the goods should have been delivered, less the unpaid transportation charges, if any." The rule which the carrier had adopted in its bill of lading supplied a convenient and ready method for the determination of the total amount of its liability; state courts of the United States, though by no means unanimous in their attitude, had on several occasions stated that the rule, which was an agreement with the shipper, was a reasonable one which did not do violence to the common law. The Cummins Amendments declared all contracts for the limitation of a carrier's liability, except under specified conditions, to be null and void. The question thereupon arose, was this rule a "limitation" of the carrier's liability? In a famous case decided in 1920, the Supreme Court declared that the rule did limit the carrier's liability, and declared that the carrier was bound to remunerate the shipper for loss and damage to property as required by the common law, which meant that value at destination, and not at point of origin, should be the proper measure of loss.[24] What the shipper was entitled to, under the common law, was what he would have had if the carrier had fulfilled its contract. Consequently, the Commission required the long-standing rule of "place and time of shipment" value to be eliminated from the domestic bill of lading.

Carriers and shippers still get into difficulty occasionally in reaching an agreement as to what actually is the value of goods at destination at the time when, in general course, they should have arrived. With respect to many commodities, where daily prices are set in exchanges by competitive bidding of traders, there is no difficulty in determining the market value, but for most articles of ordinary merchandise there is no such open, free market. The carrier does not want to pay the consignee any more than his cost of the goods, and the consignee would like to include his prospective profit on the goods as a part of his total loss. The rule which is usually employed is that the carrier should pay an amount equal to what it would cost the consignee to "replace" the lost or damaged property. This may occasionally be more or less than the invoice price of the merchandise lost or damaged, inasmuch as the consignee's purchase may have been made at a time long before the date of shipment, and

[24] Chicago, Milwaukee & St. Paul Ry. v. McCaull-Dinsmore Co., 253 U.S. 97 (1920).

prices may have risen or fallen during the interval. Under ordinary circumstances, the retail merchant obtains the wholesale value of the article lost, that is, the cost of purchasing another article of the same kind.

There have been a few cases in which a court has allowed damages based upon the retail value of what was lost. A part of an interstate carload shipment of coal was lost in Massachusetts, and the Supreme Judicial Court of that state awarded damages based upon retail price. It declared that the owner could not be expected to purchase a full carload of coal in order to replace the part of a carload which had been lost and that if he had replaced it in the local market he would have had to pay the retail price. It did not matter, the Court affirmed, that the owner did not actually make a replacement with coal purchased in the local market; the circumstances were such that he was entitled to damage equivalent to retail value regardless of what method he might employ to obtain replacement of the lost coal.[25]

THE CRAIL CASE

In another situation, in which the conditions were exactly parallel, the Supreme Court of the United States took a much different view. This case had a very interesting history. A Minneapolis coal dealer bought a carload of coal. Upon arrival the shipment was short some 5,000 pounds. He brought suit in the Federal District Court of Minnesota to recover from the carrier, the Illinois Central Railroad, the value of the lost coal. The judge awarded damages based upon the wholesale value of the coal.[26] The Circuit Court of Appeals of the Eighth District reversed the district judge, asserting that the owner of the coal was entitled to damages based upon the retail price of coal.[27] Another trial of the suit was held in the district court (necessitated because of changed stipulations by the parties to the controversy), and the judge rendered a decision consonant with the decision of the appellate court.[28] This decision was also taken to the court of appeals, and was upheld,[29] whereupon the railroad company carried the case to the Supreme Court.

The Supreme Court reversed the decision of the lower court, and the award went back to what it had been in the first decision of the district court—damages based upon the wholesale price of the lost coal.[30] Justice

[25] Leominster Fuel Co. v. New York, New Haven and Hartford R.R. 258 Mass. 149 (1927).

[26] Crail v. Illinois Central R.R., 2 F.2d 287 (1924).

[27] 13 F.2d 459 (1926).

[28] 21 F.2d 836 (1927).

[29] 31 F.2d 111 (1929).

[30] Illinois Central R.R. v. Crail, 281 U.S. 57 (1930). Oddly enough, the Massachusetts judge who handed down the decision in the Leominster Fuel Company case referred in his opinion to the Crail case, but the time was before the final decision of the Supreme Court, which reversed the decision he followed;

Stone, who wrote the opinion of the Court, refused to admit the existence of a hard and fast rule by which the amount of damage could be measured. In the actual circumstances of this case, "the cost of replacing the exact shortage at retail price was not the measure of the loss since it was capable of replacement and was, in fact, replaced in the course of the respondent's business from purchases made in carload lots at wholesale market price without added expense." He admitted that if the dealer had been obliged to replace the coal by purchasing at retail in the local market, the measure of the loss would have been based upon the retail price, but such had not been the case. Said the Justice:

There is no greater inconvenience in the application of one standard of value than in the other and we perceive no advantage to be gained from adherence to a rigid uniformity, which would justify sacrificing the reason of the rule to its letter. The test of market value is at best but a convenient means of getting at the loss suffered. It may be discarded and other more accurate means resorted to if, for special reasons, it is not exact or otherwise not applicable.

So, while the common law rule still prevails, that the claimant is entitled to that which he would have had if the carrier had fulfilled its contract, the exact manner and method of determining the amount of reimbursement a claimant should receive when a shipment is lost depends upon the circumstances of each case.

It should be mentioned here, as a matter of interest, that in the uniform through export bill of lading, which a few rail carriers still issue, there remains a clause limiting the amount which a shipper may recover for lost or damaged property to the value at place and time of shipment. The Cummins Amendments do not apply to contracts for transportation to a nonadjacent foreign country, but only to our interstate commerce and to commerce with adjacent foreign countries. Consequently, the through export bill of lading was not subjected to the same changes the Commission required to be made in the domestic bill. Moreover, in the through export bill of lading, the carrier disclaims liability for any loss, damage, or injury not occurring on its own road or water line. The Carmack Amendment likewise does not apply to commerce with nonadjacent foreign countries. Before 1906, the railroad bill of lading contained the disclaimer for liability for losses occurring on connecting lines now to be found in the export bill. After the passage of the Carmack Amendment, the railroad bill of lading declared that no carrier would be liable for loss, damage, or injury not occurring on its own line or route, or its portion of a through

---

he had read the decision awarding damages based on the retail price. Had the final word of the Supreme Court been available to him, he would doubtless have taken into consideration the manner in which it had been necessary for the dealer to replace the missing coal.

route, "except as such liability may be imposed by law but nothing contained in this bill of lading shall be deemed to exempt the initial carrier from any such liability so imposed." Whether this was a bit of "camouflage" by which the carrier hoped to impress a shipper who might be ignorant of his legal rights, it is not possible to say, but since from a strictly legal standpoint the words were without significance, the Commission required their elimination from the bill of lading.

REASONABLE DISPATCH

A railroad is bound to transport the property it carries with "reasonable dispatch," and if the shipper or owner of the property suffers a loss because of the unreasonable delay, the carrier is liable for the loss. If the grower of fruits or vegetables sends a carload of his produce to a market, and because of an unreasonable delay on the part of the carrier he is forced to accept a price lower than that which he would have received had his shipment been carried with reasonable dispatch, he can hold the carrier liable for the loss.

There are certain aspects of the responsibility of the carrier for unreasonable delay with which the shipper should be familiar. The carrier is not liable for "special" or "consequential" damages, unless it has been put upon notice of the loss which the shipper would suffer were the transportation service conducted with unreasonable delay. Under ordinary circumstances, what the carrier is liable for is the difference between the value of the goods had they been conveyed with reasonable dispatch and the value they had at the actual time of arrival. Should a gardener be unable to plant his garden because of a carrier's negligent delay in transporting the seed he planned to use, he cannot hold the carrier liable for the prospective value of the garden but only for whatever was lost in the value of the seeds. A certain canning factory in Vermont was unable to proceed with its operations because a railroad was negligently guilty of delay in the delivery of two carloads of cans which had been ordered. Because of its inability to carry on its canning operations, the canning company, to hold its losses to a minimum, sold back to the farmers the produce which it had purchased, at a much smaller price than it had paid, thereby suffering a loss of several hundred dollars. But it could not secure reimbursement from the negligent carrier for this "special" damage; all it could obtain was what the cans themselves had lost in value. A contractor who is building a bridge or other structure on a "penalty" contract cannot hold a carrier responsible for any loss he suffers because of negligent delay in the transportation of steel and other materials, unless at the time of shipment the carrier was duly notified of the loss which the contractor would suffer if delay occurred. Mere notification of a carrier that it must transport any shipment with reasonable dispatch is not necessarily enough to cause any addition to the ordinary liability of the carrier. There must be a definite certainty that there would be a loss if the property did not arrive with reasonable dispatch.

TIME FOR FILING CLAIMS AND SUITS

Subsection (b) of the second section of the terms and conditions of the bill of lading is virtually a repetition of the provisions found in part of section 20 of the Interstate Commerce Act, except that the statute is negative in its wording, stating that the time for filing claims shall not be less than nine months and the time for instituting a suit not less than two years. The carrier could, if it so desired and the Commission consented, provide for longer periods.

There have been numerous changes in this particular feature of the bill of lading. The first Cummins Amendment stipulated that the time for giving "notice of claims" should not be less than ninety days, for "filing claims" not less than four months, and for the institution of suits not less than two years. The amendment also said that "if the loss, or damage or injury complained of was due to delay or damage while being loaded or unloaded, or damaged in transit by carelessness or negligence, then no notice of claim nor filing of claim shall be required as a condition precedent to recovery." The distinction between "notice of claim" and "claim," as well as the highly ungrammatical and literally meaningless phrases about the loss or damage being due to "negligence while being loaded or unloaded," has long since been dropped from both the law and the bill of lading, and need not concern us here.[31] However, it would be well to say a few words about the limitation of time for filing claims and instituting suits.

When the Commission handed down its decision in 1919, in which it prescribed a form of bill of lading for the carriers to use, the bill of lading customarily used by the carriers followed the terms of the first Cummins Amendment, except that the time for filing claims was six months instead of four. The bill said that "any suits for loss, damage or delay shall be instituted only within two years and one day after delivery of the property, or, in case of failure to deliver, then within two years and one day after a reasonable time for delivery has elapsed." In its order prescribing the form of domestic bill of lading to be used by the carriers, the Commission left this feature of the terms and conditions unchanged. Shortly after it had issued the order, in 1919, however, it received a complaint from one Decker and Sons, charging that a railroad had denied any liability for loss or damage solely on the ground that suit had not been instituted within the statutory period. At the same time, the National In-

---

[31] The atrocious language was revised and made understandable in 1927, and the phrase dropped entirely in 1930.

dustrial Traffic League lodged a complaint with the Commission alleging that some railroads had a practice of paying some claims after the expiration of the two-year-and-one-day period but refusing to pay others, however meritorious the claims might be. Obviously such a practice on the part of any carrier was unjustly discriminatory and unduly prejudicial.

THE DECKER CASE

In its decision in the so-called "Decker case," handed down in December, 1919, the Commission took the position that it was entirely legal for a carrier to settle a meritorious claim, seasonably filed, after the expiration of the two years and one day in which suits might be instituted. The purpose of the limitation with regard to the time of instituting a suit, the Commission declared, was not to enable the carrier to escape its liability for loss or damage, and the filing of a suit was not "a condition precedent to the consideration upon its merits or the payment of a valid claim seasonably filed." [32] It meant only that, if the carrier was to be called upon to defend a suit, the suit must be filed within the two-year-and-one-day period.

Because of the lack of uniformity of practice among carriers and the possibility of undue discrimination arising from varying interpretations of the limitation provisions of the bill, the Commisson decided the section dealing with them, to which it had previously given approval, to be "unreasonable, unjustly discriminatory, and unduly prejudicial," and ordered it to be changed so as to provide that if a duly filed claim had not been declined in writing by the carrier before the beginning of the last six months of the two-year-and-one-day period, then suit might be filed within six months from the time the claim was declined. Failure to file claims within the stipulated time, as well as failure to file a suit within the proper period, was to relieve the carrier of liability, and such claims were not to be paid.

The Commission observed that it would be necessary for it to modify its order in its earlier decision prescribing the forms of bills of lading a carrier should employ.

THE LAW AMENDED

The decision in the Decker case was the occasion for much comment, adverse and otherwise, and in some quarters it was suggested that the Commission was exceeding its statutory authority and trying to do something which only Congress had the right to do. In order that any doubt about the matter might be dispelled, Congress inserted in the Transportation Act of 1920 a brief amendment to section 20 of the Interstate Commerce Act to the effect that it should be unlawful for a carrier

[32] Jacob E. Decker & Sons v. Director General, 55 I.C.C. 304 (1919).

. . . to provide by rules, contract, regulation or otherwise a shorter period for giving notice of claim than ninety days, for filing of claims than four months,[33] and for the institution of suits than two years, such period for institution of suits to be computed from the day when notice in writing is given by the carrier to the claimant that the carrier has disallowed the claim or any part or parts thereof specified in the notice.

The language is substantially the same today, except that the phrase about "notice of claim" has been dropped, and the time for filing claims is now nine months instead of four. This amendment in the law was one of the changes which led the Supreme Court to declare the Alaska Steamship Company case, in which the right of the Commission to prescribe the form of bills of lading was challenged, to be "moot."

The decision of the Commission and the wholesome change in the law put an end to the abuse on the part of carriers, who were wont to keep a claim alive by "stalling" tactics for two years and one day and then blandly inform a claimant that his case could no longer be given any consideration because of the statute of limitations. Not only had this practice subjected shippers to undeserved loss, but it had made not a few of them the victims of a peculiarly objectionable form of undue discrimination and unjust prejudice.

[33] In 1930, Congress dropped the expression "notice of claim" and extended the period of filing claims to not less than nine months. A decision of the Supreme Court had noted that there was no practical difference between a claim and a notice of claim. Georgia, Florida & Alabama Ry. v. Blish Milling Co., 241 U.S. 190 (1916). See also Minot Beverage Co. v. Minneapolis & St. Louis Ry., 65 F. Supp. 293 (1946), in which the court said, "The deletion of the requirement for a notice of claim fairly implies . . . that Congress recognized the similarity between the notice and the claim and intended to avoid much of the trouble which arose in determining whether a given communication was a claim or only a notice of claim."

CHAPTER XII

Other Terms and Conditions of the Bill of Lading: Additional Shipping Papers

The third section of the uniform domestic bill of lading now in use goes as follows:

Sec. 3. Except where such service is required as the result of carrier's negligence, all property shall be subject to necessary cooperage and baling at owner's cost. Each carrier over whose route cotton or cotton linters is to be transported hereunder shall have the privilege, at its own cost and risk, of compressing the same for greater convenience in handling or forwarding, and shall not be held responsible for deviation or unavoidable delays in procuring such compression. Grain in bulk consigned to a point where there is a railroad, public or licensed elevator, may (unless otherwise expressly noted herein, and then if it is not promptly unloaded) be there delivered and placed with other grain of the same kind and grade without respect to ownership (and prompt notice thereof shall be given to the consignor), and if so delivered shall be subject to a lien for elevator charges in addition to all other charges hereunder.

The first parts of this section are self-explanatory; they are entirely reasonable, since they serve to promote the safety of transportation and lead to greater efficiency in the use of carrier equipment. The rule with respect to grain is an especially useful one. It is difficult to see how the great annual flood of American grain which the railroads carry to market could be adequately cared for without such a rule. To "preserve the identity" of the thousands of bulk shipments of grain which go from field to elevator and mill each year would be an impossible task without a very great enlargement of our transportation and storage equipment as well as numerous changes in its character. The cultivation, harvesting, and transportation of our great grain crops constitute one of the best examples we have of the application of mass methods of production. It is mechanization at its best; it stirs the wonder and admiration of foreign visitors from lands where primitive hand methods of agriculture are still common practice; and it does something to explain how the people of this country have been able to reach and maintain a high standard of living.

BILL OF LADING CONDITIONS: SECTION 4

There are six subsections to the fourth section of the terms and conditions of the bill of lading, and it will be possible to deal with them more intelligibly if we separate them somewhat in our discussion. The first subsection is as follows:

Sec. 4. (a) Property not removed by the party entitled to receive it within the free time allowed by tariffs, lawfully on file (such free time to be computed as therein provided), after notice of the arrival of the property at destination or at the port of export (if intended for export) has been duly sent or given, and after placement of the property for delivery at destination has been made, may be kept in vessel, car, depot, warehouse or place of delivery of the carrier, subject to the tariff charge for storage and to carrier's responsibility as warehouseman only, or at the option of the carrier, may be removed to and stored in a public or licensed warehouse at the place of delivery or other available place, at the cost of the owner, and there held without liability on the part of the carrier, and subject to a lien for all freight and other lawful charges, including a reasonable charge for storage.

It will be observed that the statement of carrier's liability in this subsection is the same as that employed in the first section of the bill of lading concerning property which is destroyed by fire after the expiration of free time. But if property is unclaimed after the expiration of free time, the carrier has the choice of storing it on the carrier's own premises or of having it conveyed to a public warehouse for safekeeping at the expense of the owner. In many small communities, it is the practice of railroads to store unclaimed property for a limited time in a freight house. In larger cities, however, where the storage space in freight houses is likely to be limited, it is customary for the carrier to have nonperishable unclaimed freight carted promptly to a public warehouse where the owner may claim it after the payment of all accrued charges.

The next subsection of section 4 tells what the carrier may do with freight refused by the consignee or freight which it seems probable will remain unclaimed:

Sec. 4. (b) Where nonperishable property which has been transported to destination hereunder is refused by consignee or the party entitled to receive it, or said consignee or party entitled to receive it fails to receive it within 15 days after notice of arrival shall have been duly sent or given, the carrier may sell the same at public auction to the highest bidder, at such place as may be designated by the carrier: Provided, That the carrier shall have first mailed, sent or given to the consignor notice that the property has been refused or remains unclaimed, as the case may be, and that it will be subject to sale under the terms of the bill of lading if disposition be not arranged for, and shall have published notice containing a description of the property, the name of the party to whom consigned, or, if shipped order notify, the name of the party to be notified, and the time and place of sale once a week for two successive weeks, in a newspaper of general circulation at the place of sale or nearest place where such newspaper is published: Provided, That 30 days shall have elapsed before publication of notice of sale after said notice that the property was refused or remains unclaimed was mailed, sent, or given.

This clause of the conditions of the bill may throw some light on why the carrier provides in its classification that a shipper may be required to prepay freight charges on all property which, at a forced sale, would not yield enough to defray freight charges. All carriers are bound, through the course of the year, to be left with a certain amount of unclaimed or abandoned property in their possession. One frequently sees, in the newspapers published in cities where carriers hold the auction sales of unclaimed freight, the advertisements describing the property to be sold.

An interesting thing about this part of the bill of lading is that it introduces a new factor into the business responsibilities of a common carrier—the relation it must perforce bear to the buyer and the seller of the goods which it carries. The carrier is not at fault because the goods are refused or unclaimed, but it must have some kind of obligation to the owner, some duty to perform, before it resorts to a forced sale for the recovery of its freight charges. We are not directly concerned with the legal relations between and the mutual obligations of buyer and seller, but a question arises as to the rights of the two parties with respect to a refused or unclaimed shipment.

What should the seller do when he receives a notice from a carrier that a shipment of goods which he has sold to a certain consignee has been refused and remains in the carrier's possession? When a seller makes a contract with a buyer for the sale of certain goods or merchandise at an agreed price, and the seller turns the goods or merchandise over to a carrier for delivery to the buyer, the seller has fulfilled his obligation under the contract of sale, if the goods come fully up to the specifications of the contract.[1] The buyer refuses them at his peril; since the seller has fulfilled his part of the obligation, he has the right to collect by suit at law the amount due him from the buyer under the terms of the contract. In this case, the seller may choose to ignore the carrier's notice that the ship-

---

[1] Of course, the seller must protect the interest of the buyer in a reasonable manner. He must choose a carrier presumed to be reliable, and he must protect the buyer against loss due the seller's negligent conduct. For example, if a seller should ship by express a package the value of which is several hundred dollars, and permit it to go at a "released value" of $50, he could hardly expect to collect the full value of the goods from the buyer, in case they were lost, even though he had turned them over to a presumably responsible carrier for transportation.

ment has been refused or remains unclaimed, and endeavor to make the buyer pay. Ordinarily, however, the seller, willing to keep down a possible loss, and perhaps uncertain about the results of any legal action he might take to collect what is due from the buyer, will not abandon the goods, but will repossess them and give the carrier instructions as to their disposition, either to return them or perhaps deliver them to another purchaser. Of course the seller, under these circumstances, becomes responsible for the freight and other charges which lie against the shipment, but the loss incurred because of the necessity of meeting these obligations may be less than he would suffer if he tried to pursue his claim against the reluctant buyer. It may be, too, that the buyer has "disappeared," after the purchase was made, and the seller finds that repossession of the shipment is the most economical procedure for him to follow.

The carrier's actions with respect to unclaimed perishable property is somewhat different. The next subsection of the fourth section provides:

Sec. 4. (c) Where perishable property which has been transported hereunder to destination is refused by consignee or party entitled to receive it, or said consignee or party entitled to receive it shall fail to receive it promptly, the carrier may, in its discretion, to prevent deterioration or further deterioration, sell the same to the best advantage at private or public sale: Provided, That if time serves for notification to the consignor or owner of the refusal of the property or the failure to receive it and request for disposition of the property, such notification shall be given, in such manner as the exercise of due diligence requires, before the property is sold.

This is an entirely reasonable provision, by which the carrier obtains a measure of protection against loss of its freight and other charges, and the shipper, if time is available, can dispose of the property to his best advantage. The carrier must be on guard to send a proper notification to the consignor, if it is possible to do so, or become responsible for any loss that might result from its failure to observe the terms of this portion of the contract.

The other three subsections of the fourth section of the terms of the bill of lading are largely self-explanatory:

Sec. 4. (d) Where the procedure provided for in the two paragraphs last preceding is not possible, it is agreed that nothing contained in said paragraphs shall be construed to abridge the right of the carrier at its option to sell the property under such circumstances and in such manner as may be authorized by law.

(e) The proceeds of any sale made under this section shall be applied by the carrier to the payment of freight, demurrage, storage, and any other lawful charges and the expense of notice, advertisement, sale, and other necessary expense and of caring for and maintaining the property, if proper care of the same requires special expense, and should there be a balance it shall be paid to the owner of the property sold hereunder.

(f) Property destined to or taken from a station, wharf, or landing at which there is no regularly appointed freight agent shall be entirely at risk of owner after unloaded from cars or vessels or until loaded into cars or vessels, and, except in case of carrier's negligence, when received from or delivered to such stations, wharves, or landings shall be at owner's risk until the cars are attached to and after they are detached from locomotive or train or until loaded into and after unloaded from vessels.

Subsection (f) relieves the carrier of liability for freight which is on a platform at a nonagency station, waiting to be loaded or called for by the consignee. It also relieves the carrier of liability, except in case of negligence, for freight which is loaded in a car at such a station, until the car is attached to a train, and for freight which remains in a car at a siding at such a station previous to its unloading. In the old bill of lading, there was a provision relieving the carrier of liability for freight in detached cars at all sidings, private or public, except in case of negligence. In other words, the carrier took the position that it was liable, as a carrier, only for freight that passed through a freight house. The Commission held that the Cummins Amendments made the carrier responsible, as a carrier, for property received and delivered in cars at public and at certain private sidings, and required the last subsection quoted above to be rewritten in substantially its present form.

BILL OF LADING CONDITIONS: SECTIONS 5 AND 6

The next two sections of the terms of the bill of lading are designed to give the carrier a certain measure of protection against losses for which it should not in any event be required to assume responsibility. One of these provisions has been alluded to previously in the discussion of the rules of the classification.

Sec. 5. No carrier hereunder will carry or be liable in any way for any documents, specie, or for any articles of extraordinary value not specifically rated in the published classifications or tariffs unless a special agreement to do so and a stipulated value of the articles are indorsed hereon.

Sec. 6. Every party, whether principal or agent, shipping explosives or dangerous goods, without previous full written disclosure to the carrier of their nature, shall be liable for and indemnify the carrier against all loss or damage caused by such goods, and such goods may be warehoused at owner's risk and expense or destroyed without compensation.

BILL OF LADING CONDITIONS: SECTION 7

The seventh section of the terms and conditions of the bill of lading is one of the longest sections. A large part of it, dealing with the liability of an agent for freight charges, is taken almost verbatim from the so-called Newton Amendment, which was added to the first part of the Interstate Commerce Act in 1927.

Sec. 7. The owner or consignee shall pay the freight and average, if any, and all other lawful charges accruing on said property; but except in those instances where it may lawfully be authorized to do so, no carrier by railroad shall deliver or relinquish possession at destination of the property covered by this bill of lading until all tariff rates and charges thereon have been paid. The consignor shall be liable for the freight and all other lawful charges, except that if the consignor stipulates, by signature, in the space provided for that purpose on the face of this bill of lading that the carrier shall not make delivery without requiring payment of such charges and the carrier, contrary to such stipulation, shall make delivery without requiring such payment, the consignor (except as hereinafter provided) shall not be liable for such charges. Provided, that, where the carrier has been instructed by the shipper or consignor to deliver said property to a consignee other than the shipper or consignor, such consignee shall not be legally liable for transportation charges in respect of the transportation of said property (beyond those billed against him at the time of delivery for which he is otherwise liable) which may be found to be due after the property has been delivered to him, if the consignee (a) is an agent only and has no beneficial title in said property, and (b) prior to delivery of said property has notified the delivering carrier in writing of the fact of such agency and absence of beneficial title, and, in the case of a shipment reconsigned or diverted to a point other than that specified in the original bill of lading, has also notified the delivering carrier in writing of the name and address of the beneficial owner of said property; and, in such cases the shipper or consignor, or, in the case of a shipment so reconsigned or diverted, the beneficial owner, shall be liable for such additional charges. If the consignee has given to the carrier erroneous information as to who the beneficial owner is, such consignee shall himself be liable for such additional charges. On shipments reconsigned or diverted by an agent who has furnished the carrier in the reconsignment or diversion order with a notice of agency and the proper name and address of the beneficial owner, and where such shipments are refused or abandoned at ultimate destination, the said beneficial owner shall be liable for all legally applicable charges in connection therewith. If the reconsignor or diverter has given to the carrier erroneous information as to who the beneficial owner is, such reconsignor or diverter shall himself be liable for all such charges.

If a shipper or consignor of a shipment of property (other than a prepaid shipment) is also the consignee named in the bill of lading and, prior to the time of delivery, notifies, in writing, a delivering carrier by railroad (a) to deliver such property at destination to another party, (b) that such party is the beneficial owner of such property, and (c) that delivery is to be made to such party only upon payment of all transportation charges in respect of the transportation of such property, and delivery is made by the carrier to such party without such payment, such shipper or consignor shall not be liable (as shipper, consignor, consignee or otherwise) for such transportation charges but the party to whom delivery is so made shall in any event be liable for transportation charges billed against the property at the time of such delivery, and also for any additional charges which may be found to be due after delivery of the property, except that if such party prior to such delivery has notified in writing the delivering carrier that he is not the beneficial owner of the property, and has given in writing to such delivering carrier the name and address of such beneficial owner, such party shall not be liable for any additional charges which may be found to be due after delivery of the property; but if the party to whom delivery is made has given to the carrier erroneous information as to the beneficial owner, such party shall nevertheless be liable for such additional charges. If the shipper or consignor has given to the delivering carrier erroneous information as to who the beneficial owner is, such shipper or consignor shall himself be liable for such transportation charges, notwithstanding the foregoing provisions of this paragraph and irrespective of any provisions to the contrary in the bill of lading or in the contract of transportation under which the shipment was made. The term delivering carrier means the line-haul carrier making ultimate delivery.

Nothing herein shall limit the right of the carrier to require at time of shipment the prepayment or guarantee of the charges. If upon inspection it is ascertained that the articles shipped are not those described in this bill of lading, the freight charges must be paid upon the articles actually shipped.

Where delivery is made by a common carrier by water the foregoing provisions of this section shall apply, except as may be inconsistent with part III of the Interstate Commerce Act.

The first part of this long section dealing with the shipper's right to require the carrier to collect freight and other charges from the consignee we discussed previously, when we described the nonrecourse clause on the face of the bill of lading. The exceptional circumstances under which a consignor may still be held liable for transportation charges arrive when he makes a shipment which is handled by an agent. Many shipments of goods are consigned to "commission" men, who act as the real sellers' agents in the disposal of property. This section of the bill of lading indicates the procedure these agents must follow if they desire to escape liability for a carrier's lawful charges. Although the language seems a little more involved and circumlocutory than should be necessary, the meaning is apparent. This section of the terms of the bill should be studied carefully by all shippers who consign goods to be sold by an agent, by the agents who handle such transactions, and by consignees who become the beneficial owners of such shipments.

BILL OF LADING CONDITIONS: SECTIONS 8, 9, AND 10

The eighth section of the terms and conditions of the bill of lading provides that if "this" bill is one that, on the order of the shipper, has been exchanged for a preceding bill, the signature of the shipper to any stipulations on the prior bill of lading shall be considered a part of "this" bill.

The ninth section has to do with the liability of carriers by water. It must be understood that, as provided in the last subsection of this section, "water carriage" does not include "lighterage on or across rivers, harbors, or lakes, when performed by or on behalf of rail carriers." The great mass of freight which is lightered and floated across the Hudson River and the other waters of the Port of New York is still moving under the liability which attaches to the railroad for which the freight is being transferred about the port. The same is true with respect to the freight which the Ann Arbor and other railroads move by car ferry across Lake Michigan.

Some carriers by water which participate in through rail-and-water shipments assume the full liability of a rail carrier, and so provide in their tariffs. To the shipments moved under such tariffs the limited liability provisions of section 9 do not apply. The entire section reads as follows:

Sec. 9. (a) If all or any part of said property is carried by water over any part of said route, and loss, damage, or injury to said property occurs while the same is in the custody of a carrier by water the liability of such carrier shall be determined by the bill of lading of the carrier by water (this bill of lading being such bill of lading if the property is transported by such water carrier thereunder) and by and under the laws and regulations applicable to transportation by water. Such water carriage shall be performed subject to all the terms and provisions of, and all the exemptions from liability contained in the Act of the Congress of the United States, approved on February 13, 1893, and entitled "An act relating to the navigation of vessels, etc.," and of other statutes of the United States according carriers by water the protection of limited liability, as well as the following subdivisions of this section; and to the conditions contained in this bill of lading not inconsistent with this section, when this bill of lading becomes the bill of lading of the carrier by water.

(b) No such carrier by water shall be liable for any loss or damage resulting from any fire happening to or on board the vessel, or from explosion, bursting of boilers or breakage of shafts, unless caused by the design or neglect of such carrier.

(c) If the owner shall have exercised due diligence in making the vessel in all respects seaworthy and properly manned, equipped and supplied, no such carrier shall be liable for any loss or damage resulting from the perils of the lakes, seas, or other waters, or from latent defects in hull, machinery, or appurtenances, whether existing prior to, at the time of, or after sailing, or from collision, stranding, or other accidents of navigation, or from prolongation of the voyage. And, when for any reason it is necessary, any vessel carrying any or all of the property herein described shall be at liberty to call at any port or ports, in or out of the customary route, to tow and be towed, to transfer, trans-ship, or lighter, to load and discharge goods at any time, to assist vessels in distress, to deviate for the purpose of saving life or property, and for docking and repairs. Except in case of negligence such carrier shall not be responsible for any loss or damage to property if it be necessary or is usual to carry the same upon deck.

(d) General Average shall be payable according to the York-Antwerp rules of 1924, Sections 1 to 15, inclusive, and Sections 17 to 22, inclusive, and as to matters not covered thereby according to the laws and usages of the Port of New York. If the owners shall have exercised due diligence to make the vessel in all respects seaworthy and properly manned, equipped and supplied, it is hereby agreed that in case of danger, damage or disaster resulting from faults or errors in navigation, or in the management of the vessel, or from any latent or other defects in the vessel, her machinery or appurtenances, or from unseaworthiness, whether existing at the time of shipment or at the beginning of the voyage (provided the latent or other defects or the unseaworthiness was not discoverable by the exercise of due diligence), the shippers consignees and/or owners of the cargo shall nevertheless pay salvage and any special charges incurred in respect of the cargo, and shall contribute with the shipowner in general average to the payment of any sacrifices, losses or expenses of a general average nature that may be made or incurred for the common benefit or to relieve the adventure from any common peril.

(e) If the property is being carried under a tariff which provides that any carrier or carriers party thereto shall be liable for loss from perils of the sea, then as to such carrier or carriers the provisions of this section shall be modified in accordance with the tariff provisions, which shall be regarded as incorporated into the conditions of this bill of lading.

(f) The term "water carriage" in this section shall not be construed as including lighterage in or across rivers, harbors, or lakes, when performed by or on behalf of rail carriers.

Like railroad carriers, virtually all carriers by water for many years followed the practice of including within the terms and conditions of their bills of lading various clauses under which they were totally exempt from responsibility for loss and damage due to certain specified causes, or which, in the event of responsibility, greatly limited the amount which a shipper or owner could recover. It took the government of the United States a long time to enact any general statute dealing with the liability of carriers by water, though near the middle of the nineteenth century Congress passed laws under which shipowners received a certain measure of freedom from liability for loss and damage.

The so-called Limited Liability Act of 1851 exempted a shipowner from liability for losses due to fire on a vessel, unless the fire was caused by the negligence or design of the owner or his agent. Perhaps a more important provision of the law, so far as shippers were concerned, was that the limit of the amount recoverable by shipper who suffered a loss for which the carrier was responsible was the value of the shipowner's interest in the vessel and the freight earnings for the voyage on which the loss or damage occurred. If the ship went down in a storm because of some dereliction of duty on the part of the owner or his agents, the amount which owners of lost cargo were able to recover might be very small indeed. An odd feature of the law with respect to the carrier's liability was that the shipper of lost cargo would have no claim against any insurance the owner might carry on the ship itself. In other words, the owner might be fully reimbursed for the loss of the ship, but a shipper, whose cargo had not been insured, would suffer a total loss, even though the owner was legally responsible for the occurrence which brought about the loss.

Great Britain and other leading maritime nations have long had limited liability statutes similar to that of the United States. Since the latter part of the eighteenth century, Great Britain has had a statute which gives some measure of protection to passengers or their relatives who might suffer by reason of an accident at sea for which the shipowner could be held responsible. Even though the ship is a total loss, the owner is responsible for personal injuries to the extent of an amount equal to £5 multiplied by the figure representing the gross tonnage of the ship. For many years the United States had no such law, but after the *Morro Castle* disaster, in which so many passengers lost their lives, Congress enacted a law patterned after that of Great Britain, under the terms of which the owner's liability for personal injury and loss of life to passengers became an amount equal at least to $60 a ton of the vessel involved in the accident. This law was passed in August, 1935.

THE HARTER ACT

The Harter Act of 1893, though it did little to modify the long-standing rules of liability to which a shipowner was subject, at least made it plain that there was a limit beyond which the owner could not go in exempting himself from liability in the terms and conditions of the bill of lading. The very first section of the Act declares that it shall not be lawful for the owner of a vessel, or his agent, to insert in a bill of lading or other shipping document any clause whereby he is "relieved from liability for loss or damage arising from negligence, fault, or failure in proper loading, stowage, custody, care, or proper delivery of merchandise or property committed" to his charge. Moreover, the law stated that any such provision in a bill of lading should be "null and void and of no effect." It can be seen that this law does not go nearly so far as the Carmack and Cummins Amendments, which deal with the liability of a rail carrier. A shipowner has an unqualified and inescapable duty to cargo consisting of proper loading and stowage, care and custody, and proper delivery. If certain cargo is stowed so that it is damaged by other cargo, the shipowner is responsible for any loss. Cargo should be loaded in such a manner that it will not shift in ordinary weather. If it shifts because of improper stowage, and the ship is lost, the shipowner is liable, though, as explained before, the amount for which he is liable under these circumstances may be quite small. But if the shifting of the cargo causes the ship to take on water and results in heavy damages to the contents of the holds, and the vessel makes port safely, the amount which the owner must pay may be very large.

The Harter Act imposes no mandate on the shipowner to exercise due diligence in seeing that a vessel is seaworthy and properly manned and equipped, but by implication it says that if the owner does *not* take these precautions, he may become liable for any loss which occurs during a voyage, whatever the cause. In other words, the statute provides that "if" the owner shall exercise due diligence to carry out these duties connected with preparing a vessel for a voyage, neither the vessel nor the owner shall be held

. . . responsible for damage or loss resulting from faults or errors in navigation or in the management of said vessel, nor shall the vessel, her owner or owners, charterers, agent, or master be held liable for losses arising from dangers of the sea or other navigable waters, acts of God, or public enemies, or the inherent defects, quality, or vice of the thing carried, or from insufficiency of package, or seizure under legal process, or from loss resulting from any act or omission of the shipper or owner of the goods, his agent or representative, or from saving or attempting to save life or property at sea, or from any deviation in rendering such assistance.

One might be led to infer, from the language employed in this third section of the Harter Act, that if the shipowner was wanting in due diligence to see that his vessel was properly prepared for the voyage, he might be held liable for losses due to acts of God, the public enemy, inherent defects of the goods, or the faults of the shipper or owner. This would, of course, be an incorrect inference. Under no circumstances would a carrier, either by land or by water, be held liable for any loss due entirely and exclusively to an act of God or of the public enemy. There are certain kinds of losses for which the owner of a vessel may not be held liable, however neglectful he may have been in the performance of his common law obligations.

If the owner has exercised proper care—or due diligence—in fitting the ship for a voyage, his liability is only that which is connected with the stowage and care of cargo. The master of the ship may become intoxicated or otherwise rendered unfit for duty and steer his vessel aground, but the owner is not responsible. A driving shaft may break because of a long-standing latent defect, but if the defect was such that an inspection conducted with "due diligence" did not reveal it, the owner escapes liability for any loss due to the accident. But if a ship is sent out in an unseaworthy condition because of defects or dangerous conditions which would have been revealed by diligent inspection, and some disaster takes place, the owner is responsible for any loss the owners of cargo suffer.

Although the Harter Act states that if the owner *does* exercise due diligence to see that his vessel is properly prepared for a voyage he will *not* be liable for loss or damage due to the causes enumerated above, it does not state that if the owner *does not* exercise due diligence to prepare the vessel properly he shall be held for loss and damage due to those causes—although the second section of the Act provides that it shall "not be lawful" for the owner or his representative to insert in any bill of lading or shipping document any agreement whereby the "obligations" of the owner to exercise due diligence properly to prepare a vessel for a voyage or the obligations of the master, officers, or agents "to carefully handle and stow her cargo and to care for and properly deliver same shall be in any wise lessened, weakened or avoided." The law does not say explicitly that the owner and master have certain "obligations" with respect to the preparation of the ship for a voyage or its navigation during a voyage, but merely that they shall not evade the obligations they have, whatever they may be. Under the common law, it had long been held that the owner had certain duties with regard to the preparation of the ship and the care of its cargo, but also, under the common law, it had been possible for the shipowner to dodge some of his common law duties by contract or to limit the amount a shipper could recover in case of loss. Obviously, if it were possible for a shipowner to modify any of his supposed common law duties by contract, they were no longer obligations. The roundabout, largely negative way in which the Harter Act was worded makes it difficult to interpret, and raises some questions as to the exact character of the obligations of a carrier by water. At any rate, there is an implied obligation by the owner to exercise "due diligence" to see that his vessel has been adequately inspected for defects and properly manned and equipped; if these things have been done, his responsibilities for loss are greatly diminished. Before the passage of the Harter Act, it had been a common practice to hold shipowners liable for all loss or damage due to a vessel's unseaworthiness, even though it was caused by a latent defect which adequate inspection had not revealed. To the extent that the law made the owner responsible only if he failed to employ "due diligence" —in other words, if he were negligent—it was an act for the limitation of carrier's liability.

CARRIAGE OF GOODS BY SEA ACT

The Carriage of Goods by Sea Act—which Congress passed in 1936 and which represents the statutory embodiment of the so-called Hague Rules, adopted by the representatives of leading maritime nations in 1921 and interpreted and recommended for national legislative action by the Brussels Convention of 1924—applies to shipowners and vessels engaged in our foreign trade, and it may likewise be employed, at the option of the shipowner, in our domestic water-borne commerce. Very few of our domestic carriers by water, however, have adopted the provisions of the Carriage of Goods by Sea Act; most of them still operate under the terms of the Harter Act. Since we are not interested here in our foreign water-borne trade, it will not be necessary to discuss the terms of the Carriage of Goods by Sea Act. It might be stated, however, that the persons who drafted the law managed to avoid the negative language employed in the Harter Act and to give positive and clear mandates to shipowners and operators. For example, the law does not state that the carrier is exempt from certain liability "if" it performs certain duties with regard to preparation for a voyage. It says in plain language (section 3) that the "carrier shall be bound, before and at the beginning of a voyage, to exercise due diligence to make the ship seaworthy; properly man, equip and supply the ship; make the holds . . . and all other parts of the ship in which goods are carried, fit and safe for their reception, carriage and preservation." Liability for losses due to unseaworthiness are not incurred unless the losses were caused by a want of due diligence properly to inspect and prepare the vessel. Exemption from liability for losses due to faults of the master, pilot, or servants in the navigation of the vessel; for losses due to fire unless caused by the actual fault or privity of the owner; for losses due to perils of the sea and other navigable waters, act of God, act of war, act of the public enemy, and several other causes is complete and unqualified, without any modifying "if" phrase. The statute includes within its terms all the liabilities, and the exemptions and limitations, which were long accorded to shipowners under common law, as well as certain duties, obligations, and immunities about which there was some uncertainty under common law practice and the terms of the Harter Act. It would not be amiss for Congress to place domestic carriers by water under the Carriage of Goods by Sea Act, or at least add some clarifying amendments to the Harter Act.

GENERAL AVERAGE

Subsection (d) of section 9 of the terms and conditions has reference to a very old practice in transportation by water. Whenever a ship sets forth on a voyage, it becomes a common venture in which both shipowner and the owners of cargo have certain rights, immunities, and responsibilities. There is always danger to be encountered, the most common and the most feared danger being the "perils of the sea," a danger that cannot be avoided and sometimes cannot be escaped without severe loss. It may happen, and it has happened, times without number, that in case of danger the master of the vessel has come to the conclusion that he would have a better chance to save his ship, the crew, and at least a part of the cargo by "lightening the ship"—throwing overboard a portion of the cargo and even part of the ship's tackle. When a voluntary sacrifice of this kind is made, which is ordered or consented to by the master, the loss is regarded as "general" loss, and all parties to the venture—the owner of the ship and the various owners of the cargo—are by custom and by law required to share the loss in proportion to their interest in the total venture. The loss does not fall solely upon the shipper or the shipowner whose property was sacrificed for the benefit of all concerned in the common undertaking. Over the centuries, the maritime interests have formulated and codified rules by which the loss for which each member of the joint venture is liable can be calculated. Since the carrier must also share in the loss known as "general average," the bill of lading calls attention to the rules under which the carrier's share of responsibility is to be determined. We shall discuss general average and other kinds of maritime losses more fully in a subsequent chapter dealing with insurance.

The tenth and final section of the terms and conditions of the domestic bill of lading is very brief. It warns that any change or erasure made in the bill of lading without the special notation of the agent of the carrier shall be without effect and that the bill will be "enforceable according to its original tenor."

BILLS OF LADING OF CARRIERS BY WATER

The bills of lading issued by domestic carriers by water are similar in most respects to those issued by railroads, except with respect to the terms and conditions having to do with liability for loss and damage. Carriers by water issue both straight and order bills, and the face of a bill conveys the same information found on railroad bills concerning the shipper, the consignee, their addresses, the description of the goods, their weight, and the applicable rates for their transportation. There is, however, no nonrecourse provision on the face of the water carrier's bill of lading, and since carriers by water are not subject to the provisions of the Carmack and Cummins Amendments, they disclaim any and all responsibility for any loss or damage which a shipment of through freight may suffer on connecting lines.

Nearly all carriers by water engaged in our domestic commerce operate under the terms and conditions of the Harter Act and other Federal laws respecting the liability of water carriers. Attention is called to the fact, however, in the terms and conditions of the bill of lading that goods transported from one domestic port to another, for transshipment to a carrier which is to convey them to a foreign destination, are carried during the voyage to the foreign port under the conditions of the Carriage of Goods by Sea Act.

Although carriers by water do not always use identical language and identical terms in their bills of lading, the differences are comparatively slight. The section of the terms and conditions of the bill of lading with respect to liability for loss and damage is much longer than comparable sections in the bills of lading of railroads and motor carriers, because the water carrier is entitled to many more exemptions from and limitations upon liability than the land carriers. The following paragraph is taken from the bill of lading of one of the leading intercoastal carriers of the United States, operating under the Harter Act, and it is representative of the statements which all domestic carriers by water make in their bills of lading with respect to liability. The paragraph is somewhat long—there are many limitations—but it will repay a careful reading.

Neither carrier nor vessel shall be liable for loss, damage or delay, whether occurring before, during or after loading, transit, transshipment, discharge, delivery or other disposition of the goods, arising from any of the following causes: Act of God; act of war, or of public enemies; arrest or restraint, capture, seizure, detention by princes, rulers, governments or people; seizure under legal process; stoppage in transit; perils, dangers or accidents of the sea, rivers, canals or other waters; floating mines; dangers or accidents incident to navigation by collision, stranding, jettison, wreck, or any other kind whatsoever, even when occasioned by the negligence, default or error in judgment of the pilot, master, mariners, or other servants of the shipowner or operator of the vessel, not resulting, however, in any case, from want of due diligence by the owner or operator of the ship or any of them, or by the ship's husband or manager; explosion, bursting of boilers, breakage of shafts or machinery, or any latent defect in hull, boilers, engines, machinery, or appurtenances, even though existing at the beginning of the voyage and not discoverable by due diligence; unseaworthiness even though existing at the time of shipment or at the beginning of the voyage, provided the shipowner or operator has exercised due diligence to make the vessel seaworthy; fire from any cause on land or water, whether on board ship, on cars, lighters, in warehouse or on wharves or elsewhere; water or steam or chemicals used for the purpose of extinguishing fire; barratry of the master or crew or other servants of the carrier; enemies, pirates, robbers or thieves, pilferage, riots, civil commotions, strikes, lockouts, or stoppage or restraint of labor from whatever cause, whether partial or general, of carrier's employees or others, claims of ownership by third parties, quarantine, fumigation or disinfection, detention or accidental delay; prolongation of the voyage; causes beyond the carrier's control; ice, freshets, floods, rain, spray, fresh water, salt water, sea water, frost, or any effects of climate, weather, mildew, mould, fermentation, sifting, decay, putrefaction, decomposition, heat of hold, swelling, spontaneous combustion; want of proper cooperage or mending, chafing, insufficiency of package in strength or otherwise, insufficiency of marks, rust, stain, discoloration, dampness, loss in weight, breakage, bending, buckling, breakage of cast iron pipe and fittings, bending of pipe, injury from hooks, sweat, blowing, bursting of casks or packages from weakness or natural causes, drainage, leakage, evaporation, rats, vermin, heat, smell, taint, contact with or proximity to other goods, deterioration, decay, change of character or condition; land damage; transshipment to or from and risk of craft or storage thereon, discoloration, splits or checks of lumber, laths, staves, etc., or for number of pieces in bundles; or for loss or damage of any kind of goods packed in bales or whose bulk or nature requires them to be carried on deck or on open cars; or for the condition of packages or any deficiency in the contents thereof, if receipted by the consignee as in good order, or for injury or soiling of wrappers or containers; or for any injury that may happen under any circumstances to, or for the death of any living creature that may be embarked, or sent for embarkation, on board this vessel.

This long bill of particulars is interesting, first, because it gives a long list of the hazards to which freight shipments are subject when entrusted to a carrier of any kind, and second, because of the extent to which a carrier by water declares itself to be exempt from liability for the loss or damage which may occur as a result of these numerous hazards. There may be some question about the validity of some of these exemptions. For example, the Harter Act makes strict provision that the carrier by water is responsible for the proper loading and stowage of the property which it carries. If the carrier were so careless as to stow bags of sugar next to unclean barrels of kerosene, causing the sugar to become tainted and rendered unfit for consumption, it is doubtful that the carrier could escape liability, regardless of the clause in the paragraph quoted in which liability is disclaimed for losses due to "contact with or proximity to other goods."

Carriers by water follow a practice, which is permissible under the Carriage of Goods by Sea Act though unmentioned in the Harter Act, of limiting their liability for a single piece or package of goods to a stipulated sum, unless the shipper declares a higher value and is thereby required to pay a higher rate. It will be remembered that railroads and other common carriers by land are forbidden to impose such limitations without the express consent of the Interstate Commerce Commission. The limitation given in the bill of lading just quoted is $500 per piece or per package, which is the amount permissible under the Carriage of Goods by Sea Act. Other carriers by water may limit the extent of their liability for a single package to a smaller sum.

INSURANCE ON WATER-BORNE TRAFFIC

Obviously, the traffic manager who ships goods by water, or over a through rail-and-water route, must be familiar with the character of the liability assumed by different carriers. Moreover, since the liability of a carrier by water is so slight, he should usually follow the practice that has for many years been followed by all shippers who entrust their goods to such a carrier and who do not want to assume, themselves, the risk of loss or damage due to the many perils for which the carrier can in no way be held responsible, and see that his shipments are properly insured against loss due to such dangers. We shall discuss the matter of insurance in a subsequent chapter.

OTHER SHIPPING PAPERS

There are other shipping papers with which the industrial traffic manager is bound to become familiar. When freight reaches its destination, the carrier sends to the consignee, unless the freight is to be delivered to the consignee's place of business, an "arrival notice," which indicates the character of the freight, its origin, and the charges to be met, and of course puts the consignee on warning as to the "free time" he has before the liability of the carrier becomes the liability of a warehouseman only. When the carrier delivers the freight, it presents the consignee with a "freight bill," which the carrier's agent signs when paid, and it becomes the consignee's receipt for the freight charges. Has any loss or damage to the shipment received been noticed, the agent of the carrier should make a notation of such loss or damage on the freight bill, and if the agent has not done so upon his own initiative, he should be asked to do it by the consignee or his representative. The presence of such a notation on the freight bill is always helpful to a consignee in presenting and collecting freight claims from the carrier. Another document—one which the consignee is required to sign—is the "delivery receipt" which is retained by the carrier as evidence that it has fulfilled its contract of carriage.

THE WAYBILL

The information given in the arrival notice, freight bill, and delivery receipt is taken from the carrier's waybill, which has been mentioned previously. This document is strictly a carrier document, with which the shipper and the consignee have nothing to do. It has the same relation to a freight shipment that a ticket has to a passenger. The information it contains regarding the shipment and the names and addresses of the shipper and consignee come from the shipping order—the carrier's copy of the bill of lading. It contains also the carrier's own instructions as to how the shipment is to be transported. It names the route, gives the weight, states the charges, and contains places for the stamps of agents at junction points if the shipment is an interline shipment and must be transferred from one carrier to another. A waybill for less carload freight will indicate if the shipment has been transferred from car to car en route, and if so, where transferred, and the numbers of the cars between which the transfer was made.

The waybill is a vastly important document to the carrier. It is made out at the point where the shipment originates; it accompanies the freight to its destination, in the keeping of the freight train conductors, and is delivered to the agent at the point of destination. It is a record both of the physical movement of the shipment it represents and of the financial transactions involved in the movement of the traffic. When the agent at destination has obtained from it the information necessary to make out the arrival notice, freight bill, and delivery receipt, he sends it to the accounting office of his company—the original record of the service which the carrier has performed and the compensation it has received. The agents of the carrier, who do the paper work and collect the charges from shippers and consignees, make regular reports to the accounting office, and turn their money over to the treasurer of the carrier, either directly or by depositing it in a bank and transmitting the deposit slip to the treasurer. It is the business of the accounting office and the treasurer to check the accounts and reports of the agents for correctness, and this they are able to do from the waybills. When a carrier receives a through or interline shipment, the agent must send a copy of the waybill to all of the carriers which participate in the haul. These carriers are enabled to ascertain from these documents the amount of money due them from the originating or delivering carrier of any shipment, depending upon which collected the freight charges. The numerous coupons which go to make up a passenger ticket for a journey involving several carriers have a similar use. The coupons collected by the passenger train conductors eventually arrive at the accounting office, to be used as a check against the reports of the carrier which sold the ticket.

It is from the waybills, too, that the accounting offices of our railroads compile the voluminous statistics which must be reported to the Interstate Commerce Commission concerning the freight services of the carriers and the revenues derived from these services. Of course, the waybills are not the only source of the statistical information which the railroads are required to assemble and report, but they are a source of leading importance and provide the original record of the most important segment of the business of our chief agency of transport.

UNIT BILLING

On many railroad lines, a "unit" system of billing is employed. The waybill, arrival notice, delivery receipt, freight bill, and a copy of the waybill are all made out in a single operation at the originating freight station. Unit billing saves the labor of copying at the destination station, and it also greatly minimizes the chance of error. This type of billing is used only in the transportation of local freight, that is, freight carried between stations located on the lines of a single railroad company.

TRACING

Another transportation document for which some industrial traffic managers have frequent use is known as a "tracer." When a shipment has been delayed so long in reaching its proper destination that it may reasonably be surmised that it has been lost or otherwise gone astray, the shipper requests the railroad to trace it. The document which the carrier employs to follow, if possible, the course of the missing shipment until it is found, or given up as lost, is called a tracer. Many shippers, when requesting that a stray shipment be traced, include in their request a notation to the effect that the request is to be considered as a "notice of claim." Should the shipment not be found, the formal claim for loss will be filed later, but the notice of claim is regarded as tantamount to a claim which under the terms of the bill of lading must, as a condition of recovery for loss, be filed within nine months after a shipment is lost or damaged or after a reasonable time for delivery has elapsed.

It is somewhat difficult for a railroad to trace a less carload shipment that has been reported missing, especially if it has been transferred one or more times en route to its final destination. Although the waybill for the shipment will contain the notices of all transfers, stamped at the transfer houses, indicating the initials and numbers of the cars between which transfers were presumably made, the records kept at the transfer houses are not such that it is easy to discover whether a shipment has been placed in the wrong car. All freight agents at destination stations are required to make reports to a central office of any freight that appears to be missing or damaged and also of any freight received in excess of the amount for which waybills call. These O.S.&D. (over, short, and damaged) reports are especially useful in locating freight that has gone astray. Theoretically, every report of "over" freight should find a match in a report of "short" freight and the transportation errors speedily corrected, but not all reports of short freight can be expected to be matched by reports of over freight, because inevitably some packages are pilfered, stolen, or otherwise lost beyond hope of recovery.

The tracing of carload freight does not present so many difficulties as the tracing of less carload freight. It is bound to be easier to lose without trace a small package of freight which has been mingled with many other packages than to lose an entire carload of freight, though it happens every once in a while that a carload shipment may be "lost" for a few days, because of misdelivery, or perhaps because it has been inadvertently left on a siding without any subsequent report by the conductor. In times of national emergency, when our transportation facilities are taxed to the utmost and all shippers and receivers of freight are insistently demanding rapid service, it may be that inadequate motive power or the pressure for haste, coupled with the inability to work any mechanism beyond its capacity, may result in the delay of cars in switching yards and at junction points. Tracing becomes a heavy task for many carriers, and shippers have been known to employ "expediters," whose duty it is actually to follow cars loaded with necessary merchandise and see personally that they move through freight yards, and from train to train, as speedily as possible.

PASSING REPORTS

In normal times, railroads are likely to rely largely on "passing reports" to locate delayed carload freight and see that it is sent on its way. Every railroad yard keeps a daily record of the cars which leave the yard. The record shows the train in which any car left and the names of the members of the crew who have charge of the train. Daily passing reports are compiled from these records and transmitted to the leading traffic offices of the company. It is easy enough, with such reports, to trace the movement of a car from the point of origin to and through the various yards. When the record shows that a particular car has left a certain yard on its way to its final destination, and the record of the next yard shows that the car has not been taken from that place, it is obvious that the car must be either in the latter yard or at some place on a siding between the two yards. Telegraphic inquiry will in all probability soon reveal the location of the "missing" car, and it will be hastened on its way. Every competent industrial traffic manager is familiar with these passing reports and knows in what traffic offices they may be found in case of need.

CHAPTER XIII

Claims

Having presented a background of some of the legal and practical technicalities connected with rates and rate publication and of principles and laws relating to the liability of carriers for lost or damaged freight, we are now ready to turn to a consideration of the duties and activities of the industrial traffic manager when he is confronted with the fact that a carrier has overcharged him for transportation service, has failed to deliver a shipment at all, has delivered a shipment in a damaged condition, or has taken an unreasonably long time to make delivery. We have mentioned previously that the work of some industrial traffic departments consists in large measure of presenting claims—claims for overcharges and claims for loss and damage. Now we shall endeavor to find out how these claims may arise, how they are presented to a carrier, and how they are followed through to their final disposition.

COMMISSION WITHOUT JURISDICTION OVER CLAIMS FOR LOSS AND DAMAGE

First, however, it should be explained that the Interstate Commerce Commission has nothing to do with claims for lost and damaged freight. Such claims are made directly to the carrier concerned, and if the carrier denies responsibility or liability for any alleged loss or damage, the complainant must pursue his cause in a court of law and not before the Interstate Commerce Commission, which has no jurisdiction over such matters. On the other hand, the Commission may be appealed to in case a carrier refuses to settle a claim involving an alleged overcharge for its services. The Commission has jurisdiction over rates; it is the duty of the Commission to see that the carriers under its jurisdiction collect only those rates which are lawful, which are properly published and duly filed with the Commission. In controversies over property entrusted to a carrier's custody for transportation from one place to another, the Commission has no interest and takes no part. It can and does prescribe the forms of bills of lading which carriers use, and it requires them to indicate in the terms and conditions of a bill the nature of the carrier's liability, but when a shipment is lost or damaged, any difference between the carrier and the owner with respect to the nature of this liability and the amount recoverable by the shipper must be settled in court, if the two parties cannot reach an amicable agreement.

OVERCHARGE CLAIMS

When a shipper is subjected to an unlawful overcharge by a carrier, there is no doubt of the shipper's right to reparation for the amount of the overcharge, although he may have to appeal to the Interstate Commerce Commission if the carrier denies that an overcharge has been made.

When a shipper thinks that he has been charged a rate that is unreasonable or unduly discriminatory, he may carry his complaint to the Commission. In case the Commission sustains the shipper's allegation, it may award reparation for any damage the shipper may have suffered by reason of having been compelled to pay the unreasonable or unduly discriminatory rate, though the Commission may use its own discretion concerning the matter of awarding reparation, and in few cases will the award be more than the difference between the rate paid and the rate which the Commission declares to be either reasonable or not unduly discriminatory. But the claims for reparation because of the imposition of unreasonable or unduly discriminatory rates are in a different category from those claims based upon an allegation that the rate charged by the carrier has been a higher rate than the rate lawfully published and filed with the Commission. In the one case, before considering the matter of reparation, the Commission must exercise its quasi-judicial function of determining whether the rate complained of has actually been unreasonable or unjustly discriminatory. In the other case, no judicial function is exercised before an award is made. It is merely a matter of fact which the Commission must determine; it must simply decide whether the rate complained of was the legal rate for the carrier to apply. If the rate charged was illegal, and higher than the legal rate, reparation follows as a matter of course. But even though the Commission might decide that a certain rate was unreasonable or unduly discriminatory, it does not follow that it will award reparation to the complainant.[1]

In this chapter we are not interested in claims that may eventually flow from a case in which the Commission has decided that a certain rate was unreasonable or unjustly discriminatory. We are interested only in claims for overcharges; claims arising from the fact that a carrier has charged an amount of money for its services greater than it was lawfully authorized to charge under the provisions of its filed tariffs; and claims for lost, damaged, or delayed freight.

---

[1] It should be observed that there is a difference between a "legal" rate and a "lawful" rate, though the terms are often used interchangeably. The legal rate is the published rate, duly filed, and it is the rate which the carrier must apply. Such a legal rate may, however, be "unlawful" because it is found to be unreasonable, unduly discriminatory, or otherwise violative of the law.

There are many ways in which a carrier may make an error in its charges. First of all, there may be an error in the rating. An article may have been charged a third-class rate, for example, when its class rating in the classification book or in an exception was fourth class. Or the rate clerk of the carrier may have made a mistake in reading the tariff and charged a rate of 50 cents, let us say, when the published rate for the service in question was only 40 cents. It may be that the clerk, through error, has applied to a certain shipment the rate between stations A and B, when the shipment was billed to move from station A to station C at a lower applicable rate than that from A to B. It frequently happens that, because of an improper or inadequate description of goods listed in a bill of lading, a certain shipment or a part of it may be given a higher class rating than the one legally applicable. Perhaps some necessary notation has been left off a waybill. It will be remembered that the "follow-lot rule" of the classification provides that, in the case of many articles carried, any excess over a full carload will be transported at the applicable carload rate but handled as a less carload shipment. But the rule provides for "cross reference" on the bills of lading and the waybills employed in connection with the shipment. If the notation is omitted, the excess freight, handled as a less carload shipment, will undoubtedly be charged the less carload rate, though entitled to be charged the carload rate. Then there may be errors in the weights attributed either to a less carload or to a carload shipment.

One of the most common sources of overcharges consists of clerical errors made in copying and computing. Even though the proper rating and rate have been applied to a shipment, a clerk may have made an arithmetical error in performing the multiplication and addition necessary to ascertain the total charges on the shipment. Or, while the waybill may contain the proper rate and correct computation of charges, the clerk at destination, in making out the shipper's freight bill, has not copied the waybill figures correctly. Auditing freight bills may take a lot of time in the office of the industrial traffic manager, but it never fails to be worth while.

Once in a while a carrier's agent may, through error, bill "collect" a shipment upon which the freight charges have been prepaid. In its famous investigation of the express business in 1912, the Interstate Commerce Commission came to the conclusion that this particular form of error occurred so frequently that it was difficult to believe that it was always due to accident instead of design. Another form of overcharge may grow out of this form of error. A shipper may be denied possession of a carload of prepaid freight upon which the carrier is endeavoring to collect the freight charges a second time. The controversy lasts so long that demurrage charges accrue on the car. Badly in need of the freight, the consignee finally pays the charges and also the demurrage in order to obtain possession of the shipment. If subsequent investigation proves that the carrier was in the wrong, that the freight charges had actually been prepaid, the consignee is entitled not only to the return of the freight charges he has paid but also to the return of the demurrage charges.

Occasionally a little trouble arises because of Rule 34 of the classification, which provides that minimum carload weights shall vary with the length of a car. A shipper may order and receive a car of the length he orders and promptly dispatch the shipment in the car received. Because of some accident the carrier may find it necessary to transfer the contents of the car to another car, which happens to be longer than the car in which the freight was dispatched. If the proper notation is not made on the waybill, the consignee may be confronted with a bill for freight based upon the carload minimum applicable to the car in which the freight was received. This would be a case in which the Railway Equipment Register would prove to be useful in the settlement of the controversy.

There are doubtless other reasons for errors which result in efforts by a carrier to collect more than is justly and lawfully due. One more might be mentioned here, although it will have to be discussed again in another chapter. It will be remembered that when a shipment is charged a "combination rate," the shipper is required to pay only the lowest available combination applicable between the point of origin and the point of destination. Should the billing clerk cause a shipment, not routed by the shipper, to be dispatched over a route carrying a rate higher than a lower combination applicable over another route, and this combination is the lowest available between origin and destination, the shipper is entitled to a refund of the difference between the rate charged and the lowest combination rate. We shall discuss this matter at more length when we come to the subject of routing.

STANDARD FORM FOR OVERCHARGE CLAIMS

In presenting a claim for an overcharge, a traffic manager would do well to use the "standard form" for the presentation of such a claim, though this practice is not compulsory. But the standard form provides the blank spaces in which the carrier can be informed of all facts concerning the shipment, such as its description, the names and addresses of the consignor and consignee, the name of the carrier issuing the bill of lading, the date of the bill, the number of the paid freight bill, and the nature of the overcharge, all arranged in an orderly manner. There is likewise a space for a detailed statement of the claim, in which the shipper indicates the amount of charges actually paid and the amount which he should have been billed for. Accompanying the standard form, properly filled out, the claimant should submit, in support of his demand for refund, the original paid freight bill, which shows the amount he has paid, the original bill of lading, if not previously surrendered to the carrier, or a copy thereof, to show that the shipment was made as indicated in the claim, and such evidence as may be necessary to sustain a claim of overcharge. This evidence will consist of the proper class of an article if it has been improperly classified; the applicable rate, with tariff authority, if an incorrect rate has been applied; notations with respect to any incorrect computations that have resulted in an overcharge; evidence with regard to a mistake that has been made with respect to the weight of the shipment; or whatever information is necessary to support a claim based upon other considerations.

The use of the standard form makes it more convenient for the carrier to handle the claim and give it proper attention, and a claim for overcharge that is submitted on such a form is likely to receive more prompt consideration and speedier settlement. Forms for the presentation of overcharge claims, as well as for the presentation of claims for loss and damage, may be obtained from printing firms which regularly supply many of the forms used in business transactions. The Traffic Service Bureau of Chicago, which issues *Traffic World* and *Traffic Bulletin,* previously mentioned, is one of the many firms which print and sell these standard forms.

STATUTE OF LIMITATIONS

It is not necessary for a shipper to file a "notice of claim" for an overcharge and, in event of failure to obtain reimbursement, file a suit for recovery within a stipulated time. There is, however, a "statute of limitations" against such actions. Paragraph (c), section 16, part I, of the Interstate Commerce Act says:

For recovery of overcharges action at law shall be begun or complaint filed with the Commission against carriers subject to this part within two years from the time the cause of action accrues, and not after, subject to subdivision (d), except that if a claim for the overcharge has been presented in writing to the carrier within the two year period of limitation said period shall be extended to include six months from the time notice in writing is given by the carrier to the claimant of disallowance of the claim, or any part or parts thereof, specified in the notice.

The condition in subdivision (d) is that if the carrier brings suit to collect charges in respect to the transportation service involving the alleged overcharge, or if without action the carrier collects charges in respect of such service, the time of limitation shall be extended to include ninety days from the time such action is begun or such charges collected by the carrier.

The same statute of limitations runs against the carrier in any effort it may make to collect charges alleged to be due from a shipper; that is, it has two years from the time the cause of action accrues in which to bring suit.

It should be noticed, however, that the carrier brings a suit for its charges in a court of law. It does not file a complaint before the Interstate Commerce Commission in an effort to compel a shipper to meet what is asserted to be an obligation to the carrier.

A shipper is entitled to interest on overcharge claims, which the carrier is required to pay, on the theory that the carrier has been in wrongful possession of the shipper's money and should be required to compensate the shipper just as it would for borrowed money. If the shipper acts in a dilatory fashion, however, in meeting a carrier's request for a full and complete statement of the sums due on overcharge claims, interest may be disallowed for the time during which the shipper failed to comply with the carrier's reasonable request.

Parts II, III, and IV of the Interstate Commerce Act contain provisions with respect to the limitations of the time in which suits may be brought either for overcharges or for carrier's charges which are identical with the provisions found in part I. The uniformity in the rules now prevailing for all carriers subject to the Commission, as well as for shippers who claim to be overcharged, constitutes a marked improvement in the law, which at one time had different periods of limitation for carriers and for shippers and moreover was so worded that there was a considerable degree of confusion and uncertainty as to its precise meaning.

LOST AND DAMAGED FREIGHT

There are several varieties of claims for lost and damaged freight, according to the extent of the injury to which the claimant has been subjected. There may be a "total loss" of a shipment, that is, the entire shipment may have been stolen, burned, or otherwise made to disappear beyond chance of recovery. The loss may be a "partial loss," in which only a part of a shipment has disappeared. A partial loss may be "known," that is, visible and apparent, as when a portion of a number of packages included in a single shipment is found to be missing; but we also have many partial losses which are "concealed." A packing case may be opened, a part of its contents removed, and the case closed again in such a way as to give no apparent evidence of tampering or pilferage. In the same way we may have "total damage"; a certain shipment may be broken beyond repair and rendered entirely useless and valueless. We may also have a "partial damage," a damage of such a character that the injured article may be repaired and used. A partial damage may also be "concealed," as well as be apparent to the eye, at the time the freight reaches its station of destination.

STANDARD FORM FOR LOSS AND DAMAGE CLAIMS

There are standard forms for the presentation of loss and damage claims, just as there are for the presentation of claims for overcharges. One of these forms contains spaces for full information about the shipment and a space to indicate the amount of damage claimed and how the amount was determined. The "supporting documents" for a loss or damage claim are the bill of lading, the freight bill, the invoice of the goods which made up the shipment, or a certified copy, and such other documents as may be necessary to show satisfactory proof of the extent of the loss suffered by the claimant. If the loss or damage is of the concealed variety, it may be necessary to prepare and present other documents in support of the claim. Moreover, there are special standard forms for presentations of concealed loss or damage. A claim for concealed loss or damage is just as good as any other, if it can be shown beyond a reasonable doubt that the loss or damage took place while the goods were in the possession of the carrier. Let us say that a merchant receives a packing case supposed to contain three dozen pairs of shoes. The case shows no signs of having been tampered with, yet upon opening it after delivery to his store the merchant discovers that six pairs of shoes are missing. The procedure he will follow is to obtain affidavits from the manufacturer or wholesaler from whom the shoes were purchased to the effect that three dozen pairs of shoes were actually packed in the case for shipment. Then he obtains affidavits from the trucker or drayman who carried the case of shoes to the freight station at the point of origin and from the trucker who hauled the case from the freight station at point of destination to the merchant's place of business. If the case had been given "pick-up and delivery service" by the railroad or its agents, it would of course not be necessary for the merchant to obtain affidavits from local truckers, though the affidavit from the manufacturer or wholesaler from whom the shoes were purchased would be needed.

We discussed in a previous chapter the matter of ascertaining the value of lost or damaged shipments, and pointed out that the common law rule still prevails that the consignee is entitled to have from the carrier either that which he would have received had the carrier fulfilled its part of the contract or its equivalent in monetary compensation. Ordinarily, shipper and carrier do not have much difficulty in agreeing upon the amount of money the claimant is entitled to when goods are lost or damaged in transit, but it is well for the industrial traffic manager to know that the value which can be claimed on any lost or damaged goods is the value at destination at the time when delivery would ordinarily have been made by the carrier.

TIME FOR FILING CLAIMS

It must be emphasized again that a claim for loss or damage must be filed, under the terms of the bill of lading, within nine months after the delivery of property by the carrier or within nine months after a reasonable time for delivery has elapsed, and that suits for recovery must be filed within two years and one day after the carrier has disallowed in writing all or any part of a duly filed claim. If these time limits are not observed, the claim will not be paid. These limitations as to time of filing claims and instituting suits are in accordance with the terms of one of the several provisos of subdivision (11), section 20, part I, of the Interstate Commerce Act, which declares that it shall be unlawful for a carrier responsible under the law for lost or damaged freight

. . . to provide by rule, contract, regulation, or otherwise a shorter period for filing of claims than nine months, and for the institution of suits than two years, such period for institution of suits to be computed from the day when notice in writing is given by the carrier to the claimant that the carrier has disallowed the claim or any part or parts thereof specified in the notice.

CARRIER MUST INVESTIGATE ALL CLAIMS

Carriers are required under the law to treat all claimants alike, without undue discrimination or unjust preference for any one individual or group. On the other hand, carriers must not settle claims without investigation. The merits of each claim must be closely examined and a claim paid only if the carrier is convinced as to its liability and as to the amount which, under the law, it should be required to pay. To settle the claims of a large shipper hastily and without due investigation and subject a small shipper to a long-drawn-out process of investigation and examination would constitute a type of discrimination sternly forbidden by law.

HOW CLAIMS ARE PROCESSED AND HANDLED

The industrial traffic manager will find that the collection of valid claims against a responsible carrier will be greatly facilitated if proper attention is given to the details of filing claims and following them up until they are disposed of in one way or another. The standard form for the presentation of a claim, either for loss or damage or for an overcharge, should always be used, and care should always be taken to see that the proper supporting documents and evidentiary material bearing upon the justice and correctness of the claim are filed with the standard form.

Traffic managers have various ways of handling claims, depending largely upon the number and character of claims which must be filed. A separate folder should be maintained for each claim, and accurate copies of all the papers submitted to the carrier carefully preserved. Each claim should have a file number, and careful observation of the progress of each claim should be maintained. Active claims should be separated in the file according to the time of filing; it will often be found advantageous to use some sort of "tickler" system as a reminder to follow up on a claim the consideration of which seems to have been unduly delayed by the carrier against which it was filed. Once a claim has been disposed of, its folder is filed away in storage until the time for its destruction. Many industrial traffic managers maintain a claim index containing a complete record of all claims which it has been necessary to file. If the number of claims is small, a single index in which claims are listed in the order of their file numbers is sufficient, but if the number of claims is large a second index may be deemed advisable, in which claims are listed alphabetically according to the carriers with which they have been filed. Some traffic managers maintain a ledger account of claims. When the claim is made, the customer on whose behalf the claim has been filed is credited with the amount of the claim, and "claims" is debited; when the claim is paid, the claims account is credited and a debit is made to cash.

WHO HAS THE RIGHT TO FILE LOSS AND DAMAGE CLAIMS

Since under ordinary circumstances the title to a rail shipment passes to the consignee when received by a carrier under a straight bill of lading, it is the right of the consignee to make any claim arising because of lost or damaged freight. However, subdivision (11), section 20, of the Interstate Commerce Act requiring a carrier to issue a bill of lading to a shipper states plainly that the carrier shall be "liable to the lawful holder" of the bill for all loss or damage.[2] In the case of the order bill of lading, the lawful holder of the bill also has title to the property it represents. A straight bill of lading may remain in the possession of the shipper, and he will be regarded as the lawful holder, although he may not have a technically legal title to the property listed in the bill. But since he made the contract with the carrier, he too has the right to file claims for loss or damage. Many large industrial concerns relieve some of their customers of the labor and trouble of filing and pursuing freight claims and assume the obligation themselves. Sometimes a legal claimant may "assign" his claim to another person, giving this person the right to collect any damages which may be due from the carrier. Usually, when the customer of a large

[2] It is to the "lawful holder" of the bill of lading that the carrier is liable in case property is lost, damaged, or delayed in transit. Adams v. Croninger, 226 U.S. 491 (1913). The lawful holder of the bill of lading does not have to prove ownership of property in order to sue a carrier for loss or damage of goods. The law makes the lawful holder the representative of the real parties at interest. Pennsylvania R.R. v. Olivit Brothers, 243 U.S. 574 (1917), *affirming* 88 N.J.L. 376; Davis v. Livingston, 13 F.2d 604 (1926). It should be noted that the term F.O.B. (free on board) has nothing to do with the matter of who is the lawful holder of the bill of lading or who has title to the property. It has been said that when goods are shipped "F.O.B. point of origin" the consignee has the responsibility of making any claim arising from loss, damage, or delay, and that when the goods are shipped "F.O.B. destination" the responsibility for filing a claim falls upon the shipper. Obviously this is untrue. The carrier is liable to the lawful holder of the bill of lading, who may be neither shipper nor consignee but may still have the legal right to file a claim for loss, damage, or delay.

mail-order house notifies the concern that an ordered shipment has apparently been lost or that it has arrived in a damaged condition, the mail-order house immediately supplies the customer with duplicate merchandise and takes care of the claim itself. Some mail-order houses carry insurance on all the shipments they send out, and it may be that the insurance company will be the party to make the claim against the carrier.

RAILROAD CLAIM DEPARTMENTS

The claim department of a large railroad company is always a busy place. With the constant flow of complaints from shippers, claim agents and claim adjusters find plenty to do. It is to their own interest to settle claims promptly and satisfactorily, but it must always be remembered that their duty to their company requires them to scrutinize each claim with care and try to obtain the most favorable terms of settlement possible. The industrial traffic manager who has a thorough knowledge of the rights of the claimant and of the liability of the carrier will meet with no great difficulty in obtaining a satisfactory adjustment of his demands, but it must be admitted that the claim adjusters of carriers are often prone to take advantage of a shipper or of a traffic manager who does not know his rights. If the adjuster can "save money" for his employer by talking the claimant out of all or part of a just claim, he is not always averse to doing so. It happens, perhaps too frequently, that a shipper or consignee is induced, because of his ignorance, to sign a "release" to a carrier in return for a much smaller sum of money that he would be able to collect if he were fully acquainted with the nature of his own rights and of the obligations of the carrier.

While we are not interested so much in the operations of carriers as in the operations of shippers and receivers of freight, it should be pointed out that the carriers have taken many steps to facilitate the settlement of freight claims. The Association of American Railroads, which is the leading over-all organization of railroad companies of the United States, has a freight claim division in its operations and maintenance department. This division cooperates with shippers on all matters relating to the presentation and filing of claims. Through its activities it has succeeded in bringing a high degree of uniformity to the practices which both carriers and shippers customarily employ in their claim work. For example, in cooperation with the National Industrial Traffic (N.I.T.) League, which is the leading American shippers' organization, it has drawn up a set of rules which shippers and carriers are urged to follow in the inspection of freight alleged to be damaged and in the examination of claims for freight alleged to be lost. Although these rules do not have the effect of a tariff, and are not legally binding on carriers and shippers, they are quite reasonable in their terms; their observance leads to the limitation of controversy and to a higher degree of promptitude in the settlement or adjustment of claims.[3]

CLAIMS FOR LOST OR DAMAGED INTERLINE SHIPMENTS

The carriers frequently have some knotty problems to deal with in the settlement of claims for loss and damage. The owner of the property which is lost or damaged has the right to present his claim to the delivering carrier, to the originating carrier, or to the carrier on whose line the loss or damage took place. There are numerous cases in which the claim is presented to the originating or delivering carrier, when it is known that the loss or damage occurred on some intermediate line. Although the carrier with which the claim is filed must compensate the owner of the property for the loss suffered, it has the right to collect the amount of the claim from the carrier on whose line the loss was known to take place. But it may happen, and it does happen frequently, that the time and place of loss or damage cannot be determined. For example, if a case of goods has been opened, a part of its contents stolen, and the case closed so that no evidence of tampering is apparent, it may be impossible to find out where the theft occurred. Nevertheless, the shipper can recover from either the delivering or the originating carrier. It is only natural that neither of these carriers should feel that it should be held solely responsible for such a loss. Over the years, the claim departments of our railroads and motor carriers have worked out a plan under which these losses, paid for either by the delivering or the originating carrier, are shared equitably by all the carriers which participated in the transportation of the shipment in connection with which a claim for loss or damage has been filed.

CARRIER CASUALTY INSURANCE

Virtually all of the railroads of the United States, as well as domestic carriers by water, are the owners of a sufficient amount of property so that a shipper or passenger obtaining a judgment against one of them, because of personal injury or loss or damage of property, would have little or no difficulty in collecting the amount of the award. In other words, these carriers are regarded as self-insurers, and it has not been thought necessary to take any special precautionary measures to warrant their ability to meet any valid claims which might be enforceable against them. Like many other business concerns, some of these carriers take out casualty insurance for protection against certain kinds of losses to per-

[3] The Freight Claim Council of the American Trucking Associations has likewise, in cooperation with the National Industrial Traffic League, performed a valuable service by establishing rules and regulations under which motor carriers handle the claims arising from damage to interline motor traffic. This body has also done much excellent work on claim prevention.

sons and property, but the practice is by no means universal, and the types of coverage obtained by different carriers are not uniform.

When Congress was considering the bills which finally emerged as the Motor Carrier Act of 1935, it was pointed out that many highway carriers possessed little property—perhaps a single bus or a single truck—and in the event of an accident involving grave personal injuries or large loss of property, for which the carrier might under the law be held responsible, it might be entirely impossible to collect a judgment in which a claimant was awarded a substantial sum of money as compensation for personal injury or property loss. Consequently, the Motor Carrier Act declared that no certificate of convenience or permit issued under the law should remain in force unless the carriers complied with such rules as the Commission might prescribe governing the filing and approval of surety bonds or other securities or agreements, in such amount as the Commission might direct, to guarantee the payment within the limit of such amount any final judgment which might be obtained against the carrier "for the bodily injuries or death of any person resulting from the negligent operation, maintenance, or use of motor vehicles under such certificate or permit, or for loss or damage to the property of others." Moreover, the Commission was authorized in its discretion to require a common carrier by motor vehicle to file a surety bond or other agreement, to be conditioned upon making out line compensation to shippers whose property the carrier accepted for transportation and did not carry safely to destination. It will be noticed that the bonds to cover injuries to persons and to property not belonging to a shipper related to injury or damage resulting from negligence, while the bonds for the protection of a shipper's goods covered loss or damage whether negligence was involved or not. The law for the regulation of freight forwarders, enacted in 1942, makes similar provisions for the filing of approved surety bonds by freight forwarders.

CONVERSION

Occasionally a shipper is confronted with a loss which goes under the legal name of "conversion." This occurs when a carrier appropriates the property entrusted to it, exercises "dominion" over it, and treats it as if belonging to the carrier. An example of conversion would arise, for instance, if a carrier should sell unclaimed or abandoned freight without complying with the rules in the bill of lading with respect to notice to the consignor. When a carrier delivers property which it has transported to a person not entitled to receive it, the carrier is guilty of conversion. And occasionally a carrier has been known knowingly and deliberately to convert a shipper's property to its own use, as when during a strike or during an excessive coal shortage it uses a carload of coal belonging to a shipper for the purpose of keeping its trains moving. Needless to say, the owner of property which a carrier has taken by conversion is entitled to full remuneration for its value. There may be some controversy once in a while as to whether the appropriation of a shipper's property by a carrier legally constitutes an act of conversion, but once the question of fact is settled and the appropriation deemed to be a conversion, there is no question of the right of the shipper to recover the value of the converted shipment.

LOSSES DUE TO DELAY

While loss and damage due to carrier's delay are not so frequent as loss and damage due to theft, breakage, mishandling, and other physical causes, a great many claims for losses due to delay are filed with the carriers each year. In many cases, the damage or loss has been occasioned by the deterioration of perishable property which has not been transported with "reasonable dispatch," though, if the deterioration was due to some "inherent defect" in the shipment, and it can be shown that the deterioration would have occurred even if there had been no unreasonable delay, the carrier cannot be held responsible for the loss. Perishable property is sometimes loaded and shipped in such a condition that rapid deterioration is inevitable. A carrier is not liable as an insurer for perishable property it undertakes to transport, and it cannot be held responsible for losses to such property which are due to causes beyond the carrier's control. It frequently happens that, when there is a dispute about the causes of deterioration, the controversy must be taken to a court for the resolution of questions of fact.

It was pointed out in a previous chapter that a shipper or owner may suffer a loss because of a carrier's unreasonable delay in the transportation of nonperishable property. The traffic manager must be aware of the fact, however, that a carrier is not responsible for "special" or "consequential" damages unless it has been legally put on notice that such damages would occur if the carrier failed to perform a certain transportation service with reasonable dispatch.

There is no precise definition of "reasonable dispatch" or "unreasonable delay." It is a question of fact which a judge or jury must decide. Ordinarily, a court will say that transportation with reasonable dispatch is transportation which takes place within the time which the carrier customarily consumes in its service between the stations involved in the controversy, and that when a longer time has been taken than that customarily needed there has been an unreasonable delay. It may be, however, that weather conditions have been such as to make it impossible for the carrier to perform a certain service within the customary time, or there may have been other causes, over which the carrier had no control, which prevented it from performing a service with customary dispatch. In other words, there is no hard and fast rule for the determination of what constitutes reasonable dispatch; each case of alleged unreasonable delay will have its own particular environment of circumstances, conditions, and precedents. Conflicting testimony must be sifted and all the conditions under which the transportation took place examined. Whether there was an unreasonable delay becomes entirely a question of fact which it is the duty of a jury or judge to answer in the light of all relevant evidence. What the traffic manager should know is that the carrier owes him the duty of transporting shipments with reasonable dispatch and that he can obtain remuneration from a carrier for losses suffered because of unreasonable delay, whether the loss was due to deterioration or to shrinkage in market values.

CLAIM PREVENTION

Every industrial traffic manager should be thoroughly familiar with the legal, technical, and practical problems connected with the preparation, filing, and adjudication of freight claims. But he should be equally interested in another highly important aspect of freight claims—and overcharge claims, too—which unfortunately does not always receive the attention it deserves. This is the prevention of claims. There is no other transportation activity to which may be more appropriately applied the familiar adage, "An ounce of prevention is worth a pound of cure." Claims represent only loss—loss of property, loss of time, loss of labor, often loss of established business relations, and even loss of friendly associations. They are a part of the wastes of business enterprise, a waste which business can ill afford, a waste which every reasonable effort should be made to prevent.

COST OF LOSS AND DAMAGE

The railroads pay out each year a staggering sum of money in settlement of claims for loss and damage. Of course the amount will vary with the volume of traffic and freight revenue, with fluctuations in prices, and with the changes in the character of traffic transported. It is a noteworthy fact that the amount has been known to vary with the political and social conditions prevailing in the country. Before 1917, the largest amount the railroads had ever paid out for the settlement of loss and damage claims was slightly more than $35,000,000. In 1919, the losses soared to $104,500,000, and in 1920, to approximately $120,000,000. A better basis of comparison than the total loss each year would be the loss in proportion to the freight revenue the carriers received. Before 1917, the largest proportional loss came in 1908 when payment of loss and damage claims took 1.66 per cent of railroad freight revenue. In 1919, the carriers paid out in loss and damage claims $2.95 of every $100 of freight revenue received; in 1920 and 1921, the amounts were respectively $2.78 and $2.36. Strenuous efforts on the part of both carriers and shippers during the next few years brought about an almost spectacular decrease in the amount paid out in settlement of claims, reaching a low of 48 cents per $100 of revenue in 1941. But with the advent of unsettled conditions and the advance of prices, the claims paid on account of loss and damage grew in total amount as well as proportionally. In 1948, the losses reached $130,000,000. By the exercise of more care and labor in "plugging up holes," the loss and damage claims were reduced somewhat in 1949, although they still amounted to $109,000,000, or 1.53 per cent of the freight revenue of the carriers. In 1950, losses dropped to $89,000,000. The record of losses on Canadian railroads because of loss or damage is markedly better than the record of railroads in the United States. In no single year since 1921 have the Canadian roads paid out as much as 1 per cent of their freight revenues in settlement of claims for loss and damage, the highest amount in any year being 0.765 per cent in 1948. In part, the discrepancy is due to the fact that Canadian roads are permitted to give lower ratings or rates to much traffic carried at the risk of the shipper or owner. Railroads of the United States are not permitted under the law to make such a concession. They are not permitted to exempt themselves from liability, and they can limit the amount recoverable by the shipper in connection with only a small number of items of traffic.

PROMOTION OF SAFE TRANSPORTATION

Both railroads and shippers have done much to reduce claims for loss and damage. At times their endeavors seem to have borne fruitful results; at other times, whether because of relaxation of effort or because of conditions beyond their control, the problem seems to have gotten out of hand, and the loss and waste due to loss and damage have mounted to a formidable and discouraging level. The freight claim division of the Association of American Railroads has a Committee on Prevention of Loss and Damage, with headquarters at Chicago, which is at work constantly, educating shippers and carriers in the ways of loss prevention. Its annual reports are valuable, not only for the information they give about the amount of loss and damage which takes place each year and the analysis of known causes, but for the highly useful advice they give, by the use of precept and example, as to how the huge bill for lost and damaged freight can possibly be reduced. Shippers' organizations, such as the National Industrial Traffic League, also have committees doing highly useful work on claim prevention. The Shippers' Advisory Boards, made up of representatives of both shippers and carriers, in their regular meetings and through the work of their committees, try to discover and remove the causes of loss and damage and keep freight claims to a minimum. Individual railroads and individual shippers carry on energetic campaigns among their employees and their customers to promote greater safety in the transportation of freight, while trade magazines, newspapers, and other publications call frequent attention to the waste which excessive freight claims represent and ask for sharper and more concentrated attention upon the problem on the part of both shippers and carriers.

ANALYSIS OF LOSSES

It may be that more effective results in the movement to bring about a reduction in freight claims could be obtained if a greater effort were made to discover and analyze the causes of loss and damage to the property which railroads undertake to transport. It is a rather significant fact that the railroads' Committee on Prevention of Loss and Damage reports nearly every year that more than 60 per cent of the money paid out by the carriers in settlement of loss and damage claims is paid for loss or damage which is "unlocated." That is, there is no doubt that the loss and damage occurred, but in a great majority of cases the cause of the loss or damage was undiscoverable, or at least reported as not located. For example, of a total of $113,844,258 paid out by 129 carrier members of the Association of American Railways in 1949, representing 95 per cent of United States, Canadian, and Mexican mileage, some 64.5 per cent, or more than $73,500,000, was because of loss or damage described as "unlocated." The biggest single item in this total was $47,000,000 paid out because of "unlocated damage" to freight in packages.

There are many causes for loss and damage to freight, and it goes without saying that some of the loss is unavoidable and unescapable. Accidents are bound to happen, regardless of safety precautions that may be taken, and nobody can reasonably expect or hope to see loss and damage entirely eliminated. But when the payments in settlement of claims exceeds 1 per cent of the freight revenue of the railroads, it would seem that more intensive work is in order to plug up the leaks which lead to such a significant loss.

SHIPPERS OFTEN TO BLAME FOR LOSS

The blame for the excessive waste cannot be laid wholly at the door of either the shipper or the carrier. Both must bear a measure of responsibility, and both have a duty of seeking means to promote a higher degree of safety in our transportation service. We have spoken in previous chapters of some of the things which are done in an effort to see that shipments reach their destination promptly and in an undamaged condition. It will not be amiss to point out a few of the more important reasons why loss and damage occur and to indicate some of the steps which can be taken to bring about a reduction.

First of all, let us consider the faults of the shipper. The acts or faults of shippers which are the most prolific source of loss and damage to freight are careless billing, improper marking of packages, and poor packing. Careless billing results in the insertion of the wrong names of stations, shippers, and consignees, with the result that freight goes astray and is often lost. We have spoken previously of the necessity for marking packages correctly, and we have indicated that packages are often lost because old consignment marks were not obliterated, mistakes were made in the names of stations and consignees, the material used in marking lacked necessary durability, or shipping labels and tags were of fragile material or were not securely attached to their packages.

Of all the causes of loss due to errors on the part of shippers, poor packing is probably the greatest. The container itself may not be of sufficient strength to withstand ordinary handling—and often the container is handled in a manner that is more than ordinary—or if the container is strong enough, the material—excelsior, paper, or blocks—employed inside the container is of insufficient strength or lacking in quality or quantity or both. Poor workmanship in the construction of shipping containers is frequently found, notwithstanding the long campaign of education designed to inform shippers how containers should be made and put together. Carelessness, indifference, and ignorance in packing merchandise for shipment take an enormous annual toll in damaged freight. The damage is often so great as to bring about total loss of the shipment. The competent industrial traffic manager will find little of his work more rewarding than the framing of proper instructions with regard to packing and regular inspection to make certain that these instructions are scrupulously observed.

Another cause of loss that can be placed at the shipper's door is the careless or negligent handling of packages while they are being loaded into a car or truck or being placed in position for loading. Hooks intended to facilitate the rapid movement of packages too often find lodgment in the merchandise the packages contain; packages are piled upon platforms in such a manner that the least disturbance causes the pile to come tumbling down, resulting in damage to the merchandise and occasionally in personal injury to workmen. A final cause of loss which might be mentioned among the shipper's shortcomings is the improper stowage of carload freight. Any freight car is bound to have a certain amount of rough treatment in the course of a journey through terminals and over main-line tracks, and package freight and other articles that are not properly braced and protected against the shocks and jars to which a car is inevitably subjected are likely to arrive at destination in a damaged condition. Among nonperishable goods carried by railroads, new furniture is one upon which the greatest amount is paid in compensation for damage.

FAULTS OF CARRIERS

The carriers themselves are responsible for much of the loss and damage which freight shipments suffer. It is the duty of a carrier to see that the cars in which freight is loaded are in proper condition to receive freight, whether the cars are those in which the carrier itself is loading less carload freight or cars which are furnished on the order of a shipper for the loading of carload freight. Protruding nails and bolts in the side wall or the end wall of a car, if not removed, seem to have a persistently perverse ability to seek out bags of sugar or flour or bales of textiles and probe them until the ruin is all but complete. Leaky car roofs may be as injurious to certain kinds of freight as a leaky house roof is disconcerting to the person sleeping in a bed beneath the spot where the rain pours into the room. Loose car doors, insecure grain doors, and cracks and other openings in car floors and walls account for the loss of much freight each year, loss which proper and careful car inspection might have prevented.

It is the duty of an agent who receives less carload freight for shipment to see that the freight brought to the station is properly packed and marked. If it is not, he should refuse to accept it for transportation. It is likewise incumbent upon the carrier's agent to see that his paper work is done correctly, for a mistake in a waybill, due to errors in copying from a shipping order prepared by a shipper, may lead to loss just as may a mistake made by the shipper in preparing the original shipping document. The agent who is loyal to his job and to his employer will see to it that boxes, barrels, bags, and other freight containers are adequately coopered and mended if repairs are necessary for the prevention of loss or damage.

The mishandling of freight in freight stations by the employees of the carrier probably causes more loss than mishandling by the employees of shippers. Anybody who has watched the handling of baggage in passenger terminals can understand how necessary it is for the constant traveler to possess a sturdy trunk. Freight containers are not likely to be handled any more gently than baggage, and a package which must be transferred several times between the station of origin and the station of destination may be subjected to a succession of handlings which put a heavy strain—often one impossible to meet successfully—upon its endurance. The careless use of hooks, poor stowage in cars, and insecure piling of freight upon platforms after unloading are other forms of mishandling which add to the annual bills railroads must pay for damage.

Once a shipment of freight is adequately packed, correctly marked and billed, and successfully loaded in cars without damage, it is ready for transportation, but it is by no means sure that it will arrive at destination in sound condition. It must bear the ordinary risks of loss or damage, of course, which are due to wrecks and other accidents, or to floods, fire, and civil commotion, but beyond these it must undergo the even greater risk of damage which arises from the careless or negligent handling of the car in which it is moving. Everybody who rides on passenger trains, buses, streetcars, and the New York subways must have observed that enginemen and motormen seem to have peculiarly different methods of starting and stopping their trains. On some trains, one glides out of a terminal with a movement that is virtually imperceptible and comes to stop at a station without being aware of the fact that the movement of the train has ceased. On others, one wonders if the man in command at the front is not taking a fiendish delight in trying to dislocate the vertebrae of all the passengers entrusted to his care. The differences among the men who operate freight-carrying facilities are just as great as the differences among those who operate the motive power of the vehicles in which passengers are transported, and freight may be and frequently is damaged—especially if it has not been properly braced by the shipper—by the quick starting and stopping of trains. In many freight yards, too, loaded cars are subjected to unduly violent shocks, as car riders use hand brakes too sparingly or car retarder operators fail to check cars strongly enough as they move down a hump to a classification track. Or it may be that trainmen and yardmen are not sufficiently mindful of the hand signals they give to enginemen, and cars which are to be coupled are permitted to come together too violently. Defective brakes on engines or cars or both may cause cars of freight to be handled too roughly in switching movements in yards and on sidings.

There are many other ways in which carelessness on the part of operating employees results in loss and damage to freight. Perishable fruits and vegetables may move without adequate refrigeration; the doors and hatches of refrigerator cars may not be tightly closed; drain pipes from ice bunkers may be permitted to become clogged and freight impregnated with brine; cars may be set out at wrong sidings and loss incurred because of negligent delay; and many shipments are inadvertently misrouted.

SAFETY AIDS

The traffic manager should familiarize himself with the things that are being done to promote the safe transportation of freight. He should carefully study the packing and marking instructions contained in the Consolidated or the Uniform Classification, and he should read about the numerous experiments being conducted by such agencies as the Bureau of Forest Products of the Department of Agriculture, the Freight Container Association, the Interstate Commerce Commission, and the Association of American Railroads, not to mention the work constantly being done by container manufacturers, all designed to develop means and devices which will make it possible to move freight shipments with a greater degree of safety. New methods of binding freight containers with steel wire or straps have contributed much to the reduction of loss and damage; the palletizing of freight on loading platforms has cut the loss and damage once due to improper piling; and several manufacturers have perfected ingenious devices by which freight can be held more firmly in place in the car in which it is loaded. The railroads are helpful to the industrial traffic managers in providing them with numerous pamphlets and folders giving special instructions on packing and stowing freight, and of course shippers endeavor to point out to carriers some of the ways in which they could help in diminishing the number and amount of freight claims. Another ingenious mechanical device which has been used for some years in an effort to locate the cause of damage to freight, which might be mentioned, is the impact recorder. Placed in a car, this instrument automatically records the shocks to which cars are subjected in their movement and measures the extent of the shocks. If cars are handled too roughly, it tells the story, and operating officials can take steps to bring about an improvement in the operation of trains.

HOW TO REDUCE CLAIMS

There is one thing the industrial traffic manager should be sure to do if he finds that it is necessary to file a large number of freight claims. He should make an analysis of the causes, and while he should by no means neglect any cause of damage which can be removed, he should concentrate his greatest effort on the correction of those faults which result in the largest amount of damage. A highly successful baseball pitcher once ascribed his excellent record to the fact that he concentrated his efforts on the batters who could do him the most harm. These were not the good hitters, but the poor ones. He did not neglect to be careful with the best hitters, but they were so good that he knew that however much effort he devoted to them they were usually bound to get their quota of hits just the same. So he saved his most intense energies for the hitters who were not so good. They were the ones on which he bore down. In other words, he exercised discrimination in the expenditure of his natural talents and used them in the manner which produced the most effective results. The traffic manager who is interested in claim prevention might do well to take a leaf from this man's book, and spend his time and energy in those places which promise the largest and most fruitful results.

Finally, no traffic manager worthy of the name will fail to do all he can to aid in the work of freight claim prevention. In helping to cut down the waste caused by avoidable accidents and mishaps, of whatever kind, he is doing a genuine service to his employer. By the same token, he is doing something for his own advancement, both financially and professionally. Moreover, in helping to bring about a safer and more efficient transportation service, upon which the entire economy of the country is so dependent, he is doing something which is of immeasurable benefit to the public of which he is a part.

CHAPTER XIV

Marine Insurance

In a previous chapter, it was pointed out that carriers by water have been singled out both by custom and by law for marked favor among carriers with respect to liability for the property which they transport. While carriers by land are virtually insurers of the property they carry from place to place, if a carrier by water uses due diligence to see that his vessel is seaworthy before it starts on a voyage, his only obligation to cargo is to see that it is loaded and stowed properly and delivered to the right consignee. So far, Congress has enacted no statutes defining the liability of air carriers, and presumably their liability is determined by the age-old principles of common law, under the shelter of which they have inserted many provisions in their bills of lading the validity of which has received little test in courts of law. Some of them may have a rude awakening at some future time.

THE PREVALENCE OF RISK

The shipper who entrusts his property to a carrier by water knows that he is taking a risk—a very much greater risk than he takes when he employs the services of a carrier by land. But risk is a part—a highly important part—of all business, a part of life itself. Everybody is constantly in more or less danger. Whether we like it or not, when we walk on busy thoroughfares, in the country or in the city, we are risking life and limb; we stand at all times in danger of contracting some disease; fires, floods, and other accidental occurrences remind us daily that we are never completely safe. It is interesting to look about and see how much we do to minimize the daily risks to which we are subjected. Traffic signs and signals on highways and railroads, beacons along our airways, lighthouses and buoys which mark a safe pathway for ships, levees along large rivers, dams for flood control, building codes to lessen the danger of fire, health bureaus to control epidemics, preventive medicine and such practices as vaccination and inoculation, warnings to see the dentist twice a year— the devices which we invent and use to protect our lives and give everybody a greater measure of safety, or freedom from risk, are countless.

In business, too, we have done many things to take away some of the risk which an individual might incur. The business corporation, through which so much of the business of this country and the world is conducted, owes its origin in part, at least, to a desire of an individual to hold his risk in an enterprise to a calculated amount. How often one hears the homely adage about being careful not to put all your eggs in one basket. Shakespeare has Antonio say to his friend, "I thank my fortune for it, My ventures are not in one bottom trusted, Nor to one place. . . ."

THE PURPOSE OF INSURANCE

In business, as in many other activities, the individual cannot himself eliminate all risk and chance of loss, nor can any other agency of business enterprise do so. But the individual or the corporation can, for a price, transfer the risk or the penalty for an unforeseen loss to someone else. In other words, one can be insured against certain kinds of loss, and one of the largest kinds of business enterprise in the world today is the insurance business. Everyone is familiar with insurance and its purposes, and most of us know that fundamentally it is based upon a statistical calculation of the "probability" of death, disease, accident, or other events which endanger the safety of persons and property.

RISKS OF THE SEA

Of all the risks which a merchant or trader must take in the course of his business operations, there is none much greater than that in which he becomes involved when he turns his property over to a carrier by water for transportation. Transportation by water has from time immemorial been regarded as extremely hazardous. The sea, even when it meant only the Mediterranean Sea and a part of the Atlantic Ocean near the western coast of Europe, was regarded with awe and fear. It was the place of deep mystery, high adventure, and mortal danger. The most fearsome legends of Greece were of the perils encountered on the sea. The story of Jason and the Golden Fleece, Homer's *Odyssey*, and Vergil's *Aeneid* are examples of the tales concerning the extraordinary dangers which lay in wait for the mariner and his ship. The Psalmist said, "They that go down to the sea in ships, that do business in great waters; these see the works of the Lord, and the wonders of the deep." Our books of common prayer contain special supplications in behalf of those about to go to sea and special words of thanksgiving for those who return safely from its broad waters. In poem, gospel hymn, story, and song, writers of all ages have found in the sea and its nameless terrors a theme for their imaginative excursions.

It may be that the sea and other waters have had a peculiarly strong traditional relationship with business because for so many centuries the only large commerce of the world, worthy of the name of commerce, was water-borne. Before the invention of the steam engine and its application to transportation, carriage by land could be accomplished only by the use of the muscular power of man or beast, while in water transport the powerful natural agency of the wind drove thousands of ships about the world to effect the interchange of the products of widely separated lands. Water transportation was far cheaper than land transportation. Adam Smith, in his famous treatise, *The Wealth of Nations*, remarked that goods could be carried more cheaply from Calcutta or Bombay to London by water than from London to Edinburgh by land, and he called attention to the fact that all great civilizations, ancient and modern, had thrived in river valleys or close to the seashore where transportation by water made it possible to carry on the commerce to build a great civilization.

ORIGIN OF MARINE INSURANCE

It is not surprising, in view of the long-recognized importance of commerce by water, and because of the risk which all water transportation involved, that insurance became closely identified at an early date with this kind of commerce and that marine insurance is one of the oldest "auxiliary" business activities known, as old even as banking. It is known that both the Greeks and the Romans, as well as those first great merchants of the sea, the Phoenicians, who founded Carthage, so many years the great political and commercial rival of the Eternal City, had a form of marine insurance, consisting of "bottomry loans" and "bonds respondentia," the former applicable to ships and the latter to cargo. The insurer would lend, at agreed rates of interest, a sum of money to the owner of a ship or to the owner of a cargo, roughly equivalent to its value, the condition of a loan being that if ship or cargo were lost the loan was not to be repaid. Although we know little about insurance practices during the so-called Dark Ages, which followed the fall of Rome and during which commerce fell under a destructive blight, the chances are that the business was kept alive in a small way by traders on the Mediterranean. With the revival of European commerce and the development of the trading cities which composed the Hanseatic League, the rise to Mediterranean commercial supremacy of the cities of Venice and Genoa, and the beginning of English foreign trade at such centers as Bristol and London, marine insurance flourished anew, though it took on an appearance resembling modern insurance rather than the form of conditional loans. The term "marine insurance" seems to have been first used early in the fourteenth century. By the time Columbus made his memorable voyage, this type of business was a widespread, active, and prosperous enterprise.

LLOYD'S OF LONDON

We are likely to think of the beginning of the marine insurance business of Great Britain in connection with the establishment of Edward Lloyd's coffeehouse in the latter part of the seventeenth century. It had a flourishing existence long before that, however, so much so that as early as 1601 the English Parliament established a special court to try marine insurance cases. Lloyd unquestionably stimulated the growth of the business, however, first, because his coffeehouse supplied a meeting place where merchants and shipowners desiring protection against the risks of their ventures made contact with the "underwriters" whose business it was to sell insurance policies and assume these risks, and second, because of the other activities which he promoted, such as the publication of *Lloyd's List,* in which the movements of ships at sea were recorded, and Lloyd's *Register of Shipping,* in which thousands of vessels of all maritime nations of the world came to be classified and rated for insurance purposes.

Lloyd's of London is still the greatest marine insurance institution in the world, though the business is also conducted in many other countries and Lloyd's does not confine itself wholly to marine insurance. Of course, Lloyd's does not write or sell insurance itself. It is the market place where shipowner and merchant meet the underwriter, just as they once did in the London coffeehouse. It is comparable to the Stock Exchange of New York, which does not itself engage in the sale and purchase of securities but affords an organized and orderly market for the brokers through which this business is transacted. The merchant or shipowner transmits his need for insurance to Lloyd's; for a stated premium, he receives an insurance policy, each of the participating underwriters who assume the risk indicating the portion of the total amount of insurance for which he is liable.

INLAND MARINE INSURANCE

In the United States, there are many casualty insurance companies which write marine insurance, and there are agents who will provide a Lloyd's policy if one is desired. While we usually think of marine insurance as protection against the risks which ships and cargoes encounter on the high seas, we also have a flourishing "inland marine insurance" business which issues policies covering the risks to which merchandise is subjected when moving in domestic commerce by railroad, highway, or inland waters. The shipowner or merchant who has need of insurance can apply directly to the company which issues the policy, or he can deal through an insurance broker, who maintains contact with several insurance agencies and acts as the middleman between the insurer and the insured. It does not cost the merchant any more to secure his policies through a broker, since the latter is paid a commission by the insurer, the amount being determined by the premium which is charged for the policy.

THE OPEN POLICY

A trader may obtain a policy to cover a certain specified shipment, but the larger business concerns which are engaged constantly in the purchase and sale of commodities in many markets usually have what is called an "open policy." Such a policy is written for an amount sufficient to cover prospective commercial transactions for a certain period of time. Under such a policy, all the merchant's "ventures" are covered, though he may not know exactly when or where any particular shipment was started on its way. He is obliged under his insurance contract, however, to notify the insurer of the nature and value of the cargo covered as soon as he gets the necessary information. Sometimes, if the information is not readily forthcoming, a cargo may be transported across the sea and delivered without the underwriter having any knowledge of the precise amount for which he would be liable in case of loss, except that he knows the amount to be within the limits of the open policy previously issued.

Since we are interested primarily in the work of the industrial traffic manager, we shall not discuss the insurance applicable to vessels in which goods are carried—"hull insurance"—but only the insurance that is effected on cargo, even though it may be true that some traffic managers, whose employers have their own barges and other transportation equipment, have the responsibility of seeing that adequate insurance is maintained on these facilities.

GENERAL AVERAGE

There are many kinds of losses to cargo, which the marine insurance policy will cover. Broadly speaking, there are two general classes of losses, one of which is "general average," or a voluntary loss, and the other of which is involuntary, or accidental.[1] We have mentioned general average before, in connection with bills of lading. The distinguishing features of such a loss are that it is voluntary and intentional and that it occurs under the direction of or with the consent of the master of the vessel, representing a sacrifice made in the hope of saving the remainder of the venture. A common example of general average is the jettisoning of cargo to lighten a ship or the dismasting of a sailing ship. When a fire breaks out in a vessel's hold, the water which is used to extinguish the flames may cause damage to cargo not necessarily endangered by the fire. This loss, too, comes under general average. All participants in the entire venture—the

---

[1] Like so many other words we have met with, the word "average" has several meanings. In marine insurance, it means loss. A general average is a general loss, a particular average a particular loss. We do not speak of a "general average loss" or of a "particular average loss," for the words "loss" and "average" mean the same thing.

owners of the ship and the owners of the cargo—must bear a share of such a voluntary sacrifice, even though their own property remains intact and uninjured. The share which each participant must assume is in direct proportion to the value of his interest in the venture. General average is only a partial loss of the entire venture; if the ship goes down and the entire venture is destroyed, the sacrifice has been in vain, and no general average has resulted. On the other hand, while general average involves only a partial loss of the entire venture, it may result in the total loss of the property of one or more of the participants in the venture. But whether the loss of the party whose property has been sacrificed is total or partial, he is entitled to compensation from those others who have a share in the venture, except of course that he must bear his own proportion of the voluntary sacrifice.

Virtually all marine insurance policies give complete coverage for general average. Should all portions of the cargo be insured, and the vessel likewise, the underwriters of the insurance must bear the loss, whatever the amount may be. If one of the participants in the venture has failed, through neglect or otherwise, to obtain an insurance policy covering general average, he must himself bear his proper share of the loss occasioned by the sacrifice.

It must be understood that general average is a unique type of loss. There is nothing quite comparable to it in ordinary property and casualty insurance which covers losses on the land. Its peculiar character derives from the fact that it represents a voluntary sacrifice which is made in the midst of imminent peril for the purpose of saving life and property. If the idea of general average did not exist, however "voluntary" the sacrifice of jettisoning cargo may appear to be, it is not a particularly agreeable performance to contemplate. Those who have read *Ivanhoe* will recall how Isaac of York regretted in bitter words how "willingly" he flung over his merchandise in the Gulf of Lyons "to lighten the ship, while she labored in the tempest—robed the seething billows in my choice silks —perfumed their briny foam with myrrh and aloes—enriched their caverns with gold and silver work! And was that not an hour of unutterable misery though my hands made the sacrifice." Once in a while we hear of sacrifices on land that bear a resemblance to general average, as when blocks of city buildings are dynamited and destroyed to prevent the spread of a raging fire or when "backfires" are started to save a forest from utter destruction.

PERILS OF THE SEA; PERILS ON THE SEA

The ordinary marine insurance policy protects the insured not only against general average but also against losses which are due to "perils of the sea," such as violent storms and the sinking or stranding of the vessel, and losses due to "perils on the sea," such as theft, pilferage, "sweating," fire, barratry, or spoilage caused by the entrance of fresh or salt water into a vessel's holds. There is virtually no cause of loss, no risk, no danger, against which a shipper cannot obtain insurance, though the greater the risk assumed by the underwriters, the greater the premium the shipper must pay. The losses due to the perils encountered in water transportation may be "total" or "partial." If the loss is total, the underwriter will compensate the insured to the amount of insured value for which a premium has been paid, but if the loss is of the kind called "particular average," or a partial loss, the amount which the underwriter is required to pay may be limited, and it may be that he is not required to pay at all.

PARTICULAR AVERAGE

Some kinds of goods or merchandise are so susceptible to damage, because of their character or because of the manner in which they are transported, that the underwriter will not pay anything for a partial loss unless it is due to certain causes enumerated in the policy. The goods are declared to be "free of particular average." The F.P.A. clause in the ordinary English policy of marine insurance is different from the same clause in an ordinary American policy. Under "English conditions," the goods are "free of average, unless general, or the vessel be stranded, burnt, sunk or in collision." Under "American conditions," the goods are "free of average, unless general, or unless caused by stranding, sinking, burning or collision with another vessel." Under the English conditions, the underwriter will pay for a partial loss, even if the loss has occurred before the vessel sinks, burns, becomes stranded, or collides with another ship; under the American conditions, the underwriter will pay for a partial loss of goods insured free of particular average only if the loss has been *caused* by one of the enumerated mishaps to the vessel. The English conditions are more liberal to the insured and are now included in most policies issued by American companies. General average is paid, of course, under both sets of conditions.

Instead of giving a policy under which goods are entirely "free of particular average," and the insured is consequently entitled to no compensation for a partial loss except under the limited conditions mentioned, the underwriter may issue a policy under which the goods are insured against partial loss only if the loss exceeds a certain percentage of their insured value. The policies on many shipments therefore will read, "free of average under three percent [or under five, or some other percent], unless general, or the vessel be stranded, etc." If the partial loss is less than the stipulated fraction, the underwriter makes no payment, but if the loss exceeds this fraction, the underwriter pays the entire amount of the damage. Of course it is possible for the insurer to get a policy covering partial losses of any amount whatever, but the premium will be greater than the premium payable under the F.P.A. contract. Though bearing some resemblance to the automobile collision policy which has a "deductible clause," the F.P.A. contract is not the same. The underwriter will pay, under the automobile policy, only the amount of damage in excess of the "deduction." Under the F.P.A. contract, the underwriter will pay the entire damage if it exceeds the stipulated fraction.

The variation in the degree of responsibility assumed by an insurance company for particular average may be observed in the following excerpt from a standard form of insurance policy once issued by an American corporation:

It is also agreed, that bar, bundle, rod, hoop and sheet iron, wire of all kinds, tin plates, steel, madder, sumac, brooms, wicker-ware and willow (manufactured or otherwise), straw goods, salt, grain of all kinds, rice, tobacco, Indian meal, fruits (whether preserved or otherwise), cheese, dry fish, hay, vegetables and roots, paper, rags, hempen yarn, bags, cotton bagging, and other articles used for bags and bagging, pleasure carriages, household furniture, skins and hides, musical instruments, looking-glasses, and all other articles that are perishable in their own nature, are warranted by the assured free from average, unless general; hemp, tobacco stems, matting and cassia, except in boxes, free from average under *twenty percent.*, unless general; and sugar, flax, flax-seed and bread, are warranted by the assured free from average under *seven percent.*, unless general; and coffee, in bags or bulk, pepper, in bags or bulk, free from average under *ten percent.*, unless general.

Although insurance policies in use today may not contain so many exceptions, the traffic manager should be constantly on guard to understand just how extensively his marine insurance policy protects him against a partial loss due to the ordinary perils of water transport.

One thing the shipper must see to when obtaining marine insurance, if he wants adequate protection, is that a single shipment consisting of numerous pieces or packages of the same article is not insured as a whole but that the insurance applies to each package, piece, or unit of the shipment, or at least to a limited number of pieces. For example, if a shipment of 1,000 typewriters, each valued at $100, is insured as a whole, free of particular average under 5 per cent, and 20 of the machines are damaged beyond repair, the underwriter would not be required to give compensation for the loss because the amount of damage, $2,000, is less than 5 per cent of the total insured value of the shipment. If, however, each machine is separately insured, the shipper is protected against the entire loss. In most policies issued at the present time, there is a provision to the effect that "each case, bale or shipping package" is "separately insured," but it is well for the traffic manager, when effecting insurance on a shipment, to know all the terms of the policy under which he has protection.

CONSTRUCTIVE TOTAL LOSS

The total loss of cargo which is covered by insurance may be actual, that is, the goods may be destroyed or sunk, or it may be "constructive," meaning that the goods are so badly damaged that any attempt at salvage would probably cost more than the value of the goods after recovery and repair. It frequently happens that, when a vessel is stranded on a reef or in shoal water, it can be floated and much of the value of ship and cargo recovered by salvage operations. When the vessel is in such dire straits, however, that neither it nor the cargo can be rescued at a cost less than the value recovered, it is abandoned as a constructive total loss, and the underwriters pay the total amount of the insurance in force. In most marine insurance policies, however, may be found a clause known as the "sue and labor clause," under which the insured is required to "sue, labor, and travel for, in and about the defense, safeguard, and recovery of the said goods and merchandise, or any part thereof, without prejudice to this insurance." The insured cannot just abandon partially damaged goods and demand that the underwriters pay their full value, but must cooperate with the underwriters in reconditioning and selling damaged goods and in doing whatever else is necessary to keep the loss of the underwriters to a minimum amount.

OBLIGATIONS OF THE INSURED

There are numerous other obligations which a shipper assumes when taking out marine insurance. Since under the bill of lading issued by the carrier the shipper is required to pack goods for shipment in containers which are durable and safe, if he neglects to do so he cannot hold the underwriter responsible for any loss incurred because he failed to fulfill his own obligations with respect to packing. The shipper obtaining insurance must also be sure that the goods upon which he seeks protection are a part of a commercial venture which is entirely legal. Insurance on narcotics or other deleterious articles, being imported into a country in contravention of the country's laws or commercial regulations, would not be binding upon the underwriter in case of loss. No underwriter would be bound by a policy covering any kind of illegal shipment.

The shipper who takes out a marine insurance policy must have an "insurable interest" in the goods insured; the same is true with respect to policies taken out on vessels. In former times, insurance companies did not require that the policyholder have such an interest, and the result was that marine insurance occasionally became a vehicle for wild gambling and speculation. Speculators, hearing of a vessel in distress, would make use of insurance companies to gamble on the vessel's chance of ultimate survival. If the danger of its loss was very great, the insurance premiums would naturally be high, but if the ship went down, the enterprising gambler might reap a rich harvest. Such speculative activities represented a perversion of the use of the insurance business and resulted in legislation requiring the insured to have an insurable interest in the vessel or the merchandise for which he sought protection against loss or damage.

THREE PARTIES OF INTEREST; SUBROGATION

The transportation by water of insured merchandise involves three parties—the owner of the cargo, the carrier, and the underwriter. The owner, or shipper, makes a contract with each of the other two. While there may be no contractual relation between the carrier and the underwriter, they may nevertheless have a common interest or even a conflict of interest because of their agreements with the shipper. It will be remembered that in the bill of lading there is a provision to the effect that the carrier is to have the benefit of any insurance that may have been effected on a shipment, so far as it shall not avoid the policies or contracts of insurance. If an underwriter should insure a shipper against a loss for which the carrier under the law could be held responsible, the carrier might be greatly pleased if the underwriter would compensate the shipper for the loss and relieve the carrier of any financial responsibility to the shipper. For example, most insurance policies waive the warranty of seaworthiness which a carrier is obliged to make. Should a loss of cargo occur because of the unseaworthiness of a vessel (the unseaworthiness being of such a character that due diligence in inspection would have disclosed the fault), while the shipper's loss would be covered by his insurance policy, the carrier could be held liable. Naturally, however willing the carrier might be to let the underwriter make good the damage to the shipper, the underwriter would be of the opinion that the shipper's compensation should come from the negligent carrier. It is because of a conflict of interest such as this that the marine policy usually contains a "subrogation clause." Taken literally, subrogation would mean that the underwriter assumed the rights of the shipper with respect to any legal claim the shipper might have against the carrier. Because of certain legal technicalities, however, the subrogation clause does not, as a rule, put the matter quite so baldly, though the effect is about the same. In the first place, the insured cannot assign the policy of insurance to anybody without the consent of the underwriter. This means that the shipper cannot make a deal with the carrier under which he receives compensation for his loss from the carrier while the carrier reimburses itself from the underwriter. A second provision of the subrogation agreement forbids the shipper to give the carrier any release from a claim which the carrier might be legally bound to pay. Finally, in order that the shipper may not be deprived of funds needed in his business, which he would derive through a prompt settlement of his claim either by the underwriter or by the carrier, the underwriter agrees to make a "loan" to the shipper of an amount equal to what the shipper would receive in full settlement of the claim. If the carrier is thought to be responsible under the law for the shipper's loss, the shipper can be required, under the "sue and labor clause," to file suit against the carrier. If the claim against the carrier proves to be a valid one, the money received in settlement repays the shipper's loan from the underwriter; if the carrier cannot be held liable for the loss, the underwriter cancels the loan. In any event, the shipper receives his proper remuneration, and the responsibility for payment is lodged eventually against the party who is legally liable.

The merchant who has an "open" insurance policy must be careful, when giving the underwriter information concerning a shipment to which insurance is to apply, to state the proper value of the shipment. If he states a lower value or "underinsures" the shipment, and it is lost, he will receive in settlement of a claim an amount which bears the same proportion to the insured value that the insured value bears to the correct market value of the shipment. For example, if a shipment having a market value of $100,000 is insured for $50,000, in case of total loss the underwriter will pay the shipper only $25,000. In effect, the shipper becomes a coinsurer with the underwriter when he underinsures a shipment, and must bear his share of the loss. This arrangement is fair to the underwriter, whose earnings are derived from the premiums he obtains; the holder of an open policy should not endeavor, by a practice of undervaluation, to deprive the underwriter of premiums to which he is rightfully entitled. If the shipper does take such a chance, and a loss takes place, he may find that his mistake has cost him dearly.

EXTENT OF COVERAGE

The traffic manager who purchases insurance on a shipment of merchandise should always be careful to know how much of the shipment's journey is covered in a policy. Nearly all marine insurance is now sold on a "warehouse-to-warehouse" basis, the warehouses being at the ports between which the shipment is carried, though coverage can be obtained from a warehouse in the interior of a state or country to a warehouse in the interior of another state or country. In times past, marine policies were often written which gave coverage only when the shipment was on board a vessel, and all too often a negligent merchant woke up to the fact that his goods were not insured against losses occurring while the shipment was being transferred by barge or lighter between ship and shore.

It should be borne in mind that a "standard form" of policy issued by a company may not cover certain kinds of losses. If the insured wants further protection, he must require the insertion of additional clauses in the policy and, of course, pay a higher premium. The bill of lading of a water carrier usually provides that there shall be no deviation in a vessel's voyage except for certain specified reasons, such as docking for necessary repairs or to save life or property at sea. The ordinary marine policy will afford protection against loss in case of a deviation of the kind permissible under the terms of the bill of lading, but if deviation for other causes takes place, the owner of cargo may not be protected during the time of such deviation unless a special clause has been inserted in the policy. In the same way, many marine policies contain the statement: "Warranted free of loss or damage caused by or resulting from strikes, lockouts, labor disturbances, riots, civil commotions or the acts of any person or persons taking part in any such occurrence or disorder." If protection is wanted against such risks, a proper notation to that effect must be included in the policy. It may be said that the practices of insurance companies have undergone much change over the years, and that many risks which they once declined to assume without the payment of an extra premium are now covered in the policies ordinarily and normally issued. The Carriage of Goods by Sea Act permits a greater freedom of deviation to a vessel than was customary under the terms of the bills of lading employed before the law was passed. Ocean bills of lading have consequently been modified, and insurance policies have likewise been changed.

WAR-RISK INSURANCE

There is one kind of risk which ordinary marine policies have seldom covered and still do not cover; during the first half of the twentieth century, it was unhappily a risk that was all too prevalent on seas the world over. This was war risk. Underwriters were usually firm in their declination of responsibility for loss due to this particular type of danger. Policies often contained a clause such as this:

Notwithstanding anything herein contained to the contrary, this insurance is warranted free from capture, seizure, arrest, restraint, detainment, confiscation, preemption, requisition or nationalization and the consequences thereof or of any attempt thereat, whether in time of peace or war and whether lawful or otherwise; also warranted free from all consequences of hostilities or warlike operations (whether there be a declaration of war or not), piracy, civil war, revolution, rebellion or insurrection, or civil strife arising therefrom.

This did not mean that marine insurance companies did not give insurance against war risks, but when they did so, it was by means of a special agreement in the usual policy or, more often, by means of a special and separate policy. During times of peace, the premiums for war-risk coverage were not extremely high, and they tended to diminish as danger due to the residues of war, such as floating mines and derelicts, lessened.

During the Second World War, the problem of war-risk insurance became very difficult, especially during the height of submarine warfare when packs of German U-boats scoured the seas in search of defenseless prey. It became necessary for maritime countries to come to the aid of underwriters and assume a part of the risk. Very soon after hostilities broke out, the government of the United States made provisions for the protection of the owners of American ships and cargoes against losses due to war, although the actual policies of war-risk insurance were issued by commercial underwriters, acting as agents for the government.

INSURANCE CERTIFICATES

When a merchant holds an open policy of insurance, the underwriter does not customarily provide him with a full policy for each shipment made but issues to him instead a "certificate of insurance," which includes a résumé of the provisions of the open policy. Such a certificate is the equivalent of a policy, and in foreign trade it is usually included with the draft against a purchaser of goods, the ocean bill of lading, and such other documents as may be necessary for the completion of a commercial transaction between an exporter and an importer. Needless to say, the insurer keeps a copy of all certificates he transmits to others as well as a complete record of the actual amount of insurance certified on different shipments under the terms of his open policy.

SETTLEMENT OF INSURANCE CLAIMS

The settlement of losses for which an underwriter is responsible is much like the presentation and settlement of claims against a land carrier, except in the case of general average, when the process of settlement may be somewhat complicated, because there may be numerous parties at interest. In the case of total loss, the lawful holder of the insurance policy or certificate must present his claim directly to an agent of the underwriter or make his claim through a broker who performs such services for insurance claimants. He must present a statement from the carrier's agent indicating that the insured goods were actually loaded and dispatched, provide the underwriter with the original bill of lading for the goods as proof of ownership of the goods, submit the insurance policy or certificate, and file a commercial invoice of the goods by which the market value of the goods can be compared with the insured value. Some of these documents, including the bill of lading, if it is an order bill, and the insurance policy and certificate, must be properly endorsed.

When a partial loss occurs at sea for causes which make the underwriter responsible to the owner of the goods for the loss or damage, the master of the ship, as soon as possible after reaching port, files a "protest" with port authorities, in which he gives an official statement of the cause of the loss or damage and disclaims any responsibility on the part of the vessel. The underwriter or his agent is notified of the loss and of the proposed claim for insurance, whereupon the underwriter or the agent appoints a surveyor who, in cooperation with the insured, examines the property to find out the extent of the loss or damage. The documents filed with the claim for insurance are the same as those filed with a claim arising because of total loss, except that there must also be a certified copy of the master's protest and a statement of the amount of the claim and how it has been calculated.

It frequently happens that a shipment is landed on a pier in a damaged condition, or with a portion missing, and the master of the vessel, unaware of the loss or damage, files no protest. In the terms and conditions of the bill of lading of a carrier by water, there is usually a statement that "all claims for damage to cargo, misdelivery, short delivery, or delay in delivery thereof, or for shortage of packages or portions of packages, must be presented in writing, disclosing fully the nature and extent thereof, to the shipowner or to the vessel's agent at the port of discharge, before the cargo is removed from the carrier's custody or the final receipts signed." The rules are more strict than the rules applicable in connection with land shipment, and the time in which suit for recovery of damages may be filed is shorter. It is incumbent upon the prospective claimant for indemnity under an insurance policy to notify the carrier in accordance with this rule, both for the protection of his own rights and for the protection of the rights of the carrier. If, after the discovery of the loss, a protest is filed on behalf of the carrier, a copy of the protest must accompany the other documents which are to be filed with the insurance underwriter, as well as a copy of the written notice of loss given to the carrier and a copy of the carrier's acknowledgment of the notice.

When a vessel arrives in port after making a voluntary sacrifice of cargo or equipment, it becomes necessary to secure the services of a general average adjuster, who determines the extent of the loss, finds out which interests in the venture bore the sacrifice, and calculates the contribution which each interest in the venture must make as his share of the general average. First of all, the parties whose goods have been sacrificed must be notified and their claims for reimbursement duly filed. Since a lien exists against all cargo for the payment of general average, shipments will not be released until each interest gives a bond or other security to guarantee the payment of its contribution. If the goods which have been sacrificed are insured, the underwriter will pay the owner the insured value and assume by subrogation whatever right to payment the insured had under the general average adjustment. The general average adjuster has a vast amount of work to do before final settlement of claims can be made. All parties at interest must provide him with complete information of the nature and value of their shares in the total venture.

After all the information is assembled, since the amount of the loss or damage has been ascertained, the division of responsibility becomes merely a matter of arithmetical calculation, each interested party being called upon to pay as his share of the total loss an amount equal to the ratio which the value of his interest bore to the total value of the entire venture. As was previously explained, all marine insurance policies cover general average; an uninsured party in the venture must pay his duly assigned share of the general average himself.

CONCLUSION

We have not endeavored to do more than cover the most salient features of marine insurance in this discussion, and there are many aspects of it which we have not discussed at all or have touched upon only briefly. The study of this type of insurance, of its history as well as its practices, is a fascinating pursuit, and the ambitious traffic manager would do well to read widely and intensively on the subject. If he is engaged only in domestic commerce, he may not have any immediate use for a thorough knowledge of marine insurance, though, as indicated before, the business of inland marine insurance is a growing one, and many shippers find that it is more economical to insure against certain kinds of losses than to pursue a multitude of small claims. Furthermore, no industrial traffic manager can be unaware of the fact that his path of advancement may lead him to an employer that is engaged in foreign trade, a branch of commerce in which a knowledge of marine insurance is indispensable. Finally, though most of our domestic commerce is carried by land, on railways and highways, a valuable and substantial part of it is carried by water. Since the carrier by water in domestic commerce has a burden of liability that is little different from that of the carrier engaged in foreign trade, it is necessary for the traffic manager who deals with water carriers to know the nature of their liability and to know the need for familiarity with the principles and practices of marine insurance.

CHAPTER XV

Routing

One result of the multiplicity of railroad companies in the United States and of the competitive services offered by many different lines is that a shipper often finds that he has a wide number of routes available between many stations. There is no large commercial or industrial city in the United States which is not served by more than one railroad. Many of our seaports such as New York, San Francisco, and Seattle as well as many great interior urban centers such as Chicago, St. Louis, and Indianapolis have many lines over which freight and passenger traffic moves in and out. Connecting all of the commercial centers of the United States, which are some distance apart, there may be literally dozens and even hundreds of different rail routes. Some of these routes may be made up of a single line, as in the case of each of the four trunk lines—the New York Central, the Pennsylvania, the Erie, and the Baltimore and Ohio—connecting New York with Chicago. But there are also many routes which are composed of a combination of connecting lines. For example, the Lehigh Valley and the Delaware, Lackawanna and Western both have terminals at the Port of New York. Though these lines go no farther west than Buffalo on their own tracks, each day they originate a large amount of traffic destined for Chicago and other points west which, in order to reach its destination, must be turned over to some connecting line, such as the Nickel Plate, the Wabash, the Pere Marquette division of the Chesapeake and Ohio, or even one of the big trunk lines, for transportation beyond Buffalo. As a further illustration of the multiplicity of routes, it might be pointed out that though there are hundreds of smaller stations in Ohio, Indiana, and other central states which have only one railroad, the traffic moving to one of these stations from New York might pass over one or two or three of dozens of lines before finally being delivered to the line carrying it to its destination.

There are thousands of shipments made daily in the United States which could not possibly reach their destination by rail without passing over two or more railroad lines. Anybody familiar with the railroad geography of this country knows that we have no truly "transcontinental" railroad, that is, one owned by a single company which has a line stretching from the eastern to the western coast. Canada has two genuine transcontinentals, and it is possible there to dispatch a shipment of goods from a station on the Atlantic Ocean to one on the Pacific and have it move all the way on the tracks of a single railroad company. But such is not the case in the United States. When one travels by rail from Boston, New York, Philadelphia, or any other eastern seaport to Seattle, San Francisco, Los Angeles, or some other port on the Pacific Coast, one may find it possible to go all the way in the same car, but the car must surely pass over the lines of two or more railroads. The same is true with respect to freight shipments. Chicago is known to be the greatest railroad center in America, if not in the world. If a person were asked how many railroads pass through the Windy City, he would be likely to reply thoughtlessly that the number must be nearly forty, when as a matter of fact only three railroads actually pass *through* Chicago; the remainder terminate there. One of the most remarkable features of railroad operation in the Chicago area is the manner in which carload and less carload freight traffic is interchanged between the numerous lines which focus upon this great commercial center. The same type of operation, though not on such a grand scale, may be witnessed in the St. Louis district and in many other of our larger railroad centers.

The wide number and variety of rail routes existing in the United States keep alive a very keen competition among our many railroad companies. While this competition does not often take the form of cutting rates any more, it is extremely evident in railroad service. There are no other rival producing organizations in the United States which compete more eagerly than the railroads for the business of possible customers. In recent years, of course, this competition has been accentuated as well as modified in character because of the remarkable development of transportation by highway and by air. Every large railroad in the country maintains "off-line" offices in leading commercial cities for the solicitation of both freight and passenger business. Every industrial traffic manager who controls the routing of considerable quantities of freight will find that part of his time is taken up by traffic solicitors, not only from the competing railroads to which he might deliver traffic at the point of origin but from railroads whose lines may be hundreds of miles away, urging him to "route" some of his business their way.

RIGHT OF SHIPPER TO CONTROL ROUTING

The first thing for a traffic manager to keep in mind with respect to routing his traffic by rail is that he has the right to select the route over which he desires his traffic to move. The right is not absolute, but the exceptions are not numerous, and they usually become operative only in cases of emergency. Subdivision 8, section 15, part I, of the Interstate Commerce Act states:

In all cases where at the time of delivery of property to any railroad corporation being a common carrier, for transportation subject to the provisions of this part to any point or destination, between which and the point of such delivery for shipment two or more through routes and through rates shall have been established as in this part provided to which through routes and through rates such carrier is a party, the person, firm or corporation making such shipment, subject to such reasonable exceptions and regulations as the Interstate Commerce Commission shall from time to time prescribe, shall have the right to designate in writing by which of such through routes such property shall be transported to destination, and it shall thereupon be the duty of the initial carrier to route such property and issue a through bill of lading therefor as so directed, and to transport said property over its own line or lines and deliver the same to a connecting line or lines according to such through route, and it shall be the duty of each of said connecting carriers to receive said property and transport it over said line or lines and deliver same to the next succeeding carrier or consignee according to the routing instructions in said bill of lading: Provided, however, That the shipper shall in all instances have the right to determine, where competing lines of railroad constitute portions of a through line or route, over which of said competing lines so constituting a portion of said through line or route his freight shall be transported.

If any carrier forming a part of a through line or route fails to observe these provisions of the law and diverts a shipment to a carrier not mentioned in the through route designated by the shipper, the carrier losing the business has the right to recover the revenue it would have received (had the shipper's routing instructions been followed) from the carrier or carriers guilty of the improper diversion.

MEANING OF THROUGH ROUTE

It might be well to go into a brief explanation here of the meaning of the term "through route." The Supreme Court has provided a good definition, saying that it is an "arrangement express or implied, between connecting railroads for the continuous carriage of goods from the originating point on the line of one carrier to destination on the line of another."[1] The main point is that a through route is authorized by the participating carriers; it is the result of a specific arrangement or agreement among them. A "connecting route" does not necessarily mean a through route. While it is physically possible to send a shipment over a connecting route, the methods by which the shipment is handled and the charges the shipper must pay usually make it less desirable to use than an established

[1] See Through Rates, 12 I.C.C. 113 (1907); Ogden Gateway Case, 35 I.C.C. 131 (1915); Grain and Grain Products, 129 I.C.C. 261 (1927); Brady v. Pennsylvania R.R., 2 I.C.C. 131 (1888); Kansas City v. Kansas City Viaduct and Terminal Ry., 24 I.C.C. 22 (1912); St. Louis Southwestern Ry. v. United States, 245 U.S. 136 (1917).

through route, if one is available. The Supreme Court in another case [2] called attention to the difference between a connecting route and a through route and pointed out that a certain route may be physically open, but commercially closed. It is this fact that makes so highly important the power of the Interstate Commerce Commission to establish through routes which connecting carriers will not voluntarily establish.

It must be borne in mind, too, that a through route does not always have an applicable joint rate, although a great many of them do, and such rates are undeniably a convenience to a shipper. Nevertheless, many through routes have combination rates instead of joint rates. These combination rates, as well as joint rates, are subject to regulation by the Interstate Commerce Commission.

COMMISSION'S EMERGENCY POWER OVER ROUTING

We shall discuss at a later point in this chapter the right of the Interstate Commerce Commission to establish through routes and joint rates, but it might be mentioned here that under the subdivision 4, section 15, of the Interstate Commerce Act the Commission has the right, in times of emergency created by unusual congestion of traffic or shortage of equipment, with or without notice of hearing, to establish such temporary through routes as in the opinion of the Commission may be desirable from the standpoint of the public interest. Moreover, subdivision 16, section 1, of the Act provides:

Whenever the Commission is of the opinion that any carrier by railroad subject to this part is for any reason unable to transport the traffic offered it so as properly to serve the public, it may . . . make such just and reasonable directions with respect to the handling, routing, and movement of the traffic of such carrier and its distribution over other lines of roads, as in the opinion of the Commission will best promote the service in the interest of the public and the commerce of the people. . . .

Any action on the part of the Commission under these provisions of the law would of course temporarily deprive the shipper of the right to select his own route. The Commission has used its emergency powers over routing sparingly, though during the Second World War it did issue a few service orders establishing the routes over which certain traffic should move, regardless of the shipper's instructions or the desires of the railroads involved.

[2] Virginian Ry. v. United States, 272 U.S. 658. A footnote in this decision gives a lucid and detailed explanation of the meaning of such terms as through route, joint rate, combination rate, and through rate. The Railway Equipment Register gives ample information with regard to the "connecting routes" of American railroads, but it does not indicate which connecting routes are "through routes."

ROUTING CONSIDERATIONS OF SHIPPERS

There are many sound reasons why the shipper should have the right to route his own freight. In the first place, the exercise of the right tends to preserve a healthy condition in the transportation industry, in that it keeps competition alive and active. But the shipper often finds that he has a particular interest of his own in directing the routing of his traffic. Perhaps the most important reason is that by indicating the route to be employed he will be sure that delivery is made by the proper carrier. Receivers of freight often have their plants on the industry sidings of particular railroads, or their places of business may be near particular railroad freight houses. Should freight not be routed to the proper delivering carrier, the consignee may lose valuable time in getting a shipment delivered to his plant. It may be that he will also become involved in a switching or trucking expense which he would not have had to meet had his shipment been correctly routed. The matter of designating the correct delivering carrier is so important that a shipper dispatching property over a through route often gives no routing instructions beyond naming the carrier by which the property is to be delivered at destination. He may not be greatly concerned over the matter of which carriers participate in the road haul in advance of the delivering carrier, but the matter of how delivery is to be accomplished may be of much importance. The industrial traffic manager who designates the routing of shipments should always be careful to obey the instructions of consignees with regard to the delivering carrier to be named. Any failure to follow such instructions may result in the accumulation of needless expense at the destination point, which would quite properly be charged to the shipper by the consignee.

There are numerous other reasons why a shipper will find it advantageous to designate routing in the bill of lading and shipping order. Occasionally, though not frequently, it will be found that alternative routes between two stations bear different rates. The shipper may want to designate the route over which the rate is lower. On the other hand, it may be that the route carrying the higher rate offers much more expeditious service, and the shipper and consignee are more than willing to pay the higher charge for the sake of getting more speedy and prompt delivery. Routing may often be dictated, too, by the matter of transit privileges. One route may permit reconsignment, or the right partially to unload or complete the loading of a car, while another route does not carry such privileges.[3]

[3] Some less important reasons why a shipper prefers to route his shipments may be such matters as the availability of special equipment such as cranes, the opportunity to obtain warehousing, the use of a "package car," the contents of

Finally, a shipper may find it beneficial to favor one carrier over another just as a matter of good business relations. This carrier is more courteous than another, it carries goods with less danger of loss or damage, and if loss or damage occurs it is prompt and efficient in the consideration and settlement of claims. Just as some people prefer to ride as passengers on the trains of certain railroads because of the quality of service they receive, so do they prefer to select carriers of their freight for the same reason. It is not at all uncommon for a shipper to give a substantial part of his freight traffic to a certain carrier because of the efficient service he receives on that carrier's passenger trains. Good business relations may be found, too, to include an element of reciprocity. A railroad sells transportation, but it also buys a vast quantity of supplies and materials for use in its business. Obviously, a shipper should not be averse to the establishment of mutual relations with a railroad whereby both parties are benefited. In times past, the matter of "reciprocity" has been subjected to considerable abuse, so much so that an investigation of certain practices by the Interstate Commerce Commission gave rise to recommendations that Congress should enact legislation to put an end to some of the more unwholesome features of the mutual "accommodation" that existed between some railroads and shippers who controlled the routing of large shipments of freight traffic. Although no such legislation was enacted, the Commission gave a sharp warning to various shippers and carriers that reciprocal practices which had an element of coercion and were not based upon legitimate reasons should be discontinued.

ROUTING INSTRUCTIONS IN TARIFFS

Routing becomes a problem or a matter of controversy only in connection with shipments which move between origin and destination over the lines of two or more carriers. A local tariff does not have to indicate any routing to be followed, but a joint or interline tariff, if the rates it contains are to be restricted to specified routes, must contain adequate routing instructions. It is permissible for carriers to publish joint tariffs which do not contain routing instructions, but if this is done, a rule set forth by the Interstate Commerce Commission in *Tariff Circular* No. 20 provides that the rates shown in such tariffs shall be "applicable between the points specified via the lines of any and all the carriers that are parties to the tariff."

Where routing is restricted by the carriers which are parties to a tariff, routing instructions must be given to the shippers using the tariff. This may be done in the tariff itself, or in a publication authorized by the

which are not transferred en route, and the possibility of having trap-car or ferry-car service either at the point of origin or at destination.

Commission known as a "routing guide." The rules with regard to the publication of routing instructions are to be found in Rule 4k of *Tariff Circular* No. 20, which states explicitly that the routing over which rates apply in any joint tariff must be stated "in such manner that such routes may be definitely ascertained." The circular indicates two ways or plans in which routing instructions may be set forth in a tariff. Under the first plan, the available routes are all given some place in the body of the tariff; a notation under the heading of "routing instructions" calls attention to the tariff pages where the instructions may be found and says that the rates contained in the tariff apply only via the specified routes. Under the second plan, the routing instructions may be shortened somewhat by a statement to the effect that the rates in the tariff apply over routes made use of by the lines of any carriers named as parties to the tariff, "except as otherwise specified" on certain pages, or in connection with individual rate items or individual rates.

It sometimes happens that, instead of showing routing instructions, a tariff containing joint rates may refer to a routing guide to be used in connection with the tariff. When reference is made in a tariff to such a guide, the proper notation must be made in the tariff. The Interstate Commerce Commission allows for considerable flexibility in the publication of routing instructions, whether they are contained in the tariffs in which rates are published or in routing guides, but the rules and regulations for publication are so explicit that a traffic manager will find that he will have no difficulty in ascertaining the available routes over which the rates published in any tariff are applicable.

WHAT CONSTITUTES MISROUTING

When a shipper gives specific routing instructions, the carrier is bound to follow them, and the shipper too is bound by the instructions he has given. It must be remembered that the tariff rates applicable over any route are the rates which must be collected, and the carrier is legally obligated to observe these rates. Should a carrier send a shipment over a route carrying a higher rate than the route designated by the shipper, each carrier party to the through rate must have its correct share of the duly published rate. However, the shipper is entitled to claim an overcharge, based on the difference between the rate paid and the rate applicable over the route he selected. The loss falls upon the carrier which was responsible for the misrouting. The loss due to the refund of overcharges to the shipper may be increased if the carrier deprived of revenue because of the misrouting should demand that the carrier guilty of misrouting make good the loss. On the other hand, if a shipper indicates a certain routing on the bill of lading and shipping order, and finds out later that another route carried a cheaper rate, he has no valid claim that he has been overcharged, since the carriers who performed the service were bound by the shipper's instructions.

It seldom happens that competing routes have different rates; even though a shipment is misrouted, the shipper is not likely to suffer any loss in the line-haul charge. But it does often happen that a misrouted shipment is turned over to the wrong delivering carrier and the consignee forced to pay drayage or switching charges which he would not have had if routing instructions had been followed. Here again, the loss would fall upon the road guilty of misrouting. The consignee is entitled to have the delivery requested, and any loss he sustains because routing instructions were not observed must be made good.

WHEN ROUTE AND RATE DO NOT AGREE

Many industrial traffic departments insert both the route and the rate in the bill of lading and shipping order, which is of course quite permissible. But once in a while, it is found that the rate inserted in the bill of lading does not apply over the route indicated, though it does apply over another route. If the initial carrier observes the route, the shipper will have to pay a higher rate than that indicated in the shipping order; if it observes the rate and diverts the shipment to the route where that rate is applicable, the shipper may be deprived of some transit service he had in mind in connection with the shipment, or he may have a grievance arising from the fact that a certain carrier did not share in the haul as he had intended it to. Conflicts in rates and routes on shipping orders formerly gave rise to numerous controversies between railroads and shippers, but the Interstate Commerce Commission eventually adopted a most Solomonic attitude toward this particular complication, which did much to remove it from the field of controversy. The Commission simply called attention to the fact that the bill of lading naming a conflicting route and rate should not be signed by the railroad agent, since it represented a contract that was incapable of being lawfully fulfilled. When such a bill of lading, with its shipping order, is presented to an agent, it is his duty to get in touch with the shipper, notify him of the error, and secure proper routing instructions. If it is for some reason impossible for the carrier's agent to get in touch with the shipper, he should follow the routing instructions given in the bill of lading. Although a higher charge has to be paid than the one named in the bill of lading, the carrier will not be deemed guilty of misrouting, nor will the shipper be entitled to a refund based on a claim of overcharge.

COMMISSION POLICY ON ROUTING CONTROVERSIES

It can readily be seen that the matter of routing is of considerable importance, and that it is likely to lead to occasional controversies between railroads and shippers. Even the hastiest survey of the Interstate Commerce Commission's reports will reveal that many of its cases involve allegations of misrouting. A reading of some of the cases will show that often the Commission has some difficult knots to untangle before it can arrive at a wholly reasonable solution of a dispute over routing. Over the years, the Commission has established precedents, however, which it is able to employ in a great many routing cases. In fact, the Commission's policy has been defined with so much clarity that the up-to-date, intelligent industrial traffic manager should have to spend little time on routing controversies. One of these precedents has been alluded to in the discussion of what occurs when there is a conflict in a bill of lading between the route and the rate. The Commission has also decided that when a shipper has named in a bill of lading railroads which have a complete route between the point of origin and the point of destination no other railroads should be permitted to participate in the haul; that a railroad should not divert a shipment to a higher rated route because of a flood or storm without consultation with the shipper or consignee; and that a carrier is guilty of misrouting when it succeeds in influencing a shipper to change his routing instructions with the result that the shipper is obliged to pay a higher rate than he would have paid over the route previously chosen.

UNROUTED SHIPMENTS

The shipper or traffic manager who has no assured knowledge of routes and rates will do well to leave the routing to the initial carrier, except to the extent that, at the request of the consignee, he must specify the delivering carrier. This brings up the problem of "unrouted freight," and the responsibility of the carrier in connection with such shipments. The initial carrier is free to route such shipments as it chooses, but must bear in mind that the shipper is entitled to have the shipment move over the route carrying the lowest rate, if the route is a reasonable one and one which the agent of the carrier could reasonably be expected to know about. Where all-rail routes and rail-and-water routes are both available, it is incumbent upon the shipper, however, to indicate the "class" of route he wishes the shipment to take. In other words, if the shipper wants a shipment to move over a rail-and-water route which is cheaper than the all-rail route, he must so specify. If, in the absence of a shipper's making a choice between the two classes of routes, the initial carrier routes the shipment all-rail, even though the rate is higher than by rail and water, there has been no misrouting.

Although the right of a shipper to designate the routing of his freight represents some restriction on the freedom of the carrier, the shipper is not without obligations, too, in connection with routing. If a shipper puts different instructions in the bill of lading and the shipping order, the carrier, in following the routing given in the shipping order, even though it does not correspond to that of the bill of lading, cannot be held guilty of misrouting. If a shipper inserts a rate in a bill of lading and shipping order and does not specify a route, the carrier is justified in dispatching the shipment over the route carrying the rate given, even though there is a lower rate over another route. It is only when the terms of the shipping order are contradictory, or when for some reason the specified routing must be changed, that the carrier is obliged to consult the shipper with regard to what he wishes done. If a shipper, at a point having two or more railroads, turns a shipment over to one railroad and subsequently discovers that a cheaper route is available via another initial carrier, he cannot sustain a claim of misrouting because the carrier chosen did not turn the traffic over to the line participating in a cheaper route. If the shipment is unrouted, the initial carrier must forward the shipment over the cheapest route in which its own line is a participating carrier, but it is not bound to turn the freight over to another initial carrier merely because that carrier is a participant in a still cheaper route.

The initial carrier has the right, with certain exceptions, to select the carriers which are to participate in the transportation of an unrouted shipment, provided the cheapest reasonable route is employed. However, subdivision 10, section 15, of the Interstate Commerce Act authorizes the Commission, "whenever the public interest and a fair division of traffic require," to direct the routing beyond the lines of the initial carrier of any traffic for which the shipper has not given routing instructions.

In the absence of any routing directives from the Interstate Commerce Commission, the selection which any railroad makes among competing connecting lines for participation in the transportation of unrouted traffic is usually a matter of reciprocity. One could hardly expect a railroad to deliver many carloads of unrouted traffic to a connection from which it received no unrouted traffic in return, if another line was available which followed a practice of reciprocation. Connecting carriers often have definite arrangements with regard to the exchange of unrouted carloads of traffic at certain junction points, just as connecting roads may join in the solicitation of through traffic to be routed by the shipper. Although the third section of the Interstate Commerce Act states that a carrier shall not "unduly prejudice" a connecting line in the "distribution of traffic that is not specifically routed by the shipper," it prescribes no particular method which a railroad must follow in dividing its unrouted traffic among connecting lines, and it places no obstacle in the way of cooperative efforts among connecting lines to offer a through service to shippers who can be induced to route their traffic by way of certain roads, gateways, and junction points.

ROUTING BEFORE 1887

Before the original Act to Regulate Commerce was passed in 1887, the routing of traffic over connecting railroads was subject entirely to the control of the railroads themselves. There was no obligation on the part of one carrier to enter into any through-routing arrangement with another carrier, and no obligation on connecting carriers to establish and maintain joint rates. Many through rates and joint rates were established, but they were all a matter of mutual agreement among the participating lines; there could be no compulsion. In the early 1880's, the Denver and New Orleans Railway brought suit in a Federal circuit court for the district of Colorado to compel the Atchison, Topeka and Sante Fe Railroad to enter into an arrangement for through routes and joint rates.[4] It received a favorable decision in the circuit court, but this decision was reversed by the Supreme Court, in 1884.[5] Said Chief Justice Waite:

At common law a carrier is not bound to carry except on its own line, and we think it quite clear that if he contracts to go on beyond he may, in the absence of statutory regulations to the contrary, determine for himself what agencies he will employ. His contract is equivalent to an extension of his line for the purpose of the contract, and if he holds himself out as a carrier beyond the line, so that he may be required to carry for all alike, he may nevertheless confine himself in carrying to the particular route he chooses to use. He puts himself in no worse position, by extending his route with the help of others, than he would occupy if the means of transportation employed were all his own. He certainly may select his own agencies and his own associates for doing his own work.

This is surely a far cry from the law as it now stands, with its Carmack Amendment, the Cummins Amendments, and all the additions to the statute which give the shipper the right to route his own freight and the Interstate Commerce Commission the power to establish through routes and joint rates.

PROVISIONS OF ORIGINAL ACT

Very little was said in the original Act of 1887 about the matter of routing. It did not require the railroads to adopt through routes and joint rates, although the third section provided that every carrier subject to the act should "according to their respective powers, afford all reasonable, proper and equal facilities for the interchange of traffic between their respective lines, and for receiving, forwarding, and delivering passengers and property to and from their several lines and those connecting there-

---

[4] Denver & New Orleans R.R. v. Atchison, Topeka & Santa Fe Ry., 13 Fed. 546 (1882).
[5] Atchison, Topeka & Santa Fe Ry. v. Denver & New Orleans R.R., 110 U.S. 667 (1884).

with, and shall not discriminate in their rates and charges between connecting lines." Railroads were supposed to maintain such physical connections among their lines as were needed for the through movement of traffic, but they were not required to enter into through-routing arrangements of any kind, nor to join in single rates covering a movement over connecting lines.

The law required a carrier to keep posted for public inspection its own rates, that is, the rates applying to its local business, and in the sixth section they were directed to file with the Interstate Commerce Commission "copies of all contracts, agreements, or arrangements with other common carriers in relation to any traffic affected by provisions of the law." Furthermore, the sixth section of the law provided that

. . . in cases where passengers and freight pass over continuous lines or routes operated by more than one common carrier, and the several common carriers operating such lines or routes establish joint tariffs of rates, or fares, or charges for such continuous lines or routes, copies of such joint tariffs shall also . . . be filed with the said Commission. Such joint rates, fares, and charges on such continuous lines so filed as aforesaid shall be made public by such common carriers when directed by said Commission, in so far as may, in the judgment of the Commission, be deemed practicable; and said Commission shall from time to time prescribe the measure of publicity which shall be given to such rates, fares, and charges, or to such parts of them as it may deem practicable for such common carriers to publish, and the places where they shall be published; but no common carrier party to any such joint tariff shall be liable for the failure of any other common carrier party thereto to observe and adhere to the rates, fares, or charges thus made and published.

Another provision of the law which served to facilitate to a certain degree the through movement of traffic was to be found in section 7, declaring it to be unlawful for any common carrier subject to the Act to enter into any combination or agreement to prevent by any means or device whatever "the carriage of freights from being continuous from the place of shipment to the place of destination." Transportation by rail was not to be obstructed in any capricious or arbitrary manner, even if there were no compulsory provision for through routes and joint rates.

Since the beginning of its existence, the Interstate Commerce Commission has displayed a lively interest in securing greater freedom and fluidity in the movement of our domestic commerce, and has invariably advocated an extension of those arrangements by which traffic could move over through routes at joint rates. One of the first steps it took to enable shippers to take greater advantage of whatever through routing and rating agreements railroads might have came in March, 1889,[6] when it exercised its authority under section 6 and issued an order requiring railroads sub-

[6] Foster Lumber Co. v. Atchison, Topeka & Santa Fe Ry., 17 I.C.C. 292.

ject to the Act to file their joint rates in the same manner that their other rates were filed. Although this did not mean that any change had been made in the existing system of rating and routing, it did mean that shippers could obtain a knowledge of any through routing and rating arrangements that were available.

THE CALIFORNIA ROUTING CASE OF 1902

The Commission consistently took the position that the shipper had the right to route his through traffic and select the carriers which should participate in any through interline movement, though a carrier could not be required to short-haul itself by turning traffic over to a competing rival. In 1902, a case reached the Commission involving certain western roads which originated a large portion of the movement of the California citrus-fruit crop. The Southern Pacific and the Atchison, Topeka and Sante Fe published a joint tariff of rates on citrus fruits destined to points on and east of the Mississippi River, in which some two hundred eastern railroads were listed as participating carriers. The published rates in the tariff were "guaranteed" to shippers by the two originating carriers, but the railroads declared that as a condition of guaranteeing the joint rates named in the tariff, "the absolute and unqualified right of routing beyond its own terminal is reserved to the initial carrier giving the guarantee." Freight agents were instructed not to accept shipments under the joint rate if the shipper insisted upon the right to select the routing for the shipment. Presumably a shipper could dispatch a carload of fruit over any route he chose to designate, but if he chose to dictate the routing, each of the carriers participating in the haul would exact its full local rate, producing a combination rate considerably higher than the published joint rate. Several shippers complained that the restriction upon their right to route their own shipments under the joint tariff was a frequent cause of financial loss because of their inability to divert shipments to more favorable markets. They appealed to the Interstate Commerce Commission to have the conditional-routing rule abolished. The Commission, in a four-to-one opinion, took the position that the arbitrary rule of the carriers was of such a nature that it could easily result in unjust discrimination to shippers, and they also condemned the rule on the ground that it was an instrument for creating a traffic pool such as the Interstate Commerce Act declared to be illegal.[7]

Under the terms of the present Interstate Commerce Act, an order which the Commission issues against a carrier subject to the Act is binding upon the carrier unless set aside by a court of competent jurisdiction. But in those days (1902), a carrier could disobey a Commission order with impunity. If the Commission wanted an order which was being disobeyed

[7] Consolidated Forwarding Co. v. Southern Pacific Co., 9 I.C.C. 182 (1902).

to become effective it had to go to a Federal court to secure a decree requiring compliance. The western railroads ignored the Commission's order, and the Commission's attorneys filed suit in the circuit court of the southern district of California asking that the recalcitrant railroads be made to obey. The railroads filed a demurrer to the Commission's complaint. The judge overruled the demurrer,[8] and in a later trial of the case affirmed the order of the Commission, on the ground that the railroads' routing rule resulted in the creation of an illegal traffic pool.[9] The railroads appealed the decision to the Supreme Court, which overruled the lower court in February, 1906, several months before the enactment of the Hepburn Amendment, finding as matters of fact that the rule complained of did not result in any undue discrimination against a shipper or result in the establishment of an illegal pool.[10]

In his opinion in 1884, Chief Justice Waite had said that, in the "absence of statutory regulations to the contrary," a railroad had a right to select for itself the connecting lines with which it would enter into through-routing arrangements. The decision of 1906 strongly emphasized this position and also called attention to the fact that the Act to Regulate Commerce, as written in 1887, had done little to change the situation with respect to the carrier's right to exercise control over the through routing of traffic. Obviously, if through routes and joint rates were to be established in greater number, and if the shipper were to be permitted to have a larger measure of freedom in designating the route his traffic should take, there was a plain need for further "statutory regulations." Beginning with the enactment of the Hepburn Amendment to the Interstate Commerce Act in 1906, and lasting down to comparatively recent times, Congress has steadily added to legislative measures affecting routing, and placed greater and greater restrictions upon the freedom of the carriers to act without regard to the shipper's wishes or the public will.

ROUTING PROVISIONS OF THE HEPBURN AMENDMENT

The first change accomplished by the Hepburn Amendment was an important provision inserted in the first section of the law, which stated that "it shall be the duty of every common carrier subject to the provisions of this Act . . . to establish through routes and just and reasonable joint rates applicable thereto."

A new section 6 made some definite and specific rules with respect to

[8] Interstate Commerce Commission v. Southern Pacific Co., 123 Fed. 597 (1903).

[9] Interstate Commerce Commission v. Southern Pacific Co., 132 Fed. 829 (1904).

[10] Southern Pacific Co. v. Interstate Commerce Commission, 200 U.S. 536 (1906).

the manner in which joint rates were to be printed and filed. Every carrier subject to the Act was required to print, file, and keep open to public inspection schedules showing

. . . all the rates, fares, and charges for transportation between different points on its own route and between points on its own route and points on the route of any other carrier by railroad, by pipe line, or by water, when a through route and joint rate over a through route have been established. If no joint rate over a through route has been established, the several carriers in such through route shall file, print and keep open to public inspection as aforesaid, the separately established rates, fares and charges applied to the through transportation.

No longer was the shipper to be kept in the dark as to what the total charges might be when he dispatched his traffic over a through route for which no joint rate had been agreed upon by the connecting carriers. Finally, it was provided in section 6 that "the names of the several carriers which are parties to any joint tariff shall be specified therein, and each of the parties, other than the one filing the same, shall file with the Commission such evidence of concurrence therein or acceptance thereof as may be required by the Commission."

A new paragraph added to section 15 of the Act brought an entirely fresh note into the matter of routing. It said that

. . . the Commission may also, after hearing on a complaint, establish through routes and joint rates as the maximum to be charged and prescribe the division of such rates (in case of disagreement among the participating carriers) and the terms and conditions under which such through routes shall be operated, when that may be necessary to give effect to any provision of this Act, and the carriers complained of have refused or neglected to voluntarily establish such through routes, provided no reasonable or satisfactory through route exists, and this provision shall apply when one of the connecting carriers is a water line.

This new provision of the law represented a breaking of the ice in a most determined manner on the question of routing. It will be noticed, however, that the Commission was authorized to establish a through route and joint rate only "upon complaint," and only when "no reasonably satisfactory through route exists." The Hepburn Amendment made no mention of the shipper's right to exercise control over routing of interline freight, and for a few years the Commission was forced to continue its recognition of the right of a carrier to control intermediate routing if it chose to do so.

ROUTING PROVISIONS OF THE MANN-ELKINS ACT OF 1910

In 1910, the Mann-Elkins Act, which contained several important amendments to the Interstate Commerce Act, carried the regulation of routing still further. The provision of section 1, added in 1906, which merely said it was the "duty" of the carriers to establish through routes and joint rates, was extended by the addition of the following words: "and to provide reasonable facilities for operating such through routes and to make reasonable rules and regulations with respect to the exchange, interchange and return of cars used therein, and for the operation of such through routes, and providing reasonable compensation to those entitled thereto." This was the first time that the matter of car service was ever mentioned in the Act, and it indicated that it was the wish of Congress that carriers should put no obstacle in the way of joint operation by the establishment of unreasonable and unworkable rules concerning the interchange of freight cars. At a later date, the provisions of the law with respect to such car service were to be greatly extended.

That part of section 15 of the law which in 1906 had been modified to give the Commission authority to establish through routes and joint rates, under certain conditions, was now changed to give the Commission power to establish such routes and rates "upon its own initiative," as well as upon complaint, when carriers failed to act voluntarily, though the Commission could not require the establishment of through routes and joint rates in connection with "street electric passenger railways not engaged in the general business of transporting freight." The most important part of the modified section 15, however, was a new paragraph imposing a specific restriction on the Commission's general authority to create new through routes. This paragraph said:

And in establishing such through route, the Commission shall not require any company, without its consent, to embrace in such route substantially less than the entire length of its railroad and of any intermediate railroad operated in conjunction therewith and under a common management or control therewith which lies between the termini of such proposed route, unless to do so would make such other route unreasonably long as compared with another practicable through route which could otherwise be established.

In other words, the Commission could not require a carrier to short-haul itself, except when it meant the avoidance of an unreasonably long and circuitous route. This provision of the law was eventually to be a source of trouble—trouble which was once more to lead to a modification of the statute.

The most striking provision included in the Mann-Elkins Act, however, on the subject of routing, was a new paragraph to be inserted in section 15 (now subdivision 8 of that section) giving the shipper the right to designate the route which his shipments should follow. The new provision contained no qualification and, to be sure that the carriers would no longer be able to reserve a right of "conditional routing," which the Commission had once condemned only to be overruled by the Supreme Court, a final proviso of the paragraph stated that where "competing lines of railroad constitute portions of a through line or route" the shipper should have the right to say over which of those lines his freight should be carried. The clause covering the shipper's right to control his routing remains today substantially as it was written and enacted in 1910. It has already been quoted in this chapter.

ACT OF 1920: ROUTING PROVISIONS

Although the changes which Congress made in the law in 1906 and 1910 on the question of routing marked a wide departure from the common law which had once prevailed, Congress was not yet finished with the subject. The Transportation Act of 1920 made a small change in the routing provision of section 1 of the Act, eliminating the reference to car service—which was more fully taken care of in the provisions of the Esch Car Service Act which had been passed in 1917 and will be discussed later—and adding a clause directing carriers participating in through routes and joint rates "to establish just, reasonable, and equitable divisions" of the joint revenues, which shall not "unduly prefer or prejudice" any of the participating carriers. The paragraph in section 3 requiring carriers to "afford all reasonable, proper and equal facilities for the interchange of traffic," which had been carried in the law without substantial change since 1887, was amended by an additional clause forbidding any line to "unduly prejudice" a connecting line "in the distribution of traffic that is not specifically routed by the shipper."

The most important change brought about by the Act of 1920, however (or at least it was at the time thought to be), was the change made with respect to the Commission's power to establish through routes and joint rates. Instead of saying simply that the Commission had authority to take such action, either upon complaint or upon its own initiative, the law now said that "the Commission may, and it shall whenever deemed by it necessary or desirable in the public interest," take proper action to bring through routes and joint rates into existence. In other words, the law now became mandatory, and moreover the "public interest" as well as the interest of certain shippers or certain carriers was to be taken into consideration. The previous restriction with regard to requiring a carrier to short-haul itself was continued, though the word "company" was replaced by the word "railroad," reference was made to the provisions with regard to the interchange of traffic contained in section 3, and a railroad could be required to enter into a through-routing arrangement with a water line even though an all-rail through route might give it a longer haul. The provisions of the law previously mentioned, which gave the Commission the right to establish temporary through routes in times of emergency and the right to distribute "unrouted traffic," and which made it possible for a carrier to collect any loss which it might suffer because of failure of a connecting carrier to observe a shipper's routing instructions, were all a part of the Transportation Act of 1920.

THE SUBIACO CASE

During the years following the amendment of the Interstate Commerce Act in 1906 and 1910, and especially after the amendment of 1920, which authorized the Commission to give consideration to the "public interest" in deciding whether or not to establish through routes and joint rates, the Commission issued many orders which were designed to bring about a more unified and efficient transportation service. However, the Commission chose to regard the restrictive clause of the law, which provided that a carrier ordered to participate in a through route could not be required to short-haul itself, as applying only to carriers in possession of the traffic. The right of an originating carrier or of an intermediate carrier to its long haul was superior, in the opinion of the Commission, to the right of the delivering carrier. Its position was that the restrictive portion of the law did not cover all routes which might short-haul a carrier, but only those which would deprive a carrier of its long haul after it had obtained possession of the traffic.[11] If a certain road had a route of its own 300 miles long between two points, and another route consisting of one or more carriers covered 260 miles of the same distance, and at its terminus had a junction with the first road, it was the belief of the Commission that it could order the establishment of a through route in which the first road would be required to participate only for the final 40 miles of the haul, though it had the facilities for the movement of traffic over the entire distance. It was not being short-hauled as long as it did not get possession of the traffic before it reached the junction 40 miles distant from its terminus. The Commission embodied this interpretation of the meaning of the restrictive clause on routing in a decision handed down in 1926, in which it ordered the Missouri Pacific Railroad to participate in a through route, in which it would be short-hauled as a delivering carrier, in order that a substantial portion of the entire haul would be enjoyed by the Fort Smith, Subiaco and Rock Island Railroad, a short line which could be included as a part of a competing

[11] In Flory Milling Co. v. Central New England Ry., 93 I.C.C. 129 (1924), the Commission declared that the restrictive clauses of section 15 with respect to the Commission's power to establish through routes "has no application unless the carrier has originated the traffic or received it from a connection, in which event it should under ordinary circumstances be allowed to transport the freight as far as it can before delivering it to a connecting line." The Commission established certain through routes which it deemed to be "necessary and desirable in the public interest," even though it meant the short-hauling of delivering carriers. See D. A. Stickell & Sons v. Western Maryland Ry., 146 I.C.C. 609 (1928).

route.[12] This was the beginning of a famous case referred to for years as the "Subiaco case." The Missouri Pacific promptly sought an injunction to prevent the Commission's order from taking effect. The injunction was granted in 1927 by a three-judge statutory court of the Western District of Arkansas.[13] The court held that the distinction that the Commission endeavored to make between initial, intermediate, and delivering carriers was abstract, and that the protection which the restrictive clause gave to a carrier, to prevent it from being short-hauled without its consent, applied to the delivering carrier just as much as it applied to any other carrier forming part of a through route. The Commission carried the case to the Supreme Court on appeal, and in 1929 that court handed down a decision sustaining the district court in every particular.[14]

The outcome of this case tended to limit greatly the power which the Commission had previously exercised under its authority to establish through routes and joint rates. If two roads overlapped, neither could be required to become a part of a through route involving any part of the overlapping mileage. In several cases dealing with the establishment of through routes, the Commission was constrained to say that while it thought the route proposed or suggested would be in the "public interest," it was without power to order its establishment, because of the Supreme Court's decision in the Subiaco case.[15]

THE LAW CHANGED AGAIN

The years immediately following the decision of the Supreme Court in the Subiaco case did not witness much activity on the part of Congress in passing further legislation for the regulation of railroad practices. The effects of the pronounced and long-drawn-out business depression on the railroads were such that both Congress and the Commission devoted more energy to endeavoring to save the railroad business of the United States from abject and utter collapse than to framing more rules for the guidance of their conduct. But by 1940, the time was ripe for further consideration of the problem of routing. When Congress enacted part III of the Interstate Commerce Act, the part which deals with carriers by

[12] Ft. Smith, Subiaco & Rock Island Ry. v. Alabama & Vicksburg Ry., 107 I.C.C. 523 (1926).

[13] Missouri Pacific R.R. v. United States, 21 F.2d. 351 (1927).

[14] United States v. Missouri Pacific R.R., 278 U.S. 269 (1929).

[15] On a rehearing of the Stickell case (146 I.C.C. 609), the Commission declared in May, 1929, that it had no authority to establish the through routes requested and which it had previously ordered to be established, because of the decree of the Supreme Court in the Subiaco case handed down Jan. 2, 1929 (153 I.C.C. 759). See also Manufacturers Ry. v. Ahnapee and Western Ry., 172 I.C.C. 554 (1931).

water, it also enacted some amendments to part I, the most important of which perhaps was the revision of the paragraphs of section 15 which have to do with the power of the Commission to prescribe through routes and joint rates. There was also a minor amendment to be included in section 1, stating that a "connecting line," as the term was used in that section meant the line of any carrier subject to part I or to the provisions of part III. This change was necessitated by the transfer from part I to part III of most of the regulatory provisions having to do with carriers by water.

The language of section 15(3), giving the Commission power and even making it mandatory for the Commission to establish through routes and joint rates, whenever the Commission should deem it necessary and desirable to do so in the public interest, remained virtually unchanged, except that the portion concerning water carriers was dropped, but section 15(4) was modified to read as follows:

In establishing any such through route the Commission shall not (except as provided in Section 3, and except where one of the carriers is a carrier by water) require any carrier by railroad, without its consent, to embrace in such route substantially less than the entire length of its railroad and of any intermediate railroad operated in conjunction and under common management and control therewith, which lies between the termini of such proposed through route, (a) unless such inclusion of lines would make the proposed route unreasonably long as compared with another practicable through route which could otherwise be established, or (b) unless the Commission finds the route proposed to be established is needed in order to provide adequate, and more efficient or more economic transportation: Provided, however, That, in prescribing through routes the Commission shall, so far as is consistent with the public interest, and subject to the foregoing limitations in clauses (a) and (b), give reasonable preference to the carrier by railroad which originated the traffic. No through route and joint rates applicable thereto shall be established by the Commission for the purpose of assisting any carrier that would participate therein to meet its financial needs.

The remainder of the paragraph, giving the Commission power to establish temporary through routes in times of emergency, was unchanged.

This amendment paved the way for the Commission to act on proposals for the establishment of through routes, whether originated by some complainant or by the Commission itself, without having a too tender regard for the feelings and interests of any carrier, though it was required, when feasible, to give a "reasonable preference" to the carrier originating the traffic, and it could not rob Peter to pay Paul, by diverting traffic from one line merely for the purpose of bringing relief to the treasury of some indigent railroad. The considerations which were to govern the Commission's actions in establishing through routes and joint rates hereafter were to be the public interest in efficient and economical transportation, and the interest of the country as a whole in the smooth flowing of the great streams of American domestic trade.

THE STICKELL CASE

It was not long until the Commission put its newly defined power to the test. In a decision handed down in March, 1943,[16] in a case resembling closely the case in which it had confessed itself impotent to act in a manner consistent with the public interest, and involving the same complainant, it ordered the establishment of certain through routes and through rates, which had the effect of short-hauling certain defendant railroads. The Commission said:

It is not the province of railroads to determine what markets shall be available to sellers or buyers, or, by refusal to establish through routes or the maintenance of rate disadvantages, to restrict or circumscribe the opportunities of shippers located on other railroads to sell in the markets served by them. It is their function to transport in channels necessitated by trade conditions and not to fix limitations on commerce. The public interest demands that all shippers be accorded relatively equal opportunities to reach all reasonably available markets.

The Commission's decision was promptly appealed to the courts. Eventually it was carried to the highest Federal tribunal which, in a notable decision handed down in 1945,[17] upheld the Commission's order. Under the amended section 15, the Court declared that the Commission possessed the necessary authority, when it found that through routes were "needed in order to provide adequate and more efficient or adequate and more economic transportation," to require the establishment of such routes even though some participating carrier might be short-hauled.

We interpret that exception to mean adequate and more efficient and more economic from the public's and the shipper's as well as the participating carrier's standpoint. That such was the intent of Congress is evident from the conditions the amendment was apparently designed to correct, from the fact that in the added proviso even the preference to be accorded the originating carrier is made subservient to the public interest. . . .

The Commission's power to prescribe through routes for carriers subject to part I of the Interstate Commerce Act thus became clearly defined, and a long-standing controversy was brought to a conclusion.

[16] D. A. Stickell and Sons, Inc. v. Alton R.R., 255 I.C.C. 333 (1943). See also Beacon Milling Co. Inc. v. Akron, Canton & Youngstown Ry., 263 I.C.C. 132 (1945); Kasco Mills v. Akron, Canton & Youngstown Ry., 273 I.C.C. 175 (1948); Adrian Grain Co. v. Ann Arbor R. R., 273 I.C.C. 587 (1949).

[17] Pennsylvania R.R. v. United States, 323 U.S. 588 (1945), *affirming* Pennsylvania R.R. v. United States, 54 F. Supp. 381 (1944).

ROUTING BY MOTOR CARRIERS

There is a vast difference in the routing provisions of part I of the Interstate Commerce Act and the routing provisions of the other three parts. One of the interesting features of the routing provisions of part II, applying to motor vehicle carriers, is the different treatment accorded passenger carriers and carriers of property. The law says: "It shall be the duty of every common carrier of passengers by motor vehicle to establish reasonable through routes with other such common carriers . . . to establish, observe, and enforce just and reasonable individual and joint rates, fares and charges, and just and reasonable regulations and practices relating thereto. . . ." Of common carriers of property, however, part II says that they *may* "establish reasonable through routes and joint rates, charges and classifications with such other carriers or with common carriers by railroad and/or express and/or water. . . ." While it was the *duty* of a common carrier of passengers by motor vehicle to establish through routes in connection with other such carriers, the law says that they *may* establish through routes and joint rates with common carriers by rail or water. There is no obligation or duty to do so, and there is no obligation or duty on the part of motor vehicle common carriers of property to enter into any through-routing arrangements whatever.

The Interstate Commerce Commission receives no authority in part II of the Act to require the establishment of through routes and joint rates by motor vehicle common carriers of property, but it shall either upon complaint or upon its own initiative, whenever deemed by it to be consonant with the public interest, establish through routes and joint fares applicable to the transportation of passengers by motor vehicle common carriers. The Commission is also empowered to regulate the divisions of joint rates between motor vehicle common carriers of either passengers or property, or between these carriers and carriers by rail, express, or water, whether or not the divisions have been agreed upon by the carriers concerned, if it finds that the existing divisions are or will be "unjust, unreasonable, inequitable or unduly preferential or prejudicial" among the carriers concerned.[18]

The industrial traffic manager will find that, under the law applicable to interstate common carriers of property by motor vehicle, not only does the Interstate Commerce Commission lack the power to prescribe through routes and joint rates, but he has not been given the legal right to route his own shipments which must be transported by connecting carriers. Moreover, there is nothing in part II of the Act comparable to the provi-

[18] For a comprehensive discussion of the problem of routing by motor carriers and of the Commission's authority, see Hausman Steel Co. v. Seaboard Freight Lines, 32 M.C.C. 31 (1942).

sion in the fourth paragraph of part I which requires carriers subject to that part to provide reasonable, proper, and equal facilities for the interchange of traffic. The motor carrier which engages in the transportation of freight is at liberty to make his own arrangements with respect to through transportation, or even to refuse to enter into any arrangements whatever for the transportation of property beyond his own terminal.

If motor carriers enter into through-routing agreements, as many of them do, they are of course bound by whatever routing provisions they include in their tariffs. Presumably, where several carriers might be participants in a through haul by motor vehicle, the shipper would have the right to designate the carriers which should convey his shipment over the route. On the other hand, if precedent is to be followed, the originating carriers of through shipments might include provisions in tariffs reserving to themselves the right to dictate the intermediate routing.

When motor transportation of freight first began to assume importance in domestic commerce, it was not thought that it would be highly effective for any but short-distance or local traffic. Even when the Motor Carrier Act (now part II of the Interstate Commerce Act) was passed, in 1935, there were few who were willing to believe that highway transportation by motor vehicle would reach the scope and magnitude which characterize it today. As a consequence, the law for the regulation of motor vehicle transportation was not so comprehensive and all-embracing as the law which was applicable to railroad transportation. Just now, there seems to be a considerable amount of uncertainty and confusion as to the precise duties of motor vehicle carriers, especially in connection with the transportation of "through" shipments, and the shippers obviously do not have rights and privileges equivalent to those which they possess when their shipments are transported by railroads. There is a considerable amount of complaint in some commercial centers over the lackadaisical attitude some motor carriers seem to exhibit with respect to through shipments. It may be that in the near future we shall see action by Congress for the purpose of imposing a greater degree of responsibility upon motor carriers and defining with greater precision the mutual obligations and rights which both carriers and shippers should have. The motor carriers are subject to the same liability for loss and damage to property they carry that railroads are subject to under the Carmack and the Cummins Amendments. There seems to be no good reason why they should not have the same duties and responsibilities that railroads have with respect to all phases of the through or joint transportation of the property they accept for conveyance.

ROUTING BY WATER CARRIERS

The law bears down a little more heavily on common carriers by water in the matter of routing than it does on common carriers by motor vehicle.

Not only are water carriers required, just as railroads are, to afford reasonable facilities for the interchange of traffic with connecting lines of other water carriers and carriers subject to part I of the Act (but not with motor carriers), but they are told that it is their duty to establish through routes with other common carriers by water and with railroads. It is not their "duty" to establish through routes with common carriers by motor vehicle, but they "may" do so if they choose. The Commission has the right to require common carriers by water to establish through routes and joint rates with other such carriers and with railroads (but not with motor carriers), whenever the Commission deems the establishment of such routes and rates necessary or desirable in the public interest. Nothing is said in part III about the right of a shipper to route through traffic.

Because of the peculiar function of freight forwarders, who furnish little or none of their own transportation facilities except motor vehicles for local service, they are not subject to any of the routing provisions which, under the Interstate Commerce Act, are applicable to a greater or less extent to other carriers subject to the Act, though a part of the law deals extensively with the joint operations of forwarders and common carriers by motor vehicle.

ROUTING IN AIR TRANSPORTATION

The Civil Aeronautics Act of 1938 imposes upon carriers by air almost the same duties and obligations with respect to routing that are imposed upon railroads in part I of the Interstate Commerce Act. It is the "duty" of certificated carriers by air to "provide reasonable through service" in interstate and overseas air transportation and to establish reasonable joint rates and fares and equitable divisions thereof. Joint rates and fares must be published and filed with the Civil Aeronautics Board in the same manner that the local charges of air carriers are published and filed. The Board has the same power to establish through air service and joint charges for such service as the Interstate Commerce Commission has with regard to railroads. The Act says nothing about the right of shippers to route through traffic, but this is not a matter of great importance, since there is not the multiplicity of routes and carriers that the railway net of the country presents. Virtually all our air lines engage in joint services with other lines, some of them even having arrangements for the joint use of equipment, similar in effect to the common use of freight cars by railroads. Since few of our domestic airlines engage in overseas service, the joint arrangements for international travel and trade by air are of considerable importance.

SUMMARY

This somewhat long story of the legislative history of the routing provisions of the Interstate Commerce Act is given partly to illustrate how, over the years, public sentiment can be crystallized into law; to emphasize the fact that common carriers for hire, however "private" they may be as far as ownership and operation are concerned, are nevertheless regarded as public servants and subject to governmental control in their dealings with the public; and finally to present another of the many instances in which Congress has thought it well to clothe the Interstate Commerce Commission with a large measure of discretionary administrative power. Nothing has been said and no opinion is ventured as to the wisdom of the policy which the government has followed; that is naturally a matter of controversy about which many persons have widely differing views.

Although the industrial traffic manager is likely to have more interest in the law as it stands now, and how it affects him in his professional activities, nevertheless he will find it helpful to learn as much as he can about how the law came to be what it is. Alone and in cooperation with others, he has a part to play in the shaping of transportation policy for the future, and he will find that a knowledge of history, an awareness of how policies and attitudes have developed in the past, will enable him to cultivate a better approach to the problems which confront him in his work and give him more ability to exercise sound judgment. A spirit of understanding, a tolerant attitude toward the opinions and convictions of others, and a habit of reflecting with good humor and patience on matters upon which there is bound to be a conflict of opinion are qualities which are useful to a traffic manager, just as they are useful to all members of human society.

CHAPTER XVI

Car Service and Demurrage

It has already been mentioned that the physical facility of a railroad which produces its freight revenue is the freight car; it has also been stated that the car is fulfilling its function in this respect only when it is loaded and moving. An empty car, or a car standing still even when it is loaded, is earning nothing for the company to which it belongs. Moreover, the freight car is the chief instrument in the movement of the great flow of goods which enters into our domestic commerce. Of course, a railroad must have tracks and motive power and terminals in order to conduct a transportation service, but so far as the shipper is concerned it is the car which counts—the car in which he loads his products to have them carried to those who buy them. It goes without saying, therefore, that both carrier and shipper have a vital interest in the utilization of cars and that the efficiency and economy with which our commerce is carried on depend in a large measure upon the methods employed in the distribution, loading, movement, and unloading of railroad freight car equipment.

It is difficult for anybody familiar with the present methods which railroads employ in handling their huge volume of traffic from place to place throughout the length and breadth of the United States, with a system of freight car interchange which permits a loaded car to travel from coast to coast over the lines of several carriers, to realize that in the early days of railroad transportation in this country, a railroad company had no thought of letting its cars or locomotives leave its own rails, and that when traffic had to be moved over connecting lines it was shifted from car to car at each junction point. Passengers were obliged to change from train to train in the same manner. When the terminals of two "connecting lines" were on opposite sides of a city, teamsters and cabdrivers reaped a rich harvest from the business of transferring traffic from the station of one road to that of another. Some amusing episodes of American railroad history are connected with the indignant protests of these transfer agencies which arose when an effort was made to establish a physical union between the railroads which had separate terminals in the same city.

Even had the early railroads of America been willing to make arrangements for through transportation of freight without transfer from car to car, it would often have been physically impossible, because railroads were built with many different gauges, some with 6 feet, some with 5, some with 4 feet 10 inches, others with 4 feet 8½ inches, which was the gauge of English railroads and the present "standard gauge" in the United States, and there were even a great many "narrow-gauge" lines of 3 feet or less. It was not until some ten years after the end of our great Civil War that the movement to have the railroads adopt a uniform gauge made much headway. Like all other kinds of industry, railroad transportation was conducted on a small scale, though it was plain that, if the economic development of the country was ever to attain the scope and magnitude which the natural resources of the land and the genius of the people warranted, there would have to be some radical changes not only in the methods of production employed in field, mine, forest, and factory but also in the methods of transportation.

Three great technological changes in the railroad transportation industry, occurring during the 1870's and the years immediately following, paved the way for large-scale transportation, for the kind of transportation suitable to the needs of the United States, by which huge quantities of raw materials and finished products could be conveyed for long distances at a very low cost. It was this type of transportation which was the goal of American railroad development, in marked contrast to the transportation development of European countries where, because of the short distances commodities had to be moved, interest was concentrated largely upon the construction of facilities with which comparatively small quantities of traffic could be carried at relatively high speeds.

The three great technological changes were the adoption of a common gauge, which made it possible for the lines of numerous railroad companies to be welded, as it were, into one huge, far-flung system; the use of steel in the construction of equipment and track, which meant the introduction of cars of great capacity, locomotives with enormous tractive power, and tracks which were able to withstand the weight of burdens which our early railroads could not possibly have sustained; and the air brake, by which the movement of trains of 4,000 or 5,000 tons could be controlled by the engineer in the locomotive more easily than a train of 400 tons could be controlled by trainmen tugging at the wheels of the hand brakes with which our first freight cars were equipped. There were other mechanical innovations, too, the clasp type of car coupler, which replaced the old "link and pin," taking a rank almost equal to the rank of those mentioned, but to these three—steel, the common gauge, and the air brake—goes the chief credit for the transformation of railroad transportation from a small industry into a huge one.

CAR INTERCHANGE; FAST FREIGHT LINES

It took some time for American railroads to work out a mutually satisfactory system of car interchange. The first agency employed to facilitate
the movement of freight over connecting railroads was the "fast freight
line," which still remains in name as an advertising and soliciting device.
Such lines owned their own cars, solicited freight, loaded the cars, and
paid connecting railroads for their transportation. They were something
like the freight forwarders of today, except that they owned the cars in
which their traffic moved. The fast freight lines did not last long. Collusive
arrangements between the owners of the fast freight lines and the officers
of railroads, who were often the same persons, had the effect of transform-
ing them into devices by which the owners of the railroads were unjustly
deprived of revenue they might otherwise have received. Moreover, the
fast freight line was an anachronism. It represented a return to the primitive days of railroading when the shippers were supposed to supply the
vehicles in which their freight was carried, the railroad companies providing only the tracks and locomotives. Railroad practices in the United
States very early assumed the pattern under which the carriers not only
performed the transportation service but furnished all the equipment, or
at least the largest portion of it. Even the private freight cars we have
today are operated by the carriers just as if they were carrier owned. The
owner of the private car does not solicit the business of shippers in general and pay the railroad for hauling the car. The freight in a private car
is charged the same rate as a like kind of freight in railroad-owned cars,
and the railroad pays the owner of the private car a certain sum, based on
the mileage the car travels, for its use.

PER DIEM CHARGES; RETURN OF CARS

The chief difficulty railroads met with as the fast freight lines were
given up and a system of car interchange was put into effect was that of
devising a method by which the owners of the interchanged cars could be
satisfactorily compensated when their cars were transferred to other roads.
At first, a scheme was adopted by which the "home" cars of one line,
when on a "foreign" road, would be paid for according to mileage traveled.
This plan had two glaring defects. In the first place, there was no way
by which the home road could check up on the mileage its car had traveled
after the termination of the journey which took it to its first destination
on a foreign line. In the second place, the scheme provided no means of
expediting the return of cars to the home road. They could gather rust
on the sidetracks of the foreign road with no obligation for payment for
the time the cars were out of service. It soon became apparent that the
only feasible and satisfactory method of compensation for the use of

interchanged cars was one based on the time the cars were absent from their home line. This per diem system was adopted by the American Railway Association in the early years of the twentieth century, and it is still in use. The rate per day which each road must pay for the use of cars belonging to other roads has changed many times, once being as low as 20 cents,[1] but the method of calculating the compensation has not varied. The rate in the fall of 1952 was $2.00 a day.

The system of per diem payments was supplemented by a code of rules governing the return of home cars to the roads which owned them. We shall not go into any lengthy discussion of this code. Its chief feature was, and still is, that foreign cars, when empty, must be sent back promptly to the home road over the route by which they were received, unless the owning road consents to receive them at a different junction. If the cars are returned under load, with shipments the revenue from which is shared by the home road, they can be returned by another route. Of course, the per diem charge is ordinarily an incentive sufficient to bring about the prompt return of cars to their owners.

The car-service rules which the railroads voluntarily adopted worked in a satisfactory manner during normal times, when there was no extraordinarily large volume of traffic and consequently no shortage of freight cars. But in times of car shortage, a road in possession of foreign cars might find that it would be profitable to use such cars in its own local business despite the necessity of paying a rental. Under such circumstances, the rule requiring the "prompt" return of foreign cars was honored by nonobservance, with the result that many railroads were embarrassed because of a shortage of equipment—even though they owned sufficient cars to supply their needs, if they only had possession of them —and the shippers on lines partially denuded of cars were severely handicapped because of a lack of transportation service.

CAR SERVICE IN THE FIRST WORLD WAR

During the First World War, even before the United States entered the conflict, railroad transportation in this country fell into a sorry state. There was a tremendous demand for American goods among the allied powers ranged against Germany, not for munitions of war—the sale of which was forbidden—but for food and all kinds of "civilian" wares, which the warring countries were unable to produce for themselves. These goods were shipped to Atlantic ports in large volume for export. By the time the year 1916 was half over, the German submarine had wreaked such havoc with European merchant vessels that the supply of shipping with which to carry American products across the Atlantic was wholly inade-

[1] T. M. Kehoe & Co. v. Charleston & Western Carolina Ry., 11 I.C.C. 566 (1905).

quate to accommodate the flood of goods which day by day was started eastward from the western and central states. Since freight charges were usually paid in advance, the railroads continued to accept all the traffic that was offered regardless of the fact that no shipping was available to receive it when it reached the seaboard. By the time this country entered the war, in April, 1917, virtually every freight yard along the Atlantic Coast was choked with loaded cars. Despite the frantic efforts of railroad officials to relieve the situation, it grew steadily worse. Western lines were complaining bitterly about the detention of their cars by their eastern connections. Many of the cars, loaded and standing idle in congested freight yards, could not have been returned even had the eastern roads been inclined to return them, and when some of them were unloaded, eastern lines for the most part, glad to have them for their own use, calmly ignored the car-service rules to which they were a party, paid the per diem rental to the owners, and employed the cars in their local business.[2]

Called to Washington by the Interstate Commerce Commission, which was besieged with complaints concerning the growing shortage of cars, the officials of the leading railroads adopted more stringent car-service rules. The new rules proving to be of little use in solving the difficulty, the Commission, on its own authority, promulgated some rules that were even more strict. When these too proved to be of little effect, the Commission, a bit doubtful of its power to regulate car service, appealed to Congress, which responded with the enactment of the Esch Car Service bill of May, 1917, which, with a few amendments, is still part of section 1 of the Interstate Commerce Act.

GOVERNMENT OPERATION OF RAILROADS, 1918 TO 1920

Even with its increased power, now defined and confirmed by statute, the Commission and the railroads, which in their desperate plight promised their cooperation, were unable to bring about any improvement. Instead, matters went from bad to worse, until by the end of the year the railroad transportation system of the United States was virtually broken down, and the country was gradually becoming impotent to make felt its military strength. There were plenty of "explanations," the railroads laying the blame for the most part on the shippers and the "government," as well as on each other, but no single line displayed any particular eagerness to shoulder any of the responsibility itself. The plain fact was that the chief cause of the difficulty had been the practice of the railroads of accepting traffic consigned to destinations where there was not the remotest chance of its being delivered and unloaded. Their inability or un-

[2] For a description of the congestion in the Port of New York in 1917, see Export Free Time, 47 I.C.C. 162 (1917).

willingness to cope with the situation finally made it necessary for the government to assume control of the railroads late in December, 1917. By the use of arbitrary methods, stalled cars were soon unloaded, a system of shipping "permits" was initiated under which no freight would be received for transportation unless the shipper could give evidence that it could be cared for when it reached its destination, and in the course of a few weeks the transportation machine was moving with a much higher degree of smoothness and precision. It is a noteworthy fact that when the country became embroiled in the Second World War, the railroads, with the cooperation of the shippers and the government, immediately took steps to "control traffic at the source," and there was never the slightest need or demand for the renewal of "government operation."

There has, of course, been a long-drawn-out and seemingly never ending controversy over the many issues that arose while the government was in charge of the railroads, with entirely too much misrepresentation and distortion by virtually all who have had a part in it. Whatever the merits of the case, we at least have one inheritance left from the troubled period which preceded direct governmental control. That is the Esch Car Service Act which, with its amendments, now constitutes subdivisions 10 to 17 of section 1, part I, of the Interstate Commerce Act.

ESCH CAR-SERVICE ACT; ASSIGNED CARS

The first of these subdivisions defines "car service" as including the "use, control, supply, movement, distribution, exchange, interchange and return of locomotives, cars, and other vehicles used in the transportation of property, including special types of equipment, and the supply of trains, by any carrier by railroad subject to this Part."

Subdivision 11 declares it to be the duty of a railroad to furnish safe and adequate car service, and enforce just and reasonable rules with respect to it; unreasonable rules are declared to be unlawful.

Subdivision 12 deals specifically with cars for the transportation of coal, requiring every railroad to distribute cars equitably among the mines served by it, "whether located on its line or lines or customarily dependent upon it for the car supply." During times of car shortage, each carrier is required to apply just and reasonable "ratings" to mines, and "to count each and every car furnished to or used by such mine for transportation of coal against that mine." This paragraph bears the reflection of a stirring and protracted dispute which once took place over the distribution of cars among coal mines. It was once the custom of mining companies to have coal cars of their own, and numerous industrial establishments, such as steel mills, electric utilities, and gas-producing firms likewise formed a habit of obtaining a supply of coal cars for their exclusive use. Railroad companies followed the custom of "assigning" some of their

cars for the transportation of their own fuel supply. The privately owned
cars and the railroad cars employed in the transportation of railroad fuel
were termed "assigned" cars, while cars of railroad ownership not used
for the transportation of railroad fuel were "unassigned." It was a common
practice among railroad companies serving coal mines to issue rules for
the distribution of cars according to the producing capacity of the mines.
In other words, the mines were "rated," and each mine was presumably
entitled to the car supply which its rated capacity indicated it should
have. This system of car distribution worked satisfactorily when there
was no shortage of cars, but when the demand for coal became excessively
large and there were not enough cars to transport all the coal which the
market could absorb, there arose a troublesome question as to how coal
cars should be distributed. Previous to the enactment of the Hepburn
Amendment, in 1906, during times of car shortage, a railroad would give
to each mine all the privately owned or railroad fuel cars which were assigned to it, and then would divide the unassigned "system" cars among
the mines in proportion to their rating, the mines having assigned cars
getting their pro rata share of system cars just as the mines which received no assigned cars. This meant that the mines having assigned cars
would often be able to obtain cars in excess of their ordinary quota, as
determined by their rating, while other mines would be forced to forego
operation, or would at least curtail operations sharply, because of a lack
of cars.

After the passage of the Hepburn Amendment, the Interstate Commerce
Commission declared that the practice of the railroads in not counting
assigned cars against the distributive shares which a mine was entitled
to receive resulted in undue discrimination against those mines to which
no cars were assigned. In some notable decisions, it ordered the railroads
to modify their methods of distributing coal cars.[3] This meant that during
times of car shortage, if the number of assigned cars a mine received was
equal to or greater than the percentage of cars its tonnage rating bore
to the total number of available cars, it would receive no "system cars"
whatever. If the number of assigned cars was insufficient to fill its distributive quota, it would not receive more than enough system cars to
fill out its share. The Commission did not take the position that it could
deprive a mine of the use of private cars or railroad fuel cars specifically
assigned to it, but it did say that if the number of such cars available

---

[3] Railroad Commission of Ohio v. Hocking Valley Ry., 12 I.C.C. 398 (1907);
Glenn W. Traer v. Chicago & Alton R.R., 13 I.C.C. 451 (1908); Rail and River
Coal Co. v. Baltimore & Ohio R.R., 14 I.C.C. 86 (1908); Hillsdale Coal and
Coke Co v. Pennsylvania R.R., 19 I.C.C. 356 (1910); Chicago & Alton R.R. v.
Interstate Commerce Commission, 173 Fed. 930 (1908), *sustaining in part the
order of the Commission in* 13 I.C.C. 451; Interstate Commerce Commission v.
Chicago & Alton R.R., 215 U.S. 479 (1910), *reversing in part* 173 Fed. 930;
Interstate Commerce Commission v. Illinois Central R.R., 215 U.S. 452 (1910).

was equal to or in excess of the mine's distributive share of the limited supply of cars, it was entitled to no portion of the available system cars. The decisions of the Commission were vigorously opposed by various railroads and mineowners, but they were sustained by the courts. The Supreme Court even affirmed by implication at least, the correctness of a decision [4] in which the Commission awarded to several mineowners awards of damages amounting to some $130,000, suffered because of a loss of business arising from the unduly discriminatory methods the railroads had employed in the distribution of coal cars.[5]

After paragraph (12) was added to the Interstate Commerce Act in 1920, the National Coal Association, composed of numerous large coal-dealers, took the position that since the law required a carrier to "count each and every car furnished," there could no longer be any distinction between assigned and unassigned cars, and that during times of car shortage all available cars, whether privately owned or intended for the transportation of railroad fuel, should be distributed in proportion to mine ratings. The Commission, upon its own motion, entered into an investigation of the rules employed by the railroads for the distribution of coal cars at bituminous mines. While it did not accept the Coal Association's interpretation of "each and every car," it did change its former position to the extent of holding that during times of car shortage no mine should receive cars in excess of its pro rata allotment, and if after that allotment was reached there were any mines receiving assigned cars, "assigned cars" left over were to be considered as unassigned, or system cars, and so distributed.[6] It was not long until the Commission's ruling was challenged in the courts. A Federal district court set the order of the Commission aside on the ground that its effect was tantamount to taking private property for public use without compensation,[7] but this decision was overruled by the Supreme Court and the validity of the Commission's order confirmed.[8] It might be pointed out that in a concurring opinion, one of the ablest members of the Commission, Joseph B. Eastman, held that the plain meaning of the law was that no distinction whatever should be made between so-called assigned and unassigned cars. Other members of the Commission, however, disagreed entirely with the majority decision.

Under the next two subdivisions, 13 and 14, of section 1, the Commission is authorized to require railroads to file their car-service rules just as they file tariffs, and the Commission is empowered, either upon its own initiative or upon complaint, to prescribe the rules which railroads must ob-

[4] Hillsdale Coal and Coke Co. v. Pennsylvania R.R., 23 I.C.C. 186 (1912).

[5] Pennsylvania R.R. v. Clark Coal Co., 238 U.S. 456 (1915).

[6] Assigned Cars for Bituminous Coal Mines, 80 I.C.C. 520 (1923); *affirmed,* 83 I.C.C. 701 (1924).

[7] Berwind-White Coal Mining Co. v. United States, 9 F.2d 429 (1925).

[8] Assigned Car Cases, 274 U.S. 564 (1927).

serve with respect to car service, even to the extent of fixing the compensation to be paid for the use of interchanged equipment as well as the penalties for nonobservance of prescribed rules. Under the second part (b) of subdivision 14, the railroads and express companies subject to part I are forbidden to enter into agreements for furnishing protective service against heat or cold, or to continue any such agreement already made, unless the agreement has been approved by the Commission as just, reasonable, and consistent with the public interest. This particular provision, added by the Transportation Act of 1940, was designed to put an end to certain discriminatory practices to which there had been much objection.

Under the terms of paragraph (15), the Commission may, during times of emergency, suspend all current rules and regulations affecting car service and make such rules as it believes, under the circumstances, to be just, reasonable, and in the public interest. In time of war or threatened war, the Commission is authorized, upon the request of the President, to give preference and priority to any traffic the movement of which is essential to the national defense. The provisions of paragraphs (16), giving the Commission the authority to control the routing of the traffic of any railroad which for some reason is unable to transport properly the traffic offered to it, were mentioned in the previous chapter.

Subdivision 17 consists of two paragraphs, the first of which (a) authorizes the Commission to distribute its directions regarding car service through any agents or agencies the Commission may select for the purpose. The Commission for many years has worked in close cooperation with the Car Service Division of the Association of American Railroads, and has found it an effective agency in helping to solve some of the difficulties created by severe car shortages. The second paragraph (b) of this subdivision forbids the giving or the taking of bribes for the purpose of influencing the distribution or the movement of railroad cars. At one time, during the distressing days of the First World War, and at other times when car shortages were severe, it was virtually impossible in some freight yards to have cars moved without the expenditure of bribe money. The practice became so notorious that Congress eventually included in the Transportation Act of 1940 a provision making such bribery a crime, and fixing a penalty of fine and imprisonment for those found guilty of giving or accepting money or other rewards the purpose of which was wrongfully to influence car service.

EMERGENCY CAR-SERVICE ORDERS

The insistence of the law upon justice and fairness in the distribution and use of railroad equipment in the service of the nation's domestic commerce has had a salutary effect, and the discriminatory practices, the bribery, and the preferences, which at one time were the source of so much complaint, have largely disappeared. The Interstate Commerce Commission has used its virtually arbitrary powers with moderation and restraint, but it has not failed to make use of them when conditions in railroad transportation were such as to warrant interference on behalf of the public interest. Since 1950, with mobilization for defense causing an increase in the volume of railroad traffic and a consequent shortage of freight cars, the Commission has issued several service orders designed to speed up the movement of cars and to shorten the time of their detention by shippers and consignees.

DETENTION OF CARS BY SHIPPERS

While it has been necessary over the years to apply some pressure to railroad companies in order to bring about just and reasonable practices with respect to car service, it must not be forgotten that shippers too are able, by acts of omission or commission, to exert a marked influence upon the conditions of car service. The freight-carrying equipment of our railroads, by reason of the pattern of transportation service employed, inevitably passes, for a considerable time, into the custody of the shippers and receivers of freight. It is likely that most people think of freight transportation on American railroads much as they think of passenger transportation, and have the idea that the most important part of it passes through freight stations just as passengers pass through passenger stations. But by far the largest part of the freight traffic which our railroads carry is handled in carload quantities, and never enters a freight station. It is loaded and delivered on railroad sidings, many of them serving industries directly and many of them being "public" rather than private sidings. While freight is being loaded and unloaded on such sidings, the cars are in possession of the shippers and consignees. Once more it must be recalled that the freight car is the earning part of railroad equipment; its function is fulfilled only when it is under load and moving. It is apparent that when a shipper or consignee keeps a car out of service the railroad is being deprived of the use of its most important facility. Moreover, if a shipper or consignee fails to load and unload cars promptly and with reasonable dispatch, other shippers and consignees, as well as the public interest, which is closely bound up with the free and expeditious movement of our domestic commerce, may suffer unwarranted injury.

DEMURRAGE

It has long been the practice of railroads to impose a charge upon shippers and consignees who detained cars for loading, unloading, or other purpose, beyond a certain specified time. This charge is called "demurrage." It is not so much a charge for rental, or for any other service, as it is a penalty charge, similar to a fine which the court imposes upon a person found guilty of some infraction of the law.[9] The practice of charging demurrage seems to have been originated in connection with the detention of ships and other watercraft. Often a shipowner enters into an agreement known as "trip charter," for the transportation of certain cargo between specified ports. Obviously, if the ship is unduly delayed by the charterer, for the purpose of either loading or discharging the cargo, the shipowner is deprived of the use of his vessel beyond the time ordinarily regarded as necessary for the completion of the agreed service. For this reason, trip charters contain clauses under which the owner is compensated by the charterer for any delay beyond a specified number of days for loading and discharging. In an ordinary "time charter," the penalty of demurrage is not necessary, since the vessel is hired for a certain number of days or weeks, and the matter of the time which may be wasted by unnecessary delay in loading and unloading is no concern of the shipowner.

It seems that American railroads began to impose demurrage charges for the unreasonably long detention of cars early in the 1870's, when the progress of technological change, the steady expansion of the railroad net, and the great increase in the volume of railroad traffic testified to the transformation of the railroad transportation industry from a relatively small business into a very large one. Freight cars of railroad ownership were increasing in number, capacity, and variety, and the practice of moving raw materials and merchandise in carload lots between sidings, both private and public, where the loading and unloading were done by shipper and consignee, was growing apace. For a long time, there was no uniformity in demurrage practices, with respect either to the conditions under which a charge would be exacted or to the amount of

---

[9] The right to assess demurrage charges existed at common law. Demurrage charges were upheld on two grounds, as compensation to the carrier for storage and for loss of use of equipment and as a penalty on the offending shipper [see Turner, Dennis and Lowry Lumber Co. v. Chicago, Milwaukee & St. Paul Ry., 2 F.2d 291 (1924), *sustained,* 271 U.S. 259]. The Commission also said that it had been held by the Commission and by the courts that demurrage charges were in part compensation and in part penalty. In the Matter of Investigation and Suspension of Advances in Demurrage Charges, 25 I.C.C. 314 (1912). However, the Commission said in another case that demurrage was not based on the rental value of the car, but was rather in the nature of a penalty. T. M. Kehoe & Co. v. Charleston & Western Carolina Ry., 11 I.C.C. 166 (1905). In Chrysler Corp. v. New York Central R.R., 234 I.C.C. 755 (1939), the Commission said, "Charges for demurrage embrace two distinct elements: (1) compensation for the use of the cars and tracks; and (2) a penalty designed to prevent undue detention of cars, and insure their prompt return to public service." See also 14 I.C.C. 178; 152 I.C.C. 665. The Commission made little effort to regulate demurrage until after 1906, when its administrative authority was greatly enlarged.

the charge. Some shippers were subjected to demurrage rules and charges, some were not; some were charged one rate, some another; in fact, the widespread differences in the treatment which railroads gave their customers was the cause of numerous complaints to the effect that many railroads were guilty of unjust and unduly discriminatory practices such as were forbidden by law, after the passage of the Act to Regulate Commerce in 1887.[10]

The original Act did not mention the word "demurrage," and as a matter of fact the word is still not to be found in any part of the law. Moreover, the terms of the original law seemed to have little to do with railroad service beyond the "transportation of passengers and property." Certainly the law did not require the filing of any demurrage or storage tariffs, and while the third section made it unlawful for a carrier subject to the Act to give any undue or reasonable preference or advantage to any person or firm "in any respect whatsoever," and the first section said that "all charges made for any service rendered . . . in the transportation of passengers or property . . . or in connection therewith, or for the receiving, delivering, storage, or handling of such property, shall be reasonable and just," it seemed that the law's application was restricted to the charges for a "service" which railroads might perform, and the demurrage penalty could hardly be called a charge for a service, though occasionally it was so designated in various legal proceedings. Before 1906, the Interstate Commerce Commission did not endeavor to regulate in any manner the demurrage rules or charges which the railroads adopted.[11]

[10] Some other interesting and significant cases in which the Commission considered the subject of demurrage were: New York Hay Exchange Association v. Pennsylvania R.R., 14 I.C.C. 178 (1908); Peale, Peacock & Kerr v. Central R.R. of New Jersey, 18 I.C.C. 25 (1910); Demurrage Investigation, 19 I.C.C. 496 (1913); Pittsburgh & Ohio Mining Co. v. Baltimore & Ohio R.R., 40 I.C.C. 408 (1916); Balfour, Guthrie & Co. v. Chicago, Milwaukee, St. Paul & Pacific R.R., 223 I.C.C. 441 (1937).

[11] As a matter of fact, the Federal Circuit Court of the District of Massachusetts held in 1907 that the clause of the Act of 1887 regarding the "receiving, delivering, storage or handling of property" was broad enough in its meaning to include demurrage. Michie v. New York, New Haven & Hartford R.R., 151 Fed. 694 (1907). The court declared that certain demurrage charges imposed by the New Haven were "not unreasonable" and were not unduly discriminatory, and denied damages to the complainant who had sued the railroad because of an alleged violation of the Act to Regulate Commerce. It is worthy of note that this case was decided just one day previous to the announcement of a decision by the Supreme Court of the United States in Texas and Pacific Ry. v. Abilene Cotton Oil Co., 204 U.S. 426 (Feb. 25, 1907). In the Michie case, the judge had passed upon the "reasonableness" and the alleged discriminatory character of the demurrage charges. In the Abilene case, the Supreme Court declared that notwithstanding the provision of section 9 of the Act to Regulate Commerce, which states "that any person claiming to be damaged . . . by any common carrier . . . subject to the Act . . . may either make complaint to the Com-

The Hepburn Amendment of 1906 extended greatly the scope of the Interstate Commerce Act. Not only were the "definitions" of section 1 expanded sufficiently to permit a belief that the detention of cars might be considered a part of the "transportation" to which the law applied, but section 6 was so modified as to make it plainly evident that railroads should file demurrage tariffs, just as they file tariffs containing schedules of any other charges which shippers are required to pay.

UNIFORM CODE OF DEMURRAGE RULES

There was one thing, however, which the new law could not bring to pass. This was the adoption of uniform rules with respect to the assessment of demurrage charges, though there was plainly a need for uniformity. But every railroad went its own way. Some roads had strict rules, rigorously and fairly applied; some had rules which were vague and indefinite, often without general application; and some had no rules at all. The entire problem of demurrage was further complicated by the fact that existing rules were subject to varying degrees of regulation by the public service commissions of the states. The confusion and uncertainty which resulted from the diverse patterns of regulation finally resulted in a movement among the members of the National Association of Railway Commissioners to frame and urge the adoption of a uniform code of demurrage rules. A car shortage of unprecedented severity in 1907 served to stimulate action toward this end. At the meeting of the association in 1908 such a code was presented, approved by a large majority of the

---

mission . . . or may bring suit . . . for the recovery of damages . . . in any district court of the United States," no action for damages would be maintainable in a Federal court for an alleged infraction of the Act with respect to rates, until the Commission had passed upon the question of the unreasonableness or unduly discriminatory character of the charges complained of. To let both courts and the Commission exercise authority to pass upon these questions might cause the law to defeat itself. A shipper claiming injury can still, at his option, file a suit for damages in a Federal court, because of allegedly unlawful rates, but he can not do so until after he has made a complaint to the Commission and that body has rendered a decision with regard to the rates. This was a highly important decision. Had it been handed down earlier, the judge in the Michie case would have referred the complainant to the Commission for its opinion as to the unreasonable or unduly discriminatory nature of the demurrage charges. For further decision on this point, see Baltimore & Ohio R.R. v. United States *ex rel.* Pitcairn Coal Co., 215 U.S. 481 (1910): "Regulations which are primarily within the competency of the Interstate Commerce Commission are not subject to judicial supervision or enforcement until that body has been properly afforded an opportunity to exert its administrative function." See also Robinson v. Baltimore & Ohio R.R., 222 U.S. 506 (1912); United States v. Pacific & Arctic Ry. & Nav. Co., 228 U.S. 87 (1913); Pennsylvania R.R. v. Puritan Coal Mining Co., 237 U.S. 121 (1915).

members, and submitted to the railroads of the country for adoption. The code received the blessing of the Interstate Commerce Commission in its annual report of 1909. Within a few years it was adopted by virtually all the railroads of the country. Although it has been changed in a number of particulars, it remains basically the same as when it was adopted. It has been republished and filed many times, the current issue which became effective August 15, 1951, being known as Freight Tariff 4, issued on behalf of the railroads by Agent L. C. Schuldt of Chicago. The tariff also contains the storage rules and charges of American railroads.

FREIGHT CAR EFFICIENCY

A cursory examination of the statistics concerning railroad equipment and its movement will indicate how important as well as how necessary demurrage rules and charges are. In 1950, the Class I railroads of the United States possessed 2,277,505 freight-carrying cars.[12] Ordinarily, a trifle more than 6 per cent of the freight cars of the country are "unserviceable," being withdrawn temporarily for repair, repainting, or remodeling, which means that in that year 2,100,000 cars were in daily use. For convenience, we shall assume the number to have been 2,000,000. During the year, these cars traveled (in round numbers) 29 billion miles, 18 billion under load and 11 billion empty. The ton-miles of freight transportation reported (net, and not including the weight of cars and locomotives) amounted to 622 billion. Dividing the number of ton-miles by the number of loaded-car-miles, we find that the average load per car was approximately 35 tons. Dividing the number of car-miles (loaded and empty) by the number of cars customarily in use, we see that each car made approximately 14,000 miles for the year, or 38 miles per day. If we figure the speed of our freight trains at 20 miles an hour, it will be seen that on the average a freight car was moving not quite two hours out of each twenty-four.

Since the average capacity of the American freight car is more than 50 tons, it is apparent that many cars must have moved with a much smaller tonnage than they were capable of carrying, but it must be remembered that a great many articles of merchandise, even when occupying the available space in a car, fall short of supplying a weight equal to that which a car can withstand. Moreover, it is well known that less carload freight can seldom be loaded to much more than half the capacity of a car. It should be pointed out, however, that there has been a steady improvement over the years in the loading of freight cars. The campaigns which railroads have put on to induce shippers to load heavily but not to overload cars have borne fruit, and shippers have shown a genuine spirit

[12] Association of American Railroads, Bureau of Railway Economics, "Statistics of Railways of Class 1, United States," (October, 1951), p. 14.

of cooperation in their endeavors to have railroad equipment used more economically and more efficiently.

It can also be said that the record with respect to the average daily movement of freight cars has shown a marked improvement during the last quarter of a century, though when one reflects upon the fact that a car is moving less than two hours daily, it must seem that our freight cars lay themselves open to a charge of featherbedding. The railroads are themselves partly responsible for the idle time which cars spend, for there is still much to be desired in the way of improving the physical facilities and the operation of our freight terminals, but by far the most of the time during which car wheels do not turn elapses while the cars are in the custody of shippers and consignees for loading and unloading. It is to cut down this time that the railroads have their code of demurrage rules.

THE DEMURRAGE TARIFF

There are nine rules in the demurrage tariff. Before discussing the terms of the rules, however, we should give some attention to the "application" of the rules and to the "exceptions" to the rules, which are to be found in the first part of the tariff, following the long list of participating carriers, and the three pages devoted to the explanation of reference marks and abbreviations and to the index to the rules. The section on the general application of the rules states that they are applicable to both the interstate and intrastate traffic of the participating carriers; says that in connection with "metered mail" the meter impression of the date will be considered the postmark; and names seven days, New Year's, Washington's Birthday, Memorial Day, Independence Day, Labor Day, Thanksgiving, and Christmas, as the "holidays" referred to in the tariff.

The exceptions to the tariff are of two kinds: general, or those which apply to the tariff as a whole, as indicated, either for all participating carriers or for certain carriers as named in the exceptions; and special, which for the most part are exceptions to particular rules or parts of the rules as indicated, in connection with carriers as named.

The general exceptions are employed chiefly to show that the demurrage rules do not apply on certain cars. There are many railroads, especially in the West, which have specially equipped flatcars used for the transportation of logs. Numerous items in the general exceptions indicate railroad lines upon which such cars, when placed for loading, are not subject to the demurrage rules. One very long item shows that cars moving in milk, passenger, or mixed trains, and used for transporting milk and its products, are not subject to the rules when the individual tariffs of railroads provide other rules and charges for car detention. Another general exception exempts from the application of the rule "empty cars placed for loading coal, coal blox, coal briquettes or coal boulets on mine tracks, coal mine sidings, or at coal washing plants or for loading at coke ovens, when the washing plants or ovens are located at or adjacent to the mines producing the coal to be washed or to be used in making coke." As indicated before, the railroads have rules for distributing cars at coal mines according to daily capacity for production, and no good purpose would be served by subjecting the cars to ordinary demurrage rules. Not so many years ago, this rule for the exemption of coal cars placed for loading was included as a part of the first rule of the demurrage tariff, but for some reason it was removed from the rule and made an exception to the tariff.

Of the special exceptions, of which there are several pages in the tariff, some make provision for the extension of free time, some provide for the storage of empty cars on private tracks until they are needed for service, and others say that the rules will not apply on certain roads during the winter months to cars loaded with frozen ore or silica. One special exception reminds us that we still have an operating narrow-gauge railroad, belonging to the Denver and Rio Grande Western. This exception stipulates that if, in order to reach their destination, carload shipments forwarded in standard-gauge cars have to be transferred to two or more narrow-gauge cars, the demurrage charges will be computed on the narrow-gauge cars.

We are now ready to turn to the rules of the demurrage tariff. The first one indicates the cars to which the rules apply or do not apply. Section A says that

. . . cars of either railroad or private ownership, held for or by consignors or consignees for loading, unloading, forwarding directions or for any other purpose (including cars held for loading company material unless the loading is done by the railroad for which the material is intended and on its tracks or private sidings connected therewith), and empty cars placed on orders which are not used in transportation service, are subject to these demurrage rules, except as provided in Section B.

The exceptions mentioned in section B (and it must be remembered that certain cars were exempt from the rules under the general exceptions to the tariff) are (1) cars under load with company material for the use of and consigned to the railroad holding the cars; (2) cars loaded with livestock; (3) cars containing freight refused or unclaimed and subsequently sold by a railroad for charges, for the time the cars are held by the railroad, for its own convenience, beyond legal requirements; and (4) private cars on private tracks when the ownership of the car and the track are the same.

Some explanation concerning these exceptions may be useful. Cars loaded with livestock are not subject to demurrage rules, because the law of the country governing the transportation of livestock forbids animals to be held in cars for a longer period than twenty-eight consecutive hours.[13] Live poultry, the rule explains, is not to be considered as livestock.

DEMURRAGE ON PRIVATE CARS

It was formerly the practice of railroads to treat private cars (a private car is one having other than railroad ownership) just as railroad cars were treated. If a railroad placed a person's own car on his own private track for loading, or if he delivered to a privately owned siding a carload shipment contained in a car belonging to the owner of the siding, such cars were subject to demurrage rules and charges just the same as a car belonging to a railroad. This did not seem to be exactly fair, and as a matter of fact the Commission, in a decision handed down in 1907, declared that private cars should not be subjected to demurrage charges when on the tracks of the owners or of consignees.[14] But this was before the general adoption of the uniform code. This code, as originally written, made private cars subject to demurrage rules regardless of whose tracks they happened to be on. The Procter and Gamble Company of Cincinnati appealed to the Commission to invalidate this rule, but the Commission refused to do so.[15] Then the company appealed to the Commerce Court, a special court created by Congress in 1910 to hear appeals from the decisions of the Commission (it was abolished in 1913), on the ground that the rule was illegal and beyond the Commission's power to sustain. The Interstate Commerce Commission took the position that the courts had no right to pass upon a purely negative order of the Commission, and that consequently the Commerce Court was without jurisdiction. The court declared it had jurisdiction, but sustained the Commission's ruling.[16] An appeal was taken to the Supreme Court which, in 1912, dismissed the appeal on the ground that the Commission was correct in assuming that the courts were without authority to overrule that body's negative administrative orders.[17] Several years later, the demur-

[13] Live Stock Twenty-eight Hour Act, 34 Stat. L. 607. The time can be extended to thirty-six hours upon written request of owner or party in custody of shipment.

[14] Demurrage Charges on Privately Owned Tank Cars, 13 I.C.C. 378 (1908).

[15] Procter & Gamble Co. v. Cincinnati, Hamilton & Dayton Ry., 19 I.C.C. 556 (1910).

[16] Procter & Gamble Co. v. United States, 188 Fed. 221 (1911).

[17] United States v. Procter & Gamble Co., 225 U.S. 282 (1912). The effect of the Supreme Court's decision in this case was to give shippers and carriers a different standing before the Commission. A carrier can appeal to the courts to set aside an order of the Commission, on the ground that the order is unconstitutional or exceeds the statutory authority of the Commission. A shipper cannot appeal an adverse, or negative, order of the Commission, if the order has been properly and lawfully made. On various occasions, shippers have suggested that

rage rule regarding private cars was amended and assumed its present form. Very often the owner of a private car in which he ships goods to a customer will go through the motion of "leasing" the car to the consignee, the evidence of the lease being merely a board attached to the car giving notice of the lease. In this way the customer, if he has a private siding, can hold the car after the expiration of free time, and still avoid the payment of demurrage charges, for the lessee is considered to occupy the position of owner.

FREE TIME

The second rule of the demurrage tariff is labeled "free time." It tells how many hours shippers and consignees have, under various conditions, to hold cars for loading, unloading, or other purposes, without incurring demurrage charges. The general rule is that a shipper or consignee has "forty-eight hours (two days) free time . . . to partly or completely load, to partly or completely unload, or to partly unload and partly reload, all commodities." There are a few exceptions to this broad provision, to be noted presently, and the rule very carefully explains the meaning of the terms "loading" and "unloading." Loading is not completed when the goods are stowed in the car, and the doors closed; it "includes the furnishing of forwarding directions on out-bound cars; also advice that car is ready for forwarding after being held to finish loading." In the same way, unloading means something more than the removal of property from the car. It includes the surrender of the bill of lading for goods shipped on an order bill, the payment of lawful charges when required before the car is delivered, the furnishing of a "turn-over" order for the car if the goods contained are to be delivered to another party and there is to be no additional movement of the car beyond the siding or public yard where the car has been delivered, and advice that the car is ready for forwarding after being held for partial unloading or partial unloading and reloading. The consignee is informed in a "note" that if he wishes his car held in a receiving freight yard the car will be subject to the demurrage rules while in the yard. If the consignee gives the railroad instructions, either general or special, as to the placing of incoming cars on the tracks where

---

they too be given the right of appeal to the courts, but fortunately this has not been done. It would mean merely the further drawing out of the investigation of a shipper's complaint, and give to the courts the power to do what the Supreme Court has declared they must not do, that is, pass upon the matters of the reasonableness or the unduly discriminatory character of a rate in the first instance. That function belongs to the Commission. When shippers are disturbed because of fancied "loopholes" in the law or because of what they believe to be a misconception of duty on the part of the Commission, they can ask Congress to amend the law. This is the policy they have hitherto followed, and with striking success.

they are to be accepted, the free time begins when the car is actually placed, and the time spent in the holding yard is not counted as a part thereof.

When the same car is unloaded and then reloaded for an outbound movement, each transaction, with minor exceptions, is treated separately and independently, with forty-eight hours of free time for each operation. On cars which are shifted about a private or public delivery yard for "partial" unloading or reloading, the forty-eight hours of free time applies to the entire transaction, not to each separate portion of the loading or unloading process.

Freight cars are often detained by shippers or consignees for purposes other than loading or unloading. Only twenty-four hours of free time is allowed on cars held for reconsignment, diversion, or reshipment or held in transit on orders of the shipper, consignee, or owner. The same time is allowed on cars withheld, under tariff regulations, from a connecting line, pending the surrender of the bill of lading or the payment of lawful charges; on cars containing freight in bond for customs entry or government inspection; on cars held in transit because of conditions solely attributable to the shipper, consignee, or owner; on cars held in transit for inspection and grading of contents. No free time is allowed on cars received from another railroad and held for forwarding instructions, except that cars received between 4 P.M. and 7 A.M. will not be subject to demurrage if forwarding directions are supplied before the following noon.

COMPUTATION OF TIME

The third rule of the tariff is rather long. It is devoted to telling how the time of car detention is to be computed. It is divided into seven parts. The first part deals with cars for loading; the second with cars held for "orders" (except for placement); the third with cars for unloading. The last four parts of the rule are primarily for the purpose of explanation and clarification. It is noted, for example, that cars placed at "exactly" 7 A.M. will be treated as cars placed before that hour. "Actual placement" is determined by the "precise time the engine cuts loose." There have been many disputes in the past over demurrage rules and charges, and the carriers endeavor, in their tariff, to frame the rules in such a manner that every contingency will be cared for. One important provision in this rule is that in computing time, Saturdays, Sundays, and holidays are not counted, except in case of the use of an average agreement, which will be explained presently.

On cars for loading on "other than public delivery tracks," that is, private sidings or interchange tracks leading to plants performing their own switching and shifting services, time is computed from the first 7 A.M. after actual or constructive placement, and without notice of placement. Constructive placement of cars for loading is defined in Rule 6 as follows:

Cars for loading will be considered placed when such cars are actually placed or held on orders of the consignor. In the latter case the agent must send or give the consignor written notice of all cars which he has been unable to place because of conditions of the other-than-public-delivery track or because of other conditions attributable to the consignor. This will be considered constructive placement.

On cars for loading on public delivery tracks, time is computed from the first 7 A.M. after placement and without notice. But if they are not placed within twenty-four hours after 7 A.M. of the date for which ordered, time will be computed from the first 7 A.M. after notice of placement has been sent or given.

When a car is loaded outbound, it is the duty of the consignor to notify the railroad agent that the car is ready for movement. If the notice is sent by United States mail, it is considered as being received after 7 A.M. of the date received, even though mailed on a previous day.

The general rule with regard to cars held for such orders as for diversion or reconsignment, and to cars requiring the surrender of the bill of lading or the payment of charges, is that time is computed from the first 7 A.M. after notice of arrival is sent or given to the consignee or party entitled to receive the notice.

On cars held for unloading on public delivery tracks, the general rule is that time will be computed from the first 7 A.M. after placement and after notice of arrival has been sent or given. If a car is not placed within twenty-four hours after the notice of arrival has been sent or given, then a notice of placement is sent or given, and time is computed from the first 7 A.M. after that notice. As to cars to be delivered to other than public delivery tracks, time is computed from the first 7 A.M. after actual or constructive placement. In Rule 5 we find that

. . . when delivery of a car consigned or ordered to an industrial interchange track or to other-than-a-public-delivery track can not be made on account of the inability of the consignee to receive it, or because of any other condition attributable to the consignee, such car will be held at destination, or, if it can not reasonably be accommodated there, at the nearest available hold point, and written notice that the car is held and that this railroad is unable to deliver will be sent or given to the consignee. This will be considered constructive placement.

There are a few exceptions to the general rules of computing time given above, and a few explanatory clauses in the rule. These have to do with cars held for the surrender of bills of lading or the payment of charges, cars received from other railroads, and cars stopped in transit. On cars delivered to the interchange tracks of a plant which does its own switching, time is computed from the first 7 A.M. after the actual or constructive placement on an interchange track until the return of the car to the same or another interchange track.

NOTICES OF ARRIVAL AND PLACEMENT

Rule 4 of the demurrage tariff has to do with notification. Many disputes have arisen between railroad and shipper concerning the "sufficiency" of notice, and this rule has been worked over several times for the purpose of eliminating any uncertainty about the practices and the obligations of the railroad. A notice of arrival is customarily sent in writing, but if a consignee agrees in writing to accept notices of arrival by some other method, by telephone, for example, such method may be employed. A notice must be sent by the agent within twenty-four hours (exclusive of Saturdays, Sundays, and holidays) after the arrival of car and billing at destination, and it must show the initials and number of the car, point of shipment, contents, and, if transferred in transit, the initials and number of the original car. An impression copy of a notice must be retained, and if the notice is sent on a postal card the impression must be of both sides. Delivery of cars on other than public delivery tracks or on interchange tracks, or notification of readiness to deliver, constitutes notification of arrival. Should a consignee remove any of the contents of a car before a notice of arrival has been sent to him, the removal itself shall be considered as notice of arrival. The last part of the rule has to do with notices which under the terms of the bill of lading must be sent out when freight has been refused or is unclaimed, and indicates certain conditions and circumstances under which the carrier will not send notices regarding unclaimed shipments.

CONSTRUCTIVE PLACEMENT

Rules 5 and 6 have to do respectively with placing cars for unloading and placing cars for loading. We have already quoted the definitions of constructive placement as given in these two rules. It often happens that, because some shippers have been slow in unloading cars delivered at a public delivery track, the track becomes so crowded that other arriving cars cannot be accommodated. When it is impossible for a railroad to deliver a car to a public delivery track designated in the billing of the car, notice is sent to the consignee that delivery will be made at another point, the "nearest available to the consignee." Should the consignee prefer to take delivery at another point than the one named in the notice, and so notifies the carrier, the preferred delivery will be made. If the consignee refuses to accept delivery at the point named in the notice, the car will be held until it can be delivered at the track designated in the billing, but nevertheless subject to demurrage.

Once in a while, a shipper orders a car for loading, and then something happens which causes him to decide not to load the car. Cars ordered and not used are charged demurrage until they are released, with no free time allowed. If a car ordered for loading on a public delivery track is not used, and no notice is received from the shipper who ordered it within forty-eight hours from the first 7 A.M. after placement, the car may be removed and treated as if "released" at the time of removal. When an empty car is "appropriated" by a shipper, without being ordered, it is considered as having been ordered and placed. Should a privately owned car, loaded on the owner's track, be delivered to the railroad for movement without forwarding directions, the car is subject to demurrage charges without any free time allowance.

DEMURRAGE CHARGES

Rule 7 has to do with demurrage charges. It should be explained that demurrage charges are imposed in two ways, first as "straight demurrage," and second under an "average agreement." This rule indicates the amounts to be paid for cars subject to straight charges. The rate, after the expiration of free time, is $3 a day for the first four days and $6 a day thereafter. There are some interesting "notes" included in this rule. When under the terms of Rule 34 of the Consolidated Classification a railroad furnishes two or more cars in lieu of a car of the size ordered by the shipper, or when through no fault of the consignor or consignee the contents of a car are transferred by the railroad to two or more cars, demurrage charges, if any accrue, shall be for only one car. When two carload shipments are loaded in a single car by two different shippers, each shall have forty-eight hours of free time, and in the same way the consignees of two carload shipments arriving in a single car shall each have forty-eight hours of free time for unloading.

The rate of demurrage charges has changed many times. Until the time of the First World War, it did not exceed $1 a day, and every day of detention after the expiration of free time was charged for at the same rate. During the period of government operation, demurrage charges were advanced to a high level, reaching a figure as high as $15 a day under certain circumstances. The rate receded after the war was over, but it never reached its former low level, and the practice of charging a higher rate as the time of detention was extended was not abandoned. In recent years, under the pressure of the need of the railroads for more revenue, and because of the relative decline in the number of freight-carrying cars, there has been a tendency to advance demurrage charges just as the rates for transportation and the charges for other railroad services have been increased.

At the time this is being written, the demurrage charges are no longer those contained in Freight Tariff 4-Z, as originally published. It was stated previously that as a result of the car shortages caused by the defense mobilization program pursued by the United States in 1950, the Commission had exercised its authority to issue several "service orders" designed to speed up the movement of freight cars and shorten the periods of their detention by shippers and consignees. The most drastic step taken by the Commission was to order an increase in demurrage charges. For cars not subject to an average agreement, the charge was placed at $5 a day for the first two days, $10 a day for the third and fourth days, and $20 a day for each succeeding day. Any fraction of a day was counted as an entire day. The rate schedule for cars subject to an average agreement were also modified. These demurrage charges are the highest ever imposed by the railroads of the United States. The Commission's order became effective on September 20, 1950, was scheduled to expire on April 1, 1951, it is still in effect and will doubtless remain in effect as long as the uneasy situation in international affairs continues. A few commodities are not subject to the new rates, chiefly bulk freight for transfer to lake or ocean shipping.

CARS EXEMPT FROM CHARGES UNDER CERTAIN CONDITIONS

Rule 8 of the demurrage tariff has to do with claims. It indicates the conditions and circumstances under which demurrage charges shall not be imposed at all, even after the expiration of free time, or, if imposed, will be at a lower rate than that provided in Rule 7. The first cause for the cancellation of demurrage charges, or for their refunding, if collected, is the weather. When the temperature is so low that the lading of a car is so frozen or congealed as to require thawing before it can be unloaded, free time is extended; when, on account of floods, earthquakes, or violent windstorms, it is impossible for shippers or consignees to load or unload cars, the time lost shall be eliminated in computing demurrage charges. The relief which the shipper or consignee is entitled to under such circumstances is similar to the carrier's exemption from liability for loss or damage due to an act of God.

A second reason for the cancellation of demurrage charges is "bunching." Ordinarily, a shipper receives cars for loading or cars for unloading in an orderly stream, and is able to load or unload them with reasonable promptitude and dispatch. But because of difficult operating conditions due to weather or the congestion of traffic, a railroad may not be able to deliver cars in an orderly fashion. For a day or two, only a few of the expected number are delivered, or perhaps none at all, and then delivery is made in a single day of cars which should have been delivered over a space of two or three days or more. This accumulation of cars is called bunching, and since it is not because of any fault attributable to the shipper or consignee, the demurrage tariff provides that the shipper or consignee, as the case may be, shall be allowed such free time as he would have been entitled to had the bunching not occurred.

We have mentioned previously that any demurrage charges arising from delay caused by a demand by the railroad agent of charges in excess of tariff authority must be canceled, or if paid, must be refunded. In the same way, any error on the part of any railroad named in the bill of lading, which prevents the proper tender or delivery of a carload shipment, excuses the consignee from the payment of any demurrage charges beyond those that would have accrued had the error not been made.

When a notice of arrival transmitted by a railroad does not contain the information required under the terms of Rule 4 of the demurrage tariff, a consignee has the right to call in question the sufficiency of the notice, but he must take such action within forty-eight hours from the first 7 A.M. after the notice has been sent or given, if he is to be entitled to any avoidance of demurrage charges. Should a consignee claim relief from demurrage charges on the grounds that an arrival notice sent by mail has been delayed, the date of mailing shall be that given by the postmark.

Any delay which is caused by action of the United States customs or the Department of Agriculture, in connection with import freight, provided the delay is not caused or contributed to by the shipper, consignee, or owner, is added to the free time ordinarily allowed.

A prolific source of dispute about demurrage charges in past years was the matter of strikes which prevented the loading and unloading of cars. For a long time, the Commission took the position that strikes, even though admittedly a cause of excessive car detention, could not be accepted as an excuse for relief from the application of the rules of the demurrage tariff.[18] In 1937, however, the Commission had a change of heart on this subject. A number of automobile factories, as well as other industrial plants, were for several months plagued by the so-called "sit-down strikes." In many instances, these strikes led to car detention of such proportions that demurrage charges accrued amounting to thousands of dollars. In a case involving the Chrysler Company and the New York Central Railroad, the Commission stated that, under existing conditions of car supply (there was no shortage), there was no "good reason for the imposition of the charge so heavily penal as the existing code provides." Consequently, it held that the automobile company should be required to pay as demurrage charges upon the cars it was powerless to release a rate of $1.20 in-

[18] Wholesale Trade Association of New York v. Director General, 58 I.C.C. 15 (1920); Barker Asphalt Paving Co. v. Lehigh Valley R.R., 112 I.C.C. 4 (1926); Walford Forwarding Corp. v. Pennsylvania R.R., 87 I.C.C. 43 (1923).

stead of $2 and $5 a day.[19] The Commission adopted the same attitude in subsequent cases, with the result that the railroads now include in Rule 8 of the demurrage tariff a provision to the effect that the daily rate of charge on cars detained because of interference due to strikes shall be the rate named by the Commission in the Chrysler case.

AVERAGE AGREEMENTS

The final rule of the demurrage tariff, Rule 9, is the highly important one providing for the so-called "average agreement." Under the terms of this rule, a shipper or consignee, instead of paying "straight demurrage" for cars detained beyond free time, may enter into a written agreement, under the terms of which demurrage charges are computed on the basis of the average time of detention of cars released during a calendar month. The average detention and the charge are computed by a simple formula. One credit is allowed for each car released before the expiration of twenty-four hours of free time. After the expiration of the free time for any car, one debit per car per day or per fraction of a day is charged for the first four days. At the end of the month, credits are used to offset debits. If there is a balance of debits, the regular demurrage rate of $3 is paid for each one; if credits outnumber debits, no demurrage is paid, but the surplus credits accumulated one month cannot be used to offset debits incurred in the next month. Not more than one credit will be allowed for a single car, and when a car has accumulated four debits, it must pay the regular rate of $6 a day for any further detention, including even Saturdays, Sundays, and holidays. Credits earned on cars for loading may not be used to offset debits accumulated by cars for unloading, nor may credits earned by cars for unloading be used to offset debits charged to cars for loading. Credits cannot be earned by private cars on the tracks of the owners of the cars, but the debits charged to such cars while under constructive placement may be offset by credits earned on other cars. There are a few other features of the average agreement, but these are the most important. The charges which, in 1950, the Commission ordered to be made for cars held under an average agreement are the same as those made for cars subject to straight demurrage. However, only the $5 debits can be offset by accumulated credits, and it requires two credits to offset a single debit. These charges have the same expiration dates as the straight demurrage charges.

By the use of the average agreement, a skillful and attentive traffic manager can often manage to have demurrage charges considerably lower than they would be if straight demurrage were paid on all detained

[19] Chrysler Corp. v. New York Central R.R., 234 I.C.C. 755 (1939); Balfour, Guthrie & Co. v. Chicago, Milwaukee, St. Paul & Pacific R.R., 235 I.C.C. 437 (1939).

cars. Virtually all large plants which handle hundreds of cars in the course of a month enter into average agreements with the railroads by which they are served.

DEMURRAGE AND EXPORT FREIGHT

The demurrage rules and charges which we have been discussing are those applying exclusively to domestic commerce. They do not apply to our export traffic, and indeed they do not apply to all of our domestic traffic. We have already pointed out the fact that the tariff contains a number of "exceptions" made on behalf of certain railroads or for certain kinds of traffic. Perhaps the most important domestic traffic to which these rules do not apply is the lake cargo coal traffic, traffic of coal which is shipped to ports on Lake Erie or Lake Michigan for shipment by water to various states in the northwestern part of our country. Special rules governing this traffic provide for a longer period of free time and a different scale of charges, and there are also a few other rules which differ from the rules of the uniform code.

Because of the uncertainty of ship arrivals at our seaports and the difficulty of planning in advance for timing the transfer of cargo from car to vessel, it has long been the custom of our railroads to grant a longer period of free time to cars carrying commodities for export than that granted to cars handling commodities moving only in our domestic trade. For many years, it was customary for such cars to have unlimited free time after reaching a seaport, and the practice of the railroads in permitting this concession on export traffic persisted even after the general adoption of the uniform code of demurrage rules. Finally, the railroads brought unlimited free time to an end. However, the first limitation adopted in 1914 for the Port of New York allowed for sixty days of free time on export shipments, which was surely a far more generous allowance than that given in the uniform code. The sixty-day period was reduced to thirty days in 1915, and to fifteen days the following year. Appalled by the congestion in the port in 1917, the railroads tried to cut free time down to five days and make similar reductions at other ports, hoping that the accrual of demurrage charges would lead to a more earnest effort on the part of shippers to obtain the release of tied-up cars. The Interstate Commerce Commission suspended the five-day rule, but after investigation decided that a ten-day period of free time for export traffic at New York would be "reasonable." [20] Even this action did little to relieve the congestion, and, as we have pointed out before, conditions grew steadily worse throughout 1917, until the government felt compelled to assume control of the railroad system. The Commission has long taken

[20] Export Free Time, 47 I.C.C. 162 (1917). See also New York Harbor Storage, 47 I.C.C. 141 (1917).

the position that the difference between the conditions affecting the transportation of export traffic and the conditions under which domestic traffic moves justifies more liberal demurrage rules for export shipments.[21] Among the emergency orders issued by the Commission during 1950, however, was one limiting to seven days the free time for unloading from boxcars freight intended for further movement by water, and limiting to five days the free time for loading ex-water-borne traffic into freight cars of any kind. These orders, too, were originally scheduled to expire on April 1, 1951, but they are still in effect.

TRACK STORAGE CHARGES

While demurrage charges are relied upon for the most part to provide the penalty necessary to make shippers and consignees reasonably nimble in releasing their hold upon freight cars, it has been found that in some terminals they are not enough. In many public yards in our large cities, where fresh produce is received, it is customary for the consignees to market the shipments directly from the cars. They may find it is cheaper to pay the somewhat moderate demurrage charges than to rent store space. At many such terminals, the railroads also impose an added penalty, which they call "track storage charges." These charges are usually equal to demurrage charges, and in effect represent a doubling of the latter, though they may be less or more in different cities. At one time, an effort was made by the railroads to secure the adoption of a uniform "code" of track storage charges, but the effort did not meet with success. Such charges are neither universal nor uniform among railroads. When imposed at all, they are to be found in individual tariffs of the railroads. Track storage charges are of course not the same as railroad storage charges for unloaded freight, which will be discussed in the next chapter.

RAILROADS IN WORLD WAR II

While demurrage rules and charges alone cannot give assurance that in times of car shortage and other emergencies railroad traffic will flow with greater celerity and certainty, they have unquestionably been helpful in relieving congestion. Happily, the railroads of the country took a lesson from their distressing experience during the early months of the First World War, and did not repeat their errors when the second such war was thrust upon us. One of the most impressively brilliant achievements standing to the credit of American railroads was their handling of the nation's commerce during the Second World War. Because of the shortage of rubber, the destruction of shipping or its requisition by the government, and the diversion of the major portion of our gasoline supply to military

[21] Export Free Time, 47 I.C.C. 162 (1917); Decreased Free Time Allowance at Ports on Traffic from California, 64 I.C.C. 400 (1921).

uses, the railroads were called upon to carry not only the large burden of traffic which under ordinary circumstances they would be expected to carry but also a vast number of shipments which under normal conditions would have been transported by tankers, cargo ships, and motor vehicles. The weight of the huge demand fell upon them, moreover, at a time when because of a long and severe depression they had not been able to restore their equipment of cars and locomotives as rapidly as they had worn out and been retired from service. Despite their handicaps, the railroads carried during the war years a much greater volume of freight than they had carried in the previous banner year of 1929, and they did it with far fewer cars, fewer locomotives, and fewer employees. Their success was due in part to the cooperative spirit with which they met the task, in part to the aid received from the government in the control of traffic, and in part to the willingness of the shippers of the country to load cars to capacity and load and unload them as speedily as possible. Numerous shippers boasted with considerable pride that they had ceased for weeks at a time to incur any demurrage charges whatever. Throughout the period of the war, the statistics of transportation showed that most of the time two freight cars were performing the service which had formerly demanded the use of three cars. The effect was just the same as would have followed a sudden increase of the car supply by 50 per cent.

SUMMARY

We have already discussed in the preceding pages the part which the Interstate Commerce Commission has had in the regulation and control of car service and of demurrage rules and charges. The Commission was instrumental in securing uniformity of practice, and its interpretation of the rules in many of its decisions has been a leading factor in their modification and clarification. The Commission's most important activity, however, in shaping policy with respect to car service, has been its firm insistence on the universal observance of the rules. There was a time, and it extended even beyond the adoption of the uniform code, when there were laxity and indifference, as well as favoritism and discrimination, in the application of the rules with regard to car service and demurrage. As soon as it received the necessary power, in 1906, the Commission took the position that a demurrage tariff was like any other tariff, and that all of its terms were to be scrupulously observed; that car-service rules were to be reasonable, equitable, and adhered to without deviation. For a few years, occasional prosecutions of offenders and the infliction of heavy fines were necessary to convince some erring carriers that published rules and charges with respect to car service were to be followed with consistency and uniformity. It is seldom that one hears any more of any violation of the rules, except through inadvertence or because of an honest mistake in interpretation. Both shippers and carriers have accepted demurrage and current rules regarding car distribution as an integral and necessary part of a somewhat complex, but on the whole a fair and reasonable, process of railroad transportation service. Certainly it cannot be denied that the policies and practices worked out over a long span of years have been a solid and permanent contribution to the improvement of the flow of our domestic commerce.

CHAPTER XVII

Terminal Services: Switching and Lighterage

It has already been pointed out that most of the freight traffic carried by our railroads is received and delivered in carloads and that it is loaded and unloaded by shippers and consignees. One of the most interesting phases of railroad operation is the collection and delivery of this carload freight. These activities are much more complicated than the hauling of trains between terminals, which is, after all, a comparatively simple operation, once the schedules of train movements have been adopted and the "rules of the road" established. If one really wants to obtain a knowledge of how a railroad is operated, from a physical standpoint only, the best point of observation is a railroad terminal.

THE PECULIAR CHARACTER OF RAILROAD TRANSPORTATION

The characteristic of railroad transportation which differentiates it and sets it off completely from other forms of commercial transportation is that it is inseparably tied to a fixed highway. It moves in a groove, as it were, and unless the groove—which is a track—is provided, movement is impossible. In highway transportation, or in transportation by air, there is no fixed track which vehicles must undeviatingly follow. Trucks and motorcars can meet and pass on a highway, or one vehicle may overtake and pass another, without having specially constructed facilities for this purpose. The same thing can be said for the operation of carriers by water or by air. On ordinary highways, motor vehicles meet or pass at the will of the driver on any part of the highway (there are a few places where we have one-way roads), but railway trains, bound to the fixed track, cannot move to one side at any point to meet another train or pull out of line and pass another. In a terminal district, trucks and passenger-carrying motor vehicles operate over all streets or alleys, but railroad cars must cling to their specially built tracks. Even when a railroad car moves on a car float, the float is equipped with tracks. The movements of railroad cars are much less flexible in their nature than the movements of other surface vehicles, and they must be subjected to a much greater degree of control. It takes little reflection to understand why the original plan of railroad transportation, a system under which each shipper would provide his own vehicle and his own motive power, was quite impossible to carry out. It is futile to try even to imagine what would happen on a railroad if every shipper and traveler had the right to operate his own vehicle, yet we have thousands upon thousands of vehicle operators on our highways. The great point of difference is that highway transportation is individualized, whereas railroad transportation must be carefully organized under an elaborate system of control, with every movement carefully directed. Even where railroads are built with two or more parallel tracks, though the problem of arranging for the meeting and passing of trains is not so difficult, it is far less simple than the same problem on a highway.

WHAT SWITCHING IS

The collection and delivery of loaded cars from shippers and to consignees, the delivery of cars to shippers for loading, the recovery of empty cars from shippers after their contents have been removed, the movement of loaded and empty cars to and from railroad freight houses and team tracks, the delivery of cars to connecting lines—all these operations go under the general name of "switching." They are movements off the main line of tracks of the railroad. They are unscheduled movements, and unlike the movement of trains on the main line, they are not governed by timetables and train orders, but solely by the signals of those in immediate charge of the cars and locomotives involved.[1]

[1] It is somewhat difficult to define switching with precision. A Federal judge made this attempt: "Ordinarily in rate making a transfer service is distinguished from transportation, and switching service is usually defined as one which precedes or follows transportation upon which legal freight charges have been earned or are to be earned. The test is sometimes applied as to which branch of service in fact moves the freight; if by a yard crew or yard master, it is said to be a switching charge, but, if movement is under the direction of a train dispatcher or train master, a transportation charge." Louisville Water Co. v. Illinois Central R.R., 14 F. Supp. 301, 303 (1936).

The Interstate Commerce Commission, after refraining for many years from "defining" switching service, finally came up with this effort, which, if it does not enable a person to understand what switching service really is, at least leaves no doubt that it may be a varied and complicated operation: "Switching consists of all movements of railway cars on their own wheels other than those in road trains running between stations, and also the movement of locomotives and motor cars under their own power incidental to such car movement. It excludes movements of yard locomotives within yard limits when assisting road trains out of terminals. The elements of switching service involved in this proceeding are classification, company coal dock switching, freight house switching, industry track switching, repair track switching, team track switching and transfer. The kinds of switching service involved in this proceeding are carrier line switching (intratrain, intertrain and interchange), carrier terminal switching (origin and destination only), intermediate switching and interterminal switching and intraterminal switching." Des Moines Union Ry. Switching, 231 I.C.C. 631 (1939); Kansas City Southern Ry. v. Louisiana & Arkansas Ry.. 213 I.C.C. 351 (1935).

INDUSTRIAL SIDINGS

The track facilities employed by railroads for the collection and delivery of loaded and empty cars are of a widely varied nature, ranging from a simple siding, parallel to the main line track, to a comprehensive network of tracks serving all parts of a gigantic industrial plant. A railroad may build an industrial siding on its own land to serve one of more plants; such sidings are to be found in every industrial center. In addition to the industrial sidings which are on the property of the railroad, there are throughout the country thousands of private sidings occupying a right of way owned or leased by the shippers they serve. Any industry has a right to have a private siding or private track upon which to receive and dispatch carload traffic. Whenever an industry builds such a siding at its own expense, the railroad with which it may connect is required by law to establish a switch connection if it is reasonably safe to do so and if there is a reasonable prospect that the industry will give the railroad enough business to justify the construction and operation of the siding.[2] One would think that a railroad would not have to be compelled to establish a connection with a sidetrack if there was a prospect of development of a lucrative business, but at one time railroads were subject to persuasion on the part of shippers possessing such tracks who did not wish to see a competitor enjoying a similar facility. After the passage of the original Act to Regulate Commerce in 1887, which contained no mandate with respect to switch connections,[3] there were numerous complaints about carriers who refused to permit shippers to have facilities for handling traffic in car-

[2] Under subdivision 9, section 1, of the Interstate Commerce Act, a railroad is required to establish a switch connection with any "lateral, branch line of railroad, or private side track which may be constructed . . ." and in case of refusal to do so, after a written application has been made for the construction of a connection, the owner of the branch line or of the private side track may file a complaint with the Commission, which has the authority to require the connection to be made. As the law stood in 1906, only a shipper who was refused a switch connection after an application in writing could obtain redress from the Commission. The Commission was without authority to order the establishment of a connection with a "lateral, branch line of railroad." Interstate Commerce Commission v. Delaware, Lackawanna & Western R.R., 216 U.S. 531 (1910), *affirming* 166 Fed. 498 (1908). This situation was corrected in 1910, when an amendment to the Act gave the branch line, too, a right to appeal to the Commission. But the Commission did not yet have the authority to require a main line railroad to establish a switch connection with another main line railroad.

[3] A railroad never had any common law duty to establish switch connections with private sidings. Hocking Valley R.R. v. New York Coal Co., 217 Fed. 727 (1914). The Commission, however, had the power, even under the Act of 1887, to correct practices which were unduly prejudicial and unjustly discriminatory, and under this power could require a railroad, under some circumstances, to make a switch connection with a private siding. Red Rock Fuel Co. v. Baltimore & Ohio R.R., 11 I.C.C. 438 (1905).

loads, and one of the provisions of the Hepburn Amendment of 1906 imposed upon railroads the duty of making proper switch connections with private sidings and branch lines.

One seldom hears now of a refusal on the part of a railroad to make use of private sidings. In fact, when an industrial or commercial concern wants a private siding, and is able to provide the right of way for its construction, the siding is usually built by the railroad, though at the expense of the shipper. Nearly all railroads have a standard form of contract under which private sidetracks are built. The form used most generally provides that the railroad company shall perform the construction work, with the shipper paying the actual cost plus 15-per-cent "overhead." Such a track cannot be used by other concerns except with the consent of both the owner and the railroad, though the railroad has the right to establish other switch connections with that part of the siding which is on the railroad's land. It is usually the custom of a railroad to require the one who applies for the construction of a private siding to provide a bond or a cash deposit sufficient to cover the cost of construction. In case a cash deposit is made, any balance remaining after the work is completed is returned to the owner of the new track.

PUBLIC DELIVERY TRACKS

It is obviously highly advantageous for a shipper or receiver of carload freight to have his plant located on a siding, either an industrial siding owned by the railroad or a private siding the use of which may or may not be shared with others. Of course it is not always possible for an industry to have such a location. For the use of those industries which do not have side track delivery, the railroad provides "public delivery tracks" or "team tracks," where carload freight is received and delivered, the haul to or from the plant of consignee or shipper being accomplished by trucks, drays, or similar conveyances.

TRAP CARS

The shipper whose plant is located on a railroad siding may employ the siding not only for incoming and outbound carload traffic but often for less carload traffic, too. Ordinarily less carload freight is trucked to and from a railroad freight house, but if an industrial concern is located on a private or industrial siding, a railroad will furnish a car for the transportation of less carload shipments to the freight house, provided the combined weight of the shipments reaches a certain minimum weight, usually 12,000 pounds, though different railroads require different minimum weights. Such a car is called a "trap car" or "ferry car," and its use is quite common in American industrial plants. On some railroads, arrangements are made with a shipper to load less carload shipments in station order for a certain section of line, and the car can be incorporated directly in a local freight train without the necessity of handling and sorting the shipments at the initial freight house.

INDUSTRIAL RAILROADS AND TAP LINES

The sidetrack facilities of huge industrial plants may have many miles of track and cover hundreds of acres of ground; they comprise small railroad systems in themselves. Such systems have interchange tracks where they make connection with railroad spurs or sidings, and, as we shall see later, the railroad has no obligation to perform any switching service beyond the interchange tracks. These intraplant systems of tracks may be simply plant facilities used exclusively by the industries which own them, but in many places we find that these switching facilities are owned by an incorporated company and operated as a separate and distinct department of some industry. Such "industrial railroads" may be used solely as plant switching facilities for one or more industries, but frequently they also act as common carriers, and publish and file tariffs just as other railroads do.[4] Large logging and lumbering operators are likely to own railroad systems having several miles of track which, though built primarily for private use, are employed also to give common carrier service to the public. A "tap line" is similar to an industrial railroad, though its function is more to act as a "feeder" to the trunk line which it "taps" than to serve as a plant switching facility.

It is on tracks such as these that a railroad performs its direct switching

---

[4] A half-century ago, it was an all too common practice among American railroads to give large rebates to favored industrial shippers by granting concessions to "industrial railways and tap lines" in the form of divisions of joint rates, excessive allowances for plant switching, per diem claims and remission of demurrage charges, and also by performing for some industries costly switching services for which the line-haul revenue provided inadequate compensation. The Commission, with considerable difficulty, finally brought these unduly preferential practices to an end. The report on the general investigation of the concessions to industrial railways may be found in the Industrial Railways Case; the Matter of Allowances to Short Lines of Railroads Serving Industries, 29 I.C.C. 212 (1914). The report on the general investigation of concessions to tap lines is to be found in the Tap Line Cases, 23 I.C.C. 277 (1912). Previous reports dealing with improper concessions to tap lines were Central Yellow Pine Assn. v. Vicksburg, S. & P.R.R., 10 I.C.C. 193 (1904); Central Yellow Pine Assn. v. Illinois Central R.R., 10 I.C.C. 505 (1905); Star Grain & Lumber Co. v. Atchison, Topeka & Santa Fe Ry., 15 I.C.C. 364 (1908), 17 I.C.C. 338 (1909). The orders of the Commission issued as the result of its general investigation of tap lines were invalidated by the Commerce Court, 209 Fed. 244 (1913), and the decision affirmed by the Supreme Court, the Tap Line Cases, 234 U.S. 1 (1914). The Commission had declared the tap lines to be only "plant facilities" and not "common carriers." The adverse court decisions required further action by the Commission to remove tap line abuses. 31 I.C.C. 490 (1914). Also Wasteful Service by Tap Lines, 53 I.C.C. 656 (1919), 89 I.C.C. 327 (1924); Oakdale & Gulf Ry., 58 I.C.C. 450 (1920).

service to its patrons, where it delivers and collects carload shipments and places cars for loading. The mileage of yard tracks and sidings of American railroads is approximately one half their route mileage. In the terminal districts of a large industrial center, these auxiliary tracks are far greater in number and mileage than main line tracks. A railroad company usually establishes "switching limits" in its terminals. These limits are published in tariffs. They indicate the area in which the carrier will receive and deliver carload traffic at private or public sidings, and sometimes name the industrial plants served.

CLASSIFICATION YARDS

The switching operations of a great railroad are among the most interesting of its manifold activities. The classification of freight cars in a hump yard—in which the switches are controlled electrically from a tower located at the top of the hump, and the momentum of the cars as they move down the hump and on toward their proper classification tracks is controlled by car retarders, also operated from the tower—is a fascinating performance, though the working of an ordinary sidetrack at a local station may be no less interesting than the large-scale operations of a huge freight yard.

WAY FREIGHT TRAINS

The simplest example of railroad switching is that which takes place at a local station when the local freight train, or "way freight," picks up or delivers one or more cars on the single sidetrack, which runs for a short distance parallel to the main line and may or may not be "open" at both ends. The road engine, leaving its train or a part of it on the main line, performs the necessary shifting work, perhaps making a flying switch or a "Dutch" switch, if the sidetrack is connected with the main line at one end only, or perhaps using the sturdy pole by means of which an engine can push a car along on a parallel track. The same kind of switching work can be seen where a single long "spur" branches off to a stone quarry, sawmill, or other plant where carload traffic must be picked up and started on its way to market.

In some local stations, the work may be a trifle more complicated. There may be a freight house where less carload freight is to be delivered or taken aboard, and there may be several industrial plants, such as a grain elevator, a canning factory, a planing mill, and a fruit and vegetable warehouse, at which full cars are waiting to be taken away or empty cars are to be left for loading. While members of the train crew load and unload the way freight, the train conductor, who has received his switching instructions from the local agent, directs the movements by which the sidetrack is "pulled," the loaded cars added to the train, the empties left properly "spotted" at the industry platforms, and those cars which had to be moved in the course of the shifting operations returned to their former places. One test of the skill of the local freight train conductor is the number of "moves" the engine must make in order that all the indicated switching operations may be completed and the train hooked up and ready to proceed.

TERMINAL SWITCHING

The switching of cars at a larger industrial center, where the railroad has a terminal in which freight trains are made up and broken up, where they begin and end their runs, is more complicated than the switching at a local station. The road engine which pulls the arriving freight train into the terminal is cut off and goes to the "roundhouse" for refueling, cleaning, and minor repairs, and the yardmaster and his crew, with one or more switching engines, take over. The cars are sorted and placed on classification tracks for later distribution within the terminal district, and delivered to their destination by a switching engine. Instead of a single sidetrack, there may be several, some of them "private sidings" serving single industries, some of them "industrial sidings," on the land of the railroad, serving one or more factories, stores, or warehouses, some of them team tracks or "public delivery" tracks, and some "house tracks" alongside a freight house where less carload freight is received and delivered. Some of the cars in the train are for points farther along the line; they must be assembled on the proper track to await their dispatch in an outgoing train. Switching engines make their daily rounds of the various sidings and auxiliary tracks, delivering the cars of incoming freight or empty cars for loading, picking up for return to the freight yard the loaded cars which shippers have "released" with proper forwarding instructions, and recovering the cars which have been unloaded and are ready for further service.

The next step in the complication of switching service comes in an industrial center which is served by two railroads instead of by a single line. Each line has its own sidings and freight houses, which must be switched daily. But every day each railroad is likely to bring in cars which must be delivered to the other road, some of them loaded cars for local destinations, some of them loaded cars for further transportation by the connecting line, and some of them empty cars on their way to their home road. Moreover, each of the two roads is likely to have cars loaded each day on some of its sidings which must be delivered to the other line for transportation to destination. We arrive, therefore, in an industrial center which has two railroads, at the problem of "interchange switching," by which cars are exchanged between the carriers. The yards of the two lines are of course connected by one or more tracks and the roads make their own arrangements for interchange.[5]

INTERMEDIATE SWITCHING

Moving along to larger cities, we may find that three or four roads are conducting a daily interchange of loaded and empty freight cars. It may be that the interchange is all direct, each road delivering cars to the others over connecting tracks, but it may also happen that one road does not have a direct connection with one of the other lines. In this case, it requires the facilities of an intervening road to effect the interchange, and we have what is called "intermediate switching," in which the switching line merely performs the exchange movement and has no part in the line haul of the cars involved.

BELT LINES

In many of our larger industrial centers, the exchange of cars between railroads is all done directly, each road having direct connections somewhere in the terminal district with the other roads. In others, there may be a considerable amount of intermediate switching. In our largest industrial and commercial cities, we are likely to find that the intermediate switching is performed by a "belt line," virtually encircling the terminal district and furnishing a connection between all of the railroads in the district. This belt line, in some cases an "independent" property and in some cases owned and managed cooperatively by all or a part of the lines entering the district, is usually simply an interchange facility performing the interchange switching functions of the lines which it connects. The belt line, however, may have industrial sidings of its own for which it performs only switching movements and no actual road haul, but some belt lines, while their primary function is to provide physical connection between other carriers, also perform line-haul services between various stations located on their routes or in connection with the lines for which they perform switching services.[6]

[5] Much interchange switching involves only the exchange between connecting lines of cars which are to be transported to terminals beyond the junction where the interchange takes place. If the car is moving under a joint rate, there is no switching charge. In this chapter, we are interested only in interchange switching in which one connecting carrier receives cars for delivery at some of its terminal facilities at the interchange point.

[6] For a description of terminal switching facilities in a large industrial center, see Boston Wool Trade Assn. v. Director General, 69 I.C.C. 282 (1922); Detroit Switching Charges, 28 I.C.C. 494 (1913); Switching Rates in Chicago Switching District, 177 I.C.C. 669 (1931); Reciprocal Switching at Kansas City, 68 I.C.C. 591 (1922); Nashville v. Louisville & Nashville R.R., 33 I.C.C. 76 (1915); Des Moines Union Ry. Switching, 231 I.C.C. 631 (1939). The Roches-

The city of Chicago, which is our greatest railroad center, has three belt lines, an inner, an outer, and a middle line. The inner line virtually confines its work to switching, but the other two not only act as belt lines but perform line-haul service as well. By the use of a middle and an outer belt line, much of the interchange between the many railroads converging upon Chicago can take place at a considerable distance outside the city and away from the more congested areas of the railroad terminals. St. Louis has an interesting terminal connecting railroad; New Orleans has a belt line which is owned and operated by the city in the interests of the railroads and the shippers and receivers of freight of that port. New York does not have a belt line, but along the west bank of the Hudson River, extending from Bayonne to Weehawken, is a jointly owned and operated "marginal" line which connects the several railroads from the west which cross New Jersey to the New York port district. Before this marginal line was put into operation, and the roads in New Jersey effected their interchanges by "direct" switching, it was sometimes necessary to haul a car as much as 160 miles to transfer it from the terminal of one road to the terminal of another road barely 15 miles away.

Enough has been said to indicate that switching constitutes one of the most important parts of railroad transportation and that it is an activity which because of its very nature can give rise to numerous complicated problems as well as some lively controversies between carriers and their customers. The volumes in which the reports of the Interstate Commerce Commission are published are full of cases involving switching practices, rules, and charges.

RAILROAD CAR DELIVERY

The industrial traffic manager is interested first of all in the direct switching service given by the railroad which brings raw materials and supplies to his plant and takes finished products away. On American railroads, this direct switching has always been considered a part of the carrier's transportation service covered by the transportation rate. In England and various other foreign countries, the charges for "transportation" and for "terminal services" are separately published and are added together to make the total charge. But, as the Interstate Commerce Commission once said, "the American railroad rate has always been recognized as covering the full service which the carrier gives—in furnishing the car, a proper place at which to load it, the conveyance of that loaded car, and

---

ter Switching Case, 95 I.C.C. 30 (1924), shows how complicated switching services may become because of distances, plant locations, local topography, and the variety of patterns railroads follow in the construction and operation of freight yards and other terminal facilities.

its terminal delivery." [7] Even though the original Act to Regulate Commerce declared in section 6 that the schedules of railroad rates shall "state separately the terminal charges," and the Act now states that all "terminal charges, storage charges, icing charges, and all other charges which the Commission may require" shall be separately stated, the Commission has taken the position that the "simple delivery" of a car to an industrial or private siding is not a terminal service for which the railroad should make a separate charge. Railroads are supposed—and required—to make deliveries of carload traffic to private sidings, without an extra charge, just as they deliver carload traffic to their own public delivery tracks or to their freight houses.

Before 1910, it was a custom of the railroads serving the California cities of Los Angeles, San Francisco, and San Diego to charge their consignees $2.50 for each car delivered to a private or industrial siding. The Interstate Commerce Commission declared that this charge was "illegal and unjust" and ordered its discontinuance. [8] One member of the Commission went further than the others, declaring that since the carriers did not impose a similar charge at other California seaboard terminals, the practice at the three cities mentioned was also unjustly discriminatory. The railroads carried the Commission's order to the courts, but in vain. The Supreme Court, in a decision handed down in 1914, upheld without qualification the validity of the Commission's decision. [9]

SWITCHING ALLOWANCES

However, there is a limit to the switching service which a railroad must perform for its consignees. Even before the Los Angeles Switching case reached the Commission, it had decided that a railroad was not required to do more than deliver cars to a "convenient" place. The General Electric Company, at its Schenectady plant, had a small railroad system of its own, serving the numerous buildings in which its various operations were conducted. It was the custom of the railroads serving the plant to deliver loaded cars at certain interchange tracks, beyond which the shifting and spotting at different plant buildings were done by the company's own locomotives. The company appealed to the Commission to require the New York Central Railroad to make the company an "allowance" for the shifting and spotting which the company performed for itself, claiming that this service was a part of the railroad's obligation as a carrier. The Commission refused to take such action, saying that the carrier had com-

[7] Associated Jobbers of Los Angeles v. Atchison, Topeka & Santa Fe Ry., 18 I.C.C. 310 (1910).

[8] Associated Jobbers of Los Angeles v. Atchison, Topeka & Santa Fe Ry., 18 I.C.C. 310 (1910).

[9] Los Angeles Switching Case, 234 U.S. 294 (1914).

pleted its obligation to "deliver" loaded cars when it took them to a convenient interchange point, and it had no duty to perform switching services over the complicated, interlaced tracks within the company's plant.[10] A similar decision was made at the same time in response to a request for a switching allowance made by the Solvay Process Company.[11]

These decisions did not mean that a railroad was forbidden, under all circumstances, to withhold allowances from companies which performed some kind of switching or other terminal service. Any railroad has a right to employ an agent to perform part of the transportation service which the railroad itself can be considered as obligated to perform, and if a consignee performs such a service it is properly entitled to compensation in the way of an "allowance."[12] But there came to be a wide difference of opinion among shippers and carriers as to the exact nature of the obligations of the carrier. It was commonly accepted that a railroad was bound to "deliver" carload shipments, but what constituted delivery?[13] If the railroad performed switching services beyond that for which it was compensated by its line-haul charge, it was obviously guilty, in effect, of remitting or refunding a part of the transportation charge, a practice which was explicitly forbidden by section 7 of the Interstate Commerce Act. Moreover, if it extended to one shipper more generous treatment in the

[10] General Electric Co. v. New York Central & Hudson River R.R., 14 I.C.C. 237 (1908).

[11] Solvay Process Co. v. Delaware, Lackawanna & Western R.R., 14 I.C.C. 246 (1908).

[12] United States v. Baltimore & Ohio R.R., 231 U.S. 274 (1913).

[13] In the Industrial Railways Case, 29 I.C.C. 212 (1914), the Commission had this to say: "Under the common law as construed in practically unanimous decisions of courts, a delivery of carload freight to a shipper having a private siding is made by shunting the car upon the switch, clear of the main tracks. All services on the siding beyond that point, in placing the car for loading or unloading at a particular spot convenient to the shipper, are what may be called volunteered services in the sense that they are in addition to the main-line haul and in excess of any obligation of service by the carrier at common law. Nevertheless the custom of making delivery at the warehouse or factory door on private sidings is one of long standing in this country, and under certain language in the act it is possible that carriers may be required, upon reasonable compensation, to do spotting, as it is called. We find no authority, however, English or American, that holds or intimates that the line carrier, in connection with the main-line haul, is under any obligation to spot a car at a factory door on a private siding except upon reasonable compensation included in the rate itself or set up in the form of a special charge."

However, in Car Spotting Charges, 34 I.C.C. 609 (1915), the Commission took the position that the line-haul rate might cover the placement of a car on an industry track for loading or unloading, but that a charge should be made for each additional placement for that purpose. In other words, the established practice of giving initial spotting service at a private siding, without an extra charge, was not considered to be unlawful.

way of switching services than it rendered to another, receiving traffic under similar conditions and circumstances, it was guilty of illegal discrimination.

INTRAPLANT SWITCHING

Railroad practice was for many years far from uniform, and as a matter of fact is not uniform now. Very little difficulty arose in connection with simple switching activities such as the spotting of cars at the loading platforms of industries built along an industrial siding, or in connection with the delivery of cars to an industry located on its own private siding. The difficult problem arose at those plants which had more or less elaborate and intricate yards of their own, with a capacity for a large number of cars, many of which had to be shifted from track to track and from building to building. All these plants, as a rule, had interchange tracks where the railroad could deliver and receive cars. There were many ways in which the intraplant switching was handled. It came to be the custom of railroads throughout the South and West to assume little or no responsibility for intraplant switching and make no allowances to companies which owned and operated their own plant tracks. In the East, however, at some of these plants the railroads would perform much or all of the intraplant switching, at others it would grant allowances to plants which did their own switching, at still others the railroads merely delivered or accepted cars at interchange tracks, neither performing plant switching nor making any allowance. It was a matter of common knowledge that many railroads were suffering an unjustifiable financial loss either because of the heavy allowances they were giving some of their customers or by reason of the performance of switching services for which they were not adequately compensated by their line-haul rates.

EX PARTE 104

In 1934, at a time when the railroads were being sorely pressed financially because of depleted traffic and inability to make an adjustment of operating expenses commensurate with their loss of revenue, the Commission, on its own initiative, undertook a comprehensive investigation of all the practices of railroads which had any effect upon their revenues and expenses. Part II of the Commission's report had to do with the "terminal services" of all Class I railroads, and in particular with switching practices and the allowances made to the receivers of freight who did their own plant switching.[14] In its report, the Commission described the practices which railroads followed in their direct delivery of carload freight and reviewed numerous decisions which the Commission itself and various

[14] Ex parte 104. Practices of Carriers Affecting Operating Revenues and Expenses, 209 I.C.C. 11 (1934).

courts had made in dealing with the somewhat vexatious problems that had arisen in the past. Conceding that it was well settled that a carrier might deliver carload freight on private sidings, the Commission declared that there was no legal obligation resting upon the carrier to perform a direct switching service beyond that which could be considered equivalent to team track delivery. It condemned the practice of giving switching service beyond the interchange tracks lying between the carrier's tracks and the industrial plant's tracks, holding that such service was work for which the carrier was not compensated in its line-haul rate. Allowances which carriers made to shippers for performing switching service beyond a plant's designated interchange tracks were declared to be unlawful, in violation of section 6 of the Interstate Commerce Act.

In approximately eighty supplementary reports, more than a third of which are to be found in the volume containing the general report on switching allowances, the Commission considered individual cases, and in the large majority of them declared various allowances which many carriers had been accustomed to grant to be unlawful. In the fifty-ninth of these supplemental reports, the allowances made to the Red River Lumber Company by the Southern Pacific and Western Pacific Railroads at Westwood, California, were declared by Division 3 of the Commission to be unlawful,[15] but upon a rehearing the same division decided that the allowances were justified.[16] However, on its own motion the full Commission reconsidered the case, and reversing the second decision of Division 3, declared the allowances to be unlawful.[17]

[15] Red River Lumber Co. Terminal Service, 234 I.C.C. 287 (1930).

[16] Red River Lumber Co. Terminal Service, 256 I.C.C. 379 (1943).

[17] Red River Lumber Co. Terminal Service, Fruit Growers Supply Co., Successor, 263 I.C.C. 483 (1945). Other interesting cases dealing with direct switching and allowances are United States Cast Iron Pipe Co. v. Director General, 57 I.C.C. 677 (1920); Lehigh Portland Cement Co. v. Director General, 62 I.C.C. 231 (1921); Terminal Allowance to St. Louis Coke & Iron Co., 85 I.C.C. 591 (1923). Another case growing out of Ex parte 104 was even more long drawn out than the Red River Lumber Company case. A. E. Staley Mfg. Co. Terminal Allowances, 215 I.C.C. 656 (1936). The Commission first decided that the allowances paid to the Staley Company at Decatur, Ill., were unlawful. A few years later, an application from the Staley Company for "free spotting service, because of changes in its physical plant and operating arrangements" was denied. A. E. Staley Mfg. Co. Terminal Allowance, 245 I.C.C. 383 (1941). These decisions were sustained by the Supreme Court. United States v. Wabash R.R., 321 U.S. 309 (1944), 322 U.S. 198 (1944). In 1946, the Commission decided that one segment of the Staley plant was entitled to an initial spotting service, without charge, since the proposed service was the "substantial equivalent of a simple placement." Switching Elevator C. Staley Plant at Decatur, Ill., 266 I.C.C. 213 (1946).

This did not end the difficulty over spotting. Some shippers were fearful that if partly loaded or unloaded cars on their sidings were shifted to permit the col-

The decisions of the Commission in *Ex parte* 104 were promptly challenged in the courts. In the Federal District Court for the Western District of Pennsylvania, the orders of the Commission requiring a discontinuance of allowances granted by certain railroads to the American Sheet and Tin Plate Company and various other plants were set aside and their enforcement enjoined. The Commission thereupon appealed to the Supreme Court, which reversed the decision of the district court and held the orders to be lawful and valid.[18] In several other cases in which efforts were made to have the Commission's decisions disapproving of allowances set aside, the Supreme Court again upheld the actions of the Commission.[19] So it became a settled policy that the obligation of the carrier receiving the line-haul rate for the transportation of a carload of freight did not go beyond an act of delivery similar to what the carrier would perform in switching a car to its own freight houses or public delivery tracks. The action of the Commission plugged some of the holes through which the carriers had been losing revenue unnecessarily, and it also put a stop to numerous practices which without doubt resulted in the undue preference of some industrial plants and undue and unjust discrimination against others.[20]

INTERCHANGE SWITCHING

Thus far, we have been discussing only the switching involved in the direct delivery by a carrier of cars billed to consignees on its own network of sidings and industrial tracks. Interchange switching, or switching in which the switching carrier picks up or delivers cars which receive their road hauls by other carriers, is an entirely different thing. Obviously, if

---

lection and delivery of other cars on the same sidings, they might be subjected to "spotting charges," perhaps large in amount. Their fears were quieted when the Commission said, "We find that the shifting of empty, partly loaded, partly unloaded or loaded cars from or to any location at a shipper's shed or loading platform without charge in addition to line haul rates, if the shifting is incidental to other necessary operations, is just and reasonable." Switching Services at Western Points, 268 I.C.C. 740 (1947).

[18] United States v. American Sheet & Tin Plate Co., 301 U.S. 402 (1937), *reversing* 15 F. Supp. 711 (1936).

[19] United States v. Pan American Petroleum Corp. (together with United States v. Humble Oil & Refining Co.), 304 U.S. 156 (1938), *reversing* 18 F. Supp. 624 (1937); United States v. Wabash R.R., 321 U.S. 403 (1944), *reversing* 51 F. Sup. 141 (1943).

[20] The Commission's decision in Ex parte 104 was not unanimous. Commissioner Mahaffie recorded a dissent in that report as well as in those supplementary reports which followed. For a pungent criticism of the Commission's decisions as well as of the sustaining court decisions, see Charles S. Belsterling's article, "Freight Rates and Terminal Switching Services," *University of Pennsylvania Law Review*, Vol. 95, No. 6, June, 1947, pp. 719–738.

two or more railroads are serving the same industrial center, they cannot be expected to perform for no compensation switching movements on cars for the transportation of which they receive no line-haul revenue. Such interchange is performed at hundreds of terminals under the provisions of tariffs which are published and filed just as are the tariffs containing transportation rates, demurrage charges, storage charges, or any other charges railroads exact for their services.

It must not be supposed that every industrial community having two or more railroads has always had interchange switching among those roads such as we have today. Modern switching interchange exists as the result of a long and strenuous battle before commissions and courts. Under the common law, no railroad was obligated to open its terminal facilities to the reception of cars from other roads. The only obligation a railroad assumed was the transportation it undertook to do on its own lines, and any arrangement for through or joint transportation was entirely a matter for a railroad to settle itself. Under the original Act to Regulate Commerce, carriers subject to the law were required "according to their respective powers" to "afford all reasonable, proper and equal facilities for the interchange of traffic between their respective lines," but, the law went on to say, "this shall not be construed as requiring such common carrier to give the use of its tracks and terminal facilities to another carrier engaged in a like business." The words to be emphasized in this proviso are "give" and "use." A carrier could not be required to "give" anything, of course, and it certainly was not required to permit the "use" of its terminal facilities by another line, whether the concession was a "gift" or not. The courts for some time took the position that switching arrangements involving only delivery at a terminal meant something different from furnishing facilities for the interchange of traffic. A carrier could not be required to build a switch connection for the facilitation of through transportation; even if a connection existed, it could not be required under the common law to admit to its network of sidings the cars which were hauled by another, and possibly a rival, railroad. In many terminals, railroads freely engaged in what came to be known as "reciprocal switching," that is, each road would open its industrial sidings to the cars for which other roads had furnished the line haul. For a long time, however, they were under no legal obligation to do so, and in more than one terminal railroads stubbornly refused to admit to their terminals any cars except those which they themselves had hauled, or to permit the loading of any cars unless they were to share, in part at least, in the line haul. When reciprocal switching arrangements were made, there was usually a switching charge for any interchange movement of a car, which might be paid by the shipper or receiver, or might be "absorbed" by the carrier enjoying the line haul.

Several of the states tried to force the carriers to loosen up on their terminal operations, but the earlier efforts failed to pass muster with the Supreme Court of the United States. The state of Kentucky inserted a section in its constitution which required that

> . . . all railroads shall receive, transfer, deliver and switch empty cars coming from or going to any railroad . . . with promptness and dispatch, and without discrimination as to charges . . . and shall so receive, deliver, transfer and transport all freight from and to any point where there is a physical connection between the tracks . . . but this section shall not be construed as requiring any such carrier to allow the use of its tracks for the trains of another engaged in a like business.

THE CENTRAL STOCK YARDS CASE

In Louisville, Kentucky, the Central Stock Yards Company had a stockyard located on a siding of the Southern Railroad. The Louisville and Nashville Railroad had switch connections with the Southern, but it had a stockyard on one of its sidings, operated under contract with another stockyards company. The Louisville and Nashville refused to deliver carloads of livestock, moving either intrastate or interstate, to the plant of the Central Stock Yards Company, maintaining that it had ample facilities of its own for the receipt and delivery of livestock. In 1902, the Central Stock Yards Company asked the Federal Circuit Court for the Western District of Kentucky to issue a mandatory injunction requiring the Louisville and Nashville to deliver and receive livestock in carloads at its junction with the Southern, lying between the two stockyards, claiming that the refusal was a direct violation of section 3 of the Act to Regulate Commerce as well as in contravention of the Kentucky constitution. The circuit judge refused to issue the injunction, whereupon the stockyards company appealed to the Circuit Court of Appeals of the Sixth Circuit. The court affirmed the decision of the lower court, holding that the refusal of the Louisville and Nashville did not constitute an act of undue preference, since that road itself had adequate facilities for handling the livestock shipped on its own line, and quoting the decision of Chief Justice Waite in *Atchison, Topeka and Santa Fe Ry. v. Denver and New Orleans R.R.* (110 U.S. 667), reminded the complainant that a railroad was obligated to carry only on its own line and had no responsibility for transportation beyond its own terminus. The court made no mention of the Kentucky Constitution, declaring that the "relief sought pertains to the transportation and delivery of interstate freight," which the state had no power to regulate.[21]

The stockyards company appealed to the Supreme Court, again claim-

[21] Central Stock Yards Co. v. Louisville & Nashville R.R., 118 Fed. 113 (1902).

ing a violation of the Act to Regulate Commerce, and pointing anew to the provisions of the constitution of Kentucky. The appeal was in vain. Justice Holmes, who wrote the opinion, said that he would lay to one side the question as to whether the disputed section of the Kentucky constitution represented an attempt on the part of that state to regulate interstate commerce, because the court was "of the opinion that the defendant's conduct is not within the prohibitions or requirements of either the Act of Congress or the Constitution of Kentucky." Not even discussing the clause of section 3 of the Interstate Commerce Act about the provision of facilities for the interchange of traffic, he denied that the railroad was guilty of undue prejudice, and as to the Kentucky constitution, the requirement that railroads

. . . deliver, transfer and transport freight to any point where there is a physical connection between the tracks of railroad companies, must be taken to refer to cases where the freight is destined to some further point by transportation over a connecting line. It cannot be intended to sanction the snatching of freight from the transporting company at the moment and for the purpose of delivery.

"We have discussed the case," said Holmes, "as if the stock yards were side by side. They were not but they both were points of delivery for cattle having Louisville as their general destination." As though his mind were troubled by some slight doubt, however, he went on to say that "it may be that a case could be imagined in which carriage to another station in the same city by another road fairly might be regarded as *bona fide* further transportation over a connecting road and within the requirements of the Kentucky Constitution." [22]

Although the stockyards company had been rebuffed three times in Federal courts, it was by no means through with the controversy. So far as interstate commerce was concerned, the decision of the Supreme Court had to be accepted as final, but with respect to the part of the livestock traffic that was intrastate, the company could ask for relief in a Kentucky state court. Though Justice Holmes had interpreted the meaning of the language of the Kentucky constitution in such a way as to justify his opinion that the act of the railroad did not contravene the provisions of that document, he had not declared those provisions to be in violation of the Federal Constitution. Maybe somebody else would have a different idea about their meaning. The company secured an injunction in the circuit

[22] Central Stock Yards Co. v. Louisville & Nashville R.R., 192 U.S. 568 (1904). The weakness of the Court's decision, as embodied in Justice Holmes's opinion, lay in the employment of too much imagination. Although the stockyards were some miles apart, they were treated as if side by side. It would have been just as easy to "imagine" them much farther apart, in which case the interchange could have been said to be for the purpose of further transportation.

court of Jefferson County ordering the Louisville and Nashville to cease its refusal to perform the switching movement which was demanded. This time it was the railroad which had to appeal, which it promptly did, to the court of appeals, the highest court of the state of Kentucky. In a long and closely reasoned opinion, this court affirmed the decision of the county court, holding that even if the line-haul company did have terminal facilities capable of caring for shipments of livestock, it was nevertheless obliged by the state constitution to deliver and receive carloads of live-stock at its connections with other roads, if such roads had similar facili-ties for loading and unloading the cars. The ownership of the cars was immaterial, and even interstate shipments should be so delivered and received, since before or after reaching the terminus of the line-haul car-rier, the movement of the cars was strictly intrastate in character. The court commented sharply on the fact that the Supreme Court of the United States had "expressly declined to apply either the Constitution of the State of Kentucky or the interstate commerce act to the case," because it had chosen to treat the two stockyards as if they were "side by side." [23] The court said it was the duty of a common carrier "to accept and carry all freight tendered to it, and to make delivery to the consignee, if the point of destination is on its lines, but, if destined to a point not on its lines, it must, nevertheless, accept and carry such freight to the end of its lines, and there deliver it to a connecting line, with the instructions of the shipper." The matter of the distance the freight was to be carried on the connecting line was of no significance. It might be a mile or a hundred miles; the principle was still the same. There was a vigorous dis-sent on the part of one member of the court who thought that since the section of the Kentucky constitution under discussion did not provide for the compensation of a railroad for the use of any of its own cars it would be required to transfer to another road, there would be deprivation of property without due process.

As was to be expected, the Louisville and Nashville promptly took the case to the Supreme Court of the United States on a writ of error. Once more, Holmes was designated to write the opinion of the Court. Persisting in his former opinion that the refusal of the railroad to transfer cars involved no violation of the Interstate Commerce Act, he examined at some length the provisions of the Kentucky constitution under which the stockyards company had brought its original suit in Jefferson County. He had no difficulty in concluding that the requirement of that constitu-tion that the plaintiff in error should deliver its own cars to another car-rier, without a specific provision for compensation, was an unlawful "tak-ing of property," in violation of the Fourteenth Amendment. The decision

[23] Louisville & Nashville R.R. v. Central Stock Yards Co., 97 S.W. 778 (1906).

of the Kentucky Court of Appeals was therefore reversed.[24] But the Justice did leave a loophole:

In view of the well known and necessary practice of connecting roads, we are far from saying that a valid law could not be passed to prevent the cost and loss of time entailed in a needless transshipment or breaking bulk, in case of an unreasonable refusal by a carrier to interchange cars with another for through traffic. We do not pass upon the question. It is enough to observe that such a law perhaps ought to be so limited as to respect the paramount needs of the carrier concerned, and at least would be sustained only with the full and adequate regulations for his protection from the loss or undue detention of cars, and for securing due compensation for their use. The Constitution of Kentucky is simply a universal undiscriminating requirement with no adequate provision such as we have described. We do not mean that the silence of the Constitution might not be remedied by an act of the legislature or a regulation of a duly authorized subordinate body.

But he was adamant in the belief that, as the constitution stood, the order of the state court directing the Louisville and Nashville to transport or deliver cars to the connection with the Southern for eventual switching to the Central Stock Yards Company was an illegal exercise of judicial authority.

If the principle is sound, every railroad in Louisville, by making a physical connection with the Louisville and Nashville, can get the use of its costly terminals and make it do the switching necessary to that end, upon simply paying for the service of carriage. The duty of a carrier to accept goods tendered at its station does not extend to the acceptance of cars offered to it at an arbitrary point near its terminus by a competing road, for the purpose of using its terminal stations.

The Justice was plainly worried about the matter of distance the interchanged cars would have to be moved, and whether the cars interchanged were designed for further transportation.

Justice McKenna, who had "concurred in the result" in the first of the two cases to reach the Supreme Court, registered an emphatic dissent in this case. Not only did he hold that a state had as much right to regulate intrastate commerce as the Federal government had to regulate interstate commerce, but he insisted that the general clause for the protection of private property against public taking, which was a part of the Kentucky constitution, just as it is a part of all other state constitutions and the Federal Constitution, too, provided ample protection against any loss on the part of a railroad whose cars were turned over temporarily to another line. He made some rather biting remarks about the fact that the Interstate Commerce Act, and orders of the Interstate Commerce Com-

[24] Louisville & Nashville R.R. v. Central Stock Yards Co., 212 U.S. 132 (1909).

mission acting under that law, might require railroads to do many things with their "property," and that at no place was the matter of "compensation" mentioned.

THE MICHIGAN RAILROAD COMMISSION CASE

It would be fruitless to speculate on what would have happened in this country about railroad switching if all the restrictive implications of these decisions of the Supreme Court had been permitted to remain in effect. But they soon went into the discard. The state of Michigan enacted a railroad law creating a railroad commission which had the power to order railroads doing business within the state to

. . . receive and transport at reasonable rates all intrastate carload traffic offered for transportation under the usual conditions locally consigned between points in the same city or town, whether received from another railroad or not, and such as is offered at any junction or transfer point or intersection with another railroad within such city for delivery on team tracks or sidings therein, whether the shipment originated within or without the city or town.

The Grand Trunk Railway Company of Canada and a Detroit terminal line challenged an order of the Michigan Railroad Commission, issued under authority of this law, contending that the statute was unconstitutional. The roads asserted that the services which the Commission's order required in Detroit were merely switching services, and that intracity switching was not subject to legislative control.

The complaining roads, in their argument before the Federal District Court for the Eastern District of Michigan, relied heavily on the Supreme Court's decisions in the Louisville stockyards cases, but the court upheld the validity of the Michigan law, pointing out that there was a "valid law" such as Justice Holmes had imagined might be enacted, in which provision had been made for "compensation," and that in the Louisville cases the two stockyards had been considered as if "side by side." [25] The lower court's decision was promptly taken to the Supreme Court on appeal. Justice McKenna wrote the opinion in which the decision of the lower court was unanimously affirmed.[26] It took a little squirming to get around the Louisville decisions without appearing to reverse them, but this was managed cleverly enough by saying that the immediately preceding case (212 U.S. 132) had "turned upon the point that the roads were competitive, and that the point of delivery was an arbitrary one, and that thereby the terminal station of one company was required to be shared with the other company." Moreover, there was a "valid law." No mention

[25] Grand Trunk Ry. of Canada v. Michigan R.R. Commission, 198 Fed. 1009 (1912).

[26] Grand Trunk Ry. of Canada v. Michigan R.R. Commission, 231 U.S. 457 (Dec. 8, 1913).

was made of the implication of Holmes's remarks to the effect that inter-change freight was freight destined for further transportation and could not be "snatched" from a carrier at the "moment of delivery," it being stated that in this case the shipper was contesting for the right of "trans-portation." The opinion said:

Considering the theater of the movements, the facilities for them are no more terminal or switching facilities than the depots, side tracks, and main lines are terminal facilities in a less densely populated district. A precise distinction be-tween facilities can neither be expressed nor enforced. Transportation is the business of railroads, and when that business may be regulated and to what extent regulated may depend upon circumstances. No inflexible principle of decision can be laid down [and the terminals at Detroit are not merely] instru-ments of terminal service and delivery, but of railway transportation in the completest sense.

It is difficult to see how they differed greatly from the terminal facilities at Louisville, but for the purpose of this case they did.

TERMINALS NOT FOR EXCLUSIVE USE

Meanwhile, the Interstate Commerce Commission had been facing some problems of switching and terminal delivery. The Commission had been made to realize that under the terms of the Act of 1887 the railroads were still subject, for the most part, to the principles of common law with respect to "joint" operations, and that no carrier was "obligated" to do more than carry on its own line. But the Hepburn Amendment had wid-ened the statutory meaning of transportation and had greatly enlarged the Commission's authority. Railroads were required to furnish reasonable facilities for the interchange of traffic, and the Commission had the right to establish joint rates and routes. The Commission moved somewhat gin-gerly in the exercise of its new authority, keeping a wary eye on the Supreme Court, but it soon began to take actions which foretold the probable coming of a new dispensation with respect to switching prac-tices in railroad terminals. In 1912, taking under advisement a situation in Baltimore, where the Pennsylvania Railroad maintained an open termi-nal but imposed such excessive charges for the switching of traffic origi-nating in certain geographical regions as to make admission to its terminals for this traffic virtually impossible, the Commission declared that the railroad was guilty of unjust discrimination, and ordered a readjustment of the charges.[27] In a case considered the following year, the Commission ordered the Pennsylvania to open its terminals at Pittsburgh to traffic coming to that city over other lines.[28] The Commission granted that the

[27] Merchants & Mfrs. Assn. of Baltimore v. Pennsylvania R.R., 23 I.C.C. 474 (1912).

[28] Waverly Oil Works Co. v. Pennsylvania R.R., 28 I.C.C. 62 (Dec. 3, 1913).

courts had held it not to be a violation of section 3 of the Act of 1887 for a railroad to enter into arrangements for the exchange of freight with one or more carriers while refusing to enter into similar arrangements with other carriers.[29] It was of the opinion, however, that under the provisions of the amendments of 1906 it had the power to determine whether such exclusive arrangements were unjustly discriminatory. Though it found no unjust discrimination in this particular case, it felt obliged to take up the much broader question of whether it could require a railroad to "open" its terminals to other roads. The Pennsylvania Railroad denied that the Commission had any such authority. "But," said the Commission, in effect, "what are the rights of the public to these terminals? Can the Pennsylvania, having first acquired them, exclude from their use all persons desiring to reach the industries located on them unless they reach them through the Pennsylvania Railroad?" It was the opinion of the Commission that the "public" had the power to require the Pennsylvania to handle cars to and from its terminals, even though the line haul had been performed by other roads, but that proper compensation should be paid, not based entirely upon the immediate costs of handling the cars but "determined in view of the entire situation." Furthermore, the Commission went on to say: "We are of the opinion that the present power of the Commission is adequate to that end."

It was unquestionably with some degree of trepidation that the Commission adopted this broader interpretation of its powers. In the report, there was some animated discussion of the decisions of the Supreme Court in the Louisville cases, and it was doubtless with some feeling of relief that the Commission heard the decision of the Court in the Grand Trunk case which, though handed down five days later, still appeared in time for one member of the Commission to discuss it briefly in his concurring opinion, and for the insertion of a footnote in the Commission's report saying that the Court and the Commission were in "exact accord" in their views on interchange switching.

SWITCH CONNECTIONS BETWEEN MAIN LINES

Even before its decision in the Waverly case (28 I.C.C. 62), the Commission had made a few pointed remarks about the problems arising because of a lack of mutual accommodation among railroads in the matter of switching. In 1912, a shipper at Frederick, Maryland, had asked the Commission to require the construction of a switch connection between the Frederick Railroad, a comparatively short line on which the shipper's own plant and several other industrial plants were located, and the two trunk line roads, the Pennsylvania and the Baltimore and Ohio. Though

[29] Kentucky & Indiana Bridge Co. v. Louisville & Nashville R.R., 37 Fed. 567 (1889).

admitting that the lack of such a connection created a condition at Frederick which was "a relic of the time when railroads were administered by unenlightened selfishness," and saying that "it is difficult to understand how two great systems like the Pennsylvania and the Baltimore and Ohio can knowingly compel shippers in this community to rest under the burden which they now sustain," the Commission could only "recommend" that the trunk lines do what the shipper asked. "We have, however, no authority to require this," the Commission had to admit.[30] The duty of the railroad to establish switch connections went no further than a connection with a private siding or a lateral branch line.[31] The following year, the Commission ordered the Peoria and Pekin Union Railway, which was primarily a belt line, to "accept" cars from an electric line with which it had a switch connection, but which for some reason it had excluded from its switching arrangements although it handled the cars of other connecting lines. The Commission declared that the "terminal properties of carriers . . . are devoted to public use and must be treated exactly as all other parts of their property," and pointed out that "if the contention of the respondent to the effect that its terminal properties are absolutely subject to its determining will were to be applied, every community in the country would to that extent be absolutely at the mercy of those who control the existing terminals." [32]

These were strong words, but they were soon to be followed by words even stronger and action more positive. The Burlington road had a switch connection with the Iowa and Southwestern at Clarendon, Iowa, but refused to enter into any interchange switching arrangement, on the theory that the traffic involved was competitive. The Commission brushed this contention aside, called attention to the language of the Hepburn Amendment that railroads were to "make reasonable rules and regulations with respect to the exchange, interchange and return of cars" used in through routes, and with little ado ordered switching interchange to be estab-

---

[30] Morris Iron Co. v. Baltimore & Ohio R.R., 26 I.C.C. 240 (1912).

[31] The Commission had just been reminded sharply, in another opinion by Justice Holmes, that "its power does not extend to ordering a connection wherever it sees fit, but is limited to a certain and somewhat narrow class of lines." United States v. Baltimore & Ohio Sw. Ry., 226 U.S. 14 (1912). The Commission, apparently believing that its authority to establish through routes included the authority to order physical connections by which such routes could be operated, had ordered switch connections to be made between certain railroads in Ohio. Cincinnati & Columbus Traction Co. v. Baltimore & Ohio Sw. Ry., 22 I.C.C. 486 (1911). This order was invalidated by the Commerce Court, which declared that the power to require switch connections existed only with respect to private sidings and lateral, branch lines. Baltimore & Ohio Sw. Ry. v. United States, 195 Fed. 962 (1911). The Commerce Court's decision was affirmed by the Supreme Court.

[32] St. Louis, S. & P. R.R. v. Peoria & P.U. Ry., 26 I.C.C. 226 (1913).

lished, since it had become "well settled that a carrier could not close its terminal facilities to the public and restrict their use to shippers located on its line or to shipments originating on its own line." [33]

It was obvious that the Commission had adopted the belief that the railway transportation system of the United States should have the elasticity and freedom of operation which the public welfare required, and that the broad interests of the domestic commerce of the country should be placed ahead of the immediately selfish interest of any single transportation agency. Furthermore, the Commission displayed a complete willingness to employ its statutory authority to the utmost to see that the interests of national commerce were adequately served. It was not adverse to seeing that authority extended in order that it could correct those defects in transportation practice and policy which were beyond its reach because of statutory barriers. It was keenly aware, however, that its lack of authority to order the construction of physical connections between the main lines of railroads was a formidable obstacle in the way of obtaining complete freedom of the movement of commerce in numerous railroad terminals. It had received the power in the Panama Canal Act of 1912 to order a railroad to make physical connection with the docks of a steamship line, and it was desirous of obtaining similar authority with respect to connections between railroad lines. In its annual reports for the years 1918 and 1919, looking forward to the time when the railroads would be returned to private operation, the Commission spoke at some length of the need for a "more liberal use of terminal facilities in the interest of the movement of commerce."

TRANSPORTATION ACT OF 1920 AND SWITCHING

In response to the Commission's suggestion, Congress, in framing the Transportation Act of 1920, made some notable changes in those parts of the Interstate Commerce Act having to do with the construction, operation, and use of railroad terminals. In the first section of the law, the Commission was authorized to "require by order any carrier by railroad . . . to provide itself with safe and adequate facilities for performing as a common carrier its car service as that term is used in this Act, and to extend its line or lines." It will be remembered that car service included the "exchange, interchange and return" of cars.

The amendment of section 1 was not the only change in the law affecting the operation of terminals. The paragraph directing railroads to afford "all reasonable, proper, and equal facilities for the interchange of traffic between their respective lines" retained these words, but lost the

[33] Iowa & Sw. Ry. v. Chicago, Burlington & Quincy R.R., 32 I.C.C. 172 (1914).

provision enacted in 1887 that a carrier should not be required to "give the use of its tracks or terminal facilities to another carrier engaged in a like business." Instead, a new subdivision, at that time numbered 4 but since become 5, was added to section 3 of the law, which included a somewhat startling provision to the effect that the Commission might require one railroad to permit another not only to "use" its terminal facilities but also to make use of a part of its main line approaching the terminal. The subdivision read and still reads:

If the Commission finds it to be in the public interest and to be practicable, without substantially impairing the ability of a common carrier by railroad owning or entitled to the enjoyment of terminal facilities to handle its own business, it shall have power by order to require the use of any such terminal facilities, including main line track or tracks for a reasonable distance outside such terminal, of any common carrier by railroad, by another such carrier or other such carriers, on such terms and for such compensation as the carriers affected may agree upon or in the event of failure to agree, as the Commission may fix as just and reasonable for the use so required, to be ascertained on the principle controlling compensation in condemnation proceedings.

It was thought by some persons that under the amended section 3 the Commission would be able to bring about the complete "unification" of railroad terminal facilities, both freight and passenger, in many districts where competitive rivalry prevented such coordination as would manifestly result in improved and more economical transportation service. The clause was somewhat hard to interpret, however, and the Commission has made little use of it. It is difficult, in the face of conflicting testimony, for an administrative body or a court to determine whether a suggested operation is "practicable." Moreover, as one member of the Commission pointed out, if the Commission took action under this provision at the suggestion or on the complaint of a shipper, it might be placed in the position of trying to force a carrier to "buy" something which it did not want, which was a matter entirely different from requiring somebody to "sell" something under a law of eminent domain. It might be observed, too, that railroads did not welcome the new provision of the law with any degree of heartiness. However much one railroad might want to "share the wealth" of another road by participating in the use of its terminal facilities in some one city or industrial district, there was the inevitable danger of retaliation in some other city where the shoe was on the other foot.[34]

[34] The most notable instance of the Commission's action under this part of the law came in 1922, when it issued a report, without an order, in which it said that the Chicago, Milwaukee and St. Paul Railway would be "expected" to permit the use of its terminal facilities and part of its main line at Hastings, Minn., by the

ALABAMA AND VICKSBURG RAILWAY CASE

However lacking in hoped-for results the new subdivision was to be, the old question concerning the power of the Commission to order the establishment of switch connections between main line railroads was at last settled, and settled definitely in the interest of the public and the commerce of the nation. The affirmation of the new powers of the Commission came in a somewhat negative fashion, but its import was unmistakable. A Mississippi court of chancery authorized the condemnation of certain property of the Alabama and Vicksburg Railway to permit the construction of a connection with the Jackson and Eastern Railway, and the legality of the judgment was confirmed by the Mississippi Supreme Court. Taken to the Supreme Court of the United States on a writ of error, on the ground that the action and order represented an unlawful attempt to regulate interstate commerce, the judgment of the Mississippi Supreme Court was reversed, with an opinion written by Justice Brandeis, who took occasion to say some pertinent words concerning the authority which the Interstate Commerce Commission had acquired in the Transportation Act of 1920. While it was true, according to the words of Justice Brandeis, that the Act of 1887 required a railroad to provide "reasonable, proper and equal facilities" for the interchange of traffic, it did not confer upon the Commission authority to permit or require the construction of the physical connection needed to effectuate such interchange, and the provisions of the Panama Canal Act certainly did not extend to connections between railroads. But under the terms of the Act of 1920, the Commission "acquired full power over connections between interstate carriers." [35] There was no longer any doubt of the Commission's authority to require railroads to effect physical connections between their respective lines. Said the Commission itself, on one occasion: "We have power to require connections between carriers engaged in interstate commerce where we find that circumstances and conditions warrant such action." [36]

COMMISSION POLICY ON SWITCHING

As a matter of fact, the Commission has used its power to order the installation of switch connections quite sparingly. The very existence of

---

Chicago, Burlington and Quincy Railroad. Hastings Commercial Club v. Chicago, Milwaukee & St. Paul Ry., 69 I.C.C. 489 (1922). Four years later, the Commission "reconsidered" the complaint of the Commercial Club, decided that it had been wrong in 1922, and dismissed the complaint. 107 I.C.C. 208 (1926).

[35] Alabama & Vicksburg Ry. v. Jackson & Eastern Ry., 271 U.S. 244 (1926), *reversing* 136 Miss. 726.

[36] Wisconsin Power & Light Co. v. Chicago & North Western Ry., 220 I.C.C. 475 (1937).

the power, the pressure of public opinion, the obvious willingness of Congress to give paramount consideration to the needs of commerce, and the cultivation of a more cooperative attitude on the part of the railroad industry have all had the effect of bringing about improvement in the operation of railroad terminals in those areas where a more liberal policy with respect to interchange switching has plainly been needed. In virtually all of our great industrial centers, no obstacles are placed in the way of the free movement of cars between the switching districts of connecting lines, though, as indicated previously, interchange switching is a service for which carriers must make a charge, just as they do for the other services which they perform for the public. The Commission has not abstained from ordering switch connections, however, when it thought that "circumstances and conditions" were such as to justify the exercise of its power to do so.[37] In one instance, at least, it ordered a connection when the carrier on whose line the applicant shippers were located did not want the connection installed,[38] and on more than one occasion it has refused to order a connection because the public interest, in the opinion of the Commission, did not warrant such action.[39]

SWITCHING CHARGES

Switching charges, like all other railroad charges, must be just and reasonable.[40] Like transportation rates, they must bear some relation to

[37] Danville Board of Trade v. Danville & Mt. Morris R.R., 188 I.C.C. 580 (1922).

[38] Keyes Ry. Committee v. Beaver, M. & G. R.R., 214 I.C.C. 526 (1936). Wisconsin Power & Light Co. v. Chicago & North Western R.R., 220 I.C.C. 475 (1937).

[39] See Pittsburgh & West Virginia Ry. v. Lake Erie, A. & W. R.R., 81 I.C.C. 333 (1923); Chamber of Commerce, Breckenridge, Tex., v. Wichita Falls & Ft. W. R.R., 109 I.C.C. 81 (1926). While declining to order the establishment of a switch connection, the Commission left no doubt of its belief in its authority to do so.

[40] On the reasonableness of switching charges, see Merchants & Mfrs. Assn. v. Pennsylvania R.R., 23 I.C.C. 474 (1912); Detroit Switching Charges, 28 I.C.C. 494 (1913); Transportation Bureau of New Seattle Chamber of Commerce v. Great Northern Ry., 30 I.C.C. 683 (1914); Thatcher Mfg. Co. v. Director General, 57 I.C.C. 244 (1920); Oakes Co. v. Minneapolis St. P. & S.S.M. Ry., 77 I.C.C. 93 (1922); Jones & Laughlin Ore Co. v. Director General, 92 I.C.C. 683 (1924); Switching Charges at Kanawha Central Ry. Mines, 118 I.C.C. 468 (1926); Automatic Gravel Prod. Co. v. Burlington, M. & N. W. Ry., 151 I.C.C. 481 (1929); Switching Rates in Chicago Switching District, 177 I.C.C. 669 (1931); Reciprocal Switching Charges at Richmond, Va., 222 I.C.C. 783 (1937); Switching Charges at Jamestown, N.Y., 238 I.C.C. 383 (1940); Netherland-American Steam Nav. Co. v. Erie R.R., 241 I.C.C. 285 (1940); Denholm Packing Co. v. Baltimore & Ohio R.R., 241 I.C.C. 611 (1940); Switching at Richmond, Va., 245 I.C.C. 293 (1941).

Unjust discrimination is discussed in Switching Rates in Chicago Switching the cost of service, though again we find that it is not possible to establish an exact relationship. On the whole, however, it is easier to find the approximate cost of a switching service than the cost of transporting some single commodity, because the charge is made for the car which is moved, as a rule, and is not based upon the weight or the character of the article contained in the car. Most switching tariffs provide for a single flat charge per car for any interchange movement within the switching district, even though some cars must be moved a considerably greater distance than others. Practice is not uniform, by any means, and we find that in many industrial areas different scales of switching charges prevail, the amount increasing with the distance and complexity of the movement, and in some switching tariffs charges are based upon the class and weight of the traffic. The frequent neglect of distance as a controlling factor in the determination of switching rates arises from the fact that the actual movement of the car from one place to another accounts for only a small part of the cost of the entire switching service. Most of the cost is incurred, because of the time and effort spent in the operations at the beginning and the end of the movement—the attaching of the engine, the operation of switches, the shuffling of other cars, perhaps, and the shuffling and spotting at the point where the car is delivered. The Commission once said, "The bulk of the expense of a switch movement consists of the handling of the car at the ends of the movement. Comparatively little is added in moving the car a few miles even, when once upon the main track." [41] One is reminded of line-haul transportation rates, which are much higher per mile for short hauls than for long hauls, because of the preponderance of terminal costs in short hauls.

ABSORPTION OF SWITCHING CHARGES

Although railroads must publish tariffs showing the switching rates for the interchange movements of cars, and terminal lines, which do nothing but switch between other lines, must do the same, it does not follow that the shipper or receiver of freight always pays the switching charge. In many terminals, one will find that switching charges are "absorbed" by the road that gets the line haul and that the shipper pays only the transportation rate. For the most part, a railroad is willing to absorb switching charges only on what is called competitive traffic. When two railroads happen to serve the point of origin and also the point of destination of a carload of freight, it is obvious that either of them can perform the line haul. If the siding at the point of destination, to which the car is

---

District, 177 I.C.C. 669 (1931); Switching at Richmond, Va., 245 I.C.C. 293 (1941).

[41] Detroit Switching Charges, 28 I.C.C. 494 (1913).

eventually to be switched, is a part of the terminal delivery facilities of the road which does not perform the line haul, the road having the line haul will absorb the switching charges of the delivering road at the point of destination. The same type of absorption is frequently granted at points of origin. While the general practice is for absorption of such charges to be assumed only on competitive traffic, occasionally it will be found that the absorption of switching charges by railroads entering into reciprocal switching arrangements also applies to noncompetitive traffic. Whenever a railroad agrees to absorb switching charges, that fact must be stated, and the amount of absorption indicated, in properly filed and published tariffs, just as provisions for "allowances" which a road may make to its customers must be.

Reciprocal switching arrangements in which all switching charges are absorbed are likely to be made only between carriers between which the number of cars turned over by one road to another is approximately equal to the number received, though the exchanges do not all have to take place at the same terminal. Since at points where all switching charges are absorbed by the line-haul carrier, and what one railroad pays another is met by a return payment approximately equal in amount, the railroads have often taken the position that the rate charged for the switch movement is of no great consequence, and it may be just a nominal sum. The Commission had disapproved many times of nominal charges of this kind, however, and has said that even if the shipper or receiver does not pay the switching charge it should nevertheless be a reasonable charge, related as nearly as may be under the circumstances to the cost of the switching operation.[42] "In a proceeding to determine the propriety of switching charges," the Commission has said, "it is immaterial whether such charges are absorbed by the carrier or paid for by the shipper." While recognizing the fact that the "charges for reciprocal switching, as the term would imply, are generally established without regard to the cost of the particular service, on the theory that the services are of mutual advantage to all the carriers concerned," the Commission adhered to its position that switching charges, whether absorbed or not, should be based upon cost, and called attention to the fact that "the so-called reciprocity theory of establishing switching charges has been condemned by us in several cases." [43]

[42] Detroit Switching Charges, 28 I.C.C. 494 (1913); Switching Charges at Galesburg, Ill., 31 I.C.C. 294 (1914); Nashville v. Louisville & Nashville R. R., 33 I.C.C. 76 (1915); Nashville Switching, 40 I.C.C. 474 (1916); Reciprocal Switching at Kansas City, 68 I.C.C. 591 (1922).

[43] Reciprocal Switching Charges at Evansville, Ind., 155 I.C.C. 450 (1929); Switching and Absorption at Minneapolis, 61 I.C.C. 646 (1921); Interchange Switching at Atlanta, 63 I.C.C. 258 (1921). "Carriers should endeavor to conduct their switching operations for other carriers without loss, and charges for

Reciprocal switching agreements, under which all switching charges are absorbed by the line-haul carriers, are highly advantageous to shippers and receivers of freight who are fortunate enough to be in a switching district where they are in effect. They mean not only that the terminals of the reciprocating roads are unified physically but that regardless of which railroad obtains the line haul of a particular shipment the transportation rate covers the total charge to or from all sidings. There are not many places, however, where complete reciprocity of switching service and absorption of all switching charges are in effect.[44]

There is no common pattern which carriers follow with respect to switching absorption. The Commission cannot require the absorption of switching charges, but it may order the removal of any unjustly discriminatory charges or practices which a railroad may adopt with respect to absorption. In deciding whether unjust discrimination is present, the Commission takes into consideration all the conditions and circumstances affecting a particular situation. It has held in a number of cases that carriers may lawfully absorb switching charges on competitive traffic while refusing to absorb such charges on traffic that is not competitive.[45] It has repeatedly stated that in the absence of unjust discrimination or undue prejudice it is without power to compel a carrier to absorb charges for switching which takes place beyond its own rails.[46] On a few occasions, however, the Commission has required carriers to absorb switching charges on noncompetitive as well as competitive traffic, when the switching services were similar.[47]

It is only natural that a carrier should desire to enhance its own business,

---

the services based on cost are preferable to nominal charges based on so-called reciprocity in service." Des Moines Union Ry. Switching, 231 I.C.C. 631 (1939).

[44] The Commission refers, in Waverly Oil Works Co. v. Pennsylvania R.R., 28 I.C.C. 621 (1913), to the fact that such conditions once prevailed at Cleveland, Ohio. Although railroads in their reciprocal switching arrangements may open their public delivery tracks to one another on a basis of reciprocity, they cannot be compelled to do so. Such tracks, as well as freight houses, may be reserved solely to cars upon which the owning railroad has received the line haul. Railroad and Warehouse Commission of Minnesota v. Chicago Great Western Ry., 262 I.C.C. 437 (1945).

[45] Crown Willamette Paper Co. v. Atchison, Topeka & Santa Fe Ry., 49 I.C.C. 613 (1918).

[46] Switching Charges at Texas Points, 197 I.C.C. 513 (1913); Switching at Butte, Mont., 204 I.C.C. 6 (1934); Automatic Gravel Products Co. v. Burlington M. & N.W. Ry., 151 I.C.C. 481 (1929).

[47] Richmond Chamber of Commerce v. Seaboard Air Line Ry., 44 I.C.C. (1917). Order held valid in Seaboard Air Line Ry. v. United States, 254 U.S. 57 (1920), *affirming* 249 Fed. 268 (1918). See also Absorption Charges at Mobile, Ala., 196 I.C.C. 465 (1933); Norfolk-Portsmouth Freight Traffic Committee v. Aberdeen & Rockfish R.R., 159 I.C.C. 177 (1929).

and if it can improve its competitive position by the imposition of switching charges or by the nonabsorption of switching charges, it is likely to do so. The only requirements of the law are that neither its switching services nor its switching charges be unreasonable or unduly discriminatory and that its practices with respect to absorption be free of undue prejudice or unjust discrimination. Any carrier has the right to charge a reasonable amount for whatever switching it performs for traffic coming from or going to a connecting line, but it may not, in an effort to increase its own share of competitive traffic, impose switching charges which are so excessive as to be unreasonable.[48] Occasionally a carrier will differentiate in its switching charges according to who is responsible for their payment, making a lower charge if the shipper pays than if the line-haul carrier pays and absorbs the charge. The shipper (or receiver) is encouraged to give the line haul to the switching carrier in order to avoid the extra switching charge, and the competing carrier is discouraged in the solicitation of competitive traffic by the high switching charge it must absorb.[49]

CALCULATION OF REASONABLE SWITCHING CHARGES

The Commission has had many cases in which the reasonableness or the allegedly discriminatory character of switching charges has been brought into question. Although it has adopted no uniform rule as to how switching rates should be published, it has displayed a distinct preference for a flat rate per car.[50] The reason for this is that the Commission has held the belief that switching charges, like transportation charges, should be based as nearly as possible upon the cost of service, and the calculation of the cost of a switch movement with the car alone considered as the unit upon which the charge is to be made can be done with a much greater assurance of approximate accuracy than the calculation of the cost of a line haul on particular articles of merchandise. In fact, the Commission has devised a formula for the calculation of the "average" cost of switching movements in various terminals, and in numerous cases has applied the formula for the purpose of determining what would be a "reasonable" switching charge.[51] A thorough investigation of switching

---

[48] Roessler & Hasslacher Chemical Co. v. Baltimore & Ohio R.R., 178 I.C.C. 518 (1931); Switching at Level Siding, S.D., 270 I.C.C. 687 (1948).

[49] Switching at High Point, N.C., 203 I.C.C. 629 (1934).

[50] Mitchell Chamber of Commerce v. Chicago, Milwaukee & St. Paul Ry., 129 I.C.C. 451 (1927); Switching at St. Louis and East St. Louis, 120 I.C.C. 216 (1926).

[51] Des Moines Union Ry. Switching, 231 I.C.C. 631 (1939); Switching Charge at Texas Points, 197 I.C.C. 513 (1933); Switching at Jamestown, N.Y., 238 I.C.C. 383 (1940); Switching at Kansas City, 96 I.C.C. 538 (1925), 178 I.C.C. 97 (1931).

operation and practice in a terminal will reveal the total expenses of operating and maintaining switching facilities for a certain period of time. To this amount must be added whatever is paid in taxes and a "reasonable return" on the value of the property involved in the switching operations. The total cost is then divided by the number of cars switched during the period under study. It will be readily seen that such a cost calculation is widely different from and much more simple than the calculation of the cost of hauling a particular kind of traffic for the purpose of establishing a reasonable rate for its transportation. Moreover, in determining whether unjust discrimination exists in the switching services and charges of a terminal, the Commission is confronted with none of the numerous "exceptional" circumstances which it must take into consideration when dealing with the problem of discrimination in transportation rates.

LIGHTERAGE

The switching we have been discussing thus far has been switching done entirely by rail. In a few places in the United States, in addition to the rail switching of empty and loaded cars, we have what amounts to the switching of railroad freight by water, either in the cars themselves or in vessels known by the general name of lighters.[52] By far the most important among these places is the Port of New York, though lighterage is carried on to some extent in a few other ports. The City and Port of New York represent in an outstanding manner what has so often occurred in this country because of the unfortunate habit our people have had of underestimating the possibilities of future growth. Of course, it is not possible for anybody to foretell the improvements which invention, discovery, and technological progress will bring about, but even after we have become familiar with new devices of a revolutionary character, we have failed lamentably to make proper provision for their best use, simply because we could not believe that what was once regarded as a miracle of human ingenuity, within the reach of only a chosen few, could ever become an everyday convenience for all. One has only to look at the problems of parking and highway congestion with which we are now afflicted to understand how true this statement is.

[52] For an interesting description and history of the methods of freight handling in the Port of New York, see Lighterage and Storage Regulations at New York, 35 I.C.C. 47 (1915); the New York Harbor Case, 47 I.C.C. 643 (1917) (the latter report contains a map of the water front); New York Harbor Storage, 47 I.C.C. 141 (1917); Lighterage Cases, 203 I.C.C. 481 (1934); Constructive and Off-track Railroad Freight Stations on Manhattan Island, 156 I.C.C. 205 (1929). The "Joint Report of the New York, New Jersey Port and Harbor Development Committee" (1920) is one of the finest analyses of port and terminal problems ever prepared.

TOPOGRAPHY OF NEW YORK CITY

When New York City was first settled, Manhattan Island was an ideal spot for its location. The Battery at its lower tip, Governor's Island as a defense outpost in case of an attack by water, a short palisade or wall extending entirely across the narrow island for defense against marauding Indians—how could a safer place be found? Where could there be a location more favorable to the development of commerce? Deep water on both sides of the narrow point of land and the possibility of constructing a series of cross canals could turn the little trading post into a Venice of the Western world, an emporium of domestic and foreign commerce of unprecedented magnificence. And what city on the Atlantic seaboard had a greater hinterland than the one which the lordly Hudson, navigable as far as Albany, and the sounds and kills about Staten Island and Long Island gave to this future center of world trade? When the Erie Canal was opened, in 1825, and all the basin of the Great Lakes became a part of this hinterland, Manhattan soon fulfilled all the dreams of its most penetrating prophets—and more so. In fact, entirely too much more so, for Manhattan Island, even before the railroad became an important factor in our commerce, was getting to be a bit congested in a few spots. But nobody would believe that the island would not be able to care for the needs of all future commerce. Therefore it became a veritable magnet for railroads, which focused upon it from east, north, west, and south. Only a railroad from the north and one from "down east" could reach the island by rail. But that made no difference. If the railroads from the south and west could not reach this new center of the universe by rail, they would get as near as they could come, and transfer traffic between railhead and the magic island by water. The west side of the Hudson River opposite Manhattan Island became, for the most part, merely a railroad doorstep to the promised land across the river, and every favorable location on the island's own water front was appropriated, if possible, for use as terminals for water-borne rail traffic.

Nothing was done, nothing seemingly could be done, to check the concentration on the little island. To this day, despite frantic efforts to obtain relief, the congestion, the crowding, and the confusion have grown worse instead of better. Builders rear their tall structures to the heavens and burrow deep into the bowels of the earth to make room for the teeming thousands who earn their living in Manhattan. Subways, tunnels, and bridges appear in increasing number to accommodate the struggling crowds who enter the metropolitan center in the morning and leave at night, but the facilities for the transportation of persons and property have never caught up with the needs, and presumably never will, as long as the belief remains that Manhattan is the most desirable place in the port area for the conduct of the manifold activities of industry and commerce which originate and develop in a great urban community.

LIGHTERAGE AND CAR FLOATAGE IN NEW YORK HARBOR

So it is that much of the freight destined for Manhattan Island, and now for Brooklyn and the Bronx, whether domestic shipments or shipments intended for export in the vessels that crowd the piers, is ferried across the Hudson. Since the development of transportation by truck, the amount of traffic reaching the piers east of the Hudson is not so large relatively as it once was, but from the top of any high building which commands a view of the waters of the port, one can see dozens upon dozens of barges, lighters, and car floats shuttling hither and yon to and from all parts of the great water front. Lighterage and floatage constitute a large part of the port's activity.

Freight that is lightered is unloaded from the cars for distribution about the port. There are several kinds of lighters. Some of them are self-propelled. Most of them, however, have no propulsion machinery of their own but are pushed about by straining tugboats. Some of the lighters, used in the transportation of freight not likely to be injured by rain, snow, or fog, are merely large open scows or barges; others, employed primarily in the movement of dry cargo, are covered, and provide shelter from the weather. Car floats are equipped with tracks, a double or triple set, upon which the cars are pushed and from which they are withdrawn over float bridges. There are a few team track yards on Manhattan to which cars are brought on car floats, but most of the cars so moved are taken to railroad pier stations for unloading or loading or to private and public piers along the water front, and remain on the float until taken back to the railhead. Lightered freight goes to piers—railroad, public, and nonrailroad private—and to ships where it is transferred directly from lighter to vessel hold by ship's tackle. It is not an uncommon sight to see grain in bulk being transferred from barge to ship's hold by means of a floating elevator, equipped with two "legs," one for the barge and the other for the ship. Very frequently one sees a large freighter receiving swinging net loads of cargo from a pier on one side and from a half-dozen lighters on the other.

The lighterage service given to shippers and receivers of freight at the Port of New York is just the same as the service which shippers at inland points receive over private and public sidings. Lighterage is nothing more than a switching operation carried on by water transportation. The chief difference between lighterage and switching is that the former requires the loading and unloading of cars. There is no practical difference between switching and car floatage.

The railroads entering the Port of New York establish "lighterage limits," comparable to the "switching limits" of a dry-land terminal. Within these limits, the railroad will deliver freight either by lighter or by car float, and the compensation for the service is supposedly included in the transportation rate just as in the case of switching involving no interchange. If a shipper or consignee asks for lighterage beyond these designated limits, the carrier demands extra compensation as provided for in duly published tariffs. It has long been the custom of the railroads performing this lighterage service in New York to refer to it as "free lighterage." It was no more "free" than the switching service given to a private siding, but the impression created by the use of the word causes some confusion, and occasionally is a cause of some trouble to the carriers. Much of the carload freight entering the harbor, for which lighterage is to be provided, is destined to some designated railroad pier and will be delivered to the pier in accordance with billing. If the freight is to be lightered, and no pier delivery is designated, the shipment will be held in a freight yard, the consignee notified, and his delivery instructions obtained. It is the responsibility of the consignee to arrange for space at the private pier where delivery is to be made.

Because of the limitations of space on Manhattan Island, it was for many years the custom of railroads which lightered carload freight across the Hudson to assume the obligation of loading and unloading the cars. Since this was a service which shippers in New Jersey, with plants located on railroad sidings, did not receive, they frequently complained bitterly to the Interstate Commerce Commission that they were the objects of undue and illegal discrimination, since on all the freight coming for any substantial distance into the port district the rates were the same whether the final destination was in New Jersey or in some one of the boroughs of New York City. Here was a situation in which relative freight rates were obviously out of line with relative costs. The Commission refused to "split the port," by ordering the railroads to charge lower rates to Jersey destinations within the port district, but the railroads finally adopted the practice, in 1934, of making a charge for the loading and unloading of lightered carload freight and freight which was given floatage or trucking service in lieu of lighterage. Like all other charges of railroads, this charge for loading and unloading has been materially advanced since it was first established. At the present time it amounts to 5 cents a hundred pounds.

AN INTEGRATED RAILROAD SYSTEM

This account of the development of switching practices on American railroads has been given in some detail because it is the story of a successful attempt to change the operating methods of these railroads for the purpose of promoting the healthy prosperity of our great domestic commerce. Despite the reluctance of carriers, adverse court decisions, and other obstacles, a barrier to economic and commercial progress was gradually and steadily worn away. Our railroads, though their ownership and control remained widely diffused, were welded, from a physical standpoint at least, into a great unified and integrated system, which permits the fullest measure of fluidity and flexibility in the movement of the products of our many industries. The removal of the dams to the free flow of our domestic trade, represented by antiquated attitudes and customs with respect to routing and switching, was an achievement, the credit for which belongs to the Interstate Commerce Commission more than to any other single agency or institution. In doing what it did, that body represented government at its best, as a "servant of the people."

CHAPTER XVIII

Terminal Services: Pickup and Delivery, Storage, Weighing, Elevation

In the two preceding chapters we have been discussing the terminal delivery and collection of carload traffic under conditions in which the cars themselves, either loaded or empty, were delivered to the shipper or receiver on railroad tracks forming private, industrial, or public sidings or the freight was lightered or floated to private or public piers, as in New York and a few other ports. It was the duty of the shipper or the consignee to load or unload the carload shipments. If the shipper was fortunate enough to have his plant located on a siding, the matter of transferring freight between plant and car might be relatively simple and inexpensive; if he had to make use of a public siding, he was necessarily subjected to some expense and trouble in making the transfer. But the railroad's obligation did not extend beyond the movement of the car, except in a few terminals where the lack of space made it advisable for the railroad to load and also to unload carload freight. Even when the railroad unloaded shipments from a car, the freight was piled on a platform, and the consignee was required to call for it and haul it away.

LESS CARLOAD FREIGHT

For many years, the same rules applied to the transportation of less carload freight. The railroad transported such freight only by rail. It did the work of loading and unloading at the freight houses where freight was received for rail shipment or unloaded from cars for delivery to the consignee. Haulage between a railroad's terminal facilities and the industrial plants, warehouses, and other establishments which the railroad served was the task not of the railroad but of the shipper or consignee.

COLLECTION AND DELIVERY IN EUROPE

In Great Britain and nearly all other European countries, railroad practice was different. The railroad gave a complete service, calling for shipments at the shipper's place of business and delivering them to the consignee at destination. Freight was handled just as the express traffic has long been handled in America or as the United States mail is handled.

371

Of course, the pickup and delivery service could not be universal, that is, it could not be provided at every station. We still have many places in the United States where express packages must be called for and delivered at a railroad station. Long after the free delivery of mail became common in our larger cities, it was necessary for the inhabitants of small towns and rural communities to call at the post office for their mail; the practice is still followed in many places, although the extension of rural free delivery throughout the length and breadth of the country has made periodical trips to the post office unnecessary for many farmers and villagers.

FORMER PRACTICE IN BALTIMORE AND WASHINGTON

It was often suggested that railroads in America should follow the European example and render a complete transportation service to their patrons, but railroad management did not take kindly to the suggestion. It was the business of a railroad to give railroad service and railroad service only. Management wanted no part in a draying or trucking business that would effect local collection and delivery of freight, either carload or less carload. Transportation to and from the railroad's station and terminal facilities was entirely the business of the shipper and consignee. Of course, there had to be an exception which served to prove the rule. In Baltimore and in Washington, the railroads at an early date began a collection and delivery service, applicable to certain classes of freight, which continued for many years but was finally abandoned in 1913. Both cities expanded greatly in area, and collection and delivery had either to be abandoned or extended, if undue discrimination was to be avoided. The railroads preferred abandonment to extension, and were upheld in their decision by the Interstate Commerce Commission.[1] Of course, railroads used drays and trucks in many cities for the interchange of through less carload freight, but this was something entirely different from a collection and delivery service for a customer. It was simply a substitute for a rail haul in places where interchange by means of switching would have been slower and more expensive.

MODERN PICKUP AND DELIVERY

Eventually the time came when railroad management had to change its long-standing policy, though it was done with evident reluctance, and in a few instances only after one or more false starts. Today, nearly all of

---

[1] For a description of the Washington and Baltimore collection and delivery service and the story of its abandonment, see Casassa v. Pennsylvania R.R., 24 I.C.C. 629 (1912); Anacostia Citizens' Assn. v. Baltimore & Ohio R.R., 25 I.C.C. 411 (1912); Washington, D.C. Store Door Delivery, 27 I.C.C. 347 (1913); Merchants and Manufacturers' Assn. v. Baltimore & Ohio R.R., 30 I.C.C. 388 (1914).

our railroads offer a pickup and delivery service of less carload freight in our larger cities and towns. The service is optional, and the shipper or consignee may still call for and deliver freight at the freight house. When the shipper or receiver chooses to perform his own collection and delivery service in a terminal where the freight tariff provides that the railroad shall perform the service and the rate of transportation is fixed accordingly, the shipper receives an "allowance," similar to the allowance which some shippers receive in connection with switching operations they perform for themselves.

There were many reasons why railroad management finally broke its crust of tradition and reversed its policy with respect to the collection and delivery of freight. The two most important reasons were the emergence of competitive transportation facilities and the congestion which developed in several terminal areas where there was not sufficient space for the construction and operation of freight houses and other railroad facilities needed for efficient and economical handling of less carload traffic.

RAILROAD MONOPOLY OF COMMERCIAL TRANSPORTATION

For more than half a century, the railroads of the United States had a virtual monopoly of all commercial transportation which was not local in character, except in a few regions where water transportation facilities were available. Local collection and delivery of less carload freight, as well as of goods distributed by stores and warehouses, were made by horse-drawn drays and vans; wagons and other vehicles, drawn by horses, oxen, or mules, conveyed to the nearest railroad sidings and freight houses the products of farms and forests which were to be transported to distant markets. It is difficult for members of the present generation to picture to themselves the kinds of transportation employed in the world's domestic commerce at the turn of the twentieth century. Of course, it is the customary practice of railroad authorities to deny with some heat that the railroads ever had a "monopoly," but if somebody wanted to go from New York to Chicago or St. Louis in 1900, he did not walk, he did not go horseback, he did not make the journey in a covered wagon, there was no stagecoach or bus or reliable private automobile, and man had not yet learned to fly. Everybody was dependent upon the steam railroad for long-distance travel and trade by land. One of the reasons for the reluctance of the managers of railroads to give serious consideration to suggestions that they change their traditional methods of performing their functions was that they had little or no competition. Moreover, they refused to believe that they ever would have any. Needless to say, they were badly mistaken. Since the beginning of the twentieth century the internal combustion engine has wrought a revolution in the transportation industry as profound and significant as the revolution brought about by the introduction of the steamboat and the steam locomotive in the early years of the nineteenth century. Even the railroad is no longer a "steam" railroad; several Class I roads have banished the steam locomotive entirely, many others are more than half dieselized, and one reads almost daily of new orders for diesel-electric locomotives designed to take the place of the iron horses of bygone years. We still use the expression "steam railroad," but it is rapidly becoming a misnomer, and we are in need of another descriptive term.

THE RISE OF THE HIGHWAY MOTOR VECHICLE

When the motor truck first began to be used extensively in local transportation, replacing the horse-drawn drays, the railroad industry was urged to adopt this new contrivance and coordinate it with the freight train. It was pointed out that the motor truck was a device ideally suited for the transportation of less carload freight, the traffic which the railroad had never been able to handle with the efficiency and economy with which it transported carload shipments. The truck could be substituted for the freight train in the movement of much rail traffic, and if the railroads would only change their long-established methods of operation, it could be employed for the collection and delivery of less carload freight in urban centers. But in face of the fact that the railroad passenger business was steadily diminishing because of the mass production of cheap private automobiles, railroad management refused to believe that the motor truck would ever become a serious rival. It could and would replace the horse of flesh and blood, but never the horse of iron and steam.[2] It could be used for local hauls, but in all probability not for hauls over a distance of more than 50 miles. The railroad had nothing to fear.

It is unnecessary to dwell on what has occurred or to discuss at length the present relative positions of rail and truck transportation. The truck operator found a situation ready-made for his entrance into business. It had long been the custom of railroads to base rates to a considerable extent upon the value of the service and the value of the commodity. High-grade merchandise and small shipments of all kinds were carried at rates admittedly above the cost of service by rail, and, it was soon discovered, also considerably above the cost of transportation by motor truck. Shippers were glad to welcome the advent of the truck. Competition would mean not only an improved service but, in many instances, service at a much lower cost. The difference in cost to a shipper was not only a matter of difference in the

---

[2] The number of horses and mules on the farms of the United States declined from 26,000,000 in 1915 to 11,500,000 in 1945. Bureau of the Census, "Historical Statistics of the United States, 1789–1945" (1949), p. 101. By 1951, the number had shrunk to 7,500,000. Between 1915 and 1945, the number of tractors on farms had grown from 25 to 2,425,000.

rates of the rival carriers. Goods shipped by truck did not, as a rule, require such expensive packing as rail shipments had to have. Most important of all, shipments by truck often did not require the multiple handling and the supplementary hauling which went with rail transportation. The truck came to the shipper's door, took on a load of goods, and delivered the load at the door of the consignee. A railroad shipment of less carload freight had to be trucked to the local freight station at the point of origin and trucked from the destination station to the plant of the consignee. Finally, there was the matter of speed. Railroad cars, bound to the tracks on which they ran, had to be switched and classified at the originating terminal, and classified and switched at the terminal of destination. Such operations were not necessary for a truck moving on streets and intercity highways. It was soon found that shipments which it took a railroad two days or more to move could be transported by truck in a matter of hours. That a truck, in the transportation of certain kinds of traffic, could perform the task more speedily, more efficiently, and more cheaply than a railroad became a matter of fact which even the densest railroad management could no longer dispute. As better trucks were manufactured and better roads were constructed, the scope and diversity of truck operation were constantly enlarged. No commodity was beyond a truck's ability to handle, no distance was beyond its power to traverse. Literally hundreds of commodities, which it had been thought a motor truck could not transport in competition with a railroad, gradually abandoned the old carrier for the new. It was obvious that railroad management had to revise its ideas about the function of railroad enterprise or be condemned to "maintain unequal war"—and fight a losing battle. The belated establishment of pickup and delivery service was a part of the answer which the railroad made to the challenge of the motor truck. Other parts of the answer were the substitution of motor trucks for local freight trains, the abandonment of many miles of unprofitable branch lines, and a general stepping up of railroad service.

TERMINAL CONGESTION

The congestion of terminals in areas where space was limited began to be burdensome to railroads and shippers even before the beginning of the First World War. With the vast increase of traffic occasioned by the war, the congestion in many places became almost intolerable. We have already told how the congestion in yards finally led to the operation of the railroads by the government. The congestion around freight houses in large cities, the places where shippers and consignees came to deliver and receive less carload shipments, was as bad as or worse than the congestion in the railroad freight yards. Conditions were at their worst, perhaps, in New York City, where the pier stations, large and numerous though they were, proved to be quite incapable of caring adequately for the large volume of traffic which sought to pass through them. It frequently occurred that a trucker bent on delivering a less carload shipment to a pier station on the Hudson River front of Manhattan Island would be compelled to wait in line for as much as eight hours before he could unload the freight from his vehicle. A few shippers turned from motor trucks to old-fashioned horse-drawn drays for transportation to and from the pier stations, since the investment in such conveyances was much smaller and the loss due to idleness could be substantially reduced. Shippers who had shipments for the pier stations of several railroads abandoned attempts to deliver to individual carriers and trucked the shipments to Brooklyn, to be cared for at the "contract terminals," which acted as agents for all railroads entering New York, for the receipt and delivery of freight shipments. Various efforts were made in 1916 to induce the New York railroads to establish a system of "store-door delivery" of carload freight. The adoption of such a system was recommended by James Harlan, a member of the Interstate Commerce Commission, who investigated pier congestion in the city, but nothing came of these efforts.

THE NEW YORK AND NEW JERSEY COMMISSION

After the railroads were returned to private operation in 1920, pier congestion in New York became even worse. Because of the deplorable conditions of the port, which were making the movement of traffic in both foreign and domestic commerce slower and more expensive, the states of New York and New Jersey had appointed a joint committee in 1917 to make a thorough study of the entire port district and recommend measures for improvement. The report of this committee, which has already been mentioned, was published in 1920. It stated flatly that the "problem" of the Port of New York was essentially a "railroad problem." It recommended the reorganization and reconstruction of the facilities of the port in such a manner that freight destined for or leaving Manhattan Island could be conveyed to and from freight yards in New Jersey by an underground, automatic electric railway, connected with a series of freight stations distributed at regular intervals in the Borough of Manhattan. This project would, when completed, free the water front on both the New York and the New Jersey sides of the Hudson River for the development of piers and other facilities for handling the port's great foreign trade. That part of the great shore line which for so many years had been occupied by pier stations and float bridges could at last be used primarily to fulfill the purpose for which the shore line of any great seaport is manifestly intended.

CONSTRUCTIVE STATIONS

As might have been expected, the railroads would have no part in such a project. It was fantastic, it was costly, it was impracticable. For a time, however, they made one concession, in the establishment of so-called "constructive stations." These were an outgrowth of the inland stations which some of the railroads had found it necessary to build for the partial relief of their overburdened pier stations. The inland stations had been copied from the off-track stations which had existed in St. Louis for a number of years, to make room for the receipt and delivery of freight beyond the capacity of the on-track freight houses.[3] Freight handled at such off-track stations was trucked to and from freight yards and sidings where it was loaded into or unloaded from cars. The operation was in all respects the same as the operation of a freight house located on a track, except that the terminal movement of freight to and from the station was accomplished in drays and trucks, not in freight cars. In New York, the freight destined for an inland station was loaded into a truck at the freight yard in New Jersey and taken across the river by ferry. The cars containing this freight did not have to be switched to the float bridges as did the freight destined to the railroad pier stations on the east side of the river. The trucks which carried the freight were not owned by the railroads, the work being let out by contract to private trucking concerns.

In 1921, the Erie Railroad, one of the trunk lines which had established inland stations on Manhattan Island, had a happy thought. Why should the freight trucked across the river be unloaded at the inland station and reloaded on a truck employed by the consignee? Why not let the truck in which the freight was loaded in the Jersey freight yard carry it directly to the consignee? The railroad, of course, could not be supposed to bear the expense of trucking all the way to the consignee's place of business or be liable all the way for loss and damage. But it would establish a "constructive station" at some street corner in New York City. The consignee could make his own arrangements with the trucking company for the transportation of freight from the constructive station.[4] From the freight yard to the designated corner, the expense and liability were the railroad's; beyond that place, the expense and the matter of risk of loss and damage were the affair of the consignee and the trucking company. This innovation represented a marked improvement in the methods of handling railroad freight shipments in New York. It meant speedier deliveries, less direct expense, and the avoidance of lost time by trucks waiting to pick up and deliver shipments at pier stations. During the next six years, virtually all the other railroads entering the Port of New York, ex-

[3] For a description of the operation of the St. Louis off-track stations, see St. Louis Terminal Case, 34 I.C.C. 453 (1915); Transfer of Freight between St. Louis and East St. Louis by Dray and Truck by and on Behalf of Railroads, 155 I.C.C. 129 (1929), 177 I.C.C. 316 (1931); Off-track Stations in St. Louis, 186 I.C.C. 578 (1932). Constructive stations were also established in St. Louis.

[4] Tariffs Embracing Motor Truck or Wagon Transfer Service, 91 I.C.C. 539 (1924).

cept the New York Central, followed the Erie example, and constructive station delivery became general. Shippers and receivers of freight welcomed the change, and the trucking companies found the new business profitable.

Like many other good things, however, the constructive station did not last. Rival railroads began to make use of it to attract traffic from competitors. Constructive stations were established at numerous street corners, with a consequent lightening of trucking expense to shippers and receivers of freight. One railroad finally announced the adoption of a plan under which it offered consignees trucking in lieu of lighterage. Every lighterage point in Manhattan was designated as a constructive station. Though a consignee's shipment might be trucked for many miles from the railroad terminal, his only charges were those which were applicable from the nearest point on the Hudson or East River. To make things even better for the shipper, he was permitted to designate his own trucker, and soon the competition was so keen among truck operators, according to the Interstate Commerce Commission, that various shippers were not only escaping all trucking charges but were on the verge of being paid by trucking companies for the privilege of serving them.[5]

What had started out as a wholesome practice which might do much to ameliorate an almost intolerable terminal congestion degenerated into a fierce competitive struggle. The shipper was receiving free collection and delivery service, and the railroads were not only losing money but were becoming so angry because of the steps each line was taking to "steal" traffic from the others that they came to resemble, more than anything else, a group of snarling dogs just before the outbreak of an old-fashioned battle royal. The shippers looked upon the railroad squabble with satisfaction. Of course the multiplicity of trucks infesting the city streets, crisscrossing one another hundreds of times daily, did anything but promote the relief of vehicular traffic congestion in the city's crowded thoroughfares.

END OF CONSTRUCTIVE STATIONS

The upshot of the rumpus was that the railroads, utterly unable to reach a *modus vivendi* under which the collection and delivery service could be carried on in an orderly and peaceful fashion, decided to abandon the constructive station idea entirely and return to the *status quo*. The shippers, who would have been quite willing to forego the financial advantages which the competitive warfare had fortuitously conferred upon them if only they could retain the improved service which the operation of the constructive station had brought into being, were highly indignant at the action which the railroads took, and appealed to the Interstate Commerce Commission

[5] See Constructive and Off-track Railroad Freight Stations on Manhattan Island, 156 I.C.C. 205, 227 (1929).

for an order requiring the railroads to restore the discarded practice. Whatever sympathy the Commission may have felt for the disgruntled shippers, it had to confess that it had no authority to compel the railroads to make use of constructive stations any more than it had authority to require them to give a general pickup and delivery service. So the constructive station in Manhattan came to an untimely end after a brief existence of some nine years. The railroads went back to the primitive methods of receiving and delivering less carload freight which they had followed for so many years.[6]

HIGHWAY IMPROVEMENTS

Meanwhile, an important change had been taking place in the transportation industry. Improved vehicles and better roads had led to the discovery of the fact that the truck could compete with the railroad on more than even terms in the transportation of commodities which it had once been thought no truck could handle economically. The managers of New York railroads, who had scoffed at the suggestion of the New York and New Jersey joint commission that facilities be constructed for the all-rail movement into the greater city of traffic coming into the port district from the west, though they made some notable improvements in their individual properties, had the opportunity of witnessing the execution of a program of construction of transportation facilities in the metropolitan area which has had no counterpart anywhere in the world. It meant the expenditure of billions of dollars, many times the amount which would have been required to build the underground automatic electric railways system which the joint committee had recommended. But it was all for highways. The Holland Tunnel was opened in 1927, the George Washington Bridge in 1931. Later were to come the Lincoln Tunnel, the Queens Tunnel, the Triborough Bridge, and the vehicular tunnel from the Battery to Brooklyn. A huge network of highways constructed in northern New Jersey, some on the surface, some overhead, and some depressed, provided approaches to

[6] For an account of the rise and fall of the constructive freight station in New York, see Motor Truck and Wagon Transfer Service in Connection with Transportation by Rail or Water, 91 I.C.C. 539 (1924); Constructive and Off-track Railroad Freight Stations on Manhattan Island, 156 I.C.C. 205 (1929); Discontinuance of Off-track Stations in New York City, 173 I.C.C. 727 (1931). In 156 I.C.C. 205, the Commission said, "At common law there is no obligation on the part of a common carrier by railroad to effect personal or store-door delivery of freight." There was nothing in the Interstate Commerce Act, either, which imposed such an obligation. Moreover, the Commission declared that some of the practices in connection with the operation of constructive stations, followed by certain railroads entering New York, were clearly unjustly prejudicial and unduly discriminatory, in violation of sections 2 and 3 of the Act. This report contains an excellent brief history of the methods of freight handling in New York.

tunnels and bridges. Lighters, car floats, and ferryboats were no longer indispensable agencies for the movement of freight from New Jersey into Manhattan Island and the rest of the area which makes up greater New York.

Although the transformation was gradual, it was by no means imperceptible. Soon the time came when the congestion at the railroad pier stations on the Manhattan side of the Hudson River was no longer a traffic manager's nightmare. On the east side of Eleventh Avenue, opposite the once crowded pier stations, dozens of truck terminals made their appearance. Transportation of freight between New York City and the vast hinterland across the Hudson River was no longer a "railroad problem." The fact could not be concealed that the new kind of transportation itself created problems which demanded solution, but at least we had the stimulating influence of active and earnest competition to nourish the hope that traffic problems would be grappled with in a more forthright manner, unimpeded by a stubborn reluctance to break with tradition and an unwillingness to give any proposal of innovation a respectful hearing, even if not a hearty welcome.

BEGINNING OF PICKUP AND DELIVERY

Pickup and delivery service by railroad carriers had a modest beginning in 1931 among the lines of the South and West. In 1932, the Boston and Maine Railroad instituted a pickup and delivery service at some of its stations in New England. There were some scattered objections to the rates and practices adopted by the Boston and Maine in this strange activity, but it received a clean bill of health, as well as a green light, from the Interstate Commerce Commission. It was inevitable that other eastern roads would follow the example of the New England line, and this new variety of railroad service soon became so widespread in Official Classification Territory that the Commission felt impelled to undertake an investigation of the lawfulness of some of its aspects. The Commission did not conceal the satisfaction it felt that the railroads had at last come to a realization that the time had arrived for them to abandon some of their ancient prejudices, nor did it hesitate to point out the causes which had led them at last to take action. Said the Commission:

Among shippers and students of transportation there has been a widespread belief that the movement of less-than-carload freight from the premises of the consignor to those of the consignee should be completely under the control of the line-haul carrier or carriers under some kind of pick-up and delivery arrangement, but the compelling force of competition was required to extend this conviction to railroad traffic officials, who in the past have been reluctant to assume any obligation for transportation beyond their rail terminals.[7]

[7] Pickup and Delivery in Official Territory, 218 I.C.C. 441, 444 (1936).

The Commission remembered that in an extensive report dealing with motor vehicle transportation, which it had issued nearly ten years previously, it had said:

Store-door delivery is today receiving the earnest consideration of railroad executives and shippers' representatives, as well as ours. Store-door delivery would mean quicker and better service to the shipper with a great saving of time, elimination of terminal congestion, consolidation of freight into fewer cars, and reduction in use of stations and cars for storage.[8]

The Commission has never wavered in its position that the transportation service of the United States could be greatly improved by a greater degree of coordination among the numerous agencies which now provide carrier service for the public. It has recommended the establishment of "universal" stations, such as the one operated by the Port of New York Authority on Manhattan Island, and has sharply criticized the railroads entering the port district for their reluctance or outright refusal to cooperate with one another and with the Authority in making use of this modern facility, which has served to cut down the cost and time of handling less carload traffic in New York. Although the Commission has not been unanimous in its decisions with respect to the lawfulness of the rates and practices adopted by the carriers in their pickup and delivery operations, it has invariably given its approval to the establishment of a "complete" transportation service by the railroads, and has encouraged them to continue its development.[9]

THE SUCCESS OF PICKUP AND DELIVERY

It cannot be said that the pickup and delivery services of the railroads have met with an unqualified success. Some railroad managers are still disposed to deprecate the establishment of the auxiliary operations and even suggest that they be abandoned, while others are in favor of their continuation and even their extension. It is usually noticeable that the managers who regard pickup and delivery with approbation come from lines where a genuine effort has been put forth to try to make it work and where all trucking operations, whether in pickup and delivery service or in substitution-for-rail service, have been managed so efficiently that they show a substantial profit. The adverse opinion usually originates with persons who took up the new service only under the compulsion of the competitive activities of motor vehicle lines and rival railroads, who never regarded the innovation with any substantial measure of belief in its ultimate success. Despite the revolutionary changes which have taken

[8] Motor Bus and Motor Truck Operation, 140 I.C.C. 685 (1928).
[9] See Motor Club of Massachusetts v. Boston & Maine R.R., 206 I.C.C. 18 (1934); Master Truckmen of America v. Pennsylvania R.R., 225 I.C.C. 516 (1937); Empire Carpet Corp. v. Boston & Maine R.R., 258 I.C.C. 697 (1944).

place in the transportation industry in the past fifty years, even upon the railroads themselves, transportation to some people is still synonymous with steam railroad; they will continue to cling to this belief even after the long familiar blast of the steam locomotive whistle has become only a poignant memory.

FREIGHT STORAGE

In addition to pickup and delivery service, there are several other terminal services provided by railroads and other carriers to which attention should be called, if only briefly. Perhaps the most important of these services is storage.

It has already been noted in the discussion of the bill of lading that the tariffs of our carriers provide for a certain amount of free time allowed to the consignee to take delivery of a shipment after a notice of arrival has been sent or given; attention was called to the fact that, after the expiration of this free time, the liability of the carrier is no longer the liability which makes the carrier virtually an insurer, but instead is the liability of a warehouseman only. That is, if the shipment is lost or damaged after the expiration of free time, the carrier can be held responsible only if it has been negligent in caring for the property involved.

The storage which a carrier gives during the period of free time is presumably compensated for in the transportation rate. But for the storage afforded by the carrier after the expiration of free time, the carrier is entitled to compensation which is not included in the transportation charges. Needless to say, these storage charges must be just, reasonable, and not unduly discriminatory, and the same may be said of the rules and regulations which a carrier adopts with respect to storage.

While storage is included in the several items listed in the definition of "transportation" found in subdivision 3 (a) of section 1 of the Interstate Commerce Act, it must not be thought that storage services given by a carrier are the same as transportation services. The Commission has said on several occasions that the business of a carrier is transportation and not storage, and that storage service which the carrier gives to its shippers and consignees is only "incidental" to its primary function of transportation.

There is some similarity between storage and demurrage. Just as the charge for withholding a car from service is in part a penalty charge, so does the charge for storage partake of the nature of a penalty.[10] Its primary

---

[10] The storage charges discussed in this chapter must not be confused with the "track storage" charges mentioned in the preceding chapter. The storage under consideration here is the storage of the actual freight, and the rules and charges are fairly uniform throughout the country. Track storage charges are, in effect, just additional demurrage charges applicable to cars. They are imposed in only a few terminals, where space for delivery tracks is at a premium and the problem of congestion is likely to be a difficult one.

purpose, like the purpose of demurrage, is to prevent the congestion of terminals. It is imposed in the interest of both the carrier and the shipping public—in the interest of the carrier in order that it may use its premises for the purpose of fulfilling its primary function of transportation, and in the interest of the public in order that all shippers and consignees may have an opportunity to employ the services of our common carriers, unimpeded by the selfish or thoughtless acts of those persons who sometimes give little evidence of willingness to consider the rights and privileges of others. The fact that storage charges by carriers are considered to be in part penalty charges carries with it the implication that it is the duty of consignees promptly to remove their property from carrier premises and also the duty of shippers promptly to provide forwarding instructions for shipments turned over to a carrier for transportation.

STORAGE CHARGES

For the most part, storage charges are incurred on account of shipments which have not been picked up by consignees or have not been accepted by consignees during the period of free time. They are met with most frequently in connection with freight, carload or less carload, which passes through freight houses. However, a shipper too may find it necessary to pay storage charges on freight awaiting shipment, and storage charges may be imposed on carload shipments which have been consigned to public delivery tracks. Storage charges are not imposed upon freight received or delivered at private sidings; the storage for which the carrier makes a charge must be upon the premises of the carrier. Storage charges are for the most part levied only against freight which has been unloaded from a car or freight that has not been loaded into a car, though certain kinds of freight are subject to storage charges even while remaining in a car.

THE STORAGE TARIFF

Virtually all the railroads of the United States follow a uniform pattern in their storage charges. The tariff containing the rules and rates with respect to storage are to be found in the same publication which contains the national demurrage rules and rates, Freight Tariff 4, published by Agent L. C. Schuldt, of Chicago. Like the demurrage tariff, the storage tariff contains a number of "general exceptions" and several "special exceptions" applicable at different places and on different railroads, as indicated in the tariff. The tariff contains seven "rules," showing what freight is subject to the tariff, indicating the amount of free time to which shipments are entitled, telling how the time for which a charge is made is computed, setting forth the scale of charges, and giving the conditions under which storage charges, otherwise applicable, will not be imposed. The charges for the storage of explosives and other dangerous articles are considerably higher than the charges for the storage of ordinary merchandise freight, and storage charges are imposed upon explosives and dangerous articles even when such shipments are held in cars. In general, storage charges are applicable to freight "received for delivery, or held to complete a shipment, for forwarding directions, or any other purpose of the consignee, consignor, or owner, stored or held in or on the premises or tracks" of the carrier. Carload freight upon which the free time under demurrage rules has expired while in the cars, if unloaded on railroad premises, is subject to storage charges, without any free time allowance. When carload freight is unloaded by the carrier for the purpose of releasing equipment, the storage charge on the unloaded freight is the same as would have accrued under the demurrage tariff had the freight remained in the car. When carload freight is unloaded on railroad premises at the request of the consignee, the storage charge will not exceed the amount that would have been due under straight demurrage charges had the freight remained in the car.

A substantial portion of the storage charges which railroads collect each year arises because of refused or unclaimed freight. The storage tariff contains a rule relating to the carrier's duty to notify the consignor of such freight. The free time allowed before storage charges begin to accrue is usually forty-eight hours, though under certain conditions it may be less. The charges, as given in the current tariff, on freight held in excess of the free time allowed are 3 cents a hundred pounds for the first five days, and 5½ cents a hundred pounds for the sixth and each succeeding day. There is a minimum charge of 48 cents for freight held beyond free time for five days or less, and of 93 cents for freight held beyond free time for more than five days. The tariff calls attention to the rule of the bill of lading, which we have previously mentioned, that the carrier can, at its option, send to a public warehouse any freight upon which the free time has expired. On shipments sent to a public warehouse, the carrier has a lien for all freight and other charges which have been incurred.

WEIGHING OF FREIGHT

Another service performed by railroads, which may be designated as a terminal service though it is not one in the same sense that switching and storage are terminal services, is the weighing of freight. It has been explained previously that virtually all railroad charges, as well as the charges of other carriers, are based upon the weight of shipments and that rates are usually quoted as so much per ton or per hundredweight. It must be remembered, though, that since carload shipments and many less carload shipments are subject to "minimum weights," the charges applicable to shipments are not always based on actual weight. But weight is invariably an important element in the computation of freight charges. As was pointed out in a previous chapter, the fact that freight charges for hauling any particular commodity vary in direct proportion to the weight of shipments is conclusive evidence of the high importance of the cost of service as a factor in the determination of the "reasonableness" of rates. The ascertainment of the weight of a shipment is an indispensable part of virtually every transportation transaction.

There is no problem in connection with the weighing of less carload freight. Every freight house is equipped with tested scales, upon which small shipments can be weighed, though most less carload freight is weighed by the shipper and the weight entered on the bill of lading and shipping order which the shipper himself prepares. It is always the privilege of the railroad to check the weights entered on shipping papers by a shipper, and, as was mentioned previously, each railroad has a weighing and inspection service of some kind, which is constantly active in an effort to see that freight is properly described and accurately weighed.

TRACK SCALES

Carload freight is for the most part weighed on track scales, most of which belong to the carriers, though numerous large shippers have their own track scales as a part of their plant facilities. Everybody has noticed that a freight car carries on its side, in stenciled letters, figures indicating the weight of the car and its loading capacity. When freight is weighed on track scales, the "tare," or weight of the car, is subtracted from the gross weight of car and lading to obtain the weight of the car's contents. All cars are weighed at regular intervals and their tare weights accurately recorded.

Many shippers maintain weight agreements with the carriers which serve them. This is particularly true of shippers whose products are ordinarily shipped in standardized containers. It is necessary with such freight only to count the packages in order to secure the total weight. It is customary for both carrier and shipper occasionally to check the weight of the packages to which weighing agreements apply to see that the shipper is not being undercharged or overcharged.

The weighing practices of railroads, like all other rules and practices affecting their relations with shippers, must be reasonable and not unduly discriminatory, and of course they are subject to the supervision of the Interstate Commerce Commission. The Commission has had numerous cases involving weighing rules and customs, though disputes over these matters do not arise so frequently as disputes concerning rates and several other kinds of carrier service.

CODE OF WEIGHING RULES

There is no "official tariff" governing the weighing and reweighing of carload freight, but the Association of American Railroads has adopted a code of weighing rules which has received the endorsement and approval of the Commission. These rules tell how, when, and where the weight of carload freight is ascertained and indicate the amount of "tolerance" allowed, that is, the discrepancy which may be permitted without correction in the billed weight should different track scales not show the same results. The rules acknowledge the right of either consignor or consignee to have a car reweighed, both loaded and empty, in order to check the accuracy of the billed weight upon which freight charges have been computed. They indicate the practices to be followed when a request for reweighing has been received by the carrier. There is also a rule governing the weight agreements which carriers and shippers may enter into. The code of rules has been highly beneficial to shippers and carriers alike, in that it has led to the avoidance of disputes which would be likely to arise if weighing practices were not uniform.

ELEVATION OF GRAIN

One other kind of terminal service provided by many of our railroads deserves a brief discussion. This is the service known as elevation, which, according to the Interstate Commerce Commission, "as commonly understood among elevator men and among buyers and sellers of grain, signifies the unloading of grain from cars, or from grain-carrying vessels, into a grain elevator and loading it out again after storage for a period of not to exceed ten days." [11] This definition applies only to "transportation elevation" as distinguished from "commercial elevation" and "storage." When grain, in the course of its transportation, is held in an elevator for a period exceeding ten days, it becomes grain in storage; if the grain is given treatment of any kind, such as cleaning, mixing, drying, or clipping, while in an elevator, it is being subjected to commercial elevation.

As passed in 1887, the Interstate Commerce Act did not impose upon any carrier any "duty" to transport property for shippers. The duties of a carrier were simply those that had long been recognized in the common law. The word "elevation" did not appear in the Act at all. In 1906, the Hepburn Amendment made some interesting and significant changes. It became the "duty of every carrier subject to the provisions of this Act to provide and furnish such transportation upon reasonable request therefor." [12] By the same statute, the word "transportation" acquired a much broader meaning than had hitherto been attached to it. It was made to "include locomotives, cars, and other vehicles, vessels and all instrumentalities and facilities of shipment or carriage . . . and all services in connection with the receipt, delivery, elevation, and transfer in transit,

[11] Allowances to Elevators by the Union Pacific R. R., 10 I.C.C. 309 (1904).

[12] The language of this part of the law was modified in a few unimportant particulars by the Transportation Act of 1920, but restored virtually to the form adopted in 1906 by the Transportation Act of 1940.

ventilation, refrigeration or icing, storage, and handling of property transported."

Examined in the light of the broad and sweeping definition of transportation, the duty of the carriers "to provide and furnish transportation upon reasonable request therefor" meant something vastly more than the duty of carriage which had been imposed upon them by the common law. Among the obligations which railroads were required to assume was that of "elevation." The agricultural interests of the country had come a long way in the regulation of the transportation business since the time of the granger laws and the first somewhat feeble Act of 1887.

It has been noted previously that the methods by which the enormous crops of American grain are planted, cultivated, harvested, and carried to market constitute one of the outstanding triumphs of large-scale or mass production. The varied processes through which grain passes on its way from the harvest field to the dining table are among the most remarkable achievements of modern mechanization and organization of productive activities. The grain elevator is one of the most useful mechanisms we have for the speedy and regular movement of grain. It permits grain to be hauled with fewer cars, and it permits it to be placed under shelter within a short time after it has been threshed.

OWNERSHIP OF GRAIN ELEVATORS

Not all grain elevators are owned by the railroads, of course. In fact, most of the "country elevators," where the crops of wheat, oats, barley, rye, corn, and other cereals are first cared for, belong to grain dealers. The railroad elevators are to be found, for the most part, in the great cities of the grain belt, such as Chicago, St. Louis, and Kansas City, where the grain is first concentrated on its way to domestic milling centers or to the seaboard for export. Railroads have long employed, and continue to employ, different methods of providing elevator service. They may own and operate elevators directly, or they may own them and have them operated by a subsidiary corporation or a lessee. In many grain-marketing cities, a railroad may furnish land for the construction of large elevators which are built, owned, and operated by other interests.

Although a railroad is bound under the terms of the Interstate Commerce Act to furnish elevation upon a reasonable demand therefor, it does not have to provide and operate the elevator itself but can employ others to do the work. The operator of an elevator not owned by a railroad, which performs transportation elevation for one or more carriers, is more than likely to be a grain dealer himself; often his own shipments make up the major portion of the grain passing through his elevator. Both the elevators owned and operated by railroads and those owned and operated by nonrailroad interests often furnish commercial elevation as well as transportation elevation, but if such service is performed by a railroad-owned elevator, the carrier must charge the shipper a reasonable amount for the service. Only transportation elevation can be given by a carrier without making a special service charge.

ELEVATION ALLOWANCES

When a railroad utilizes the services of an "outside" elevator to perform transportation elevation, it compensates the owner for the service, even making an "allowance" for the elevation of the operator's own grain. But just as a carrier may not give free commercial elevation, so must it refrain from granting an allowance for this work. Several years ago, various railroads, shippers, elevator owners, and milling interests engaged in an animated controversy over the allowances paid by railroads to elevator owners. Both the Commission and the Federal courts had to be appealed to before all differences were settled.[13] It was during the course of this controversy that the Commission found it necessary to make the distinction between transportation elevation and commercial elevation. It changed its collective mind over the matter of allowances, and finally ordered the cancellation of allowances, even for transportation elevation, to those elevator owners whose business consisted chiefly of handling their own grain, to which it gave both varieties of elevation, on the theory that the practice resulted in an unjust discrimination against those shippers who had no elevators. However, the Supreme Court held that the Commission, in making the order for the cancellation of the allowances for transportation elevation, had exceeded its statutory power. The Court declared that a railroad had the right to employ other agencies for the performance of

[13] The following Commission reports and court decisions give the complete details of the controversy over allowances: Allowances to Elevators by the Union Pacific R.R., 10 I.C.C. 309 (1904), 12 I.C.C. 85 (1907), 14 I.C.C. 315 (1908); Traffic Bureau, Merchants' Exchange of St. Louis v. Chicago, Burlington & Quincy Ry., 14 I.C.C. 317 (1908); F. H. Peavey & Co. v. Union Pacific R.R., 176 Fed. 409 (1910); Interstate Commerce Commission v. Diffenbaugh, 222 U.S. 42 (1911); Union Pacific R.R. v. Updike Grain Co,, 222 U.S. 215 (1911); Traffic Bureau, Merchants Exchange of St. Louis v. Chicago, Burlington & Quincy Ry., 22 I.C.C. 496 (1912); Elevator Allowances at Points Located on the Missouri, Mississippi and Ohio Rivers and on the Great Lakes, 24 I.C.C. 197 (1912); Grain Elevation Allowances at St. Louis, 30 I.C.C. 696 (1914); Grain Elevator Allowances at Kansas City, 34 I.C.C. 442 (1915). The Commission made an interesting point in Milwaukee Maltsters Traffic Association v. Grand Trunk Western Ry., 28 I.C.C. 489 (1913). It denied an allowance to maltsters who did their own transportation elevation, on the ground that the malt which was "loaded out" was a different product from the grain that was "unloaded in." Commercial elevation does not change the character of the grain treated.

any of its carrier functions, and that any agency so employed was lawfully entitled to proper compensation. It became necessary for the Commission to determine what compensation was fair and reasonable; it ruled that there should be no allowance whatever for commercial elevation and that the allowance made for transportation elevation should be no greater than the actual cost of the service to the elevator.

CHAPTER XIX

Reconsignment and Diversion: Transit Privileges

To a person who has only a brief acquaintance with the history of railroad transportation in America, the record of the changes which have taken place, both in the mechanism of the railroad and in the services it provides for the public, invariably excites wonder and admiration. It is difficult to believe that the great locomotives—steam, diesel, and electric—which now pull our trains; the luxurious passenger train equipment with its dining cars, club cars, coaches, and numerous kinds of sleeping cars; the capacious freight-hauling cars, including not only the long familiar box, flat, open-top, and stock cars, but many specialized cars for hauling liquids —acid, oil, wine, milk, and mineral water—and for hauling all kinds of fruit, vegetables, meat, and other perishable products; the heavily ballasted track with chemically treated crossties and rails of a hundred pounds and more to the yard; the signal systems; the automatic crossing gates; the huge passenger terminals with their varied facilities; the sprawling freight terminals whose tracks and structures cover hundreds upon hundreds of acres of ground—it is difficult to believe that all these things had their origin only a little more than a century ago in a small 5-ton steam locomotive drawing a stagecoach with flanged wheels over a road whose rails were iron-plated wooden stringers laid on blocks of granite.

But it is not only in its mechanical, technological aspects that the railroad has undergone an enormous transformation. There has been an equally important transformation in the character and in the quality of transportation service. Some of the changes we have already noted, such as the interchange of cars, through routing, intercarrier switching, and pickup and delivery. A few of the improved services of railroads have required a little nudge by public authority to cause them to become practices of ordinary everyday occurrence, but for the most part they have eventually become accepted. Once established, they have been developed and enlarged with the enterprise and ingenuity that have characterized the introduction and development of many mechanical features of the modern railroad.

RECONSIGNMENT AND DIVERSION

There remain a few more specialized transportation services of which the industrial traffic manager should have knowledge, services which were initiated long after the railroad was a demonstrated mechanical success and which have been of great importance in facilitating the movement of our domestic commerce. One of these services is that known as reconsignment, or diversion, or sometimes diversion and reconsignment. These two terms are usually considered to be synonymous. In its administrative rulings governing the publishing and filing of tariffs, contained in *Tariff Circular* No. 20, the Commission says:

Some carriers do not consider a change of consignee which does not involve a change of destination as a reconsignment, while others do consider it a reconsignment and charge for it as such. The commission holds the view that when not specifically qualified in tariffs, the terms "reconsignment" or "diversion" include changes in destination, routing, consignor, or consignee. If a carrier wishes to distinguish between such changes in its privileges or charges it must so specify in its tariff rules.

We shall use the single term "reconsignment," taking it to mean the same as diversion, but bearing in mind that some carriers hold that there is a technical difference between them, though when such a view is held, it must be specifically indicated in a tariff.

Reconsignment of shipments is a privilege which railroads have extended to their patrons for many years. It is the privilege of making a change in the name of the consignee, a change in the name of the consignor, a change in the destination of a shipment, a change in routing, or any other change which requires the billing of a shipment to be modified or necessitates an additional or a different movement, which was not definitely planned or contemplated when the shipment was turned over to the railroad for transportation. To quote the Commission again:

Frequently a shipper desires to forward a shipment to a certain point and have the privilege of changing the destination or consignee while shipment is in transit or after it arrives at destination to which originally consigned, and to forward it under the through rate from point of origin to final destination which is generally lower than the combination of intermediate rates.[1]

Reconsignment privileges, as the Commission goes on to say, "are of value to the shipper." Consequently they must be clearly described and set forth in appropriate tariffs "in terms that are not open to misconstruction," with a clear statement as to the "conditions under which they may be used and the charges that will be made therefor."

The type of reconsignment described in the preceding quotation from the Commission's administrative rulings is probably the most common

[1] Even the Commission slips occasionally in the use of technical terms. What it means here is obviously a "single through rate" or a "specific through rate," either joint or local. The "combination of intermediate rates" is also a "through rate."

type of reconsignment with which railroads have to deal, though, as we shall find later, there can be other kinds of reconsignment. But reconsignment by the original shipper is a wide practice in American domestic commerce. The owner of a coal mine in the Pocahontas district may send a whole trainload of coal westward, without knowing the ultimate destination of a single car. The coal is sold, en route, to brokers, commission men, wholesalers, and others, after the train has started on its way. By the time the train gets to a certain reconsignment point, the coal has been sold, and the carrier has received orders giving the names and addresses of the consignees to whom the coal is to be delivered. Many other commodities are shipped under the same conditions. We have previously mentioned how shiploads of bananas arriving at New Orleans may be started on their way north by rail before they are sold. Lumber, shingles, cotton, livestock, hay, grain, and many other commodities are reconsigned in the same manner.

VALUE OF RECONSIGNMENT PRIVILEGE

This privilege of reconsignment is of great benefit to many shippers. It enables them to keep their products moving; it makes for greater fluidity and flexibility in trade; it enables shippers to divert their wares from markets where prices may be sagging to markets where prices are firm and strong. It was explained in a previous chapter how, by the use of an order bill of lading, a shipper may secure credit at the bank for shipments which he has dispatched on their way but which he has not yet sold. There is still another great advantage which a shipper may derive from the privilege of reconsignment. On a shipment which, under a duly published tariff, is entitled to be reconsigned en route, he is not required to pay a combination of rates based upon the reconsignment point, if an applicable specific, single through rate, either joint or local, exists. He is obliged to pay the through rate from point of origin to final destination, plus a reconsignment charge, if any is due, the total charge being generally less, as the Commission observes, than the sum of the intermediate rates. The shipper not only obtains speedier service, but speedier service at a lower charge than he would find it necessary to pay if it were not possible to reconsign his shipment. If the shipper fails to give his reconsignment order in time to "catch" a car before it passes the point at which it is to be reconsigned, he must pay the "back-haul" charge to and from the place where the car has been held for return to the reconsignment point.[2]

It should be mentioned at this point that reconsignment can be, and sometimes is, effected at intermediate points via which there is no single

[2] Permissible back-haul or out-of-line movements of reconsigned shipments, either with or without charge, must be provided for in the reconsignment tariffs, just as other reconsignment practices must be provided for.

through rate from point of origin to destination. If this is so, it is obvious that the through rate applicable to the reconsigned shipment would be a combination rate based upon the reconsignment point. When a reconsignment of this nature takes place, the carrier may not impose a special reconsignment charge. The service given is no greater than would have been given had the goods been stopped at the reconsignment point and billed to destination as a new shipment, and the transportation charges would be the same.[3] Needless to say, a railroad may not extend reconsignment privileges except by authority of duly filed and published tariffs to which it is a party. If a car is rebilled and forwarded from its initial destination, and no reconsignment privileges exist at that point, the second movement is regarded simply as a new shipment, and the combination of rates based upon the rebilling point will apply, even though there is a single through rate applicable from the point of origin to the point of ultimate destination.

Although the privilege of reconsignment is employed, as a rule, only in connection with carload shipments, there are some railroads which permit less carload freight to be reconsigned, though usually the minimum charge imposed is so high that the privilege is not often used.

WHO HAS THE RIGHT TO GIVE RECONSIGNMENT ORDER?

It is not only the shipper who can take advantage of the right to have a shipment reconsigned. And the shipper, except when he is exercising the right of stoppage in transitu because of the insolvency of the named consignee, cannot always exercise the right. Broadly speaking, it is the owner of a shipment who has the right to direct the movement of the shipment after it is turned over to the carrier for transportation. But this is true only "broadly speaking." Anybody who is lawfully entitled to the possession of a shipment may reconsign it. A freight forwarder, for example, is seldom the owner, either in whole or in part, of a shipment which he turns over to a railroad. Yet if the forwarder is both the shipper and the named consignee, the railroad will be justified in accepting from him a reconsignment order. The initial deal which a carrier makes concerning a shipment is with the shipper, who may or may not be the owner. But if the shipper is not the owner, if somebody else is lawfully entitled to

---

[3] Chessnut Lumber Co. v. Director General, 89 I.C.C. 236 (1924); Traffic Bureau, Chamber of Commerce v. Southern Ry., 115 I.C.C. 625 (1926). The Commission pointed out on more than one occasion that the right of reconsignment was of little if any value, if the reconsigned shipment was assessed the full combination of rates to and from the point of reconsignment, declared a reconsignment charge under such circumstances to be unreasonable, and ordered it refunded to the shipper. A. S. Nowlin & Co. v. Norfolk & Western Ry., 155 I.C.C. 465 (1929). See also Wilgus v. Pennsylvania R.R., 113 I.C.C. 617 (1926); Brown Hoisting Co. v. Pennsylvania R.R., 115 I.C.C 218 (1926).

possession of the goods shipped, and *the carrier is aware of this fact,* obviously it is the duty of the carrier to accept a reconsignment order only from the owner of the goods or from one entitled to their possession. If a carrier executes a reconsignment order given by a person who the carrier knows is not entitled to make the order, and ultimately makes delivery of the property to a party not entitled to receive it, the carrier is guilty of conversion, and is liable to the lawful owner of the shipment for the value of the property converted.[4] Even if the carrier does not lose possession of the property, under such circumstances, it can collect from the rightful owner no extra freight charges incurred by reason of transportation movements not lawfully authorized.

It must be understood that the Interstate Commerce Commission has no jurisdiction over the matter of losses due to conversion or to the execution of reconsignment orders unlawfully made, any more than it has jurisdiction over claims for lost or damaged freight. Controversies over the ownership or the alleged conversion of property are for the courts to settle, if they cannot be settled amicably by the parties concerned. The Commission has the power to supervise the publication and filing of reconsignment tariffs and to see that the provisions of the tariffs are complied with, but these terms have to do with the movement of shipments and the charges therefor, and not with the ownership of property.

We can now see again why the bill of lading is such an important document, and we can see once more the vital differences between a straight and an order-notify bill of lading. When goods are shipped under an order bill of lading, there is likely to be no dispute over the matter of reconsignment. An order bill of lading is documentary evidence of title to the goods which it covers, it is negotiable, and the holder is presumed to be the owner of the goods or at least entitled to their possession. Under the Pomerene Bills of Lading Act, a carrier is justified in delivering goods covered by an order bill of lading to the holder of the bill, unless it has knowledge that the holder is not entitled to their possession or has been requested by one having the "right of property or possession of the goods" not to make such delivery. Just as a carrier demands the surrender of an order bill of lading as a condition of delivery of goods, so it requires the surrender of an order bill as a condition of executing an order of reconsignment, though if the agent of the carrier is satisfied that the person who seeks delivery, or who makes a reconsignment order, is lawfully entitled to do so, he may make delivery or execute the reconsignment order, if proper bond is posted. Ordinarily, the carload shipments which are sent

---

[4] "Where ownership . . . was known to the carrier . . . by diverting goods at an intermediate point, although directed to do so by those in whose care the shipment was addressed, carrier rendered itself liable for conversion." Estherville Produce Co. v. Chicago Rock Island & Pacific R.R., 57 F.2d 50 (1932).

on their way, to be reconsigned at some point in their journey, are shipped under order bills of lading, the bills are surrendered to the carrier for proper notations before the cars are rebilled, and no difficulty is likely to arise over the question of who has the right to make the reconsignment order. Even if the original shipper has sold the goods to a broker, or a customer, he has turned the bill over to the buyer as evidence of ownership, and the buyer presents the bill if a reconsignment order is to be made.

When goods are shipped under a straight bill of lading, the ·question of who has the right to make a reconsignment order may be a trifle more difficult to answer. If a shipper contemplates placing a reconsignment order while the goods are en route, and does not want to use an order bill of lading, he consigns them to himself, under a straight bill. Since he is both shipper and consignee, little question is likely to be raised about any reconsignment order he may place if he presents the bill of lading as proof of his authority. If the shipper is not the consignee named in the straight bill of lading, the title to the goods presumably rests in the designated consignee. The bill of lading law says that a carrier is justified in delivering goods shipped under a straight bill to the named consignee, unless it knows that the consignee is not lawfully entitled to their possession. If the named consignee makes a reconsignment order, even though not lawfully entitled to do so, before the carrier is put upon notice or has otherwise received information that this consignee has no lawful claim to the goods, the carrier is justified in executing the order. It is not often that any trouble arises over this matter, but there have been difficulties which were settled only by litigation. A named consignee, other than the shipper, may sell goods in transit to a third party or may resell them to the shipper, and thereby lose his lawful right to reconsign, but may go ahead and reconsign just the same. The carrier must be on its guard and take reasonable precautions to see that the person who has placed a reconsignment order for a shipment carried under a straight bill of lading has the right to make the order. Certainly, the carrier must not execute such an order if it knows that the one who makes it has no lawful right to do so.

F.O.B. AND RECONSIGNMENT

Here again, the industrial traffic manager is warned not to be led astray by the trade expression "F.O.B." If goods are shipped on a straight bill of lading, "F.O.B. destination," it does not necessarily mean that the title to the property rests in the shipper until the goods reach the end of their journey. The shipper may not have—in fact, as a rule, does not have— the right to reconsign them, and the carrier must be very careful about accepting a reconsignment order from the shipper of goods so shipped, if a charge of conversion is to be avoided. It may be that the shipper does retain title, or he may have the right to reconsign because of the named consignee's insolvency. But the term "F.O.B." has nothing to do with title. If the shipper has repurchased the goods in transit, if it is the "custom of the trade" with this particular consignee to regard the title to the goods as resting in the shipper until their journey is completed, or if the contract of sale provides for the retention of title by the shipper, then the shipper may have the right to reconsign. But, under ordinary circumstances, it is the consignee who has the right to reconsign goods shipped under a straight bill of lading. We learned in a former chapter that the "lawful holder" of the bill of lading is the person to whom the railroad is responsible for lost or damaged shipments and that this lawful holder need not be the owner of the goods. We might have a situation under reconsignment practices in which the "lawful holder" of the bill of lading, regardless of his right to file claims for loss or damage, does not retain the right to give a reconsignment order for the goods represented in the bill of lading. As we said before, broadly speaking, it is the owner of goods who has the right to reconsign, but there are exceptions.

RECONSIGNMENT BY CONSIGNEE

Thus far, we have been discussing chiefly reconsignment orders made by the shipper. But it is often the consignee who places the reconsignment order, either directly or through a duly authorized agent. Reconsignment orders are frequently made by consignees who are brokers, commission merchants, or wholesalers, who do not make use of the shipments consigned to them but transfer them to their customers. Very often a broker or a wholesale dealer finds it possible to save both time and money by making use of the privilege of reconsignment. A New York broker dealing in wood flour, for example, may regularly purchase carloads of this product from manufacturers in Michigan or Wisconsin and have them started eastward, consigned to him at some rail terminal on the New Jersey side of the Hudson River. Informed that the shipment is on its way, if he makes a sale of a carload before it reaches some intermediate point, such as Buffalo or Pittsburgh, he may order the car reconsigned to his customer, located, let us say, in Newark. The applicable rate will be the through rate to Newark and not a combination based upon the original terminal. It may be that a sale has been made to a customer whose plant is a considerable distance west of New York, at a point taking a lower rate than the rate to the port. The purchaser of the wood flour gets quicker service, and the freight charges are lower. Some eastern railroads make a practice of notifying New York brokers and wholesalers, when cars consigned to them have reached certain intermediate terminals, and telling them when they may expect arrival at the port, giving them plenty of time either to reconsign or to arrange in advance for pier delivery in the metropolitan area. Commission men who handle shipments of livestock always have their fingers on the pulse of the markets in different livestock-purchasing centers, and often make use of the reconsignment privilege to direct the movement of incoming carloads to the market where prices are the most favorable.

RECONSIGNMENT PRACTICE ON AMERICAN RAILROADS

Although the practices of American railroads with respect to reconsignment are fairly uniform, there are some variations. There is no general reconsignment tariff comparable to the demurrage tariff and the storage tariff. Reconsignment privileges may vary according to the railroad or the commodity involved. On some shipments, only one reconsignment is permitted; on others, two or even more reconsignment orders will be accepted and executed. Reconsignment charges vary with the amount of work, both clerical and physical, which must be done before the order of reconsignment is carried out. In some instances there may be no charge whatever for a reconsignment. For example, if an order for reconsignment is received at the initial billing point before the car involved has been moved from the freight yard, there will be no charge unless the carrying out of the order requires some extra movement of the car, such as reclassification or switching. In the same way, no charge is made at the point of destination of a car for a single change in the name of the consignee, or a single change in the delivery destination, provided the reconsignment order has been received in time for freight yard employees to be notified of the change before the car arrives in the yard. Very often, a car is placed on a public delivery track for unloading, and the consignee named in the bill of lading sells the contents of the car before unloading begins. No charge is made for carrying out the order of the named consignee to deliver the lading of the car to another party.

When a charge is made for reconsignment, the amount of the charge usually depends upon whether the reconsignment order reaches the reconsignment point before the train containing the reconsigned car arrives at that point. If the order is received in such time that the yard employees have to classify it only once to get it to the track from which it will be started on its way to the rebilled destination, the charge is only about half the amount charged if the order for reconsignment is received after the car has been switched to the classification track designated for cars bound to the original destination, and it has to be switched again in order that the reconsignment order may be carried out.

If a car has been placed for unloading at its original billed destination, and before unloading has started, the owner of the lading orders the car moved to another destination, the movement is not regarded as a reconsignment movement but as a reshipment. There is no reconsignment charge, but the freight charges applicable to the car will be based upon the rate to the original destination plus the rate to the rebilled destination. The transaction is regarded as two separate shipments, and even though there is an existing single through rate from the point of origin to the eventual destination, and even though the right of reconsignment is duly provided for at the first destination, the charges applicable will be computed upon the combination of rates based on the first destination point.

INTERSTATE COMMERCE COMMISSION ON RECONSIGNMENT

Since the authority of the Interstate Commerce Commission was increased by the enactment of the Hepburn Amendment of 1906, it has made several investigations of reconsignment rules and charges and has had to deal with a number of controversies between shippers and carriers in which the matter of reconsignment was involved. For a time, the Commission seemed to regard reconsignment as a privilege voluntarily extended by the carriers to the shippers and not a service which shippers had a right to demand in the same way that they could demand elevation or protective services for perishables.[5] Once a carrier extended reconsignment privileges, the Commission had the authority to see that rules and charges were reasonable and the service given without undue discrimination, but it doubted if it had the power to order the establishment of reconsignment practices where they were wanting, however advantageous they might be to shippers and to carriers, too.

In the course of time, the Commission abandoned its early position and adopted the view that reconsignment was a service which, under the law, a carrier may properly be expected to provide and furnish.[6] In effect, reconsignment came to be regarded as coming within the scope of the definition of transportation as set forth in the first section of the Interstate Commerce Act, just as elevation, storage, and icing did. The carriers never challenged this view. A few railroad officials once suggested, when the railroads were financially in a deplorable condition, that the revenues of the carriers could be substantially increased if reconsignment charges were abolished and combination rates based upon reconsignment points charged on all reconsigned shipments. There was an immediate protest from many shippers, who had long since come to regard reconsignment as a right and not a privilege, and the Commission too quickly frowned

[5] See Cedar Hill Coal & Coke Co. v. Colorado & Southern Ry., 16 I.C.C. 387 (1909); Bayou City Rice Mills v. Texas & New Orleans R.R., 18 I.C.C. 490 (1910); Dietz Lumber Co. v. Atchison, Topeka & Santa Fe Ry., 22 I.C.C. 75 (1911).

[6] Charles Becker v. Pere Marquette R.R., 28 I.C.C. 645 (1913); Reconsignment and Storage Rules of Lumber and Shingles, 27 I.C.C. 451 (1913); Doran & Co. v. Nashville, Chattanooga & St. Louis Ry., 33 I.C.C. 523 (1915); Commercial Exchange of Philadelphia v. New York Central & Hudson River R.R., 38 I.C.C. 551 (1916).

upon the suggestion. The idea did not meet with approval even among the majority of the carriers, and no attempt was ever made to carry it into effect. There have been many occasions upon which the Commission has required railroads to grant or enlarge reconsignment privileges.

In a long series of reports and decisions, the Commission has explained the nature of reconsignment, showed how reconsignment orders are handled by the carriers, and has expounded upon the benefits and advantages of reconsignment to both carriers and shippers and to the commerce and industry of the United States.[7] It has held steadfastly to the belief that reconsignment is something to which the shipper is of right entitled; it has condemned the exaction of reconsignment charges at points via which there is no single through rate and the shipper is obliged to pay a combination of rates. The Commission has held to the theory that reconsignment charges should be based upon the cost of service, with a reasonable allowance for a profit on the capital value of the facilities employed, and has recognized that there may be a wide variation in the cost of reconsignment because of differences in the amount of clerical and physical work required.[8] Because of the policy which the Commission

[7] See Detroit Traffic Association v. Lake Shore & Michigan Southern Ry., 21 I.C.C. 257 (1911); Doran & Co. v. Nashville, Chattanooga & St. Louis Ry., 33 I.C.C. 523 (1915); Reconsignment Case, 47 I.C.C. 590 (1917); Reconsignment Case No. 3, 53 I.C.C. 455 (1919); Reconsignment and Diversion Rules, 58 I.C.C. 568 (1920), 61 I.C.C. 385 (1921).

[8] Perhaps the most thorough discussion of reconsignment by the Commission is to be found in the Reconsignment Case, 47 I.C.C. 590 (1917). In this report, the Commission even listed the steps which the clerical force of a railroad found it necessary to take in order to comply with a reconsignment order. They were as follows: "(1) Agent receives request to reconsign. (2) Agent writes message ordering the reconsignment. (3) Message is checked with request. (4) Message is sent to telegraph office. (5) If request was made by telephone, agent receives confirmation by letter. (6) Agent checks written confirmation with telephone order and files them together. (7) Operator sends reconsignment message. (8) Operator at point of reconsignment receives the message. (9) Message is sent to yard clerk. (10) Yard clerk books the order. (11) Yard clerk examines record of cars previously passing station. (12) If record fails to show that car has already passed, yard clerk next checks record of cars in yard. (13) If car is not in yard, yard clerk examines record of all trains arriving from direction in which the car originates until it is received. (14) Yard clerk finds waybill and makes necessary changes thereon. (15) Yard clerk makes memorandum against his order record. (16) Yard clerk writes message to agent from whom order was received advising that reconsignment has been effected. (17) Message is sent to telegraph office. (18) Operator sends message. (19) Operator at destination receives message. (20) Message is delivered to agent. (21) Agent checks message with original order. (22) Agent advises party who requested the reconsignment and files paper." This clerical work does not include the steps which must be taken to see that the reconsignment order has been placed by proper authority or the work involved in making proper notations on the bill of lading if the shipment is an order-notify shipment. It must be remembered that, if car-

has long followed, reconsignment has become as much a part of standard railroad practice in the United States as any other of the manifold operations which have in the course of time been added to the mere duty of carriage.

TRANSIT PRIVILEGES

The last special railroad service with which we shall deal is not a single service, but rather a group of services, which all go under the general name of "transit services," "transit privileges," or just "transit." Reconsignment is, as a matter of fact, a transit service, and is often spoken of as reconsignment in transit or diversion in transit. There is one outstanding difference, however, between reconsignment and the other transit services to be discussed, which has led to the consideration of reconsignment as being in a separate and distinct category. In reconsignment (of goods shipped in carloads), the car is not unloaded, and the lading is not subjected to any process, manufacturing or otherwise. Reconsignment has to do only with the movement or the transportation of traffic. The stoppage is only temporary—usually but a brief interruption—for the transmission and execution of the orders concerning the further movement of the cars involved. When goods are granted a "transit service," they are virtually always unloaded from the cars and subjected to some process or operation, after which they are reloaded, though seldom in the same car, and carried forward to their destination. The Interstate Commerce Commission has said that transit is the

. . . right of a shipper to stop at an intermediate point and change the form or substance of the commodity shipped, and afterwards reship the commodity so changed to point of final destination at a total charge for transportation not exceeding that which would have applied if the changed commodity had been shipped from point of origin to final destination without being stopped in transit.

Like many other terms, however, the term "transit" has not been defined with complete accuracy. But a transit service usually involves a stoppage in the movement of freight which is intended to be more than just temporary, and ordinarily the goods stopped are unloaded and subjected to some treatment or process before reshipment.[9] It might perhaps be better if

---

load shipments are held in transit at the order of the owner, the cars are ordinarily subject to demurrage rules and charges after only twenty-four hours of free time. The checking of the time of a car's arrival and departure and the computation of demurrage are other clerical duties which must receive attention.

[9] Cottonseed, Its Products and Related Articles, 188 I.C.C. 605 (1932). This definition emphasizes the fact that goods receiving transit service are changed in "form and substance." However, when goods are given storage-in-transit, they are not necessarily processed during the period of storage. That the Commis-

all halts in the transportation of any commodity, made with some particular need or purpose of the owner in mind and made on the order of the owner, were called transit services. Such halts would include diversion, reconsignment, and commercial elevation, but they would not include stops for transportation elevation or for weighing made solely upon the orders of and for the purposes of the carrier.

HOW TRANSIT WORKS

The understanding of transit in its commonly accepted meaning will be aided by an illustration. A great deal of the wheat purchased by millers to be converted into flour for sale to the baking industry is "milled" in transit. After leaving a primary elevator, where it has been purchased, the wheat is transported to a flour mill, turned into flour, and shipped forward to market. In the same way, corn is converted into meal; logs into lumber; lumber into the materials for making boxes or crates; and steel bars, billets, and channels into the members of the framework of a building.

The essential feature of transit, as the Commission points out, is that the raw product which is milled, fabricated, or otherwise processed or serviced in transit moves from its point of origin to its final destination at the through rate applicable between those points to the secondary products, and is not subjected to any combination rate made upon the transit point. Just as in the case of reconsignment, a transit service would be of little value to a shipper or manufacturer if the full rates were charged to and from the transit point. In fact, it was to avoid the imposition of the combination of rates on the processed commodities that the practice of granting transit privileges was initiated.

---

sion is not invariably precise in its language can be seen by reading Rule 10a of *Tariff Circular* No. 20, which says: "Each carrier or its agent shall publish, post, and file tariffs which shall contain in clear, plain, and specific form and terms all the rules governing and rates and charges for demurrage, switching, floating, lighterage, wharfage, and other terminal services, storage, transfer and drayage, weighing, diversion, reconsignment, icing, refrigeration, heat, elevation, feeding, grazing, and other transit services. . . ." Here diversion, reconsignment, storage, and elevation are classified as transit services. Yet the Commission almost invariably regards diversion and reconsignment as something different from "transit." Minneapolis Traffic Assn. v. Chicago, Milwaukee & St. Paul Ry., 46 I.C.C. 685 (1917). Obviously, there are two kinds of storage, one of which is a terminal service and the other a transit service. The storage tariff, previously discussed, is never considered to be a transit tariff; there are, however, numerous storage-in-transit tariffs. In the same way, "transportation elevation" is not regarded as a transit service unless the grain elevated is held for more than ten days. Commercial elevation may be a transit service, even if the grain is held for less than ten days.

TRANSIT CHARGES

The carrier often makes a small charge for the transit privilege, the amount varying with different commodities and with different railroads. This charge must be added, of course, to the other transportation charges which the shipper must pay. At many places, however, if carrier competition is exceptionally keen, there is no charge for transit service. It is not unlawful to grant a transit service free of charge, so long as there is no undue discrimination and no unjust prejudice.

PROCESSING IN TRANSIT

It will be readily understood that there must be some limit to the amount of processing or servicing which will be permitted under a transit privilege. Wheat may be made into flour while in transit, but this does not mean that flour may be made into bread and cake in a similar manner. Logs may be converted into lumber in transit, and lumber into slabs for boxes, but there will be no transit tariff under which lumber can be made into furniture and forwarded at the through rate applicable to lumber. Steel bars and billets may be sawed to proper lengths and punched with rivet holes under a transit arrangement, but not manufactured into such articles as shovels, picks, rakes, and similar tools. In other words, the permissible processing under transit must be of a somewhat elementary nature; the product which emerges must be closely related to the product which enters a plant operating under a transit privilege; there must be no such change that the processed article is something completely new and different as compared to the article which was subjected to processing.[10] From a practical standpoint, the limitation upon the amount of processing which may be given to a commodity in transit does not cause a great deal of difficulty. This is because, from the very character of the service, there

[10] "The underlying principle of all transit arrangements is that the same commodity which moves to transit points shall move therefrom in a more or less changed form." Maley & Wertz v. Louisville & Nashville R.R., 36 I.C.C. 657 (1915). The transited commodity does not *have* to be changed, but the fact that it *is* changed more or less does not deprive it of transit privileges. The change is a matter of degree. To "require absolute identity of inbound and outbound shipments would destroy the value of transit." But "it is reasonable to withhold transit from a product which is essentially different from the raw material." Douglas & Co. v. Chicago, Rock Island & Pacific Ry., 16 I.C.C. 232 (1909). For an interesting discussion of when a transited article becomes a new commodity, see Judge Learned Hand's opinion in Baltimore & Ohio R.R. v. United States, 15 F. Sup. 674 (1936), *reviewing the Commission's order in* Thomas Keery Co. v. New York, Ontario & Western Ry., 206 I.C.C. 585 (1935), 211 I.C.C. 451 (1935). The case bore primarily, however, upon the power of the Commission to establish a through rate on a transited article, if one part of the haul was intrastate.

must not be a great deal of difference between the rate on the article which moves into the transit point and that on the commodity which moves out. The through rate is, as a general rule, the rate applicable to the outgoing commodity. The difference between the rates on the raw materials of manufacture and the highly finished products is usually so great that in-transit rates would be of no advantage to the shipper. It is cheaper to pay the low rate on the raw material to the manufacturing plant and the high rate on the finished article from manufacturing plant to market than to pay the high rate on the entire movement. However, this may not always be true, and on a few occasions the Interstate Commerce Commission has denied transit privileges when the manufacturing process was such as completely to change the character of the article upon which transit privileges were desired.

Transit, therefore, is one of those activities in the regulation of which the Commission must exercise "judgment." There is no hard and fast rule which may be drawn and applied to all situations. It will be remembered that the Commission denied the right of a maltster to claim an allowance for transportation elevation because the malt which was loaded out was so greatly different from the barley which was unloaded in at the malting plant. There can be no objection, however, to extending a transit privilege to a maltster, any more than there can be a valid objection to giving transit privileges to the miller who turns wheat into flour.

POLICING OF TRANSIT

It will be apparent to anybody that the transportation of commodities under a transit arrangement will require a substantial amount of "policing" by the carrier, similar to the policing of freight which is shipped for export under an export rate lower than the domestic rate on the same freight. A flour mill or other manufacturing plant may draw its raw materials from many different sources, and the through rates from the various sources to the final destinations of the product may not be the same. This means that a careful account must be kept of the volume of materials arriving from each source, as well as a careful record of the amount of finished product shipped out. It is not possible to preserve the identity of each shipment, of course, any more than it is practicable to preserve the identity of the large number of shipments of wheat and other grains which find their way to public and other terminal elevators. But it is possible to check the amount of inbound wheat with the amount of outbound flour, or the amount of outbound meal with the amount of inbound corn. Not only is it necessary to check on the volume of shipments, but care must be taken to see that inbound traffic and outbound traffic match properly. In the identification of transited shipments and in calculation of total freight charges, wheat is not matched with corn meal, nor corn with wheat flour; in a lumber mill, oak logs must produce oak lumber, and not lumber of walnut or pine, if total transportation and transit charges are to be accurately calculated.[11] Then, too, we have the matter of time. Ordinarily an inbound commodity entitled to transit must be moved out within a year, though either a longer or a shorter time may be established for different commodities.

CALCULATION OF CHARGES ON TRANSIT FREIGHT

The methods by which the total charges on transited articles are computed are not uniform. Ordinarily, when grain is milled in transit, the shipper or owner pays the full rate from the point of origin to the transit point, local, joint, or combination, as the case may be. When the flour or other grain product is shipped out from the transit point, he pays the balance of the through rate from the point of origin to the final destination. On the other hand, when steel is fabricated in transit, it is customary for the shipper or owner to pay the full rate to the transit point and the full rate from the transit point to destination. Then he makes a "fabrication-in-transit reclaim" upon the carrier, based on the difference between the through rate from origin to destination and the sum of rates which he has paid.

BACK HAUL

Occasionally the matter of "back-haul" or "out-of-line" movement becomes involved in the practice of extending transit privileges, just as it does in reconsignment. Ordinarily, a transit privilege is established only at a point located on a direct route between the point of origin and the ultimate destination of the commodity enjoying the privilege. Transit is regarded, for the most part, simply as "suspended transportation," and the movement via the transit point is supposed to be direct and over a reasonably short route, with no reverse or unduly long circuitous movement. The Commission has said that a "back-haul is contrary to the purpose of transit, and should generally be permitted only to meet unusual situations, and when to do so does not result in unjust discrimination or other violation of law." Unusual situations do arise occasionally, however, commonly created by reason of the rivalry of competing lines, competing

---

[11] In Administrative Ruling No. 76 of *Tariff Circular* No. 18–A, which was the predecessor of *Tariff Circular* No. 20, the Commission said that "oats or products of oats may not be substituted for corn, nor corn or the products of corn for wheat, nor wheat or the products of wheat for barley, nor may shingles be substituted for lumber, or lumber for shingles . . . oak lumber may not be substituted for maple lumber, nor pine lumber for either oak or maple, nor may hard wheat, soft wheat, or spring wheat be substituted either for the other." For substitution "abuses," see Substitution of Tonnage at Transit Points, 18 I.C.C. 280 (1910); Transit Case, 26 I.C.C. 204 (1913).

producing regions, or competing markets. Consequently, some transit tariffs permit back hauls or out-of-line movements. Such movements are usually charged for, just as are similar movements of reconsigned cars, though under some competitive conditions a carrier may permit the back hauling of a transit shipment without exacting any extra charge beyond the through rate and the transit charge.[12]

THE INDUSTRIAL TRAFFIC MANAGER AND TRANSIT

The railroad agent at a point where a large tonnage of freight moves in and out under transit privileges has something more to do in the way of calculating rates and keeping records and accounts than an agent at a point where there are no industries operating under transit privileges. The industrial traffic manager of a plant which processes or fabricates commodities in transit finds that his duties are a bit more complicated than those of the industrial traffic manager of a plant which does not find it necessary to make use of transit privileges. The tariffs which he must read and apply are more complicated, the records he must keep are greater in number and variety, and there are more operations upon which he must keep a watchful eye, if he is to hold his transportation costs to a minimum. The traffic department of a large food-producing enterprise or of a steel-fabricating plant may have a subdivision which has no counterpart whatever in the traffic department of an enterprise whose products are not shipped subject to transit privileges.

TRANSIT AND THE LOCATION OF INDUSTRY

Transit privileges have been of peculiar importance in the United States, and have had more to do with shaping the pattern of our industrial development than is generally acknowledged. Until comparatively recent times, our chief products were those of the extractive industries which exploited the rich resources of our fields, forests, and subsoil. The vast stretch of territory over which domestic enterprise was scattered made it inevitable that for many articles there would be a great distance between the producing center and the consuming market. If there was any one dominant feature in the planning and construction of our railroad system it was that the system would be able to haul huge quantities of relatively cheap products for long distances at a low cost. Many of our raw products had to be processed or put through some simple manufacturing operations before they were ready for consumption. From the

---

[12] F. W. Stock & Sons v. Lake Shore & Michigan Southern Ry., 31 I.C.C. 150 (1914); Montgomery Cotton Exchange v. Louisville & Nashville R.R., 112 I.C.C. 325 (1926); Grain and Grain Products, 164 I.C.C. 619 (1930); Out-of-line and Back-haul Charges, 169 I.C.C. 105 (1930); Pillsbury Flour Milling Co. v. Great Northern Ry., 198 I.C.C. 642 (1934).

very beginning of our economic development, our enterprisers, the men who conceived, planned, and carried out the establishment of the industries which processed our raw materials, were confronted with the problem of industrial location. Where could these industries be best established so that they could perform their function effectively and at the same time provide a profit for the owners and operators?

There are many factors which economic geographers and economists must take into consideration in their study of the location of industries. We shall not venture to discuss the general problem at all. But when one considers the problems of economic development in this country of "magnificent distances," one cannot help being aware of the fact that the costs of transportation must have been of vital significance in any deliberations having to do with the matter of industrial location. Should a particular industry be located near the source of its raw materials or near the consuming market? If other considerations were not compelling, it was a matter of indifference, if the costs of transportation of the raw product and of the processed product were substantially the same. The industry could be located either near the point where the raw materials were turned out or near the market where the processed material found its market. But could such an industry be located at some point, or at many points, *between* producing region and market? If the industry could not be so located, the tendency toward the geographical concentration of industry in America, which many factors affecting industrial location have long made a marked feature of our economic development, would have been much stronger. There are few who will deny that a diffusion of industry, when it can be accomplished without the dislocation of the economy as a whole and without waste, is conducive to the development and maintenance of a higher degree of economic, political, and social health for the nation. Probably no feature of our economic system has done more to promote the diffusion of primary industry than the establishment and enlargement of transit privileges by our railroads. Our transportation has always been so cheap and efficient that we have experienced only slight difficulty over the years in hauling to market the vast quantities of grain, livestock, cotton, lumber, and other products which field, mine, and forest have yielded to business enterprise. But because of the character of freight rates it has not been necessary to establish our flour mills at the edge of the wheatfield or at the door of the baker, nor sawmills and planing mills either in the shade of the forest or at the outskirts of our largest cities. With transit privileges, any "local" businessman who had the capital, the knowledge, and an available supply of labor could establish a flour mill or a planing mill at a point far removed, though in direct line between them, from the source of the raw material and the market for the processed product. He could compete on even terms, in so far as transportation rates were a factor, with the miller or planer who otherwise would have had a distinct advantage of location. Transit has been of incalculable value to thousands of so-called small-business concerns. More than that, it has served to create employment at places where otherwise it would not exist, it has helped to equalize "opportunity," and it has permitted a healthy diffusion of population and of wealth and all the social advantages which follow such diffusion.

OTHER VARIETIES OF TRANSIT

Up to this point, we have confined our attention largely to transit privileges which involve some mechanical processing of the commodity in transit. There are, however, numerous transit privileges under which no manufacturing operation takes place, no processing takes place, and in some cases little or no change whatever is made in the commodity. One of the most common forms of transit, as a matter of fact, is the storage-in-transit of grain and many other products, which are simply held in storage, awaiting perhaps a hoped-for turn in the market, waiting until they are needed by the owner to whom they represent raw materials, or waiting for satisfactory transportation facilities. It frequently happens that great quantities of grain are stored in Buffalo elevators for the winter, to be exported in the spring. Everybody is familiar with the fact that at all times we have a "hold-over" supply of grain and cotton, much of which, though by no means all of which, may be stored in transit. These storage facilities, intermediate between the source of production and the market, offer an illustration of how a transit privilege, employed in connection with a through rate, leads to the diffusion of that highly important commercial activity known as warehousing. Concentration in transit, by which different shipments of such commodities as cotton, eggs, and butter and other dairy products are assembled, to be shipped from the primary market to large centers of consumption, and stopping to complete loading or stopping partly to unload, are other transit privileges in which no significant change is made in the commodity. The same can be said of feeding-in-transit and grazing-in-transit, though the animals shipped out of the transit point are usually much larger than they were when they arrived, on their way from ranch to packing house. Some of the other transit privileges which permit the processing of the product are refining-in-transit (usually of oils, though other liquids and some minerals are also refined under transit privileges), packaging-in-transit (sacking, barreling, boxing), cleaning-, grading-, mixing-in-transit, and creosoting-in-transit. All of these privileges—any transit privilege—must be provided for in duly filed tariffs, with rules, regulations, and transit charges clearly set forth.

REGULATION OF TRANSIT

The attitude of the Interstate Commerce Commission toward transit, like its attitude toward reconsignment, has undergone a substantial change since it first began to deal with the subject. Although the Commission recognized the possible value of transit to both shippers and carriers, even in the early years of its existence, it disclaimed any authority to regulate the transit rules of a carrier, except to the extent necessary to remove any unjust discrimination or undue prejudice.[13] Moreover, the Commission did not look with favor upon the granting of transit privileges by railroads. This was true even after the legislation of 1906 and 1910 enlarged the Commission's authority. Its policy was to "curtail" transit privileges rather than to enlarge them;[14] transit privileges, declared the Commission, "savor of a gratuity";[15] they did not exist as a matter of right, but were more in the nature of a voluntary gift.[16]

As the years passed, however, and the Commission became more acutely aware of the vast reach of its administrative authority, its views with respect to transit, like its views with respect to many other aspects of the transportation business, as well as its attitude toward the advisability of exercising its enlarged powers, began to change. Transit ceased to be a privilege which a railroad could grant or withhold at will so long as no undue prejudice resulted from its action. The Commission took the position that under section 15 of the Interstate Commerce Act, as amended in 1906 and 1910, its power to "determine and prescribe . . . what individual or joint classification, regulation or practice is just, fair and reasonable, to be thereafter followed" included the power to regulate transit in all respects, and that it could order the establishment of transit privileges whether or not there was a question of undue discrimination or undue prejudice involved.[17] Though its policy for a time was not to order a carrier to grant a transit privilege "except to remove unjust discrimination or undue prejudice,"[18] it never hesitated to assert that its authority over transit was as extensive as its authority over all other railroad practices and charges. Its views on the matter were unequivocally sustained by the

[13] Crews v. Richmond & Danville R.R., 1 I.C.C. 401 (1888); Douglas & Co. v. Central R.R. of N.J., 16 I.C.C. 232 (1909).

[14] Traugott Schmidt & Sons v. Michigan Central R.R., 19 I.C.C. 535 (1910); Middletown Car Co. v. Pennsylvania R. R., 32 I.C.C. 185 (1914).

[15] Douglas & Co. v. Chicago, Rock Island & Pacific Ry., 21 I.C.C. 97 (1911).

[16] Plano Milling Co. v. St. Louis Southwestern Ry., 22 I.C.C. 360 (1912).

[17] Southern Rice Growers' Assn. v. Texas & New Orleans R.R., 53 I.C.C. 197 (1919). See also Transportation of Wool, Hides and Pelts, 23 I.C.C. 151 (1912); Spiegle v. Southern Ry., 25 I.C.C. 71 (1912); Fabrication-in-Transit Charges, 29 I.C.C. 70 (1914).

[18] Procter & Gamble Co. v. Alabama & Vicksburg Ry., 112 I.C.C. 381 (1926).

Supreme Court, which declared in 1921 that transit was one of the "just and reasonable regulations and practices . . . relating to or connected with the . . . transporting . . . of property . . ." mentioned in section 1 of the Interstate Commerce Act, which it was the "duty" of carriers to establish and observe.[19] Oddly enough, in this particular case, the Court sustained an application for an injunction to prevent the enforcing of an order which the Commission had made requiring the establishment of creosoting-in-transit at Newark, New Jersey, because the Commission had based its order on the provisions of section 3 of the Act, which forbade railroads to subject a shipper to undue prejudice. The Court held that the Commission had made a "mistake of law," and that the carrier's refusal to establish the desired transit service had not, under the attendant circumstances and conditions, created any undue prejudice. The Court pointed out, however, that if the Commission had acted under section 1, and ordered the establishment of the transit service as a "reasonable" practice, the enforcement of its order could not have been enjoined. This was one of the few cases in which the Court seemed to be ahead of the Commission, in defining the latter's power and authority.

[19] Central R.R. of N.J. v. United States, 257 U.S. 247 (1921). This is a very interesting case and presents what perhaps has been the Court's best exposition of the conditions that must prevail, with regard to carrier operations, in order that undue prejudice may be said to exist. The Commission quoted that part of the decision referring to its power to order the establishment of transit in Montgomery Cotton Exchange v. Louisville & Nashville R.R., 112 I.C.C. 235 (1926).

CHAPTER XX

Freight Forwarding

Freight forwarding is a hybrid enterprise. Like some other hybrid institutions and organisms, it is, as somebody quoted, from one of John Heywood's better known proverbs, "neither fish, nor flesh, nor good red herring." The freight forwarder, as he is most familiarly known as an agency of our domestic commerce, is both a shipper and a carrier. But he is not a "common carrier," and he is a somewhat uncommon shipper. He has assumed a place of considerable significance in the internal transportation scene, especially since the advance of the motor carrier to a position of high importance among our transportation facilities. Indeed, he finally became so important that, like virtually all other carriers engaged in interstate commerce, he was subjected to Federal regulation and control, in 1942, when Congress enacted what is now part IV of the Interstate Commerce Act. This part is devoted almost exclusively to forwarders, just as parts II and III are devoted almost exclusively to motor vehicle carriers and carriers by water respectively, and part I is devoted to railroads, pipelines, express companies, and sleeping car companies.

WHAT IS A FREIGHT FORWARDER?

According to this law

. . . the term "freight forwarder" means any person which (otherwise than as a carrier subject to part I, II, or III of this Act) holds itself out to the general public to transport or provide transportation of property, or any class or classes of property, for compensation, in interstate commerce, and which, in the ordinary and usual course of its undertaking (A) assembles and consolidates or provides for assembling and consolidating shipments of such property, and performs or provides for the performance of break-bulk and distributing operations with respect to such consolidated shipments, and (B) assumes responsibility for the transportation of such property from point of receipt to point of destination, and (C) utilizes, for the whole or any part of the transportation of such shipments, the services of a carrier or carriers subject to part I, II, or III of this Act.

EXPRESS COMPANY NOT A FORWARDER

It will be noticed, perhaps, that if carriers subject to part I of the Act were not specifically excluded, this definition might cover an express com-

410

pany, though the express agency does not, in the ordinary and usual course of its business, do any assembling, consolidating, and breaking bulk. Even before the law was enacted, however, it was customary to exclude express companies from the category of freight forwarders, though, as Commissioner Eastman said, "forwarding companies are certainly very similar to express companies in their operations." [1] Certainly there was never any thought in 1906, when express companies were brought under Federal regulation, that the term "express companies" included freight forwarders. Moreover, the business of the express company is quite different from the business of the ordinary freight forwarder. Express traffic which moves by rail is carried almost entirely on passenger trains, the express company has a "system" of rates which is all its own, and the system of rates bears no necessary relationship to railroad charges. The manner in which an express company compensates a carrier for transporting express traffic is altogether different from the method employed by the forwarder. Before the express business came under the direct operating control of the railroads, the railroads were compensated by receiving a percentage of the gross revenues of the express companies; now a somewhat complicated system of pooling is employed, in which each railroad shares in express revenues according to the amount of express traffic it hauls. The freight forwarder pays the railroad the regular freight tariff rates for whatever tonnage the railroad carries on the forwarder's behalf. There are other differences between the express business and freight forwarding, but these are enough to show that their dissimilarities are more marked than their similarities.

FREIGHT FORWARDER A CONSOLIDATOR

The general practice of the freight forwarder today, as we employ the term, is "to assemble into carload lots numerous shipments of merchandise for individual consignors. It tenders the shipments to rail lines as a carload and pays the carload rates. At destination it distributes the individual consignments to the ultimate consignees for whom they are intended." [2] In other words, the freight forwarder is a "consolidator" of less carload shipments into carloads. Some of our largest freight forwarding companies are known as "carloading companies." "At the heart of the forwarder's business," as Commissioner Eastman remarked, "lies the consolidation of many small shipments into a quantity which can be tendered as a single carload shipment and move at the carload rate." [3]

[1] Freight Forwarding Investigation, 229 I.C.C. 201, 317 (1938).
[2] Freight Forwarding Investigation, 229 I.C.C. 203, 317 (1938).
[3] Freight Forwarding Investigation, 229 I.C.C. 201, 309 (1938). In Acme Fast Freight v. United States, 30 F. Supp. 968 (1940), *affirmed*, 309 U.S. 638 (1940), Judge Augustus Hand said, "The business of forwarders is to collect small shipments of goods, consolidate them and ship them in bulk. In their busi-

The freight forwarder in domestic commerce must perform his function for "compensation." In other words, he is engaged in a business enterprise from which he hopes to obtain a profit. A cooperative forwarding arrangement entered into by individual shippers as a nonprofit undertaking, under which they may "pool" their less carload traffic and ship it as a carload, is not a freight forwarding business within the legal meaning of the term. If the cooperative organization employed an agent to supervise the pooling, he would not assume the status of a freight forwarder if the various shipments were consigned in the name of the nonprofit organization, since he does not assume responsibility for the transportation, either as shipper or as consignee. If the cooperative undertook to handle the shipments of nonmembers, however, and made a charge for the service, it would surely be regarded as a freight forwarding enterprise and subject to all the provisions of part IV of the Interstate Commerce Act.

A FREIGHT BROKER

A freight broker, who "arranges" for transportation, and because of his knowledge of routes and rates is peculiarly qualified to act as a kind of "middleman" between a shipper and a carrier, and receives a compensation for his services, either from the shipper or from the carrier or from both, is not a forwarder within the meaning of part IV, any more than one of the numerous travel agencies or travel bureaus, which arrange for foreign and domestic tours, can be said to be engaged in actual transportation. The person who is a freight forwarder under the law issues a bill of lading to the actual shipper of property, for which the forwarder assumes responsibility, and the forwarder in turn receives a bill of lading from the actual carrier. We have many "foreign freight forwarders" who are perhaps better described as "brokers." They may engage steamship space, look after marine insurance, clear imports through customs, and perform other services of a similar nature, but if they performed similar functions in interstate commerce, they would not qualify as freight forwarders under part IV. They are agents or middlemen in the transactions between ship-

---

ness they employ rail and water carriers and also trucks. In their railroad operations, which are the largest part of their business, their profit is derived from the spread between the carload rates under which they ship and the less-than-carload rates which the owner would have to pay. In their truck operations their profit is derived from a division of freight receipts between themselves and the truck companies." For other attempts at determining the exact nature of a freight forwarder, see Judson-Sheldon Corporation, 260 I.C.C. 473 (1945); Universal Transcontinental Corporation, 260 I.C.C. 521 (1945); Universal Carloading and Distributing Co., 260 I.C.C. 33 (1943); Howard Terminal, 260 I.C.C. 240 (1944), 260 I.C.C. 773 (1946); J. Nelson Kagarise, 260 I.C.C. 745 (1946); Pacific Coast Wholesalers Assn., 264 I.C.C. 134 (1945), 269 I.C.C. 504 (1947); Definition of Freight Consolidators, 43 M.C.C. 527 (1944).

per and carrier, and not the principals. In his relation to the actual carrier, the freight forwarder of part IV is a principal; he makes the contract of carriage in his own name. Of course, the foreign freight forwarder seldom arranges for "consolidating."

ORIGIN OF FREIGHT FORWARDING

Freight forwarding as a consolidating activity owes its origin to the difference between carload and less carload rates which railroads have long been accustomed to charge on the same commodity. The consolidator took his profit originally from the "spread" between these different rates.[4] He would charge the actual shipper something less than the less carload rate the shipper would be obliged to pay to the railroad, and he would pay the railroad the regular carload rate. The shipper would make a saving, the railroad would suffer no loss, and the forwarder, if he could secure enough traffic, would have a prosperous business. He would have overhead and office expenses to pay, but he would have no investment in actual transportation facilities, except to the extent that he provided terminal stations and performed the work of collection and delivery with his own vehicles. Often he had no such physical equipment. The shipper and consignee did their own cartage, and the railroad might furnish the space for assembling the consolidated shipments. Obviously, such a business could be carried on successfully only over routes where there was a fairly regular movement of small shipments, and of course the greater the spread between carload and less carload rates on the consolidated shipments, the greater the possibility of substantial earnings for the enterprising forwarder. One of the most profitable early forwarding operations in the United States was one which specialized in transcontinental traffic. On much of this traffic, especially household goods, the less carload rates were high, while the carload commodity rates on the same traffic were extremely low. One enterprising New York forwarder was for a time engaged in taking advantage of the "spread" between carload freight rates and parcel-post rates. He found that there was a parcel-post movement of books between publishing houses in New York and Chicago book purchasers sufficient to fill a freight car each fortnight. By consolidating the shipments, he was able to save the publishers a large amount of transportation charges, and his own margin on a consolidated car would usually be more than a thousand dollars.

MINIMUM CHARGES

It was not only because of the spread in rates that the forwarder was able to make a profit. The matter of the minimum charge on less carload

[4] Forwarders have long made use of the mixed carload rule of the freight classification, as well as of many all-commodity rates which numerous railroads have published.

shipments also permitted him to turn a few honest dollars. It will be remembered that the minimum charge, less carload, on articles having a rating first class or higher is the charge for 100 pounds first class, and the minimum charge on an article below first class is 100 pounds at the class to which it belongs. Since the forwarder too imposed a minimum charge, one can see that if he could consolidate four hundred 50-pound shipments of first-class carload freight, his earnings on the carload would be considerably greater than if each individual shipment weighed 100 pounds. Many industrial establishments take advantage themselves of the minimum weights and minimum charges prescribed in transportation tariffs. When one ships a parcel-post package, if it weighs "but in the estimation of a hair" more than the even pound, the hair is charged for as a pound. Many mail-order houses find it profitable to consolidate parcel-post packages into a single large carton and dispatch them either by post or by express to a distant zone where an agent drops them in the local post office. The savings derived from such a "forwarding" operation may amount to a large number of dollars in the course of a few years. When the local postage rates on letters was 2 cents, as compared to 3 cents on letters destined to points beyond the local post office delivery zone, a certain department store in Manhattan found that it could save a substantial sum each month by having the driver of one of its delivery trucks drop letters for Brooklyn addresses at the Brooklyn post office. The advance of the local letter rate to 3 cents put an abrupt end to the opportunity to achieve this bit of economy. Automobile manufacturers add to the profits they obtain on each car sold by taking advantage of the difference between carload and less carload rates. A car manufactured in Detroit and sold at any other place in the United States is sold F.O.B. Detroit, and the purchaser pays the established price of the car plus the less carload railway freight charges on the car from Detroit to the place where the car is purchased. It is seldom that the car manufacturer actually pays out this less carload rate for the transportation of the car. He ships by rail in carload quantities, ships over the highways in the long trucks, which take up so much room, at a charge usually less than the rail rate, or, more often still, ship the parts of many cars in carload quantities to various assembling points throughout the country. The car purchaser frequently pays a very substantial sum for "transportation" which the car manufacturer or dealer did not buy and did not pay for, though he puts it on the customer's bill just the same.

RAILROADS AND FREIGHT FORWARDERS

The early freight forwarders who acted as consolidators, and made their earnings from the "spread" between carload and less carload rates, were not looked upon with favor by the railroads. Though they were offering a service of which many shippers were glad to take advantage, and were probably saving the railroads money by making possible a more efficient use of freight cars and by bringing about a reduction in claims for loss and damage, nevertheless railroad management was inclined to regard the business as parasitic, and displayed a distinct unwillingness to afford it any encouragement or cooperation. Of course, the railroads might have regarded the express companies as they regarded the freight forwarders, but the relations between express companies and railroads were entirely different from the relations between railroads and forwarders. By the time the forwarders were getting well started, the express business had become a virtual monopoly. It was parceled out among a limited number of large companies, and each one had exclusive rights on the railroads over which it operated. Moreover, the express company shared its gross receipts with a railroad. It did not make its way, as a forwarder did, by "shaving" the margin between two different kinds of railroad rates. To a railroad, an express company did not stand in the relation of a shipper, as a forwarder did; the express company partook of the nature of a subsidiary railroad agency, performing a certain function or duty "on the shares." The present Railway Express Agency, which developed from a combination of the once well-known and powerful companies, such as the Adams, the American, Wells-Fargo, United States, Southern, and others, is now, in fact, a subsidiary railroad agency.

As the railroads increased the number of commodities upon which they quoted different rates for carload and less carload shipments, the freight forwarding business flourished and expanded. Railroad animosity against it continued to grow, as the forwarder traffic increased in volume. The forwarder was regarded as a competitor, as well as a parasite, and the railroad industry began to take steps by which it hoped to crush the "viper" which it had "nourished in its bosom." In 1899, a rule was introduced into the Official Classification which stated that carload shipments would be accepted only when the "consignor or consignee is the actual owner of the property." Another rule declared that shipments tendered by a freight forwarder would be accepted only when the names of the individual consignors and consignees were declared. The property would be billed as separate shipments and the less carload rate applied to each consignment. At about the same time, the express companies, which had long charged lower rates on so-called "bulk" shipments, declared that these rates would not apply on bulk shipments which were in fact "consolidations" of several small shipments belonging not to the nominal consignors but to a number of different shippers or consignees.

For a time, little effort seems to have been made to enforce the provisions of these rules and regulations. But after the enactment of the Hepburn Amendment in 1906, the carriers decided that if they were to be held to the letter of the law in their own operations they would endeavor to hold their customers also to the letter of the law. A freight forwarding company in Chicago shipped three carloads of consolidated freight to New York. The delivering railroad collected the less carload charges on each individual consignment. About the same time Wells, Fargo and Company enforced its rule with respect to bulk shipments against a California forwarding establishment. The forwarders, in both instances, appealed to the Interstate Commerce Commission, which handed down decisions in both cases on the same day in June, 1908.[5] It can readily be seen that if the controversy in these cases finally had been resolved in favor of the carriers, the freight forwarding business of the United States would have come to an abrupt and untimely end.

INTERSTATE COMMERCE COMMISSION ON FREIGHT FORWARDING

A majority of the Commission decided, however, that a carrier could not properly look beyond goods tendered to it for transportation to the "ownership of the shipment." The forwarding agent was just as much entitled to make use of a published carload rate as any other shipper, and the ownership of the property was none of the business of the railroad or the express company. By its refusal to permit the forwarder to take advantage of the lower carload rate, the railroad was violating the second section of the Interstate Commerce Act, which sternly forbade the unequal treatment of shippers. In both cases, there was a vigorous dissenting opinion, joined in by Commissioners Knapp and Harlan. Harlan, who wrote the dissent in the Wells-Fargo case, took the position that a carrier could not be required to provide sustenance for a competitor. Moreover, he observed, freight forwarding ought to be discouraged, since "it is not an economically sound proposition to interpose a new factor in transportation between the shipper and the carrier." He apparently forgot that to be consistent he should have suggested the abolition of all express companies, since they too were a factor in transportation between the shipper and the actual carrier, just as much as a forwarder was.

The dissent in the other case, written by Chairman Knapp, was a long and closely reasoned argument, in which he called upon numerous precedents in English and American law and jurisprudence to confirm his opinion that the railroads and express companies were acting entirely within their rights when they refused to accept the consolidated shipments of freight forwarders as single shipments.

The decisions of the Commission were promptly appealed to the courts. The Circuit Court of the United States for the Southern District of New York declared the Commission to have been wrong and invalidated its decision. The court did not write an opinion, merely saying that it ac-

[5] California Commercial Association v. Wells, Fargo & Co., 14 I.C.C. 422 (1908); Export Shipping Co. v. Wabash R.R., 14 I.C.C. 437 (1908).

cepted *in toto* the lengthy and brilliant dissent of which Chairman Knapp had been the author. The Commission then appealed to the Supreme Court, which considered not only the railroad case, upon which the appeal was made, but the express case as well.

The Supreme Court reversed the lower court, and upheld the decision reached by the majority of the Commission.[6] Said Chief Justice White, who delivered the opinion of the Court:

The contention that a carrier when goods are tendered to him for transportation can make the mere ownership of the goods the test of the duty to carry . . . is so in conflict with the obvious and elementary duty resting upon a carrier, and so destructive of the rights of shippers as to demonstrate the unsoundness of the proposition by the mere statement.

The decision of the Commission that the rules adopted by the carriers were unduly discriminatory against the forwarders was, according to the Court, a "finding of fact," and it was the settled policy of the Court that no such finding, when based upon properly received and competent evidence, should be set aside. In a number of subsequent cases, the Court reaffirmed, in unmistakable language, that as far as a railroad was concerned, a freight forwarder had the same standing as any other carload shipper.[7]

FREIGHT FORWARDING AND THE MOTOR VEHICLE

Impregnably intrenched behind the decisions of Commission and Court, the forwarding business continued to thrive, though for a time there was nothing spectacular about its growth. After the First World War, however, when the motor truck began to come into its own as a facility for the transportation of local and intercity freight, the freight forwarding

[6] Interstate Commerce Commission v. Delaware, Lackawanna & Western R.R., 220 U.S. 235 (1911).

[7] See Great Northern Ry. v. O'Connor, 232 U.S. 508 (1914); Lehigh Valley R.R. v. United States, 243 U.S. 444 (1927). In the first of these cases, a woman had turned over some household furniture to a forwarding company which had shipped the goods under a "released value rate." The shipment was destroyed, and the owner, who declared that the forwarder had neglected to follow shipping instructions, sued for "full value" and got a judgment for the amount of damage claimed in the state courts of Minnesota. The Supreme Court reversed the judgment. The actual carrier did not have to look "beyond the shipper" as to the character of the property shipped, and the owner's remedy, if any, was against the forwarder. The second case indicated that the freight forwarder was not only being accepted by carriers, but was regarded with a measure of esteem. The Lehigh Valley was paying both a salary and a commission to a forwarder for the privilege of being the exclusive carrier of the forwarder's consolidated shipments. The Court declared that such an arrangement constituted an illegal rebate, that it was not an "allowance," since the forwarder performed no necessary part of the actual "carriage."

business entered a period of rapid expansion. Gross receipts began to compare favorably with the gross receipts of the railway express business. The motor vehicle was an instrument admirably adapted to the forwarder's needs. With it, he could perform local collection and delivery service with much greater speed and facility, and since the rail movement of the forwarder's traffic in solid carloads meant greater safety, greater speed, and greater certainty, a very large number of shippers soon found that it was more to their advantage to turn their small shipments over to a forwarder for transportation than to endeavor to deal directly with a railroad for the transportation of less carload freight. The freight congestion and the refusal of railroads for many years to establish a pickup and delivery service, which we discussed in a previous chapter, favored greatly the development of freight forwarding activity. Like all other transportation agencies, the forwarder fell upon woeful times during the long years of economic depression which came in the wake of the financial collapse of 1929. But even during the depression, the forwarding business showed a tendency to hold its own, since it offered many shippers an opportunity to make a saving in transportation charges, and in those days all shippers were on the lookout for any and all means of reducing their costs of operation and distribution to the lowest point possible.

RAILROAD CONTROL OF FREIGHT FORWARDING

The railroads, which had once looked upon freight forwarding with disapproval and disdain, now began to regard it with a feeling of envy, tinged to some degree with a feeling of hope. Since the forwarders were performing a service which was obviously welcome to the shipping public, and since the railroads did not want to establish a door-to-door service of their own, why should they not try at least to build up their own receipts by encouraging and cooperating with the forwarders? Here was one way in which a railroad might compete successfully with the motor vehicle, whose star was steadily rising. The thought behind the new carrier attitude was doubtless a good one, but unhappily the establishment of a working partnership between forwarder and railroad soon led to the development of numerous abuses, which brought both forwarders and railroads into disrepute. Favored forwarders began to receive "special" privileges from certain railroads in the way of free terminal space and preferred movement of cars. Jealousy among forwarders soon created dissension. Since the forwarder was subject to no regulation as far as rates and services were concerned, unduly discriminatory rates and practices began to develop, which though arising in connection with rail transportation, were not subject to legal condemnation because they were manipulated indirectly through forwarders.

The forwarder quickly became an agency by means of which rival railroads joined in a vigorous competitive struggle for the purpose of securing a larger share of less carload rail business as well as of the business which was showing a tendency to abandon the railroad for the motor truck. Some of the leading railroads, deeming it necessary, for the consolidation of their position, to cement more closely their alliances with favored forwarders, took the step of buying up control of some of the larger, well-established carloading companies. They did not do it directly, but through the device of holding companies. As Commissioner Eastman said, "Attempts have been made to conceal or disguise the control by the childish humbuggery in which lawyers indulge for the purpose of confusing the courts, but which does not deceive those in practical contact with the situation." [8]

It was often a matter of indifference to the controlling railroad whether the forwarding company itself made any money or not. Since the railroad was in fact the owner of the business, any net revenue of the forwarder merely meant taking money from one pocket and putting it in another. The forwarding company became little more than a competitive weapon in the struggle for a lion's share of less carload freight, and in the rough-and-tumble scramble it soon came about that many shippers who turned their freight over to forwarders were obtaining what amounted to carload rates on less carload shipments. At the same time, the shippers who tendered less carload freight directly to the railroads were compelled to pay the full less carload charges. Undue discrimination—but undue discrimination contrived in such a fashion that it could not for a time be corrected by existing law—became a common practice in a number of large commercial and industrial centers. Some of the persons who suffered most cruelly from this new dispensation, who were not even mentioned in the subsequent investigation of the freight forwarding business by the Interstate Commerce Commission, were men who had employed their capital, ability, and industry to found carloading companies and build up their business. Forwarding companies under railroad domination ceased to make any profits, and their founders and organizers saw their investment lose all its former value; some of them were even "frozen out" of their positions with the companies they had founded, and had to go elsewhere to find employment for their talents.

FREIGHT FORWARDING INVESTIGATION OF 1938

Conditions finally became so notorious in the freight forwarding industry that the Commission, on its own initiative, undertook a thorough investigation of the business.[9] The Commission had no authority, of course, to

[8] Freight Forwarding Investigation, 229 I.C.C. 201, 321 (1938).

[9] The Commission was well aware of some of the abuses in the freight forwarding business, and in its annual report for 1930 had recommended regulation. Similar recommendations were made in its annual reports for 1931, 1936, and 1937.

investigate the forwarding companies as such, but they had ample authority to investigate all railroad corporations and all phases of their relationships with the carloading concerns. After a series of hearings held at many places throughout the country, the Commission issued a report of more than two hundred pages, in which it described the forwarding business as it was being conducted at the time and made various recommendations as to what action should be taken to eliminate some of the abuses found to exist.[10] A great many forwarding companies welcomed the investigation, especially those which were not under railroad control and which were finding the going hard in competition with companies in which direct profits from forwarder operation were a matter of little or no moment.

We shall not attempt to analyze or even summarize the Commission's long and exhaustive report. Suffice it to say, the Commission had no difficulty in reaching the conclusion that certain railroads:

(1) [are] rendering the public a service, by indirection, which is unauthorized by tariffs on file, (2) are collecting and receiving a different compensation for the transportation of such forwarder freight than the rates and charges specified in governing tariffs, in violation of section 6 of the act, (3) are charging and collecting from some shippers a different compensation than from others for substantially like transportation services, in violation of section 2 of the act.

The Commission adhered to its previously established opinion that the forwarder, in its relation to rail lines, was a shipper, but asserted that if the railroads did not voluntarily modify their practices with respect to forwarding so that all shippers of less carload traffic would receive equal treatment, the existing abuses should be corrected by the enactment of appropriate legislation designed to prevent and prohibit "unreasonable, unjustly discriminatory, and unduly prejudicial rates, charges, rules and practices, and regulating specifically the relation between the forwarder and other transportation agencies."

Although the report of the Commission was not a unanimous expression of opinion, and several individual views were presented, partly concurring and partly dissenting, it was the consensus of thought among all members that freight forwarding as an independent activity should be brought to an end, and that the railroads themselves should provide a service similar to that which the forwarders were giving. Commissioner Eastman repeated, in effect, the recommendations he had made in one of his reports as Federal Coordinator of Transportation, and said that if the railroads would take the necessary steps to modify their antiquated operating prac-

---

[10] Freight Forwarding Investigation, 229 I.C.C. 201 (1938). This report was supplemented later, and a few minor changes made in the original findings and recommendations, 232 I.C.C. 175 (1939); 243 I.C.C. 53 (1941).

tices and revise their obsolete rate structure, "the forwarding companies will disappear from the scene and not need regulating." It was also the view of all members of the Commission that if the railroads did not assume the functions of existing forwarders, the business would have to be regulated and more wholesome relations established between forwarders and the carriers they patronized. The Commission had no hesitation in saying that the freight forwarder was performing a useful and highly commendable service, a service which was of great value to individual shippers and to the commerce of the country as a whole; it merely thought that the public interest would be better served if the "wheel within a wheel" setup were abandoned and the railroads assumed direct responsibility for the activities which heretofore had been within the province of the forwarder.

REGULATION OF FREIGHT FORWARDING

If railroad management heard the recommendations of the Commission with a sympathetic ear, it gave no evidence to that effect in its conduct. The rail carriers displayed no more enthusiasm for assuming the functions of the freight forwarder that they had formerly displayed for store-door delivery, coordinated rail-truck service, or any other activity which did not involve, in the most literal sense of the term, railroad and only railroad transportation. Regulation of the forwarding business, therefore, was inevitable, and with somewhat more than its customary celerity, Congress responded to the recommendations of the Commission by enacting part IV of the Interstate Commerce Act in 1942. The forwarding business passed under the jurisdiction of the Commission in a law the terms of which were similar in nearly all respects to the provisions of the first three parts of the Act, which applied to other types of carriers. The Commission soon issued rules and regulations by which the activities of freight forwarders were henceforth to be governed.[11] Railroad domination of a favored segment of the business came to an end, and the unjustly discriminatory practices which had the effect of discrediting both railroads and forwarders were perforce abandoned. Part IV was amended in minor particulars in 1943, 1945, and 1946, primarily to take care of the joint arrangement freight forwarders might make with carriers subject to the first three parts of the Interstate Commerce Act.

Freight forwarding has continued, then, as an independent business activity, and its functions have not been absorbed by the railroads or by motor vehicle carriers. Some of the forwarders also arrange for the consolidation of shipments which are transported by air, in both domestic and foreign commerce. The leading air transportation companies tried at one

---

[11] See Consolidating of Shipments by Forwarders, 256 I.C.C. 305 (1943); Bills of Lading of Freight Forwarders, 259 I.C.C. 277 (1944); Terminal to Terminal Charges of Liberty Motor Freight Lines, Inc., 44 M.C.C. 591 (1945).

time to organize their own "forwarding company," and withhold plane-load rates from independent forwarders, but the Civil Aeronautics Board eyed this attempt to establish a monopoly in much the same manner that the Interstate Commerce Commission, years previously, had regarded the efforts of the railroads to destroy the forwarding business by rules providing that traffic would be accepted only from the owners of the shipments tendered.

FREIGHT FORWARDERS AND SHIPPERS

It may have been just as well that the railroads did not follow the Commission's suggestion that they take over the work of the freight forwarders. The shipper of small lots of merchandise is likely to get more consideration and more careful treatment of his business from a forwarder than he does from a railroad or any other carrier. While to the actual shipper the forwarder is a carrier, the forwarder is nevertheless himself a shipper in his dealings with the carriers which perform the actual transportation of forwarder traffic. The forwarder seems to have the attitude of the shipper rather than of the carrier, regardless of his dual character. He seems to give more sympathetic consideration to the traffic problems of the actual shipper than a railroad or any other carrier seems to give. In fact, one reason which many shippers have for turning their business over to a forwarder is that the forwarder readily and cheerfully gives reliable, expert advice on traffic and transportation problems, not only in connection with forwarder traffic but in connection with the traffic going directly to a carrier. For some reason, a forwarder seems to handle loss and damage claims more expeditiously and with less controversy and argument than does a railroad or other carrier. The "extra" services, the courtesy services, which a forwarder gives to its customers have proved to be of such value to shippers, and are regarded so highly, that recent years have witnessed a somewhat remarkable change in the charges which forwarders make for their services. Whereas the forwarder once obtained his profits from the difference between less carload and carload rates, we now find that the forwarders in some parts of the country actually charge the shipper more on a less carload shipment than the shipper would have to pay if he dealt directly with a carrier. Shippers seem willing to pay an extra sum because of the greater amount of personal attention their shipments receive, because the transportation service is faster and safer when obtained through a forwarder, and because the forwarder is always ready to offer counsel and guidance in connection with many kinds of traffic problems. The forwarder has made a real place for himself in the business of the physical distribution of the products of American industry.

Freight forwarding is an interesting kind of business, and it has had an interesting history. One cannot escape the conclusion that it persists and thrives because it performs a highly useful function, because it does something which shippers want and are willing to pay for. It is a good illustration of the truth that in America opportunity in business enterprise consists, more than anything else, of the ability to discern a public or private need and the initiative, ambition, and industry necessary to supply that need. It is not necessary, in order to achieve success in business, to resort to unethical practices. One often wonders why some business interests willfully persist in conduct which violates the spirit if not the letter of the law, in conduct morally so indefensible that the public, in self-defense, is obliged to take steps to render it punishable by law. It is a peculiar fact that more often than not the persons who shriek the loudest about the "intolerable" bureaucracy in Washington are the ones who, more than anyone else, have been responsible for its creation.

CHAPTER XXI

Regulation of Transportation by the Federal Government

Throughout all the preceding chapters of this work, we have had occasion to speak many times of the Interstate Commerce Act and the Interstate Commerce Commission, of other regulatory measures and administrative bodies, and of courts, through which the policies of Congress with respect to the great transportation industry have been given effect, have been interpreted, and have been applied. It is the purpose of this chapter to give a brief historical review of the origin and development of transportation regulation by our Federal government. There will unavoidably be some repetition of what has previously been said, but an effort will be made to keep the repetition to a minimum. For example, the constitutional questions involved in the legislative regulation of transportation have already received adequate consideration and will not be discussed further, but some attention will be given to the attitude toward the Commission which our courts have adopted over the years. We shall not discuss in detail all the various amendments of the legislative measures which Congress has enacted in giving expression to transportation policy, but we shall devote the inquiry primarily to the great landmarks of legislation, administration, and court review, the events and actions by which our transportation policy was molded and brought to its present form.

In the chapters immediately following, there will be given, in outline form, the provisions of the four parts of the Interstate Commerce Act and of the Civil Aeronautics Act, with special attention only to the provisions which are of prime importance to the industrial traffic manager. A final chapter will deal with the organization of the Interstate Commerce Commission, its methods of administration, and the rules of procedure it has adopted for the guidance of those who appeal to it either by written communication or by personal appearance.

INTERSTATE COMMERCE ACT REGULATES TRANSPORTATION

Before starting out on the brief historical survey, it might be well to explain away certain misconceptions concerning our transportation laws and their administration which, over the years, seem to have gained a measure of acceptance. One of these misconceptions is a belief that our transportation laws have been written for the regulation of both carriers and shippers. The fact that the leading law has been known throughout its history as the Interstate Commerce Act, though its technical title before 1920 was the Act to Regulate Commerce, has led some people to think that it has for its purpose the control and regulation of commerce, in the ordinary sense of the word, and that it has to do with all the operations of trade and exchange, of which transportation is only a part, albeit a highly important part. There is no foundation for a belief of this kind. It may have arisen because of the name which Congress gave the law. The name was probably chosen because the Constitution says quite plainly that Congress shall have the right to regulate "commerce with foreign nations, and among the several States and with the Indian tribes," but it does not say that Congress shall have the right to regulate transportation. The founding fathers could not have included in the original Constitution a provision saying that Congress should have the right to regulate railroads, since, at the time the document was framed in Philadelphia, it is doubtful if more than a half-dozen members of the convention had ever given any thought to the possibility of the application of steam power to transportation, either by water or by land. Though Chief Justice John Marshall declared in 1824 that "transportation" was "commerce,"[1] it could not be denied that there was a large part of commerce which most certainly was not transportation. In 1887, Congress apparently wanted to take no chances on the matter of technical definitions. Since that time, the term "interstate commerce" has been stretched to include a great many activities which were once thought not to be included in its scope, and Congress has not had to tread so gingerly. Indeed, beginning with the law enacted in 1920, Congress has given the name "transportation act" to the chief amendments of the Interstate Commerce Act, distinguishing between them by giving the dates of their enactment; of course, there was no pretense that the Motor Carrier Act or the Civil Aeronautics Act was anything but a law for the regulation of a particular variety of transportation.

That is just what all the legislation under consideration here has been. It has been legislation for the regulation of the business of transportation, of the carriage of persons and property from place to place, and not for the regulation of those operations of trade and exchange, of buying and selling, to which the term "commerce" is much more generally applied than it is to the business of transportation. The Interstate Commerce Act was not framed to control the activities of shippers. In only a few parts of the law are shippers admonished to refrain from certain actions or to perform certain actions; the law is addressed almost entirely to carriers. It was originally passed to give shippers a measure of protection against objectionable practices in which our railroads had long freely indulged, and though the law has been modified over the years for the purpose of

[1] Gibbons v. Ogden, 9 Wheat. 1 (1824).

giving railroads and other surface carriers aid, support, and encouragement in their operations, the primary and pervading purpose of the law is to regulate the business of transportation so that shippers will not be subjected to unreasonable or unjustly discriminatory rates or practices and so that the internal commerce of the country shall flow smoothly and freely, unimpeded by arbitrary actions on the part of those who manage and direct the transportation industry. Even the Civil Aeronautics Act, which goes so much further than the Interstate Commerce Act in providing for "promotional" work, which will serve to encourage the development and growth of civil aviation, consists very largely of provisions designed to effectuate the "economic regulation" of the industry, by giving shippers and travelers the same kind of protection against carriers by air that they receive in the Interstate Commerce Act against carriers by land and water.

COMMISSION NOT A RATE BUREAU

Another misconception, and this one is for some reason more common than the preceding one, has to do with the functions of the Interstate Commerce Commission. It is surprising to find how widespread is the belief that the Interstate Commerce Commission is a sort of glorified carrier traffic department, and that it "makes" all the rates which our surface carriers charge. Many people seem to think that the Interstate Commerce Commission must either prescribe the rates which railroads charge or set its seal of approval on all these rates. Nothing could be further from the truth. There are thousands—hundreds of thousands—of rates to which the Commission never gave any direct consideration, which were never subjected to close scrutiny by the Commission. They were made by the carriers, published and filed according to law, and put into effect as provided by statute, without any affirmative action whatever on the part of the Commission. Of course, when the Commission issues an order permitting a general percentage increase or ordering a general percentage decrease in all rates, both class and commodity, it may be said that it is "making" all the rates charged by the railroads, but we are thinking here not of general increases or decreases but of the rates which are made and applied to individual articles of traffic.

It is not the business of the Commission to act as a rate-making agency for the carriers under its jurisdiction. Its function is not to originate and promulgate rates. Its function with respect to rates may be said to be "correctional." It modifies rates which, because of some complaint by a shipper or because of an investigation it has itself initiated, it finds are violative of those provisions of the Interstate Commerce Act which forbid unreasonable or unduly discriminatory rates. Only once, in the history of railroad regulation, has the Interstate Commerce Commission ever been directed to take the "initiative" in rate making. In the original Act to Regulate Commerce, the Commission had no rate-making power; in the Act as amended by the Hepburn Law of 1906, if the Commission found any rate to be unreasonable or unjustly discriminatory, it had power to prescribe a maximum reasonable rate or one which would remove the discrimination. In other words, its function was purely a corrective function. But in the Transportation Act of 1920, which added section 15a to the Interstate Commerce Act, Congress said that "in the exercise of its power to prescribe just and reasonable rates the Commission shall initiate, modify, establish or adjust such rates" so that the carriers might earn a fair return upon the value of their property devoted to transportation service. In the Transportation Act of 1933, this famous "rule of rate making" was repealed. The Commission was still authorized, when it found a rate to be unreasonable or unduly discriminatory, to prescribe a rate which would correct the injustice, but "in the exercise of its power to prescribe just and reasonable rates" the Commission was no longer directed to "initiate," "modify," or "adjust" rates in such a way as to give the carriers any particular rate of return. It was not directed to initiate, modify, or adjust rates in any fashion whatever. It was simply told that in the exercise of its correctional authority over rates, it should give "due consideration, among other factors, to the effect of rates on the movement of traffic by the carrier or carriers for which the rates are prescribed; to the need, in the public interest, of adequate and efficient railway transportation at the lowest cost consistent with the furnishing of such service; and to the need of revenues sufficient to enable carriers, under honest, economical and efficient management, to provide such service." The "initiative" in rate making was restored to the carriers, where it had been before 1920. This does not mean that the Commission, if it believes rates to be unduly high or unduly low, may not take the initiative in bringing about a proper readjustment. It is simply no longer under a "mandate" to take the initiative. If there is no complaint or petition from shipper or carrier, and if the Commission is not of the opinion that the rate situation is such as to demand initial action on its part, it is not required or obliged by law to make any changes in the level of rates for the purpose of having it conform to some particular design or pattern. With respect to rates on individual articles, the Commission has never been required to act on its own initiative. If it chooses to do so, it has the necessary authority, and of course it must always act on a shipper's complaint. As indicated before, however, there are many individual rates upon which the Commission has never taken any action whatever.

It is because of the existence of many rates which are not made by the Commission, as well as the existence of rates which the Commission has made, together with the existence of the Commission's power to suspend proposed changes in rates, that appeals of railroads for a general, across-the-board increase of rates are usually handled as they are by the Commission. The railroads have the right, in the case of rates upon which the Commission has not passed judgment, to file notices of increase. Unless the Commission interposes a suspension order, the rates become effective within the statutory time limit of thirty days. But with respect to rates which the Commission has ordered into effect as the maximum charges to be collected by the railroads, the carriers naturally cannot at once file notices of increases. Consequently, a notice of a general increase of all rates cannot always be filed. Even if it were possible to do so, the chances are that the Commission would issue a suspension order, and conduct an investigation of the proposed changes before permitting them to become effective. There is a time limit upon the duration of a suspension order of seven months, and if the investigation is not completed by that time, the carriers may put the proposed rates into effect. But in case the Commission has not completed its investigation within the statutory period, or sees that it cannot do so, it can order the carriers to keep a strict account of all monies collected under any increased rates, and if they are eventually found to be unreasonable may order the carriers to return the amounts collected from shippers in excess of reasonable rates. The bookkeeping task which carriers would confront in the face of such an order is sufficiently formidable so that they have refrained from any attempt to give effect to proposed increases of rates concerning which the Commission has not had the necessary time to complete its investigation.

EX PARTE PROCEEDINGS

Because of the trying and time-consuming difficulties which the carriers would have to meet in the event of an attempt to make a general increase of rates simply by filing new schedules, and going through the long-drawn-out process which would follow an investigation and suspension order, it has become customary for them, when feeling the need of raising the general level of their charges, to appear before the Commission and request permission in advance to file desired percentage increases. The Commission will then undertake an investigation of an *ex parte* nature, though objections and protests against proposed increases may be invited, received, and considered during the course of the investigation. At the conclusion of its deliberations, the Commission may refuse the carriers permission to file their proposed schedules of increased rates, it may give them permission to file schedules in which all proposed advances of rates are included, or it may permit the filing of schedules in which only a part of the proposed increases appears. During the inflationary period which has come in the wake of the Second World War, the railroads have appealed frequently to the Commission for permission to make general increases in their rates. They have seldom met with refusal, though they have seldom secured in the first instance all they asked for.

PRESIDENT CLEVELAND AND THE ACT OF 1887

When the Act to Regulate Commerce passed both houses of Congress in 1887 and was submitted to President Cleveland, he signed it with much trepidation. Although he had taken notice of the transportation problem with which our agricultural and industrial interests were confronted, he realized that the law which had been enacted for the control of railroads represented a new departure in American political policy and practice. It was not only the first Federal statute for the regulation of transportation enterprise; it was the first law which Congress had enacted for the regulation of any kind of purely private enterprise. Laws had been passed for the regulation of banking, but from almost the beginning of our national history, banking had not been regarded as a private enterprise. The first and second United States banks had not only been creatures of Congress; they had been owned in part by the government of the United States, and representatives of the government sat upon their boards of directors. The Act to Regulate Commerce did not mean that the government was to participate either in the ownership or in the management of our railroads, but it did mean that for the first time an administrative commission or bureau was to have a voice in the guidance and control of a private business undertaking. The Act really marked the beginning of a fourth branch of our government, a branch created not by the Constitution, as the other three branches had been created, but created by a legislative act of Congress. What worried President Cleveland was not so much this beginning, which he recognized as more or less necessary in the interests of our national economy, but what this beginning should lead to in the way of administrative control of all forms of business enterprise. Needless to say, there are many persons who believe that his fears and suspicions were more than justified.

THE ACT'S RECEPTION

While the new law was warmly welcomed by agricultural interests and certain industrial interests, it was severely criticized by the more conservative section of the press and in numerous financial periodicals. The constitutionality of the entire Act was widely questioned, on the grounds that it represented a delegation by Congress of power which under the Constitution Congress alone could exercise, that the Commission was clothed with judicial power which the Constitution vested in "one Supreme Court, and in such inferior courts as Congress shall from time to time ordain and establish," that it violated the Seventh Amendment of the Constitution by denying the "right of a trial by jury" in suits subject to common-law proceedings, and that its effect might be, under certain conditions, to give preference by regulation of commerce to the ports of one state over the ports of another. John R. Dos Passos, a leading member of the New York bar, summarized his criticism of the law by saying: "It is the first attempt on the part of Congress to concentrate into the hands of a Commission powers that are at once judicial, commercial and inquisitorial, and the decision of the Supreme Court of the United States upon this important subject will be awaited with the most intense anxiety and interest by the people of the United States." [2]

It is a noteworthy fact that, although the Supreme Court gave many "interpretations" of the Interstate Commerce Act which were somewhat at variance with the meaning which several members of Congress, members of the Interstate Commerce Commission, and others thought the language of the law to have, it has never at any time declared any part of the law to be in violation of any part of the Federal Constitution. In entrusting an administrative body with the duty of applying the general rules laid down in the Act, even though the administrative body was given a fairly wide area within which to employ administrative discretion, Congress was neither "abdicating" nor "delegating" its own constitutional authority. On several other occasions, similar "delegations" of authority by Congress have been challenged, but the Supreme Court has uniformly held that when Congress establishes the rules or, as it were, sets the metes and bounds, within which a duly created administrative or executive authority may operate, it is acting within the boundaries of its constitutional powers.

Mr. Dos Passos was entirely right when he declared that the "most important portion of the Inter-State Commerce Act" was the part "which relates to the creation of the Commission, and its general functions and powers." The Commission represented a new departure in our system of government. Although the law declared that rates must be "reasonable" and not "unduly discriminatory," these provisions merely meant that long-standing rules of common law were at last embodied in a statute. It was in the means adopted for administering, for enforcing, the law that Congress was injecting something new and untried into the framework of the Federal government. It was so new that Mr. Dos Passos felt impelled to say:

A study of the powers of the Commission shows that Congress has clothed it with more important and extensive judicial attributes than have ever been conferred upon any tribunal created under the laws of the Federal Government. The Commission becomes, under the Act, not only a suitor or party, but it is a

[2] John R. Dos Passos, "The Inter-state Commerce Act" (1887), p. 99.

judge in its own causes. It not only possesses all the powers of a petit jury, but has conferred upon it all the inquisitorial attributes of a grand jury.

STANDING OF THE COMMISSION

But the Commission came into being despite the fears that, if it were not destroyed by the courts, its creation would mark the beginning of the disintegration of constitutional law and government in the United States. It still abides, with powers so vastly increased over the years that it is without doubt the most powerful and influential administrative body ever established in the United States or in any other country possessing a constitutional form of government.

The Commission, of course, is a creature of Congress. It came into existence by virtue of a law duly enacted by Congress and signed by the President. It could be abolished in the same manner in which it was created. Moreover, its powers are strictly limited by law, either the law under which it was created or other laws which give it additional authority. Just as Congress can exercise only such power as it is duly authorized to exercise by the Constitution of the United States, so can the Commission exercise only such power as is duly conferred upon it by statute. Because of the lack of precision in the use of words, or because of the lack of precise and exact definitions of all words, we have never been entirely sure of the meaning of various parts of our Constitution and of our statutes, and many times the Supreme Court has been called upon to deal with problems arising largely from linguistic difficulties. We have noted previously that the Supreme Court has interpreted the meaning of the word "transportation," as used in the Interstate Commerce Act, in such manner that the Commission found itself possessed of authority which it was not sure it had. In the same way, Congress and the President have frequently found that their powers, under the Constitution, were sometimes more and frequently less than they had thought them to be before the Supreme Court had its say about the matter. One may not always be sure that any point of difference is definitely settled, however, for the Supreme Court may, and occasionally does, change its collective mind. The minority opinion of today may become the majority opinion of tomorrow.

There is one advantage which an administrative body such as the Interstate Commerce Commission has over Congress if its powers are called into question before the Court. Once the Court decides that Congress has taken action in excess of its constitutional powers, unless the Court changes its mind, it takes an amendment of the Constitution to give Congress any power denied it by the Court. In the case of the Interstate Commerce Commission or of any other similar administrative tribunal, any power which the Court declares to have been unlawfully exercised—so long as it is not a power the exercise of which is forbidden by the Constitution—may be given to it by a simple legislative enactment. The enactment of a law by Congress is a much easier process than the amendment of the Federal Constitution.

As a matter of fact, many of the obstacles which the Commission has met, in its endeavors to regulate the transportation industry, obstacles created largely by judicial action, have been effectively removed by acts of Congress. The story of the development of the Interstate Commerce Act from the form in which it was passed in 1887 to its present form is in large measure the story of amendments passed to fill unsuspected gaps or loopholes in the law, a great many of which were brought to light in court proceedings. The Act has been amended and added to almost fifty times since it first became a law in 1887. During the same period of time, the Federal Constitution has been amended seven times, and one of the amendments had for its purpose the repeal of another of the seven.

THE COURTS AND THE ACT OF 1887

It did not take the Interstate Commerce Commission long to find out that the law by which it was created did not vest it with as much authority as both Congress and the Commission thought it possessed. Since the Commission had the right, under the statute, to declare a rate unreasonable or unduly discriminatory, it blandly assumed that it had the complementary right of naming the rate which would take the place of a rate found to be violative of the law. But when the Supreme Court scanned the various sections of the law, it could not find—and neither could anybody else— a single phrase which gave the Commission any authority to name a rate which a railroad was obliged to charge.[3] It has been explained in a previous chapter how the "weasel words" of the fourth section deprived it of any vitality,[4] and it must be added that the interpretation which the courts gave to the second and the third sections rendered them as ineffectual, for regulative purposes, as the fourth section. The Commission could assert, as often as it chose to do so, that certain rates were unreasonable or unduly discriminatory, but it had no power to prescribe rates which in its judgment were reasonable and not unduly discriminatory.

While the failure of the law to give the Commission any corrective power with respect to rates was its greatest—in fact, its fatal—defect, in

[3] Cincinnati, New Orleans & Texas Pacific Ry. v. Interstate Commerce Commission, 162 U.S. 184 (1896); Interstate Commerce Commission v. Cincinnati, New Orleans & Texas Pacific Ry., 167 U.S. 479 (1897). In denying the Commission the authority to make rates for the future, the Court said, "It is one thing to inquire whether rates which have been charged and collected are reasonable—that is a judicial act; but an entirely different thing to prescribe rates which shall be charged in the future—that is a legislative act."

[4] Cincinnati, New Orleans & Texas Pacific Ry. v. Interstate Commerce Commission, 162 U.S. 184 (1896).

so far as effective regulation of railroad charges was concerned, the law was also lamentably weak because of the procedure the Commission was compelled to follow. Its orders were not binding on the railroads to which they were addressed. The Commission might find a certain rate to be unreasonable or unduly discriminatory. Although it could not correct the unlawful rate, it could order the offending carrier to cease charging a rate thought by the Commission to be unlawful. The railroad served with such an order could figuratively thumb its nose at the Commission with undisguised impunity. It was not obliged to obey and suffered no penalty for disobedience. The only thing the Commission could do was to go to a Federal court and seek an order from the court directing the recalcitrant carrier to obey the Commission's command. Here the Commission, in its early days, met with another extremely trying obstacle to any attempt it might make to see that the law requiring rates to be reasonable and not unduly discriminatory was given the effect which Congress doubtless intended it should have. It was the practice of the courts to which the Commission appealed for enforcement orders to give little or no heed to the record of the case which had been compiled at the hearings before the Commission. Instead, the case was heard *de novo* before the court. Under such circumstances, it became the custom of railroads hauled up before the Commission for violation of the Act to Regulate Commerce to put in merely a *pro forma* appearance and save all pertinent and relevant testimony for presentation in court. This frequently put the Commission in an embarrassing and even a ridiculous position. But this was not the only thing the courts did to hamper the work it was hoped the Commission would be able to do. The court would accept no "finding of fact" which the Commission had made, and freely substituted its own judgment for that of the Commission on all matters under dispute. Under such conditions, it would obviously have been a time-saving procedure for a shipper to go to a court in the first instance with any complaint about the unreasonable or discriminatory character of a railroad rate.

By 1897, the Interstate Commerce Act was virtually a dead letter. The Commission collected statistics and made annual reports in which it set forth its recommendations for the improvement of the law, but as an agency before which a shipper could secure the redress of any wrongs due to railroad violations of the law, the Commission was virtually impotent. The southern basing point system took on the appearance of immutability, the intermountain shippers complained in vain about their grossly discriminatory freight rates, and the more powerful shippers of the country enjoyed rebates and other unjustly discriminatory practices which became more pronounced and more obnoxious with each passing year.

THE ELKINS ACT OF 1903

Oddly enough, it was the railroads themselves which made the first breach in what appeared to be a legislative log jam. They finally grew weary of seeing their revenues dissipated by the payment of enormous rebates to large and powerful shippers. They were not in a position abruptly to refuse to pay, however much they might have desired to do so, because a large shipper, by playing one carrier against another, was in a position to precipitate a rate war which would have been even more costly to the carriers than the pervasive custom of granting rebates. But such blackjacking practices might be stopped by adequate legislation. The determination of the railroads to bring an end, if possible, to excessive rebating found expression in the Elkins Act, which was passed by Congress in 1903. This was not an amendment to the Interstate Commerce Act. It was a separate measure directed almost solely against unjust personal discrimination in any form, whether by rebates, discounts, or other concessions. The law made the mere departure from a published railroad rate the equivalent of an unjust discrimination, punishable by a fine of not less than $1,000 or more than $20,000 for each offense; it made the receiver of a rebate equally guilty with the giver.

Few statutes have accomplished their intended purpose more effectively than the Elkins Act. It did not bring an immediate discontinuation of the vicious practice of rebating, but it had a salutary effect in that direction, which became more pronounced when the penalty of imprisonment for violation, which was omitted in 1903, was restored in 1906.[5] Much to the satisfaction of the railroads, rebating for the purpose of attracting traffic became largely unnecessary, and the elimination of special favors to large shippers was also a source of gratification to many shippers who had suf-

[5] It was under the Elkins Act that the Standard Oil Company of Indiana was fined $29,240,000 by Judge Kenesaw Mountain Landis of the Federal District Court for the Northern District of Illinois. United States v. Standard Oil Co. of Indiana, 155 Fed. 305 (1907). Landis later became the high commissioner of professional baseball. A Federal jury in his court found the oil company guilty, under an indictment of 1902 counts (441 of which were quashed by the judge), of shipping numerous carloads of oil from Whiting, Indiana, to St. Louis at an unfiled rate of 6½ cents a hundred pounds, when the published and filed rate was almost three times as much. The Circuit Court of Appeals reversed the verdict on the grounds that certain evidence, which might have shown that the company did not know that the rate paid was not properly filed, was excluded from the jury, and because the fine imposed was for each separate carload shipped at the illegal rate instead of each separate "shipment." One of the appellate judges, in a concurring opinion, held that there was no evidence of "intent" to violate the law. Standard Oil Co. of Indiana v. United States, 164 Fed. 376 (1908). The case was remanded for retrial. The Supreme Court refused the government a writ of certiorari for which it petitioned. 212 U.S. 579 (1909). The Department of Justice did not seek to retry the case.

fered gross injuries because of the disparity between their rates and those granted to their overgrown competitors.

THE HEPBURN ACT OF 1906

Although the Elkins law tended to bring to an end the practice which railroads had so long followed of granting unjustly discriminatory rates and other concessions to favored shippers, it had no effect whatever upon the practice of unjust discrimination against places, nor did it remove any of the difficulties the Commission had encountered in its efforts to give effect to that part of the Interstate Commerce Act which said that railroad rates should be "reasonable." The struggle to secure the necessary legislation to correct the defects of the law was long and bitter. It ended in at least a partial victory, not with the aid and encouragement of the railroads, but over their strenuous and extremely powerful opposition. It took all the personal prestige and political sagacity of President Theodore Roosevelt to bring about favorable action by Congress on the Hepburn Amendment to the Interstate Commerce Act, which became a law in 1906 and which was, without doubt, the most important and significant law that Congress has ever enacted for the regulation and control of business enterprise in the United States. Not only did it bring about effective regulation of the transportation industry, but it established a precedent in legislation which has served as the constitutional foundation for many other laws of a related nature.

The Hepburn Amendment made several changes in the old Act to Regulate Commerce, with two changes being of outstanding importance. The first of these new provisions authorized the Interstate Commerce Commission, if it found any rate under investigation to be unreasonable or unduly discriminatory, to prescribe another rate in its place, which should be observed as a maximum by the carrier. In other words, the Commission received the power to make railroad rates—or at least maximum railroad rates.

The second important change in the law stipulated that the orders of the Commission, except orders for the payment of money, should be of binding effect upon the carriers to which they were addressed, within a reasonable time to be determined by the Commission itself, unless modified or rescinded by the Commission, or "set aside by a court of competent jurisdiction." Heretofore the Commission had been obliged to go to court to test the legality and the validity of its orders. The Hepburn Amendment transferred the burden of initiating court action to the carriers involved. If a railroad company chose to treat an order of the Commission with brazen disregard, as formerly it could do without penalty, it found itself subject to a fine of $5,000, and each day of continuing noncompliance was regarded as a separate and distinct offense. If a carrier wanted to challenge the validity of a Commission order, it was obliged to initiate the court proceedings by which it hoped to obtain relief.

The practice which the railroads had long followed of giving free transportation in their passenger trains to editors, lawyers, judges, legislators, politicians, and others whose favors might be sought was brought to an end by the Hepburn Act, passes being confined under the law to railroad officers and employees and a few other persons. A "commodities clause" forbade railroads to transport any article which they themselves might produce or manufacture, except timber and the manufactured products thereof. The Commission received the authority necessary for full and complete control of railroad accounting practices. We have previously mentioned other important portions of the Hepburn legislation, such as the Carmack Amendment and provisions for Commission control of through routes and rates and methods of rate publication. The law increased the membership of the Commission from five to seven.

JUDICIAL REVIEW

Although the law was transformed in many respects, with nearly all changes clearly designed to give the Interstate Commerce Commission a much greater degree of control over railroad charges, it made no mention of the future relationship to be established and observed between the Commission and the courts. Were the courts to continue to act as appellate commissions, substituting their own judgment for that of the Interstate Commerce Commission if they so desired? Or were they to give the decisions of the Commission the measure of respect they should have if the body was to function in the manner which Congress obviously desired? No mention was made in the law about judicial review of Commission decisions and orders. The Federal Constitution vests the judicial power of the United States in the courts, and while Congress has the right to create new courts and indicate their field of jurisdiction, it has no right to limit or modify "judicial power," which rests on the same foundation as the power of Congress or of the President. Many leaders in business, law, and politics awaited with much interest the word the Supreme Court would speak with respect to the authority of the vitalized and enlarged administrative body. Of course, there was no lack of opinions among members of the legal profession that Congress had gone entirely too far in granting both judicial and legislative powers to the same tribunal, and it was predicted quite freely that the Supreme Court would quickly declare those parts of the law which gave the Commission rate-making power to be unconstitutional and void.[6]

___

[6] For a lucid and brilliant discussion of the constitutional as well as the economic questions involved in rate regulation by an administrative commission, one should read Walter C. Noyes, "American Railroad Rates" (1905). This work

Even before the Hepburn Act was passed, the Supreme Court had frowned upon the practice followed by lower Federal courts of admitting entirely new evidence in the review of Commission orders, declaring that all material facts should be disclosed in the hearings held by the Commission.[7] But of much greater importance was the question of how the courts were to regard the orders of the Commission. Upon what grounds should they be set aside? The Supreme Court gave a definite answer to this question in 1910,[8] stating that an order of the Commission would not be set aside unless the Commission had exceeded its constitutional or its statutory authority. Reaffirming its position two years later, the Court said:

It has been settled that the orders of the Commission are final unless (1) beyond the power which it could constitutionally exercise; or (2) beyond its statutory power; or (3) based upon a mistake of law. But questions of fact may be involved in the determination of question of law, so that an order, regular on its face, may be set aside if it appears that (4) the rate is so low as to be confiscatory and in violation of the constitutional provisions against taking property without due process of law; or (5) if the Commission acted so arbitrarily and unjustly as to fix rates contrary to evidence, or without evidence to support it; or (6) if the authority therein involved has been exercised in such an unreasonable manner as to cause it to be within the elementary rule that the substance, and not the shadow, determines the validity of the exercise of the power.[9]

These decisions and a few others of similar tenor definitely fixed the status of the Interstate Commerce Commission as an administrative body with real power and authority. It has been told in previous chapters how the Supreme Court further clarified questions about the Commission's

---

appeared at the time when Congress was earnestly, and often violently, debating various bills which finally emerged as the Hepburn Amendment. Noyes was an extremely able lawyer, the president of the New London Railroad, and at the time he wrote the book, a judge of the Court of Common Pleas in Connecticut. He was clearly of the opinion that a law authorizing an administrative commission to declare a rate unreasonable and then to name a reasonable rate to take its place would be unconstitutional. He felt, however, that some legislation was necessary to protect shippers from the unjust and unduly discriminatory rates to which they had been subjected for years. He proposed that a special court should be created which would be authorized to deal with the matter of the unreasonableness of existing rates, and a commission created to make rates for the future to take the place of rates declared by the court to be unreasonable. There are many persons who still believe that Noyes's position was legally sound. However, the Supreme Court took an opposite view.

[7] Cincinnati, New Orleans & Texas Pacific Ry. v. Interstate Commerce Commission, 162 U.S. 184 (1896).

[8] Interstate Commerce Commission v. Illinois Central R.R., 215 U.S. 452 (1910).

[9] Interstate Commerce Commission v. Union Pacific R.R., 222 U.S. 541 (1912).

authority by asserting that negative orders of the Commission were not subject to court review and that a Federal court would not pass upon the question of the reasonableness of a rate under dispute until the question had been properly submitted to the Commission to pass upon in its administrative capacity.

MANN-ELKINS ACT OF 1910

The next landmark in the legislative history of railroad regulation by commission in the United States was the enactment of the Mann-Elkins Act, in 1910. There was very little opposition to the passage of the Act, for by this time railroad regulation had been firmly established and generally accepted as a part of our government policy. It will be remembered, too, that the chief feature of the law was the result of a sort of bargain, entered into by Congress, the railroads, and the Department of Justice, under which Congress would give the Commission the authority to suspend proposed changes in rates pending an investigation as to their reasonableness, the railroads would withdraw the tariffs which they had filed calling for a general increase of 10 per cent in nearly all railroad freight rates, and the Department of Justice would withdraw the suit it had filed under the Sherman Antitrust Law to prevent the increases from taking effect.

Although the power of suspending proposed increases or rates, which the Commission received, was the most important feature of the Mann-Elkins Act, there were a few other additions to the Interstate Commerce Act which served to round out the system of Federal regulation of railroads which Congress was endeavoring to perfect. The words "under substantially similar circumstances and conditions" were erased from the fourth section, and thereafter violations of the long-and-short-haul rule of rate making could come only with the express authorization of the Commission. The powers of the Commission were clarified in a few particulars by changes which explicitly gave it the right to regulate freight classification as well as freight rates, and also the right to prescribe maximum rates after hearings held on its own initiative. Shippers finally received the unqualified right to designate the route over which their through shipments should move. A clause which was subsequently repealed required a railroad, under penalty of a fine, to give a shipper written information concerning freight rates, when a proper request was received by the carrier.

Another feature of the Act of 1910, which was included chiefly because of the desires of President Taft, was the creation of a Federal Commerce Court, to which was given the duty of trying cases involving appeals to set aside orders of the Commission. In theory, the court represented an admirable addition to the Federal judiciary, for such a court would have an expert acquaintance with the law under which the Commission operated, and the existence of a special court would serve to expedite the trial of appeals from the Commission's decisions. Unfortunately, the court did the very thing which the Supreme Court declared the Federal judiciary should not do. It presumed to act as a sort of appellate Interstate Commerce Commission, substituting its own judgment for that of the Commission on matters of fact as well as matters of law, when it chose to do so. It soon became highly unpopular with shippers and the public in general, it was not regarded with favor or admiration by the Commission, and its most important decisions were promptly and emphatically overruled by the Supreme Court. It was formally abolished after three years of troubled existence, its *coup de grâce* being due largely to the discovery that one of its members had engaged in some reprehensible financial transactions with certain railroads and coal companies, for which he was impeached by the House of Representatives, tried before the Senate, found guilty, and removed from office. The duties of the court were restored to the Federal district courts.

LEGISLATION FROM 1910 TO 1920

Between 1910 and 1917, a few additions were made to the Interstate Commerce Act, as events brought to light real or fancied weaknesses in the law. The valuation provisions were added in 1913, the Cummins Amendments came in 1915 and 1916, and the car-service regulations appeared in 1917; all of these additions have been discussed in previous chapters. In 1917, the membership of the Interstate Commerce Commission was increased from seven to nine, and since the Commission's labors had increased so enormously in volume, because of the added authority it had received in 1906 and 1910, it was authorized to organize itself into "divisions" of not less than three members each, with each division having the power of Commission, though the decisions of any division were always to be subject to review by the entire body. Other laws enacted by Congress affected the conduct of the railroad business. The Panama Canal Act of 1912 regulated the railroad control of competing carriers by water. The Clayton Antitrust Act of 1914 contained provisions designed to check the monopolization of the railroad business through the creation of so-called "interlocking directorates," or "communities of interest," and to require competitive bidding in business transactions involving more than $50,000 which a railroad should enter into with a concern in which the directors or officers of the railroad might have an interest.

TRANSPORTATION ACT OF 1920

The next important chapter in railroad regulation by the Federal government was written primarily as a result of experience with government operation of our railroads during the First World War; in fact, the law was signed by President Wilson only a couple of days before the roads were returned to their owners. There were three parts to the Transportation Act of 1920, as it was called. One part dealt with the arrangements to be made between the government and the owners of the railroads following the termination of government operation. The most important feature of this part was the guarantee of railroad income, to railroads which desired to accept it, for a period of six months following the relinquishment of the railroads by the government, during which time it was thought that the Interstate Commerce Commission could study the rate situation and initiate a system of rates which would give the railroads an adequate net return. Because advances in railroad rates had lagged far behind the advance of costs of operation during the war period, the railroads were in a desperate financial plight.

The second part of the Act represented an attempt on the part of the government to deal with future railroad labor disputes through the employment of a cumbersome organization designated as a Railway Labor Board. This feeble attempt to deal with the railroad labor problem proved to be entirely ineffectual and was repealed within six years.

The third part of the Transportation Act of 1920 consisted of amendments to the Interstate Commerce Act. It was thought at the time the law was passed that two provisions of this part were of transcendent importance, that they constituted a new charter of freedom and progress for the railroad industry. One was the fair value—fair return "rule of rate making," and the other was a clumsy and unworkable scheme for the consolidation of all the railroads of the United States into a "limited number" of great systems of fairly equal size and competitive strength. The rule of rate making, though it served as a screen behind which the Commission was able to give the carriers the largest single advance in rates they have ever enjoyed, either under unrestricted private management or under government control, was not the appropriate medicine for the illness which overtook the railroads during the great depression. It was repealed, along with the recapture clause, in 1933. The consolidation scheme proved to be conducive to widespread financial manipulation and speculation rather than to the creation of large integrated railroad systems. It, too, was quietly repealed in 1940, after a complete and convincing demonstration of its utter uselessness for the purpose for which supposedly it had been written.

There were some other amendments to the Interstate Commerce Act which proved to be highly effective, virtually all of which have been referred to with more or less detail in previous chapters. Among these were the provisions with regard to the liability of water carriers, changes in those parts of the law which dealt with routing, and slight modifications with regard to the times in which claims and suits arising out of loss and damage might be filed. The Commission received, among other additions to its power, the right to regulate intrastate rates which might have a discriminating effect on interstate commerce, the power to name minimum as well as maximum rates, and authority over the capitalization of railroads and over the construction of new lines or the abandonment of old lines. The Commission's power to suspend rates was slightly curtailed, but under such qualifications that it remained virtually unchanged if not, indeed, enhanced. The membership of the Commission was increased once more, this time to eleven, where it still remains.

The Transportation Act of 1920 changed the system of numbering which had previously been used to designate different sections and paragraphs of the Interstate Commerce Act. The system of consecutively numbered sections, with numbered subsections and lettered subdivisions of subsections, adopted in 1920, is still in use.

ACT OF 1933; MOTOR CARRIER ACT OF 1935

The Emergency Transportation Act of 1933 was a not overly successful effort to enable the railroads to weather the financial storms which came in the wake of the economic depression. Perhaps one of its most important results was the final crystallization of sentiment in favor of the Federal regulation of highway transportation. Commissioner Eastman, who was appointed Federal Coordinator of Transportation under the terms of the Act of 1933, believed such regulation to be necessary. The Motor Carrier Act, which was passed in 1935 and which is now officially part II of the Interstate Commerce Act, was framed largely along lines that he suggested in some of his reports as coordinator. We have mentioned frequently some of the terms of this law, which subjects interstate motor vehicle carriers to regulatory provisions patterned to a considerable degree after the provisions of part I, which are applicable to railroads. The provisions of the Motor Carrier Act—or of part II of the Interstate Commerce Act, as it should properly be called—will be summarized in a later chapter.

CIVIL AERONAUTICS ACT OF 1938

It was in the United States that air transportation in heavier-than-air vehicles had its origin, when Wilbur and Orville Wright made their first successful flights at Kitty Hawk, North Carolina, in 1903. It must be admitted that foreign governments and foreign business enterprise displayed a much greater interest in the early work of the Wrights than was displayed in the United States, but eventually the time came when the use of the airplane in commercial transportation, for the speedy carriage of persons, mail, and valuable parcels, began to receive in this country the same measure of recognition as that given its use in the destruction of property and human life. Like many other "new" mechanisms, which had possibilities for the promotion of economic progress and political power, the airplane became an object of governmental solicitude. Both as an instrument of war and as an influential agency of peaceful communication and commerce, its construction and operation began to receive government encouragement and aid in the form of direct and indirect subsidies. Several acts were passed by Congress in the 1920's and 1930's to promote the development of civil aviation, most of the laws having to do with the transportation of United States mail by air. Finally, in 1938, came the comprehensive Civil Aeronautics Act, under which the government adopted a program of aid for civil aviation as well as rules for its regulation and control. Although the organization of the regulatory authorities created in the Act of 1938 has been changed somewhat by executive action, the purposes of the Act have not been changed, and the main lines of regulatory policy remain the same. In a subsequent chapter, we shall summarize the provisions of the Civil Aeronautics Act.

TRANSPORTATION ACT OF 1940

Domestic transportation by water was placed under the control of the Interstate Commerce Commission by the Transportation Act of 1940, which for the most part became part III of the Interstate Commerce Act but which contained some amendments of the first two parts. Previous to the year 1916, we had little regulation of interstate commerce by water except that which was carried on under common management and control in connection with transportation by rail. The Shipping Act of 1916 contained certain provisions for the regulation of water carriers engaged in foreign and domestic commerce, and several subsequently enacted laws extended these regulatory provisions, especially as they applied to our intercoastal trade by way of the Panama Canal. Since we are interested here primarily in industrial traffic management, we shall not endeavor to examine the provisions of the statutes by which the rates of water carriers were subjected by these earlier laws to a certain degree of control. In a later chapter will be found a summarization of the provisions of the Transportation Act of 1940, as they affect the regulation of the rates and services of our domestic water carriers. We shall also summarize the provisions of part IV of the Interstate Commerce Act, passed in 1942, by which freight forwarders also were placed under the supervision of the Interstate Commerce Commission.

.SUMMARY AND CONCLUSION

The development of the present system of transportation regulation in the United States has been a long and often a painful process. Few would venture to claim that it is entirely satisfactory. Criticism is sharp and frequent, but there are many opinions, and many shades of opinion, as to what is wrong with regulation as practiced at present. There are persons who think there should be no regulation at all and persons who think that regulation should be more strict and more embracing; one of the most common criticisms is that the system of regulation now employed is uneven, that certain types of carriers are favored at the expense of others, or, to put it another way, that certain carriers are subjected to regulation which is unjustly discriminatory in character.

Perhaps there is one thing that might be said in favor of transportation regulation in the United States. All countries have met with the very same problems that have confronted the people and the government here. This country has at least been able to maintain a program under which the ownership of the facilities of transportation is still in private hands. There are many people who seem inclined to think that this condition has not long to last, that in the not too distant future the United States will follow the example of nearly all the other industrial countries of the world, as well as of many countries which have made little progress toward industrialization, and enact legislation for the purchase of our railroad system and some other transportation facilities by the government. Virtually all the railroads of Europe are now state-owned; the same is true of Australia, New Zealand, Africa, and Asia. While some of the railroads in Latin America are still privately owned, most of the lines have been built and operated by the state or have passed into the possession of the state. Even in Canada, our neighbor to the north, where there has been general adherence to the principle and practice of private enterprise, one of the two great railroad systems is owned and operated by the government.

It is the duty of every traffic manager to familiarize himself with the transportation policy of this country and of other countries. Not only is it a matter of importance to him in his professional activities to become acquainted with the law under which our transportation system is required to operate, but as a citizen and voter, he should have a knowledge of our public policy and be able to formulate reasonable opinions with respect to what he conceives to be its strength and its weakness. Moreover, every traffic manager is likely to become a member of some organization composed largely of "traffic men," such as a traffic club or a shippers' conference. Some of these organizations are local, some of them state or regional, and some of them national in scope and membership. All of them are interested in traffic problems, and all of them are deeply concerned with the laws, rules, and policies under which our great transportation system operates. Not only do these organizations make frequent appearances before regulative bodies to present their views on matters affecting the relations of carriers and shippers, but their representatives are frequently called into consultation by commissions and legislative bodies to give counsel and advice with respect to proposed modifications of transportation law and policy. The national and state organizations of traffic managers, representing both carriers and shippers, have exerted great influence in shaping transportation legislation. They have likewise been of assistance to the Interstate Commerce Commission and other commissions in reaching decisions on knotty controversial questions. Many of the organizations provide a forum where differences of opinion between carriers and shippers may be thoroughly aired, where matters of the gravest concern can be examined and discussed, and where attempts can be made to form a common front with respect to many problems and difficulties of mutual interest. The individual traffic manager should not fail to acquire membership in important traffic organizations, and he should be able to partake intelligently in all of their deliberations and discussions. To do this he needs far more knowledge than he is likely to gain in the day-to-day experience of his immediate position. He must read, he must study, he must think. And he should keep in mind that a thorough knowledge of the history and background of the transportation industry and of the current transportation policy of the government is essential to an intelligent understanding of their present aspects.

CHAPTER XXII

The Interstate Commerce Act: National Transportation Policy and Part I [1]

NATIONAL TRANSPORTATION POLICY

Occasionally, Congress includes in a statute a declaration of the purpose of the statute or of the government policy which the statute embodies. The Act of 1887 contained no such declaration, nor did any of the laws amending the Interstate Commerce Act which were passed before 1920. In one of the "miscellaneous provisions" of the Transportation Act of 1920, Congress declared it "to be the policy of Congress to promote, encourage and develop water transportation" and to "foster and preserve in full vigor both rail and water transportation." We have discussed previously how the Commission interpreted this provision of the Act as a mandate under which it was to limit the discrimination against Intermountain Territory which formerly had been permitted in the transcontinental rate structure. The next declaration of transportation "policy" by Congress appeared in the famous Hoch-Smith Resolution of 1925, in which a "true policy of rate making" was prescribed for the Interstate Commerce Commission, which was obviously designed to result in especially favorable rates for the products of agriculture.

There was no declaration of policy in the Motor Carrier Act of 1935, but the second section of the Civil Aeronautics Act, which became a law in 1938, did have such a declaration, in which the Civil Aeronautics Authority was instructed that in the "exercise and performance of its powers and duties" it was to do all it could to promote and encourage the development of civil aviation.

By the time Congress was ready to add a third part to the Interstate Commerce Act in 1940, under which the regulation of water carriers was to be effected, it was thought desirable to give expression to a policy which should be followed with respect to all kinds of transportation. Since the declaration, in its opening sentence, mentions "modes of transportation subject to the provisions of this Act," it seems to have been the opinion of a great many persons, including at times members of the Civil Aeronautics Board, that this declaration did not apply to aviation, regardless of the

[1] The Government Printing Office publishes from time to time a booklet containing the Interstate Commerce Act, as amended, and other acts and parts of acts relating to surface transportation and its regulation. The booklet can be ob-

inclusion of the phrase "as well as other means" at a later point in the declaration.

The declaration of policy, though a portion of the Interstate Commerce Act, is not a numbered section of the law and does not belong to any one of its four enumerated parts. It is a preliminary statement, or preamble, to the Act, similar in nature to the opening paragraphs of the Declaration of Independence and the Federal Constitution. The declaration reads as follows:

It is hereby declared to be the national transportation policy of the Congress [2] to provide for fair and impartial regulation of all modes of transportation subject to the provisions of this Act, so administered as to recognize and preserve the inherent advantages of each; to promote safe, adequate, economical, and efficient service and foster sound economic conditions in transportation and among the several carriers; to encourage the establishment and maintenance of reasonable charges for transportation services, without unjust discriminations, undue preferences or advantages, or unfair or destructive competitive practices; to cooperate with the several States and the duly authorized officials thereof; and to encourage fair wages and equitable working conditions;—all to the end of developing, coordinating, and preserving a national transportation system by water, highway, and rail, as well as other means, adequate to meet the needs of the commerce of the United States, of the Postal Service, and of the national defense. All the provisions of this Act shall be administered and enforced with a view to carrying out the above declaration of policy.[3]

---

tained at a small price from the Superintendent of Documents. Not only does it contain the text of the law, but it has volume, page, and date references to the published statutes of the United States, for the use of those who desire the exact wording of the numerous acts passed since 1887 for the regulation of our surface carriers. Under the terms of an Act passed in 1926, the laws of the United States are now codified under fifty titles. Title 49 is Transportation, and under it appear the four parts of the Interstate Commerce Act, the Civil Aeronautics Act, and various other statutes dealing with the transportation system. Other titles of the United States Code, such as Agriculture, Army, Commerce, Postal Service, Railroads, and War, also contain statutes affecting the transportation industry and its control by the government. The "catch-line subtitles" in this summary did not appear in part I of the law as it was enacted by Congress, but were supplied by the persons who framed the United States Code.

[2] There is no uniformity of practice with respect to the use of the definite article "the" before the word "Congress." The Constitution itself, and the amendments, have it both ways. In various statutes, the article is sometimes employed and sometimes omitted. The Presidents, in their messages on the state of the Union, have not followed a uniform practice.

[3] There are many persons who believe that not nearly enough has been done, either by Congress or by regulative agencies, to give effect to this declaration. As an illustration, Senator Bricker of Ohio is reported in *The New York Times* of Dec. 13, 1951, p. 57, to have said in a speech delivered in Cleveland the day before that the regulation of transportation in the United States is by no means "fair and impartial." The Senator was merely echoing some of the views

INTERSTATE COMMERCE ACT: PART I

Regulation in General; Car Service; Alteration of Line

Section 1. Paragraph (1) names the kinds of carriers to which this part applies—rail, rail-and-water under common control, and pipelines, except those carrying water and artificial gas. It indicates the points between which the part applies, primarily points located in different states.

Paragraph (2) says that this part shall apply only to transportation within the United States, but not to intrastate transportation or transportation wholly by water.

Paragraph (3) explains that the term "common carrier" as used in this part shall include pipeline companies, express companies, sleeping car companies, and "all persons, natural or artificial, engaged in transportation" as described in the first subdivisions. The term "railroad" includes all railroad facilities; the term "transportation" includes not only transportation services but transportation facilities; the term "person" applies to corporate as well as natural persons; the term "control" includes actual as well as legal control, whether direct or indirect.

Paragraph (4) describes the duties of carriers subject to this part, including the common law duty to carry, upon reasonable request, at charges which are "just and reasonable," and the duty to provide through routes, with reasonable facilities for their operation.

Paragraph (5) requires that all charges for the transportation of persons or property shall be just and reasonable, and forbids charges which are unreasonable or unjust.[4]

Paragraph (6) expands the previous subdivision by requiring just and reasonable classifications, regulations, and practices of many kinds.

Paragraph (7) deals with "free" transportation, which is, for the most part, strictly forbidden.

Paragraph (8) is the commodities clause.

---

expressed in the report of an investigation held under Senate Resolution 50, 81st Congress, by the Senate Subcommittee on Domestic Land and Water Transportation, of which he was a member. The report (Senate Report No. 1039, 82d Congress, 1st Session) has not been approved or disapproved by the Senate Committee on Interstate and Foreign Commerce, under whose auspices the inquiry was held.

[4] It is frequently said that the Interstate Commerce Act of 1887 and many of its subsequent amendments "copied" British transportation legislation of 1854, 1873, and 1888. This is true only in part. The British laws of those years had virtually nothing to say about "reasonable rates," which in Great Britain were provided for in maximum rate laws enacted directly by Parliament. The British regulatory acts were directed almost entirely against unjust discrimination. The second section of our Interstate Commerce Act was copied almost word for word from the earlier British statute.

Paragraph (9) deals with switch connections (see Chapter XVII).

Paragraphs (10) to (17) constitute the Esch Car-Service Act of 1917, with some amendments (see Chapter XVI).

Paragraph (18) requires a railroad desiring to extend its line or to construct a new line to obtain a certificate of convenience and necessity from the Commission. A similar certificate must be obtained for abandonment of a line or a part of a line.

Paragraph (19) describes the procedure to be followed in application for certificates.

Paragraph (20) authorizes the Commission to grant or withhold certificates in whole or in part, and attach conditions to their issuance.

Paragraph (21) authorizes the Commission to require a carrier by railroad to provide itself with "safe and adequate facilities" for performing its car service, and to extend its line or lines if the public convenience and necessity require such action by the carrier.

Paragraph (22) states that the preceding requirements with respect to construction and abandonment shall not extend to the "spur, industrial, team, switching or side tracks, located or to be located wholly within one State," or to electric railways not operated as a part of a steam railway system.

Special Rates and Rebates Prohibited

Section 2. This section, which was quoted and discussed in Chapter IX, defines and prohibits a certain kind of unjust discrimination. This section and sections 1 and 3 are often described as the heart of the Interstate Commerce Act.

Preferences; Interchange of Traffic; Terminal Facilities

Section 3. This section was quoted and discussed in Chapter IX. Paragraph (1) forbids undue or unreasonable preference or advantage and undue prejudice.

Paragraph (1a) requires that shippers of farm commodities for export shall be granted export rates on the same principles as are applicable in the case of rates on industrial products for export.

Paragraph (2) has to do with credit arrangements which a carrier may make with a shipper and the responsibility of an agent or shipper for freight charges.

Paragraph (3) has to do with responsibility for freight charges when consignor is also consignee and delivery is to be made to another party.

Paragraph (4) requires carriers to provide facilities for the interchange of traffic, without prejudice to a connecting line.

Paragraph (5) authorizes the Commission to require common use of terminals and tracks. This part of the law has been little used (see Chapter XVII).

Long-and-short-haul Charges; Competition with Water Routes

Section 4. This is the famous "long-and-short-haul" section, which was quoted and discussed in Chapter IX.

Combinations and Consolidations of Carriers

Section 5. This section has to do with pooling, which was forbidden by the Act of 1887 but which is now permissible under Commission supervision, and with the merger, consolidation, or combination of carriers, or the control of one carrier—rail, highway, or water—by another carrier. Designed to prevent the monopolization of transportation service, it nevertheless permits the formation of combinations deemed to be in the public interest.

Rate Agreements

Section 5a. This section is the much debated Reed-Bulwinkle Act passed over presidential veto in 1948 (see Chapter VI).

Schedules and Statements of Rates, etc.; Joint Rail-and-water Transportation

Section 6. This section has to do primarily with the publication, filing, and posting of the rates of all carriers subject to the terms of part I.

Paragraph (1) requires the publication of local and joint rates and all other charges, and the rules and regulations which may affect the aggregate of such charges. The duty of publication and the supervision of such publication was discussed in Chapter II.

Paragraph (2) requires the publication of the through charges applicable to shipments originating at some point in the United States and shipped through a foreign country to another point in the United States. If such rates are not published, such shipments, upon re-entry into this country, are subject to customs duties as if the freight "were of foreign production."

Paragraph (3) fixes the time limit within which rates and other charges may be changed at thirty days, though the Commission may permit a shorter period.

Paragraph (4) requires that joint tariffs contain the names of all participants, with evidence of the concurrence of those carriers which do not do the filing.

Paragraph (5) requires that contracts or agreements between carriers relating to any "traffic affected by the provisions of this part" be filed with the Commission.

Paragraph (6) says that all tariffs must be filed and posted in such manner as the Commission may prescribe and gives the Commission authority to reject any tariff not so filed and posted.

Paragraph (7) states that no carrier, "unless otherwise provided in this part," shall engage in transportation as defined in this part unless its tariffs have been properly published and filed with the Commission. It also states that published rates must be strictly observed, that a carrier shall not refund any portion of its published rates, once collected, nor extend any privileges or facilities to shippers or passengers, except as provided in published tariffs.

Paragraph (8) gives preference to military traffic in time of war or "threatened war," and provides that, even in time of peace, shipments consigned to agents of the United States shall not be subject to any embargo.

Paragraph (9) authorizes the Commission to reject tariffs which do not give proper notice of their effective date.

Paragraph (10) provides a penalty of a fine for the refusal of a carrier to comply with instructions the Commission may issue under the terms of this section, the fine being $500 for each offense and $25 for each and every day of the continuation of the offense.

Paragraph (11) gives the Commission certain additional powers with regard to rail-and-water traffic of common carriers, if the transportation is not wholly within a single state. The Commission may require the construction of physical connections between rail lines and the docks of the water carriers, if public convenience and necessity require such construction. The Commission may require the establishment of proportional rates to and from the ports where rail-and-water traffic is transferred from one type of carrier to the other for further transportation. It is pointed out that a proportional rate differs from "corresponding local rates" to and from the ports, and is to be employed only as a part of a combination rail-and-water through rate.

Paragraph (12) says that if any common carrier subject to this Act (not this part) enters into any "arrangements" with a water carrier operating between any port of the United States and a foreign country, for the handling of through business between interior points of the United States and the said foreign country, the Commission can direct such carrier to "enter into similar arrangements with any or all other lines of steamships operating from said port to the same foreign country." In other words, the Commission may prevent a domestic carrier by land or water from maintaining a "preferential" arrangement with a steamship line carrying our foreign commerce.

Combinations to Prevent Continuous Carriage of Freight Prohibited

Section 7. Freight transportation must be considered as continuous from point of origin to destination, unless stoppage is made in good faith and not for the purpose of "defeating" what would otherwise be a through service. A through interstate shipment may not be stopped and "reshipped" merely for the purpose of enabling the shipper to take possible advantage of a lower combination rate, of which one component may be a low intrastate rate.[5]

Liability in Damages to Persons Injured by Violation of Law

Section 8. A carrier subject to this part doing anything declared by this part to be unlawful shall be liable for the full amount of damage suffered by a person by reason of the carrier's unlawful act.

Remedies of Persons Damaged; Election; Witnesses

Section 9. A person claiming to have been damaged by reason of any act of a carrier, declared in this part to be unlawful, may make a complaint to the Commission or may bring suit for recovery of damages in a Federal district court. The complainant shall not, however, have the right to pursue both remedies, but must elect which method he shall adopt. Officers of a defendant carrier may be compelled to testify, even though the evidence given shall be of an incriminating nature. Such evidence, however, shall not be used against the witness in any criminal proceeding. The procedure followed in connection with complaints to the Commission is set forth in sections 13 and 16 below. It has been previously explained that a Federal court will not hear a suit for damages brought because a carrier has charged an allegedly unreasonable or unduly discriminatory rate until the Commission, in the exercise of its administrative functions, has passed upon the matter of the alleged unreasonable or unduly discriminatory character of the rate or rates involved.[6]

Violation of Regulations by Carriers; Discrimination; Penalties

Section 10. This section is often called the "penalty clause" of the Interstate Commerce Act.

Paragraph (1) provides penalties for carriers and for their officers or agents who "shall willfully do or cause to be done, or shall willingly suffer or permit to be done, any act, matter, or thing in this part prohibited or declared to be unlawful" or who shall fail to do anything required by this part to be done. This paragraph contains the penalty of imprisonment for agents of carriers who willfully violate the law. This penalty, which was originally established in 1889, but omitted when the Elkins law of 1903 was enacted, was restored by the Hepburn Amendment of 1906.

[5] See Kanotex Refining Co. v. Atchison, Topeka and Santa Fe Ry., 34 I.C.C. 271 (1915), 46 I.C.C. 495 (1917); Baltimore & Southwestern R. R. v. Seattle, 260 U.S. 166 (1922).

[6] See note 11, Chapter XVI.

Paragraph (2) provides penalties of fine or imprisonment or both for carriers or their agents who bill shipments falsely or do any other act enabling a shipper to obtain transportation at less than the published rates.

Paragraph (3) provides similar penalties for shippers or their agents who "shall knowingly and willfully, directly or indirectly," misrepresent their shipments for the purpose of obtaining transportation at rates lower than those lawfully published and filed. This is one of the few portions of the Interstate Commerce Act which contains provisions for the "regulation" of shippers as well as of carriers.

Paragraph (4) establishes penalties for anybody who shall, by the offer of bribes or other favors, induce or attempt to induce a carrier to engage in unjustly discriminatory practices. Should discrimination result from such inducement, the person giving the bribe or favor and the carrier involved shall be jointly and severally liable for any damages suffered by the consignor or consignee against whom the discriminatory practice was directed.[7]

Interstate Commerce Commission; Appointment, Term, and Qualifications of Commissioners

Section 11. This is the section of the original Act to Regulate Commerce by which the Interstate Commerce Commission was created. With the exception of minor amendments adopted in 1935, the section remains as originally enacted, though it has been amended with respect to the number of members, the term of office, and other matters, in section 24.

The original Commission was to consist of five members, to be appointed by the President, "by and with the advice and consent of the Senate." The term of office, except for the first appointees, was fixed at six years. Any Commissioner could be removed by the President for inefficiency, neglect of duty, or malfeasance in office. The only qualifications for membership were that not more than three should belong to the same

---

[7] This section affords a shining example of how a collection of words, under the direction of legislative draftsmen, can gather size like a rolling snowball. Despite the fact that in section 1 a "person" is said to include "an individual, firm, copartnership, corporation, company, association, or joint-stock association; and includes a trustee, receiver, assignee or personal representative thereof," this section and several others monotonously repeat "person, corporation, company, or any agent or officer thereof." It is said that in olden times, when few people could read or write, those who could not do so employed the services of artisans who went under the name of "scriveners." These gentlemen were not only expert in the art of penmanship, but since they charged for their labors by the word, they became equally expert in the art of inventing synonymous words and phrases, which members of the legal profession have persistently and tenaciously clung to, in order presumably to preserve the "mystery" of their calling. In many warranty deeds one does not sell something; one "doth grant, bargain, sell, remise, release, alien and confirm."

political party, and that no person should enter upon his duties as a Commissioner if he were at the time in the employ of, had any official relation with, or had any pecuniary interest in any carrier subject to the Act. In case of a vacancy, the remaining Commissioners retained the right to act for the Commission. An amendment of 1935 provided that upon the expiration of his term of office a Commissioner might continue to serve until his successor was appointed and qualified.

Authority and Duties of the Commission; Witnesses; Depositions

Section 12. Under the terms of paragraph (1), the Commission is "authorized and required to execute and enforce the provisions of this part." In the exercise of its duty of enforcement, the Commission has authority to inquire into the management of carriers subject to this part and obtain whatever information it deems needful for the performance of its duties. It is the duty of all United States district attorneys, at the request of the Commission, to initiate whatever proceedings are necessary to secure enforcement of this part and punishment for its violation. The Commission is also authorized to transmit to Congress whatever recommendations it deems necessary, including recommendations for additional legislation.

Paragraphs (2) and (3) provide for the compulsory testimony of witnesses summoned by the Commission. In case of contumacy on the part of a witness, a Federal district court may order the testimony to be given, and disobedience involves the recalcitrant witness in contempt of court proceedings. The claim by a witness that his testimony might be self-incriminating is no excuse for refusal to testify, though such testimony shall not be used in any criminal proceeding against the witness. It took the Compulsory Testimony Act of 1893 to give the Commission complete authority to require witnesses to testify, previous legislation having been declared by the courts insufficient to guarantee the immunity provided for in the Fifth Amendment of the Constitution.

Paragraphs (4) to (7) provide for the taking of testimony by "deposition," and prescribe the procedure to be followed.

Complaints to and Investigations by Commission

Section 13. Paragraph (1) provides that virtually anybody or any organization may file a complaint with the Commission,[8] charging violation of the Act by a carrier. The Commission calls upon the carrier to "satisfy" the complaint, within a reasonable time to be designated by the Commission. Should the common carrier against which the complaint was filed

---

[8] Under the Agricultural Adjustment Act of 1933, the Secretary of Agriculture receives special standing as a complainant in behalf of or as a representative of agricultural interests.

make reparation for alleged injury, it is relieved of further liability for the violation of the law complained of. If the carrier does not satisfy the complaint, and there appear to be reasonable grounds for its investigation, it is the "duty" of the Commission to undertake such an investigation in any manner it thinks proper.

Paragraph (2) directs the Commission to investigate complaints filed by state commissions. It gives the Commission power to institute an inquiry on its own motion, even if no complaint has been filed, and proceed in the same manner employed when a complaint has been received. However, the Commission is prohibited from making any orders for the payment of money in proceedings instituted on the Commission's own motion. An interesting provision of this paragraph is that no complaint is to be dismissed "because of the absence of direct damage to the complainant."

Paragraphs (3) and (4) deal with the power of the Commission to regulate intrastate rates which create an undue discrimination against interstate commerce. These paragraphs were discussed in Chapter IX.

Reports and Decisions of Commission

Section 14. The three paragraphs of this section make it the duty of the Commission to make reports of its investigations, with statements of its conclusions, decisions, and orders, and to supply a copy of reports to complainants and to the carriers involved. If the Commission awards damages, the report must contain the findings of fact upon which the award was made. The Commission provides for the publication of its reports and decisions in "such form and manner as may best be adapted for public information and use," and these published reports and decisions shall be "competent evidence" in all state and Federal courts. The Commission is also authorized to have its annual reports "printed for early distribution."

Determination of Rates, Routes, etc.; Routing of Traffic; Disclosures, etc.

Section 15. This is the section which gives the Interstate Commerce Commission the power to make rates and establish through routes.

Paragraph (1) states that whenever the Commission, acting on its own initiative or on complaint as provided for in section 13, shall find any rate, classification, or practice by a carrier subject to this part to be unreasonable or unjustly discriminatory, or "otherwise in violation of any of the provisions of this part," it shall have the right to correct the violation by naming the "maximum or minimum, or maximum and minimum" rate to be charged thereafter as well as to prescribe such reasonable rule, regulation, or practice as it thinks proper in the circumstances.

Paragraph (2) states that orders prescribed by the Commission under this part, other than orders for the payment of money, shall take effect in such reasonable time, not less than thirty days, as the Commission may direct, and shall continue in effect for such time as the Commission may prescribe, unless set aside or modified by the Commission itself or "suspended or set aside by a court of competent jurisdiction." [9]

Paragraphs (3) and (4), giving the Commission power to establish through routes and joint rates, with certain qualifications, were discussed in Chapter XV.

Paragraph (5) requires railroads transporting livestock destined to or received at public stockyards to perform necessary loading and unloading services, without extra charge to the shipper or consignee, except when the loading or unloading is done on request. The Commission may establish reasonable rules and rates with respect to exceptional services.

Paragraph (6) gives the Commission power to prescribe the "division" which each participating carrier may receive from a joint rate. Certain considerations are listed which the Commission must observe in prescribing such divisions.

Paragraph (7) gives the Commission power to suspend proposed changes in rates. This was the leading feature of the Mann-Elkins Act of 1910. At any hearing involving a change in rate or other charge, the burden of proof is upon the carrier to show that the proposed change is "just and reasonable."

Paragraphs (8) to (10), which give the shipper the right to route his traffic and make certain other rules with regard to routing, were discussed in Chapter XV.

Paragraph (11) forbids a carrier to disclose information concerning the nature of the traffic of a shipper or consignee to another "person," without consent. This part of the law was enacted to give a measure of protection to various shippers who suffered injury because carriers had a habit of disclosing information concerning their business to their competitors. There is a proviso to the paragraph to the effect that it is not to be construed to prevent giving information to government officials seeking evidence for the prosecution of persons suspected of criminal activity or the exchange between carriers of information necessary for the adjustment of traffic accounts.

Paragraph (12) provides a penalty of a fine for violation of the provisions of paragraph (11).

Paragraph (13) permits a carrier to give "allowances" to shippers who

[9] Under the District Court Jurisdiction Act (United States Code, title 28, Judicial Code and Judiciary), section 47, applications for injunction to set aside orders of the Commission are presented to a district judge, who thereupon requests the assistance of two other district judges to hear the application. A majority of such a statutory court may allow a temporary stay of a Commission order. Final decisions of such a court may be appealed directly to the Supreme Court, bypassing the Circuit Court of Appeals.

perform services or provide facilities which would ordinarily come within the obligations of the carrier. Such allowances must be just and reasonable, and are subject to the jurisdiction of the Commission.

Paragraph (14) states that the enumeration of powers in this section shall not exclude any power which the Commission would otherwise have under the provisions of this part. In other words, the powers of the Commission listed in this section are not to be regarded as its only powers.

Fair Return for Carriers

Section 15a. The "catch title," provided by the codifiers of the laws of the United States, cannot be said to apply to this section any longer, for it makes no mention of a "fair return." This section was added to the law in 1920, and radically modified in 1933. It has been discussed previously in Chapter VIII.

Orders of Commission and Enforcement Thereof; Forfeitures

Section 16. Paragraph (1) authorizes the Commission to award damages to a complainant who has been injured because of violation of the law by a carrier and who has filed a complaint as provided in section 13.

Under the terms of paragraph (2), if a carrier does not comply with a Commission order awarding damages to a complainant, the complainant may bring suit for recovery in a Federal district court or in a state court. The order of the Commission is to be regarded as prima-facie evidence of the facts stated in the order. If the complainant prevails in the suit, he is allowed a reasonable attorney's fee, to be taxed and collected as a part of the cost of the suit.[10]

---

[10] The Commission has asked Congress, on several occasions, to be relieved of the duty or power of awarding damages for violation of the law, preferring that the task of doing so be entrusted entirely to the courts. Congress, however, has never made the necessary change in the law, and the Commission is still frequently called on to award "reparation" for which a carrier may be liable under the terms of section 8. Ordinarily, the reparation awards of the Commission consist merely of the difference between the rate a shipper actually paid and the rate which under a proper construction of the law he should have paid. However, reparation awards are not confined to differences in rates, and it does not follow that reparation will always be allowed even when the rate payable at the time a shipment moved has been found to be unreasonable or otherwise unlawful. Section 8 permits an award of damages for any act of omission or commission of a carrier if the act violates the statute, and the carrier which is guilty of the unlawful act is "liable to the person or persons injured thereby for the full amount of damages sustained." For example, awards of damage may follow misrouting, improper distribution of cars, or improper assessment of demurrage or storage charges. The Commission may not, however, award damages because of "breach of contract" if no violation of the law is involved, nor may it award punitive or exemplary damages. The entire matter of damages—the reasons for an award, the measure of the damage, and related questions—is a long and complicated problem. Those interested in the problem will find it fully discussed, with hun-

The eight lettered subdivisions, (a) to (h), of paragraph (3) constitute a statute of limitations with respect to the time in which a carrier may file suit for recovery of its charges or a complainant may file suit for recovery of overcharges or for damages other than overcharges. In general, the time limit for both kinds of actions is two years, though there are certain designated conditions under which the time for a complainant is extended. A complaint for the enforcement of a Commission order for the payment of money must be filed in a Federal or state court within one year from the date of the order.

Paragraph (4) permits all parties in whose favor the Commission has made an award of damages to be "joined as plaintiffs" in a suit for recovery, and all carriers party to the order to be joined as defendants.

Paragraph (5) directs that every order of the Commission shall be "forthwith" served upon the carrier's agent in the city of Washington, or "in such other manner as may be provided by law." The Mann-Elkins Act of 1910 had a clause directing carriers subject to the Interstate Commerce Act to maintain an agent in Washington upon whom all notices and orders could be served.

Paragraph (6) authorizes the Commission to suspend or modify any of its orders upon "such notice and in such manner as it shall deem proper."

Paragraph (7) declares it to be the duty of common carriers and their agents to comply with Commission orders so long as the orders are in effect.

Paragraph (8) represents one of the notable changes which the Hepburn Amendment made in the Interstate Commerce Act. The Commission's orders, made under sections 3, 13, and 15, are of binding effect and failure or neglect to obey is punishable by a forfeiture of $5,000 to the United States for each offense. Every violation is to be considered as a separate offense, and in case of continued violation each day is considered as a separate offense.

Paragraph (9) provides for the recovery of "forfeitures" by civil suit in a Federal court.

Paragraph (10) makes it the duty of Federal district attorneys to undertake prosecutions for the recovery of unpaid forfeitures.

Paragraph (11) authorizes the Commission to employ whatever legal counsel it may need in the pursuit of its duties. The Commission, of course, maintains a permanent legal staff, but if occasion requires, it may employ special, additional counsel.

Paragraph (12) makes it possible for the Commission to bring legal

---

dreds of references to the decisions of the Commission and of the courts in *Interstate Commerce Acts Annotated,* Vol. 2, pp. 1545–1670; Vol. 3, pp. 1731–1824, 2129–2147; Vol. 7, pp. 5281–5377; Vol. 9, pp. 7527–7581; Vol. 11, pp. 9240–9246; Vol. 12, pp. 10289–10295; Vol. 13, pp. 10998–11002; Vol. 14, pp. 11501–11504.

proceedings for the enforcement of its orders, other than those for the payment of money to a complainant. A carrier may stubbornly refuse to obey a Commission order. In such case the Commission, through the Attorney General of the United States, or even a party injured by the carrier's violation of the law, may apply to a Federal district court for the enforcement of the order. If the court finds that the order has been properly issued and served, and that the carrier is guilty of disobedience, it may order compliance by mandatory order. Of course, the failure of a carrier or its agents to obey such a court order involves contempt proceedings.

Paragraph (13) provides that all rate schedules, all contracts and agreements among carriers, and all statistical material collected and published by the Commission shall be received as prima-facie evidence in judicial proceedings, and that certified copies of all or parts of such documentary material shall be received with like effect as the originals.

Commission Procedure; Delegation of Duties; Rehearings

Section 17. Just as the Commission has a large measure of discretion in dealing with the problems with which it is confronted in the performance of its administrative functions, so it has a large measure of discretion in making its own rules of procedure. We shall discuss the organization and the rules of procedure of the Commission in the final chapter of this book. This particular section of the law has to do with the operations of the Commission to the extent that Congress desired to control and direct them. The Commission is governed, too, by the terms of the Administrative Procedure Act of 1946.

Paragraph (1) of this section authorizes the Commission to divide itself into divisions of not less than three members each, a division to have the same power as the entire Commission. The Commission may designate one or more of the divisions created as "appellate" divisions. Since the original authorization of divisional organization was made by Congress in 1917, the Commission has received further authority to divide and delegate its manifold duties.

Paragraph (2) states that the Commission may direct any of its "work, business or functions" to be assigned "to any division, to an individual Commissioner, or to a board to be composed of three or more eligible employees of the Commission." Among the "eligible" employees are the "examiners, directors or assistant directors of bureaus, chiefs of sections, and attorneys."

Paragraph (3) authorizes the Commission to conduct its proceedings "in such manner as will best conduce to the proper dispatch of business and to the ends of justice." The Commission has a seal, which is to be "judicially noticed"; any member of the Commission or of a "board" or the Secretary of the Commission may administer oaths. A majority of the

Commission, or of a division or of a board, constitutes a quorum. The Commission may make or amend its general rules at any time, but the rules should conform, as nearly as may be, to "those in use in the courts of the United States." A party may appear before the Commission personally or by attorney; hearings are to be public upon the request of any interested party; no Commissioner or employee is to take part in any proceeding in which he may have a pecuniary interest. (Part II of the Act, under which highway transportation is regulated, provides for joint boards in which state officials are participants. These boards will be discussed in the outline summary of part II.)

Paragraph (4) gives a division, an individual Commissioner, or a board authority with respect to matters referred equal to the authority of the Commission.

Under paragraph (5), matters referred to an individual Commissioner or to a board, upon which public hearings have been held, must be reported on to the Commission, the report to be accompanied with a recommended order. Copies of the proposed order are served upon interested parties, who may file exceptions within twenty days. If no exceptions are filed within twenty days, or within such time as the Commission or a designated division may prescribe, the proposed order becomes the order of the Commission and becomes effective, unless stayed by the Commission or a division. If exceptions are filed (or on the Commission's own motion), the order may be reviewed either on the record or after further hearings.

Paragraph (6) provides for the rehearing of orders made by an individual Commissioner or a board, as well as of orders made by the Commission or a division, if the Commission deems such rehearing to be advisable. The appellate procedure is prescribed.

Paragraph (7) empowers the Commission to reverse or modify orders which have been given by any agency of the Commission. The modified orders are likewise subject to the provisions with respect to rehearing.

Paragraph (8) requires that when application for a rehearing has been made with regard to an order that has not yet become effective, the order shall be stayed pending disposition of the appeal.

Paragraph (9) makes provision for suits in Federal courts to enforce, enjoin, suspend, or set aside orders of the Commission.

Paragraph (10) provides for reference to a Commission examiner of any matter arising under the administration of part II of the Act as to which a hearing is to be held.

Paragraph (11) permits the employees of carriers to intervene in proceedings under the Act which may affect their interests.

Paragraph (12) authorizes the Commission to promulgate rules and regulations relating to admission to practice before it, and authorizes the charging of a reasonable fee for admission to the Commission's "bar" of practitioners.

Employees; Appointment and Compensation; Witness Fees; Expenses

Section 18. Paragraph (1) of this section originally named the salary of the members of the Commission, but that part of the law has been changed by section 24, under which the membership of the Commission has been enlarged. Originally, the Commission was authorized to employ such assistants as it needed and fix their compensation. Most of the Commission's staff now come under civil-service regulations. Originally, the Commission was authorized to "hire suitable offices"; now it is permanently housed in a commodious building. The fees of witnesses summoned to appear before the Commission are the same as those paid to witnesses in the Federal courts.

Paragraph (2) provides for the necessary expenses of the Commission, which are now audited by the General Accounting Office.

Offices and Sessions

Section 19. The principal office of the Commission is in Washington, but the Commission is truly a peripatetic organization, and can pursue its inquiries "in any part of the United States."

Valuation of Property of Carriers

Section 19a. This long and considerably amended section is the well-known La Follette Valuation Act of 1913, which directs the Commission to "investigate, ascertain, and report the value of all the property owned or used by every common carrier subject to the provisions of this part," with minor exceptions.

Although this Act cost the government millions of dollars, and the railroad companies even more millions than the government spent on valuation work, it is difficult to see that the effort or the results were of much value. For the past ten years, the valuation division of the Commission has been little more than a skeleton organization, with personnel far too small in number to carry on the work the Commission is directed to do under this section. Congress has failed to appropriate funds necessary for valuation to be kept up to date, and on a few occasions has specifically reduced the amounts requested in the Commission's proposed budget to enable the valuation division to perform the task presumably assigned to it. As conditions are now, this entire section could be repealed with only a few persons being the wiser, and with injury to nobody.

Reports, Records, and Accounts of Carriers; Mandamus; Liability of Initial Carrier for Loss, etc.

Section 20. The first eight paragraphs of this highly important section give the Commission complete control over the accounting practices of all carriers subject to this part, including agencies which supply protective services such as heating or refrigeration for property in transit. The Commission prescribes the accounting system to be followed, has full power to "police" all carrier accounting practices, and may require carriers to make such annual, periodical, or special reports as it may deem necessary. It is from these reports that the Commission obtains the data for the numerous statistical bulletins it issues, as well as for its well-known annual, *Statistics of Railways in the United States.* Penalties are provided for disobedience of Commission rules and directions with respect to accounts and reports.

Paragraph (9) gives the district courts of the United States jurisdiction

. . . upon the application of the Attorney-General of the United States at the request of the Commission, alleging a failure to comply with or a violation of any of the provisions of the said Act to regulate commerce or of any Act supplementary thereto or amendatory thereof by any common carrier, to issue a writ or writs of mandamus commanding such common carrier to comply with the provisions of the said Acts, or any of them.

Paragraph (10) authorizes the Commission to employ "special agents or examiners" to carry out and give effect to the acts passed for the regulation of commerce.

Paragraph (11) consists chiefly of the Carmack and the two Cummins Amendments, with some modifications, which were discussed in detail in the chapters dealing with bills of lading and claims.

Paragraph (12) provides that, if the carrier issuing the bill of lading is held liable for the loss of or damage to a shipment, it may recover from the carrier on whose line the loss or damage occurred "the amount of such loss, damage, or injury as it may be required to pay to the owners of such property." It is also entitled to recover any expense reasonably incurred in defending an action at law brought by the "owners" of lost or damaged property.[11]

Securities of Carriers; Insurance, etc.

Section 20a. This long section, which will not be discussed, gives the Interstate Commerce Commission authority to control the issuance of

[11] This paragraph probably contains another instance of careless or inept legislative draftsmanship. The initial carrier of a joint shipment is responsible not to the "owner" of the property but to the "lawful holder" of the bill of lading, who may or may not be the owner. Does this paragraph mean that the initial carrier cannot recover from a connecting line damages which have been paid to a "lawful holder" who is not the owner? For example, under this section, strictly construed, the initial carrier could not recover from a connecting carrier any sum paid out on a loss and damage claim of a freight forwarder. There is little excuse for such faulty draftsmanship (if that is what it is), for this paragraph was amended twice after the Supreme Court handed down its decision in Pennsylvania R.R. v. Olivit Brothers, 243 U.S. 574 (1917). See Chapter XIII.

securities by railroad companies. Included in the law originally in 1920, it was passed long after the evil deeds it was designed to prohibit and prevent had been perpetrated. Had it been included in the Act of 1887, it is possible that many railroad companies and thousands of investors in railroad securities would have been saved from grievous and irreparable loss.

Railroad Reorganizations

Section 20b. This section, added to the Interstate Commerce Act in 1948, will likewise not be discussed. It permits the Interstate Commerce Commission, under certain conditions, to aid and supervise the modification of the "capital structure" of railroad companies. Almost since their inception, the railroads of the United States have suffered from the blight of misguided and faulty financial policies resulting in the creation of a capital structure in which bonds and other fixed interest-bearing obligations far exceeded stocks and other securities having only a contingent obligation. Because of the preponderant importance of fixed costs in railroad operating and nonoperating expenses, it was inevitable that in times of acute depression railroad corporations would meet with severe and unavoidable financial difficulties. There are comparatively few railroads in the United States which at one time or another have not passed through a bankruptcy court, and on a few occasions nearly half the railroad mileage of the country has been in the hands of receivers. By an amendment of section 77 of the Bankruptcy Act, in 1933, the Interstate Commerce Commission received authority to participate in the reorganization of railroads which were either in bankruptcy or threatened with insolvency. This section of the Interstate Commerce Act gives the Commission additional powers to employ in the assistance of financially indigent railroad corporations.

Annual Report of Commission

Section 21. This section directs the Commission to render to Congress an annual report of its activities. The report must be made on or before the third day of January. In it, the Commission also makes its recommendations for legislation. In the original Act to Regulate Commerce, the Commission was directed to render its annual report to the Secretary of the Interior, for transmission to Congress, but since 1889 the Commission has been responsible directly to Congress. It is worthy of note that in passing laws permitting the reorganization of governmental executive and administrative agencies by presidential action, the Interstate Commerce Commission has invariably been specifically excluded from the provisions of such laws. It is the creature of Congress and responsible only to Congress.

Restrictions

Section 22. This section is interpretative in nature, and enumerates several things which the law does *not* do. It does not prevent a carrier from providing transportation free or at reduced rates for national, state, or local governments or for "charitable purposes." It does not forbid the issuance and sale of mileage, excursion, or commutation tickets, nor does it prohibit giving reduced rates to ministers of religion, to municipal governments for the transportation of indigent persons, to inmates of soldiers' homes, to members of our military forces, or to the officers and employees of carriers. A blind person and an accompanying seeing-eye dog may be carried at the fare charged for a single person. The law does not forbid granting reduced rates for the transportation of property to or from areas suffering from some calamity such as drought, earthquake, famine, or pestilence, provided such reduced rates and the scope of their application have been established by the Commission. A carrier is not to be held guilty of undue discrimination by granting free transportation or transportation at reduced rates, such as this section declares not to be "prevented" or "prohibited" by the act.

Mandamus to Obtain Equal Facilities for Shippers

Section 23. The district courts of the United States are to have jurisdiction for the purpose of compelling a carrier to furnish to a shipper facilities equal to those provided for other shippers, and at the same rates.

Enlargement of Commission; Salaries of Commissioners and Secretary

Section 24. The membership of the Commission has been increased in number on three different occasions, from five to seven in 1906, seven to nine in 1917, and nine to eleven in 1920. The term of office, originally six years, is now seven. The "political" qualification of Commissioners still remains, that is, not more than six are to belong to the same party. When this condition was first established, the nation was fairly well wedded to a two-party system, but with the occasional rise of a strong third party, such as the "Bull Moose" Progressive party of 1912, a President was able at times to make appointments which disarranged the customary division of posts on the Commission between the two major parties. The method of appointment in the original Act, and in the acts which have provided for an increase of membership of the Commission, was such that appointments could be "staggered" in such a way that there was always a fairly large number of "continuing" members. However, the provision of the law which permits a duly appointed member to serve until his successor is appointed and has qualified permits a larger number of simultaneous appointments that was originally contemplated in the law. The law fixes the annual salary of a Commissioner at $12,000. The salary of the secretary of the Commission is set in this section at $7,500 a year, but since the enactment of the Classification Act of 1923, the salary of the secretary has been determined in accordance with the terms of that statute.

Safety Appliances, Methods, and Systems

Section 25. It has been noted before that the former section 25 of the Act, which made it the duty of railroads to inform inquiring shippers about ocean steamship schedules, was repealed in 1940, and what was formerly section 26 is now, in amended form, the present section 25. It gives the Commission authority to require the installation of safety devices on railroads, inspect them regularly, and supervise the rules of the carriers for their installation, inspection, and maintenance. The use of unsafe and uninspected devices is prohibited.

There are many other statutes dealing with railroad equipment, such as the Safety Appliance Act of 1893, requiring all cars moving in interstate commerce to be equipped with air brakes and automatic couplers; the Ash Pan Act of 1908, by which steam locomotives must have ash pans which can be emptied and cleaned without the necessity of an employee going under the locomotive; the Accident Report Act of 1910, which requires railroads to report to the Commission all train accidents which result in injury to persons or property and authorizes the Commission to make an investigation of train accidents; and the Boiler Inspection Act of 1911, which directs the Commission to inspect locomotive boilers and, if necessary, require locomotives with defective boilers to be withdrawn from service until properly repaired.

The Commission has an enormous burden of administrative work which is not directly concerned with the regulation of transportation rates and services. Many persons think it should be relieved of some of these duties in order that it can give more of its time to the purposes for which it was originally created.

Citation

Section 26. This section, which was formerly section 27, and still bears that number in the United States Code, merely states that this "part may be cited as part I of the Interstate Commerce Act." Until 1920, the title of the entire statute was the Act to Regulate Commerce. All four parts of the law, according to the brief statement which precedes the declaration of national transportation policy, may be cited as the Interstate Commerce Act.

CHAPTER XXIII

The Interstate Commerce Act: Part II

The Motor Carrier Act, which constitutes part II of the Interstate Commerce Act, became a law in 1935. Although it was patterned largely after the earlier law for the regulation of railroads, there are several differences, some of which have already been pointed out. On the whole, our motor carriers are not regulated by the Federal government in such detail or so extensively as our rail carriers. Because of the highly individualized character of highway transportation, much of it escapes regulation entirely. The law does not pretend to deal with private carriers, and many commercial carriers are specifically excluded from the provisions of the law. Moreover, the contract carriers which operate in interstate commerce on our highways are not regulated to the same extent or in the same fashion that common carriers are regulated. The law has been amended in a few particulars since it was first enacted, but for the most part it still retains its original form.

Like part I of the law, this part is administered and enforced by the Interstate Commerce Commission. Because of the large number of commercial motor carriers and because the operations of so many of them are limited in scope, the problems of administration have been varied and often difficult. While the Commission exhibited its customary commendable zeal in the early performance of its manifold duties under the new law, it also displayed a spirit of patience and toleration without which a law of the scope of this one could have been made effective only with the greatest friction and ill feeling. The large measure of success with which the law has met and its eventual cheerful acceptance by those whom it touches most closely have been due more than anything else to its able administration.

Short Title

Section 201. "This part may be cited as Part II of the Interstate Commerce Act."

Application of Provisions

Section 202. Paragraph (a) applies to the transportation of passengers or property by motor carriers engaged in interstate or foreign commerce, and the regulation of such transportation is vested in the Interstate Commerce Commission.

Paragraph (b) does not affect the powers of the states to tax or to regulate motor vehicle transportation which is entirely intrastate in character.

Paragraph (c), with certain exceptions having to do with safety regulation, does not apply to motor vehicle operations conducted by railroads, water carriers, or freight forwarders in their various terminal collection, transfer, and delivery services, whether performed directly or under contract. Such services are regulated under other parts of the Act.

Definitions

Section 203. This section consists entirely of definitions. Such terms as person, board or state board, Commission, joint board, certificate, permit, license, state (here this word includes the District of Columbia), express company, interstate commerce, foreign commerce, and highway are defined.

The term "motor vehicle" means "any vehicle, machine, tractor, trailer, or semi-trailer propelled or drawn by mechanical power and used on the highways in the transportation of passengers or property." It does not include vehicles operated on rails or trolley buses.

The term "common carrier by motor vehicle" means a person who "holds itself out to the general public to engage in transportation by motor vehicle in interstate or foreign commerce . . . for compensation. . . ." A contract carrier, however, is one which operates under individual contract or agreement. A "private carrier of property by motor vehicle" is one which is neither a common nor a contract carrier. A "broker" is one which sells or negotiates for the sale of transportation by motor vehicle, but does not actually furnish the service.

One long paragraph of this section indicates several kinds of equipment and services which are not included in the preceding definitions and are not subject to regulation under this part. School buses, hotel buses, motor vehicles operated in national park service, and taxicabs, or other "motor vehicles performing a bona fide taxicab service, having a capacity of not more than six passengers and not operated on a regular route or between fixed termini," are excluded, as are motor vehicles operated by farmers for the transportation of their farm products and farm supplies. The vehicles of cooperative farm organizations are likewise excluded, as well as vehicles used in "carrying property consisting of ordinary livestock, fish (including shell fish), or agricultural commodities (not including manufactured products thereof), if such motor vehicles are not used in carrying any other property, or passengers, for compensation." Also in the excepted list are motor vehicles used exclusively for the distribution of newspapers and vehicles used in transportation "incidental" to air transport. Another highly important service that does not come within the terms of this law is what may be considered "local" transportation within the municipality or between contiguous municipalities, even though it may be concerned with interstate or foreign commerce.

A great deal of such transportation takes place between New York City and numerous cities and towns in New Jersey, between St. Louis and points in Illinois, between Chicago and the Indiana suburbs of that city. It is the duty of the Commission to delineate the "zone" in which this local transportation, when interstate or foreign, does not come within the terms of this part. Of course, if the local haul is part of a longer joint service under common control or arrangement, it is subject to regulation just as any other interstate movement is. A final exception is made for "the casual, occasional or reciprocal transportation of passengers or property . . . for compensation by any person not engaged in transportation by motor vehicle as a regular occupation or business," unless the transportation is arranged for through a broker. For example, if a farmer should transport the driver of a stalled car to a destination in another state, and accept compensation for his effort, the service would not come under the terms of this part of the Interstate Commerce Act.

General Duties and Powers of the Commission

Section 204. This section has to do with the general powers which the Commission exercises over highway transport.

Paragraph (1) directs the Commission to regulate common carriers by motor vehicle and authorizes it to establish "reasonable requirements with respect to continuous and adequate service," uniform systems of accounts and records, qualifications and maximum hours of service for employees, and safety of operation and equipment.

Paragraph (2) gives the Commission the same general authority over contract carriers by motor vehicle.

Paragraph (3) authorizes the Commission, "if need therefor be found," to establish reasonable safety requirements, including maximum hours of employment and standards of equipment, for private carriers of property —but not for carriers of passengers.

Paragraph (4) authorizes the Commission to regulate brokers, with respect to licensing, financial requirements, accounts, reports, and other practices.

Paragraph (4a) is a somewhat long but highly interesting paragraph. There are many carriers by motor vehicle whose operations take place entirely in a single state. But these carriers, even though their physical operations are so confined, may engage in interstate or foreign commerce as a part of their business, when they take part in through services. This paragraph authorizes the Commission to determine, either on its own motion or on the application of such a carrier, a state board, or any other interested party, whether the interstate or foreign business of such an intrastate carrier is of such a nature as to affect the regulation of the transportation by motor carriers physically engaged in foreign or interstate commerce. If the business is not of such a nature, the Commission can issue a certificate exempting the intrastate carrier from regulation under this part. Such a certificate is subject to revocation at any time at the will of the Commission. Provision is made for automatic exemption, under certain conditions, on the presentation of a certificate from a state board. When an exemption certificate is granted, any regulation of the "exempt" services by a state shall not be regarded as a burden upon interstate or foreign commerce, which is in general prohibited.

Paragraph (5) provides that the Commission may make use of any of the research agencies of the Federal government in carrying out its functions with respect to the safety of motor vehicle operations.

Paragraph (6) authorizes the Commission to "administer, execute, and enforce all provisions of this part, to make all necessary orders in connection therewith, and to prescribe rules, regulations, and procedure for such administration."

Paragraph (7) gives the Commission blanket authority to inquire into the business of motor vehicle carriers and brokers similar to that which it has with respect to the railroad business. It authorizes the Commission to establish reasonable classifications of brokers, common carriers, and contract carriers. Either on its own initiative or on the complaint of a person, state board, organization, or body politic, the Commission may undertake an investigation to see if any broker or carrier subject to this part has failed to comply with the terms of the law or with any requirement established according to its terms. If after notice or hearing the Commission finds a broker or carrier guilty of noncompliance with the law, it may issue an order appropriate to the situation, and compel the offender to comply with such order. With respect to reports, decisions, and other records, the Commission exercises the same power it has under the provisions of part I. It also has the same powers over motor carriers that it has over railroads when there is a shortage of equipment or congestion of traffic or other emergency. Finally, the Commission has authority to modify, suspend, or change any order or certificate which it may make under the provisions of this part.

Administration

Section 205. This section has to do almost entirely with Commission procedure in its administration of this part. Congress was confronted with the fact that there were many motor vehicle operations which, though interstate in character, were relatively small in their scope and importance, but so numerous that something should be done to make it possible for the Commission, if need be, to relieve itself of some of the inevitable mass of administrative labor. Consequently, provision was made in this section for the creation of joint boards of state representatives to consider matters of motor vehicle regulation in which the brokers or vehicles concerned did not involve more than three states. Such a joint board is made up of one representative from each state, and the Commission may assign one or more examiners to work with any joint board. The first part of this long section tells how the joint boards are formed, how they carry out their functions, and how they cooperate with the Commission. It must be understood that the creation of a joint board is entirely optional with the Commission. It is not mandatory for the Commission to refer any duty to such a board.

There are four final paragraphs to this section which are not concerned with the organization and functioning of joint boards.

Paragraph (g) gives any party at interest in a case arising under this part the same right to judicial relief that is provided with respect to orders of the Commission issued under the provisions of part I. Any order may be appealed to a court of "competent jurisdiction." There is, however, one interesting difference between this part and part I. It will be remembered that under part I a "negative order" of the Commission is not subject to judicial review. If under this part the Commission should issue a negative order, "solely because of a supposed lack of power," a party at interest may file a bill of complaint with a Federal district court, and if the court decides that the Commission does have the power "supposed" to be lacking, it may order the Commission to take jurisdiction in the matter about which the negative order was issued.

Paragraph (h) states that all the provisions of section 17, part I, shall apply to proceedings under this part. Section 17 describes in detail the procedure which the Commission may employ.

Paragraph (i) provides that members of the Commission, its examiners, and members of joint boards shall hold no official relation to, own securities of, or have any pecuniary interest in "any motor carrier or in any carrier by railroad, water, or other form of transportation."

Paragraph (j) authorizes the Commission to employ such assistance as it may deem necessary for the administration of this part.

Application for Certificate of Public Convenience and Necessity

Section 206. We now come to the provisions of the law which are substantive in nature.

Paragraph (a) provides that, with certain exceptions to be pointed out later, every common carrier by motor vehicle subject to the provisions of this part must secure from the Commission a "certificate of convenience and necessity" as a condition to operation. A "grandfather clause" protected bona fide carriers which were in operation on June 1, 1935.

Paragraph (b) indicates how applications for certificates may be filed with the Commission.

Issuance of Certificate.

Section 207. This section provides that a certificate shall be issued to any qualified applicant, authorizing the whole or part of the operations applied for, if it is found that the applicant is "fit, willing and able" properly to perform the proposed service, and that the proposed service, to the extent to be authorized, "is or will be required by the present or future public convenience and necessity." Common carriers of passengers receive certificates, only for operations over regular routes and between fixed termini, except as they may be authorized to engage in charter operations.

Terms and Conditions of Certificates

Section 208. Paragraph (a) states that a certificate must describe the services which it authorizes, giving the territory in which the services are to be provided. The Commission may establish such reasonable terms and conditions as the public convenience and necessity may require. Each carrier receiving a certificate has the right to add to its facilities as the development of its business may require.

Paragraph (b) permits reasonable "deviation" under such rules as the Commission may prescribe.

Paragraph (c) permits a certificated carrier to offer chartered services under such rules as the Commission may issue.

Paragraph (d) authorizes a carrier having a certificate for the transportation of passengers to transport mail, express, and baggage in the same vehicle with passengers, or to transport baggage in a separate vehicle.

Permits for Contract Carriers by Motor Vehicle

Section 209. Paragraph (a) explains that the contract carrier does not procure a "certificate" from the Commission, but a "permit," by which it is authorized to operate. There is a grandfather clause for the contract carrier, too.

Paragraph (b) states that applications for permits are made in the same manner as are applications for certificates, and a permit will be issued if the applicant is "fit, willing and able" to perform the operations described in the application, and if the operation, as authorized, will be "consistent with the public interest and with the national transportation policy." It is not necessary to show that the operation will be required by "public convenience and necessity." Each permit will indicate the nature and scope of the business operations allowed, and the Commission may at any time indicate the terms, limitations, and conditions of the permit. A contract carrier, like a common carrier, has the right to add to its equipment and facilities as the demands of its authorized operations may require.

Dual Operations

Section 210. This section provides that, unless the Commission finds it to be consistent with the public interest and the national transportation policy, no person shall have both a certificate and a permit for the transportation of property by motor vehicle over the same route or within the same territory.

In all requirements concerning certificates and permits, Congress showed that a part of its purpose in enacting this part was to prevent too much competition or a wasteful duplication of transportation service.

Temporary Operation of Motor Carrier Properties Pending Action on Application for Consolidation, Merger, and So Forth

Section 210a. This section authorizes the Commission to grant temporary authority, without hearings, for common or contract motor vehicle operation, in order to provide service to points having no carrier service meeting their urgent needs. It also permits the "temporary merger" of motor carrier properties pending hearings on applications for a definitive merger.

Brokerage Licenses

Section 211. A considerable amount of motor vehicle transportation, of both passengers and property, is arranged for through brokers, just as steamship space is engaged in foreign travel and trade. Paragraph (a) states that a broker must obtain a license from the Commission before engaging in the sale of transportation. A broker may not actually engage in transportation unless it has a certificate or permit, and its bona fide employees are not required to have a broker's license, even for the sale of transportation it conducts under joint arrangements with another carrier having a like certificate or permit or with a common carrier by railroad, express, or water.

Paragraph (b) states the qualifications necessary for an applicant to obtain a broker's license, and provides a grandfather clause.

Paragraph (c) directs the Commission to prescribe reasonable rules and regulations for the protection of shippers and travelers who deal with licensed brokers, and requires a broker to furnish a bond to ensure financial responsibility in the conduct of his business.

Paragraph (d) gives the Commission the same authority with respect to the accounts and records of brokers that it has with regard to motor carriers.

Suspension, Change, Revocation, and Transfer of Certificates, Permits, and Licenses

Section 212. Certificates, permits, and licenses may be suspended or revoked by the Commission for willful failure on the part of a holder to comply with this part. With minor exceptions, a certificate or permit may be transferred under such rules and regulations as the Commission may make.

Issuance of Securities

Section 214. [1] Common and contract carriers by motor vehicle and corporations authorized by the Commission to control such carrier or carriers are subject, with regard to the issuance of securities, to paragraphs 2 to 11, section 20a, part I, under which the issuance of securities by railroads is regulated, except that the provisions will not apply to motor carriers with a capitalization of $500,000 or less or to the issue of notes of a maturity of two years or less and aggregating not more than $100,000.

Security for the Protection of the Public

Section 215. This section was discussed in Chapter XIII. It provides that the Commission may require a motor carrier to take out insurance, file surety bonds, or make other arrangements to ensure its ability to pay valid claims or judgments growing out of the injury to persons or property.

Rates, Fares, and Charges of Common Carriers by Motor Vehicle

Section 216. Paragraph (a) states that the fares and other charges of common carriers of passengers by motor vehicle must be just and reasonable, and so must all regulations, rules, and practices. It is the duty of such carriers to establish reasonable through routes at fares which are reasonable and unprejudicial to participating carriers.

Paragraph (b) says that common carriers of property by motor vehicle must provide safe and adequate equipment and service and must enforce just and reasonable rates and practices.

Under the terms of paragraph (c), common carriers of property by

[1] When enacted, in 1935, the Motor Vehicle Act had a section 213 dealing with the matter of the merger and consolidation of motor vehicle carriers with other carriers. In 1940, the rules and regulations with regard to these matters were made a part of section 5, part I. Since no other matter was substituted for that which was transferred, there is no section 213 as the part now stands.

motor vehicle may establish reasonable through routes and joint rates, in connection with other carriers by highway, rail, or water, but they have no duty to do so. Common carriers of passengers by motor vehicle are required to establish through routes and joint rates with other carriers of passengers by motor vehicle. Under this paragraph they "may" establish through services in connection with carriers by rail and by water, but there is no obligation to do so.

Paragraph (d) forbids unjust and unreasonable charges and all undue and unjust discrimination, preference, and prejudice. It is worthy of note that the provisions with regard to these matters, which take up a large portion of the first four sections of part I, are here confined to one short paragraph. There is nothing in this part resembling sections 2 and 4 of part I. The provisions with respect to discrimination are virtually the same as those contained in section 3 of part I.

Paragraph (e) tells how complaints may be filed alleging violations of this part and who may file them, and authorizes the Commission to act on its own initiative if it believes the law is being violated. This paragraph gives the Commission corrective powers over common carrier motor vehicle rates found to be unreasonable or unduly discriminatory, but the Commission is denied the power to regulate intrastate rates or fares even for the purpose of removing discriminations against interstate commerce.

Paragraph (d) authorizes the Commission to prescribe the divisions of joint rates established by a motor vehicle common carrier, in conjunction with other carriers, if current divisions are found to be inequitable or prejudicial.

Paragraph (g) gives the Commission the power to suspend proposed rates and practices pending an investigation of their reasonableness or lawfulness. The time of suspension is limited to seven months, but the Commission is not authorized, as in the case of railroads, to require motor vehicle carriers to keep an account of increased charges collected if at the end of the seven-month period of suspension the Commission has not concluded its investigation and the rates go into effect. The burden of proof rests upon the carrier to show the reasonableness of a proposed change.

Paragraph (h) explains that if, in a proceeding to determine the reasonableness of a rate, the Commission gives consideration to the "value" of the property of the carrier as a base upon which return is calculated, it shall not allow as elements of that value either good will, earning power, or the certificate under which the carrier operates. This is a far cry from *Smyth v. Ames*, in which all elements of value, tangible and intangible, including earning power, were entitled to consideration.

Paragraph (i) is the rule of rate making to be observed by the Commission in the regulation of the rates of common carriers by motor vehicle.

It is similar to the rule prescribed in section 15a, with respect to railroad rates, except that here the Commission is required to give due consideration "to the inherent advantages of transportation by such carriers."

Paragraph (j) is a saving clause, declaring that nothing in this section shall extinguish any "remedy or right of action not inconsistent herewith."

Tariffs of Common Carriers by Motor Vehicle

Section 217. This section makes provision for the publication and filing of the tariffs of motor vehicle common carriers. It is copied largely after section 6, part I. Published tariffs must be scrupulously observed; rebates are forbidden; the rules with respect to free or reduced-rate transportation are as found in sections 1 and 22 of part I. Changes in rates are to be made only on thirty days' notice, except by permission of the Commission. A common carrier by motor vehicle is forbidden to engage in transportation unless rate schedules are properly filed and published.

Schedules of Contract Carriers by Motor Vehicle

Section 218. The provisions with respect to the rate schedules and practices of contract carriers are widely different from the provisions applicable to the rates and practices of common carriers by motor vehicle. The contract carrier is required to observe only "reasonable minimum" rates and charges for services performed. Schedules of such minimum rates must be filed with the Commission, published, and kept open for public inspection. Contract carriers may not operate unless rates are properly published and filed; reductions may not be made except on thirty days' notice, except with permission of the Commission; published rates must be collected, and no contract carrier shall accept less than its duly published charges. It is provided, however, that the Commission may excuse a contract carrier from the general duty to publish and file its minimum charges, if the Commission should deem such action consistent with the public interest and the national transportation policy.

The Commission has corrective powers over the charges of contract carriers and may establish a minimum rate or charge to be observed in place of one found to be unreasonable.

One of the most interesting provisions of this section, and of the entire part, states that no minimum rate prescribed by the Commission shall give any undue advantage or preference to a contract carrier in competition with a common carrier by motor vehicle. As it was explained previously, the general provisions with respect to undue discrimination practiced by common carriers by motor vehicle, set forth in section 216, are not to be construed "to apply to discriminations, prejudice, or disadvantage to the traffic of any other carrier of whatever description." But the Commission may not give a contract carrier an undue advantage over a common carrier by motor vehicle.

A "rule of rate making" for contract carriers directs the Commission, in regulating the charges of such carriers, to give due consideration to the cost of service and to the effect which the minimum rate or charge shall have upon the movement of traffic by such carriers.

The Commission has the power to suspend a proposed reduced charge or any new charge of a contract carrier, similar in all respects to the powers of suspension it exercises over the rates and charges of other carriers. Here, too, if the Commission has not concluded its investigation within seven months, the charge goes into effect. The burden of proof rests upon the carrier to show the reasonableness of any proposed change.

Receipts or Bills of Lading

Section 219. This section says simply that the provisions of paragraphs (11) and (12), section 20, part I, shall apply to transportation by common carriers by motor vehicle. This means that all these carriers have the duties, obligations, and liability imposed upon rail carriers by the Carmack and the two Cummins Amendments. These matters were discussed at length in Chapters XI and XII.

Accounts, Records, and Reports

Section 220. As is the case with carriers subject to part I, the Commission may require such regular and special reports as it deems necessary from common and contract carriers by motor vehicle, as well as from licensed brokers, subject to part II. It may prescribe the methods of accounting to be employed, and has full policing power to see that its rules, regulations, and orders are properly observed.

Orders, Notices, and Service of Process

Section 221. Paragraph (a) states that, whereas a railroad is required to appoint an agent with offices in Washington upon whom an order or a notice of the Commission may be served, it is the duty of a carrier or broker subject to part II to file with the board of each state in which it operates, and also with the Commission, the name and post-office address of the person upon whom service of notice or orders may be made. Service may be made directly upon the carrier or upon the designated agent, or may be made by registered mail to the designated agent. If no agent has been designated, service may be made by posting in the office of the clerk of the board of the state in which the carrier maintains headquarters and in the office of the secretary of the Commission.

Paragraph (b) provides that Commission orders issued under the provisions of this part shall take effect "within such reasonable time, not less than thirty days, as the Commission may prescribe" and shall continue in force during the pleasure of the Commission, unless modified, suspended, or set aside by the Commission, or set aside by a court of "competent jurisdiction."

Paragraph (c) requires a motor carrier to file with the board of each state in which it operates the name and address of an agent upon whom service of judicial process may be made. In case of failure to designate such an agent, service may be made upon any agent of the motor carrier in such state.

Unlawful Operation

Section 222. Paragraph (a) provides that any person who knowingly or willfully violates any provision of this part or any terms of certificate, permit, or license, for which a penalty is not otherwise in this part provided, shall upon conviction be subject to a fine of not more than $100 for the first offense and not more than $500 for each subsequent offense. Each day of violation is to be considered as a separate offense.

Paragraph (b) states that if any motor carrier or broker subject to this part violates the terms of the part (except as to the reasonableness or unduly discriminatory character of charges) or any rule or regulation, requirement, or order thereunder, or any condition of certificate or permit, the Commission is authorized to apply to a Federal district court for enforcement of the part of the law or the condition or order violated. The court has power to issue an injunction or mandatory order requiring compliance with the law.

Paragraph (c) provides penalties for rebating or transporting passengers or property at less than the applicable charges as provided in published tariffs.

Paragraph (d) forbids agents of the Commission to divulge any fact or information which they may obtain in the course of any investigation of the accounts and business operations of a motor carrier, except as directed to by the Commission or by a court. A penalty of fine and imprisonment is provided for disobedience.

Paragraph (e) makes it unlawful for a motor carrier or broker, or its agents, to make any unauthorized disclosure of information concerning the property received for transportation from any shipper.

Paragraph (f) states that the preceding paragraph shall not be construed to prohibit the disclosure of information sought by a duly authorized agent of the government, if such information is desired for the purpose of the prosecution of crime.

Paragraph (g) provides penalties for the failure on the part of a motor carrier to make reports such as the Commission may order.

Paragraph (h) admonishes the motor carrier to do its business on a cash basis, but permits credit arrangements under rules and regulations which the Commission may prescribe. However, the United States and each state or political subdivision thereof is entitled to credit. An agent to whom goods are shipped is not liable for transportation charges, if he is not the beneficial owner and discloses to the carrier the name of the beneficial owner. The agent is liable, however, if the information given turns out to be erroneous.

Identification of Interstate Carriers

Section 224. Vehicles subject to the provisions of this part must bear an identifying plate as described by the Commission. The owner of the vehicle must pay the cost of the license plates, the receipts going to the United States Treasury.

Allowances to Shippers for Transportation Services

Section 225. A motor carrier, like a railroad, may make allowances to a shipper for the performance of a service which, in the ordinary course of its business, the carrier would perform at the published rate. Such allowances must be reasonable, and must be published in properly filed tariffs.

Investigation of Motor Vehicle Sizes, Weights, and So Forth

Section 226. The Commission is authorized by this section to investigate and report upon the need for Federal regulation of sizes and weights of motor vehicles and of the qualifications and maximum hours of service of the employees "of all motor carriers and private carriers of property by motor vehicle."

Separability of Provisions

Section 227. This section is a precautionary measure found in many laws enacted by Congress, providing that if one part of the Act is declared to be invalid, other parts shall not be affected.

Time Effective

Section 228. This final section, rendered obsolete by the passage of time, made this part effective December 1, 1935, but authorized the Commission to postpone the effective date of any provision, but not beyond April 1, 1936.

CONCLUSION

A study of parts I and II of the Interstate Commerce Act shows that the general purpose of both sections is essentially the same, though because of the difference in the types of carriers there are some differences between the two parts. For example, there are no "contract" carriers by railroad, and such carriers are not mentioned in part I. Because of the similarity of the objects to be achieved by both parts, some of the provisions of part I are in effect written into part II, such as the provisions with respect to liability for loss or damage. These provisions apply to contract carriers as well as to common carriers by motor vehicle. It was explained above that the provisions of the law with respect to combinations and consolidations of motor carriers, which once formed a separate section of part II, were transferred to section 5 of part I. Under the terms of the Reed-Bulwinkle Act (section 5a, part I), motor vehicle carriers, as well as rail carriers, motor carriers, and freight forwarders, are sheltered against prosecution for making rates by the "conference" method.

There are some dissimilarities in the two parts of the statute, however, which do not necessarily arise from the fact that there is a difference in the types of carriers. Some of these differences give rise to the belief that the regulation of our transportation facilities is not in all respects "fair and impartial." For example, while the orders of the Commission are made binding in both parts, the penalty for noncompliance, except in connection with keeping accounts and records, is less for the motor vehicle carrier than for the rail carrier. Another difference, which doubtless receives approbation by the members of the Commission, is that part II makes no reference whatever to a shipper's right to recover damages from a motor vehicle carrier for violation of the statute, except of course in case of loss of or damage to a shipment. The Commission is not authorized to "award" damages to a shipper because the Act has been violated by a motor vehicle carrier. Although the subject is not mentioned, there can be no question of the right of a shipper to bring suit in a court for damages sustained because a motor carrier has failed to observe the terms of the statute. Congress probably acted wisely in not inflicting upon the Commission the power and the duty of awarding damages to a complainant, in a motor vehicle case. As indicated before, the Commission would be pleased if part I were amended to put it in the same position with respect to other carriers. Another difference, which is somewhat difficult to explain, is that the Commission is specifically denied authority to regulate any intrastate rates which may create a discrimination against interstate or foreign commerce.

CHAPTER XXIV

The Interstate Commerce Act: Parts III and IV

PART III

The third part of the Interstate Commerce Act, dealing with the regulation of water carriers engaged in the interstate and foreign commerce of the United States, was embodied in the Transportation Act of 1940. Although that law contained certain amendments to the previously enacted parts, by far the largest portion of it was devoted to the regulation of water carriers, which now joined railroads, pipelines, express companies, motor vehicle carriers, and carriers by air in being subjected to control by the Federal government. Perhaps it would be better to say that the carriers by water were subjected to a larger degree of control, for ever since the passage of the Shipping Act of 1916 their business operations had been regulated, but not to the extent that they were to be regulated under this part. It will be remembered that a portion of the Transportation Act of 1940 consisted of the declaration of national transportation policy, which now appears as a preamble to the entire Interstate Commerce Act.

Short Title

Section 301. "This part, divided into sections according to the following table of contents, may be cited as Part III of the Interstate Commerce Act." The table of contents is omitted here, since it consists of the catch titles appearing at the heads of the various sections.

Definitions

Section 302. This section contains the definitions of certain terms as they are employed in the statute, such as person, Commission, United States, state, common carrier by railroad, and common carrier by water. Although the term "state" is defined so as to include the District of Columbia, the draftsmen forgot this fact occasionally and piled up some of the superfluous verbiage found in so many of our statutes. Some of the definitions should be given with some detail.

The term "water carrier" means a common carrier or a contract carrier by water.

A "common carrier by water" holds itself out to serve the general public for compensation, but it is not to include transportation by water by an express company subject to part I.

A "contract carrier by water," with the same exception as to the express business, engages in transportation by water under individual contracts or agreements. When a vessel is chartered to a person not subject to the Interstate Commerce Act, for the transportation of its own property, the chartering shall be considered as a contract carrier operation. The Commission may, however, in its discretion, exempt such chartering from the terms of the Act.

A "vessel" is any watercraft or "other artificial contrivance" which may be used in transportation by water.

The term "transportation facility" includes terminal facilities and other equipment employed in transportation by water, as well as vessels.

The term "transportation" embraces all services in or in connection with transportation, including such services as icing, storage, transit, and handling.

The term "transportation in interstate or foreign commerce" means the transportation of persons or property (1) wholly by water from one state to another whether or not the transportation takes place wholly within the United States; (2) partly by water and partly by railroad or motor vehicle from a place in one state to a place in any other, except that any movement by rail or motor vehicle outside the United States is not included; (3) wholly by water, or partly by water and partly by railroad or motor vehicle, from or to a place in the United States to or from a place outside the United States, but only in so far as the movement by rail or motor vehicle takes place within the United States, and the movement by water takes place to a place for transshipment outside the United States, or from a place where transshipment takes place for entry into the United States.

Application of Provisions; Exemptions

Section 303. Paragraph (a) states that, if transportation is subject to both part I and part III, part I shall apply only to the extent that it imposes requirements not imposed by part III.

Paragraphs (b) to (h) provide for the exemption of numerous water transportation services from the impact of this part. The exemptions are so numerous and so extensive that it can readily be seen that a very large part of our domestic transportation by water is not subject to regulation under this law. The exemptions include transportation by a water carrier of commodities in bulk "when the cargo space of the vessel in which such commodities are transported is being used for the carrying of not more than three such commodities." This particular exemption does not apply, however, to intercoastal carriers. The next exemption applies to transportation by a contract carrier by water of commodities in bulk in a non-ocean-going vessel, if the cargo space is occupied by not more than three such commodities and if the vessel passes through waters which have been made international for purposes of navigation. Tank vessels carrying liquid cargo in bulk are exempt. In addition to the foregoing exemptions, there is a declaration of Congressional "policy" to exclude from the terms of this part that transportation by contract carriers by water which, "by reason of the inherent nature of the commodities transported, their requirement of special equipment, or their shipment in bulk, is not actually and substantially competitive with transportation by any common carrier subject to this part or part I or part II." The Commission is authorized to issue an order of exemption for carriers engaged in such noncompetitive transportation.

This part does not apply to transportation by water by a railroad or by a motor carrier if such transportation is "incidental" to terminal transfer services, such as floatage or towage. This exemption extends to those who may be performing such terminal services under contract. All these services are subject to regulation under part I or part II, being considered an integral part of rail or motor vehicle service.

Unless the Commission finds regulation necessary in order to give effect to the national transportation policy, this part does not apply to water transportation within harbors or between places in contiguous harbors if the transportation is not part of a through service, or to

. . . transportation by small craft of not more than one hundred tons carrying capacity or not more than one hundred indicated horsepower, or to vessels carrying passengers only, and equipped to carry no more than sixteen passengers, or to ferries, or to the movement by water carriers of contractors' equipment employed or to be employed in construction or repair for such water carrier, or to the operation of salvors.

Finally, this part does not apply to a water carrier engaged in transporting the property of a person who owns all or substantially all of the voting stock of such carrier. The Commission has the power to determine whether any carrier is entitled to this exemption, and if so to issue a revocable certificate of exemption.

Paragraph (i) states that water carriers owned or controlled by the United States are subject to the same general rules and regulations as carriers not so owned or controlled.

Paragraph (j) reserves to each state the right to regulate intrastate commerce by water carriers within the jurisdiction of such state.

Paragraph (k) follows a similar clause in part II by declaring that the Commission is not authorized to regulate any charges for intrastate transportation, for the purpose of removing discrimination against interstate commerce "or for any other purpose."

Paragraph (1) provides that if a certain kind of water transportation, which has been exempted, becomes subject to this part, the carrier has one hundred and twenty days of grace to operate without certificate.

General Powers and Duties of the Commission

Section 304. This section gives the Commission the same authority over water carriers subject to this part that it exercises over motor vehicle carriers subject to part II. It can investigate, require reports, classify carriers, and order them to comply with all provisions of the law. In addition, paragraph (d) authorizes the Commission, should it find that the charges or practices of persons engaged in transportation by water to or from a port or ports of any foreign country in competition with common or contract carriers of the United States cause undue disadvantage to such carriers, to relieve such carriers from the provisions of this part to the extent necessary to avoid the disadvantage.

Rates, Fares, Charges, and Practices; Through Routes

Section 305. Paragraph (a), following the general pattern of parts I and II, requires common carriers by water to furnish adequate service at just and reasonable rates.

Paragraph (b) states that, like railroads, but unlike motor vehicle carriers of property, common carriers by water have the "duty" of establishing through routes at reasonable rates with other common carriers by water and with railroads. The establishment of through routes in connection with common carriers by motor vehicle is optional.

Paragraph (c) forbids common carriers by water to charge rates which are unjustly discriminatory or unreasonably prejudicial. A special clause states that differences of water carrier rates from rail rates is not prohibited, and such differences shall not be deemed to constitute undue discrimination.

Paragraph (d) requires common carriers by water to afford reasonable facilities for the interchange of traffic with other common carriers by water and with railroads, without discriminating against any connecting line.

Tariffs and Schedules

Section 306. Common carriers by water are required to publish and file their rates in the same manner and make the same rules as common carriers by rail or motor vehicle. Contract carriers by water are required to file their scales of minimum charges in the same manner as contract carriers by motor vehicle.

Commission's Authority over Rates, and So Forth

Section 307. The Commission has corrective power over the rates of water carriers in all respects similar to the power it has over the charges of railroad and motor vehicle carriers. The Commission has authority to establish through routes and joint rates applicable to the transportation of both passengers and property by common carriers by water and by water and rail. This power extends only to the transportation of passengers by motor vehicle common carriers. The Commission also has the power to prescribe the divisions of joint rates. The rule of rate making applicable to transportation by common carriers by water is the same as that prescribed in connection with transportation by common carriers by motor vehicle. Likewise, the Commission's authority with respect to the suspension of proposed charges of both common and contract carriers by water is virtually the same as that possessed with respect to the same carriers by motor vehicle.

Reparation Awards; Limitation of Actions

Section 308. If any carrier by water engaged in transportation through the Panama Canal, or a common carrier by water on the high seas or Great Lakes on regular routes from port to port, shall permit to be performed anything declared in this part to be unlawful, or omit to do any act it is required to do under this part, it shall be liable for the "full amount of damages sustained in consequence of such violation." Here part III follows part I, in so far at least as the carriers mentioned are concerned, and differs from part II, in which reparation is not mentioned. Just as in part I, the person seeking reparation for damages due to violation of the law may appeal either to the Commission or to a Federal district court, but shall not have the right to pursue both remedies. Orders by the Commission for the payment of monetary damages may be enforced by a district court.

All complaints against carriers for the recovery of damages or overcharges shall be filed with the Commission within two years from the time the cause of action accrues. The time limitation for such complaints in part I is two years in case of damages other than overcharges, and the same for overcharges, with certain qualifications. A complaint for the enforcement of an order of the Commission for the payment of money must be filed within one year after the date of the order.

Certificates of Public Convenience and Necessity and Permits

Section 309. The Commission issues certificates of convenience and necessity to common carriers by water and permits to contract carriers by water just as it does to carriers by motor vehicle. There are the usual grandfather clauses, and the carriers are forbidden to operate without a certificate, or permit, as the case may be. The methods of filing applications and issuance and the terms and conditions of the documents are virtually the same as for motor carriers.

Dual Operations under Certificates and Permits

Section 310. Under ordinary circumstances, the same person shall not hold both a certificate and a permit, but the Commission may make an exception if it is thought to be consistent with the public interest.

Temporary Operations

Section 311. In case of urgent need, the Commission may authorize emergency operations to a point not having adequate transportation service.

Transfer of Certificates and Permits

Section 312. These documents may be transferred under such regulations as the Commission may prescribe. In the corresponding section of part II (212), provision is made for the suspension or revocation of certificates and permits by the Commission. The Commission has recommended the amendment of this part to give it equal powers with respect to the permits and certificates of carriers by water.

Accounts, Records, and Reports

Section 313. This section follows corresponding sections in the first two parts, giving the Commission virtually complete authority over the accounting practices of water carriers, with policing power as well as authority to require any regular or special report needed, and to require the filing of all contracts or agreements which a water carrier may make with any other carrier.

Allowances to Shippers for Transportation Service

Section 314. Like carriers by rail or highway, a carrier by water may permit a shipper to perform certain services which ordinarily fall within the duty of the carrier and are compensated for in the transportation rate. The carrier has the right to make proper allowances for such services, when performed by shippers, but such allowances must be authorized by duly published tariffs and are subject to regulation by the Commission.

Notices, Orders, and Service of Process

Section 315. This section follows the pattern of part II. The carrier by water must designate agencies upon which notices may be served, but they are not required, as railroads are, to maintain an agent in Washington upon whom legal papers may be served. Here, too, are provisions stating that the Commission shall issue a finding that a carrier has violated this part only after hearing, authorizing the Commission to modify or set aside its own orders, and stipulating that all orders of the Commission, other than for the payment of money, shall take effect within such reasonable time, not less than thirty days, as the Commission may direct, and shall remain in force either for a specified time or until modified or set aside by the Commission or a court.

Enforcement and Procedure

Section 316. Witnesses may be compelled to give testimony, but only under immunity from prosecution. In case a carrier refuses to obey an order of the Commission, the Commission may apply, through the Attorney General, to a Federal district court for an order requiring obedience. Provisions with respect to the Commission's duty as to its hearings, orders, and awards follow the provisions of the first two parts.

Unlawful Acts and Penalties

Section 317. This section likewise follows the provisions of parts I and II with regard to penalties for rebating, acceptance of rebates or concessions, false billing or other misrepresentation, failure to make correct reports, and unauthorized divulgence of information by agents of the Commision or by a carrier.

Collection of Rates and Charges

Section 318. Common carriers by water are required to transact their transportation business on a cash basis, giving credit only as the Commission may permit.

Repeals

Section 320. This section repeals certain parts of previously enacted laws, the provisions of which are superseded by this part. Attention is called, however, to the fact that certain features of these previously enacted statutes are not repealed.

Transfer of Employees, Records, Property, and Appropriations

Section 321. Before the enactment of this part, virtually all of the regulatory statutes applicable to water carriers in domestic commerce had been administered by the Shipping Board or by its successors, the Shipping Board Bureau and the United States Maritime Commission. In this section, employees, property, records, and files of the Maritime Commission were to be transferred, as the President might determine, to the Interstate Commerce Commission.

Existing Orders, Rules, Tariffs, and So Forth; Pending Matters

Section 322. This section provides for the continuation in effect of existing orders, contracts, and rulings until changed or modified by the Interstate Commerce Commission. It transferred all pending proceedings before the Maritime Commission to the new regulatory authority.

Separability of Provisions

Section 323. This is the customary provision that the invalidation of one part of the law would not be construed as affecting the validity of the remainder of the statute.

PART IV

This part of the Interstate Commerce Act was added to the law in 1942. It has for its purpose the regulation of the freight forwarding business.

Short Title

Section 401. This part is to be cited as part IV of the Interstate Commerce Act. A table of contents is included in this section, consisting of the catch titles of the various sections of the part.

Definitions and Exemptions

Section 402. Here we find repeated several of the definitions given in other parts of the Act, such as those of person, state, United States, Commission, interstate commerce, and control. However, we meet with some new definitions, the most important being that of a freight forwarder as

. . . any person which (otherwise than as a carrier subject to part I, II, or III of this Act) holds itself out to the general public to transport or to provide transportation of property, or any class or classes of property, for compensation, in interstate commerce, and which, in the ordinary and usual course of its undertaking, (A) assembles and consolidates and provides for assembling and consolidating shipments of such property, and performs or provides for the performance of break-bulk and distributing operations with respect to such consolidated shipments, and (B) assumes responsibility for the transportation of such property from point of receipt to point of destination, and (C) utilizes, for the whole or any part of the transportation of such shipments, the services of a carrier or carriers subject to part I, II, or III of this Act.

It should be noted that a freight forwarder, as defined by this part, is one utilizing the services of carriers subject to the first three parts of the Act. There is nothing to prevent a forwarder from using the services of a carrier by air. If a forwarder uses only air transportation in its business, it is not subject to this part but to the Civil Aeronautics Act as an "indirect carrier" by air. In conjunction with this section, however, consideration must be given to section 418, which forbids a freight forwarder, except in the performance of terminal services, to employ or utilize the services of any carriers except those subject to the first three parts of the Interstate Commerce Act, subject to the Civil Aeronautics Act, or specifically exempted from regulation under parts II and III. In other words, there can be no "unregulated" freight forwarders, though their business may be subject to the control of the Interstate Commerce Commission or of the Civil Aeronautics Board or both.

Subsection (7), paragraph (a), of this section specifically exempts from this part the operations of a freight forwarder in connection with an air carrier or an "exempt" motor vehicle carrier.

Paragraphs (b) and (c) of this section give some highly important exemptions. Among these are the services of agricultural cooperative associations as defined by the Agricultural Marketing Act of 1929, services in connection with the transportation of ordinary livestock, fish (including shellfish), agricultural commodities, or used household goods, if the services of the forwarder are conducted with respect to not more than one of these classes of property. In addition, this part does not apply to the operations of a shipper or an association of shippers consolidating and distributing freight for themselves on a nonprofit basis, for the benefit of securing carload or other "volume" rates, or to the operations of a warehouseman or other shippers' agent in consolidating and distributing pool cars, if the operations are confined solely to a terminal area. As may well be imagined, the Commission has occasionally had some difficulty in deciding whether particular services come within the scope of these exemptions.

General Powers and Duties of Commission

Section 403. The Commission has powers and duties similar in all respects to those exercised over motor vehicle carriers, including the power of investigation, of requiring adequate service, and of requiring forwarders to provide surety bonds or other evidences of financial responsibility for injury to persons or loss and damage to property.

Rates, Charges, and Practices

Section 404. Like the rates of common carriers subject to the Act, the rates of forwarders must be reasonable and not unduly discriminatory. Common carriers subject to the first three parts are forbidden to give to one forwarder any undue advantage or preference over another, whether or not such forwarder is controlled by the carrier. Forwarders may enter into ageements for joint loading, subject to Commission supervision and control.

Tariffs of Freight Forwarders

Section 405. The tariffs of freight forwarders must be published and filed, just like the tariffs of carriers, and must be prepared in accordance with the rules and instructions of the Commission.

Commission's Authority over Rates and Practices

Section 406. The Commission's powers over the rates and practices of freight forwarders are virtually the same as its powers over the rates and practices of rail, highway, and water carriers. It can correct rates found to be unlawful, and it has the power of suspension, for a limited period, of new rates and proposed changes in rates. It has the same authority over intrastate rates of freight forwarders that it has over the rates of railroads but not over the rates of highway and water carriers, that is, it can correct intrastate rates which would have the effect of causing undue discrimination against interstate commerce, regardless of the laws or regulations of a state.

Section 406a. This section was not included in this part as it was passed originally, but was added as an afterthought, in 1949. With regard to the matter of reparation for damages suffered because of violation of the law or overcharges, this part follows part II rather than parts I and III. The Commission is not authorized to award reparation. This section sets the time within which "actions at law" may be brought by freight forwarders for undercharges or actions brought against forwarders for overcharges. The time limit is in general two years, but under certain circumstances it may be longer in case the action is for overcharges.

Motor Carrier Rates Applicable to Small Parcel Forwarding

Section 407. Common carriers by motor vehicle, subject to part II, are authorized to give consideration to the type of property tendered for transportation by a forwarder, with respect to parcels not exceeding 70 pounds in weight or 100 inches in length and girth combined.

Authority for Assembling and Distribution Rates

Section 408. Common carriers subject to the first three parts are authorized to extend to freight forwarders (and others) assembling and distribution rates different from assembling and distribution charges ordinarily applied, if the difference in the charge is justified by a difference in the service extended. An assembling rate is one charged for the transportation of less carload or less truckload shipments to a point for consolidation, and a distribution rate is one for the movement of less carload or less truckload shipments from a point into which they have moved as a carload or truckload. The assembling and distribution charges do not apply to line-haul movements between concentration and break-bulk points.

Freight Forwarders and Motor Vehicle Carriers

Section 409. When this part was enacted, in 1942, many freight forwarders had joint or cooperative arrangements with carriers by motor vehicle, the legality of which under the new law was subject, to say the least, to some doubt. This section originally made temporary provision for the possible continuation of the joint arrangements of freight forwarders and motor carriers in force at the time the law was enacted. In February, 1946, the section was rewritten to prescribe the conditions under which the joint operations of freight forwarders and common carriers by motor vehicle might be carried on, subject to the direction and control of the Commission.

Permits

Section 410. This section states that no person shall engage in a forwarding service subject to this part without obtaining a permit from the Commission. Grandfather rights are preserved. The methods of application, the conditions under which permits are granted, and the terms of permits are similar to the methods, conditions, and terms mentioned in connection with the permits given to contract carriers by motor vehicle. No forwarder permit will be issued to a carrier subject to part I, II, or III of the Act, though no application for a permit made by a corporation controlled by, or under common control with, a carrier subject to any one of the first three parts will be denied merely because of such relationship. Prospective competition with another forwarder will not cause the denial of any application for a permit. Permits may be transferred under Commission rules and, unlike the permits and certificates of carriers by water, may be revoked or suspended by the Commission. If the transfer of a permit affects the interests of the employees of a forwarder, the Commission may require, as a condition of the transfer, some equitable arrangement for the protection of such interests. A forwarder controlled by a common carrier or under common control with a common carrier subject to part I, II, or III is forbidden to abandon operation without the consent of the Commission.

Relationships between Freight Forwarders and Other Persons

Section 411. Paragraph (a) forbids a forwarder, any person controlling, controlled by, or under common control with a freight forwarder to acquire control of a carrier subject to part I, II, or III. This does not affect the right of a carrier subject to one of those parts to acquire control of another carrier subject to one of the same parts, in accordance with the provisions of section 5 of part I.

Paragraph (b) contains a "commodities clause" for freight forwarders, which forbids a person whose principal business is manufacturing or merchandising "commodities" to engage in any forwarding service subject to this part, though the Commission may make an exception, if the exception is deemed to be "consistent with the public interest."

Paragraph (c) forbids officers, directors, employees, and agents of carriers subject to parts I, II, and III to have any direct or indirect pecuniary interest in a freight forwarder, except to the extent of holding a director's qualifying shares of stock.

Paragraph (d) authorizes the Commission to investigate and determine whether there is any violation of the preceding three paragraphs, and require the violation to be discontinued.

Paragraph (e) permits the Commission to appeal to a Federal district court for the enforcement of any order issued under the authority granted by the preceding paragraph.

Paragraph (f) authorizes the Commission to make supplemental orders to any order issued under the terms of the preceding paragraphs.

Paragraph (g) states that nothing in this Act is to be construed as forbidding a common carrier subject to part I, II, or III to acquire control of a freight forwarder; in case such control is acquired, none of the charges or practices of either the controlling carrier or the controlled forwarder are to be held to be unlawful merely because of the relationship.

Accounts, Records, and Reports

Section 412. This section gives the Commission virtually the same authority with respect to the accounting practices and reports of freight forwarders that it has in connection with carriers subject to the first three parts.

Bills of Lading and Delivery of Property

Section 413. The liability of a freight forwarder for lost and damaged shipments is by this section made the same as the liability imposed upon rail carriers in section 20 of part I. The forwarder is subject to the Carmack and Cummins Amendments. The forwarder is to be regarded as both the receiving and the delivering transportation company for the purposes of section 20.

When a forwarder utilizes the services of a common carrier by motor vehicle subject to part II for the receipt of shipments from consignors, the motor carrier may execute the bill of lading or shipping receipt on behalf of the forwarder. Similarly, if a motor carrier is employed to deliver forwarder traffic to a consignee named in the forwarder's bill of lading, it may deliver on the freight bill and on the delivery receipt of the forwarder.

Collection of Rates and Charges

Section 414. Like other persons subject to the provisions of the Interstate Commerce Act, freight forwarders are required to operate on a cash basis, except when a body politic is the customer, though the Commission may permit the granting of credit under rules that preclude any unjust discrimination.

Allowances to Shippers for Transportation Service

Section 415. Forwarders may make allowances for services or facilities provided by shippers, under the same conditions prescribed for other transportation agencies subject to the Act.

Notices, Orders, and Service of Processes

Section 416. Forwarders need not have an agent in Washington, but are required to indicate agents upon whom legal papers may be served in the same manner as motor carriers subject to part II. This section also follows corresponding sections in the other parts of the Act in giving the Commission authority to suspend, modify, or set aside its own orders.

Enforcement and Procedure

Section 417. This section follows the pattern set in parts II and III with regard to enforcement and procedure.

Carriers the Services of Which Freight Forwarders May Utilize

Section 418. This section has already been mentioned. Except in their terminal services, forwarders subject to this part may utilize only the services of carriers regulated under other parts of the Act and under the Civil Aeronautics Act.

Liability for Past Acts and Omissions

Section 419. This section constitutes an act of pardon, grace, and absolution. Under it, no person is subject to punishment or liability for any previous act of commission or omission in connection with "establishment, charging, collection, receipt, or payment of rates of freight forwarders, or joint rates or divisions between freight forwarders and common carriers by motor vehicle subject to this Act."

Special Powers during Time of War or Other Emergency

Section 420. This section applies the emergency provisions of part I to freight forwarders.

Unlawful Acts and Penalties

Section 421. This section provides penalties for violation of this part, for such offenses as rebating, accepting rebates, misrepresentation, failure to make accurate reports, falsification of records, and unauthorized disclosure of information. The provisions of the Elkins Act of 1903, directed against rebating in all forms, is made applicable to freight forwarders "in addition to, and not to the exclusion of, the provisions of this part."

Separability of Provisions

Section 422. The invalidation of any provision of this part shall not affect the validity of other provisions.

CHAPTER XXV

The Civil Aeronautics Act

We come now to the last of the major statutes for the regulation of the transportation systems and services of the United States. Although the Civil Aeronautics Act of 1938 follows generally the pattern of the various parts of the Interstate Commerce Act, it has some important differences both in the scope of its application and in the details of its numerous provisions. It is in many respects a much more elaborate document than the Interstate Commerce Act, and deals with matters for which one finds no counterpart in the latter statute.[1]

One major difference is that the Civil Aeronautics Act has to do not only with domestic commerce but also with overseas foreign commerce. Several foreign air transportation companies engage in the transportation of mail, persons, and property between the United States and other nations throughout the world, and this measure sets forth the manner in which arrangements are made for the right of foreign air carriers to participate in our commerce.

Another difference between this aviation law and the laws applicable to surface transportation is that it has many more provisions which can be characterized as "promotional." From the time the Wrights demonstrated, in 1903, the possibility of flight in machines heavier than air, the United States, as well as many other nations, took a lively interest in the development of air transportation, partly because of the effect it might have on military operations and partly because of its probable importance as a future agency of peaceful commerce. The direct interest of the government of the United States in commercial transportation by air was chiefly in connection with the carriage of mail. Before the Civil Aeronautics Act became a law, Congress had enacted several measures whose primary purpose was to bring about the development of a nationwide air mail service. Since the Civil Aeronautics Act superseded virtually all of these previously enacted statutes, it was necessary to include in the new law

[1] The Government Printing Office issues from time to time a booklet containing the Civil Aeronautics Act, other statutory provisions, executive and administrative orders, and certain nonstatutory material relating to civil aeronautics. This booklet may be obtained, for a moderate price, from the Superintendent of Documents in Washington, D.C.

numerous provisions with respect to the transportation of mail, a subject that is seldom mentioned in the various parts of the Interstate Commerce Act.

Another interesting difference between the Civil Aeronautics Act and the Interstate Commerce Act, with the exception of part III, is that the former has nothing whatever to say, of a positive nature, about the liability of an air carrier for injury or death of persons or for loss and damage to property. This omission has been previously noted. Commercial air lines write into their receipts and airbills numerous "limitations" of their liability, which certainly have no statutory sanction and may or may not be regarded as valid under the common law.

Finally, the Civil Aeronautics Act, unlike the four parts of the Interstate Commerce Act, which deal almost exclusively with the services of carriers whose operations are confined to the surface of the earth, is administered not by the Interstate Commerce Commission but by a separate agency, or agencies, the most important one being what is now known as the Civil Aeronautics Board.

The administrative machinery now responsible for the enforcement of the provisions of the Civil Aeronautics Act is not that prescribed by the original and present language of the law. Originally, this administrative organization consisted of three separate agencies. These agencies were designated in the law as the Civil Aeronautics Authority; an Administrator who, though declared to be "in the Authority," nevertheless was assigned functions to be carried on independently of the Authority; and, finally, an Air Safety Board which, like the Administrator, was directed to "cooperate" with the Authority in the "administration and enforcement of the Act." Under authority granted by the Reorganization Act of 1939, President Roosevelt, with the consent of Congress, as required by law, issued a series of reorganization "plans," under which the administrative machinery created by the Civil Aeronautics Act was modified with respect both to its form and to its functions. The five-man Civil Aeronautics Authority was renamed the Civil Aeronautics Board, retaining the powers and duties which the Authority had possessed and receiving some new duties besides. Though nominally linked with the Department of Commerce for accounting and budgetary purposes, the Board remained a completely independent body with regard to its powers of regulation and supervision of the aviation industry. Under the reorganization plan the Administrator, now termed the Administrator of Civil Aeronautics, was definitely separated from the Civil Aeronautics Board and became an official in the Department of Commerce, directly responsible to the Secretary. The Air Safety Board was abolished, and the functions which the Act had assigned to it were entrusted to the Board. The expression "Civil

Aeronautics Authority" lost the official significance given it by the Act, but continued to be employed as a general term to designate both the Board and the Administrator. The expression "Civil Aeronautics Administration" is frequently used rather than Civil Aeronautics Authority.

In the summary of the Civil Aeronautics Act, which is to follow, the term "Civil Aeronautics Board" is used in the discussion of functions and duties which are now lodged in the Board, even though the law still employs the term "Civil Aeronautics Authority." The form in which the Civil Aeronautics Act was drafted and published differs somewhat from the form of the Interstate Commerce Act. It has eleven "titles," under each of which are found numbered and lettered sections and subsections. Each has its own catch title, as in the Interstate Commerce Act.

THE CIVIL AERONAUTICS ACT OF 1938

An introductory paragraph states that "this Act, divided into titles and sections according to the following table of contents, may be cited as the Civil Aeronautics Act of 1938." The table of contents is omitted, the titles and catch titles, of which it consists, being given for the most part in the summary outline.

TITLE I: GENERAL PROVISIONS

Definitions

Title I consists of three sections, the first section giving the definitions of numerous terms as used in the Act. Such terms as person, interstate air commerce, and United States follow the definitions of the Interstate Commerce Act. Most of the definitions, however, are for terms used solely in aviation, and some of these should be briefly explained.

"Aeronautics" is the science and art of flight.

An "air carrier" is a citizen of the United States, who undertakes, directly or indirectly, to engage in air transportation. This definition includes a freight forwarder or any other agency which makes use of air transportation, even though it does not operate aircraft directly. The Board has the authority to exempt indirect carriers from the provisions of the Act.

"Air commerce" includes foreign and domestic air commerce, the transportation of mail by air, and the operation of aircraft which directly affects or which may endanger safety in air commerce.

"Aircraft" is a contrivance used or designed for aerial flight.

"Airman" includes persons who serve as commanders or as members of the crew of aircraft in flight, individuals in charge of the maintenance and inspection of aircraft and appurtenances, and any individual who serves as an aircraft dispatcher or control tower operator.

"Air navigation facility" is a term applied to all mechanical facilities and apparatus used in guiding, take-off, navigation, and landing of aircraft.

"Appliances" means the instruments and apparatus, including parachutes, which are parts of an aircraft or its appurtenances and employed to facilitate flight.

"Air space reservation," under the law, does not mean a reserved seat on a plane, but a space on the earth's surface in which the flight of aircraft is prohibited or restricted.

"Citizen of the United States" means not only an individual citizen but a partnership, of which each member is a citizen, and a corporation, of which the president and two-thirds of the directors are citizens and in which 75 per cent of the voting interest is owned or controlled by citizens.

"Civil aircraft" means aircraft other than public aircraft, while "civil aircraft of the United States" means any aircraft registered as provided by the Act.

"Public aircraft" means aircraft used exclusively in the service of any governmental agency of the United States, but does not include government-owned aircraft used in commercial transportation.

"Foreign air carrier" means a person, not a citizen of the United States, who engages directly or indirectly in foreign air transportation.

Declaration of Policy

The second section of this title is a "declaration of policy," in which the Civil Aeronautics Board is adjured to consider, as being in the public interest, the encouragement and development of a system of air transportation adapted to the commercial needs of the United States; the regulation of air transportation in such a manner as to preserve its inherent advantages, foster sound economic conditions in air transportation, and coordinate transportation by air carriers; the promotion of adequate service at rates which are reasonable, not unduly discriminatory, and free of destructive competitive practices; the maintenance of such competition as is essential to the sound development of air transportation; the promotion of safety in air navigation; and the encouragement and development of civil aeronautics.

It will be noted that this declaration of policy mentions only coordination between air carriers, and is silent on the subject of cooperation between air carriers and surface carriers.

Public Right of Transit

The third section of this title declares that any citizen of the United States has the "public right of freedom of transit in air commerce through the navigable air space of the United States."

TITLE II: ORGANIZATION OF AUTHORITY

Creation of Board; Appointment of Members of Board

Section 201. Paragraph (a) creates the Board of five members, appointed by the President, each for a term of six years, with the advice and consent of the Senate. They are subject to removal by the President for inefficiency, neglect of duty, or malfeasance. No more than three shall belong to the same political party. The salary of each member is fixed at the rate of $12,000 a year.

Administrator

Paragraph (b) provides for the appointment of the Administrator.

Qualifications of Members

Paragraph (c) states that members of the Board shall be selected with due regard to their fitness for the performance of duties imposed by the Act. Members of the Board and the Administrator must be citizens of the United States, none of them shall have any pecuniary interest in an aviation enterprise, and none of them shall have any other business or employment.

Quorum, Principal Office, and Seal

Paragraph (d) states that three members of the Board shall constitute a quorum, names Washington as the place in which the Board's principal office is to be, and authorizes the Board to have an official seal.

Organization of Board

Section 202. This section provides for the appointment by the Board of needed temporary and permanent personnel, including the heads of such divisions or sections as the Board may establish, a secretary for the Board, and a secretary for each member. The Administrator is likewise authorized to appoint necessary aids.

Personnel, Property, and Appropriations

Section 203. This section, of which there are two paragraphs, provides for the transfer to the Board of certain personnel, property, and appropriations previously employed in the regulation and promotion of the aviation industry by other government agencies.

Authorization of Expenditures and Travel

Section 204. Paragraph (a) makes provisions for the expenditure by the Board and the Administrator of such funds as may be necessary for travel, rent, books, magazines, automobiles, and other property needed in the execution of their duties.

Paragraph (b) authorizes the Board, within the limits of Congressional appropriations, to purchase aircraft for experimental purposes.

Paragraph (c) provides that travel by the personnel of the United States government on commercial aircraft, domestic or foreign, may be allowed at public expense, when approved by proper authority, the expenses to be allowed without regard to the comparative costs of transportation by other agencies.

General Powers and Duties of the Board

Section 205. This section, containing four paragraphs, empowers the Board to conduct investigations, to issue orders, and to make such rules and regulations as may be necessary for the enforcement of the Act. The Board may cooperate with state agencies and may exchange information with foreign governments. It is required to issue reports of proceedings and investigations in which formal hearings have been held, just as is the Interstate Commerce Commission.

Annual Report

Section 206. The Board reports annually directly to Congress. The annual report contains such information as the Board and the Administrator have collected which may be considered as having value in the shaping of Congressional policy with respect to aviation and such recommendations with respect to legislation as the Board feels constrained to make. It is authorized, too, to make recommendations with respect to legislation at any time it chooses to do so.

TITLE III: POWERS AND DUTIES OF ADMINISTRATOR

This title, consisting of sections 306 to 309 of the Act, empowers the Administrator to "foster and encourage the development of civil aeronautics and air commerce in the United States," and indicates several ways in which this may be done. A few of the suggested activities are establishing airways, with navigational aids; training control tower operators; conducting research and developmental work; suggesting improvements of meteorological service.

TITLE IV: AIR CARRIER ECONOMIC REGULATION

Certificates of Public Convenience and Necessity; Certificate Required

Section 401. No air carrier shall engage in air transportation without having a certificate from the Board. Grandfather rights are preserved, especially those existing under air mail contracts previously authorized by the Postmaster General. Directions are given on methods of applying for certificates. The Board grants a certificate to an applicant who is "fit, willing, and able" to perform the proposed service, if the Board believes that the service is required by "the public convenience and necessity." The terms and conditions of a certificate are set forth. Each certificate indicates the privileges to be enjoyed by its holder, and states the terminal and intermediate points between which operation is authorized. Any air carrier may engage in special or charter service, without regard to the terms of its certificate. The Board has the right to suspend, modify, or revoke any certificate, and with the Board's permission a certificate may be transferred. An air carrier must not abandon all or any part of a route for which it has a certificate without the consent of the Board, though a temporary suspension may be permitted. Pilots and copilots receive certain protection with respect to compensation and working conditions, and their relationships with employers come within the provisions of title II of the Railway Labor Act. Certificated carriers are required to transport mail on the request of the Postmaster General, and if the Postmaster General believes any extension of air mail service to be desirable, the Board is directed to make provision for it, if public convenience and necessity require it, by the issuance of proper certificates.

Permits to Foreign Air Carriers

Section 402. A foreign air carrier, to engage in air transportation between the United States and a foreign country, must obtain a permit from the Civil Aeronautics Board. The terms and conditions of such permits are given, and the methods by which an applicant may obtain a permit. It should be mentioned here that all permits of foreign air carriers and all certificates authorizing domestic air carriers to engage in foreign air transportation service, according to section 801, title VIII, of the Act, may be issued only subject to the approval of the President of the United States. The modification, revocation, and transfer of such certificates and permits are likewise subject to his approval.

Tariffs of Air Carriers

Section 403. This section follows closely the provisions of the Interstate Commerce Act with respect to the tariffs of surface carriers. Tariffs of both domestic and foreign air carriers must be published and filed in accordance with the rules of the Board. Rates and fares must be given in terms of lawful money of the United States, but they may be stated also in terms of foreign currencies, and the tariffs may contain such information as is required by the governments of foreign nations. All provisions of published tariffs must be rigidly observed, and there must be no rebating. Free transportation or transportation at reduced rates may be enjoyed by certain designated classes of persons under such terms as the Board may prescribe. Tariffs may be changed only on thirty days' notice, except with the consent of the Board. All carriers must file with the Board their agreements for the division of joint rates, fares, and other charges.

Rates for Carriage of Persons and Property

Section 404. Air carriers must provide service, as authorized by their certificates, upon reasonable request, at charges which are just, reasonable, and not unduly discriminatory. Joint charges must be equitably divided among participating carriers.

Transportation of Mail

Section 405. This somewhat long section has to do with the arrangements which the Postmaster General, in cooperation with the Board, may make for the transportation of mail, both domestic and foreign, by air. It authorizes the continuation of "experimental" air mail service, and directs that air carriers transporting mail give free transportation to accredited agents of the Post Office Department traveling on official business.

Rates for Transportation of Mail

Section 406. This section authorizes the Civil Aeronautics Board to fix the compensation an air carrier shall receive for transporting mail and to prescribe the methods by which the said compensation is to be computed.

In determining the rates of compensation for the transportation of mail by air carriers, the Board is authorized to take into consideration the conditions peculiar to each carrier, and it may fix different rates for different carriers. It must give consideration to the "need" of the air carrier for compensation sufficient to enable it to perform the service desired. This is a polite way of saying that if under efficient and economical management an air carrier possessing an air mail contract does not earn enough from its passenger and other commercial business to enable it to transport mail at a rate of compensation based on cost, the Board may order that it receive what amounts to a mail payment subsidy. Many of our air lines have been subsidized through air mail compensation authorized by the Board.

The Postmaster General is directed, in making arrangements for the transportation of mail between the United States and a foreign country by a foreign air carrier, to pay such carrier no more for the service than it would receive from the foreign country for a like service.

Accounts, Records, and Reports

Section 407. The Board regulates the accounting practices of air carriers much as the Interstate Commerce Commission regulates those of surface carriers. Each air carrier is required to supply the Board with a list of the persons holding more than 5 per cent of its capital stock or capital. Officers and directors of air carriers are required to report their holding in stock or other interests in air carriers and in all kinds of common carriers.

Consolidation, Merger, and Acquisition of Control

Section 408. It is unlawful, without the consent of the Board, for two or more air carriers to merge their properties, or for an air carrier to consolidate with another common carrier. In general, common control of air transport enterprises is prohibited, unless the Board gives its consent.

The Board is not to approve of any merger, consolidation, or other acquisition of control if the action would result in the creation of a monopoly, restrain competition, or jeopardize the interest of another air carrier not a party to the proposed combination. If the applicant seeking approval of a combination with an air carrier is a carrier other than an air carrier, that is, a surface carrier, the applicant shall be regarded by the Board as an air carrier, and the proposed transaction shall not be approved unless the Board finds that the proposed transaction will promote the public interest "by enabling such carrier other than an air carrier to use aircraft to public advantage in its operation and will not restrain competition." The Board has adopted and strictly followed a policy of preventing surface carriers by land and water from entering into the business of air transportation either by certificate or by acquisition of control of an existing air carrier. Air carriers and their officers and directors are not forbidden, however, to have an interest in landing areas, ticket offices, hangars, and other ground facilities.

Prohibited Interests

Section 409. This section prohibits, without the approval of the Board, all interlocking relationships between air carriers which may be effected through common directors. An officer or director of an air carrier may not profit in any manner from the sale or hypothecation of the securities of the carrier.

Loans and Financial Aid

Section 410. The Board has the right to approve or disapprove of any application an air carrier may make for a loan from the United States or any agency thereof. In case of the Board's disapproval, no loan shall be granted.

Methods of Competition

Section 411. The Board has the right to investigate the competitive practices of air carriers, domestic or foreign, and if it finds, after proper hearing, that any competitive practice is unfair or deceptive, it may order such practice to be discontinued.

Pooling and Other Agreements

Section 412. All pooling and other cooperative agreements entered into by air carriers must be filed with the Board. The Board may approve or disapprove of any agreement, as the public interest may require, but it may not approve of any agreement between an air carrier not directly engaged in the operation of aircraft and a common carrier subject to the Interstate Commerce Act governing the compensation to be received by such common carrier for transportation services performed by it.

Forms of Control

Section 413. The word "control," as used in this title, refers either to direct or to indirect control.

Legal Restraints

Section 414. This section exempts from the operation of the antitrust laws any person affected by an order made by the Board under sections 408, 409, and 412, with respect to mergers, interlocking relationships, or pooling and other cooperative agreements.

Inquiry into Air Carrier Management

Section 415. The Board is authorized to inquire into the management of the business of air carriers to the extent necessary to obtain needed information about their operation.

Classification and Exemption of Carriers

Section 416. The Board is authorized to establish reasonable classifications of air carriers.

The Board has the power to exempt any class of air carriers from the provisions of this title or from any rules or regulations promulgated under this title, except that under certain conditions it may not exempt an air carrier from any of the provisions with respect to labor found in subsection (1) of section 401.

TITLE V: NATIONALITY AND OWNERSHIP OF AIRCRAFT

This title provides that all aircraft of the United States, either privately or publicly owned, except aircraft operated by national defense forces, must be registered with the Civil Aeronautics Board. Under certain circumstances, the Board may permit temporary operation of nonregistered aircraft.

The title also makes provision for a recording system, under the supervision of the Administrator. All conveyances, leases, mortgages, and other documents bearing upon the ownership of aircraft must be recorded. The entire system of registration and recording is similar to that maintained by most states with respect to motor vehicles.

There is one paragraph in this title having to do with liability. Persons having a "security interest" in civil aircraft under a contract for conditional sale or chattel mortgage, and the lessor of such aircraft under a lease of thirty days or more, shall not be liable, by reason of such interest, for the injury or death of persons or the loss or damage to property caused by such aircraft. This is only a negative provision. The law contains no positive clauses with regard to liability such as those found in section 20 of the Interstate Commerce Act.

TITLE VI: CIVIL AERONAUTICS SAFETY REGULATION

This title authorizes the Board to establish mimimum standards governing the "design, materials, workmanship, construction, and performance of aircraft, aircraft engines, and propellers." It can also establish rules and standards with respect to maintenance and inspection of aircraft and all their physical appurtenances. The Board may issue, upon application, "airman certificates," "type certificates," and "production certificates" for aircraft and aircraft engines, propellers, and appliances, and "airworthiness certificates" prescribing the type of service in which the aircraft may be used, and such other "terms, conditions, and limitations as are required in the interest of safety."

The Board also may issue air operating certificates and establish minimum safety standards for the operation of the air carrier to which a certificate is issued.

One section of this title imposes upon each air carrier the duty of proper inspection and maintenance of all equipment used in air transportation. The Board is directed to employ inspectors who shall inspect all aircraft and their appurtenances, both during their manufacture and after they are put into service. The inspectors are required to cooperate with air carriers in their work. If an inspector finds that any aircraft or appurtenance thereof is not in condition for safe operation, he shall so notify the air carrier, and "for a period of five days thereafter, such aircraft, aircraft engine, propeller, or appliance shall not be used in air transportation, or in such manner as to endanger air transportation, unless found by the Board or its inspector to be in condition for safe operation."

The Board is authorized to establish "ratings" for air navigation facilities, for civilian flying schools, repair stations and shops, and other air agencies.

The certificates granted under this title may be suspended, modified, or revoked by the Board.

From the standpoint of safety, perhaps the most important section of this title is section 610, which sets forth certain "prohibitions." It is declared to be unlawful for any person (1) to operate any civil aircraft in air commerce for which there is not currently in effect an airworthiness certificate; (2) to serve as an airman without proper certification of his ability to serve in the capacity for which he is employed; (3) to employ in connection with civil aircraft an airman who is not properly certificated; (4) to operate an air carrier without an air carrier operating certificate; and (5) to operate aircraft in air commerce in violation of any rule, regulation, or certificate of the Board.

These prohibitions do not apply to foreign aircraft and airmen, except with respect to the proper observation of air traffic rules, and except to the extent and under such terms and conditions as the Board may prescribe.

TITLE VII: AIR SAFETY BOARD

This title created an Air Safety Board, the chief function of which was to investigate accidents involving aircraft, report thereon, and make such recommendations as in its judgment would tend to prevent other accidents. As was explained previously, under the reorganization plans promulgated by President Roosevelt and acceded to by Congress, this board was abolished and its functions given to the Civil Aeronautics Board.

TITLE VIII: OTHER ADMINISTRATIVE AGENCIES

It has already been noted that under this title the President of the United States must give his approval to certificates or permits authorizing carriers to engage in the foreign air commerce of this country before such documents become effective.

The Secretary of State is directed to advise with the Board concerning the negotiation of agreements with foreign governments for the establishment and development of air navigation.

The Weather Bureau is required to employ all its facilities to the fullest extent possible for the development and advancement of air transportation.

TITLE IX: PENALTIES

Civil Penalties; Safety and Postal Offenses

Section 901. This section provides as a civil penalty a fine of $1,000 for violations of any provision of titles V, VI, and VII of this Act, for violating a section of the Air Commerce Act of 1926 which forbids flight over airspace reservation, except in conformity with executive orders, and for violating orders of the Postmaster General made under the provisions of this Act. The Postmaster General and the Board are authorized to "compromise" any such civil penalty which may be imposed.

Criminal Penalties

Section 902. This section imposes penalties of fines, and in some instances of imprisonment, for various violations of the law, including disobedience of rules and regulations, forgery of certificates, interference with air navigation, rebating, failure to file required reports, falsification of records, divulgence of information to persons not authorized to receive it, and refusal to testify.

TITLE X: PROCEDURE

The Civil Aeronautics Board has the same freedom in the conduct of its proceedings as has the Interstate Commerce Commission, and the various provisions of this title follow closely corresponding provisions of the four parts of the Interstate Commerce Act. The Board may initiate investigations, either on complaint or on its own motion, and after any investigation, if it finds, after hearing, that any provision of the law has been violated, it may issue the orders necessary to compel compliance.

The Board has rate-making authority over air carriers similar in all respects to the authority which the Interstate Commerce Commission possesses over surface carriers subject to the terms of the Interstate Commerce Act. It can suspend proposed rates, name the rate to take the place of any rate found to be unreasonable or unduly discriminatory, and prescribe the division of joint rates. It has one power which the Interstate Commerce Commission does not have; it may order the removal of any rate discrimination found to exist in our foreign air commerce.

The Board may require the establishment of through routes and joint rates and charges for both interstate and overseas air transportation.

Under section 1003, air carriers, except indirect air carriers, may establish through routes and joint rates in connection with other common carriers. Such routes and services are subject to the jurisdiction of the Interstate Commerce Commission and the Civil Aeronautics Board, and the chairmen of these two bodies are authorized to create joint boards to give consideration to matters arising because of joint services established by carriers subject to the jurisdiction of both agencies.

The members of the Board or its examiners may issue subpoenas, administer oaths, and receive evidence. Evidence may also be taken by deposition. Although witnesses may be compelled to testify, they are entitled to complete immunity from prosecution because of anything disclosed in the testimony.

The orders of the Board are of binding effect unless set aside by judicial process.

Unlike orders of the Interstate Commerce Commission, which are subject to review by Federal district courts, the orders of the Civil Aeronautics

Board are subject to review by circuit courts of appeals or by the United States Court of Appeals for the District of Columbia. Moreover, a negative order of the Board, as well as an affirmative order, "except an order in respect of any foreign carrier" subject to presidential approval, is reviewable.

The Board has powers similar to those of the Interstate Commerce Commission to compel obedience to its orders through judicial process in Federal district courts, and while it is the duty of the Attorney General to conduct enforcement proceedings, the Board has the right to participate in such proceedings.

TITLE XI: MISCELLANEOUS

Hazards to Air Commerce

Section 1101. The Board may require, by rule or by order, that persons give adequate notice of the construction or proposed construction of any structure along or near a civil airway where such notice will promote the safety of air commerce.

International Agreements

Section 1102. The Board is required to give due attention to any treaty or convention between the United States and foreign nations.

Nature and Use of Documents Filed

Section 1103. The copies of all tariffs, reports, and other documents filed with the Board by air carriers and others are to be preserved as public records, and be accepted as prima-facie evidence in Board investigations and in judicial proceedings.

Withholding of Information

Section 1104. The Board is authorized to withhold the publication of secret information affecting public defense, and also to withhold from public disclosure any information contained in any application or report filed with the Board if the person filing the same makes written request that it be withheld.

Cooperation with Government Agencies

Section 1105. The Board is authorized to avail itself of the assistance of research and technical agencies of the government in all matters having to do with aviation.

Remedies Not Exclusive

Section 1106. This Act does not abridge other remedies existing by reason of statute or common law.

Amendments and Repeals

Section 1107. Various sections and clauses of many acts are repealed or amended to bring them into conformity with this Act.

Effect of Transfers, Repeals, and Amendments

Section 1108. Existing orders, regulations, and rules issued before the enactment of this statute are to continue in effect until modified or terminated by authority of the Board or by proper judicial process. Pending administrative and judicial proceedings are not to be affected by this Act. All records transferred to the Board are to be available for use by the Board.

Separability

Section 1109. The invalidation of one part of the Act is not to affect the validity of other parts.

Effective Date

Section 1110. The statute was to become effective within sixty days after passage, except that the Board could, in its discretion, postpone the effective date of nearly all provisions, but not beyond the one hundred and eightieth day following enactment.

CHAPTER XXVI

Administrative Procedure

It has been pointed out previously that the bureaus, boards, commissions, authorities, and other agencies which, beginning with the creation of the Interstate Commerce Commission in 1887, have been brought into existence by numerous Federal statutes constitute, in effect, a fourth branch of our national government—which may be termed the administrative branch. It owes its origin and being not directly to any specific articles of the Constitution, as do the executive, legislative, and judicial departments of our government, but solely to acts of Congress. Its steady proliferation and constant growth have been a matter of grave concern to many persons, but so long as the public insists upon entrusting new and varied functions to government it will be impossible to restrict its expansion. Congress is too large and unwieldy to act in a direct administrative capacity for the application and enforcement of the laws which it passes for the regulation and promotion of various kinds of business enterprise or for the direction of the enterprise which Congress believes should be operated by the government instead of by private agencies, and there are numerous reasons why it has been thought desirable not to entrust some functions of regulation and management to the executive departments of the government.[1] Those who shudder the most violently at the spread of bureaucracy may find some comfort in the fact that all highly industrialized and urbanized countries have met with the same administrative problems that have confronted our own government and have endeavored to cope with them in similar fashion. Indeed, several European countries have far outdone this country not only in the number of bureaucratic agencies that have been created but in the variety of function and scope of authority that have been bestowed upon them.[2]

[1] The recent removal of the collectors of internal revenue from the exclusive jurisdiction of the Treasury and their placement under civil service is illustrative of the present trend in the administrative activities of the government.

[2] For an account of the flowering of British bureaucracy and a severe castigation of the entire system and its methods of operation, see Lord Hewart of Bury, Lord Chief Justice of England, "The New Despotism" (1929). Since this work was written, the socialization of various industries and the enlargement of the functions of the government in the field of social activity have led to an increase in the number of British administrative agencies.

FORMER METHODS OF ADMINISTRATIVE PROCEDURE

Like the Interstate Commerce Commission, most of the administrative agencies created by Congress during the past half-century have been given a large measure of freedom with respect to the procedure employed in carrying out their work. The statutes defined—though sometimes with such a lack of accuracy that judicial interpretation of the language was necessary—the powers, duties, and obligations of Federal bureaus and contained some directions with regard to procedure, but for the most part the bureaus were permitted to conduct their manifold activities pretty much as they chose. Each agency was usually authorized to employ its own assistants and officers and in most cases be the judge of the qualifications of those employed. Each bureau was the architect of its own internal organization and the author of its own rules of practice. It was true that the decisions of bureaus were subject to judicial review, but the manner in which a bureau was to conduct its operations, so long as it did not violate the Constitution or overstep its statutory authority, was subject to little interference or control by either the executive, the legislative, or the judicial branch of the government.

It was inevitable that under such a system—or lack of system—of procedure, complaints would eventually arise with regard to the methods which some bureaus employed in the exercise of their assigned functions. It was charged that the acts of some bureaus were arbitrary or capricious, and too often lacking in consideration of the rights which persons appearing before them thought they possessed. We are not interested here in the nature of these complaints and charges or in the matter of their foundation or justification. Suffice it to say that Congress finally took cognizance of the somewhat unwholesome situation which developed over the years, and enacted a law whose purpose was to give a greater degree of uniformity to administrative practice and procedure and at the same time ensure a strict observance of the rights and privileges of all who came in contact with a bureau as an applicant, a complainant, a respondent, a defendant, or in any other capacity. This law is the Administrative Procedure Act, which was passed in 1946.[3] Its purpose, as stated in the title of the law, was "to improve the administration of justice by prescribing fair administrative procedure."

ADMINISTRATIVE PROCEDURE ACT

The Act applies to all Federal administrative agencies except a designated few created because of the exigencies of war to serve for a fixed period of time. It does not apply to military tribunals such as courts-martial or to military authority exercised in "occupied territories."

[3] 60 Stat. 237; United States Code, Title 5, Chapter 11; *Interstate Commerce Acts Annotated,* Vol. 13, pp. 11171–11179.

Each administrative agency to which the law applies was required to publish in the Federal Register a description of its organization and a statement of its rules and methods of practice, and in the course of time the rules were modified if found not to be consonant with the provisions of the law. All agencies are directed to make available for public inspection their opinions, orders, and rules, and in the making of rules of general or special application any parties who might have an interest are to have an opportunity to participate in the deliberations held for the purpose of formulating the rules.

In the adjudication of all matters required by statute to be determined on the record, after opportunity for an agency hearing (with a few minor exceptions), interested parties are entitled to receive due and timely notice of hearings, and are to have opportunity for the submission and consideration of facts, arguments, offers of settlement, or proposals of adjustment, where time, the nature of the proceeding, and the public interest permit.

Each agency is directed to proceed with reasonable dispatch in its consideration of any matter presented to it; persons compelled to appear before an agency or its representative are entitled to be accompanied by and advised by counsel; interested parties can appear in person or by or with counsel; and nothing in the Act is to be construed "either to grant or deny to any person who is not a lawyer the right to appear for or represent others before any agency or in any agency proceeding."

HEARINGS

In any hearing before an agency, at the taking of evidence, it is directed that the entire agency, one or more of its members, or an examiner shall preside. This provision does not apply to certain proceedings which are by statute permitted to be conducted by boards or officers of the agency. The presiding officer at any hearing has the powers to administer oaths, issue subpoenas, rule upon the relevance of evidence, and exercise other functions of a similar nature. While the provision of the law with respect to the admissibility of evidence is not so strict or so exacting as the rules of evidence in civil and criminal procedure, it is declared that every agency shall "as a matter of policy provide for the exclusion of irrelevant, immaterial, or unduly repetitious evidence." Any order, rule, or sanction issued by an agency must be based on the record of the hearing and be "supported by and in accordance with the reliable, probative, and substantial evidence." Every interested party in a proceeding shall have the right to present his case by documentary or oral evidence, and to conduct such cross-examination as may be necessary "for a full and true disclosure of the facts." The record of a hearing shall include a transcript of testimony and all papers filed in the proceeding, and the record shall be made available to interested parties on the payment of lawfully prescribed costs.

DECISIONS

In cases in which the agency has not itself presided, the presiding officers shall "initially decide the case" or the agency shall "require (in specific cases or by general rule) the entire record to be certified to it for initial decision." In the absence of review by the agency, either on appeal of an interested party or on the agency's own motion, the initial decision of the presiding officer or officers shall become the decision of the agency.

The parties at interest in any case have the opportunity, prior to any initial or recommended decision or decision upon agency review of the decisions of subordinate officers, to submit proposed findings or exceptions to proposed decisions of subordinate or tentative agency decisions. All decisions (including initial, recommended, or tentative decisions) shall become a part of the record, and must "include a statement of (1) findings and conclusions, as well as the reasons or basis therefor, upon all material issues of fact, law, or discretion presented for the record; and (2) the appropriate rule, order, sanction, relief, or denial thereof."

JUDICIAL REVIEW

The law makes careful provision for the judicial review of the acts and decisions of an administrative agency. Any person suffering a legal wrong because of agency action, or adversely affected by such actions, is entitled to judicial review. Every agency action made reviewable by statute and every final agency action for which there is no other adequate remedy shall be subject to judicial review. Pending judicial review, an agency is authorized to postpone the effective date of any action it may have taken.

This section has a very interesting paragraph on the "scope of judicial review." The reviewing court "shall decide all relevant questions of law, interpret constitutional and statutory provisions, and determine the meaning and applicability of the terms of any agency action." A court may compel an agency to act, when it unlawfully delays or refuses to take action. The reviewing court may set aside agency actions found to be:

(1) arbitrary, capricious, an abuse of discretion, or otherwise not in accordance with law; (2) contrary to constitutional right, power, privilege, or immunity; (3) in excess of statutory jurisdiction, authority, or limitations, or short of statutory right; (4) without observance of procedure required by law; (5) unsupported by substantial evidence . . . ; or (6) unwarranted by the facts to the extent that the facts are subject to trial de novo by the reviewing court.

The provisions with respect to judicial review mark a departure from the customary clauses with regard to such review found in the laws by which administrative agencies are created and their powers defined, but it should be noted that in effect they merely repeat what the Supreme

Court has said over and over on the matter of judicial review of agency decisions and actions. In other words, as one Federal judge pointed out, the section of the Administrative Procedure Act dealing with the question of judicial review is merely declaratory of existing law; it does not confer any jurisdiction above and beyond that which the courts already possessed, and it does not confer to aggrieved parties any rights they did not already have.[4]

EXAMINERS

Perhaps the most interesting part of the Administrative Procedure Act, and certainly the part that created the greatest amount of controversy and confusion, was the eleventh section, which put hearing examiners of administrative boards unrestrictedly under the control of the Civil Service Commission with respect to appointment, salary, and removal. The section applied only to examiners who were authorized to conduct hearings and render initial decisions, thereby creating a distinction between "examiners" and "hearing examiners" which had not previously existed. Heretofore, administrative agencies had selected their own examiners, and some of these officers had acquired "status." The new act apparently permitted the Civil Service Commission to review the qualifications of all persons acting as hearing examiners with Federal boards as well as to have charge of the selection of new hearing examiners to be assigned in the future to the various agencies.

Unhappily, the method which the Civil Service Commission adopted for the resurvey of the staff of hearing examiners already in office was open to much question with regard both to its wisdom and to its legality. More than 25 per cent of the examiners were found to be "unqualified," and orders were sent to the various agencies for their summary dismissal.[5] There was a wave of protest, in which legal action by the dismissed examiners, indignant objections on the part of hundreds of "practitioners" who appeared more or less regularly before various boards, and the threat of a Congressional investigation all had a place. The Civil Service Commission hastily reviewed its somewhat precipitous action, virtually all of the "disqualified" examiners were restored to duty, and the commotion came to an end.[6]

[4] Olin Industries Inc. v. National Labor Relations Board, 72 F. Supp. 225 (228) (1947).

[5] The chief objection to the action of the Civil Service Commission was that to obtain an opinion as to the qualifications of the hearing examiners currently in service it enlisted the services of a board of "outsiders" whose qualifications for the task and complete disinterestedness were, to say the least, open to question.

[6] For an account of this somewhat curious incident in the management and direction of public affairs, see Morgan Thomas, "The Selection of Federal Hearing Examiners: Pressure Groups and the Administrative Process," *Yale Law Journal*, Feb., 1950, pp. 431–475; Ralph F. Fuchs, "The Hearing Examiner

A hearing examiner of an administrative board holds a highly important position, for he presides at many hearings, rules upon the admissibility of evidence, often listens to oral argument, and makes the report upon which decisions are to be based. An examiner needs the same qualifications that should be possessed by a judge of a court of law, and these qualifications go far beyond a mere knowledge of the letter of the law. His selection is a matter of much concern both to the agencies which he serves and to the parties which appear before him. Before the Administrative Procedure Act was passed, a Committee on Administrative Procedure, appointed by the Attorney General, submitted a report to Congress in which attention was called to the importance of the hearing examiner's position and function and to the necessity for making provision for the careful selection of the persons who were to receive appointment. The committee advised the creation of a permanent Office of Federal Administrative Procedure whose function it would be to work constantly for the improvement of administrative agency processes. Among its duties was to be the appointment of hearing examiners upon the nomination by the agency concerned. Congress chose to disregard this recommendation. However, it decided that the matter of appointment should no longer be left solely to the agencies but should be largely under the control of the Civil Service Commission. It must be admitted that the Commission's initial contact with this new task was not productive of satisfactory results, and while there may have been some advantage gained in relieving the examiner of complete subservience to his agency with regard to such matters as salary, advancement, and assignment of work, there is still some question in the minds of many persons if the method of appointment provided for by the Administrative Procedure Act is the right solution to the problem of securing suitably qualified examiners.

THE ADMINISTRATIVE PROCEDURE ACT AND THE INTERSTATE COMMERCE COMMISSION

Of all the Federal administrative agencies, the Interstate Commerce Commission was probably the least disturbed either in its organization or in its methods of procedure by the Administrative Procedure Act. It is true that of the Commission's forty-eight trial examiners twelve, or exactly 25 per cent, were "disqualified" by the initial processing of the Civil Service Commission and its advisers, but the disqualification was not in effect long enough to cause any serious interruption in the performance of the normal functions of the agency.

Over the years, the Interstate Commerce Commission had built up an

Fiasco under the Administrative Procedure Act," *Harvard Law Review*, Vol. 63, No. 5, March, 1950, pp. 737–768.

organization and a system of procedure which had been subjected to a long period of trial and had been modified, as occasion demanded, to meet the needs of the Commission. There had been many times when the Commission was admonished by the courts that it was presuming to exercise powers which were lacking the necessary basis of constitutional or statutory authority. Many times, in previous chapters, attention has been called to amendments made in the Interstate Commerce Act which Congress passed for the purpose of conferring upon the Commission authority which the courts had declared it did not possess under existing law. It was seldom necessary for the Commission to make any significant change in its organization or rules of procedure because of adverse court decisions. It was inevitable, of course, that as its duties grew in number and in scope its staff had to be enlarged, just as the membership of the Commission itself had to be enlarged. Its organization had perforce undergone certain changes, but it had readily adjusted itself to any situation brought about by the enactment of new legislation. Its methods of conducting its manifold activities had been systematized and reduced to a workable pattern, so that there was little in the Administrative Procedure Act which required it to make any change whatever in its customary routine. Indeed, the Commission said itself that while some difficulty might be encountered in reconciling certain provisions of the Interstate Commerce Act and of other acts with the provisions of the Administrative Procedure Act, "the latter act is in part merely repetitious of what has long been the Commission's established procedure" and that it did not contemplate any radical changes.

The Commission, in accordance with the law, designated a number of its examiners who were to be regarded in the future as hearing examiners, and it made one change in its Organization and Assignment of Work, which had been published in the Federal Register in 1942, four years before the Administration Procedure Act became a law. This change assigned to the Commission itself the "initial decision" in the cases dealt with in accordance with those sections of the Administrative Procedure Act having to do with hearings and decisions. There were a few exceptions, and the Commission reserved the right to assign the task of making the initial decision to a division of the Commission, to an individual Commissioner, or to a board, as provided in the Interstate Commerce Act. This rule did not preclude the right of the Commission to require a hearing officer to render a recommended or tentative report such as hearing officers had previously been accustomed to submit. Although the rule was in technical compliance with the terms of the Administrative Procedure Act, it is difficult to see that it made any substantial change in the procedure which the Commission had long followed.

OTHER ADMINISTRATIVE AGENCIES

The changes in the organization and procedure of other Federal administrative agencies were likewise neither revolutionary nor far-reaching. As a matter of fact, the greatest change which the Act made was in the matter of selection and appointment of hearing examiners and the assignment of them to a class somewhat different from and superior to examiners in general.

Perhaps the chief reason for the lack of any pronounced transformation in these other agencies was that, for the most part, they had followed the pattern of organization and procedure which had been originated, established, and tested by the oldest of our administrative agencies, the Interstate Commerce Commission. However different the functions and activities of these agencies might be, there was no good reason for a wide variation in the methods in which they should conduct their deliberations and other activities, and it was almost inevitable that as each new agency was called into existence, however much freedom it might be granted in shaping its own organization and framing its own rules and regulations, it would follow the example and precedent which the Interstate Commerce Commission had established. We have already pointed out how Congress, in enacting the many measures it has passed for controlling and regulating different forms of transportation, as well as other kinds of business enterprise, has showed a tendency to follow the pattern first laid down in the Interstate Commerce Act, even to the extent often of repeating verbatim in other regulatory acts the provisions of that law.

The following pages will be devoted, for the most part, to a description and discussion of the organization and Rules of Practice of the Interstate Commerce Commission. No such description of the organization and rules of the Civil Aeronautics Board or other Federal administrative body will be given, but it should be borne in mind that they follow largely the model which the Interstate Commerce Commission originated. Because of differences in function, there are bound to be differences in the details of organization, but the underlying patterns are the same, and procedures are now the same, by virtue of the provisions of the Administrative Procedure Act. Even without this statute, the differences would have been of only minor significance. Administrative processes, like judicial processes, have been evolved by experience, by trial and error, and while these processes are now dictated by statute, it should be remembered that ordinarily the fact preceded the theory, and custom came before law.

CHAIRMAN OF THE THE COMMISSION

The Interstate Commerce Commission selects its own chairman. Formerly, a member elected to the chairmanship served in that capacity until his term of service ended, but for many years it has been the usual custom for the chairmanship to rotate annually among the members in order of their seniority in service. The chairman is the executive head of the Commission, and his most important duty is to see that the work of the Commission is performed with promptness and efficiency. He presides at all full meetings of the Commission, sees that the minutes are properly recorded, and as a rule represents the Commission in all matters involving contacts with other agencies of the government. For example, it is usually the chairman who appears before committees of the House or the Senate to give expression to the official views of the Commission on legislative or other matters.

STANDING COMMITTEES

The Commission has two standing committees, one of which deals with the formulation of rules and reports and the other with legislation and proposals for additional and amendatory legislation in which the Commission might have a direct interest.

SECRETARY OF THE COMMISSION

The Secretary of the Commission, who is appointed by the Commission, is its chief administrative officer. He is the custodian of the Commission's seal, has charge of the Commission's records, papers, and property, and signs all orders which the Commission issues. He is, in effect, the public-relations officer of the Commission, and is the person to whom application must first be made for information concerning the Commission's activities.

The reports and orders of the Commission, which are prepared in the Secretary's office, appear at first in mimeographed form for service on all parties at interest. All mimeographed reports and orders are kept in the Secretary's office and are available for public inspection. Subsequently, the more important reports are printed in the Government Printing Office and are for sale in sheet form by the Superintendent of Documents. They are issued later in bound volumes, with the less important cases merely summarized. The Commission issues three series of reports of its decisions and orders: the ICC reports, dealing with the cases and investigations arising under parts I, III, and IV of the Act; the MCC reports, dealing with cases arising under part II of the Act (the Motor Vehicle Act); and valuation reports. The first twenty-one volumes of the valuation reports were included in the regular ICC reports, but later volumes have been published in a separate series. The ICC reports now number nearly three hundred volumes, and the MCC reports nearly one hundred.

DIVISIONS OF THE COMMISSION

In 1917, the Commission was authorized to organize itself into divisions for the facilitation of the large volume of work which its manifold tasks and duties imposed upon it. The Commission has five numbered divisions, four of them having three members each and one having four members. This means, of course, that some Commissioners must serve on more than one division. The varied administrative duties of the Commission are parceled out among these divisions, each having supervision over the administration and enforcement of designated sections of the Interstate Commerce Act.

Division 1, of which the Chairman of the Commission is a member ex officio, is known as the Administrative Division. Among its duties are the supervision of personnel, salaries and Commission finances, the admission and disbarment of practitioners, and the preparation of the Commission's annual report to Congress and of the reports in which the decisions and orders are recorded and published. Division 2 is known as the Rates, Valuation and Tariff Division. It has jurisdiction over the filing of carriers' tariffs of freight, passenger and other charges, released rate applications and applications for fourth section relief, and any rate agreements which may be negotiated under the provisions of the Reed-Bulwinkle law. Division 3, the Rates, Service and Safety Division, deals with various carrier services, such as routing, switching, and car service, and it also supervises the enforcement of the numerous statutes having to do with the safety of operation of railroads. Division 4 is the Finance Division, and has to do with the administration of that part of the Act which has for its purpose the regulation of the financial operations of carriers, including the issuance of securities, loans, reorganization, and mergers and consolidations. Division 5 is the Motor Carrier Division; as its name implies, it finds its chief duties in matters arising from the administration of part II of the Act.

All divisions may hold hearings and render decisions in complaints and investigations arising from the provisions of the law to the administration of which they are particularly assigned. Any formal case having to do with railroad rates may be assigned to any one of the divisions or reserved to the Commission as a whole. If not so assigned or reserved, such cases, and all cases arising under parts II, III, and IV of the Act, if they have involved taking testimony at public hearings, are assigned to Divisions 2 and 3, sitting alternately in monthly rotation.

BUREAUS OF THE COMMISSION

To take care of routine administrative work, of which there is necessarily a vast amount, the Commission has created within its internal organization several bureaus, at the present time fifteen in number, to each of which are assigned certain administrative duties. Each bureau reports through a designated individual Commissioner to that division of the Commisssion which is charged with the administration of that part of the law under whose provisions the bureau functions.

The Bureau of Administration, under the leadership of the Secretary of the Commission, is responsible for the preparation of the Commission's budget and the supervision of personnel. The Bureau of Accounts and Cost Finding prepares the rules and regulations under which carrier accounts are to be kept and makes cost studies which the Commission employs in its deliberations with respect to the reasonableness of rates. A Bureau of Transport Economics and Statistics is responsible for collecting, analyzing, and tabulating the statistical information which all carriers are required to file with the Commission, and for the preparation of the reports in which the collected and tabulated statistics are made available to the public. The Bureau of Finance concerns itself with studies necessary for the work which comes under the jurisdiction of Division 4, and the Bureau of Valuation has charge of the valuation of carrier property. Its work, once requiring a large staff of engineers, accountants, and analysts, has been very greatly limited in scope in recent years, because of the lack of necessary financial appropriations. There are two bureaus dealing with the proceedings arising from the complaints which come to the Commission and from the Commission's own investigations. They are, respectively, the Bureau of Formal Complaints and the Bureau of Informal Complaints. Their functions will become clearer later, when we discuss the Commission's Rules of Practice. A Bureau of Inquiry makes the necessary inquiries into alleged infractions of the Interstate Commerce Act which come to the Commission's attention and institutes actions leading to the criminal prosecution of offenders. A Bureau of Law, headed by the Chief Counsel, represents the Commission in court proceedings resulting from any attempt to challenge the legality of the Commission's orders, and advises the Commission on all matters of law about which the Commission requires information and expert guidance. The Bureau of Traffic receives and cares for the thousands of tariffs which, under the law, must be filed with the Commission each year, and also prepares the rules and regulations which carriers must observe in the publication and filing of their tariffs. It is in this bureau that may probably be found the most experienced and competent rate and tariff experts in the country, whose duty it is to provide the Commission with all requested information concerning the rates and other charges for which shippers are legally responsible. Three bureaus deal with matters affecting railroad operation and railroad safety. They are the Bureau of Safety, the Bureau of Locomotive Inspection, and the Bureau of Service. The Bureau of Motor Carriers takes care of all the routine work connected with the administration and enforcement of part II of the Act, while the Bureau of Water Carriers and Freight Forwarders performs a similar service in connection with parts III and IV.

FIELD ORGANIZATION

In addition to its central organization in Washington, the Commission finds it necessary to maintain a fairly large and scattered field organization. The Bureau of Motor Carriers, the Bureau of Safety, the Bureau of Locomotive Inspection, and the Bureau of Service have the largest network of field offices, located at strategic points throughout the United States. The Bureau of Inquiry, the Bureau of Accounts and Cost Finding, the Bureau of Valuation, and the Bureau of Water Carriers and Freight Forwarders also maintain small field organizations.

RULES OF PRACTICE

The Interstate Commerce Commission has for many years published its Rules of Practice for the guidance of those who appear before it in one capacity or another, either in person, by counsel, or by correspondence. The Commission bears much resemblance to a court, but it is not a court. It is an administrative body. It can conduct proceedings either on complaint or on its own initiative. Ordinarily, a court action implies controversy, and there are two opposing parties in most court proceedings. The Commission, while it has many proceedings arising out of controversies between shippers and carriers, between carriers, or between public agencies and carriers, also deals with many matters in which the element of controversy may not appear at all. Applications by carriers for fourth section relief or for permission to file tariffs on less than statutory notice, to issue new securities, to construct new track or abandon old trackage, or to secure approval of rate-making agreements among competing lines may be a few of the matters arising before the Commission in which the carriers may have no opposition.

In framing its Rules of Practice, the Commission has from the very beginning endeavored to establish conditions that would permit the conduct of its business with the greatest possible dispatch, at the same time carefully guarding the rights and privileges of all interested parties. Its rules are much more flexible than those followed by courts of justice, and it has done its best to create a system of procedure under which many controversies can be settled without formal hearings, and even in the case of some formal hearings, under rules which permit much abbreviated proceedings. Both Congress and the Commission have endeavored, one by the law and the other by Rules of Practice, to make the settlement of controversies arising under the Act as inexpensive as possible to all parties at interest. The Commission has sometimes been called a "poor man's court," not because it is a tribunal to which only the poor can appeal, but because in all of its administrative labors it has tried consistently to conduct its activities in such a manner as to involve the least possible expenditure of money and time by those who seek its help.

The present Rules of Practice of the Commission were first published in the Federal Register in 1942, and they have since been changed only a little.[7] The Administrative Procedure Act, as was previously noted, required only a few minor changes either in the Commission's plan of organization or in its Rules or Practice.[8] The ensuing brief discussion of the rules will be made under the headings employed by the Commission.

GENERAL INFORMATION

This part of the Rules of Practice consists largely of general instructions and definitions. Only a few of the definitions need be noted. A "practitioner" is a "person authorized by the Commission to appear before it in a representative capacity." The word "representative" is the important word in this definition. Any person who is an interested party in a proceeding before the Commission has a right to appear, whether he is a "practitioner" or not.

Another group of interesting definitions classifies the "interested parties" who ordinarily appear before the Commission:

The term "complainant" means a person filing a complaint; "applicant" means a person filing an application; "respondent" means a person designated in an investigation; "protestant" means a person opposed to a tentative valuation, to the granting of an application, or to any tariff or schedule becoming effective; "intervener" means a person permitted to intervene as provided in Rule 72; and "petitioner" means any other person seeking relief otherwise than by complaint or application.

One of the most important paragraphs of this part is that which says: "These rules shall be liberally construed to secure just, speedy and inexpensive determination of the issues presented."

PRACTITIONERS

For many years, the Commission did not have a "bar" to which some kind of formal admittance was required, as all the courts of the United States have long had. Anybody could appear before the Commission in a representative capacity. It has been mentioned before that on several occasions there has been a movement among various bar associations and

[7] Annual Report of the Interstate Commerce Commission for 1946, pp. 58–59.

[8] The Commission's Rules of Practice can be found in the Federal Register of Aug. 14, 1942, p. 6395, and in *Interstate Commerce Acts Annotated*, Vol. 11, pp. 9782–9813. They are available in pamphlet form from the Superintendent of Documents, in Washington, D.C. They have been published in many manuals and reference books dealing with the subject of traffic management.

other groups of lawyers to confine practice before administrative bodies such as the Interstate Commerce Commission to "members of the bar" of the courts, but thus far these efforts have met with failure. An attempt was made during the discussion preceding the enactment of the Administrative Procedure Act to have such a restriction embodied in that statute, but the law states specifically that none of its terms shall be construed as withholding or granting the right of a person who is not a lawyer to represent others before administrative boards.

The Commission has found it advisable, however, to require that the right to practice before it be conferred only upon persons who have proper qualifications. It now maintains a "register of practitioners," in which are entered the names of all persons entitled to practice before it. There are two classes of practitioners: first, attorneys at law who have been admitted to practice before the highest court of a state or of the District of Columbia; and second, persons not attorneys at law, who are citizens of the United States and who have satisfied the Commission that they have necessary legal and technical qualifications. These qualifications are determined by examination which test an applicant's knowledge of the "structure and history of the Interstate Commerce Act and related acts, our rules of practice, the general rules of evidence, the leading cases involving interstate commerce and their significance, and the principles of legal ethics." After passing the required examination, as a further condition of admission to practice, the applicant must submit a satisfactory report as to his moral qualifications attested by members of the Commission's bar. The Commission reserves the right to deny admission to a person not properly qualified and to suspend or disbar any practitioner for cause after hearing.

In several of its annual reports, the Commission has called attention to the fact that a growing number of its practitioners are persons who are not attorneys at law, and has ascribed the tendency to the steady growth of the number and quality of the courses in traffic management now offered in our colleges, universities, and other schools.

SPECIAL RULES RESPECTING BOARDS

These rules have to do with the organization and procedure of joint boards, consisting of state regulatory authorities and representatives of the Commission, as authorized by the Interstate Commerce Act.

PLEADING SPECIFICATIONS GENERALLY

Pleading, as defined in the first section of the rules, means a complaint, answer, reply, application, protest, petition, and various other documents filed with the Commission. This part of the rules deals chiefly with the mechanical aspects of the preparation and filing of pleadings, designating the kind and size of paper to be employed, the methods of preparing exhibits, and how to compute time under the rules.

COMMENCEMENT OF PROCEEDINGS; INFORMAL COMPLAINTS

Proceedings before the Commission must be initiated by complaint, application, protest, or petition or by the Commission's own action. There are two kinds of complaints, formal and informal. The latter may or may not seek damages. If not seeking damages, it may be disposed of merely by correspondence, but the fact that the complainant is not content with the result of such proceedings does not prejudice his right to file a formal complaint. Informal complaints in which damages are sought by the complainant must contain data in substantiation of the claim. Very often, a carrier is willing to satisfy a complainant seeking damages without the filing of a formal complaint. Under these circumstances, the carrier must file a petition asking for the necessary authority. Of course, if the claim arises merely from an overcharge due to errors in calculation or failure to apply the proper rate, no Commission authorization is needed for refunding the overcharge. If the claim arises because of an admittedly unreasonable or unduly discriminatory rate or other charge, however, the matter of reimbursement must be taken up with the Commission. Special forms are prescribed by the Commission for the filing of such petitions.

FORMAL COMPLAINTS

In filing a formal complaint, as might be expected from the descriptive adjective, there must be a close observance of certain directions, because such a complaint requires a prescribed administrative procedure. A formal complaint may or may not include a demand for damages. It must charge a violation or violations of the Interstate Commerce Act, describe fully and accurately in what respects the Act is alleged to be violated, state the facts upon which the allegation is based, and indicate the nature of the relief desired for the future. In the appendix to the Rules of Practice may be found an approved form for use in making a formal complaint. The Commission serves a formal complaint upon those against whom it is lodged, and the defendant or defendants must file an answer within a prescribed time. An approved form for use in filing an answer is also found in the appendix. Other documents may be required before the complaint proceeds to adjudication. There may be cross complaints, amended or supplemental complaints, motions to have the complaint made more definite, and petitions to intervene. If after the filing of a formal complaint the defendant agrees to grant satisfaction without making answer or proceeding to a hearing, there must be filed with the Commission a statement telling when and how the complaint has been satisfied.

Applications for certificates or permits and protests against the granting of an application must be filed in much the same manner that complaints and answers are filed, and the same is true with respect to petitions.

When the Commission institutes an investigation on its own initiative, it serves copies of the order upon all respondents concerned. A respondent is given a certain specified time in which to meet any requirement of the order, and in case of failure to do so is deemed to have waived any right to a hearing.

DISPOSITION OF COMPLAINTS

Shortened and Modified Procedure

Many of the complaints reaching the Commission, and many of its investigations, require long-drawn-out proceedings, with batteries of lawyers and expert witnesses, the taking of thousands of pages of testimony, the assembling of scores of exhibits, the preparation of numerous briefs, and the presentation of much oral argument. But the Commission has developed methods of procedure in which many controversies arising because of formal complaints can be adjudicated without recourse to long and tedious proceedings.

There are two varieties of short cuts which the Commission has developed, called respectively shortened procedure and modified procedure. Under the former, there are no oral hearings. The complainant and defendant, by consent, agree to file their pleadings, and a decision is arrived at which is based entirely upon scrutiny of the pleadings.

Modified procedure may be followed either on the Commission's own initiative or on its approval of a petition of one of the parties at interest. All parties are notified that modified procedure is to be followed, and are required to observe the rules adopted by the Commission for such proceeding. The complaint is filed in the customary manner. An answer is not required, and if none is filed, the Commission proceeds to adjudication. However, statements may be filed by both the defendant and the complainant specifying the statements of fact of the opposite party to which exception is taken. A hearing, if one is ordered, will be confined to a consideration only of those matters upon which the parties at interest are not in agreement. Modified procedure, though it may consume more work than shortened procedure, nevertheless makes possible the saving of time and effort both by the Commission and by the parties to the controversy.

Full Hearings

If a full hearing on any complaint is to be held, the Commission sends out notices to the interested parties designating the time and place of the hearing. Witnesses may be summoned by subpoena, and depositions may be taken for inclusion within the record.

If it chooses to do so, the Commission may require a prehearing conference of parties at interest or their representatives. At such a prehearing, an effort is made to simplify the issues at stake, effect, if necessary, the amplification or clarification of pleadings, and permit certain stipulations or averments of fact which will serve to limit the record. Agreement is reached as to the procedure to be followed at the hearing, an attempt is made to keep the number of witnesses within reasonable limits, and an arrangement is made, if possible, for the exchange of exhibits and prepared testimony between the contesting parties. In fact, everything is done that can be done to shorten and simplify the subsequent formal proceedings.

During the course of the hearing, the opposing parties may make stipulations of agreement on certain facts, thereby avoiding the necessity of presenting some testimony. The Rules of Practice go on to indicate how interveners may be permitted to participate, how and in what order witnesses are to be examined, and how exhibits are to be prepared and presented. The general rules with respect to evidence are set forth at some length, and all persons appearing are admonished that they must abide by the standards of conduct required by the code of ethics of the Association of Interstate Commerce Commission Practitioners.

After all testimony has been taken, oral argument may be had before the hearing officer if proper request has been made. At the conclusion of the oral proceedings, the parties are permitted to file briefs. Careful directions are given in the rules with respect to the preparation of such briefs and the time of filing. If no report is to be made by the hearing officer, the parties are permitted to file reply briefs.

If a report is to be made by the hearing officer, it is prepared after the expiration of the time for filing briefs, and a copy of the report is sent to all parties at interest. These parties have the right to file "exceptions" to the report within a specified time. Exceptions stay the effectiveness of any recommended order until the Commission has reached a decision on the basis of a study of the record, the report, and the exceptions. If no exceptions are filed, the proposed report of the hearing officer will not necessarily become the decision of the Commission, though under ordinary circumstances the statement of facts and of the issues at stake will be taken as the basis for the Commission's final action.

It is possible for the contestants to have oral argument before the Commission after the conclusion of any formal hearing. If no officer's report is to be filed, the request for such argument must be made within ten days after the hearing. If an officer's report is to be prepared and served, the request for oral argument must be included as a part of the "exception" which has been taken to the report.

ORDER COMPLIANCE

It will be remembered that the orders of the Commission are "binding" upon the carriers to which they are addressed, unless set aside by a "court of competent jurisdiction." If the carrier refuses to obey an order, in the absence of judicial relief, it becomes subject to severe penalties. The Commission therefore requires that a defendant or a respondent must notify the Commission on or before the date the order becomes effective if the order has been properly complied with. If the order involves a change in rates or other charges, the notification must nevertheless be filed, and proper tariffs also filed.

DAMAGE STATEMENTS

In many complaints, the complaining party asks that the Commission make an award of damages against the carrier for its nonobservance of the law. It may be that the complaint does not contain a statement as to the amount of damages the complainant believes to be due. In almost the last one of the Rules of Practice, it is provided that if the Commission believes damages should be awarded, the complainant is to file a complete statement, fully documented, as to the amount claimed. An appropriate form for such a statement is given in the appendix to the rules.

The Commission has the right, of course, to reopen any investigation which may have been "closed," and either on petition or on its own initiative it may reopen for further hearing or for rehearing any case to which it has given previous consideration.

As may be surmised, the number of cases which the Commission disposes of informally is far greater than the number of cases which it considers under formal procedure. It is worth while to look at the annual reports of the Commission to see how it has disposed of the complaints and applications which have come before it. In the fiscal year 1950, to give an example, the Commission received 2,318 informal complaints and disposed of 1,900 complaints of this nature. During the same year, it received some 14,000 letters, many of which were in the realm of informal complaints but were not so classified. It also received 3,477 "special-docket" applications from carriers asking authority to make refunds of amounts collected under lawfully filed tariffs, but acknowledged by the carriers to have been unreasonable. Orders authorizing refunds amounting to $1,483,255 were issued during the year. The formal complaints filed during the same period numbered 415. Complaints to the number of 326 were disposed of by formal decision, and 126 dismissed by stipulation. Almost half of the cases settled were disposed of through shortened or modified procedure.

Every industrial traffic manager should study and become thoroughly familiar with the Rules of Practice of the Commission. If he is a practitioner, he must have a detailed and accurate knowledge of the rules. If he is not a practitioner but aspires to become one, the rules must be one of the chief objects of his study. Even if he is not a practitioner and does not plan to become one and thereby be able to represent any complainant before the Commission, he may find it advisable to appear before the Commission, either by correspondence or in person, as a "party in interest" in some proceeding. The rules are not particularly difficult to master. One of the most commendable acts of the Commission has been the formulation and adoption of procedures and practices which will permit the shippers of the country to avail themselves of the protective shelter of the Interstate Commerce Act without the need of spending a great deal of time or assuming a heavy burden of expense.

RECORD OF THE COMMISSION

We have had occasion, at several points in this book, to mention the fact that the Interstate Commerce Commission has been a public servant of outstanding merit. We can think of no better way in which to close this discussion of traffic management than to say something once more about the distinguished record which this oldest and probably most important of our administrative bodies has made. In its long career, now well past its semicentennial and hurrying toward its three-quarter-of-a century mark, it has pursued a course in which it has been noted for faithful service, adherence to duty, unflagging industry, impartial administration, and unquestioned rectitude. It has never endeavored to arrogate to itself the function of making governmental policy, and while it may have been mistaken now and then in the interpretation of the statute in which its powers are defined, its legislative recommendations have invariably been directed toward the implementation of the policy which it honestly believed Congress to have in mind, without the slightest hint of an attempt to usurp the prerogative which the Constitution bestows upon the legislative branch of our government. No breath of scandal, no taint of corruption, has ever dimmed its reputation for integrity. It has earned and held the confidence of Congress, the approbation of the courts, and the esteem of the public at large. While it may not always have been regarded with undiluted affection by carriers, shippers, travelers, and the critical press, it has never failed to command their trust and respect.

Bibliographical Note

The literature of transportation, especially of railroad transportation, is singularly rich and varied. Those who are interested in more study of this branch of our economic activity may find some suggestions for further reading to be helpful. It must be understood that the list of books which follows is selective and not exhaustive. In many of the works mentioned, the reader will find much additional bibliographical material.

There are many general works on transportation dealing with what may be called the economics of the subject. Most of these books, but by no means all of them, were written for use as textbooks. They follow pretty much the same pattern, having sections dealing respectively with history, services, rates, and government regulation. One of the first American books of this character was Arthur Twining Hadley's "Railroad Transportation" (New York, 1885). Although it apeared nearly three-quarters of a century ago, this book is surprisingly modern in its approach and analysis. A more exhaustive treatment is to be found in William Z. Ripley's two companion volumes, "Railroads: Rates and Regulation" (New York, 1912) and "Railroads: Finance and Organization" (New York, 1915). This work, too, though published early in the twentieth century, shows that fundamentally the economic, political, and social problems arising by reason of the development of the steam railroad and other forms of mechanized transportation have changed little. The following list gives the titles of some books of comparatively recent vintage. Nearly all of them, even those devoted primarily to railroad transportation, contain sections dealing with all the various forms of transportation.

Baker, Morris B., "Air Transportation: Traffic and Operations" (New York, 1947).

Bigham, Truman C., and Merrill J. Roberts, "Transportation: Principles and Problems," 2d ed. (New York, 1952).

Bryan, Leslie A., "Principles of Water Transportation" (New York, 1939).

Daggett, Stuart, "The Economics of Transportation" (New York, 1940).

Fair, Marvin L., and Ernest W. Williams, "Economics of Transportation" (New York, 1950).

Frederick, John H., "Commercial Air Transportation," 3d ed. (Chicago, 1951).

Henry, Robert S., "This Fascinating Railroad Business" (Indianapolis, 1943).

Locklin, D. Philip, "Economics of Transportation," 3d ed. (Chicago, 1947).

Mason, Linton W., "Local Trucking" (New York, 1951).

Owen, Wilfred, "Automotive Transportation: Trends and Problems" (Washington, 1949).

Parmelee, Julius H., "The Modern Railway" (New York, 1940).

Taff, Charles A., "Commercial Motor Transportation" (Chicago, 1950).

Van Metre, T. W., "Transportation in the United States," 2d ed. (Brooklyn, 1950).

Wilson, G. Lloyd, and Leslie A. Bryan, "Air Transportation" (New York, 1949).

Wolfe, Thomas, "Air Transportation: Traffic and Management" (New York, 1950).

For those who want to read further about the history of transportation in the United States there is a vast amount of material. There are numerous works of a general character, and there are many books dealing with individual enterprises, regional developments, and the personalities who have been important in transportation history.

Of the older works, which because of their age alone if for no other reason may be regarded as historical in character, perhaps the first that should be mentioned is J. L. Ringwalt's "The Development of Transportation Systems in the United States" (Philadelphia, 1888). Consisting largely of articles taken from magazines and newspapers, showing transportation progress in America decade by decade, this book is a rich storehouse of information. Another book of almost equal interest, but dealing entirely with railroads, is "The American Railroad" (New York, 1892), made up of several highly interesting and informative essays written by men who, nearly three-quarters of a century ago, were the outstanding authorities on all phases of railroad transportation. The book has numerous pictures, many of them by that former prince of American illustrators, A. B. Frost.

Preceding these two books was Henry V. Poor's "History of Railroads and Canals in the United States" (New York, 1860), which was the precursor of the well-known "Poor's Manual of Railroads," the first annual issue of which appeared in 1868. Preceding Poor were hundreds of "guides," published and sold in every large eastern city, to tell emigrants bound for the "great West" the best routes to follow on their journey to the promised land. Mitchell's "Compendium of Railroads and Canals" (Philadelphia, 1835) and Appleton's "Railroad and Steamboat Companion," prepared by Wellington Williams and published under several different titles between 1847 and 1860, contain maps, travel instructions, and information about inns. Henry S. Tanner published his "American Traveler: A Guide through the United States, Containing Brief Notices of Canals and Railroads" in Philadelphia, in 1834. His better known "Description of Canals and Railroads in the United States" (edition of 1840), while not exactly a guide for prospective settlers, gave much information they were glad to have. The "Rise and Progress of Internal Improvements in America" in "Poor's Manual of Railroads" (New York, 1881) is one of the best brief histories we have of early transportation enterprise in the United States. Caroline E. MacGill's "History of Transportation in the United States before 1860," prepared for the Carnegie Institution under the editorial supervision of Balthasar H. Meyer, then a member of the Interstate Commerce Commission, contains an abundance of factual matter. It contains one of the best bibliographies available on the history of transportation during the early years of our republic.

Of later works on American transportation history, Seymour Dunbar's "History of Travel in the United States" (Indianapolis, 1915) is among the best. It is especially valuable for its excellent illustrations. A more recent work on railroads is Stewart H. Holbrook's "The Story of American Railroads" (New York, 1947). Though not too well organized, and often rambling and discursive, it contains a good running account of the development of the American railroad system, with emphasis on the dramatic elements of the story, the clash of personalities, and the titanic accomplishment of some of our great railroad builders. It contains a well-chosen list of books of interest to the historian.

As one may imagine, transportation has been the inspiration of a swelling flood of government documents. Statutory enactments, decisions of commissions and courts, reports of Congressional "investigations," and monographs of executive agencies fill hundreds of volumes. One of the earliest Congressional reports on transportation (House Document No. 18, 22d Congress, 1st Session, 1831–1832) contains some highly entertaining comments by American civil engineers on the respective merits of railroads and canals. Perhaps the greatest "classic" among Congressional reports on the the subject of transportation is the Windom Report of 1871 (Transportation Routes to the Seaboard, Senate Report No. 307, Part 1, 43d Congress, 1st Session. This report, together with the Cullom Report of 1886 (Senate Report No. 46, 49th Congress, 1st Session), formed the background against which the Act to Regulate Commerce was framed and passed in 1887.

In nonscientific and fictional literature, it is only transportation by water that has had a conspicuously important place. From the story of Jonah and the great fish, the Greek myth about Jason and his quest for the Golden Fleece, Homer's account of the wanderings of Ulysses, and Vergil's epic tale of Aeneas, down through "Robinson Crusoe" and "Swiss Family Robinson," to the works of Melville, Verne, Stevenson, Conrad, and McFee, the sea and its mysteries have had a peculiar fascination for the weavers of tales of high adventure. There have been short stories by the thousand about adventures connected with railroads, trucks, airplanes, and watercraft of all kinds. There have been a few novels dealing with surface transportation other than that by water, but most of them, such as "Black Beauty" and "The Covered Wagon," have had to do with transportation in which the motive power was provided by animals. Frank Norris's "The Octopus" had for its central theme the transportation of wheat, with the railroad playing the part of the villain in the plot. All sorts of transportation have been the inspiration of poetry and song, but here again the sea has been most effective in stimulating the imagination of the writer, from Homer to John Masefield. Many people, however, have enjoyed the stirring lines of such short poems as Browning's "How They Brought the Good News from Ghent to Aix," Woolson's "Kentucky Belle," and Read's "Sheridan's Ride." Even the railroad has been celebrated in "Casey Jones" and in a few of the recent vehicles for the talents of popular radio crooners.

In painting, as in fiction and poetry, the mechanized facilities of transportation do not seem to have had a strong appeal to the artist. However alive a steam or diesel locomotive, a steamboat, a motor vehicle, or an airplane may seem to be as it speeds along, its moving parts flashing and flying, its motion cannot be made to live in a painting. There is no change of shape, as there is in the animal or the sailing ship, when they move, and a picture of a locomotive speeding along at a hundred miles an hour looks just like one that is standing still, unless some conventional symbol is used to indicate movement. On the other hand, the photographer finds some of his best subjects in the man-made machines and structures of today, and we have many albums of locomotives and other vehicles which provide transportation service for this busy, bustling world.

Questions and Topics

CHAPTER I

1. What conditions have led to the increase in the importance of traffic management in the general field of business management?

2. What are some of the ways in which a competent traffic manager may be of help to the managers of other departments of a business enterprise?

3. Freight forwarders occasionally show some resentment at being called "middlemen." This resentment may arise because there is a somewhat widely held opinion that middlemen are parasitic encumbrances to trade and industry. Is there any justification for such an opinion?

4. What are the chief factors which control a traffic manager's decision in the selection of a carrier?

5. Why does the law provide that the shipper is "presumed" to know a railroad freight rate and cannot hold a carrier responsible for any loss suffered because of the misquotation of a rate by the carrier's agent?

6. What is meant by "reciprocity" in business dealings? How might it become a source of abuse?

7. Why are proper packing and marking of freight shipments so important?

8. What is a "transit privilege"?

9. What are the leading causes of "claims" against carriers?

10. Draw up three or four different organization "charts" of a traffic department.

11. The general manager of a business enterprise may not have knowledge of traffic work sufficient to enable him to evaluate correctly the worth to the enterprise of a competent traffic manager. Can you suggest any ways in which a traffic manager might diplomatically and not too obtrusively "educate" the general manager as to the importance of traffic management?

CHAPTER II

1. What are the leading reasons for the legal requirement that the rates of common carriers be published and kept open to "public" inspection?

2. Althought this matter will be discussed later, can you suggest any reason why the rate per hundred pounds on a less carload shipment of a certain commodity should be greater than the rate per hundred pounds on a carload shipment of the same commodity?

3. Select any two large cities with which you are familiar and which are served by several different railroads, for example, New York and Chicago. See how many different routes (up to twenty-five) you might have between the cities. The routes may be all rail, all water, or rail and water.

4. Be sure that you know the meaning of class rate, commodity rate, local

rate, joint rate, combination rate, proportional rate, export rate, import rate, and through rate.

5. What is a freight rate tariff?

6. What is a "tariff circular"?

7. If you have a copy of *Tariff Circular* No. 20, explain the differences between the different forms of "concurrences." How does a "power of attorney" differ from a "concurrence"?

8. How long does a rate, once published, remain in effect?

9. What are some of the reasons for the requirement of uniformity in the publication of tariffs?

10. Would the consolidation of our railroads into a small number of systems, or even into one large system, result in the simplification of tariffs?

CHAPTER III

1. What is the chief purpose of freight classification?

2. Why is it difficult to attain complete uniformity of freight classification in this country?

3. Before the Uniform Classification replaces the Consolidated Classification entirely, the latter must be formally "canceled." Can you suggest how this might be done without issuing a new classification?

4. Why is it necessary for railroads to provide carload minimum weights?

5. Why do carriers publish exceptions to the classification?

6. What is the difference between a rating and a rate?

7. In both the Consolidated and the Uniform Classifications, potatoes, other than sweet, have a carload minimum weight which varies with the season of the year. See if you can find out the reason for the variation.

8. Here are a few articles upon which to find the applicable ratings. Use either the Consolidated Classification or the Uniform Classification or both.

Boxes, bottles, or cans, fiberboard, paperboard, or pulpboard, with or without metal tops or bottoms, noibn, measuring outside (*a*) 20 by 20 by ½ inches, (*b*) 6 by 6 by 3 inches, (*c*) 10 by 10 by 2 inches, (*d*) 12 by 12 by 1 inches.

Poles used in pole vaulting, l.c.l.

Tobacco cigarettes.

9. Using the Uniform Classification, and assuming a Class 100 rate of 60 cents a hundred pounds, what would be the charge on 1,000 pounds of stone statuary?

10. If the "stone statuary" consisted of a single piece of marble sculpture having a value of $15,000, what would your answer be?

CHAPTER IV

1. In the regulation of transportation, it has frequently been deemed advisable to supersede long-established rules of common law by statutory enactments. Can you think of some instances of the substitution of statute for common law rule? One example of such substitution would be the rules with regard to employer's liability.

2. If a "dry or solid" article has a certain rating when shipped in "boxes,"

what would be its rating if shipped in barrels? Would the charges on a shipment of such an article be any different if shipped in crates?

3. Can you think of any reason why goods shipped under an order bill of lading must be marked with an identifying symbol?

4. The story has been told that a man offered a somewhat decrepit horse and a dilapidated vehicle for transportation from Kansas City to New York. Without paying any fare, he accompanied the shipment as a caretaker, as he had a right to do. When they all reached New York the man abandoned the shipment and departed, destination unknown. The railroads involved found that they were quite a bit out of pocket as a result of their efforts. What error had the agent in Kansas City made?

5. Using either of the classifications, make up a number of mixed carload shipments, assume certain carload and less carload rates, and calculate total charges, under Rule 10 both as published in the classification and as given in eastern and southern exceptions.

6. With respect to the caution a carrier must exercise in making delivery, what is the chief difference between a straight bill of lading and an order bill of lading?

CHAPTER V

1. Do utilities other than carriers have minimum charges? What are some of the ways in which they are computed?

2. Can you think of some "invention" which, not specifically classified or subject to classification as noibn, would have to be classified by "analogy"? Proceed with its "classification."

3. Look up some articles that are classified "not nested," "nested," and "nested solid." Assuming applicable rates, calculate the difference in transportation charges. Do you suppose the design of any receptacles has ever been modified in order to permit "nesting"?

4. What is the justification for giving different ratings to the same article according to whether it is "in the white" or "finished"?

5. A contractor wishes to ship his derrick, which is permanently mounted on a railroad flatcar, to another location. The derrick boom is 60 feet long. The weight of the derrick engine, base, and car upon which they are mounted is 80,000 pounds; the weight of the boom is 12,000 pounds. Upon what weight will the total charges be computed? Use either classification.

6. A manufacturer ships a carload of airplane propellers. On arrival it is found that some of the propellers have been damaged because of inadequate packing. Is the carrier responsible for the damage?

7. What in general are the characteristics of most of the articles which are shipped subject to Rule 34?

8. Examine some carton made of fiberboard and make a note of the specifications required by Rule 41. What is meant by bursting test? How is such a test made?

9. What is meant by fourth section relief?

10. What is the outstanding difference between the classification provisions

applicable to the movement of railway cars on their own wheels and virtually all the other articles listed in both classifications?

CHAPTER VI

1. Construct a "class-rate scale" for six classes, those below first having the following percentage relationships to first class: 85, 70, 50, 35, 25. Assume a first-class rate of 30 cents per hundred pounds, for the first 5 miles. Progress at the rate of 2 cents for each additional 5 miles up to 50 miles, at the rate of 4 cents for each additional 10 miles up to 150 miles, and at the rate of 3 cents for each additional 10 miles. Do not carry the scale beyond 250 miles.

2. Imagine twelve different freight stations, and give each a name. Assume distances between stations of varying mileage, but in no case in excess of 20 miles. Using the scale constructed under the directions given in the preceding question, construct a class-rate tariff, showing the rates between each pair of the twelve stations on each of the six classes.

3. What is the "intermediate rule" of tariff application?

4. What is meant by the expression "rate structure"?

5. What can a railroad traffic association now do that the law forbids an industrial "trade association" to do?

6. What are some other fields in which the terms "association," "conference," "league," and "federation" are used to designate an organization?

7. Can you think of any way in which freight rate tariffs could be further simplified and systematized?

8. If an *Official Guide* is available, make up the schedule of a journey from New York to Seattle by three different routes, indicating the railroads employed and the times of the departure and arrival of trains at point of origin, junction points, and destination.

9. A traffic manager must keep a strict watch on the rates applying to and from his own plant and also on the rates applying to and from competitive plants. Suppose he found that the rates enjoyed by a competitor were obviously "out of line" with the rates applicable to his own shipments. What procedure should he follow to obtain a more reasonable relationship?

CHAPTER VII

1. How are prices determined in a "free market"? Can you mention any practices now followed in our economic system which prevent the market from being "free"?

2. Have you heard the expression "normal price" in your study of economics? Under conditions of a free market, at what point does the normal price settle in the long run? Is there a tendency to have "regulated prices" settle at the same point?

3. Does labor in an industrialized nation tend to become more or less "mobile"? Why?

4. In an effort to bring about the establishment of "reasonable prices," a government can try to compel producers to compete with one another or can

actually name the prices which they charge. Which method of regulation do you think is likely to be more effective? Why?

5. Explain the difference between fixed costs and joint costs.

6. What is the essential difference between contracts which are legal, extra-legal, and illegal?

7. What change of attitude on the part of Congress with respect to the general problem of economic regulation was indicated by the fact that pooling contracts, once declared illegal, were eventually legalized?

8. Is this change of attitude reflected in any way in the present efforts to enact "fair trade" laws?

9. Why is industrial competition more difficult to subject to control than intercarrier competition?

10. What effect might the "gasification" of coal in the ground and the transportation of the gas by pipeline have upon railroad transportation?

11. If you were the minister of transport in a small island country, such as Cuba, which would you urge more strongly, the development of railroad transportation or the development of highway transportation? Why?

12. Describe some one of the most important rate structures that have been developed in the United States, and comment on its most outstanding characteristic.

CHAPTER VIII

1. If you have access to the reports of the United States Supreme Court, read the dissenting opinion in *Munn v. Illinois*. Do you think the reasoning in that opinion was more or less "logical" than the reasoning in the majority opinion? Why?

2. Is there likely to be any difference between a "valuation" for taxing purposes and valuations for condemnation proceedings and rate making? Which valuation is likely to be the lowest, if there is a difference? Which the highest?

3. Why did Congress fix a fair rate of return which might vary from time to time, but provide for the "recapture" of part of the earnings in excess of a fixed rate of 6 percent?

4. What is meant by "circular reasoning"?

5. What is meant by "pragmatic adjustment"?

6. Explain the phrase "zone of reasonableness."

7. It is frequently said these days that the railroads "lose" over a half-billion dollars a year on their passenger business. Do you think their net income would increase by a half-billion if they dropped their passenger operations entirely? Give your reasons.

8. A member of the Interstate Commerce Commission once said that the chief considerations in rate regulation were the three C's—comparison, competition, and compromise. What did he mean?

9. It has been said that the railroads of the United States were constructed for the purpose of "overcoming distance" but that the present policy of the Commission is such that we seem to be "surrendering" to distance. What effect might this surrender to distance have upon American industry with respect to

the matter of "centralization"? Has such an effect been evident in recent years?

10. A Canadian railroad official once said that railroad traffic formerly consisted of three parts, one which paid little more than its variable or "out-of-pocket" costs, one which paid all its variable costs and its "fair share" of constant or fixed costs, and another which not only paid its variable costs but considerably more than its fair share of fixed costs. What would be the effect of such a setup for motor carrier competition?

CHAPTER IX

1. Explain how a rate can be "reasonable" but not "unduly discriminatory"; "unreasonable" but not "unduly discriminatory"; "reasonable" but "unduly discriminatory"; both "unreasonable" and "unduly discriminatory."

2. Make a short list of practices which are regarded as "discriminatory." Upon what grounds are they so regarded? Which of them are considered to be "unduly discriminatory"? What is the test?

3. For the past few years, the Federal government has imposed a tax of 15 per cent on all passenger fares in excess of 35 cents. If you are coming from Newark to New York on the Pennsylvania Railroad, you can buy a ticket for 50 cents which brings you to the Pennsylvania Terminal. The tax on the ticket will be 8 cents. If you buy a ticket good on the Hudson Tube to Cortland Street, the price is 35 cents, and there is no tax. You can use this ticket on a Pennsylvania Railroad train and get to the Pennsylvania Terminal by the payment of a cash "tunnel toll" of 15 cents. Does the difference of 8 cents in the fares of two passengers, perhaps occupying the same seat, constitute an unjust discrimination?

4. How may a quantity discount bring about undue discrimination, even though the discount fairly represents a difference in costs?

5. Do you think the fourth section should be repealed, and the long-and-short-haul problem administered under the third section?

6. It has been said that all discrimination in transportation rates is "personal," since rates are paid by persons, and not by regions, gateways, or other geographical units. Do you think we can have "place" discrimination?

7. Explain and comment on the Shreveport case.

8. Why do you think Congress did not apply to motor carriers the same rules with respect to discrimination against interstate commerce that it applied to railroads? Do you think the law should be changed to bring all carriers under the same rule in this matter? In which direction should it be changed?

9. What would happen if a traffic manager, who had charged only that a certain rate was unreasonable, should endeavor, at a hearing before the Commission or an examiner, to present evidence that the challenged rate was also unjustly discriminatory?

10. If the Interstate Commerce Act were to be amended so as to drop either the requirement that rates should be reasonable or the requirement that they should not be unjustly discriminatory, which requirement do you think should be dropped? Why?

CHAPTER X

1. What is the advantage of "uniformity" in domestic bills of lading?

2. What is the difference between "prepaid" charges and "advanced" charges?

3. What is meant by "nonrecourse"?

4. You make a shipment by express at a released value of $50. The shipment is lost. Its actual value is $100. How much can you recover from the carrier? How much if the actual value is $25? Suppose the actual value is $2,000 and you declare a value of $1,000. You own a house having a value of $20,000, you insure it against loss by fire to the amount of $10,000, and it is totally destroyed by fire. How much can you recover? How much if there is only a partial loss, amounting to $5,000?

5. What is the most important difference between a straight and an order bill of lading?

6. What is the meaning of "negotiability"?

7. Does the expression "F.O.B." have anything to do with the matter of the passing of title?

8. Explain how an order bill of lading is handled in business transactions.

9. Why do some shippers prefer to consign goods to themselves under a straight bill of lading rather than make use of an order bill of lading?

10. Can you think of any reasons why the liability of a carrier by water should differ from the liability of a carrier by land?

CHAPTER XI

1. Why do you think Congress has refrained from enacting legislation defining the liability of an air carrier?

2. What was the chief purpose of the Carmack Amendment? What effect did it have which was not contemplated at the time of its passage?

3. In reading paragraph (11), section 20, of the Interstate Commerce Act, you will notice that the carrier is liable to the "lawful holder" of the bill of lading. The last part of the section, paragraph (12), provides that the initial carrier can recover from the connecting carrier, but only for losses for which compensation has been paid to the "owner." Under this statute, could the initial carrier recover from a connecting carrier for compensation paid out because of the loss of a shipment of a freight forwarder?

4. How is the "value" of a lost or damaged shipment measured?

5. Does a rate based upon "actual value" act as limitation of a carrier's liability?

6. Indicate some of the ways in which carrier's liability under the common law has been increased by reason of statutory enactments.

7. A potato grower in Maine shipped a carload of potatoes to New York. The delivering carrier negligently held the car in its yard for several days, and when delivery was finally made the potatoes had deteriorated to such an extent that the loss on the carload amounted to $1,500. The shipper filed a claim seasonably with the delivering carrier. The carrier said that it would pay only

half the claim, since it had had possession of the car for only half the time it was in transit from the point of shipment. Comment.

8. What are "special damages"? Under what conditions will a carrier reimburse a shipper for such damages?

9. What is meant by "reasonable dispatch"?

10. Do you think that the liability of water carriers should be the same as that of rail carriers with respect to goods transported in domestic commerce? Give your reasons.

CHAPTER XII

1. What must a rail carrier do before it sells unclaimed nonperishable freight?

2. How does the liability of a warehouseman differ from the liability of a common carrier? If a hotel guest leaves money and jewels in a rented room and they are stolen, is the hotel responsible for the loss? If you store an automobile in a public garage, under what conditions is the owner of the garage responsible for its destruction by fire while it is in storage?

3. Should a traffic manager have some knowledge of the laws applicable to sales and to warehousing? Why?

4. A carload of freight is placed on a public delivery track and the consignee duly notified. The car is destroyed by fire within the free time allowed for its unloading. Is the carrier responsible for the loss? Would the carrier's responsibility be any different if the destruction took place after the expiration of free time?

5. What is a "beneficial owner?"

6. What was another provision of the Transportation Act of 1920 which led the Supreme Court to declare the Alaska Steamship case to be moot?

7. An interesting exercise would be to look up the story of the *Vestris* and find out how the claims arising from its loss were eventually settled.

8. Do you think that the provisions of the Carriage of Goods by Sea Act should be applied in domestic trade?

9. Secure an "airbill" from some aviation company, and compare its provisions with regard to liability with the provisions of a railroad bill of lading.

10. What are the various uses of a railroad waybill?

CHAPTER XIII

1. What is the difference between a legal rate and a lawful rate?

2. Make a list of ways in which errors may creep into freight bills.

3. What documents should be submitted with a claim for the refund of an overcharge?

4. Describe the procedure to be taken in preparing a claim for concealed loss or damage.

5. Does the one who files a claim against a carrier for loss or damage have to be the owner of the goods?

6. A shipment made under a straight bill of lading is lost. The shipper files a claim with the carrier. How can the carrier protect itself against the possibility of a claim on the part of the consignee?

7. A manufacturer of grape juice in New York made numerous contracts for

the purchase of grapes, and made other contracts for the delivery of the juice. For the manufacture of the juice he was depending upon a machine he had purchased in St. Louis. The machine was seasonably shipped, but because of the negligence of the carriers it did not arrive in time for use as the grapes were delivered. The manufacturer disposed of the grapes as well as he could, and purchased grape juice to fulfil his contracts. He lost some $25,000 in the various transactions, and brought suit against the carriers for this amount. Was he able to recover?

8. Try to get some literature from the Association of American Railroads on the matter of claim prevention.

9. What are some of the more common causes of loss and damage to freight? Which of these are most "preventable"?

10. What is meant by "palletizing"?

CHAPTER XIV

1. Look up in a good dictionary the meaning of the word "average," as used in marine insurance.

2. How does the liability of a stockholder of a corporation compare with the liability of a member of a business partnership?

3. What is an "open" policy of marine insurance?

4. What are the distinguishing features of "general average"? Why can such a loss not be "total"?

5. What is the meaning of the expression "free of average under 10 per cent unless general"?

6. Explain the "sue and labor" clause of a marine insurance policy.

7. What is a "certificate" of insurance?

8. What is a master's "protest"?

9. You ship a cargo worth $1,000,000 in a vessel valued at $3,000,000. There are three other shippers of cargo carried in the same vessel, each shipment having a value of $1,000,000. Your cargo is voluntarily sacrificed in order to save the remainder of the venture. Each shipper and the shipowner are insured, but each with a separate insurance company. How much will your insurance company pay you? To what extent, if any, will your company be reimbursed by the other insurance companies?

10. What is the advantage, if any, of insuring shipments made by rail or by motor carrier in domestic commerce?

CHAPTER XV

1. What is an "off-line" office of a railroad? Why are such offices maintained?

2. What is the difference between a "connecting route" and a "through route"?

3. What are some of the reasons for giving the shipper the right to route his traffic?

4. If a shipper inserts both route and rate in a shipping order, and the rate is not applicable over the route named, what procedure should be followed?

5. What rule should a railroad agent follow with regard to a shipment not routed by the shipper?

6. In connection with routing, we have another example of how common law may be modified by statute. What change was made?

7. What was the Subiaco case?

8. Do you think that motor carriers of freight should be required to establish through routes? Give your reasons.

9. What have been the leading changes in part I of the Interstate Commerce Act with respect to routing?

10. Why have railroads so often opposed the liberalization of the law with regard to routing?

CHAPTER XVI

1. What are some of the "technological" changes which have contributed to the rapid development of motor vehicle transportation?

2. Explain the operation of the early fast freight lines.

3. What are the leading provisions of the Esch Car Service Act?

4. Every once in a while, a situation arises in which fancied "rights" are not protected by law. An industrial concern has sidings served by two different railroads. It orders and receives from one of the roads a car for loading, and then dispatches the loaded car over the other road. You can imagine the feelings of the road which supplied the car. But has it any grounds for legal redress?

5. Since the word "demurrage" is not mentioned in the Interstate Commerce Act, how can the Commission exercise jurisdiction over demurrage charges and practices?

6. What is a "private" freight car? How does a railroad charge for freight carried in private cars? How is the owner of a private car compensated for its use?

7. What is meant by "constructive placement"?

8. Because of rearmament, it has been necessary for the Commission to make many changes in the rules and charges affecting car service. The principles of the rules remain the same, but practices differ because of recurring emergencies. See if you can find out what demurrage charges are at the present time.

9. Explain how an average agreement works.

10. A potato grower in Idaho took the precaution to order, several weeks in advance of shipping time, the number of cars he thought he would need to ship his crop. When shipping time arrived, there was a severe car shortage. He received only his "fair share" of available cars. He complained to the Interstate Commerce Commission, asserting that since he had ordered his cars long before other growers had placed their orders, he was entitled to have his order filled before the others received any cars at all. How do you think the Commission disposed of his complaint?

CHAPTER XVII

1. What is a public delivery track?

2. "What was once the greatest competitive advantage of a railroad has become its greatest competitive handicap." What does this statement mean?

3. How does a belt line facilitate switching operations?

4. How much "switching service" is a railroad ordinarily required to give as a part of its line-haul service?

5. Explain interchange switching, reciprocal switching, switching absorption.

6. Has the Commission the power to order the construction of a switch connection between two main line railroads?

7. Why is it easier to establish a "reasonable" charge for switching than a reasonable charge for hauling a particular commodity from one point to another?

8. If you make a through shipment under a joint rate, does the rate cover the charge for any necessary interchange switching, or must you pay extra for such a service?

9. What peculiar advantage has the City of New York enjoyed as a great center of commerce? What have been its disadvantages, if any?

10. How has the modification of railroad switching practices contributed to the prosperity of our domestic commerce?

CHAPTER XVIII

1. Since American railroads followed European railroad practice in so many ways, how do you account for the fact that they did not establish pickup and delivery service when railroad transportation first began in this country?

2. What caused the railroads finally to offer pickup and delivery of less carload freight?

3. What are some of the chief advantages which motor transportation has over railroad transportation? What are some of the advantages possessed by railroads?

4. We have had a long-standing controversy in this country as to whether motor vehicles, and especially motor trucks, pay their fair share of the costs of highway construction and maintenance. What are the chief arguments on both sides of this question?

5. What is your opinion of the advisability of confining intercity motor trucks to toll roads?

6. Do you think any of our railroads would benefit financially if they converted some of their branch lines into toll highways?

7. Explain the device known as the constructive station.

8. How does storage differ from demurrage?

9. What is the difference between transportation elevation and commercial elevation of grain?

10. What are some of the various "allowances" which railroads give to shippers? Must allowances have tariff authority for their payment?

CHAPTER XIX

1. Of what benefit to a shipper is the privilege of reconsignment in transit?

2. Who has the right to order the reconsignment of a carload of freight?

3. Why is there less likely to be a dispute over the reconsignment of a shipment covered by an order bill of lading than over a shipment moving under a straight bill?

4. Has the Interstate Commerce Commission the right to order the establishment of a reconsignment privilege?

5. Name several of the transit privileges which are offered by American railroads.

6. Tell how a transit privilege may be used by a shipper.

7. What are the methods by which the total charges on transited shipments are computed?

8. What are some of the industries which are most likely to make use of transit privileges?

9. How can the existence of a transit privilege affect the location of industry?

10. What is meant by "creosoting-in-transit"?

CHAPTER XX

1. Is a freight forwarder a common carrier in the same sense that a railroad or a motor carrier is a common carrier?

2. How does the express agency differ from a freight forwarder?

3. Which rule of the classification is of particular interest to freight forwarders?

4. How does a freight forwarder differ from a freight broker?

5. Can you tell where the quotation "but in the estimation of a hair" is to be found?

6. How could a railroad use a controlled freight forwarding company as an instrument of competition with other roads? How might unjust discrimination arise?

7. Why did the railroads not adopt the recommendation of the Interstate Commerce Commission and offer a service which would render the freight forwarding business obsolete?

8. What are some of the services a forwarder may give a shipper, in addition to transportation service?

CHAPTER XXI

1. How do railroads usually proceed to get authority to make a blanket increase of their rates?

2. Why was President Cleveland somewhat reluctant to sign the Act to Regulate Commerce?

3. What were some of the "constitutional" objections to the Act of 1887?

4. What were the leading defects of the Act of 1887?

5. What were the chief provisions of the Elkins Act of 1903?

6. What were the chief changes which the Hepburn Amendment made in the Act of 1887?

7. On what grounds will a Federal court set aside an order of the Interstate Commerce Commission?

8. What were the leading provisions of the Mann-Elkins Act of 1910?

9. Compare the rule of rate making of the Transportation Act of 1920 with the rule adopted in 1933.

10. What were the chief reasons for the failure of the planned railroad consolidation provided for in the Act of 1920?

11. What are the purposes of parts II, III, and IV of the Interstate Commerce Act?

12. In what ways does the Civil Aeronautics Act seem to differ from the Interstate Commerce Act?

13. Do you think that all transportation agencies in domestic commerce should come under the regulatory supervision of the same government agency? Give your reasons.

14. What are some of the "inequities" of regulation about which railroads and their friends now complain? Do you believe the complaints to be justified?

15. What changes do you think should be made in our present laws for the regulation of the transportation industry?

CHAPTERS XXII TO XXVI

Since these chapters represent for the most part a digest of our transportation statutes, no lists of questions are given.

The reader is urged to secure copies of the Interstate Commerce Act, the Civil Aeronautics Act, and the Interstate Commerce Commission's Rules of Practice, and read the full text of these documents.

A rewarding study would be the comparison of the provisions of the different parts of the Interstate Commerce Act and Civil Aeronautics Act. This may be done topically. For example, take the topic "through routing." Then place in parallel columns the "duty," with respect to routing, which is imposed upon each carrier. Other topics, which could be similarly treated, are discrimination, rate reasonableness, rules of rate making, penalties, and liability for loss and damage. The powers and duties of the Interstate Commerce Commission and of the Civil Aeronautics Board may be compared in the same way under appropriate topical headings.

Another study might be the framing of an imaginary complaint to be filed with the proper commission. It should be properly prepared and followed through the various stages of presentation, hearing, argument, and decision. A part of the exercise would be the preparation of exhibits and briefs. Rules of Practice must be carefully observed.

Index

A

Absorption of switching charges, 362
Act of God, 215
Act to Regulate Commerce (*see* Interstate Commerce Act)
Actual value rates, 55, 211
Adams v. Croninger, 204
Administrative agencies, decisions of, 511
    judicial review of, 511
    hearings before, 510
Administrative procedure, former methods of, 509
    of Interstate Commerce Commission, 513
Administrative Procedure Act of 1946, 508–526
Advanced charges, 71
Agency and agent's tariffs, 104
Agreements, average, in demurrage, 330
Aids to safety in transportation, 263
Air competition, 122
Air transportation, routing in, 304
Alaska Steamship Company case, 181
Allowances, elevation, 388
    switching, 344
Analogy, classification by, 79
Arbitraries, 98
Arrival notice, of cars, 326
    of shipments, 241
Assigned cars, 311
Associations, railway traffic, 101
Attendants accompanying shipments, 86
Auditing of freight bills, 13

Average, general, 237, 270
    particular, 272
Average agreements in demurrage, 330

B

Back haul, 404
Baltimore, former pickup and delivery at, 372
Bases of classification, 50
Belt lines, 342
Bibliographical note, 527–529
Bill of lading, 11, 175–244
    carrier must issue, 176
    definition of, 175
    face of, 185
    form of, adopted, 183
        alternative, 189
        prescribed, 179
        short, 66, 188
    government, 196
    order, 194
    required by Harter Act, 177
    straight, 191
Bills of lading of carriers by water, 238
Bills of Lading Act, Pomerene, 178, 190
Broker, freight, 412
Bulk and weight, 52
Bureaus, of Interstate Commerce Commission, 517
    weighing and inspection, 67

C

California routing case, 293
Cancellation of tariffs, 99

543